CAPITALIST DICTATORSHIP

Studies in Critical Social Sciences Book Series

Haymarket Books is proud to be working with Brill Academic Publishers (www.brill.nl) to republish the *Studies in Critical Social Sciences* book series in paperback editions. This peer-reviewed book series offers insights into our current reality by exploring the content and consequences of power relationships under capitalism, and by considering the spaces of opposition and resistance to these changes that have been defining our new age. Our full catalog of *SCSS* volumes can be viewed at https://www.haymarketbooks .org/series_collections/4-studies-in-critical-social-sciences.

CAPITALIST DICTATORSHIP

A Study of Its Social Systems, Dimensions, Forms and Indicators

MILAN ZAFIROVSKI

Haymarket Books
Chicago, IL

First published in 2021 by Brill Academic Publishers, The Netherlands
© 2021 Koninklijke Brill NV, Leiden, The Netherlands

Published in paperback in 2022 by
Haymarket Books
P.O. Box 180165
Chicago, IL 60618
773-583-7884
www.haymarketbooks.org

ISBN: 978-1-64259-773-8

Distributed to the trade in the US through Consortium Book Sales and
Distribution (www.cbsd.com) and internationally through Ingram Publisher
Services International (www.ingramcontent.com).

This book was published with the generous support of Lannan Foundation and
Wallace Action Fund.

Special discounts are available for bulk purchases by organizations and
institutions. Please call 773-583-7884 or email info@haymarketbooks.org for more
information.

Cover design by Jamie Kerry and Ragina Johnson.

Printed in the United States.

10 9 8 7 6 5 4 3 2 1

Library of Congress Cataloging-in-Publication data is available.

Contents

Acknowledgements   IX
List of Figures and Tables   X

1 Introduction   1
  1   The Concept of Capitalist Dictatorship   1
  2   A Sociological Study of Capitalist Dictatorship—General
       Outlines   9

2 Capitalist Dictatorship as an Economic System   15
  1   Negative Definition and Specification of Capitalist Dictatorship   15
  2   Positive Definition and Specification of Capitalist Dictatorship   19
  3   Economic Forms and Agents of Capitalist Dictatorship   22
       3.1   *Capitalist Autocracy*   22
       3.2   *Capitalist Dynasty*   25
       3.3   *Capitalist Plutocracy, Oligarchy, and Aristocracy*   29
       3.4   *Secondary Forms and Agents of Capitalist Dictatorship*   39
       3.5   *Plutocracy and Secondary Forms and Agents of Capitalist
              Dictatorship*   43
  4   Economic Indicators and Proxies of Capitalist Dictatorship   52
       4.1   *Indicators and Proxies of Economic Coercion, Oppression and
              Non-democracy*   53
              4.1.1   Suppression of Unionization   53
              4.1.2   Restriction of the Scope of Unionization   57
              4.1.3   Suppression of Collective Bargaining   59
              4.1.4   Suppression of Codetermination   65
       4.2   *Indicators and Proxies of Economic Inequality, Degradation and
              Deprivation*   68
              4.2.1   Extreme Concentration of Wealth   68
              4.2.2   Extremely Unequal Income Distribution   77
              4.2.3   Economic Degradation, Deprivation and
                       Hardship   82
              4.2.4   Economic Exploitation and Non-protection and
                       Insecurity   87

3 Capitalist Dictatorship as a Political Regime   96
  1   Moving from Economy to Polity, Transforming Economic to Political
       Domination   96

2   Negative Definition and Specification of Capitalist Dictatorship as a
     Political Regime   98
3   Positive Definition and Specification of Capitalist Dictatorship as a
     Political Regime   102
4   Political Forms and Agents of Capitalist Dictatorship   104
     4.1   *Capitalist Autocracy as a Political Regime*   106
     4.2   *Capitalist Dynasty as a Political Regime*   109
     4.3   *Capitalist Plutocracy, Aristocracy and Oligarchy as a Political
            Regime*   110
     4.4   *Secondary Forms of Capitalist Dictatorship as Political
            Regimes*   111
5   Political Indicators and Proxies of Capitalist Dictatorship   115
     5.1   *Suppression of Political Freedoms and Rights*   115
            5.1.1   Suppression of Voting and Related Political
                     Freedoms and Rights   117
            5.1.2   Suppression of Free Political Competition for
                     Power   122
            5.1.3   Suppression of Political 'Voice'   125
     5.2   *Concentration of Political Power*   126
            5.2.1   Mistreatment and Subordination of Non-capital
                     Groups   127
            5.2.2   Denial of Equal Political Freedoms and Rights   130
            5.2.3   Suppression of Political Pluralism and Imposition
                     of Ideological Monism   132
            5.2.4   Unequal Legal Treatment   139
     5.3   *Severe Penal Repression and Punishment*   143
            5.3.1   'Law and Order' for Non-capitalists, Lawlessness for
                     Capital   144
            5.3.2   Political Terror: Mass Imprisonment, Executions,
                     Violations of Human Rights   146
     5.4   *Militarism*   151
            5.4.1   The Military-Capitalist Complex and Aggressive
                     Wars   152
            5.4.2   Militarized Political Repression   155

4 Capitalist Dictatorship as Civil Society   162
  1   Capitalist Dictatorship and Civil Society   162
  2   Negative Definition and Specification of Capitalist Dictatorship as
       Civil Society   165

3 Positive Definition and Specification of Capitalist Dictatorship as
  Civil Society   168
4 Forms and Agents of Capitalist Dictatorship as Civil Society   177
  4.1   *Capitalist Autocracy and Dynasty in Civil Society*   177
  4.2   *Capitalist Plutocracy, Oligarchy, and Aristocracy in Civil
        Society*   179
  4.3   *Secondary Forms of Capitalist Dictatorship in Civil Society*   183
5 Indicators and Proxies of Capitalist Dictatorship as Civil Society   188
  5.1   *Suppression of Individual Liberty and Other Civil Liberties*   188
        5.1.1   Denial of Personal Freedom of Moral Choice   189
  5.2   *Negation of Civil and Other Human Rights*   193
  5.3   *Criminalization and Severe Sanctioning of Moral Offenses*   197
  5.4   *Moralistic-Religious Terror*   199
        5.4.1   Massive Populations of Prisoners of Ethical
                Conscience   200

5 **Capitalist Dictatorship as a Cultural System**   204
  1   Capitalist Dictatorship and Culture   204
  2   Negative Definition and Specification of Capitalist Dictatorship as a
      Cultural System   206
  3   Positive Definition and Specification of Capitalist Dictatorship as a
      Cultural System   211
  4   Forms and Agents of Capitalist Dictatorship as a Cultural
      System   214
  5   Indicators and Proxies of Capitalist Dictatorship as a Cultural
      System   218
    5.1   *Suppression of Artistic and Cultural Liberties and Devaluation
          of the Arts and Culture*   219
    5.2   *Extreme and Compulsory Religiosity*   223
    5.3   *Obstruction and Suppression of Scientific Progress and
          Freedom*   226
    5.4   *Persistence of Widespread Religious Superstitions*   234

6 **Degrees of Capitalist Dictatorship for Contemporary Societies**   241
  1   Summary and Specification of Societal Indicators of Capitalist
      Dictatorship   241
    1.1   *Economic Indicators*   241
    1.2   *Political Indicators*   246
    1.3   *Civil-Society Indicators*   249
    1.4   *Cultural Indicators*   252

2   Measures of Capitalist Dictatorship   255
     2.1   *Economic Measures*   255
     2.2   *Political Measures*   260
     2.3   *Civil-Society Measures*   264
     2.4   *Cultural Measures*   267
3   Calculation of the Degrees of Capitalist Dictatorship   270
4   Degrees of Capitalist Dictatorship for Western and Comparable
     Societies   273

7 **Conclusion**   296

Appendix 1   Capitalist Dictatorship in the Literature   319
Appendix 2   Data on Capitalist Dictatorship Measures   342
References   422
Index   449

Acknowledgements

I thank Prof. David Fasenfest for giving his generous and helpful editorial assistance, advice and time.

Figures and Tables

Figures

1   Degrees of capitalist dictatorship, OECD countries   280
2   Indexes of liberal/capitalist democracy, OECD countries   283

Tables

1   Capitalist dictatorship as a total social system   12
2   Capitalist/liberal democracy as a total social system   13
3   Features of capitalist dictatorship and its social systems   14
4   Economic forms and agents of capitalist dictatorship   23
5   Economic indicators and proxies of capitalist dictatorship   52
6   Political forms and agents of capitalist dictatorship   106
7   Political indicators and proxies of capitalist dictatorship   116
8   Forms and agents of capitalist dictatorship as civil society   177
9   Indicators and proxies of capitalist dictatorship as civil society   188
10   Forms and agents of capitalist dictatorship as a cultural system   215
11   Indicators and proxies of capitalist dictatorship as a cultural system   218
12   A summary of the above measures of capitalist dictatorship   271
13   Measures and degrees of capitalist dictatorship, OECD countries   274
14   Ranking in capitalist dictatorship by average degrees, OECD countries   281
15   Indexes of capitalist/liberal democracy, OECD countries   282
16   Ranking in capitalist/liberal democracy by average indexes, OECD countries   290
A1   Trade union density and inverse, OECD countries, 2017 or nearest year   342
A2   Collective bargaining coverage and inverse, OECD countries, 2017 or nearest year   344
A3   Works councils and councils' inverse, OECD countries, various years   346
A4   Board-level employee representation (BLER) and inverse, OECD countries, 2019 or nearest year   348
A5   Share of top one percent of wealth and wealth concentration scores, OECD countries, 2016 or nearest year   350
A6   Gini coefficient on disposable household income and income inequality scores, OECD countries, 2018 or latest available   352
A7   General poverty rates after taxes and transfers, age group 17–66 years, and general poverty scores, OECD countries, 2018 or latest available   354

A8   Child poverty rates after taxes and transfers, age group 0–17 years, and child poverty score OECD countries, 2018 or latest available   356

A9   Average annual hours actually worked per worker and annual work hours scores, OECD countries 2018 or latest available   358

A10   Statutory minimum and collectively agreed paid annual leave and vacation inverse, OECD countries 2016 or latest available   360

A11   Real GDP per hour, hourly wages (US dollars) and labor exploitation rates and scores, OECD countries, 2016   362

A12   Coefficients of strictness of employment protection, individual dismissals (regular contracts) and protection inverse, OECD countries, 2014 or latest available   364

A13   Unemployment benefits, net replacement rates in unemployment (single person without children, duration of 60 months), and benefit inverse, OECD countries, 2018 or latest available   366

A14   Government spending on social protection as % of GDP and social protection inverse, OECD countries, 2018 or latest available   368

A15   Voter turnout, parliamentary elections, as % of voting age population, and voter turnout inverse, OECD countries, 2019 or most recent elections   370

A16   Voice and accountability ranking and voice inverse, OECD countries, 2018   372

A17   Constraints on government powers and constraints inverse, OECD countries, 2018   374

A18   Electoral process and political pluralism indexes and inverse, OECD countries, 2019   376

A19   Political stability and absence of violence/terrorism, percentile ranks and inverse, OECD countries, 2018   378

A20   Rule of law percentile ranks and inverse, OECD countries, 2018   380

A21   Control of corruption percentile ranks and inverse, OECD countries, 2018   382

A22   Open government factor scores and inverse, OECD countries, 2018   384

A23   Prison population rates (per 100,000) and scores, OECD countries, 2019   386

A24   Death sentences and executions numbers and scores, OECD countries, 2018   388

A25   Political terror scale and scores, OECD countries, 2018 or nearest year   390

A26   Military expenditure as a percentage of GDP and scores, OECD countries, 2019   392

A27   Personal freedom indexes and inverse, OECD countries, 2017   394

A28   Civil liberties indexes and inverse, OECD countries, 2019   396

A29   World Press freedom indexes and scores, OECD countries, 2019   398

A30   Fundamental human rights factor and inverse scores, OECD countries, 2018   400

A31   National privacy rankings, indexes and inverse, OECD countries, 2007   402

A32   Global Peace Index and peace inverse score, OECD countries, 2019   404

A33   Death penalty for drug offenses, OECD countries, 2018   406

A34   Share of drug offenders of total prisoners, estimates, OECD countries, 2019   408

A35   Government spending on culture as % of GDP and inverse, 2018 or latest available   410

A36   Beliefs in 'God', OECD countries, various years   412

A37   Importance of religion In daily life, OECD countries, 2018   414

A38   Daily prayer, OECD countries, 2018   416

A39   Public acceptance of evolution and evolution inverse, OECD countries, various years   418

A40   Belief in the existence of 'Satan', OECD countries, various years   420

CHAPTER 1

Introduction

> Outgrowing ... capitalist dictatorships
>
> —MANCUR OLSON (2000)

∴

1 The Concept of Capitalist Dictatorship

As the opening citation[1] suggests, 'capitalist dictatorships' are a reality and need to be outgrown, along with all others.[2] However, this is the only known explicit mention of capitalist dictatorship in the scholarly literature, although its concept is often implied in sociology and related social science such as economics. In addition, the concept is implicit through its equivalents or essential elements such as 'plutonomy' or the concentration of wealth and power in some non-academic analyses and among certain segments of the capitalist class concerned about these tendencies.[3]

This book is precisely a study of capitalist dictatorship: of its social systems, dimensions, forms and indicators. It seeks to introduce, expand and establish what is still a rarely employed, mostly unknown or latent concept and term in the sociological and related literature and perhaps to popularize it beyond to become more used and better known. It aims to contribute to making

---

1 Even a neoclassical economist like Olson (2000) urges 'outgrowing' not only 'communist' but also 'capitalist dictatorships' and generally examines the relations between 'capitalism, socialism and dictatorship' (see also Sandler 2001).
2 Segal (2000, p. 569) suggests that 'all dictatorships are equally bad'.
3 Kapur, Macleod and Singh (2005) observe that the 'U.S., UK, and Canada are the key Plutonomies—economies (dominated) by the wealthy', especially that the 'U.S.is a Plutonomy' that is an apparent synonym for plutocracy as a particular form of capitalist dictatorship and more broadly non-democracy. In addition, the prominent economist Frank (2007) embraces and redefines this notion of 'Plutonomy' as a 'country that is defined by massive income and wealth inequality', adding that according to this definition, 'the U.S. is a Plutonomy, along with the U.K., Canada and Australia'. Further, the US Patriotic Millionaires state that '"Proud 'traitors to their class', members of the Patriotic Millionaires are high-net worth Americans, business leaders, and investors who are united in their concern about the destabilizing concentration of wealth and power in America'.

capitalist dictatorship as a matter of course and a generalized concept in the academic literature and partly public discourse as are dictatorships in general because it is, after all, a special case of the latter. In so doing, the book opens a Pandora's box of capitalist dictatorship, which encloses and hides the latter as a non-entity, impossibility theorem and taboo, as most of orthodox, especially 'libertarian' economics treats this mutation of capitalism. It does this in light of the observed resurgence of capitalist dictatorship or its equivalents in some Western and comparable societies and many non-Western countries during recent times, most recently after the 2016 US Presidential elections. Therefore, the book captures and does full justice to an emergent, salient and, as in the US post-2016, predominant reality of contemporary society. Specifically, it captures and does justice to capitalism's mutation into capitalist dictatorship and related authoritarian, typically conservative-fascist or radical-right and theocratic, regimes in some Western and comparable societies such as OECD countries, just as in the non-Western world. In this respect, this book represents both a document and product, a witness and reflection of the social space and time, especially OECD countries, post-2016.

The shadow of capitalist dictatorship in the scholarly literature and beyond may seem at first glance unlikely, surprising and incongruous in light of the recent triumph of capitalism over its alternatives and its typical association, especially within Western societies like the US and Great Britain with democracy. This association yields the notion of capitalist democracy as the presumed rule with hardly any undemocratic aberrations in these societal settings.[4] Nevertheless, the implicit idea of capitalist dictatorship persists or reappears as a certain undercurrent—below and versus that of capitalist democracy—in parts of the scholarly literature and among some non-academic analysts and members of the capitalist class. In this sense, capitalist dictatorship becomes a latent concept that is less known and relevant than capitalist democracy and non-capitalist dictatorships with which most neoclassical, particularly 'libertarian', economics continues, along with non-academics and the capitalist class, to preoccupy despite their effective extinction or comparative rarity.

The problem is that social science, particularly economics, does not study capitalist dictatorship in a sufficient and satisfactory amount and fashion comparable to studying non-capitalist dictatorships. When some economists

---

4 For instance, Acemoglu and Robinson (2006a), Arrow (1969), Fearon (2011), Morck, Wolfenzon, and Yeung (2005), Frey and Stutzer (2010) adopt and focus on the notion of 'capitalist democracy'.

explicitly employ the expression 'capitalist dictatorships'[5] and propose 'over-growing' them along with their 'communist' counterparts they do not define and analyze the first, instead centering and elaborating on the second even if these are extinct or rarified after the early 1990s. Other economists admit to the existence of 'noncommunist dictatorships' and 'noncommunist dictators' of which capitalist dictatorships and dictators are primary cases, but do not define and study the latter, aside from partial and implicit exceptions.[6]

Most neoclassical economists consider capitalist and more generally non-communist dictatorships and dictators a lesser evil, minor disturbance or rarity compared to their non-capitalist variants. Still, using the term 'capitalist dictatorships' or its synonyms and admitting their existence is telling of an actual phenomenon and its reluctant recognition by some staunch theorists of capitalism. The latter more precisely means for these economists laissez-faire unregulated and inegalitarian capitalism as the Panglossian world versus regulated welfare capitalism that especially Chicago-style US economics opposes and equates with 'European' socialism.[7]

In addition, many other economists while not explicitly employing the expression imply or approximate the concept of capitalist dictatorship in expressions such as autocracy, dynasty, oligarchy, plutocracy, plutonomy, kleptocracy, military and other juntas and related phenomena within capitalism. Others alert to the concept more broadly by the process of extreme concentration of wealth and power, compulsion, oppression, and encompassing domination by capital over non-capital social strata such as labor, as do even some members of the capitalist class.

Further expressions conveying the concept include dictatorial, authoritarian, undemocratic, predatory, robber, mafia, crony and similar elements and forms of capitalism. In this respect, capitalist dictatorship as an implicit concept and partial reality becomes an undercurrent beneath capitalist democracy, albeit not established and studied as non-capitalist dictatorships, in parts

---

5 In addition to Olson's reference to 'capitalist dictatorships', Lindbeck (1971) refers to 'non-communist dictatorships' and Mulligan, Gil and Sala-i-Martin (2004) to 'noncommunist dictators' (see also, Acemoglu and Robinson 2013; Acemoglu, Egorov, and Sonin 2018; Besley and Kudamatsu 2006; Rajan and Zingales 2004; Rodrik 1999; Sen 1995).

6 Such exceptions include Hirschman (1977), Hodgson (1999), Sen (1999) and Solow, Budd, and Weizsacker (1987).

7 They thereby follow early hardcore pro-capital economistic 'libertarians' Mises, Hayek and Friedman advocating laissez-faire capitalism as what Merton (1968) ironically calls the Panglossian 'best of all possible worlds' and condemning the welfare state, including Scandinavian social democracy as well as the American 'New Deal', as the 'road to serfdom' (in Hayek words).

of economics. The latter especially involves sociologically minded social and institutional economics and political economy in the modern meaning, as distinct from purist and apologetic economics[8] such as Chicago-style 'libertarianism' where capitalist dictatorship is a non sequitur, non-entity and taboo and only non-capitalist dictatorships are a legitimate notion, matter and exist.

While partly admitting it as a latent concept and occasionally an expression, modern economics does not sufficiently and satisfactorily study capitalist dictatorship. First, it treats the latter as a lesser problem and secondary phenomenon compared to non-capitalist dictatorships not only when they exist and are prominent as before the 1990s, but even when becoming extinct or rare and impertinent especially in Europe since the 1990s after the collapse of communism, instead obsessing with the latter.[9]

Much of the economic literature omits or downgrades capitalist dictatorship to comparative irrelevance and continues, as does particularly 'libertarianism',

---

8 Knight (1923, p. 589) uses the term 'apologetic economics' and Schumpeter (1956, p. 12) the expression pure 'market economics'. Knight (1923, p. 589) states that in the 'conditions of real life no possible social order based upon a laissez-faire policy can justify the familiar ethical conclusions of apologetic economics'. Specifically, Knight (1960, p. 34) alerts that if wealth distribution in capitalism 'is made arbitrary to any large degree', the result is that 'general social freedoms will then undoubtedly contract or disappear'. For his part Schumpeter (1950, p. 298; 1956, p. 115), while describing democracy and capitalism as 'twins' and characterizing the view that 'true democracy' is impossible in the capitalist order as 'an obvious overstatement', notes the failure of 'bourgeois society' to fulfill some preconditions for functioning of the 'democratic method' and the 'apparent ease' of 'bourgeois democracy' in some situations to surrender to 'dictatorship'. For instance, he observes that in capitalism 'in some cases political life all but resolved itself into a struggle of pressure groups and in many cases practices that failed to conform to the spirit of the democratic method have become important enough to distort its *modus operandi*' (Schumpeter 1950, p. 298). So, Schumpeter (1950, p. 298) concedes that 'capitalism is rapidly losing the advantages it used to possess' with respect to democracy so that 'bourgeois democracy which is wedded to that ideal of the state has for some time been working with increasing friction. In part this was due to the fact that (the) democratic method never works at its best when nations are much divided on fundamental questions of social structure'. Yet, displaying his old pro-capitalist instinct he laments that the bourgeoisie 'did not produce a successful political stratum of its own' (Schumpeter 1950, p. 298), which appears an odd statement even within Pareto's anti-Marxian framework in which this class not only produced but constituted itself such a stratum, namely plutocracy as the new aristocracy or oligarchy, simply elite, of capital. At any rate, Schumpeter (1950, p. 298) almost in despair concludes that 'all these facts together seem to suggest a pessimistic prognosis for this type of democracy' and explain the 'apparent ease with which in some cases it surrendered to dictatorship'.
9 Some examples in contemporary economics are Acemoglu and Robinson (2006a), Glaeser and Shleifer (2002), Kornai (2000), Lucas (2009), McGuire and Olson (1996), and Olson (2000).

to make a drama of and be obsessed with communist and other non-capitalist dictatorships even when these are essentially extinct or so scarce and unimportant that are hardly worthy of sustained theorizing or studying. On this account, it deserves the label of 'apologetic economics' by both the fallacy of omission through dogmatic exoneration of capitalism from actual or potential dictatorship and that of commission via the continued obsession with and attack on what is practically the ghost of communist dictatorships (equivalent to beating a dead horse or strawmen).

Second, it continues to do so even in the face of the persistence, expansion and intensification of certain elements, forms or proxies of capitalist dictatorship, such as oligarchy and plutocracy in contemporary societies, including some Western and many non-Western countries, precisely after the demise of most non-capitalist dictatorships.[10]

Third, in historical terms, the economics literature that admits the concept mostly regards capitalist dictatorship or its equivalents as a short and transient phenomenon characteristic only for early capitalism and disappearing during its mature phases. Therefore, it regards capitalist dictatorship as a long-term non-entity in a variation of the 'end of history' (or Hollywood-style happy end[11]) in the Western world, especially the US and Great Britain. Fourth, in comparative terms and as a corollary, it considers capitalist dictatorship almost exclusively a non-Western system by relegating it to the third world and, as 'libertarianism' does, ruling it out as non-existent and even impossible among contemporary Western societies, especially the US and Great Britain. Alternatively, it asserts that in these societies 'capitalist democracy' reasserts itself, prevails and as 'self-enforcing' lasts into infinity.[12] In view of these and related treatments, aside from some pertinent but implicit exceptions, much of economics is unable or unwilling to properly study capitalist dictatorship as a legitimate concept and increasingly manifest and salient phenomenon in contemporary Western and other societies

---

10   For the identification of oligarchy and plutocracy or 'plutonomy' and related phenomena in contemporary Western societies, especially the US and to some extent other Anglo-Saxon countries, see Formisano (2015), Frank (2007), Kapur, Macleod and Singh (2005), Piketty (2014), Pryor (2002 and Stiglitz (2012).

11   Some examples of such views are Acemoglu and Robinson (2006a), Fearon (2011), Rajan and Zingales (2004).

12   See Acemoglu and Robinson (2013), Fearon (2011), Morck et al. (2005), Rajan and Zingales (2004).

during recent times, particularly America post-2016 and to some degree Britain after Brexit.[13]

Like economics but more satisfactorily, sociology recognizes the concept of capitalist dictatorship, even though does not fully establish and widely use the term. Some contemporary sociologists use such expressions as 'a dictatorial business class' linked with a 'hyperactive police and penal state' as the coercive instrument of its assumed dictatorship with special reference to the US, as well as 'workplace dictatorships' and 'authoritarian firms' within modern capitalism.[14] Other sociologists employ substantively equivalent notions or expressions like 'despotism', 'tyranny' and 'totalitarianism', along with coercion, constraints on freedom, and repression, with reference to contemporary capitalism, especially its unrestrained, laissez-faire ('neoliberal') variation in the US, Great Britain and a lesser degree elsewhere.[15]

More broadly, among earlier sociologists, Mannheim especially envisions and actually experiences during interwar times the possibility of 'dictatorship' in capitalism under certain conditions such as the capitalist class' own devices for waging and winning class struggle proving 'insufficient'. His contemporary Schumpeter holds a similar view but from a premise of the sufficiency of 'bourgeois democracy' despite its 'apparent ease' to surrender to 'dictatorship'. Specifically, Mannheim predicts that such dictatorship will assume the form of fascism, which he characterizes as the 'exponent of bourgeois groups' aiming to substitute 'one ruling group for another within the existing class arrangements', and points to Mussolini praising capitalism in the manner of social Darwinism as the 'choice of the fittest' and 'not just a system of oppression'. Mannheim[16] implies that fascism, after some initial, transient and superficial or

---

13   Observations of these tendencies are in Bonikowski (2016), Garrido (2017), Gorman and Seguin (2018), Hahl, Minjae and Zuckerman (2018), Jouet (2017), Kranton and Sanders (2017) and Lamont (2018).

14   Wacquant (2002, p. 1521) identifies 'a dictatorial business class' and a 'hyperactive police and penal state' in the US and Wright (2013, pp. 6–7) alerts to 'workplace dictatorships' and 'authoritarian firms' in modern, especially American, capitalism.

15   Such examples among sociologists are Bourdieu (1998), Burawoy (2005), Dahl (1985), Dahrendorf (1979), Kristal (2010), Martin and Dixon (2010), Piven (2008), Sutton (2013) and Tilly (2000).

16   Mannheim (1936, p. 143) envisions and in fact personally witnesses that when the political mechanisms 'devised by the bourgeoisie for carrying out the class struggle (e.g. parliamentarianism) prove insufficient (then) a dictatorship becomes possible' (see also Kettler and Meja 1984). Mannheim therefore both echoes and generalizes or updates Marx's prior historical observations of 'bourgeois dictatorship' or the 'dictatorship of the bourgeois republicans', for example, in France during 1848. In this regard, Mannheim seems the proximate inventor of capitalist dictatorship as a general and modern sociological concept and Marx the identifier of it as a particular and distant historical occurrence.

nominal anti-capitalist 'socialist' overtones by Mussolini and Hitler's 'national socialism'.[17] represents ultimately a variant of dictatorial capitalism, a merged capitalist-conservative 'right' dictatorship.

Later sociological and other research vindicates Mannheim's prediction and personal experience in this regard. Mannheim witnesses Hitler's 1933 promised 'broad coalition' of the conservative right with major German capitalists such as Krupp, Thyssen and others. The latter financed the rise of Nazism to counter democratic socialism or social democracy and liberal democracy, just as capitalist firms benefited from their Nazi connections through the stock market as the essence of modern capitalism, which Nazism preserved despite its 'national socialism' pretensions. In addition, Mannheim's contemporary Polanyi implicitly identifies capitalist/fascist dictatorship as the totalitarian 'solution' to the systemic breakdown of laissez-faire capitalism, and Moore implies it as the outcome of the latter moving through the conservative 'reactionary' political phase to eventuate in fascism.[18]

---

17 Gastil (1989, p. 4) comments that 'it is surprising how many well-informed persons believe that since the 'German Democratic Republic' also uses the term democracy in its label, we must include regimes of this type within our definition. It would be like saying that since the German fascists called their party 'National Socialist', discussions of socialism must use definitions that would include the Nazis'. The above implies that 'National Socialism' had as much to do with socialism as the 'German Democratic Republic' did with democracy—almost nothing or approximately a minimum. This especially applies to its later stages and once seizing power, as after 1933, and then launching persecution of socialists or social democrats and labor unions, while allying with capitalists like Krupp et al. who financed its rise to power and merging with conservatism through Hitler's 'broad coalition of the right', as Ferguson and Voth (2008, p. 105) note. Also, Mann (2004, p. 177) finds that 'like the Italian fascists, the Nazis actually seized (state) power with help from the country's elites' involving both capitalists and traditional conservatives, with Nazism presenting itself as the 'new conservatism'. See also Blinkhorn (2003), Burawoy (2005), Riley (2005), Riley and Fernández (2014), and Satyanath, Voigtländer, and Voth (2017).

18 Polanyi (1944, p. 239) considers fascism to be the 'process of the extirpation of all democratic institutions, both in the industrial and in the political realm' and so a dictatorial resolution of the impasse' of laissez-faire capitalism by its 'reform' rather than its supersession, thus raising and operating de facto as capitalist dictatorship. Moore (1993, pp. xvii-xxiii, 413) finds that under certain conditions capitalism 'culminate(s) in fascism' by passing through conservatism such as 'reactionary political forms'. Mann (2004, p. 237) registers that 'fascism diffused widely—not only as a distinct movement, but also as a corrosive radical force within more conservative authoritarian regimes' and that authoritarians during the interwar period formed 'a fractious family' of reactionary (conservative), corporatist (capitalist), and fascist members' seeking 'overall dominance'. Mann (2004, p. 353) concludes that fascists were members of the 'forward surge of a broader family of authoritarian rightists who swept into power across one-half of interwar Europe, plus a few swaths in the rest of the world', and so fascism part of 'authoritarian rightism' as

Overall, like political and social economists, most sociologists refrain from explicitly using and formally establishing the expression capitalist dictatorship and instead imply, intimate or anticipate the concept through identical or similar expressions. These expressions include especially authoritarian, undemocratic capitalism, including oligarchy and plutocracy within the latter, extreme concentration of wealth and power, coercion, oppression, and comprehensive domination by capital over non-capitalist social strata, and the like. Going further, this book aims to introduce, establish and generalize capitalist dictatorship not just as a latent concept but as an explicit expression in sociology so that sociologists can use it as commonly and routinely as the terms, capitalist democracy and non-capitalist dictatorships.

By contrast to economics, even if not using and establishing the explicit expression sociology approaches capitalist dictatorship in a more complete and satisfactory manner. Thus, it rectifies the four deficiencies of economics' treatment of capitalist dictatorship. First, considers capitalist dictatorship, as theoretically relevant as non-capitalist dictatorships. Second, it takes account of the persistence or resurgence and prevalence of capitalist dictatorship and the demise or rarity of non-capitalist dictatorships. Third, it treats capitalist dictatorships as more than short, transient historical phenomena that arise in early capitalism and persist or reappear in its later phases. Fourth, it posits that capitalist dictatorships exist and identifies them in both Western and non-Western societies. Despite these comparative advantages over economics, but just like the latter, sociology features both a void and need of a systematic, explicit and elaborate study of *capitalist dictatorship* precisely so called. (An appendix considers in more details the place of capitalist dictatorship in the literature.)

The book aims to offer such a study that is according to the author's best of knowledge among the first in sociology and related social science. While building on the 'shoulders of giants' such as previous contributions from sociology and related literatures, the study is both formally and substantively novel, original and unique. Formally, it is such by its formulation as the 'study of capitalist dictatorship' that appears new in sociology and other social science. Conversely, it is not a study of capitalism or dictatorship—though with implications for both—but only of their peculiar conjunction into a capitalist type of the second or a dictatorial variant of the first. At the minimum, the

conservative-reactionary 'response to both general problems of modernity and particular social crises left by World War I'. In this sense, fascism emerged as totalitarian conservatism or 'rightism' intensifying the latter's intrinsic authoritarianism (see also Giddens 1979, pp. 144–5).

designation as its stands is atypical, new and rare in sociology and related literatures.

Substantively and more importantly, the book has the above features by virtue of being a sociological and thus holistic study, thus becoming novel, original and unique. This holds especially compared to the economics literature that usually avoids or lacks such studies in favor of claiming narrower 'economic origins of dictatorship' and neglecting the wider complex of non-economic determinants. In substantive theoretical terms, the study is integrative with respect to sociological and related theories. With respect to sociological theories, it is both a conflict and functionalist, coercion and integration, study and theory, including those of relevant classical and contemporary sociologists. With respect to related economic theories, it is both an orthodox or neoclassical and heterodox study and theory, including political economy in the modern sense.

2   A Sociological Study of Capitalist Dictatorship—General Outlines

Against the background of the literature and certain processes and events in contemporary society, notably post-2016 America and via contagion beyond, the following outlines a sociological conception of capitalist dictatorship in general terms. In this study, capitalist dictatorship constitutes a 'sociological system' in the sense of the total social system or society, just as capitalism does historically and empirically.[19] Generally, the sociological system is more comprehensive, complex and consequential than and incorporates economy as its integral element and thus subsystem, along with polity, civil society and culture as other subsystems. Accordingly, the study of capitalist dictatorship as a sociological system is more holistic and complete and thus realistic and satisfactory than economics' models. This holds compared to these models because they mostly exhibit economism through economic determinism, which the Chicago School, including its all-encompassing 'economic approach to human behavior', epitomizes.[20] Especially such a sociological study is preferable to economics' models that conceive capitalist dictatorship and its elements and

---

19 Classical sociologist-economist Pareto (1932, p. 1313) uses the expression 'sociological system' in the sense of that of society and Durkheim (1965, p. xxviii), Mauss (1967, p. 1), Parsons (1951, p. 190) and other sociologists 'total social system(s)', 'total society,' or 'total social phenomena'. In particular, Braudel (1979), Collins (1988) and Mills (1957) consider capitalism such a social system.

20 For direct or implicit criticisms of economism see Bourdieu (1998) and Piketty (2014).

forms, for example, autocracy and oligarchy, and non-capitalist dictatorships, as purely economic systems.[21] Relatedly, it is preferable because these models center on and overstate the 'economic origins of dictatorships' and by doing so overlook their non-economic conditions, aside from some pertinent exceptions.[22] The present study moving beyond its supposed exclusive or main economic origins hence studies capitalist dictatorship as the system of 'sociological factors'[23] spanning from ideology and polity to culture and religion.

Accordingly, such a study represents an application of sociological economics[24] to capitalist dictatorship and of theoretical, especially economic, sociology, as Pareto suggests with respect to pre-capitalist and capitalist dictatorships and elites qua aristocracies, oligarchies, plutocracies, and theocracies. It applies sociological economics and its equivalent economic sociology that considers the economy, including capitalism and its democratic and undemocratic types, a social structure, including an institutional arrangement, political entity, ideological blueprint and cultural pattern, rather than, as pure economics does, a purely economic mechanism and a set of markets. This is consistent with sociological economics or economic sociology as the study of institutions and other social structures and their consequences for the economy, which Durkheimian institutionalism epitomizes.[25] Economic sociology as defined contrasts with 'pure' market economics that neoclassical economists (for example, Schumpeter) define as the analysis of 'economic mechanisms' of which markets are presumably exemplars. Thus understood, sociological economics or institutionalist economic sociology provides the compelling theoretical grounds for studying capitalist dictatorship holistically as a broader and complex sociological system rather than only an economic system, as in economics' models if they acknowledge or imply it.[26] Even when they do, in comparative or geographic terms, these models mostly theoretically

---

21   Some examples of such economic conceptions are Acemoglu and Robinson (2006a), Besley and Kudamatsu (2006), Fearon (2011), Mulligan et al. (2004), and Morck et al. (2005).

22   Such exceptions include Hodgson (1999), Piketty (2014), Rodrik (1999) and Sen (1995).

23   Akerlof (2002) is the probably the most prominent, consistent and explicit among contemporary economists in incorporating sociological factors and assumptions in economic analysis.

24   See also Collins (1986) and Hodgson (2000).

25   On institutional definitions of economic sociology and generally institutionalism, see also Boulding (1957), Fligstein (2001), Granovetter (2017), Merton (1998), Parsons (1935), Rutherford (2001), Schumpeter (1954), and Swedberg (1991, 1998).

26   For some earlier economists' broader insights into capitalist and related dictatorship as a social system see Mitchell (1917), Wieser (1967) and in part Schumpeter (1950).

exorcise capitalist dictatorship from and construe it as non-existent in Western capitalism and relegate it and regard it as unique only to non-Western countries such as third-world autocracies, oligarchies, military dictatorships and other pro-capital 'dictatorial regimes'.[27]

The holistic sociological study of capitalist dictatorship remedies these and related deficiencies, including extra-scientific ingredients, of its economic models, especially overtly ideological 'libertarian' economics as the foremost apologetics of unrestrained capitalism even in its dictatorial and other authoritarian modalities. It does this by studying this phenomenon as a total dictatorial social system,[28] including an economic system, political regime, peculiar civil society and cultural pattern, within the framework of contemporary global capitalism. In consequence, it studies capitalist dictatorship as a such system existing and functioning within both Western and non-Western capitalism, thus with a comparatively wider domain and longer life cycle in contemporary society than its narrow economic models suppose. The study

---

27   Especially, 'libertarian' economics such as the Chicago School categorically denies that capitalist dictatorship, including autocracy/dynasty and oligarchy/plutocracy, exists or even could and did ever exist within Western, especially American, capitalism, instead obsessing with dead 'communist dictatorships. It does this because of its establishing an invariant equation of the latter with democracy and 'freedom' (Friedman 1982; Hayek 1991; Lucas 2009; Simmons 1951; also, Kornai 2000). Moreover, going beyond some other economists, by universalizing such an equation to all societies, 'libertarian' economics denies the existence of capitalist dictatorships in non-Western, third world countries. These include South America's, particularly Chile under 'free market' military dictatorship that it reportedly helped install and zealously supported, including Friedman's and Hayek's personal visits of support for their 'free-market' dictator Pinochet (Barber 1995). To that extent, these models of dictatorship from economics manifest an analytical bias, distortion and unrealism, as well as seemingly, as with especially the Chicago School, pro-Western ideological commitment, pro-capital and conservative 'libertarian' partisanship (Krugman 2009; Palley 2006; Tirole 2015; Tilman 2001). Further, they expound or endorse overt or covert ethnocentrism, nationalism and imperialism, including 'Americanism' (Beck 2000; also, Lipset 1955). Historically, by so doing they continue or revive orthodox economics' reported role of an apologetics for laissez-faire, especially unrestrained, plutocratic American, capitalism, and most economists as 'servants' of capitalist power in America and other Western societies during the Cold War (e.g., the Kuznets thesis of decreasing economic inequality in these) and before. This period includes the time prior to and during the Great Depression when Keynes and Keynesians identity and deplore various classical and neoclassical pro-capital 'apologists' (Bowles 1974; Bowles and Gintis 2000; Piketty 2014; Samuelson 1994).

28   Dewey (1940) already uses the expression 'a dictatorial (social' system' to denote 'fascism or authoritarianism', particularly the 'German system' for 'Nazism'. Frey and Stutzer (2010) distinguish 'a dictatorial' social-political system from 'democratic' and 'authoritarian' systems.

thereby transcends the narrow economic models that construe this phenomenon as a mere 'third-world' economy or even deny it altogether and absolve
Western capitalism from autocratic, oligarchic, plutocratic and more broadly
authoritarian tendencies, as erupting in America and via contagion other societies post-2016.

In structural terms, the holistic study of capitalist dictatorship and more
broadly authoritarian capitalism as a sociological system incorporates certain
elements as partial systems existing and operating in interaction and reciprocal reinforcement, with some variations. In short, they form component
social systems or subsystems of capitalist dictatorship in interconnection
and mutual reinforcement. The first social system of capitalist dictatorship
is an authoritarian, coercive and inegalitarian economy, including industrial
non-democracy in capitalism. The second social system is an authoritarian,
repressive and exclusionary polity, or political non-democracy in capitalism.
The third social system is an illiberal and repressive civil society, including suppression of individual liberty. The fourth social system is an irrational and anti-
rationalist culture, including suppression of cultural freedom.

The preceding hence form four respective economic, political, civil-society
and cultural subsystems of capitalist dictatorship as a total social system.

The subsystems of capitalist dictatorship contrast with those of capitalist or
more precisely liberal democracy as a total social system. These latter are, first,
a democratic economy, including industrial democracy, second, democratic
polity or political democracy, third, liberal civil-society, including preservation
of individual liberty, and four liberal, rationalistic culture including protection
of cultural freedom. While the remainder of the book centers on the subsystems of capitalist dictatorship, it occasionally contrasts them with those of
capitalist or liberal democracy.

TABLE 1   Capitalist dictatorship as a total social system

Economy	Polity
authoritarian, coercive, inegalitarian economy (industrial non-democracy)	authoritarian, repressive, exclusionary polity (political non-democracy)
Civil society	Culture
illiberal and repressive civil society (suppression of individual liberty)	irrational and anti-rationalist culture (suppression of cultural freedom)

TABLE 2   Capitalist/liberal democracy as a total social system

Economy	Polity
democratic economy	democratic polity
(industrial democracy)	(political democracy in capitalism)
Civil society	Culture
liberal civil-society	liberal, rationalistic culture
(preservation of individual liberty)	(protection of cultural freedom)

In formal terms, capitalist dictatorship represents a total social system by virtue of representing a totality of these specific economic and non-economic partial systems, as capitalism does. Substantively, it constitutes or approximates a totalistic, 'totalitarian' social system, as capitalism does in some views.[29] It is totalistic by constituting a totality of dictatorial subsystems spanning from economy and polity to civil society and culture. It thus has a virtually infinite scope of operation and control within society, extending beyond the economic sector to non-economic sectors and manifesting a high intensity in its adverse treatment of non-capitalist social strata.[30] Both formal and substantive characteristics of capitalist dictatorship conform to the pattern of most dictatorships. This is that they represent formally total social systems of economic and non-economic components and constitute substantively 'totalitarian' regimes with multiple dictatorial segments and an almost unlimited domain in society, including its economy and other domains, and to feature a high intensity of repression. At this point, as a total/totalistic social system capitalist dictatorship looks hardly different, new and exceptional in the context of dictatorships, past and present.[31]

This holds with prudent adaptations and secondary modifications that especially its Western instances or proxies perform by aiming to obscure or temper

---

29   Giddens (1981) and MacIver (1964) characterize capitalism as a 'totality' of social systems or elements. Marcuse (1960) and Mills (1957) consider capitalism a 'totalitarian' social system.

30   On this matter, see Beck (2000), Bourdieu (1998), Burawoy (2005), Cohen (2003), Giddens (1981) and Hodgson (1999).

31   For dictatorships overall, see Acemoglu and Robinson (2006a), Acemoglu et al. (2018), Adorno (1991), Arendt (1951), Binmore (2001), Giddens (1979), Moore (1993) and Riley and Fernández (2014).

TABLE 3   Features of capitalist dictatorship and its social systems

negative dimension, definition and specification of capitalist dictatorship
positive dimension, definition and specification of capitalist dictatorship
forms and agents of capitalist dictatorship
indicators and proxies of capitalist dictatorship

capitalist dictatorship's formal and especially substantive totality of scope, as well as its intensity. The reported exemplar is the American-style ideological, political and cultural, including especially religious, rationalizing, sanctifying and sweetening of capital's overwhelming systemic power, comprehensive control and domination and intense repression of non-capital social strata.[32] In theoretical terms, the proposition that capitalist dictatorship constitutes formally a total and substantively totalistic social system is consistent with holistic or multidimensional sociological frameworks. In these frameworks, democracy and dictatorship both represent encompassing social systems, but crucially differ in that the first is a totality of democratic subsystems and the second one of their opposites.

Finally, the present study defines, specifies and identifies each subsystem of capitalist dictatorship in certain relevant terms. These are negative and positive dimensions, definitions and specifications, forms and agents, and indicators and proxies. Such properties of capitalist dictatorship and its subsystems tend to be complementary, interrelated and mutually reinforcing, with certain variations. Negative and positive definitions and specifications of capitalist dictatorship's subsystems complement one another, and its forms and agents and its indicators and proxies interrelate with and reinforce each other, with some variations.

With the above in mind, the structure of the remainder of the book is as follows. Chapter 2 studies capitalist dictatorship as an economic system. Chapter 3 analyzes capitalist dictatorship as a political regime. Chapter 4 examines capitalist dictatorship in terms of civil society. Chapter 5 treats capitalist dictatorship as a cultural system. Chapter 6 estimates the degrees of capitalist dictatorship for contemporary Western and comparable societies such as OECD countries. The last chapter constitutes conclusion.

---

32   For these issues, see Beck (2000) and Wright (2013).

CHAPTER 2

Capitalist Dictatorship as an Economic System

The first and probably most apparent integral element or subsystem of capitalist dictatorship as a total/totalistic social system represents a coercive,
oppressive, inegalitarian and generally authoritarian economy within capitalism. In this respect, capitalist dictatorship appears, as its models from economics conceive it but mostly for non-Western societies, as a purely economic
system. However, the latter, as Pareto, Durkheim and other sociologists would
caution, does not exhaust it as a sociological system and represents only a part
of it, approximately a quarter of its equation, the other three parts being its
non-economic subsystems. This is important to emphasize because in a holistic sociological study capitalist dictatorship constitutes an economic system
having a definite scope of operation in the economy and a broader set of non-
economic systems, including a political regime, civil-society and culture, and
has an infinite domain in the rest of society.[1] The study acknowledges that
capitalist dictatorship most visibly and saliently—near-axiomatically given
the term—appears and functions as an economic system or mode of production, just as capitalism does.[2] Hence, it starts with the latter while balancing
economics' models' proclivity to conceive capitalist dictatorship or generally
capitalism in terms of economic determinism (economism) and disregard or
downplay its non-economic elements and factors.

1 Negative Definition and Specification of Capitalist Dictatorship

In terms of a negative dimension, definition and specification, capitalist
dictatorship constitutes a system of devaluation, negation and suppression
of economic freedom or agency for non-capital production factors or social
classes versus its affirmation and promotion for capital. Especially it depreciates, negates and suppresses collective freedom, organization, action and thus

---

1 For capitalist and related dictatorship as a social system, especially a political regime, see
   Bourdieu (1998), Burawoy (2005), Jacobs and Dirlam (2016), Murray (2017), Piven (2008),
   Wodtke (2016), and Wright (2013).
2 More broadly, Collins (1988, p. 352) remarks that the 'dominant mode of production' gives
   the 'name to a particular social formation' as 'capitalist' or other (see also Chase-Dun 1992;
   Habermas 1989; Parkin 1980; Popper 1973; Wright 2002).

power or 'power resources' for labor as a coerced, oppressed or subordinate production factor and social class, including union organizations, collective bargaining and worker participation in corporate governance, while exalting and protecting these properties for capital.

What therefore typifies capitalist dictatorship is that it treats principal production factors or social classes in capitalism in a differential, indeed opposite manner, by subjecting their non-capital types to a negative treatment in relation to capital. In Weber's words, it regards, indeed renders and maintains non-capital in the sense of labor as a 'negatively privileged', 'disprivileged' production factor or social class while privileging capital in this dual form in a positive manner. In this respect, it becomes a negative, unfavorable production regime or class system, almost pure negativity of productive processes and economic stratification from the experience, interests and standpoint of non-capital production factors in relation to capital.[3]

As a consequence of such an unbalanced, asymmetrical condition and treatment of production factors or classes, notable the disprivilege of labor, a negative defining core of capitalist dictatorship is the intrinsic absence or ultimate elimination of the balance or symmetry of freedom, agency and power between capital and non-capital. More precisely, this condition tends to disfavor non-capital, such as shifting away this balance from workers to employers in the US since Reaganism and reminiscent of the Gilded Age of unrestrained capital power over labor. By contrast, the presence of such a balance defines both economic and political democracy within capitalism, a power constellation that social democracy or welfare capitalism primarily demonstrates.

In Hobbesian terms, capitalist dictatorship negatively defined represents Leviathan for non-capital through an adverse condition and treatment of labor and systematic and severe coercion and repression of its freedom and action. While by contrast representing the state of nature or anarchy for capital, Leviathan in this regard includes the 'tyranny of the market' and the 'New Leviathan' of financial markets in some accounts and relatedly 'intolerable tyranny and violations of liberty'.[4]

---

3 Generally, Parsons (1949, p. 329) admits that 'everywhere that modern industrial society has existed there has been a class system in this sense', adding that 'there are, however, considerable variations from one society to another, particularly between the European versions of industrial capitalism and the American'. Furthermore, Dahrendorf (1959, p. 61) suggests that 'much of modern social history can be understood in terms of 'war' between 'citizenship rights' (which are equal rights) and the 'capitalist class system' (see also Steinberg 2003).

4 On this duality of anarchy for capital, Leviathan for non-capital, see Bourdieu (1998), Burawoy (2005), Habermas (2001), MacLean (2018), McDonnell (2017), Musgrave (1997), Sen

In democratic terms, capitalist dictatorship amounts to negative, non-existent democracy within capitalism, namely economic and political non-democracy, a system of negation and elimination of democratic freedoms in the economy and society.[5] In purely capitalist terms, it forms negative, pathological capitalism, even its terminal 'cancer stage' in some accounts.[6] This holds especially in relation to prevailing democratic or egalitarian welfare capitalism within contemporary Western society, above all Western Europe and within it Scandinavian/Nordic social democracies.[7]

In general, just as pre-capitalist dictatorships were to coerced, oppressed non-aristocratic social strata, capitalist dictatorship is, with secondary variations, a pure and total negativity—denial, adversity, indignity and mistreatment—for non-capital. This includes the imbalance of freedom, agency and power disprivileging labor and hence economic, political and social non-democracy within capitalism. The above holds, however, for capitalist dictatorship and not necessarily for capitalism as a whole. Indeed, it definitely does not hold for regulated and egalitarian or advanced welfare capitalism in most of Western Europe, especially what some earlier political economists propose as 'a rationally regulated social economy' in Scandinavia and early US institutional economists imply for America in the midst of the Great Depression.[8]

By contrast, compared to welfare capitalism, laissez-faire or unrestrained and inegalitarian capitalism represents an 'irrationally unregulated' economy. It exemplifies itself in the US, to some degree Great Britain and most third-world countries, such as South America, Africa, much of Asia, Islamic plutocratic theocracies, and Eastern Europe under capitalist oligarchy. Unrestrained capitalism manifests itself as 'economic anarchy' that is a facet of societal irrationalism by disprivileging and oppressing non-capital versus capital and in

---

(1999), Somers and Block (2005), and Steinmetz (2005), from a radical-right perspective, see Buchanan (1975).

5   For the relations between economic and political democracy, see Dahl (1985; also, Acemoglu and Robinson 2006a; Gompers, Joy, and Andrew 2003; Ellman and Pezanis-Christou 2010; Mulligan et al. 2004).

6   McMurtry (1999) diagnoses the 'cancer stage of capitalism'.

7   For Scandinavian/Nordic welfare capitalism, see Blanchard (2004), Glass, Simon, and Andersson. (2016), Kalleberg (2009), and Roemer and Trannoy (2016), with some qualifications for Sweden in Wright (2013).

8   An early Swedish political economist, Cassel (1928) proposes 'a rationally regulated social economy' in Scandinavia and the US institutional economist Commons (1931) implies the concept for America during the Great Depression.

that sense as capitalist dictatorship.[9] In Keynes' framework, laisses-faire capitalism is an irrational and even self-destructive economy because of its 'failure to provide for full employment' due its recurring catastrophic economic crises such as the Great Depression, the Great Recession and others. And it forms composite economic-sociological irrationalism because of what Keynes detects as its 'arbitrary and inequitable distribution of wealth and incomes' and consequently power, approaching capitalist dictatorship that shares the last property with pre-capitalist dictatorships.[10]

Furthermore, this primarily American and more broadly Anglo-Saxon model of capitalism epitomizes irrationalism in its own right irrespective of its comparison with 'a rationally regulated' capitalist economy. It does this by its tendency to not just economic self-destructiveness through such crises but even to non-economic, including military and environmental, self-destruction. During post and present times, its irrationalism includes especially potential 'mutually assured destruction' via offensive imperial wars and the huge and expanding US military-capitalist complex ('defense spending') and ultimately self-destructive militarism and aggressive nationalism. In addition, it involves the specter of 'environmental disaster' through causing catastrophic climate change, as by persisting in the use of 'dirty' versus 'clean' technology or resisting rational collective action to remedy the problem that it reproduces or aggravates.[11]

With regard of such self-destructiveness, laissez-faire American and similar capitalism resembles suicidal religious sects and cults in America and elsewhere. Its ultimate effects from military self-destruction to an environmental catastrophe, let alone catastrophic economic crises in the way of Great Depression/Recession, seem analogous to their Judgment Day 'sacrificial violence' and mass suicides. Indeed, it merges or allies with such groups, as through the uniquely American 'Christian Right' alliance between the capitalist rich and poor religious strata in revolt against liberal-secular democracy and scientific rationalism.

---

9   Keynes (1960, p. 305) and Parsons (1935, p. 427) use the word 'economic anarchy' and 'anarchism', respectively, for laissez-faire capitalism and Mannheim (1936, p. 127) detects and emphasizes 'complete irrationalism' in conservatism, including fascism.

10 Keynes (1960, p. 375) identifies 'two outstanding faults' of laissez-faire capitalism in 'its failure to provide for full employment and its arbitrary and inequitable distribution of wealth and incomes' (see also Allais 1997; Bourdieu 1998; Piketty 2014; Wright 2013).

11 On such economic and social self-destructiveness of laissez-faire American and similar capitalism, see Acemoglu and Yared (2010), Acemoglu et al. (2012), Frank (2007), Habermas (2001), Parsons (1935), Stern (2013), Schelling (2006), Steinmetz (2005), and Trigilia (2002).

Most importantly in the present context, laissez-faire capitalism inherently moves toward, as Keynes implies by the diagnosis of its 'arbitrary and inequitable distribution' of wealth and consequently power, and eventually turns into capitalist dictatorship, as later theorists suggest.[12] In any event, while not necessarily capitalism such as its regulated, egalitarian Western European versus its American and non-Western type, capitalist dictatorship represents an adverse economic system for non-capital production factors or social classes in respect of their freedom, organization, action and influence in the economy, just as pre-capitalist despotism did for non-aristocratic strata.

2   Positive Definition and Specification of Capitalist Dictatorship

In a positive dimension, definition and specification, capitalist dictatorship becomes a system of appreciation, affirmation and protection of economic freedom and agency, plus material resources ('economic power'), exclusively for capital versus non-capital—'free enterprise' in apologetic economics' and American terminology.[13] In particular, such a system includes appreciating, affirming and protecting exclusive and near-absolute collective freedom, action and power for capital, which it hence establishes, exerts and sustains as a dominant production factor or social class against non-capital. This includes capital organization in various powerful 'associations of capitalists' aiming to devaluate and suppress labor and to establish and sustain monopolistic control or oligopoly collusion, and its complete dominance in corporate governance through 'authoritarian firms' and 'workplace dictatorships'.[14] In this regard, capitalist dictatorship is an exclusively positive condition and treatment of capital, literally treating it, thus making and sustaining it as a 'positively privileged' social class in Weber's sense, as in the US South after slavery, versus non-capital classes as the opposite.[15] As a result, capitalist dictatorship forms the process of distribution, concentration, monopolization and exertion

---

12 Some of these theorists are Beck (2000), Bourdieu (1998), Perelman (2000), Piketty (2014), and Piven (2008).

13 For the praise of 'free enterprise', see Friedman (1982), Kornai (2000), and Rajan and Zingales (2004), for a skeptical sociological interpretation see Parsons (1967).

14 The term 'associations of capitalists' is from Clark (1892, p. 144) and terms 'authoritarian firms' and 'workplace dictatorships' from Wright (2013, pp. 6–7; see also Walker, Martin and McCarthy 2008; Wodtke 2016).

15 For the US South after slavery, see Acemoglu and Robinson (2006b, 2008), Amenta, Bonastia, and Caren (2001), Hoff and Stiglitz (2004), Lloyd (2012), Morck et al. (2005), and Ruef (2014).

of unconstrained and arbitrary power, alongside social status, and hence near-total domination by capital over non-capital in the economy. Such a process enfolds in conjunction and mutual reinforcement with the same processes with respect to wealth and income—their arbitrary and inequitable distribution and concentration. Taken together, the intertwined and self-perpetuating concentration of power and wealth in capital is the twin core of capitalist dictatorship positively defined and more broadly of unrestrained capitalism.

Consequently, the extreme imbalance, asymmetry of freedom, agency or power in favor of capital versus non-capital especially as collective agents positively defines and typifies capitalist dictatorship. Such an imbalance hence reveals the latter as the antithesis of economic as well as political democracy within capitalism. In Hobbes' terms, capitalist dictatorship positively defined manifests itself as the state of nature or the Hobbesian 'state of anarchy' for capital through its nearly absolute, unrestrained and arbitrary freedom approaching the figurative or literal 'license to kill', coerce and oppress, to monopolize and destroy competition, all under the guise of 'free enterprise'. In this sense, capitalist dictatorship epitomizes and resurrects rather than, as the defenders of unrestrained capitalism allege, overcome the 'dead hand of the past', including the property 'dead hand of the past generations'. Specifically, this involves resurrecting the 'dead past' of the 'law of the strongest' and the 'law of the jungle' that typifies the Hobbesian state of nature and its anarchy in the new form of 'capitalistic despotism',[16] along with that of inherited wealth/power and patrimonialism resurrected as patrimonial, inheritance-based capitalism.

More broadly, laissez-faire, unrestrained capitalism operates in accordance with and enforces the 'law of the strongest' or the jungle and thus represents economic anarchism. This explains why laissez-faire capitalism ultimately moves toward capitalist dictatorship and its equivalents, even if embellished with 'economic freedom' or free enterprise for capital as 'free' to coerce, oppress and exploit non-capital and impose monopoly. The difference is that what Pareto considers the new aristocracy of capital or plutocracy substitutes and ultimately incorporates (in Michels' words) the 'old master-caste', including the military caste and its warlords, to become the strongest in laissez-faire capitalism and the creator and enforcer of the 'law of the strongest' and the jungle within the latter turned into capitalist dictatorship. In short, laissez-faire

---

16   The 'law of the strongest' is from Durkheim (1965) and Mises (1957). In addition, the 'state of anarchy' is from Durkheim (1965), the 'dead past' from Mannheim (1936), the 'dead hand of the past' from Harrod (1956), the 'dead hand of the past generations' from Milanovic (2014) and Piketty (2014), the 'law of the jungle' from Kimeldorf (2013) and Mises (1957), and 'capitalistic despotism' from Wieser (1967).

capitalism is *pax capitalis*, hence 'laissez-faire authoritarianism' and ultimately capitalist dictatorship.[17]

Thus, Spencer's sociological evolution of military to industrial society, more precisely laissez-faire capitalism, seems actually—contrary to his expectations—one from the 'old master-caste' aristocratic to capital's plutocratic form of the 'law' of the jungle reportedly governing capital-labor conflict in American capitalism during the Gilded Age and since Reaganism. This is what the compounded military-capitalist complex, so 'military capitalism' in America indicates and indeed (as a US President alarmed in the early 1960s) poses a grave threat to democracy, by capitalism blending with militarism which Spencer, like Jefferson and Madison, could not predict. Relatedly, in Spencer's terms, this is an evolution from a military to a capitalist 'system of status' and 'coercion', rather than, as he predicts, from the first to the 'system of contract' and 'voluntary cooperation' that becomes a fiction in the sense of that between capital and labor in capitalist dictatorship and laissez-faire capitalism. This system of coercion involves its paternalistic form in the style of theocratic or moralistic Prohibition and its sequel through continuing alcohol prohibitions and restrictions such as Southern 'dry' states and the highest legal drinking age in the Western world and the Reagan Puritanical 'war on drugs' in America under religious extremism and conservatism.

In this sense, capitalist dictatorship positively defined and more broadly laissez-faire capitalism merely perpetuates, with prudent adaptations, and strongly resembles pre-capitalist despotism, including feudalism. Both systems function according to the 'law of the strongest' or the jungle, although the 'strongest' and so the creator/enforcer of this law is a different social stratum in either case. Just as pre-capitalist despotism and along with fascism, capitalist dictatorship looks as the positive rule of the 'strongest' after the model or image of the 'law of the jungle', as in American capitalism during the Gilded Age, since Reaganism and post-2016. Both economic systems, together with fascism, exalt and use as the first—and not last—resort physical, including military and other state, strength or what Weber calls 'naked force' against lower social classes, as in American Gilded-Age capitalism, during Reaganism and post-2016 times. (In this connection, Weber during his visit to America also identifies a 'naked plutocracy' in the sense of nakedly or literally purchasing power with 'mere money'.)

In democratic terms, as its pre- and non-capitalist versions, capitalist dictatorship represents positively an ersatz form or simulation and placebo of

---

17   *Pax capitalis* is from Ayres (1933).

economic and political democracy, an extreme system of non-democracy in the economy, just as a repressive regime in the polity. In capitalist terms, it self-evidently constitutes an authoritarian and anti-egalitarian modality of capitalism in contrast and opposition to democratic and egalitarian welfare capitalism within Western society, above all Western Europe and within it Scandinavian/Nordic social democracies.

In sum, with certain variations, capitalist dictatorship is a pure positivity or total appreciation, affirmation, privilege, wealth and honor for capital, including the severe imbalance of freedom, agency and power in its favor and economic, political and social, coercion and oppression, as pre-capitalist dictatorships were for the aristocratic class. In this respect, as pre-capitalist dictatorships did for the aristocratic class, capitalist dictatorship forms a purely, consistently and near-totally positive economic system for capital in terms of freedom, action and power in the economy, plus wealth and income. Capital never reigns more privileged and supreme than in capitalist dictatorship, as in its American variation during its 'golden' time, the Gilded Age with its 'naked plutocracy' that a US President deplores as the 'tyranny of mere wealth' and more recently since Reaganomics through its post-2016 plutocratic and autocratic reenactment.

3   Economic Forms and Agents of Capitalist Dictatorship

3.1   *Capitalist Autocracy*
In terms of its forms and agents, capitalist dictatorship represents a manifold and various economic system and a set of multiple and varying systems and actors. One of its forms and agents consists of autocracy and autocrats or the 'full autocratic power of the ruler' that arises and functions in capitalism.[18]

Historically, such a power is distinct from the prevalent pre-capitalist 'autocratic state' or 'autocratic regimes' in pre-capitalism and from their post-capitalist variations. Such autocratic power hence yields capitalist autocracy and autocrats as a particular form and agent of dictatorship within capitalism. In some statements, capitalist autocracy and autocrats while distinct from their pre-capitalist variants since the Roman Empire (Julius Caesar) display a certain continuity with the latter in that the 'President of the United States

---

18   Simmel (1950, p. 206) identifies the 'full autocratic power of the ruler' (also, Dal et al. 2017; Dixit, Grossman and Faruk 2000; Fearon 2011). Wieser (1967) notes that autocratic power operates within capitalism, as do Bourdieu (1998), Cole (2005), Gurvitch (1945), and Lee (2007).

TABLE 4   Economic forms and agents of capitalist dictatorship

---

capitalist autocracy and autocrats
capitalist d.nasty and dynastic families
capitalist plutocracy, oligarchy, and aristocracy/plutocrats, oligarchs and
aristocrats
secondary forms and agents of capitalist dictatorship
    capitalist kleptocracy and kleptocrats
    predatory, robber and mafia capitalism and capitalists
    capitalist police states
    capitalist military dictatorships and dictators
    capitalist theocracy and theocrats

---

acquires in certain conditions a power that makes him to all intents and purposes a dictator in the Roman sense'. This statement—aside from expressing
the reported animus to FDR and the New Deal—anticipates unwittingly the
post-2016 capitalist-autocratic demagogic and plutocratic replay of 'authoritarian politics'.[19]

Generally, what axiomatically defines capitalist autocracy is the dictatorial rule or regime in the economy and society of an individual extremely
wealthy ruler—as, with rare exceptions, most US Presidents have been since
the Gilded Age through post-2016—to be distinguished from non-wealthy or
historically pre- and non-capitalist rulers. Such a ruler exerts autocratic power
either single-handedly or more typically in association with a family and what
Simmel denotes an oligarchical clique' like 'old boy networks', as reportedly
pervasive and seemingly perpetual in the US South.[20]

More broadly, what defines and typifies capitalist autocracy is 'dictatorship
of the rich' in some definitions that contrast it to democracy as 'dictatorship
of the poor'.[21] In this context, capitalist autocracy is 'dictatorship of the rich'

---

19   Schumpeter (1965, pp. 96–7) refers to the prevalent pre-capitalist 'autocratic state' or
      'autocratic regimes' in pre-capitalism but implicitly denies the existence of such states
      or regimes in capitalism (also, McGuire and Olson 1996; North 1990; Olson 2000). This
      is what Schumpeter (1950, 296) states about the 'President of the United States' during
      WW II (see also Bonikowski 2016; Hahl et al. 2018; Lamont 2018; Redbird and Grusky 2016;
      Schilke and Rossman 2018).
20   For such closed social networks' in the US South and elsewhere, see Levy and Razin (2017),
      Mailath, Samuelson, and Shaked (2000), Ruef, Aldrich and Carter (2003).
21   Such definitions are in Acemoglu et al. (2018) and Besley and Kudamatsu (2006).

in the sense of an individual agent rather than a social group as representing other forms and agents of capitalist and pre-capitalist dictatorship such
as oligarchy, plutocracy, aristocracy, and dynasty. This demarcation avoids the
frequent conflation especially within economics of capitalist and pre- and
non-capitalist autocracy with aristocracy, oligarchy, plutocracy and dynasty
within capitalism and pre- and non-capitalism and generally dictatorship by
reducing the latter to the former. This is an unacceptable reduction of a set to
a subset committing an individualist fallacy so long as dictatorship can be not
only autocratic power through a single agent but also collective rule via class
and other group agents, for example, military dictatorships as mostly juntas
rather than personal.[22]

Thus understood, capitalist autocracy and autocrats amount to an opposite and opponents of economic and political democracy, although probably
not the most salient within contemporary Western society when compared
to collective, class forms and agents like oligarchy, plutocracy or plutocratic
aristocracy. Comparatively, capitalist autocracy hence typifies and prevails in
and autocrats are common for and rule many non-Western societies. The latter
consist of much of South America which Chile's Pinochet autocratic 'free market' (Chicago economics-style) dictatorship epitomizes historically and that in
Brazil does presently.[23] They also include post-socialist Eastern European and
non-European countries such as Hungary and Poland under conservative and
religious domination, Turkey under Islamic governance, Saudi Arabia and other
Gulf capitalist-theocratic states with their 'commonness of autocratic rule'.[24]

However, capitalist autocracy and autocrats are not a non-existent phenomenon and an extinct species within Western society. The latter involves the US
post-2016 and in part via contagion or confluence some other countries such
as in part Brexit Britain, along with Nazi Germany and fascist Italy and Spain as
autocratic merged capitalist-conservative dictatorships during interwar and to
some degree, as with the last country, postwar times.[25] In particular, this is what
some interwar laissez-faire economists like Schumpeter suggest—although

---

22 On military dictatorships as mainly collective or juntas, see Acemoglu, Egorov, and Sonin
    (2009).
23 For more on these non-European capitalist autocracies, see Acemoglu, Egorov, and Sonin
    (2012), Acemoglu and Robinson (2013), Huber and Stephens (2005), Kerrissey (2015),
    Kuran (2018), and Mueller (1996).
24 The observation is from Kuran (2004, 86).
25 On these autocratic capitalist dictatorships in fascist Europe, see Ferguson and Voth
    (2008), Friedman (1982), Riley (2005), and Riley and Fernández (2014).

probably driven by the anti-New Deal animus for wrong agents such as FDR and other liberal/Keynesian presidents—for the US Presidency. They suggest that the latter intrinsically or under certain conditions constitutes capitalist autocracy and so personal dictatorship resembling that of Roman emperors, as the description 'imperial presidency' indicates, including president-driven economic and militaristic imperialism or wielding proxy 'monarchical power' in the style of English monarchs. Following this account, it appears that most postwar US conservative presidents act as would-be autocrats and 'dictators' against whom the Constitution's celebrated best checks-and-balances become helpless or ineffective and who indeed exploit these supposed constraints as 'a technique of divide and rule' in a 'virtually dictatorial way' and during times of 'rigid (capitalist) dictatorship'. This is a pattern that Reagan et al. as 'uncompromising' and 'rigid extremists' and their successors post-2016 reportedly demonstrate. The post-2016 Presidency qualifies in some views as probably the most egregious instance of effective or potential capitalist autocracy through the personal 'authoritarian', populist and irrational rule of the 'lying demagogue' among Western societies and in American history after the Civil War and Tocqueville's visit.

The prevalence and visibility of capitalist and non-capitalist autocracies and autocrats in non-Western societies has probably misdirected many economists and some sociologists to reduce dictatorship and dictators and more broadly non-democracy to autocracy and autocratic rulers, including military ones. This has induced them to conflate autocracy and autocrats with, or overstate their importance in relation to, collective dictatorial forms and agents, notably oligarchy and plutocracy, oligarchs and plutocrats in these and Western countries. At any rate, autocracy and autocrats raising and operating within capitalism, including its Western and non-Western variations exemplify an individual form and personal agent of capitalist dictatorship from the US post-2016 through Brazil, Poland and Hungary to Turkey and Saudi Arabia and other Gulf states.

3.2   *Capitalist Dynasty*

The preceding anticipates another corollary form and agent of capitalist dictatorship—family and related dynasty and dynastic agents or 'despotism of dynastic usurpers' and 'dynastic leadership'. Frequently, capitalist dynasty emerges as an eventual extension of autocracy in capitalism, just as pre- and non-capitalist dynasties do as extensions of autocracies in pre- and non-capitalism. Dynastic families as 'usurpers' can arise as extended arms of autocrats descending from a certain privileged family and effecting the transmission of wealth, political power and social status across generations via a 'sequence of dynasties' in a 'long, dynastic horizon'.[26]

Conversely, capitalist and pre- and non-capitalist autocratic rulers often come from dynastic families and reproduce and expand dynastic leadership, property and wealth. This is a pattern that monarchies and even republics in capitalism and pre-capitalism exemplify, such as feudal and later royal dynasties and autocrats in England and their capitalist and presidential equivalents in America. In the latter reportedly dynasties are 'self-perpetuating' within a 'new plutocracy' and create a reservoir of potential demagogic autocrats or authoritarian rulers, as during post-2016 years.[27]

Hence, dynastic wealth and monopolistic closure is pervasive and chronic since the property and unrestrained power of the robber barons during the Gilded Age through their later and current heirs or analogues (including a self-proclaimed 'business genius' turned would-be 'total power' president). In this connection, one can adduce at least one instance of the sequence of dynasties. This is the succession of dynastic conservative-theocratic presidents resembling a 'nepotistic succession'[28] and thus the transmission and expansion of dynastic property, power and status in the US during postwar times—the 2001–2009 Presidency. This example evidently dispels as a 'myth' supposed 'American exceptionalism' in this regard. It contradicts the claim to America's exceptional absence of and 'freedom' from capitalist and other dynasty, autocracy, oligarchy, plutocracy, class structure overall and related undemocratic or inegalitarian phenomena such as lack of equal opportunity and of social mobility, which 'American exceptionalism' proponents relegate to the 'old world' of Europe.

While this extension of autocracy is usually limited in formal terms within the narrow or extended family of autocrats and relatively impertinent substantively, dynasty in capitalism assumes a partially primary-group character. In that sense, dynasty becomes the most elementary collective form of capitalist dictatorship or its proxy—indeed of what some neoclassical economists (Wieser) denote 'capitalistic despotism'—although it typically serves only as such an instrument or complement of a ruling autocrat already in power. Relatedly, when this autocratic rule ends with its agent's demise,

---

26   Wieser (1967, p. 405) points to the 'despotism of dynastic usurpers' and 'dynastic leadership'; related insights are found in Atkinson (1997), Cox (2007), Farhi and Werning (2007), Hällsten and Pfeffer (2017), and Kremer (1997), and Mueller and Philippon (2011).

27   For these and related tendencies in America post-2016 and earlier, see Bonikowski (2016), Hahl et al. (2018), Jouet (2017), Lamont (2018), Piketty (2014), and Stiglitz (2012).

28   'Nepotistic succession' is from Cox (2007, p. 95).

capitalist dynasty may begin as what Weber would call dynastic (and bureaucratic) routinization of autocratic charisma or a charismatic autocrat from a dominant family, thus as intergenerational familial transmission of autocracy within capitalism, as other dynasties do in pre- and non-capitalism. Capitalist dynasty develops as Clausewitz's style continuation of the politics of autocracy by other or identical means of coercion, oppression, exclusion and elite closure, thus dynastic families in dominance and wealth continuing the policy and inheriting the power and property of autocrats from a certain family. In short, the 'despotism of dynastic usurpers' within capitalism continues and extends that of single 'capitalistic despots' by the same or slightly different means.

On the other hand, dynasty and dynastic families in capitalism can be a stand-alone form and agent of capitalist dictatorship by not deriving from or not closely associating with autocracy and autocrats, but instead resulting from or linking with and developing and functioning within its larger collective forms and agents. Capitalist and other dynasty may result from the dissolution, dilution or fragmentation of aristocracy, oligarchy and plutocracy as such collective forms. This holds so long as what Mosca, Michels, and Pareto postulate and other sociologists imply as a certain strong tendency operates within capitalism, as well as in pre- and non-capitalism. The tendency consists in that the proportion of the ruling class/elite to the ruled tends to diminish with the size of the social-system and reach a dynastic and, under certain conditions, autocratic level, more broadly that of oligarchy. It generally consists in what Simmel calls the 'numerical insignificance of the ruling class'. For illustration, reportedly the ruling class in the form of a 'new plutocracy' in America eventually reduces itself to a small set of dynasties (500 or so families) that perpetuate themselves within it and even to personal demagogic authoritarian and populist rule after 2016. In short, if Mosca's sociological law is valid, 'plutonomy' moves toward capitalist dynasty and ultimately autocracy, as apparently happened in the US post-2016.

In addition, capitalist dynasty may ensue from internal conflicts, divergences or tensions between various factions of aristocracy, oligarchy and plutocracy as collective forms of dictatorial rule, with one faction, as Mosca suggests, sustaining 'a dictatorship by a leader' as autocratic 'tyranny' or emerging victorious and effectively becoming a ruling dynasty among 'warring elite factions'. While essentially united for long since Reaganism and before, after 2016 the nativists, theocratic or hyper-religious factions apparently prevail over the globalist and non-religious within the 'new American oligarchy or plutocracy'. They thus yield 'self-perpetuating' dynasties or sustain what appears as an attempted 'dictatorship by a leader', such as the 'lying demagogue', at least personal 'authoritarian' or 'populist' rule.[29]

More broadly, Mannheim implies such collective origins of dynasty and autocracy envisioning that when the capitalist class' devices for effecting inter-class and perhaps intra-class struggles prove 'insufficient', then a 'dictatorship' in a dynastic or autocratic-fascist shape becomes 'possible'. Mannheim envisions capitalist class' dictatorship by the agency and in the shape of fascism. In his account and experience, fascism arises as the 'exponent of bourgeois groups' that consequently substitutes one 'ruling group' in capitalism, including a dynasty or set of dynasties, for another within the 'existing class arrangements', citing to that effect Mussolini's exaltation of capitalism as the 'choice of the fittest', and 'not just a system of oppression'. Mannheim thus suggests that fascism arises as bourgeois and conservative (and religion-based) autocratic and dynastic dictatorship through Hitler's promised wide alliance of authoritarian conservatism or 'rightism'. His contemporary Polanyi and most later scholars[30] generally agree with Mannheim's characterization of fascism as, after some initial anti-capitalist 'socialist' disguises, capitalist-right dynastic, autocratic and oligarchic dictatorship driven by the idea of history as the 'circulation of elites'. Further, capitalist dynasty can develop, function and perpetuate itself within and indicate oligarchy, plutocracy and generally an elite. A reported case in point consists of US dynasties arising, functioning and self-perpetuating within and marking the 'new American oligarchy or plutocracy' and America as a 'land of an inherited oligarchy'.[31]

In comparative terms, like and usually conjoined with autocracy, capitalist and other dynasty typifies and dynastic-oligarchic families dominate the economy and society especially in non-Western settings. The latter include most of Latin America and Africa, much of Asia, including Japan and South Korea, and

---

29   The 'new American oligarchy or plutocracy' and 'self-perpetuating' dynasties are from Stiglitz (2012), the 'lying demagogue' from Hahl et al. (2018; see also Lamont 2018).

30   Polanyi (1944, p. 239) identifies the 'fascist solution to the impasse' of *laissez-faire* capitalism by reforming, but not eliminating, the latter, along with the 'process of the extirpation of all democratic institutions, both in the industrial and in the political realm'. Moore (1993, p. 413) states that capitalism culminates in essentially fascist dictatorship by passing through an anti-liberal 'reactionary' political stage, by implication conservatism. Giddens (1979, pp. 144–5) implies that modern capitalism experiences a dictatorial 'type of system degeneration' such as conservative, 'right totalitarianism', simply fascism. Mann (2004, pp. 177, 353) observes that both the Italian fascists and the Nazis captured power helped by capitalist and conservative elites and generally that fascism arose within authoritarian conservatism ('rightism').

31   The 'land of an inherited oligarchy' is from Stiglitz (2012, p. 75).

virtually the entire Islamic world mixing primitive capitalism with stringent theocracy, as with Saudi Arabia and other Gulf states and Turkey during recent times. Nevertheless, it is far from being an exclusively non-Western phenomenon, so long as elements or proxies of capitalist dynasty persist and dynastic families still exist and enjoy high wealth, power and status in the societies of Western capitalism, including England, Italy, Spain, France, in part Germany and others. Moreover, they reappear, indeed expand and reinforce, as in America after the 2016 Presidential elections effectively ushering in yet another instance of a long-standing pattern of dynastic, family-powered and autocratic capitalism which dynastic wealth and elite closure typifies. This is a pattern reportedly causing the 'country's sharply rising levels of wealth inequality' and in which the top 1 percent ever-growing share involving 'a small number of families and individuals' that are 'disproportionately rich' reportedly threatens and indeed harms the 'health of political institutions', simply democracy.[32]

As with autocracy, the comparative prevalence of capitalist and other dynasty in non-Western countries has misled many economists to attribute it exclusively to them. Conversely, its persistence and reappearance in many Western societies, notably the US post-2016 and before, contradict their absolving and theoretically purifying the latter from dynastic familial and autocratic capitalism. More precisely, many economists, aside from some exceptions, tend to attribute or link dynastic familial and in part autocratic capitalism to Italy, Spain, Greece, France and other Southern European countries, as to Eastern Europe, the third world and Japan and South Korea. By contrast, they are prone to detach it from America and England despite these countries' long tradition of persistence and prevalence and even, as in the first post-2016, resurgence of capitalist dynasty and an Anglo-Saxon variation of the 'despotism of dynastic usurpers'. In sum, capitalist dynasty and dynastic families are the primary-group, proto-collective form and agent of capitalist dictatorship persisting or reappearing within non-Western and Western capitalism from Latin America and the Gulf states through Japan and South Korea and Eastern Europe to Italy, France, Germany and the UK perpetually and to the US post-2016.

3.3   Capitalist Plutocracy, Oligarchy, and Aristocracy

The above anticipates an additional, formally larger and substantively more important group form and collective agent of capitalist dictatorship as an economic system. This is plutocracy, oligarchy, and aristocracy, so plutocrats,

---

32   Hällsten and Pfeffer 2017, p. 355) note the US's 'sharply rising levels of wealth inequality' and Acemoglu and Robinson (2015, p. 24) warn about the negative effect on the 'health of political institutions'.

oligarchs and aristocrats, respectively, when emerging and persisting within capitalism as distinct from pre-capitalism. In terms of the sociological classification of groups, if autocracy and dynasty and their holders are its respective non-group and primary-group forms and agents, capitalist plutocracy or its equivalent oligarchy and aristocracy and plutocrats and their equivalents represent a secondary and tertiary-group, form and agent of capitalist dictatorship. Moreover, if one wishes to identify the essential form and main agent of capitalist dictatorship, this is probably plutocracy and plutocrats in capitalism and their functional equivalents, as Pareto, Weber and other sociologists and economists, as well as business analysts, suggest.[33] The functional equivalents of plutocracy and plutocrats are typically what MIchels[34] denotes plutocratic oligarchy ('oligarchy of plutocrats') and aristocracy and wealthy oligarchs and aristocrats.

Still, some economists representing apologetic economics' ideal of laissez-faire, unrestrained capitalism defend plutocracy by claiming that Hitler attacked plutocracy. This seems historically inaccurate in light of the historical evidence that precisely plutocratic 'influential industrialists' like Friedrich Karl Flick, Alfried Krupp, and I. G. Farben executives (convicted in the Nuremberg trials) and most other major German capitalist firms 'financed the Nazi party's rapid rise after 1930', with Fritz Thyssen's stating 'I Paid Hitler'. Moreover, reportedly, measured by market capitalization in 1932, 'more than half of listed firms on the Berlin stock exchange enjoyed close links with the Nazi movement' and after Hitler's seizure of power on January 30, 1933 the firms and so plutocrats that had financed Hitler 'benefited substantially'. It is also inaccurate in view of the fact that Hitler promised essentially an encompassing alliance of plutocracy and so capitalism, traditional conservatism and Nazism as the 'new conservatism' in the form of 'a broad coalition of the right'[35] or the wider family of 'authoritarian rightism'. Other strands of apologetic economics such as Chicago, Austrian and related schools categorically deny or overlook the existence or relevance of plutocracy and oligarchy in capitalism and generally capitalist dictatorship among Western societies, above all, Great Britain

---

33   On plutocracy or plutonomy with a special reference to America see also Baxter and Margavio (2000), Formisano (2015), Frank (2007), Kapur et al. (2005), Rajan (2009), Stiglitz (2012), and Tilman (2001).
34   See Michels (1968, p. 79).
35   Kornai (2000, p. 30) complains that Hitler 'railed against plutocracy'. However, Ferguson and Voth (2008, p. 102) cite one of the latter's representatives Fritz Thyssen saying 'I Paid Hitler'. Overall for the close links between German capitalists and Nazism see Ferguson and Voth (2008), also, Mann (2004).

and the US—for them 'there is no such thing'. Conversely, they reluctantly recognize or imply and relegate it to non-Western countries in Africa, Asia, South America and post-socialist Eastern Europe.[36]

Among earlier economists and sociologists especially Pareto and Weber, along with Michels and Mosca, identify plutocracy or its equivalents oligarchy and aristocracy as the core form and chief agent of capitalist dictatorship and more broadly the dominant class of undemocratic or unrestrained capitalism. Pareto during the early 20th century identifies plutocracy as the 'ruling power in civilized countries', notably the 'present plutocratic regime in the civilized countries of the West', especially large Western countries like France, England and the US, in which plutocracy is 'dominant'. Consequently, he characterizes Western putative democracies as increasingly becoming effective capitalist dictatorships and generally non-democracies in the form of 'demagogic plutocracies' as the 'way of radical transformations', invoking those in France, England, Germany and the US.[37] Pareto probably implicitly includes into 'demagogic plutocracies' demagogic autocracies as their special cases or segments and seemingly anticipates the reported rise of plutocracy and the autocracy of the 'lying demagogue' in the US post-2016. In class terms, Pareto conceptualizes and redefines plutocracy in capitalism as the new aristocracy and oligarchy of capital existing in a substantive continuity with and a formal distinction from old aristocracies based on land estate. This is what his precursor Taine also suggests by pointing to the 'aristocracy of fortune' as effective plutocracy with reference to England.[38]

Similarly, Weber identifies 'a 'plutocratic' recruitment of the leading political strata' continuing and expanding from pre-capitalism to capitalism, including the 'plutocratic acquisition of charisma' leading to the 'monopolization of charismatic education' by plutocrats in both economic systems. For example, later research vindicates Weber in this last respect in that it finds that in the US before the creation of a public educational system private education was 'outside the reach of many families', thus of social classes not belonging to plutocracy or aristocracy. In particular Weber identifies the 'naked plutocracy' as the ruling class in American capitalism in which consequently 'mere money' effectively purchases and thus translates into power—although not social honor

---

36   Examples of such denials for Western societies are Friedman (1982), Hayek (1991), and
     Mises (1966), also Lucas (2009). Instances of this relegation to non-Western countries see
     Brender and Drazen (2009), Morck et al. (2005), Muligan et al. (2004), Olson (2000), and
     Rajan (2009).
37   See Pareto (1963, pp. 1217–23, 1587, 1863; 2000, pp. 40, 69).
38   See Pareto (2000, p. 87) and Taine (1885, p. 242).

requiring more than wealth to obtain—and through its exercise control and domination in society. Like Pareto, Weber implies that such plutocracy represents or eventually seeks to belong to 'aristocratic status groups' characterizing 'contemporary American development' and developing in conjunction with (and partly in contrast to) it. This is what Weber notes as the penchant of Southern plutocrats to live like European-style 'lords' indicate, including their striving for social status through conspicuous consumption, as the plutocratic 'robber barons' did during the Gilded Age and via their would-be-aristocrats proxies up to present days.[39]

Like Pareto and Weber, Michels observes that aristocracy in capitalism maintains its 'essentially plutocratic character' and alerts to the 'danger of plutocracy' through the rise and dominance of 'an oligarchy of plutocrats' in contemporary capitalist societies. Particularly, Michels suggests that in the United States—that he describes as the 'land of the almighty dollar' in that 'in no other country in the world does public life seem to be dominated to the same extent by the thirst for gold'—'plutocratic rule' turns 'supreme'. Further, he observes that 'corruption' continues and expands due to the 'unrestricted power of capital', with even the American labor movement by 'merely' following the 'lead of the capitalism' dominating the country becoming 'essentially plutocratic'.

In a similar vein, Mosca envisions the advent of a 'plutocratic dictatorship' and other dictatorships or their combination as the product of the accelerated or continued decline of a 'moderately well-to-do middle class'. Furthermore, like Pareto, Mosca posits that plutocracy or plutocratic oligarchy represents a norm both within capitalism and pre-capitalism, while democracy not even being an exception, stating that the many, if 'poor and ignorant', have never ruled the few, especially 'fairly rich and intelligent'. Mosca's prediction linking a 'plutocratic dictatorship' with middle-class decline seems almost prophetic in light of the steady decline of US middle and working classes especially since Reaganism and the associated 'plutocratic excesses of capitalism'. These excesses reportedly entail the rise of 'a new American oligarchy or plutocracy' because of the extreme wealth concentration in the 'upper 1 percent (or the upper 0.1 percent)' making America 'a land of an inherited oligarchy', with Congress and a conservative-dominated Supreme Court catering to 'a hydra-headed plutocracy'.[40]

39   See Weber (1958, pp. 84–6; 1968, pp. 1145–6; 1976, p. 310), also, Long and Ferrie (2013, p. 1109), plus Acemoglu and Robinson (2008), Akerlof (2007), Formisano (2015), Mizruchi and Marshall (2016), Piketty (2014), Tilman (2001), and Wright (2013).
40   See Michels (1968, pp. 76–9, 109, 188) and Mosca (1939, pp. 391–2), also, Baxter and Margavio (2000), Jacobs and Dirlam (2016), Kalleberg (2009), Kimeldorf (2013), Solow et al. (1987), plus Formisano (2015, p. 3) and Stiglitz (2012, pp. 79, 219).

Moreover, more explicitly than these classical sociologists, their contemporary US President Theodore Roosevelt condemns what he witnesses as the 'tyranny of a plutocracy' in America. He suggests that the 'tyranny of mere wealth' consists, indeed is the 'most vulgar' of 'all forms of tyranny', in that money in America (as Weber puts it) purchases and converts itself into power in society. This conversion of wealth into power sets in motion a reverse alchemy from the 'thirst for gold' in Michels' account to that for social control and domination. Then the 'thirst for gold' alchemy via the conversion of power into wealth reasserts itself, as the post-2016 government shows in a myriad of ways and means of apparent monetary profiting from political office, as unprecedented in its scale and scope for Presidents and families since the 20th century. Relatedly, Roosevelt implies that the 'tyranny of a plutocracy' becomes the primary form and agent of capitalist dictatorship (without using the term) or undemocratic capitalism. This is in the sense of capitalist dictatorship as what his contemporary, institutional economist Mitchell denotes 'economic oppression' and 'industrial despotism' resulting from the 'despotic might of capital' and belonging—together with the 'physical and moral degradation of the lower classes'—to the 'socially irrational, anti-economic' phenomena of American capitalism versus 'industrial democracy'. In this context, Mitchell concurs with Wieser. The latter states that the capitalistic class has 'a certain social compulsion to despotism' and a crushing despotism attaches to 'entrepreneur's capital', which thereby produces 'capitalistic despotism' and creates 'capitalistic despots', concurring with Marx in a striking departure (unless interpreting this as a sarcastic statement) from the fervently pro-capitalist 'Austrian school'.[41]

In general, capitalist dictatorship primarily assumes the form of plutocracy or its equivalents oligarchy and aristocracy within capitalism and mainly operates via the agency of plutocrats or plutocratic oligarchs and aristocrats especially in contemporary Western societies. This holds so long as the latter as Pareto's nominal democracies rule out pure autocracy—even if not entirely so, as in the US post-2016 and interwar fascist Europe—and mitigate brazen dynasty, although not completely, as in many Western countries, including England, France, Italy, Germany and America. Hence, as the sociological essence and epitome of capitalist dictatorship, plutocracy rather than autocracy, as many economists and political scientists believe, functions as the most comprehensive and serious antithesis and nemesis of economic and political democracy particularly in Western societies and to some extent their

---

41   For early insights see Mitchell (1917, pp. 107–8) and Wieser (1967, pp. 405–6), for later and recent observations see Bourdieu (2000), Gorman and Seguin (2018), Hahl et al. (2018) and Lamont (2018).

non-Western counterparts. Moreover, plutocracy often persists and operates together and in conjunction and mutual reinforcement with theocracy, as in the blended capitalist-theocratic 'American regime' and its counterparts in Catholic-dominated South America and Poland and in Islamic countries like Turkey, Saudi Arabia and other Gulf states.

Hence, when referring to dictatorship and economic and political-social non-democracy among both societies or within capitalism, plutocracy rather than autocracy is the most appropriate reference point, except for some non-Western countries like Hungary, Poland, Russia, China, Brazil, Saudi Arabia, Turkey and most other Islamic states, along with the US post-2016. The same applies to plutocracy's functional equivalents in Pareto-Michels' and related sociological and economic frameworks, namely capitalist oligarchy and aristocracy. While being a paradigmatic exemplar of capitalist dictatorship and the gravest antithesis of democracy within capitalism, nevertheless plutocracy does not fully exhaust the latter in view of its additional complementary and often intermingled forms and agents. Any plutocracy and plutocrat in capitalism especially in its Western version represents capitalist dictatorship and agent playing 'dictator games', but not all such dictatorships and dictators in these and particularly non-Western settings are plutocracies and plutocrats due to comprising autocracies, dynasties and other forms and agents.[42]

The same holds, with minor variations, for its equivalents. This suggests that oligarchy and aristocracy and their representatives within capitalism in its Western and non-Western versions represent or approximate capitalist dictatorship and dictators, even if not all instances of the later are oligarchies and aristocracies, plutocratic oligarchs and aristocrats. In this connection, one should distinguish, as Pareto, Michels and Mosca do, plutocracy and plutocrats, oligarchy and oligarchs from aristocracy and aristocrats, simply governing/ruling classes or elites, in capitalism from those in pre-capitalism, including slavery, caste, feudalism or the master-servant system.

However, what typifies all these capitalist and pre-capitalist plutocracies is, with some secondary variations, their substantive continuity and identity or functional equivalence. This is what Pareto precisely suggests by the historical 'circulation of elites'[43] and history as the 'graveyard of aristocracies', so of oligarchies as their perverted forms spanning from pre-capitalism to capitalism

---

42   On capitalist and other 'dictator games', see Andreoni, Rao, and Trachtman (2017), Henrich et al. (2004), Opp (2011) and specifically Stiglitz (2012), for the 'hardnose' dictator Cherry, Frykblom and Shogren (2002).

43   On the 'circulation of elites' and related matters, see also Benhabib and Bisin (2018), Lange (1935), Lenski (1994), Lerner (1955), and Tilly (2000).

and socialism that he envisions and in part witnesses, along with his contemporaries Schumpeter and Wieser. In this context, plutocracy reappears in capitalism as what Pareto denotes the 'new aristocracy and oligarchy' of capital or money—which his predecessor Taine identifies as the 'aristocracy of fortune' in England—rather than as completely different from and opposite to the old aristocracy and oligarchy, plus family and royal dynasty, of estate. Furthermore, US President Thomas Jefferson suggests this by defending emergent liberal and egalitarian democracy and the legal system from a rising plutocracy by hoping to defeat in its 'birth the aristocracy of our monied corporations' that 'dare already to challenge our government to a trial of strength and bid defiance to the laws of our country'. In other words, Jefferson as 'a democratic republican' denounces these plutocratic forces as new 'aristocrats' wanting to dominate and separate from the 'great majority' as their 'inferiors' by demonstrating their wealth through with Veblenian-Weberian luxury status consumption.

Plutocracy, oligarchy and aristocracy can coexist with and complement, incorporate or expand capitalist autocracy and dynasty. This is a pattern that especially typifies non-Western settings such as large sections of Latin America, the vast majority of Eastern Europe during the transition to oligarchic capitalism, much of Asia, most of Africa and virtually all Islamic capitalist-theocratic countries, especially Saudi Arabia, other Gulf states, and Turkey. In addition, the pattern characterizes some Western societies displaying both plutocratic or oligarchic and autocratic or dynastic tendencies in unison, alliance or cooperation like Great Britain traditionally and the US post-2016 and Germany. Italy and Spain during interwar years. For example, the 'new American oligarchy or plutocracy' reportedly coexists with and incorporates self-perpetuating dynasties and, as apparent for post-2016, actual or potential demagogic autocrats.

On the other hand, plutocracy can contest with, dilute, mitigate and substitute capitalist and pre-capitalist autocracy or dynasty, just as conversely, the latter seeking to dominate, intensify and replace the former. The tendency to the substitution of plutocracy for autocracy typifies most Western societies, including postwar Germany and Italy and for a longer time France, England and the US, but seemingly reversed post-2016, in respect of the autocratic form and Scandinavia with regard to both forms, as well as probably Australia, Canada and New Zealand. Overall, capitalist plutocracy, oligarchy or aristocracy exists and functions in dual and more broadly diverse relations to autocracy and dynasty within capitalism ranging from their complementarity and mutual reinforcement to their contestation and substitution. Regardless of their relations, including contestation, capitalist plutocracy, oligarchy or aristocracy, along with autocracy and dynasty, unite in or converge on their compulsion and exclusion of non-capital strata, which labor coercion epitomizes, and opposition to and elimination of economic and political democracy. In short, they remain just different forms and agents of capitalist dictatorship and more broadly non-democracy in capitalism—plutocratic-oligarchic and autocratic-dynastic, respectively.

In comparative terms, capitalist plutocracy or oligarchy characterizes both Western and non-Western societies presently and at various points of their history. Moreover, if autocracy or dynasty prevails in non-Western countries like South America, parts of Eastern Europe, Africa, Asia and Islamic states, plutocracy or plutocratic oligarchy and aristocracy and plutocrats continue to be the prevailing form and agent of capitalist dictatorship and non-democracy among Western societies. This holds as a general tendency with such seemingly aberrant or transient exceptions as the US under the proxy autocratic and dynastic regime or attempt after 2016 and interwar fascist autocracies or dynasties in Germany, Italy and Spain. This is what Pareto and Michels propose in their time and prophetically predict for present times. They characterize formal Western democracies as effective 'plutocracies' and 'plutocratic' oligarchies and aristocracies and to that extent exemplary capitalist dictatorships because they consider plutocracy, like oligarchy or aristocracy, an exemplar of dictatorship or non-democracy, as do later sociologists. In particular, Weber and President Roosevelt predict this result for the US by detecting and deploring the 'naked plutocracy' and its 'tyranny' in America during their life, as do Michels and Mitchell diagnosing the 'unrestricted power' and 'despotic might' of capital and related 'irrational' phenomena, notably the 'degradation' of non-capital classes in American capitalism.

Furthermore, evoking these early observations, some contemporary business analysis rediscover, along with 'a new American' plutocracy or oligarchy, 'plutonomy' which they define as an economic system and political regime powered or dominated, by the wealthy, invoking the U.S., UK, and Canada as the 'key Plutonomies'. 'Plutonomy' is evidently the equivalent of plutocracy and to that extent of capitalist dictatorship or non-democracy in the US and other Anglo-Saxon countries. This indicates that in America the plutocratic system has substantively persisted and solidified or reappeared and reaffirmed, as after the New Deal and early postwar partial disruption of capital power, since Pareto's diagnosis of 'demagogic plutocracies' and President Roosevelt's warning of plutocratic 'tyranny'. Moreover, Western and especially American-style plutocracy or oligarchy evidently expands and moves to prevail, though in association and reinforcement with autocracy and dynasty, in many non-Western societies. Among these latter, an exemplar is South America as the US government's regular field for experimentation in and imposition of capitalist and conservative dictatorship from Chile's and other free market' dictatorships during the 1970–90s—whose effects still persist judging by the recent mass demonstrations in this country—to Brazil's authoritarian rule post-2016. In addition, they include most Eastern European countries during the transition to oligarchic capitalism and illiberal democracy, including Hungary, Poland, most Baltic states, and Russia and Ukraine, which form capitalist plutocracies or oligarchies, along with autocracies, dynasties and, as with Catholic-dominated Poland, theocracies. Simply, they are all ruled by plutocrats as what Michels and their own populations call 'plutocratic oligarchs'.

Its continuing prevalence in putatively democratic Western societies, most notably and persistently in America and Britain, and its expansion beyond suggests that capitalist plutocracy functions in these settings as what Simmel would call a collective 'compensatory substitute' for or structural-functional equivalent of autocracy/dynasty. This occurs once the latter have suffered demise or discredit, as with autocracy during postwar times, apart from American exceptionalism since 2016, and decline, as with dynasty, aside from some exceptions, including persistent and growing 'dynastic' wealth and 'elite closure' in the US in contrast to Scandinavia. Hence, this is the process of substitution of one larger group form and agent of capitalist dictatorship for others rather than completely overcoming it—a variation on the choose own poison or, as in conservative America, execution method theme. As Wieser deplores, in spite of such shifts in its forms and agents, 'capitalistic despotism' persists in dominating 'wide fields of enterprise' in Western societies, particularly in Mitchell's account 'industrial despotism' or 'economic oppression' pervading unrestrained American capitalism.

In this process, capitalist dictatorship displays an exceptionally high level of adaptability to changed social conditions and new historical conjunctures and consequently a strong continuity, persistence and tenacity through Schumpeter's style non-democratic institutional 'creative destruction'. The latter process consists of substituting and reincorporating capitalist dictatorship's autocratic and dynastic structures and creating and reproducing the plutocratic and oligarchic, as in nominally democratic Western societies after the episodes of interwar fascist and other earlier conservative autocracies like Austria, Germany, Spain and others, and entrenched family and royal dynasties. In Pareto's framework, capitalist dictatorship appears and operates as the process of 'circulation of (antidemocratic) elites' from their autocratic and dynastic to their plutocratic and oligarchic variants—and back under certain conditions such as internal struggles and splits within plutocracy and oligarchy.[44]

---

44   On institutional 'creative destruction, see Massey (2009), on antidemocratic elites and similar tendencies, see Adorno (2001), Atkinson (1997), Benhabib and Bisin (2018),

In this framework, capitalist dictatorship converges and ultimately merges with fascism that, as Mannheim suggests and personally experiences, construes societal history as a 'circulation of elites' and as the 'exponent of bourgeois groups' and the creation of conservatism merely substitutes 'one ruling group for another within the existing class arrangements' of capitalism. This is what Mannheim, Polanyi and other interwar observers precisely witnessed in and other scholars report for Nazi Germany and Austria and fascist Italy and Spain that ultimately became capitalist dictatorships.[45] Further, even some 'libertarian' economists reluctantly admit this, noting that in all of them 'private enterprise was the dominant form of economic organization', thus merging 'fundamentally capitalist' economic systems with unfree 'political arrangements'.

In passing, Schumpeter downplays the anti-democratic institutional 'creative destruction' of capitalist dictatorship which he nevertheless admits as a potentiality, and extols, following ironically Marx, capitalism's economic 'revolutionizing' as market and technological 'creative destruction'. Overall, most modern economics exalts what it sees as the unprecedented and unrivalled economic and technological adaptability and endurance of capitalism in the face of economic and social changes as the reason of why it has not collapsed contrary to Marx's predictions of its demise. Yet, it overlooks the parallel fact that capitalist dictatorship is adaptable to and enduring in changed conditions, apparently more so than its non-capitalist opposites in view of their disappearance or rarifying, even as pro-capital economists continue to obsess with this *caput mortuum* post mortem.[46] It neglects that this adaptability provides the explanation of the longevity and indeed perpetuity of capitalist dictatorship. This applies to Great Britain from the 19th century, the US since the Gilded Age, most of Africa and South America, much of Asia, and Islamic countries like Turkey, Saudi Arabia and other Gulf states and Eastern Europe during its movement to unrestrained oligarchic capitalism. Furthermore, capitalist dictatorship's adaptability, tenacity and consequently longevity approaches that of theocracies as the most obstinate and lasting type of dictatorships due to claiming 'Divine' mandate, which the capitalist-theocratic 'American regime' from Puritan to evangelical America in the West and Islamic 'theocratic' regimes among non-Western settings demonstrate.

Brender and Drazen (2009), Piketty (2014), Polanyi (1944), Riley and Fernández (2014), and Wright (2013).

45 For example, Friedman (1982, p. 9).
46 Some instances are Kornai (2000), Lucas (2009), and Olson (2000), on Marx's predictions about capitalism see Acemoglu and Robinson (2015).

In terms of studying the phenomenon, the persistence and predominance of autocracies in non-Western countries misdirects economists to reduce dictatorship to autocracy and regard the latter as the main opposite of democracy, aside from some exceptions.[47] Alternatively, they fail to capture and do justice in their models to the continuity, obstinacy, resurgence and prevalence of capitalist plutocracy and so the new aristocracy of capital among many Western societies. The latter include especially those that Pareto, Michels, Weber and President Roosevelt identify in their time, above all the US under oligarchic rule, although probably excluding Scandinavian/Nordic countries like Sweden. Thus, many economists not only keep reducing dictatorship to third-world autocracy and viewing the latter as the key threat to democracy. They in their models absolve, disassociate and thus theoretically purify Western societies, notably America and Great Britain as their darlings of unregulated capitalism, from plutocracy and oligarchy that, like capitalist dictatorship or non-democracy generally, they attribute exclusively and relegate to non-Western settings. By contrast, the current study views plutocracy and plutocrats represent as continuing, obstinate, resurging and prevailing Western, as well as persistent non-Western, form and agent of capitalist dictatorship and more broadly of undemocratic, antiegalitarian and unrestrained proxy laissez-faire déjà vu capitalism.

In sum, plutocracy, oligarchy and aristocracy and its agents when developing and operating within capitalism constitutes the genuine collective and thus the sociologically most relevant form and agent of capitalist dictatorship. This especially holds for Western societies experiencing the demise of autocracy and the comparative decline of dynasty during postwar times, aside from the 'American exceptionalism' of resurging autocratic-dynastic tendencies post-2016.

3.4   *Secondary Forms and Agents of Capitalist Dictatorship*

Additionally, capitalist dictatorship can assume and involve some other, largely secondary forms and agents. These include what economists and sociologists denote and identify as kleptocracy and kleptocrats, predatory, robber and mafia capitalism and capitalists, police states and military dictatorships and dictators, theocracy and theocrats and other coercive and oppressive economic and political systems and rulers existing and acting within capitalism, including its Western and non-Western variations. At first glance, all these appear as formally illegitimate or illegal and thus non-institutional and

---

47   Such exceptions include Piketty (2014), Sen (1999), and Stiglitz (2012).

degenerate forms and agents of capitalist dictatorship—and yet so does the latter. It does this in the sense of a stage of 'dictator games' by unconstrained, laissez-faire domination of capital from the prism of non-dictatorial, egalitarian and 'rationally regulated' capitalism and liberal democracy as legitimate, institutional and normal systems within contemporary Western society. In substantive terms, these secondary forms and agents are structurally generated or enabled and often widespread within capitalist dictatorship. This holds for kleptocracy or predatory, rapacious, robber or crony capitalism in the familiar face of the American robber barons and their unrestrained power, and related incarnations in America and to some extent other Western and even more non-Western societies.

Furthermore, some of these secondary forms and agents of capitalist dictatorship tend to be extremely coercive, repressive, violent and terrorist—even by its own standards—in the sense of state terror, as with merged capitalist-fascist and capitalist-theocratic police states with mass incarceration and widespread executions. Such regimes span from Nazi Germany and fascist Italy through Pinochet's Chile to Turkey under Islamic rule and Saudi Arabia, Hungary and Poland under conservatism and effective theocracy and conservative America since Reaganism's 'tough on crime' crusade. The latter comprises the reportedly disastrous 'war on drugs' and other wars on sins-as-crimes, including persistent alcohol prohibitions in the style of the 'Bible Belt' converging with Islamic theocracies like Iran and Saudi Arabia and ever-new restrictions (e.g., the highest legal drinking age among all OECD countries) reenacting moralistic, religiously driven Prohibition.

Related secondary forms and agents consist of capitalist military dictatorship and dictators spanning from Latin America, Africa, and Asia to parts of Europe such as Greece, Portugal and Spain during early postwar times. Cases in point include capitalist military dictatorship in South Korea and the Korean military dictator President Park, those of Paraguay during Stroessner's rule, Chile and its dictator Pinochet, and of Argentina, Brazil and Uruguay in South America during the 1960–90s. All these were 'harshly repressive' capitalist military dictatorships. They were either autocratic, as with Stroessner in Paraguay, Pinochet in Chile and Park in South Korea, or juntas consisting of a clique of military leaders, as in some other countries in South America, Africa, Asia and Europe, for example, Greece's military dictatorship with the US government's support during the 1960–70s.

Alternatively, as the above and other examples indicate, aside from some anti-capitalist exceptions increasingly rarifying (e.g., Cuba, North Korea), since the 1990s most military dictatorships, including their autocratic variants and juntas, tend to be capitalist or pro-capitalist. Military dictatorships and dictators are the most repressive, violent and extreme forms and agents of capitalist dictatorship that becomes militaristic through militarized repression when all others, including kleptocracy, predatory capitalism and police states, fail to sustain it and protect its rulers. Just as in Mannheim's account and experience capitalist dictatorship becomes a possibility when capital's devices for conducting class struggles prove insufficient, so do military dictatorships when all its forms and agents do not suffice to enforce and perpetuate it. This is what Mosca implies by predicting 'a bureaucratico-military dictatorship' arising when a 'plutocratic dictatorship' itself proves, for various reasons, insufficient to maintain capitalists as the 'ruling class' or in combination with the second, especially during the decline of middle classes, which anticipates the latter's adverse fate in the US since Reaganism.

If and when military dictatorships prove themselves insufficient to perpetuate capitalist dictatorship, the latter may assume the form and agency of capitalist theocracy[48] and theocrats or theocratic capitalism and capitalists. Where the earthly most brutal force fails, 'divine power' via religion succeeds to perpetuate the unconstrained domination of capital, just as (as with medieval Christianity) perpetuating slavery, caste and serfdom in pre-capitalism, including, by functioning as the 'second estate' to aristocracy, European feudalism. In this respect, capitalist theocracy by claiming to be (in Simmel's words), the 'divine world order' and so (as Veblen puts it) 'divinely instituted' and theocrats proclaiming to have 'divine rights'—even if these for Pareto have not the 'slightest experimental validity'—represent the ultimate, perpetual, total and most potent form and agents of capitalist dictatorship. Consequently, even military dictatorship within capitalism seems partial, transient and weak by comparison to capitalist theocracy. Thanks to its alleged 'divine' origin and glory, the latter becomes a definitive and strongest solution to the problem of capitalist dictatorship's enforcement and perpetuation into seeming eternity when all other devises, forms and agents, including police states and military dictatorships, prove deficient for that purpose.

Capitalist theocracy therefore accords with and epitomizes the tendency of theocracies as 'divine' dictatorial governments to be more enduring, indeed eternal in the minds of their rulers and rank-and-file, and more total, persistent and obstinate than non-religious dictatorships. This holds insofar as one does not include into the latter fascist dictatorships. These dictatorships are in most cases religiously driven, linked or supported spanning from Nazi

---

48   Davis and Moore (1945, p. 245) intimate capitalist theocracy ('theocratic regimes'), although regard it mostly as a pre-capitalist and premodern phenomenon.

Germany and fascist Italy, Spain and other Catholic countries in Europe to neo-fascist Chile and Latin America and more recent cases such as Hungary under conservatism. For instance, Hume deplores the 'unreasonable obstinacy' of Puritanism and its theocracy in England, as Taine does later. They thereby anticipate the obstinacy of Puritanical evangelicalism and its invention of what Weber would call capitalist 'Bibliocracy' in America through the 'Bible Belt' of 'Money and God' belonging, alongside Islamic theocracies like Iran, to the 'protototalitarian' antitheses to individual liberty in some accounts.[49] Exemplars of capitalist theocracy range from, besides the regional case of Southern capitalism-bibliocracy, the 'American regime'[50] merging substantively plutocracy and theocratic religion through the 'Religious Right' against scientific progress and personal freedom to the Islamic legally merged capitalist 'theocratic regime' in the style of Saudi Arabia and other Gulf states. Both regimes fundamentally differ from and vehemently oppose the secular European regime combining egalitarian welfare capitalism with liberal democracy and scientific progress.

Moreover, some forms and agents of capitalist dictatorship represent both predatory, 'kleptocratic regimes' and repressive, violent systems, such as 'mafia' or 'gangster' capitalism, including state and non-state violence, that some observers detect or predict in American capitalism, with the other similar alternative being 'Hobbesian anarchy'.[51] According to this prediction, in 'mafia capitalism', 'Hobbesian anarchy' and generally in any future rendition of American capitalism with its 'inhuman face', 'repression of the population' will be ever-harsher as if it were not already harsh enough since Reaganism's anti-labor, anti-liberal, anti-secular and temperance wars. Indeed, such social repression is reportedly the harshest and most moralistic and religiously driven among Western societies in a striking continuity with repressive Puritanism and by the impetus of Puritanical evangelicalism. As regards mafia or gangster capitalism, it appears that 'dictators and mafias' often ally and blend, literally go hand in hand, in capitalist dictatorship by enforcing and sustaining the latter through state violence and extra-legal mob boss-style activities.[52]

---

49   See Bauman (1997, p. 184).

50   See Bénabou, Ticchi and Vindigni (2015, p. 347).

51   Giddens (2000, p. 35) characterizes 'gangster capitalism' as a 'specifically abnormal and unstable form of market structure' in which 'rent-seeking is backed by the use of violence' (see also Pryor 2002). For 'kleptocratic regimes' or kleptocracy', see Acemoglu (2005) and Mesquita et al. (2005).

52   'Mafia capitalism', 'Hobbesian anarchy', and generally American capitalism's 'inhuman face' come from Pryor (2002, pp. 364, 367).

3.5   Plutocracy and Secondary Forms and Agents of Capitalist Dictatorship

Overall, most of these secondary forms and agents of capitalist dictatorship arise and function as modes of perpetuation, escalation and intensification of plutocracy, oligarchy and aristocracy, as well as autocracy and dynasty, in capitalism. More broadly, they perpetuate, escalate and intensify the latter, specifically laissez-fare, 'irrationally unregulated' (in Cassel-Commons-Keynes' sense), inegalitarian and authoritarian capitalism, above all its American version. In that sense, they appear logical and normal rather than illogical and pathological forms and agents in relation to capitalist dictatorship, especially its primary plutocracy and plutocrats. This holds so long as capitalist dictatorship, as any other, is an economic and sociological pathology or 'morbidity' in its own right in Durkheim's societal sense (his other term is 'monstrousity') and an irrationality in that it tends to create what Mannheim connotes a 'new irrational sphere' similar to conservative-fascist 'irrationalism'. For example, these economic-social pathologies and irrationalities of capitalist dictatorship include, aside from rising income and wealth inequalities and perpetual widespread poverty, literally morbid health outcomes such as the recurrence and diffusion of once-eradicated contagious diseases (meningitis, tuberculosis, measles) and consequently, ceteris paribus, comparatively higher mortality and lower life expectancy especially in its American version.

Most strikingly, capitalist dictatorship looks as an economic-social pathology or irrationality when compared to its antithesis and antidote, Cassel-Commons-Keynes' 'rationally regulated', egalitarian and non-authoritarian capitalism primarily in Western Europe and within it Scandinavia and to liberal democracy in the same setting. Thus, Mitchell applying Wieser's theoretical ideas portrays unrestrained American capitalism owing to the 'despotic might of capital' as a system of 'socially irrational, anti-economic' phenomena, including profit-making through the 'sheer financial control over markets without the exercise of social leadership', the 'physical and moral degradation of the lower classes', exploitation of the 'weak' and 'economic oppression'.

Like Clausewitz's offensive wars, these secondary forms and agents of capitalist dictatorship are the continuation of plutocracy and oligarchy, as well as autocracy and dynasty, by other, marginally different means and agents. The latter range from predation, extortion, robbery and robbers ('robber barons'), corruption and 'corruptors' (Michels' word) in kleptocracy to violence, terror and dictators in pro-capitalist police states, military dictatorships and theocracies, while involving both sets in mafia or gangster capitalism. For example, kleptocracy and predatory robber-baron and mafia capitalism continue by their own means and agents, thus escalate and intensify plutocracy, oligarchy and

aristocracy, as well as autocracy and dynasty, rather than pathologically deviating from these forms because the latter are pathological from the standpoint
of non-authoritarian capitalism and liberal democracy. At this point, the 'robber barons' and their later and present mutants in America since Reaganism
or post-2016 reappear as the ultimate faces and embodiments of plutocracy,
oligarchy and the aristocracy or nobility of capital and its 'tyranny' that the US
President deplores or its 'economic oppression' that Mitchell identifies. Simply,
they look, as Weber, Veblen and Merton describe them, like 'super-men', rather
than aberrations ('rotten apples'), among capitalist plutocrats.

In addition, police states and military dictatorships within capitalism continue by their own specific means and agents and thus perpetuate, escalate
and intensify especially capitalist autocracy or dynasty through personal
dictatorial rule and plutocracy or oligarchy via military juntas and generally
militarized repression and terror. Along with police states, capitalist military
dictatorships in many non-Western countries usually either maintain and reinforce autocracy and dynasty or derive from and enforce plutocracy and oligarchy, and moreover in some situations can depose and replace the latter, as in
Chile and the rest of South America during postwar times.

Similarly, capitalist theocracies continue, intensify, perpetuate and sanctify plutocracy and oligarchy, as well as autocracy and dynasty, as 'Divinely
ordained' and their agents with 'divine rights'. An exemplar within Western
society is the substantively theocratic 'American regime' (especially the 'Bible
Belt') in which religious forces ally and indeed merge with the wealthy through
the 'Christian Right' alliance. A paradigmatic instance in the non-Western
world consists of Islamic pure 'theocratic regimes' blending strict theocracies
with autocratic rule, specifically capitalist or rich autocrats.

On one hand, military dictatorships are the extreme 'profane' (in Durkheim's
sense), worldly continuation and enforcement of plutocracy and oligarchy,
autocracy and dynasty in capitalism via brute force, which capital reportedly
used in Gilded-Age America according to sociological studies. On the other
hand, capitalist theocracies are the final 'sacred', transcendental mode of perpetuation and sanctification of them through 'divine' power, command and
glory. Consequently, capitalist-military dictatorships tend to be more partial,
transient, unstable and contested, as in South America, including Chile under
Pinochet, let alone postwar Europe (e.g., Greece), with the exception of those
in Portugal and Spain, yet even these while rooted in a long tradition of conservative authoritarian rulers eventually ended with the dictators' death.

By contrast, capitalist theocracies have a tendency to be more total,
enduring, stable and virtually uncontested—not many humans dare to contest a 'Divinely instituted' system—and broadly embraced. This is what the

'American regime' demonstrates by being all-encompassing, perpetuated and sanctified in a lineage from proto-capitalist Puritan theocracy to capitalist-evangelical America. The pattern also holds for the non-Western 'theocratic regime' such as Islamic capitalist theocracies and autocracies in Turkey, Saudi Arabia and other Gulf states. This difference from capitalist military dictatorships is consistent with theocracy's tendency to be the most total, enduring, obstinate and indeed, by its rulers and rank-and-file construing and enforcing it as 'divine power', the eternal type of dictatorship compared to its secular counterparts. This holds with secondary variations in which some secular dictatorships (e.g., the Soviet Union, Eastern Europe) may approach but hardly ever reach the totality, longevity and tenacity of capitalist and other theocracies (the US 'Bible Belt', Saudi Arabia, etc.).[53]

This pattern helps explain why the substantively theocratic 'American regime' and Islamic legal theocracies have been so long-lasting, for example, enduring for centuries, as with Puritan New England or the evangelical South and Islamic Saudi Arabia, both the sites of religion-based coercive capitalism. It relatedly explains why they have been tenacious, stable, virtually uncontested and widely accepted as eternally given, valid and obligatory systems and truths, including various theocratic or theocentric syndromes ('in God we trust', the 'one nation indivisible under God' pledge of allegiance) in postwar conservative America. Conversely, the pattern helps account for the fact that, aside from rare exceptions, most military and other nominally non-religious dictatorships end sooner or later, as in South America, Africa and Asia, and are mostly capitalist, with Pinochet's Chile dictatorship remaining a prototype for them.[54]

In this connection, Pareto's statement that aristocracies/elites 'do not last' in long terms applies to military and other secular dictatorships but less to their religious variants so long as theocracies, at least their American-evangelical and Islamic variations, evidently do last long or claim to be ever-lasting and indeed evergreen. Secular dictatorships might be 'gone with the wind' but capitalist theocracies keep on standing strong against the wind, even if they, namely their American-evangelical variations, may make the last stand of theocracy within Western society in which the secular European regime prevails.

---

53 For America and Islamic countries, see Barro and McCreary (2005), Friedland (2001), Habermas (2001), Juergensmeyer (2003), Kaufman (2008), Kuran (2018), Mueller (2009), and Munch (2001).

54 This excludes Cuba and North Korea as the virtually only remaining and peripheral anti-capitalist dictatorial regimes lacking multi-party systems and so competitive elections, with which 'libertarian' economists still obsess.

This suggests that theocracies within capitalism especially their evangelical and Islamic variants ranging from the US 'Bible Belt' to Iran and Saudi Arabia tend to be the most lasting form and agent of capitalist, conservative and indeed any dictatorship, surpassing pro-capitalist military and other dictatorships. Furthermore, they develop and function as functional equivalents in terms of proto-totalitarian 'solutions' to the supposed problem of individual liberty, including penal repression via religiously driven executions and mass imprisonment.

On the other hand, capitalist military dictatorships and theocracies can continue, perpetuate and enforce plutocracy/oligarchy and autocracy/dynasty in capitalism in conjunction, unison and mutual reinforcement and by merging into a single system. This is what various historical and current instances show. They include the merger or alliance of fascist/radical-right dictatorship and Catholic and Protestant theocracy in interwar Europe, including Germany, Italy and Spain, that in Chile and most of Latin America and to some degree Hungary recently and Poland since the 1990s. Additional cases are the mergers of militarized repression with Islamic theocratic rule and rulers in Turkey during recent times, especially after the failed 2016 military coup, and Saudi Arabia and other Gulf and Muslim states for long. A proxy among contemporary Western societies seems to be the persistent and even intensifying effort by American conservatism to merge what a US President deplores as the potentially undemocratic military-industrial complex with theocratic religion. This involves evangelicalism via religious nationalism rooted in 'manifest destiny' sanctifying militarism, imperialism and destruction, including the 'near extinction of the Native American population', and creating a pure 'Christian' army trained for 'crusade for Christ' and 'holy' warriors. Taken together, militarism and religious extremism facilitate the perpetuation, extension and intensification of plutocracy/oligarchy and even, as after 2016, autocracy/dynasty in conjunction and indeed unison.

Moreover, Pareto predicts the advent of a 'military dictatorship' among some Western nations serving as an extremely violent instrument of continuation and imposition of plutocracy as the elite in capitalism, just as arising as the explicit result of colonial and other wars between them. This effectively predicts both the outbreak of WW I and the rise of fascist regimes—which he inspired according to Mannheim—from Italy to Germany and Spain as precisely such dictatorships. By continuing plutocracy and autocracy among these and other nations, military dictatorships, including individual dictators and juntas, in capitalism effectively continue, intensify and enforce capitalist dictatorship through militarized coercion, just as police states and theocracies do by state and religious repression and terror, respectively. Furthermore,

Pareto implicitly detects elements of a moralistic Puritanical or evangelical, medieval-style theocracy in the US as the final 'divine' instrument of continuation, perpetuation and sanctification of plutocracy. He observes in America— and predicting Prohibition and similar acts—the theocratic or moralistic 'mass of hypocritical laws for the enforcement of morality that are replicas of laws of the European Middle Ages'. Like military dictatorship, this theocracy by perpetuating plutocracy and conceivably, as after 2016, autocracy perpetuates, sanctifies and enforces capitalist dictatorship and indeed merges with it to become Weber's capitalistic-Puritan Bibliocracy as the 'Money and God' 'Bible Belt'. More broadly, it operates in this manner in connection with 'unfettered', authoritarian and anti-egalitarian American capitalism as a 'divine' design and 'manifest destiny'.[55]

As a coup de grace, mafia capitalism fusing the predation of kleptocracy and the robber barons with the repression and terror of military dictatorships, police states and theocracies continues, escalates and intensifies all these forms and agents of capitalist dictatorship from plutocracy and oligarchy to autocracy and dynasty. It does so by its own peculiar double set of means and agents of robbery and violence. In a sense, mafia capitalism exemplifies plutocracy and capitalist dictatorship in general without the cloths of deceptions, manipulations and pretensions, and instead 'gone wild' into a mix of predation and robbery and of violence and terror. Mafia capitalism looks as a terminal 'cancer stage' of capitalist dictatorship, just as the latter's political basis, conservatism with its intrinsic and 'militant authoritarianism' becomes a 'cancer' in America.[56]

In general, kleptocracy, robber and mafia capitalism, pro-capitalist military dictatorships, police states and theocracies and other oppressive systems usually coexist with and perpetuate via continuation and intensification autocratic and plutocratic forms and agents of capitalist dictatorship. This holds as a prevailing tendency, with the outbreak of occasional frictions, tensions and conflicts between the first and second forms and agents—and within each of them—that are analogous to feuds within and between pre-capitalist aristocracy and aristocrats (land proprietors and barons in Hume) or, as with mafia capitalism, to 'mafia wars'.[57] Comparatively, among these additional forms and agents, capitalist and other kleptocracy and kleptocrats seem to typify and prevail especially in non-Western settings from Africa, Asia and Latin America

---

55   See Pareto (1963, p. 1429), also, Gorman and Seguin (2018), Hahl et al. (2018), Lamont (2018), Jouet (2017), Munch (2001), and Slater and Smith (2016).
56   See Altemeyer (2007) and McMurtry (1999).
57   The term 'mafia wars' is from Bolle, Tan and Zizzo (2014, p. 93).

chronically to most of Eastern Europe in the transition to capitalism under oligarchy.

Still, as dynasties, kleptocracies and kleptocrats are far from being an extinct specimen or rare phenomenon among Western societies spanning from Italy and Southern Europe overall to the US and the UK, and consequently widespread corruption and its agents persist and even expand in these settings as well. Michels remarks that because of plutocratic and by implication kleptocratic rule being 'supreme' in the US, corruption 'persists unchanged' so that only the 'corruptor' is different—the new sanctimonious all-American plutocrat/kleptocrat as distinct from the old decadent European aristocrat. Moreover, Michels[58] observes that due to the 'unrestricted power of capital', plutocrat/kleptocratic corruption and corruptors in this country surpass any others in terms of expansiveness and social acceptance and indeed institutionalization. He observes that in America corruption exhibits itself on a 'gigantic scale' and becomes a 'recognized institution' regarded with 'indifference' or provoking 'an indulgent smile' by contrast to arousing in Europe 'censure and anger'. Michels apparently refers to the Gilded Age that historically marks the birth or expansion of kleptocracy and kleptocrats in America in that kleptocratic and other plutocratic abuse and corruption was 'rife' during this era, along with 'evidence of continued corruption' in 19th century England.

Moreover, various proxies or correlates of kleptocracy and kleptocrats like corrupt plutocratic families and 'crony capitalists' reportedly continue to operate in some Western societies, including Italy, the UK and the US since Reaganism and after 2016. Evidently, while pervading non-Western countries from South America perennially to Eastern Europe under oligarchy, 'kleptocratic regimes' or tendencies arise and persist in some Western societies, including the US during the Gilded Age and post-2016, contradicting the claims of Western, especially American, ethnocentrism to pure, uncorrupted capitalism and democracy.[59]

Relatedly, predatory, robber, crony or political capitalism and capitalists as the analogue or variants of kleptocracy and kleptocrats pervade not only non-Western, including Asian, Eastern European, African, and South American, countries as their preferred method of wealth appropriation and expropriation. Further, such capitalism and capitalists characterize some Western societies in reportedly comparable degrees. For example, 'crony capitalists' enjoying 'extreme concentrations of economic power' and 'corporate political

58   See Michels (1968, p. 247).
59   See Michels (1968, p. 188).

connections' reportedly exist not just in third-world countries but in Western societies such as Italy, Great Britain and the US whose economic system in some accounts resembles more 'crony capitalism' than its competitive version. In fact, the concepts of robber and mafia capitalism and capitalists initially pertain to American capitalism during the Gilded Age and recent and present times since Reaganism and under conservatism, just as capitalist predators or kleptocrats like the robber barons and their later reincarnations are its exceptional creation within the West.

By contrast, capitalist military dictatorships during postwar and present times primarily emerge and exist in non-Western and non-European societies, including South America, most of Africa, parts of Asia, and many Islamic states, except for some Southern European counties like Greece, Portugal, and Span until the 1970s. In particular, capitalist military juntas or dictators have become a characteristic feature of South America since the 1950–60s, culminating in Chile's murderous 'free market' (Chicago 'libertarian' economics-style) dictatorship that even if being economically 'disastrous' serves as the prototype and inspiration for dictatorial capitalism and conservative militarized murder, repression and counterrevolution. Capitalist military and other dictatorships are presently non-existent and probably an 'impossibility theorem' among Western societies in the foreseeable future. However, even these societies have historically experienced these regimes, as Nazi Germany and fascist Italy and Spain did during interwar times. These outcomes thus fulfilled Pareto-Mosca's prediction of a rising military dictatorship among Western nations resulting from their imperial wars or as the instrument of and in combination with its plutocratic form. Further, some correlates or bases of such dictatorships reemerge in some Western societies during postwar and current times, most notably with the rise and expansion of a military-capitalist complex in the US since the 1950s and a 'Christian army' in the making due to the infiltration of evangelicalism. This holds so long as by its militarism and imperialism this compound poses, as even a US President warned, a serious threat to democracy and thus forms a potential stepping-stone to a military dictatorship in the service of imposition and preservation of unrestrained, repressive capitalism merged with authoritarian conservatism and its design of theocracy.

The preceding about capitalist military dictatorships also holds in comparative terms for police states and theocracies within capitalism in that the latter also represent primarily non-Western phenomena, with some qualifications. Compared to military dictatorships, capitalist police states and theocracies appear more resilient and even resurge among some Western societies, in particular the US and to a lesser extent Great Britain under conservatism since the 1980s or the 2000s. Elements or proxies of a capitalist police state reportedly

reappear in these two Western societies, especially the first featuring the highest imprisonment rate not only in the West but in the entire world of global
capitalism, thus supplying the indicator of such a form of government. These
tendencies include near-totalitarian intrusive surveillance, the ever-expanding
size and unparalleled brutality and egregious violence of the police force, dramatically growing and mass incarceration, widespread executions, including
those of innocent people, and more broadly intensified penal repression.

Moreover, this trend assumes the form of a recurring religiously driven vice-
police state in America because it devotes the most police resources to eradicating Puritan-style vices and sins or Orwellian crimes generating the dystopian
outcome of decreasing actual crime and growing severe punishment. As a result,
a large proportion (between 20 and nearly 50 percent of the exploding (especially
Federal) prison population comprises moral sinners and so prisoners of ethical
conscience such as non-violent drug users redefined and punished as criminals through Reaganism's 'war on drugs' and related Puritanical wars on sins-as
crimes. In this sense, aside from minor exceptions (Las Vegas), the government
at all levels in conservative—as distinct from liberal—America still looks as a
self-perpetuating moralistic Puritan policing, penal, and repressive state modeled
after the 'Puritan policeman' and the repression of Puritanism. Consequently, it
continues to obsess with, fight and exorcize 'witches' spanning those at Salem
to those produced by Prohibition, the war on drugs and other Puritanical wars
on sin-as-crime, committing 'sacrificial violence' by staging equivalents of witch-
trials for sinners (e.g., non-violent drug, alcohol, sexual and other offenders).[60]

Pareto already detects the existence and predicts the persistence of
such a moralistic repressive state by observing in America 'a mass of hypocritical laws for the enforcement of morality', including the constitution-
ally enforced Prohibition with its punishments up to life in prison, just as
his contemporaries Scheler and Sombart and the US dissident journalist
Mencken do. Comparatively, the Puritan-style vice-police state in the US—
including special anti-alcohol units in the 'dry' South[61] due to its persistent

---

60   'Less crime, more punishment' comes from Cooney and Burt (2008), 'sacrificial violence'
     from Gorski and Türkmen-Dervişoğlu (2013), see also Earl, McCarthy, and Soule (2003),
     Kaufman (2008), Levitt (1997), Merril (1945), and Wagner (1997).
61   Merton (1968, p. 133) remarks that it 'would be peculiar to argue that prior to 1920
     (Prohibition) the provision of liquor constituted an economic good, that from 1920 to
     1933 (not) and that from 1934 to the present (does) once again. It would be economi-
     cally (not morally) absurd to suggest that the sale of bootlegged liquor in the dry state
     of Kansas is less a response to a market demand that the sale of publicly manufactured
     liquor in the neighboring wet state of Missouri'. Relatedly Merton (1968, p. 134) deems it
     absurd to argue that 'in European countries with registered and regulated prostitution the

alcohol prohibitions or restrictions—operates as a functional equivalent of Islamic states. Evangelical America and Iran or Saudi Arabia qualify as probably the two most extensive and severe capitalist or anti-secular police states in Western and non-Western societies, respectively, judging by both standards: the proportion of police resources devoted to wars on sins-vices and imprisonment and execution levels, notably such punishment for these moral offenses redefined as crimes.

Relatedly, while the secular 'European regime' prevails as a norm in Western societies, the exceptional 'American regime' merging capitalism and theocracy or religion reportedly persists since Puritanism and intensifies through the Religious Right alliance between plutocracy and religious masses against both science and personal freedom. To that extent, this regime perpetuates itself as the strongest and most obstinate deviation from liberal-secular modernity rather than a supreme model for all countries to adopt or emulate. In this account, the 'American regime' remains the substantively sole outstanding, even if formally diluted, system of capitalist theocracy—in which 'money and God' rule—of a Puritanical evangelical variety or theocratic capitalism, as in the 'Bible Belt' as almost half of the country, among Western societies. More broadly, it persists as such a system in the world as a whole, along with Catholic-dominated Poland and most of South America and Islamic plutocratic theocracies.

At the minimum, some Western societies like the US and to a certain extent Great Britain retain vestiges of capitalist police states and, as with the first, theocracies, while most, above all Western European and especially Scandinavian countries, supersede these systems. While diverging in terms of military dictatorship but keeping in mind its potential in the American ever-expanding military-industrial complex and growing militarism, some Western societies such as the US converge with non-Western countries, including Catholic-dominated Poland/South America and Islamic states, in respect of capitalist theocracy or religiously sanctified capitalism. Moreover, on account of capitalist theocracy and a vice-police state, the US in its predominant or expanding pole of conservative America seems closer to non-Western countries, including Islamic plutocratic-theocratic states (Kuwait, Saudi Arabia, Emirates, Qatar, Turkey), than to Western societies, especially liberal-secular Western Europe, notably Scandinavia.

---

prostitute contributes an economic service, whereas in this country lacking legal sanction the prostitute provides no such service.

TABLE 5   Economic indicators and proxies of capitalist dictatorship

indicators and proxies of economic coercion, oppression and
non-democracy
    suppression of unionization (union density)
    restriction of the scope of unionization (collective bargaining coverage)
    suppression of collective bargaining between capital and non-capital
    suppression of labor collective participation in enterprise management
    (codetermination)
indicators and proxies of economic inequality, degradation and deprivation
    extreme concentration of wealth
    extremely unequal income distribution.
    economic degradation, deprivation and hardship
    economic exploitation and non-protection and insecurity

In sum, kleptocracy, predatory and mafia capitalism, police states and military dictatorships, theocracies and similar oppressive systems represent extreme variations of plutocracy, oligarchy and aristocracy, as well as autocracy and dynasty, rather than their deviations. Conversely, these latter forms and agents, including plutocracy and autocracy and their rulers, continue, intensify and enforce capitalist dictatorship through kleptocracy or predatory capitalism and thus predation, robbery and corruption, via military dictatorships, police states and theocracies and so force and terror, and by mafia capitalism using all these means.

4   Economic Indicators and Proxies of Capitalist Dictatorship

Economic indicators and proxies of capitalist dictatorship are multiple, interconnected and usually mutually reinforcing. Consistent with the double character of capitalist dictatorship (economically considered) as an authoritarian system of coercion and oppression in the economy and more broadly industrial non-democracy and an anti-egalitarian structure of economic inequality, degradation and deprivation, they can accordingly be divided into two groups. Correspondingly, the first group comprises indicators and proxies of coercion, oppression and non-democracy in the economy, and the second those of economic inequality, degradation and deprivation, thus authoritarianism and anti-egalitarianism, respectively.

4.1 *Indicators and Proxies of Economic Coercion, Oppression and Non-democracy*

Indicators and proxies of economic coercion, oppression and non-democracy within capitalist dictatorship include the suppression of unionization, restriction of the scope of unionization, suppression of collective bargaining between capital and non-capital, and suppression of labor participation in enterprise management, simply of codetermination.

4.1.1 Suppression of Unionization

A salient and typical feature of capitalist dictatorship involves prohibition and suppression of labor collective organization and action, simply unionization. As a consequence, a low level of unionization or minimal union density typifies capitalist dictatorship, specifically the unfreedom of non-capital in the economy, while its high levels typifying economic and political democracy. Suppression of unionization is therefore indicative of capitalist dictatorship's high degrees of economic coercion, oppression and industrial non-democracy. Specifically, it indicates, all else being equal, the minimal and maximal structural and organizational power and freedom or collective agency of labor and capital, respectively, hence an extreme imbalance or asymmetry between the two production factors and social classes disfavoring the first in violation of democracy that such a balance characterizes.

Alternatively, capitalist dictatorship reveals itself as what Mitchell calls a system of 'economic oppression' in negation of 'industrial democracy' in the manner of early and post-Reagan American capitalism owing to the 'despotic might of capital' by low unionization and the minimal power and freedom of non-capital, as a result of the denial and suppression of labor collective organization and action. Consequently, due to its inherent logic and system of economic compulsion and oppression of non-capital, capitalist dictatorship invariably tends to have extremely low union density and to grant minimal power, freedom or agency to labor as a collective agent versus that of capital as maximal, structural, exclusive and arbitrary. Especially in American capitalism, union density since Reaganism has fallen to around 10 percent and that in the private sector to less than 7 percent. This is mostly the result of that reportedly the US is 'one of the few industrial democracies in violation of the International Labour Organization's principles for safeguarding the right to organize' and other anti-union strategies such as a 'striker replacement strategy' spreading like a contagion from the anti-union deep South to the entire economy.[62]

---

62 See Kimeldorf (2013, p. 1056), also, Clawson and Clawson (1999), Fligstein (2001), Goldstein (2012), Hung and Thompson (2016), Jacobs and Dirlam (2016), Kalleberg (2009), Kristal (2013), and Wright (2013).

Empirically, capitalist dictatorships and related repressive systems confirm and exemplify this pattern of labor organization suppression and hence
low unionization. Instances range from 19th-century English and Gilded-Age
American capitalism until the New Deal through Nazi Germany and fascist
Europe to South Korea and Latin America over the 1960–80s and Britain
and America déjà vu under Thatcherism and Reaganism. Further examples
include most of Eastern Europe, especially autocratic Hungary, along with the
Baltic states, during the transition to oligarchic capitalism and the post-2016
US under the plutocratic radical-right government and via global contagion
or confluence other OECD countries such as Turkey during anti-labor Islamic
rule. (An unexpected case is France with its low unionization level at barely 9
percent, but its near-maximal union coverage of almost 99 percent apparently
compensates for this, by stark contrast to the other cases, including Eastern
Europe, the US and Turkey, that feature both extremely low union density and
coverage.)

Thus, 19th-century English and American capitalism basically perpetuated
a despotic master-servant, common-law system and even, as in the US postbellum South, slavery through what Wieser laments as 'capitalistic despotism'.
Later Nazi Germany, Reaganism and Thatcherism and Pinochet's Chile dictatorship emerge as particularly egregious exemplars of union suppression and
generally labor coercion, thus as functional equivalents ('brothers in arms')
in this regard. For example, consistent with Hitler's promise of forming a
capitalist-conservative 'broad coalition of the right', specifically the 'broader
family of authoritarian rightists', in Germany, the Nazi government immediately after seizing power dissolved in May 1933 labor unions and imprisoned
'numerous members'.[63] Similarly, forming broad coalitions of the right through
a capitalist-conservative populist mobilization, Reaganism's and Thatcherism's
'right-wing leaders' reportedly launched a direct attack, indeed a class war on
organized labor, including 'Thatcher's defeat of the coal miners' strike in 1984–
85, and Reagan's crushing of the air traffic controllers' strike in 1981'. Applying
the capitalist, anti-labor prescription of 'libertarian' Chicago economics and
personally instructed by its exponents Friedman and Hayek, Pinochet with his
'free market' dictatorship immediately after seizing power acted accordingly,
thus learning from Hitler, Reagan and Thatcher.[64] Reportedly, the 'Pinochet

---

63   See Ferguson and Voth (2008, pp. 105–6), Mann (2004, p. 353).
64   To confirm that they were allies, 'brothers in arms' not only did 'libertarian' econo-
      mists Friedman and Hayek personally visit and instruct Pinochet in the economics
      of capitalist anti-labor mass repression and murder. Also, Thatcher met, welcomed

dictatorship between 1973 and 1990' attempted to destroy 'worker organiza-tions' that represented the 'main political opposition' by outlawing unions and brutally oppressing their activists, combined with other acts of 'mass repres-sion and murder', including thousands of persons killed for political reasons and tens of thousands imprisoned and tortured (plus hundreds of thousands fired from their jobs).[65]

Furthermore, unionization appears minimal and suppressed in other past and current capitalist and related 'right' conservative, fascist or religious, dic-tatorships. These include most of Africa and Latin America, much of Asia, Eastern Europe under oligarchic capitalism, Islamic states that mix oppressive capitalism—and decreasingly, as Saud Arabia, other Gulf states and Iran show, despotic feudalism—with proto-totalitarian theocracy almost in the man-ner evangelical America like the 'God and Money' Southern 'Bible Belt' does. Unionization and more broadly widespread and effective labor collective orga-nization and action and economic democracy is virtually non-existent or min-imal and repressed in most 'Latin American, Caribbean, and African (and also Asian) countries' subjected to the 'iron law' of oligarchy and to that extent cap-italist or conservative-religious dictatorship. With rare exceptions (Slovenia with a union density of around 20 percent), labor organization and action has suffered a dramatic weakening and irrelevance mainly due to the attack and

---

and fervently shielded the dictator when detained in London on an extradition war-rant for crimes against humanity during the early 1990s. Yet, the British Conservative government displaying its Thatcherite legacy predictably chose not to extradite an apparently ideological ally, 'brother in arms' within the extended family of authori-tarian conservatism. It hence showed clearly that for it, as for most conservative gov-ernments, fascism or military dictatorship is perfectly fine so long as it is 'free market' capitalism, so fascists or military dictators are 'decent' people (as Thatcher defended Pinochet) if they are capitalist or anti-socialist. After all, modern conservatism and neo-fascism continue to belong to a 'broader family' of 'authoritarian rightism' (and populism), just as traditional conservatism and fascism did through the interwar period (see Mann 2004).

65   See accounts in Acemoglu and Robinson (2013) and Kerrissey (2015). In this regard, the Pinochet dictatorship's depriving hundreds of thousands from employment and thus subsistence contradicts and exposes as a deception 'libertarian' economics' assertion that authoritarian cum laissez-faire capitalism ('private enterprise') is the best and sole pro-tection against the government arbitrary firing of people from their jobs and deprivation of their sustenance. The same holds, ceteris paribus, for pro-capitalist McCarthyism and more broadly the 'red scare', by firing and black-listing thousands of Americans from their job and thus depriving them from the means of material existence because of their 'un-American' ideas and activities.

opposition by the rising oligarchy in most of Eastern Europe, especially the Baltic states and Hungary, during the transition to oligarchic or crony dependent capitalism and in that sense capitalist dictatorship. To compound and reinforce this process, the latter or oligarchy typically emerges and operates in association with pro-capital, anti-labor conservative political regimes. These include theocracy or religion-driven governance, as in Catholic-dominated and illiberal Poland, and nationalist populism, repression and xenophobia, as in Hungary, or neo-fascism, as in Croatia reenacting the ww ii Nazi-puppet state with Germany's critical assistance continuing its ww i and ii Balkans policy.

Moreover, while declining but still existing in Eastern Europe under oligarchic capitalism, unions, labor collective organization and action and economic democracy are virtually unknown and non-existent, nearly taboos in most Islamic capitalist-theocratic or autocratic states, especially Iran, Saudi Arabia and other Gulf states, or weak and repressed in Turkey by the Islamic government (with union density falling under 10 percent). By contrast, unions are traditionally more salient or visible in less theocentric Islamic countries like Egypt and in part Algeria and Tunisia under secular or less religious governments. Therefore, such Islamic states as Iran and especially intensively capitalist Saudi Arabia and other Gulf states converge with evangelical America cum the 'Bible Belt' on the suppression of unionization, labor rights and economic democracy—indeed, public unions are nonentities and taboos both in these Muslim theocracies and most of the deep South and similar regions. Furthermore, the two states, as reported, converge on the proto-totalitarian elimination of individual liberty as the 'burden' and 'agony of choice' and liberal democracy. Applying Mill's method of identity, while they differ in formal, demographic, geographical and theological respects the two reappear as substantive identities or function as functional equivalents on what is an essential dimension presently and in functionalist terms. This is manifesting convergence on suppressing labor collective organization and economic democracy, just as converging on eliminating individual liberty and liberal-secular democracy, including Draconian punishment by widespread executions and mass imprisonment.[66]

In sum, the suppression of and consequently low unionization represents, with minor variations, a typical indicator of capitalist dictatorship in terms of economic coercion, oppression and non-democracy, specifically of the minimal organizational and structural power of non-capital versus capital.

---

66   For the notion of functional equivalence see Luhmann (1995) and Merton (1968).

4.1.2   Restriction of the Scope of Unionization

A related typical property of capitalist dictatorship represents the restriction of the scope of unionization, hence restricted union coverage, as a facet or correlate of the suppression of labor collective organization and especially action. The restricted scope of unionization through low levels of union or collective bargaining coverage characterizes capitalist dictatorship, namely the unfreedom and exclusion of non-capital strata in the economy, while its high level characterizing economic democracy and inclusion. Low and often minimal union coverage therefore indicates capitalist dictatorship's high degree of economic coercion and oppression and non-democracy. Specifically, it expresses the minimal structural and bargaining power and collective agency as well as exclusion of labor in relation to capital, thus the severe imbalance between their powers and actions violating industrial and political democracy. Moreover, for evident reasons low union coverage provides a more complete indicator of capitalist dictatorship than union density, especially being a good measure of labor minimal collective rights and bargaining power. Conversely, its high level by extending collective agreements to nonunion workers more completely reflects economic democracy and measures the balance between capital and non-capital in these terms.

These reasons consist in that in quantitative terms collective bargaining coverage is typically among OECD countries, aside from some exceptions (Japan, Lithuania, Mexico, New Zealand, Turkey), higher than union density, as in all of Western Europe (plus Australia, Canada and marginally the US with a 1.5 percent differential). Substantively, collective bargaining coverage expresses the freedom and so agency of labor, regardless of being organized in unions or not, to negotiate with capital or to be included in the collective contract with the latter and share in its provisions about wages, benefits, job security, work conditions, etc. In these terms, the narrow scope and impact of unionization through minimal union coverage expressing equivalent labor structural and bargaining power even more fully than its low density captures and does justice to capitalist dictatorship in its coercive, oppressive and non-democratic dimension.

Alternatively, capitalist dictatorship shows that it represents a system of economic coercion, oppression and non-democracy as well as exclusion of non-capital by narrow union coverage and thus the minimal freedom and agency of non-capital. This is consequent to suppressing labor collective action, including its free group-level transaction, negotiation and contracting with capital and the extension of its terms to all laborers, contrary to the exalted essence of capitalism as the voluntary complex of transactions, negotiations and contract, the 'free enterprise' system.[67] As a result, capitalist dictatorship invariably features extremely narrow union coverage and thus sustains minimal freedom and agency for labor as a collective agent, while endowing capital with the maximum in these terms. Both results are consistent with its nature and system of economic coercion, oppression and exclusion of non-capital.

In empirical terms, contemporary capitalist dictatorships and similar oppressive systems exhibit the tendency to exceedingly narrow union coverage resulting from the suppression of labor collective action and coercion overall. Such instances span from the non-Western world, including most of South America and Africa, much of Asia, Eastern Europe under oligarchic capitalism, Turkey and other Islamic countries, to some Western societies, especially the US since Reaganism and post-2016 consistently having the lowest coverage rate by far (12 percent) among them. For instance, not only is the level of unionization lower in the US than in most other Western countries, but its 'collective bargaining coverage statistics' is the lowest among them expressing the fact that such bargaining only covers unionized workplaces in which moreover individual worker-employer contracts predominate over collective contracting. To that extent, this statistic makes American capitalism's system of industrial relations since anti-labor Reaganism appear as or approximate capitalist dictatorship according to this criterion, as the observation of 'workplace dictatorships' and 'authoritarian firms' in this context precisely suggests.[68]

The same holds for most non-Western variations, extensions or emulations of unrestrained American capitalism such as those in Latin America and Africa, Mexico, parts of Asia, Eastern Europe under the new capitalist oligarchy, Turkey and some other Islamic countries. All these countries qualify as capitalist dictatorships judging by their extremely low collective bargaining coverage rates, aside from rare exceptions. Strikingly, the union coverage rate is virtually the same in the US (12 percent) and Mexico (12.5 percent), more precisely even slightly higher in the latter. On this criterion, American capitalism converges with and appears closer to the capitalist third world (Mexico) than to the Western European model from which it strikingly deviates in union coverage

---

67 Examples of such exaltation of capitalism as the 'free' enterprise and contract system include Friedman (1982), Kornai (2000), Rajan and Zingales (2004), Shleifer (2009), for a more nuanced view see Parsons (1967).

68 Expressions 'workplace dictatorships' and 'authoritarian firms' come from (Wright 2013, pp. 6–7; also, see Blau and Kahn (2000), Kimeldorf (2013), Kristal (2013), Western and Beckett (1999), and Wodtke (2016).

(98.5 percent in France, 56 percent in Germany, 90 percent in Sweden) and related terms. It therefore displays another, genuine facet of conservatism's sustained 'American exceptionalism' as a deviation from Western regulated welfare capitalism—although US 'libertarian' economists and conservative politicians construe and denounce the latter as 'European socialism'—and not from the despised third world.

To take a reverse example, by having a considerably higher coverage rate due to collective contracts and agreements between the 'three main labor market parties: trade unions, employer associations, and works councils', German capitalism's system of industrial relations does not qualify as capitalist dictatorship using this criterion but as economic democracy.[69] This applies to most other Western European, especially Scandinavian or Nordic, societies, including France, Austria, Belgium, Iceland, Sweden, Finland, Denmark, Italy, and the Netherlands. They qualify as and indeed epitomize capitalist-economic democracies by their highest coverage rates in the Western and whole world (reaching often 80, 90 and approaching 100 percent) because of such collective contracts and agreements between labor and capital. Moreover, as for and stemming from the suppression of unionization and severe labor repression, union coverage hardly exists in many capitalist and similar dictatorships in Africa and the Islamic world. In addition, it is, aside from partial exceptions like Chile (21 percent), comparatively low in many Asian, South American and Eastern European oligarchic states from South Korea (12 percent), Turkey (7 percent) and Mexico (12.5 percent) to most Baltic states (14 percent in Latvia, 7 percent in Lithuania) and Poland (15 percent), forming a rock-bottom OECD subgroup in union coverage which the US joins.

In sum, the restriction of the scope of unionization and consequently low levels of union coverage resulting from the suppression of labor collective action and industrial democracy provide another, more complete invariant indicator of capitalist dictatorship with respect to economic oppression. It particularly represents a proper measure of the minimal freedom or collective agency of non-capital production factors and classes in relation to capital.

4.1.3   Suppression of Collective Bargaining

As a corollary, the suppression and consequent non-existence or rarity of collective bargaining between capital and non-capital, as another result of suppressing labor collective action, marks capitalist dictatorship, particularly its

---

69   See Dustmann et al. (2014, p. 176; also, Goldschmidt and Schmieder 2017; Lyness et al. 2012; Nickell 1997).

unfreedom and exclusion in the economy. Such a tendency violates the principle and observation that the permission, promotion and hence presence and strength of collective bargaining (as Webb and Webb[70] classically argue) between the two characterizes economic democracy and inclusion and constrains unrestrained capitalism. The labor freedom and right to group-level—not just individual—negotiation through collective bargaining with capital and to inclusion in its provisions hence determines and predicts the scope of union coverage, although the latter not necessarily relate to unionization levels. After all, capitalism represents, as most economists since Smith exalt it, what Spencer (following the legal historian Maine) denotes the voluntary 'system of contract' and free negotiations and transactions versus pre-capitalism as the coercive 'system of status'. Consequently, narrow union coverage reflects equivalently low labor collective contracting or bargaining power versus capital within capitalism, violating the 'equality of bargaining power' between the two.[71]

Conversely, by suppressing the labor freedom and agency of collective bargaining and generating minimal union coverage, capitalist dictatorship perpetuates the pre-capitalist system of coercion and suspends non-coercive capitalism as Smith-Spencer's glorified 'system of contract' and free group-level negotiations (as some early neoclassical US economists admit[72]). Such a system includes what Durkheim denotes 'contractual solidarity', although unlike orthodox economists, he identifies the institutional 'non-contractual' bases of commercial contracts.

The suppression and consequently non-existence or rarity of collective bargaining even more specifically indicates capitalist dictatorship's dimension of economic coercion, oppression and exclusion of non-capital production factors and social classes.[73] It does this by expressing labor's low degree of freedom or collective agency and exclusion from the system of collective

---

70   Webb and Webb (1902, pp. xxii, xxxv–vi, 172) invoke the 'Method of Collective Bargaining' as one of the two 'alternative Methods' of enacting industrial democracy (the other being 'legal enactment'), preferring it to 'free and unfettered Individual Bargaining' that leads to 'sweating'.

71   Commons (1931) and Laski (1936) point to and Parsons (1967) implies the 'equality of bargaining power'. See also Acemoglu and Robinson (2015), Beck (2000), Blau and Kahn (2000), Dustmann et al. (2014), Esping-Andersen (2003), Halac (2012), Hallock (2009), Kristal (2013), Lee (2007), and Rogers and Streeck (1995).

72   This is J. B. Clark (1892), see also Kalleberg (2009), Somerville (2000), and Western and Beckett (1999).

73   This is what Web and Web already imply above, see also Esping-Andersen (2003), Rogers and Streeck (1995) and Western and Beckett (1999).

contracting with capital, thus their imbalance of power and action and industrial non-democracy, including 'workplace dictatorships' and 'authoritarian' enterprises ruled by a 'dictatorial' plutocratic class.

In particular, thereby capitalist dictatorship negates, eliminates and indeed rules out labor's collective bargaining power as a legitimate, institutionalized influence and its agency and capacity to engage in group-level negotiation, contracting and transaction with capital. Tönnies classically suggests this observing that early coercive capitalism reduces 'all non-capitalists' either to 'inanimate tools—the very essence of slavery' or to legal 'nonentities' hence 'unable to make contracts valid within the system'.[74] Therefore, capitalist dictatorship delegitimizes non-capital—as does unrestrained American capitalism that 'never completely institutionalized' labor relations—as an institutional contracting partner to capital, and makes non-capitalists-negotiators groups non grata.

In the process, it contravenes and suspends the hallmark of capitalism as the presumably free and universal 'system of contract'. Therefore, by eliminating collective bargaining capitalist dictatorship deprives non-capital as a group actor of the 'freedom of contract' that it generously bestows on and monopolizes for capital. It thus contradicts capitalism as the presumed realm of universally free contracting in Smith-Spencer's vision between both individuals and groups, including capitalists and non-capitalists.[75] Conversely, by this criterion capitalism becomes or approaches capitalist dictatorship so long it rules out and eliminates collective bargaining and the group freedom of contract for non-capital.

Hence, the hallmark of capitalist dictatorship is not just suppressing or rendering labor's collective bargaining power, versus that of capital, weak but negating and ruling it out altogether by eliminating collective bargaining as a legitimate institutionalized procedure involving capital and non-capital as group actors, not mere individual agents. It seems immaterial or futile to talk of labor's collective bargaining power and group freedom of contract, including Durkheimian 'contractual solidarity' between capitalist and non-capitalist classes, in the absence of its free collective bargaining and contracting with capital. This is the case with the anti-union US South, especially the public

---

74   See Tönnies (2001, p. 71), also, Beck (1999), Kristal (2010), Lin and Tomaskovic-Devey (2013), Martin and Dixon (2010), Rogers and Streeck (1995), and Walker, Martin, and McCarthy (2008).

75   Examples of such depictions of capitalism are in Hart (2017), Kornai (2000), La Porta, Lopez-de-Silanes, and Shleifer (2008); for skeptical views, see Bowles and Gintis (2000), also Laski (1936), and Simpson (1934).

sector where such a procedure is non-existent and taboo hardly ever considered, as well as in non-Western countries from most of Latin America to much of Eastern Europe during oligarchic capitalism to virtually all Islamic theocratic states. In short, such situations of 'collective bargaining prohibited', as literally stated in the US South's public sector and most third-world countries, make labor's group bargaining power and freedom of contract versus capital a non sequitur, an impossibility theorem. Further, like the 'freedom of contract' in some views, free collective contracting may be irrelevant or inefficient and distorted without the approximate balance of collective bargaining power between capital and labor and with severe 'wealth constraints'.[76]

At any rate, compatible and entwined with restricted union coverage, the suppression of collective bargaining supplies a proper, concrete indicator of capitalist dictatorship, in particular a useful yardstick of labor minimal collective freedom and structural and bargaining power. By contrast, its permission and pervasiveness indicate developed and pervasive economic democracy and freedoms, particularly measuring the proximate balance between capital and non-capital in this respect. The non-existence or scarcity of collective bargaining is the mirror and proof of capitalist dictatorship negating and suppressing the freedom and right of non-capital to collective transaction and economic negotiation with capital as an aspect of its negation and suppression of free labor collective action. Non-existent or scarce collective bargaining seems particularly revealing of capitalist dictatorship, because it reveals the latter's denial and suppression of non-capitalists' freedom and right to collectively bargain with capitalists and extend the terms of such negotiations to all, including nonunion, workers, as in most of Western Europe. Moreover, such a situation of 'collective bargaining prohibited' in the US South and most of the third world exposes the plutocratic, indeed aristocratic, elite distaste for and resistance to labor classes (the populace) collectively contracting as co-equal with the capitalist class AS what Pareto deems the new aristocracy of capital. The latter instead forces in a classic dictatorial manner non-capital production factors and strata to accept or resign to the will and interest of capital under the threat of severe economic degradation, deprivation, hardship and other sanctions.

Alternatively, capitalist dictatorship indicates that it represents a system of economic oppression and exclusion of non-capital by its suppression or limitation of collective bargaining and thus of democratic and cooperative versus

---

76   See Halac (2012), also Commons (1931), Hart (2017), Laski (1936), Lin and Tomaskovic-Devey (2013) and Simpson (1934), for the anti-union US South, see Kimeldorf (2013; Lloyd (2012) and Rao, Yue, and Ingram (2011).

undemocratic and antagonistic industrial relations between capital and labor. It does so by negating the freedom and right of non-capital to negotiate and contract collectively, as a particular facet of its negation of free labor collective action. In so doing, it is dictatorship precisely by denying and displaying an aristocracy-style plutocratic, oligarchic and autocratic disgust for and resistance to the same kind of freedom or agency for non-capital as a production factor or collective actor with which it lavishes and exalts capital in the same capacity—'free' enterprise, bargaining, contracting, action. It thereby shows that it is a pathological or irrational system in its own right even in terms of capitalism as Smith's 'system of natural' universal economic liberty and Spencer's system of free contract'.[77]

Capitalist dictatorship therefore treats non-capital social strata as equivalents to slaves and servants by labor coercion or as legal non-agents denied as production factors or collective actors the agency and capacity for bargaining and contracting. It therefore reduces, in Tönnies' account, 'all non-capitalists' to 'inanimate tools' as the 'essence of slavery' or makes them 'legally nonentities, deemed incapable of exercising rational choice, therefore unable to make contracts valid within the system'.[78] As a consequence of its logic and system of suppression of and aristocratic-style distaste for labor free collective action in relation to capital, capitalist dictatorship exhibits the non-existence or rarity of collective bargaining and thus the lack of freedom of Tönnies' 'non-capitalists' to collectively transact, negotiate and contract with capital.

Empirically, capitalist dictatorships and similar oppressive systems fully conform to the pattern of suppression and non-existence or rarity of capital-labor collective bargaining and related democratic and cooperative industrial relations. The empirical settings involve the same range of such systems from non-Western settings like most of South America, much of Asia, Eastern Europe during oligarchic capitalism, Turkey under Islamic governance to some Western societies, above all the US where collective bargaining has suffered near-demise to become a rarified procedure since Reaganism and post-2016. This especially applies to the anti-union South where collective bargaining has become virtually an extinct practice and taboo hardly anyone dares to advocate in the public sector (state schools and universities) or steadily diminishing in the private industry in which contracting between individual employees and employers functions as a bogus substitute, as in much of the country.

---

77 For such interpretations of capitalism, see Buchanan (1991), Commons (1931), and Grampp (2000).

78 See Tönnies (2000, p. 71).

Furthermore, collective bargaining is virtually unheard of and does not exist as an institutionalized practice or is extremely rare among capitalist-conservative dictatorships in Africa and the Islamic world of oppressive capitalism and strict theocracy, for example Iran, Saudi Arabia and other Gulf states, just as in the public sector of the 'Bible Belt' of 'money and God'. This shared feature shows that these theocracies suppress even this facet of labor collective action and economic democracy with no necessarily adverse bearing on religion and 'holy' repression, affirming the common proto-totalitarian core.[79]

Taken together, all these capitalist/theocratic dictatorships from most of South America and Eastern Europe under oligarchic capitalism to Turkey, Saudi Arabia and other Islamic states and to conservative America, at least the 'Bible Belt', display a strong linkage between the preceding indicators. Specifically, this is the link between the suppression and absence or weakness of labor unions and the prohibition and non-existence or rarity of collective bargaining between capital and non-capital, with the first generating and predicting the second. A classic historical case in point is Germany during Nazism where consistent with Hitler's promised conservative pro-capitalist and anti-labor 'broad coalition of the right', notably 'authoritarian rightism', shortly upon seizing power the Nazi state dissolved labor unions and imprisoned its members. A more recent exemplar is Chile's Pinochet dictatorship that following this fascist template immediately eradicated worker organizations and murdered and persecuted their activists. Thatcherism in Great Britain and Reaganism in America seemingly follow both templates in launching their violent or repressive anti-union and anti-labor class-driven warfare, with prudent adaptations to their different environments. This warfare crucially contributes to and explains the near-demise of collective bargaining and contracting between capital and non-capital especially in much of American capitalism since the 1980s through present days.

In sum, ensuing from the plutocratic negation of and disgust for free labor collective action versus capital, the suppression of collective bargaining between the two production factors as collective actors furnishes an indicator of capitalist dictatorship in its facet of economic coercion, exclusion and closure. It especially supplies a good metric of the denial of the freedom and capacity of non-capitalists to transact, negotiate and contract collectively with capitalists on existential and related questions, thus reducing the first to legal

---

79   The term 'proto-totalitarian' is from Bauman (1997, p. 184).

non-agents not capable of making valid collective contracts with the second within the capitalist system.

4.1.4   Suppression of Codetermination

In addition, the suppression and resulting absence or weakness of the freedom and right, practice and mechanisms of labor collective participation in the management of enterprises—briefly, codetermination—typifies capitalist dictatorship, just as its extensiveness and strength are for economic democracy. Consequently, the suppression or restriction of labor codetermination in corporate governance is an additional indicator of capitalist dictatorship in its facet of coercion, oppression and exclusion of non-capital and non-democracy in the economy, reaching the point of 'workplace dictatorships' and 'authoritarian firms'.

Specifically, non-codetermination indicates the sharp inequality, imbalance, or asymmetry of power and influence between capital and labor in favor of the first, which violates economic democracy and cooperative industrial relations. It instead reproduces their antagonistic variants in which the first production factor invariably enjoys superior positional or structural power over and dominates the second, as reported especially for American capitalism, and to that extent becomes a 'dictatorial business class' or acts according to the 'dictator game' script. For instance, the absence or scarcity of works councils as mechanisms of labor codetermination in firm management is typical for capitalist dictatorship, just as their existence, frequency and importance typify economic democracy. This holds for some other mechanisms of labor codetermination involving its 'real right' of intervening in corporate decision-making such as worker seats on the company's board of directors implementing board-level employee representation.[80]

Alternatively, capitalist dictatorship reveals that it represents an economic system of coercion, non-democracy and closure in relation to non-capital by the non-existence or irrelevance of labor codetermination in corporate governance, including works councils, employee board representation and similar mechanisms, and generally of democratic and cooperative capital-labor industrial relations. As a consequence of its built-in structure of economic coercion and exclusion, capitalist dictatorship tends to display the lack or extremely low levels of labor codetermination, including works councils, employee board representation and other methods of economic democracy.

---

80   Piketty (2014, p. 397) suggests that 'without a real right to intervene in corporate decision-making (including seats for workers on the company's board of directors), transparency is of little use'.

In empirical terms, capitalist dictatorships and related coercive economic systems confirm the tendency toward the suppression, absence or weakness of labor codetermination in company management, including works councils and employee board representation. For example, labor codetermination through works councils or employee board representation is nonexistent and almost unheard of, at most an extreme rarity, among capitalist and related dictatorships in Africa, Asia (except for, in part, South Korea), Latin America, and the Islamic world, including Iran, Saudi Arabia, other Gulf states and Turkey. In addition, it is relatively limited and weak in much of Eastern Europe, particularly the Baltic states, under oligarchy, albeit with exceptions like Czech Republic, Hungary, Slovak Republic and especially Slovenia.

Further, aside from some exceptions, labor codetermination is almost nonexistent or ephemeral in some Western societies, above all the US, particularly the anti-union South. Thus, works councils and employee board representation, with rare exceptions, do not exist or matter and are largely unknown and proxy taboos in most American companies. A particularly egregious and recent notorious instance reportedly involves a European company's (Volkswagen's) unsuccessful attempt at introducing a works council in the deep South (Tennessee) mainly because of the virulent anti-union opposition of Southern conservative authorities. By contrast, the company reportedly considers the participation of such councils in management decision-making 'a cornerstone of successful firm policy that helps furthering common interests' and indeed seeks to establish them in all of its operations, ranging from Europe to Mexico and elsewhere.[81] Judging by this report, it turns out that the Mexican Volkswagen plant has a works council but not that in the US South due to the vehemently adverse reaction of its ultra-conservative anti-labor rulers, and is in that sense ahead of its Northern counterpart in labor codetermination. This episode reaffirms the unparalleled pro-capital, anti-labor intransigence of American conservatism as the most vehement and ultimately violent enabler and defender of capitalist dictatorship, including capitalist 'Bible-Belt' theocracy, and labor coercion in the Western world.

In light of such abortive attempts to introduce works council as a common form of labor codetermination in Western Europe, giving US workers seats on the 'company's board of directors' may seem even more of a 'mission impossible', dream, fantasy or utopia within American capitalism, in spite or precisely because of the fact such worker representation would provide them with a 'real right to intervene' in corporate decisions. In stark contrast to the

---

81   See the report in Dustmann et al. (2014, p. 177).

above non-American company, most US companies choose not to introduce and actively oppose the introduction of works councils and employee board representation, rendering both forms of labor codetermination and economic democracy nonentities in American capitalism and beyond the apparently anachronistic South At least on this account, such a model of capitalism approximates capitalist dictatorship and manifests economic non-democracy in that it constitutes a system of 'workplace dictatorships' and most companies represent 'authoritarian firms'. Overall, labor codetermination as a dimension of industrial democracy has historically been and continues to be exceedingly rare and weak in the US economy, with minor exceptions, and further rarifying and weakening, effectively disappearing. This process enfolds in unison and mutual reinforcement with the dramatic fall of union density and coverage and the near-demise of collective bargaining since anti-labor Reaganism and during conservatism as a whole.

Furthermore, the preceding about negative labor codetermination through its two mechanisms in the US applies, with some qualifications, to most other Anglo-Saxon countries. Among these countries, works councils exist as an institutionalized and widespread mechanism only, in part, in Great Britain, employee board representation is essentially non-existent in the latter, Australia, Canada and New Zealand, while Ireland features extremely limited cases of both forms of labor codetermination. In this regard, these countries justify their characterization as reemerging 'plutonomies' and to that extent capitalist dictatorships, albeit with some differences in degree between America as the leader and the others, including Great Britain in light of its partial incidence of labor codetermination through works councils. Altogether, with secondary variations, the suppression or scarcity of labor codetermination via works councils and employee board representation appears to be primarily a syndrome of non-Western/non-European and American/Anglo-Saxon capitalisms. They stand in sharp contrast to their Western European counterpart featuring the highest level of this dimension of democracy, including both mechanisms of labor participation in corporate governance. Judging by this criterion, the first two modalities of capitalism consequently exemplify or approximate capitalist dictatorship, while the second variety epitomizing capitalist-economic democracy, ceteris paribus.

In sum, the suppression and lack or irrelevance of the freedom and practice of labor codetermination in corporate governance, including work councils, employee board representation and similar mechanisms, is yet another complementary indicator of capitalist dictatorship in respect of economic coercion, non-democracy and closure. Especially it indicates the extreme imbalance of power and influence between capital and labor disfavoring the second, thus negating and suppressing industrial democracy which the balance in this respect typifies.

4.2 Indicators and Proxies of Economic Inequality, Degradation and Deprivation

4.2.1 Extreme Concentration of Wealth

Indicators and proxies of capitalist dictatorship as the anti-egalitarian system of economic inequality, degradation and deprivation are also multiple, interconnected and mutually reinforcing. They include extreme wealth concentration, extremely unequal income distribution, widespread material deprivation, hardship and poverty, and intense labor exploitation, economic non-protection and insecurity.

First, the massive distribution and consequently extreme concentration of wealth in favor of capital typifies and pervades capitalist dictatorship in all its forms and agents from autocracy and dynasty to aristocracy, oligarchy and plutocracy, just as that privileging aristocracy typified pre-capitalist despotism. In this respect, expressions 'unequal distribution' and 'great concentration' of wealth characterizing capitalism and pre-capitalism and to a lesser degree post-capitalism appear as understatements and partly imprecise statements with regard to capitalist dictatorship. Such a distribution is not just unequal and this concentration great but reaches and persists at extremely high levels in capitalist dictatorship, precisely and exclusively privileging a definite production factor and social class of capital and disfavoring 'all non-capitalists', even though this is axiomatically given and understood in the system.

This distributive process initially involves original, 'natural' wealth distribution inherently favoring capital over non-capital during long periods: large, virtually unlimited or exponentially growing capitalist returns prevail over relatively small, limited or slowly increasing labor incomes. This process thereby generates and perpetuates an extreme inequality between the two classes, a sharply unequal class distribution of wealth and thus economic resources. Such wealth distribution inherently privileges capital primarily because of the sociological factor of class stratification, notably the differential systemic power of social classes. Specifically, this difference consists in that, as Tönnies' suggests, capitalists represent the 'natural lords and masters' of capitalism that 'exists for their sake and is their tool', while 'all non-capitalists' within this system being either akin to 'inanimate tools' and so emanations of 'slavery' or 'legally nonentities'. Such an extreme duality of power between the two social classes in capitalism coexists and co-functions with certain economic and technological factors, the aggregate effect being that in long terms capital returns grow at a considerably higher rate (4–5 percent per year) than labor incomes and the economy (1–1.5 percent).[82]

By analogy, Tönnies implies that wealth distribution also inherently privileges slave owners and aristocrats in slavery and feudalism, respectively, because they are the 'natural lords and masters' of these pre-capitalist systems that exist only for their sake and are their tool, while all other classes within them being either 'inanimate tools', simply 'slaves or legal 'nonentities' like servants. This suggests that wealth distribution in capitalism and the latter as an economic system displays a fundamental continuity with that in slavery and feudalism and these ancient regimes rather than a profound rupture with them by being almost as power-based and thus arbitrary. This contradicts 'libertarian' and other apologetic economics' glorification of such wealth distribution as completely 'impartial' and 'fair' governed by "natural' and iron' market-economic laws and the capitalist system as the Panglossian 'best of all possible worlds'.[83]

Furthermore, the process of distribution in capitalist dictatorship comprises the derivative and often coercive redistribution of wealth from non-capitalist classes to capital, expressing an inverse Robin-Hood transfer of economic resources from poor to rich strata, especially from laboring classes to plutocracy.[84] Overall, unequal initial wealth distribution seems axiomatic, intrinsic

---

82 This is what Piketty observes and postulates for the long-term evolution of capitalism. Specifically, Piketty (2014, p. 388) that with respect to wealth distribution the 'principal destabilizing force has to do with the fact that the private rate of return on capital, r, can be significantly higher for long periods of time than the rate of growth of income and output, g. The inequality $r > g$ implies that wealth accumulated in the past grows more rapidly than output and wages. This inequality expresses a fundamental logical contradiction. The entrepreneur inevitably tends to become a rentier, more and more dominant over those who own nothing but their labor. Once constituted, capital reproduces itself faster than output increases. The past devours the future'. Further, he predicts that given 'an average return on capital of 4–5 percent, it is therefore likely that $r > g$ will again become the norm in the twenty-first century, as it had been throughout history until the eve of World War I. In the 20th century, it took two world wars to wipe away the past and significantly reduce the return on capital, thereby creating the illusion that the fundamental structural contradiction of capitalism ($r > g$) had been overcome'. (Piketty 2014, p. 398). For wealth concentration in the US in relation to social mobility, see also (Benhabib, Bisin, and Luo 2019).

83 For skeptical views, see Baumol (2000), Merton (1968) and Nelson and Sheffrin (1991), also, Schumpeter (1954).

84 Samuelson (1983a, p. 203) states that under certain conditions 'any interference (a la Robin Hood) with perfect competition which transfers income from rich to poor would be beneficial'. See also Acemoglu et al. (2008), Feagin (2001), Martin (2010), and Stiglitz (2010).

to capitalism, just as to pre-capitalism. In particular, such redistribution from non-capital to capital, especially when massive, compulsory and systematic, is even more typical of capitalist dictatorship and related inegalitarian and nondemocratic, including conservative, fascist and theocratic systems, as of ancient anti-egalitarian and despotic regimes like slavery, caste, and feudalism.

A reported paradigmatic exemplar is the redistribution of wealth 'in favor of the wealthy', just as of power 'in favor of the powerful'—thus from non-capitalists to capitalist 'lords and masters'—that forms the program of Reaganism launching the 'conservative revolution' in America.[85] This exemplar epitomizes a broader pattern of 'redistributing toward the rich' such as 'expensive transfers' to this class through the 'politics of upward-redistributive policy', including "radically inegalitarian tax policies', in its favor, especially typifying American capitalism during conservatism since the 1950s through the 21st century. This time includes Reaganism and post-2016 as the second and third apogee in this process—with transient interruptions like the New Deal and wartime—of enriching the wealthy and so capitalist plutocracy, autocracy (the 'lying demagogue') and dynasty, combined with empowering the powerful, after the Gilded Age as the first.

Crucially, both the initial economic distribution and subsequent non-economic, coercive redistribution of wealth generate and sustain, in conjunction and reciprocal intensification, as a consequence its extreme and perpetual concentration in capital versus non-capital within capitalist dictatorship. Indeed, this process of wealth distribution, redistribution to and extreme concentration in capital as a ruling class in Mosca-Pareto's sense especially in the US economically defines and grounds the sociologically most relevant and persistent form and agent of capitalist dictatorship among Western societies. This form and agent is plutocracy or plutocratic aristocracy and oligarchy in Michels' meaning and its holders within capitalism, such as 'plutonomy' and its agents reemerging and entrenching in America and other Anglo-Saxon countries during recent times.

Furthermore, by the intrinsic tendency to nearly infinite expansion of wealth its concentration tends to reach or approach its monopolization, in Weber's words, its 'full appropriation' and 'monopolistic closure' by capitalists such as plutocracy or plutocratic oligarchy, autocracy and dynasty within capitalist

---

85   Solow et al. (1987, p. 182) observe that Reaganism as the 'conservative revolution' in
      America 'cares about the distribution of wealth and power and its program is and has
      always been in favour of.the redistribution of wealth in favour of the wealthy and of
      power in favour of the powerful'. See also Jacobs and Dirlam (2016), Hung and Thompson
      (2016), and Stiglitz (2012).

dictatorship and capitalism generally. This especially holds for the productive, permanent or investment segment of wealth, such as means of production (in Marx's and Menger's context) or capital goods (in Tönnies' words), simply capital that the capitalist class attempts to fully appropriate, monopolize and close against non-capitalists. This is what after all makes this class 'capitalist' and its members 'capitalists', so 'natural lords and masters' in capitalism.

Like its concentration but more manifestly, the monopolization of wealth by capitalist plutocracy resembles, often parallels and results from monopolizing or controlling the market and economy. The latter process entails what Weber designates as domination 'by virtue of a position of monopoly', specifically 'capitalistic monopolies' or in Wieser's words, 'capitalistic monopoly-organizations' aggregating to form monopoly capitalism[86] and power. Hence, wealth monopolization coexists with an anticompetitive and partially coercive or predatory—as most economists since Smith deplore monopoly—form of economic-market distribution invariably privileging and, as Weber suggests, imposed by the capitalist class on non-capitalist strata, as distinct from pre-capitalism in which 'monopolies of status groups' predominate. For example, the monopolization or concentration of wealth and power by large capitalists named the 'robber barons' in Gilded-Age American capitalism reportedly parallels and mostly results from their monopolizing or controlling the market.

Conversely, wealth monopolization by the capitalist class would seem incompatible with a non-monopolistic, open market and economy such as free competition that should presumably diffuse or dilute wealth by dispersing profits and other capital incomes among many competing capitalists and even non-capitalists. Nevertheless, a competitive market does not invariably rule out and indeed can lead to wealth monopolization as well in that competing, just as monopolistic, capitalists may monopolize or concentrate wealth and income versus and deny or restrict it to non-capitalists as a social class, as they evidently do in capitalist dictatorship and capitalism as a whole. On this account, economic monopoly in capitalism while the sufficient is not the necessary condition of wealth monopolization by the capitalist class. Conversely, free competition in capitalism while perhaps the necessary is not the sufficient antidote to wealth monopolization or concentration by the capitalist class as a whole versus other classes. Taken together, monopoly enables but is not strictly indispensable for and competition may but does not necessarily disable capital's wealth monopolization. This implies that purely market-economic

---

86   See also Adorno (1991), Baran and Sweezy (1966), Braudel (1979), Morgan and Prasad (2009).

explanations and theories of wealth monopolization or concentration in capitalism are at best insufficient or partial and need to combine with sociological
conceptions that include political, cultural and other social factors in a holistic
and thus more realistic explanation.

Relatedly, economic-political oligarchy corresponds to and ultimately fuses
with what Wieser and Schumpeter designate as 'monopoloids' such as market oligopoly. This is what the 'oligarchical control of both the state and the
economy' and the resulting fusion of political and economic oligarchies ('old
boy networks') demonstrate in contemporary American capitalism.[87] Also,
Mitchell identifies the monopoly or oligopoly source of wealth observing
that US capitalists make profits from the 'sheer financial control over markets without the exercise of social leadership', as the prevalent mechanism of
wealth acquisition and a 'socially irrational, anti-economic' phenomenon in
early American capitalism. Consequently, Mitchell paints the latter as effective capitalist dictatorship in the form of 'economic oppression' and 'industrial despotism' that the 'despotic might of capital' exerts over labor and hence
suppresses 'industrial democracy. His contemporary, US President Theodore
Roosevelt also implies the link between the concentrated wealth and monopoly or oligopoly of the robber barons by deploring the 'tyranny' of plutocracy
through that of 'mere wealth', as do other observers alerting to monopolistic
'malefactors of great wealth' and another President, Franklin Roosevelt later
denouncing 'economic royalists'.[88]

It follows that the monopolized or concentrated wealth, just as the reported
'power and abuses', of the robber barons connect with and indeed derive from
their economic monopoly or oligopoly. Furthermore, the latter often expands
into double, bilateral monopoly or oligopoly by also involving monopolistic
control of labor markets, simply monopsony or oligopsony. An exemplar is the
postbellum US South in which reportedly 'monopsonistic arrangements' substituted for slavery and persisted, along with the 'persistence of labor repression',[89] for long, partly up to the present.

In addition, and conjunction, the robber barons' concentrated economic
and political power is reportedly both the cause and product of criminal 'innovation' (in Merton's words). This includes, as MIchels already alerts, 'gigantic',
socially accepted and institutionalized corruption, with monopoly/monop-
sony being often a form, cause and result of the latter. It also involves the lax

---

87   See Pryor (2002, p. 364), also, Levy and Razin (2017), Mailath et al. (2000), for more gen-
      eral observations see Morck et al. (2005).
88   See also Formisano (2015).
89   See Acemoglu and Robinson (2008, pp. 286–7).

'regulation of private political activity' and the robber barons' suppression of labor organization often using violence, including violent capitalist militias, leading to the condemnation of these predatory and repressive specimens of capitalists during the Gilded Age.[90] In Smith's terms, this provides an instance of capital monopolization or concentration of wealth effected through what he deplores as capitalists' constant tendency for 'conspiracy against the public',[91] including monopolistic restrictions of competition, as perhaps the only valid 'conspiracy theory' in capitalist dictatorship and generally capitalism by protecting it primarily from capitalists.

Relatedly, the monopolization of wealth by capital in capitalist dictatorship relates to and indeed derives from the coercive political and ideologically-driven extraction and redistribution of economic resources from non-capitalist strata to the capitalist class. This involves reverse Robin-Hood transfers from the poor to the wealthy and in that sense corporate 'welfare assistance' or 'relief' for capitalists via extensive transfers from non-capitalists. Due to being typically coercive and involving corruption resulting from what Michels denotes the 'unrestrained power of capital' and predation or extortion, this mode of redistribution approximates the 'method of extraction' of wealth from society in kleptocracy and predatory capitalism and its twin 'mafia capitalism'.

On account of this method of redistribution, capitalist dictatorship effectively operates and overtly exposes itself as kleptocracy and predatory capitalism, which confirms that the latter belong to its component forms and agents and especially represent consummate continuations and intensifications of plutocracy or oligarchy. Within Western society, such a method especially typifies Reaganism and generally conservatism in America since, notably post-2016, along with Thatcherism and its legacy in Great Britain, through the coercive and persistent 'redistribution of wealth in favour of the wealthy'.[92]

Consequently, such wealth redistribution succeeds in only evermore enriching the rich and so the capitalist class in America, Great Britain and other Anglo-Saxon plutonomies, as well as in non-Western, including old South American, African and Asian and new Eastern European, plutocracies, oligarchies, autocracies and dynasties. The process looks as an absurdity, anomaly or irrationality from the standpoint of 'rationally regulated' and egalitarian

---

90   See Isaac (2002, p. 396), Kimeldorf (2013, p. 1035), and Mizruchi and Marshall (2016, pp. 144–5).
91   See also Bruni and Sugden (2013) and Eggertsson (2012).
92   See Solow et al. (1987, p. 182), also, Atkinson (1997), Auclert and Rognlie (2017), Beck (2000), Hodgson (1999), Hung and Thompson (2016), Jacobs and Dirlam (2016), Kristal (2010), Martin (2010), Stiglitz (2010).

capitalism in Scandinavia and most of Western Europe, just as laissez-faire capitalism does. The latter typically enables and rationalizes this inverse Robin-
Hood extraction in the name of capital unrestricted 'freedom' as Hobbesian
anarchy in which the 'law of the strongest' rules and determines—instead of
the 'law' of marginal productivity that neoclassical economics postulates—
through 'power resources' wealth shares for capitalists and non-capitalists, and
commands massive transfers from the second to the first.[93]

However, this reverse wealth redistribution constitutes the inner economic
logic and normal pattern of capitalist dictatorship or plutocracy in these and
other societies, just as represented the inherent element of pre capitalist dictatorships from slavery and caste to feudalism or master-servant systems in
various settings. This indicates a basic continuity running from pre capitalist to
capitalist dictatorships rather than a rupture in this direction. While being the
essence and symbol of capitalist and related dictatorship, such wealth redistribution amounts to an insult to the injury of extortion and predation from
the standpoint of non-capital classes. It does so by, first, expropriating from
non-capitalist classes their already minimal and even, as in America since
Reaganism and under conservatism, relatively declining share of the original
distribution of wealth. Then it transfers this wealth to the capitalist class that
already enjoys a maximal amount in many diverse shapes, including profits,
dividends, capital gains, and rents, by 'upward-redistributive policy' such as
'radically inegalitarian tax policies' in favor of capital.[94]

Such a reverse wealth redistribution represents a variation (to cite the main
actor's statement in an atypically critical and sociologically-minded American
movie) on the theme of always giving 'plenty to the few' and 'few to the plenty'
and the consequent 'paradox of poverty in the midst of plenty'. The latter forms
an inherent feature and accurate indicator of capitalist and similar dictatorship, including plutonomy in Anglo-Saxon societies and autocracy in third-
world countries, as of pre-capitalist despotism from slavery and caste to feudal
master-servant systems. This confirms that capitalist dictatorship on account
of reverse redistribution is continuous with and perpetuates in a modified
shape rather than, as its 'libertarian' apologists allege while not admitting the
term, supersedes pre-capitalist despotism. Further, such reverse redistribution
in capitalist dictatorship is consistent with the logic, operation and outcome

---

93   Laissez-faire capitalism's Hayekian rendition is rejected in Knight (1967), see also Bowles
       and Gintis (2000), Hodgson (1999), and Samuelson (1983b). For 'power resources' and
       transfers to capital see Auclert and Rognlie (2017), Jacobs and Dirlam (2016), Martin
       (2010) and Piven (2008).
94   See Martin (2010, pp. 2–4).

of dictatorships or oligarchies of the rich—systems and methods of expropriation, extortion or extraction of wealth from non-wealthy to wealthy strata.

The preceding also reaffirms that capitalist dictatorship, in particular plutocracy, not just fundamentally diverges from regulated, egalitarian and democratic capitalism. It also perverts and deviates from contemporary capitalism in general. This holds so long as wealth redistribution from the rich to other classes a la Robin Hood has become an established norm and institutionalized procedure—'redistribution' means exactly this—in most variants of capitalism. The latter involve virtually all Western societies, albeit in differing ways and degrees, and many non-Western countries, except for Africa, Latin America and Eastern Europe under oligarchy. The above holds as a rule, while keeping in mind the standard conservative 'American exceptionalism of redistributing from the non-wealthy to the wealthy and the partial exception of Great Britain under Thatcherism. As a rule, ideal-typical or generalized contemporary capitalism does not redistribute wealth in the poor-to-rich inverted Robin-Hood form, including from labor to capital.

Yet capitalist dictatorship such as plutocracy evidently does even in some Western societies like the US and Great Britain. This renders capitalist dictatorship an aberrant case even within the broader system and modalities of Western capitalism, as are relatedly U.S. pro-capital, exceptionally ungenerous social policies. In so doing, it also appears as a historical near-equivalent of pre-capitalist dictatorships that perform such wealth redistribution, in particular that from slaves and servants to masters and aristocracy. Relatedly, capitalist plutocracy or 'corporate capitalism' in America reportedly deviates from the classical Jeffersonian liberal-republican ideal of 'a wide diffusion of economic resources among citizens' as the necessary condition of democracy. It does so by the 'concentration of ownership' allowing the allocation of 'great financial rewards' to a 'small minority' of property owners and so economic inequality being 'more extreme' than Jefferson ever anticipated for 'a people with democratic aspirations'.[95]

In sum, both the originally unequal economic distribution of wealth between capitalists and non-capitalists and its derivative non-economic coercive redistribution from the second to the first inevitably generate its extreme concentration and approximate monopolization and closure by capital against non-capital in capitalist dictatorship such as plutocracy in America, Great Britain and other Anglo-Saxon societies and oligarchy, autocracy and dynasty in most third-world countries.

---

95   See Dahl (1985, p. 108).

In economic terms, therefore capitalist dictatorship, plutocracy in particular as its crucial sociological form and agent among Western societies since
Pareto, constitutes a corresponding phenomenon. It is an anti-egalitarian system of distributed, redistributed, extremely concentrated and approximately
monopolized wealth in capital as the dominant production factor and ruling
class, so the 'new aristocracy' versus non-capital as the aggregate of other factors and classes, as was pre-capitalist despotism ruled by old aristocracies of
estate against slaves or servants. It thus represents an economic system of
maximal and maximizing, potentially unlimited, wealth for the first class and
of minimal and minimizing, including zero or negative, wealth for the second.
This is what the share of the top one percent of the population in America
demonstrates—approaching half of financial and even total wealth—as an
embodiment of the capitalist class or plutocracy versus that of other social
strata. Historically, the wealth share of the US capitalist class tends to equal
or approach the shares of the European pre-capitalist aristocracy, namely the
1 percent or so of the population, as sometimes estimated.[96] This confirms
that all-American plutocracy represents the truly new aristocracy of capital a
la Pareto and its members merely emulate, indeed, as Weber notes, want to live
like 'European lords', as in the ante- and post-bellum South and beyond.

Generally, on these grounds the distribution/redistribution and concentration of wealth privileging capital against non-capital qualifies as an accurate
and plausible indicator of capitalist dictatorship, notably plutocracy, indicating its logic and system of permanent severe economic inequality and anti-
egalitarianism. Alternatively, capitalist dictatorship exposes itself behind the
veil of pretense, 'cheap talk', discourse and simulation of 'equality', especially
'equality of opportunity' and 'ownership for all' in American capitalism, as a
system of economic inequality by the distribution, redistribution, concentration and ultimately monopolization of wealth and power in capital as its
indicative syndrome. Simply, it reveals itself as classical plutocracy or recent
'plutonomy'.

Consequently, capitalist dictatorship generates the most extreme level
of wealth concentration in the ruling class among comparative economic
systems—excluding pre-capitalism such as slavery, caste, and feudalism—
including the variants of capitalism. Its wealth concentration tends to be
drastically higher, as in conservative America since Reaganism, than that

---

96   See Lenski (1984), also, Acemoglu and Robinson (2015), Akerlof (2007), Alvaredo et al.
      (2013, 2017), Atkinson, Piketty, and Saez (2011), Bivens and Mishel (2013), Bonica et al.
      (2013), Corak (2013), Piketty, Postel-Vinay and Jean-Laurent (2006), Saez and Zucman
      (2016), and Wolff (2002).

of democratic and egalitarian or welfare capitalism such as that in Western Europe, most notably Scandinavian and Nordic countries.

Empirically, capitalist and related conservative-fascist 'right' dictatorships manifest, with slight variations, the syndrome of extreme wealth concentration in capital versus non-capital, including the top 1 percent and so plutocracy's share of wealth and relatedly income. In the Western setting, instances range from 19th-century England and America in the Gilded Age and the 1920s through these two déjà vu during Thatcherism and Reaganism with the resulting 'plutonomy'. Notably, under and since Reaganism the US's wealth share of the top one percent (42.5 percent) has become by far the largest among Western societies and even all OECD countries.

In sum, the extreme concentration and proximate monopolization of wealth in capital is a pertinent indicator of capitalist dictatorship in its anti-egalitarian facet as the system of severe economic inequality, notably plutocracy.

4.2.2   Extremely Unequal Income Distribution

Relatedly, the extremely unequal distribution, redistribution and consequently high concentration of income privileging capital characterizes capitalist dictatorship, including autocracy, dynasty, aristocracy, oligarchy and plutocracy. The preceding about these processes in respect of wealth applies, with certain qualifications, to them with regard to income. Like that of wealth, the 'unequal distribution of income' understates and too abstractly expresses economic inequality in capitalist dictatorship for the same reason. It is not merely unequal, as is to some degree by not being absolutely equal even in egalitarian welfare capitalism and socialism, but extremely, massively or severely so, and specifically favoring a definite production factor and social class over others.

As with respect to wealth, this process involves the economic mode of extremely unequal, permanent and essentially (as Keynes and other theorists suggest) arbitrary distribution of income between capital and non-capital favoring the first. Just as that of wealth, such distribution of income is the result of (what Wieser, Michels, and Mitchell consider) the unconstrained, near-absolute and arbitrary structural power of capital. As with wealth, the process encompasses income distribution in the Weberian and Smithian manner. The latter consists of a position of capitalist monopoly or 'conspiracy against the public' as the species of extreme and arbitrary market power in its own right and the monopolistic closure of the 'opportunities for income' to non-capitalists as in Tönnies' framework, including profit to other capitalists in Smith's context.

The aforesaid about monopoly in its double form as a major, even if not only, source and domain of wealth concentration in favor of capital applies essentially to that of income distribution within capitalist dictatorship. What Weber denotes as 'capitalist monopolies' and the consequent 'monopolistic closure' of 'opportunities for income' operate as the condition of and predict the distribution and concentration of income, just as wealth, in capital, and conversely the second presupposes and depends on the first. This is what Mitchell applying Wieser's theoretical insights suggests. Mitchell observes that capital in America obtains profits from the 'sheer' monopolistic 'financial control over markets without the exercise of social leadership' but instead exercising its 'despotic might' and thus arbitrary power, which he classifies among the 'socially irrational, anti-economic' phenomena of early 20th-century American capitalism. More generally, Smith suggests the above by diagnosing the monopolistic 'conspiracy against the public' as a constant and indeed preferred means and source of profit for capitalists. Mitchell evidently implicates and Wieser intimates the notorious robber barons making exorbitant profits from their monopoly and thus arbitrary power and its abuses, and Smith alerts to all capitalists due to their diagnosed constant tendency for such monopolistic and other antisocial actions against society.

They imply that monopolistic control/conspiracy secures and predicts high capitalist profits and reproduces the income distribution and concentration that favors capital, unless it pursues (as Schumpeter) implies, 'monopoly power' for its own sake. However, Weber considers such an intrinsic motivation and pursuit more typical for political power involving 'domination by virtue of authority' than for its economic variant consisting of 'domination by virtue of a constellation of interests', including a 'position of monopoly', primarily in the service of 'opportunities for income' as an extrinsic incentive. Mitchell specifically suggests applying Wieser's theory of capitalism that the high concentration of income and wealth in capital through obtaining massive profits associates with monopolistic control and abuse and generally with the concentration of market and political power rampant in early 20th-century American capitalism.

Moreover, as if almost nothing substantively changed since these times presumed to be the 'dead hand of the past', such an association reappears in American capitalism during its later stages, especially since the 1980s through the present. Just as in the Gilded Age, during this period the growing concentration of income and wealth or ownership of the means of production clearly and consistently associates with the increasing monopolization and more broadly market concentration in the US economy.

Specifically, such income concentration appears to be the likely effect of economic monopolization or market concentration, ceteris paribus, since a reverse causation is less empirically probable and theoretically sensible while allowing for some recursive, reinforcement effects. For example, reportedly 'a remarkably consistent upward trend in concentration' pervades the entire US economy, from manufacturing to finance, since the 1980s, and notably causes income concentration in favor of capital and at the expense of labor in that from 2007 to 2012 an one percentage increase in an industry's concentration index generates a 0.4 percentage decrease in its labor share.[97] Overall, monopolization and market concentration typically generates or sustains the growing concentration of income and wealth, as well as power, although the first process is not necessary to produce the second that also can result from other processes inherent to capitalist dictatorships. These processes include both those falling short of and going beyond monopoly ranging from laissez-faire 'free enterprise' for capital generating an extremely unequal distribution of income and wealth in its favor to predation, robbery, coercion, repression, violence and terror enabling redistribution from non-capitalists to capitalists.

At the minimum, by its 'arbitrariness of power' over the market/economy and as an instrument of the 'conspiracy against the public', monopoly, including that in the labor market (monopsony), epitomizes and sustains the extremely unequal and arbitrary distribution of income between capital and non-capital and its high concentration in the first within capitalist dictatorship. Conversely, this distribution and concentration is such at least because of monopolistic (and monopsonistic) control and closure characterizing capitalist as well as pre-capitalist dictatorships in Weber's and other settings. However, as just an extreme case of Weber's economic 'domination by virtue of a constellation of interests' or market power, monopoly does not exhaust the domain and conditioning of such a distribution and concentration. This holds so long as the latter process does not limit to but goes beyond monopoly and the 'conspiracy against the public' in capitalist dictatorship. Monopoly or the monopolistic 'conspiracy against the public' does not constitute a necessary condition and imperative, while being a sufficient one, for the extremely unequal, persistent and arbitrary distribution of income between capital and non-capital and its concentration in the first. For such distribution and concentration privileging the ruling class is intrinsic to and pervasive in capitalist and pre-capitalist dictatorships, as Mosca, Pareto and other sociologists suggest, and would persist even if these regimes conceivably abolished capitalist and status monopolies, respectively—but which they never do in reality. In sum, capitalist dictatorship involves and yet consists of more than monopoly and other conspiracy against non-capitalists

---

97   This finding is reported in Autor et al. (2017), see also, Kristal (2010).

and inherently constitutes a coherent and self-reproducing economic system of extremely unequal and arbitrary distribution of income privileging the ruling class versus others.

More broadly, the extreme inequality and arbitrariness of income distribution stemming from capital superior and arbitrary, including monopoly, power over non-capital contradicts the presumption that this process enfolds according to 'natural' laws a la the 'law' of marginal or total productivity of these production factors in neoclassical or apologetic economics rationalizing such extreme inequalities as 'fair' and 'necessary'. Even if assuming that they operate in ideal-typical egalitarian and democratic capitalism and distribute income fairly among capital and labor according to their productive contributions, economics overlooks that these 'laws' in reality operate as the 'law of the strongest' and the jungle in capitalist and all dictatorships, as in American Gilded-Age and contemporary capitalism. These 'laws' hence generate an arbitrary, extremely unequal and unjust distribution between these production factors yielding income concentration in capital. Capitalist dictatorship rules out or suspends any 'natural', 'objective' laws of income and wealth distribution of ideal-typical capitalism, including neoclassical economics' celebrated law of marginal and total-factor productivity, just as pre-capitalist despotism did. Instead, capitalist dictatorship reinstitutes and imposes its own law intrinsic to itself, which is that of dictatorships and their rulers such as Pareto's elites or aristocracies—the 'law of the strongest', coercion and force as the sole or prime method of domination that they know and apply.

In conjunction and mutual reinforcement, the process of income concentration comprises the non-economic arbitrary and coercive method of its redistribution from non-capitalist classes to the capitalist class by expropriation of the first or extraction of their incomes and massive transfers to the second through state coercion. A vehement pro-capital, anti-labor ideology and politics in the style of Reaganism and Thatcherism and generally neo-conservatism ('neo-liberalism') rationalizes—as 'libertarian' and similar economics does as well—this reverse Robin-Hood poor-to-rich redistribution. These rationalizations are in the name of 'efficiency', 'freedom', 'free enterprise', 'meritocracy', meritocratic 'defense of the one percent' and implicitly Divine 'intelligent design' reminiscent of religious conservatism's justification of slavery in America and elsewhere. Conversely, they vehemently condemn and eliminate Robin-Hood rich-to-poor redistribution as 'distortionary', 'inefficient', 'coercion', and 'wasteful'. In passing, Reaganism, Thatcherism and other neo-conservatism misleadingly, because of being explicitly anti-liberal in antagonism to comprehensive and consistent liberalism and oppressive, becomes 'neo-liberalism', although in the limited sense of unrestricted freedom, adapted laissez-faire or proxy Hobbesian anarchy for capital versus labor subjected instead to growing oppression and deprivation.

As with that of wealth, in capitalist dictatorship the high and recently growing concentration of income in capital therefore typically follows from both its original extremely unequal and arbitrary distribution (as Keynes emphasizes) in favor of the latter and its derivative massive redistribution from non-capitalist to capitalist strata. Consequently, this is an outcome not only of purely market-economic distributive processes—as 'pure' and 'libertarian' economists believe—but also of coercive non-market and non-economic forces. These include especially conservative pro-capital, anti-labor plutocratic politics and ideology emerging in America during the Gilded Age and the 1920s and resurging since the 1980s with the capitalist-populist and religious mobilization of Reaganism, alongside its ideological twin Thatcherism in Great Britain. Furthermore, the trend seemingly culminates after the 2016 US elections and the ensuing plutocratic and growingly autocratic regime contaminating and motivating via global contagion and alliance many other regions from South America (Brazil, Colombia) to parts of Europe (Austria, Hungary, Italy briefly, Poland) and beyond to reimpose conservative repressive and populist regimes. In short, capitalist dictatorship arises and functions at this point as the severely anti-egalitarian economic system of distribution, redistribution, and high concentration of income, just as of wealth, in capital.

Accordingly, the originally unequal distribution, derivative coercive redistribution and consequent concentration of income privileging capital plausibly indicates and identifies capitalist dictatorship as the system of extreme economic inequality typically in substantive conjunction, complementarity and mutual reinforcement with that of wealth. This holds as a general tendency, albeit with some variations or moderations, including moderate correlations between some of their measures such as wealth and income Gini coefficients. Especially, while within capitalist dictatorship and capitalism overall, the concentration of income in capital is typically lower than that of wealth, it tends to be severe compared to its levels in democratic and egalitarian welfare capitalism or its structural equivalent social democracy where it is considerably lower. Further, the concentration of income complements and reinforces that of wealth, in particular reproducing or exacerbating the latter, just as conversely, in capitalist dictatorship. This dual process therefore renders the latter a pure, consistent and self-perpetuating system of economic inequality.

Alternatively, in spite of some egalitarian simulations ('ownership for all'), capitalist dictatorship manifests itself as a coherently anti-egalitarian economic system due to the distribution, redistribution and concentration of income in capital, conjoined and mutually reinforced with the same processes of wealth. Hence, it tends to reach the highest level of inequality of income in favor of capital among economic systems—thus excluding pre-capitalism like slavery and feudalism—and the varieties of capitalism,[98] in particular a drastically higher one than that in regulated, welfare capitalism.

Contemporary and historical capitalist dictatorships consistently exemplify this tendency by having high and indeed the comparatively highest income inequalities. Among Western societies, the most salient instances include the US, the UK, and other Anglo-Saxon 'plutonomies' like Australia, Canada, New Zealand, and in part Ireland with their high-income inequality since Reaganism and Thatcherism in a continuity with such earlier times as laissez-faire capitalism during the Gilded Age and the early 19th century. Another déjà vu consists of the post-2016 US under remerging plutocracy/autocracy spreading via contagion to other countries, including Brexit Great Britain and beyond. Especially during these years, the US (39) and the UK (35.7) continue to have the first and second highest Gini Index of income inequality among Western societies, while being followed by other Anglo-Saxon countries such as Australia (33) and New Zealand (34.9). Additional, non-Western cases are most of South America ruled by plutocratic and conservative dictatorships, Eastern Europe under capitalist and right-wing oligarchy, much of Asia under authoritarian rule, African predatory states and Islamic regimes mixing capitalism and theocracy, especially Turkey, Saudi Arabia and other Gulf states. For example, Chile has the single highest Gini Index (46) among OECD countries and is followed by Mexico (45.8), Turkey (40.4), Lithuania (37.8), South Korea (35.5), and Latvia (34.6).

In sum, the distribution, redistribution and massive concentration of income in capital represents a complementary and pertinent identifier of capitalist dictatorship in its anti-egalitarian facet as a system of extreme, arbitrary and persistent economic inequality and to that extent, all else being equal, injustice.

4.2.3   Economic Degradation, Deprivation and Hardship

Large-scale and persistent economic degradation, deprivation and hardship, including poverty, of non-capital represents a complementary indicator of capitalist dictatorship as an anti-egalitarian system to wealth and income concentration in capital. Aside from rare exceptions, widespread and chronic poverty, more broadly material deprivation, degradation and hardship of non-capital

---

98   On the 'varieties of capitalism'—rather its duality since there are only two in this classification—see Hall and Soskice (2001).

strata pervades capitalist dictatorship, in conjunction and reciprocal intensification with wealth/income concentration in capital.

Typically, wealth and income concentration in capital generates and perpetuates, ceteris paribus, economic deprivation, degradation and hardship of non-capital production factors and social classes, including their pervasive and enduring poverty—and conversely, the second, especially the degrading of non-capitalists, reinforces and sustains the first. Both the initial economic distribution of wealth and income privileging capital and their derivative non-economic redistribution to the capitalist class from non-capitalist strata reproduce the latter's degradation, deprivation and hardship, particularly generating deep and widespread poverty. The latter may ultimately reach the threshold of existential unviability. This occurs when capitalists under certain conditions reduce wages to (what even a neoclassical economist deplores as) 'a starvation limit' while themselves enjoying 'an ultimate safeguard against starvation' due to the 'permanent fund of productive wealth', or (as another laments) deprive 'thousands of workers of their bread' and inflict them with 'misery'.[99] Yet, despite almost one fifth of Americans and nearly one quarter of American children being perpetually afflicted by poverty and thus degradation, deprivation and misery, the highest rates among Western societies, 'libertarian' economists postulate 'no one at misery' in unregulated US capitalism as their best of all possible worlds or nirvana.[100]

In this sense, non-capitalist classes' degradation, deprivation and hardship, especially extensive and persisting poverty and existential insecurity like famine and starvation, along with coerced or long work, are primarily the product of processes in and inherent to capitalist dictatorship, just as those of other strata being intrinsic to pre-capitalist dictatorships. These factors consist of the combination of capital's extreme wealth/income concentration with its unrestrained power, domination and oppression of non-capital strata and to that extent are primarily sociological, including political, ones. Hence, they are just secondarily narrow economic, technological and natural causes, including absolute scarcity of material resources such as food supply and caprices of nature like failing harvests, disasters, or unfavorable weather, as most economists believe, aside from some exceptions that earlier sociologists like Sorokin prefigure.[101]

---

99   See J. B. Clark (1892, p. 1899), also, Böhm-Bawerk (1959) and Wieser (1967), plus Baudrillard (1994).

100   'No one at misery' is stated in Farhi and Werning (2007, p. 366), see also Lucas (2009).

101   These exceptions include North (2005), Ó'Gráda (2007), Ravallion (2018), and Sen (1995, 1999), see also Sorokin (1975).

Therefore, far from being a novelty, capitalist dictatorship continues pre-capitalist despotism such as slavery, caste, and feudalism, and converges with non-capitalist dictatorships on this and related dimensions. In these systems, the degradation, deprivation and hardship, notably poverty and existential unviability, including famine, starvation and coerced or hard long work, of low classes are mainly the effect of extreme wealth concentration in the ruling class and its unrestrained power over and oppression of others, as are in capitalist dictatorship, with differences in degree. In this respect, the above negative process of capitalist dictatorship is consequent to and generally compatible with the first two positive processes. The degradation, deprivation, hardship, and poverty of non-capitalist strata mostly derive from and usually go hand in hand with the elevation, enjoyment, riches and well-being of the capitalist class—'poverty in the midst of plenty', mass urban/rural squalor and aristocracy-style splendor. This duality of material condition completes the identification of capitalist dictatorship as the dual economic system of pervasive and persistent material degradation, deprivation, hardship, and poverty of non-capital classes and the extreme concentration of wealth/income in capital, identifying the other side of the latter's opulence and privilege.

Conversely, the degradation and deprivation of non-capital classes, such as (what Tönnies and Wieser call) depriving most workers of 'property' and 'pecuniary means' and even work in American capitalism during the Gilded Age, McCarthyism and Reaganism tends to reinforce and sustain wealth and income concentration in capital. Hence, the first process can be both the effect and cause of the second, as in the link between 'social degrading across the distribution' and the 'sharply rising levels of wealth inequality' favoring capital and its consequent 'elite closure' in the US.[102] Moreover, such extensive social degrading, notably what Mitchell identifies as the 'physical and moral degradation of the lower classes' in early American capitalism, reportedly operates through Reaganism's class-driven attempt to degrade. demonize and demolish organized labor by attacks on unions and suppressing their actions as a major factor of growing wealth and income inequality since the 1980s. Further, the growing economic inequality in favor of capital and its resulting elite closure resumes, after some interludes like the New Deal, the 'physical and moral degradation', devaluation and depredation that US non-capitalist classes inherit as an unwanted bequest from early American capitalism and continue to experience, with transient and secondary exceptions, in its later phases. This hence forms a vicious and virtuous circle, respectively, enfolding between the two

---

102   These findings are from Hällsten and Pfeffer (2017) and Redbird and Grusky (2016).

processes—degradation and devaluation of non-capitalist classes and wealth concentration in the capitalist class and its monopolistic closure.

In particular, the large-scale and mostly perpetual poverty of non-capital classes is not only the obverse of and complementary with wealth and income concentration in capital but as intrinsic to and systematic and salient in capitalist dictatorship as these two tendencies are. Capitalist dictatorship by its logic and operation as the system of economic inequality and degradation, deprivation and devaluation of non-capital strata intrinsically and systematically tends to impoverish, disfavor and disenfranchise the latter and keep them in perpetual hardship, poverty and disadvantage, just as to enrich and favor capital and maintain it in permanent wealth and privilege. For example, 'kleptocratic regimes' invariably impoverish all groups not belonging to kleptocracy and the formula of all capitalist and pre-capitalist dictatorships from autocracies to plutocracies, with some variations, seems to be 'relative poverty and dictatorship' or repression in opposition to that of 'relative prosperity and democracy'.

Consequently, what characterizes capitalist dictatorship in aggregate economic or class terms is impoverishing, degrading and depriving non-capital strata of material resources and keeping them in that condition as disprivileged classes in Weber's sense, while enriching and privileging capital and maintaining it in such a state of affairs as a positively privileged class. In so doing, capitalist dictatorship does not really supersede and appears consistent and continuous with pre-capitalist despotism, including slavery, caste, patrimonialism, feudalism or the master-servant system—a kind of neo-feudalism or new patrimonialism.[103] It does this by sharing their pattern of impoverishing and dis-privileging low classes and enriching and privileging the ruling class, while being convergent with, rather than supplanting, non-capitalist dictatorships that show a similar though less salient or manifest tendency.

In light of the preceding, the large-scale and near-perpetual poverty and material hardship, degrading and depriving of non-capital strata negatively indicates and identifies capitalist dictatorship as the system of economic inequality, degradation and deprivation, just as wealth and income concentration in capital do it positively. Conversely, capitalist dictatorship actually identifies itself as such a system by non-capitalist strata's poverty, degradation and deprivation as its negative identifier, just as by capital's concentrated wealth and income as its positive identifiers. Mitchell considers the 'physical and

---

103   On neo-feudalism and new patrimonialism, see Beck (2000), Binmore (2001), Cohen (2003), and Piketty (2014).

moral degradation of the lower classes', along with its complement, capital-ist profits resulting from the 'sheer financial control over markets without the exercise of social leadership', an instance of 'socially irrational, anti-economic' phenomena of American capitalism and a negative identifier of 'economic oppression' or 'industrial despotism'. Insofar as he regards the degradation of these classes as interconnected with this capitalist profit-making within the set of these irrational phenomena and the result of the 'despotic might of cap-ital', he anticipates the link of the continuous 'social degrading' and increasing deprivation and hardship of non-wealthy groups with rising wealth inequality and elite closure in later American capitalism.

More broadly, his contemporary Wieser predicts as if emulating (or satiriz-ing) Marx 'a lasting, physical and moral degradation of the proletarian strata' following a 'concentration of many in a proletariat of working-people' within capitalism as a whole. In addition, Toynbee alerts to the existing 'degradation of a large body of producers', as Polanyi does to the 'general degradation of existence' in capitalism. They treat such degradation as resulting from or con-necting with capital's extreme concentration of wealth and power. It results from, in Wieser's account, the unequal 'distribution of incomes and property' in favor of the 'capitalistic despots', in Toynbee's, 'a great increase of wealth' for capitalists together with 'an enormous increase of pauperism' for others, in Polanyi's, 'economic inferiority' causing the weaker class to yield.[104]

In any event, capitalist dictatorship tends to have high and indeed compar-atively the highest levels of poverty and more broadly material degradation, deprivation and hardship among the types of capitalism and other compar-ative economic systems, notably being drastically higher than those of dem-ocratic, egalitarian welfare capitalism. Further, capitalist dictatorship's level of poverty, degradation and deprivation of non-capitalist classes historically approaches, although with differences in degrees by being lower than, that of pre-capitalist despotism, such as caste and feudalism with regard to lower castes and subordinate strata like peasants and substantively and partially slavery. This striking continuity forms the obverse of capital's share of societal wealth approximating that of pre-capitalist aristocracy.

Empirically, aside from minor and transient exceptions, capitalist dictator-ships implement the logic and design of the large-scale and perpetual poverty, generally economic degradation, deprivation and hardship, of non-capital strata, in conjunction with extreme wealth and income concentration in capital,

---

104   See Mitchell (1917), Polanyi (1944), Toynbee (2002), and Wieser (1967), also Ramirez (2013).

as Wieser and Mitchell suggests for early capitalism with its 'degradation' of laboring classes. Among Western societies, this holds in a historical sequence and a comparative context spanning from Gilded-Age America and 19th-century master-servant England through these two déjà vu since Reaganism and Thatcherism having consistently, along with the other Anglo-Saxon countries, high (usually double-digit) and higher poverty rates than most of these societies.[105] Especially, the US features the single highest general poverty rate (17.8) among Western societies and even OECD countries (after Israel's 17.9) and the fourth largest child poverty rate (21.2) among the latter. Non-Western examples are Chile and other Latin America under 'free market' dictatorships with their 'disastrous' poverty and related outcomes, most African predatory states, much of Asia under authoritarian capitalism, including South Korea, most Islamic capitalist countries like Turkey, with minor exceptions such as the rich Gulf states, yet inflicting degradation and hardship on non-capitalist or non-theocratic strata, as in Saudi Arabia and others. Further, they include growingly many Eastern European countries, especially the Baltic states, ruled by the new capitalist and conservative oligarchy. For example, South Korea has the third highest general poverty rate (17.4) among OECD countries (after Israel and the US), followed by Turkey (17.2), Lithuania (16.9), Latvia (16.8), Mexico (16.6), Chile (16.5) and so on.

In sum, the large-scale poverty or systematic impoverishing and thus material hardship of non-capitalist classes is an additional identifier of capitalist dictatorship in its facet as the system of economic inequality and especially degradation and deprivation. In turn, this represents mostly a consequence of and a complementary process to that of wealth and income concentration in or enriching and privileging of capital.

4.2.4   Economic Exploitation and Non-protection and Insecurity

An additional complementary indicator of capitalist dictatorship as an anti-egalitarian economic system of inequality and of degradation and deprivation of non-capital is extensive and intense economic exploitation, non-protection and insecurity, specifically of non-capital production factors and classes, simply of labor. This especially involves, in Polanyi's words, the 'exploitation of the physical strength of the worker' or 'economic exploitation', along with the

---

105   For Western societies such as the US and the UK, see Bénabou and Tirole (2006), Chetty et al. (2014), Kimeldorf (2013), Naidu and Yuchtman (2013), Newman and Massengill (2006), Redbird and Grusky (2016), and Smeeding (2006); for non-Western, including post-communist, examples see Hamm, King, and Stuckler (2012), Hoff and Stiglitz (2004), Rodrik (2010), and Roland (2002).

non-protection and insecurity of labor. Like the previous features, this is a systemic institutionalized feature of capitalist dictatorship through institutional forms and patterns of exploitation, joined with non-protection and insecurity, in 'capitalist labour processes', which capital exerts over and reproduces for non-capital.

In capitalist dictatorship and generally capitalism, the exploitation of labor reportedly exists when its real wages fall substantially below its (total, average, marginal) productivity or productive contribution and performance. This forms an essential and persistent pattern in this and related, conservative-fascist dictatorships subjecting labor to constant and severe exploitation and relatedly coercion, non-protection and economic insecurity. Consequently, due to its pattern of exploitation and coercion, capitalist dictatorship constitutes an economic system of injustice, specifically distributive injustice or unfairness in terms of labor income, just as of non-protection and economic insecurity. This holds in view of the general rule that (as even a neoclassical economist admits) when workers are 'exploited' by being paid less than their (marginal net) productivity, their wages are 'unfair'.[106] Such a situation tends especially, but not solely, to occur in employer monopoly and oligopoly (a monopsonic labor market and oligopsony) or bilateral monopoly (mixed monopoly and monopsony) thanks to capital's superior structural and bargaining power over labor.[107]

Overall, all pre-capitalist dictatorships from slavery and caste to feudalism or the master-servant system represent exploitative and unjust systems with regard to laboring and similar classes by inflicting them with exploitation, along with non-protection and economic insecurity. To that extent, capitalist dictatorship substantively perpetuates this long-standing tradition of exploitation and injustice, non-protection and economic insecurity, rather than, as its 'libertarian' and conservative defenders allege, supersede it. This holds in substantive terms despite some formal differences such as between non-monetary incomes and money wages and unfree forced and legally free labor in pre-capitalist and capitalist dictatorships, respectively. Compared to this substantive continuity, such formal differences seem mostly irrelevant and insufficient in that money wages and legally free labor evidently do not to eliminate or even mitigate exploitation, as well as coercion, non-protection and economic insecurity, of labor. Instead, they just endow exploitation with

---

106   See Pigou (1960, p. 551), also, Bils, Klenow, and Malin (2018), Fishback (1998), McGrattan and Prescott (2014), and Stiglitz (2016).

107   See Chamberlin (1957), also, Acemoglu and Robinson (2008), Bhaskar et al. (2002), and Boal and Ransom (1997), for broader insights, see Akerlof and Shiller (2015).

a different, monetary measure and legal form in capitalist dictatorship relative to pre-capitalist dictatorships, as, for example, during the Gilded-Age of American capitalism and later, including the post-bellum South.

Historically the exploitation, just as non-protection, insecurity and oppression, of labor in early capitalist dictatorship and more broadly capitalism equals and occasionally surpasses that in pre-capitalism such as feudalism and approaches that in slavery. This later tendency yields what Weber refers to as the "masterless slavery' of the modern proletariat' and Wieser laments as 'capitalistic power' and 'capitalist exploitation' of workers and posits that such economic domination tends to abolish 'once for all the freedom of the oppressed' and renders legal 'freedom into slavery'. To be sure, slavery even if reemerging in some new forms or leaving vestiges in global capitalism may be just a formal hyperbole or metaphor for capitalist dictatorship.[108] What is substantively relevant is that the latter continues and expands through its global expansion—as through the emergence of Eastern European oligarchic capitalism and the post-2016 contagion of the US plutocratic and autocratic regime—the tradition of labor exploitation, non-protection and insecurity of pre-capitalist dictatorship with its forced, unprotected and insecure labor. This holds with such modifications as money wages, legally free labor and quantitative differences in the degree of exploitation.

Moreover, capitalist dictatorship sometimes perpetuates unfree, coerced labor from pre-capitalism and the consequent form of its intertwined exploitation, coercion, non-protection and insecurity in a unified structure of control, power and domination. It does this through perpetuating the common-law coercive master-servant economy in Great Britain until the late 19th century and America up to the New Deal, along with the long-lasting Southern slavery and its legacy. Reportedly, repressive capitalism emerged in the postbellum South that while granting legal freedom to all laborers continued the pre-Civil War system of entwined labor exploitation and repression through 'monopsonistic arrangements', 'political disenfranchisement, intimidation, violence and lynching'[109] for long after the official abolition of slavery and its forced labor.

The process of labor exploitation, non-protection and insecurity in capitalist dictatorship relates to and complements both the degradation, deprivation

---

108   See Weber (1968, p. 600) and Wieser (1967, p. 62), also, Acemoglu and Robinson (2006a), Braudel (1979), Naidu and Yuchtman (2013), Perelman (2000), Somerville (2000), Steinberg (2003), Steinfeld (2001), Wacquant (2002), and Wallerstein (1974), plus Popper (1973).

109   See Acemoglu and Robinson (2008, pp. 286–7).

and poverty of non-capital and the distribution and concentration of wealth and income in capital. Specifically, the exploitation of labor in the sense of its real wages being lower than its product operates as the effective process of generating or sustaining both the poverty, degradation and deprivation of non-capital strata and the distribution and concentration of wealth and income in the capitalist ruling class. It functions as the efficient and perpetual mechanism of impoverishing, economically degrading and depriving non-capital from material resources and of enriching, 'upgrading' or empowering and privileging capital.

Conversely, these processes allow exploitation, non-protection and insecurity through non-capital strata's degradation, deprivation and resulting dependence and vulnerability inviting the exploiter, and enable exploiting them via capital's concentrated wealth, including exclusive ownership of the means of production, and consequent unrestricted and arbitrary power. This is what Tönnies signifies by characterizing capital in the sense of a production factor as the means for the 'exploitation of workers' defined as the 'appropriation of products of labor' and resulting from the fact that capitalists are the 'masters' of capitalism. Also, Parsons acknowledges that labor exploitation is the result of the 'factor of differences of power', in particular 'bargaining power', between workers and capitalist classes (which he admits as the 'permanent importance of the Marxian exploitation theory').[110]

Simply, the exploitation, non-protection and insecurity, of labor go hand in hand with both its degradation and deprivation and with capitalist wealth and power, thus domination and oppression of non-capital even if formally unforced and free. Such 'capitalist exploitation' joins with labor degradation and deprivation to form a vicious circle, collective bad for non-capital strata, such as the large class of working, powerless and oppressed poor in America, and together with capitalist wealth and power forming an unmitigated virtuous circle, class good for capital. This holds so long as labor exploitation, along with non-protection and insecurity, both generates and follows the degradation and deprivation of non-capitalist classes. Alternatively, it reproduces and derives from the wealth, especially ownership and control of the instruments and processes of production, and power of the capitalist class and its domination of non-capitalists. In consequence, labor exploitation, non-protection and insecurity, typically emerge and enfold in interaction and mutual reinforcement with the previous processes of capitalist dictatorship.

---

110   See Tönnies (2001, p. 26) and Parsons (1967, p. 109), also, Braudel (1979), Sen (2009), Wallerstein (1974), and Wright (2002).

In general, the extensive and intensive exploitation, non-protection and insecurity of labor typifies capitalist dictatorship as the system of economic injustice and coercion. Moreover, this exploitation, non-protection and insecurity inheres to and defines in a way axiomatically capitalist dictatorship as such a system, specifically one of distributive economic injustice. This holds so long as capitalist dictatorship merits its designation precisely by its intrinsically exploitative and thus unjust and oppressive treatment of non-capital afflicted also with non-protection and insecurity. If all pre-capitalist dictatorships from slavery and caste to feudalism were inherently exploitative and non-protective of lower strata in various degrees and ways, capitalist dictatorship follows this syndrome with respect to non-capitalist classes and involves labor exploitation, non-protection and insecurity, in a substantive continuity with its antecedents, with formal modifications and differences in degree.

In other words, non-capital class exploitation, joined with non-protection and insecurity, and hence unjust class distribution of wealth is the inner logic, working and outcome of capitalist dictatorship, as of pre-capitalist dictatorships, which renders the first substantively a sequel of the second, even if formally novel. At this point, to paraphrase Clausewitz, capitalist dictatorship appears as a continuation of the politics and practice of class exploitation, non-protection and insecurity of pre-capitalist dictatorships such as feudal bondage by other or identical means. The latter include formally free labor and money wages versus forced labor and non-monetary income, together with extreme wealth concentration, notably exclusive ownership and control of the instruments and processes of production and coercion. In short, it substantively continues rather than supersedes, despite formal modifications, what Michels calls the exploitative, oppressive pattern and 'conservative spirit of the old master-caste'.[111]

Counterfactually, capitalist dictatorship is probably a non sequitur, impossibility theorem and non-entity without, all else being equal, such exploitation, non-protection and insecurity, coercion, oppression and exclusion of non-capital, conjoined with the wealth, power and domination of capital. Historically, it is so just as pre-capitalist despotism, including feudal bondage, was impossible without the same treatment of non-aristocratic strata and the equivalent privilege, position and mastery of aristocracy. Capitalist plutocracy, including its resurgence as plutonomy in America and other Anglo-Saxon countries, is probably just as impossible and unsustainable without the

---

111   See Michels (1968, p. 11), also, Braudel (1979), Perelman (2000), Samuelson (1983a), Sen (2009), Somerville (2000), Wodtke (2016), and Wright (2002).

exploitation, non-protection, insecurity and oppression of other classes, as was Michels' 'old master-caste' of aristocrats, not to mention slave masters. Hence, pervasive and intense labor exploitation, non-protection and insecurity fully captures, accurately indicates and precisely identifies capitalist dictatorship, specifically its system of distributive injustice in the economy and its method of unjust economic distribution, as well as coercion, oppression and exclusion. Their pervasiveness and intensity express capitalist dictatorship's unjust and coercive income distribution between capital and non-capital disfavoring the second and thus distributive injustice and coercion.

Alternatively, capitalist dictatorship reveals itself as a system of distributive injustice, notably unjust wage distribution, by pervasive and intensive labor exploitation in the sense of the level of non-capital income being substantively lower than that of its productivity (in money equivalent) or wage movements below productivity growth, compounded with non-protection and insecurity. In consequence, capitalist dictatorship, aside from secondary variations, tends to feature high and indeed comparatively the highest levels of labor exploitation and coercion and thus distributive injustice in the economy among contemporary economic systems or the variants of capitalism, in particular a drastically higher level than that in egalitarian and democratic capitalism. Relatedly, capitalist dictatorship's level of non-protection and economic insecurity of non-capital has a tendency to be extremely high and the highest among these systems or variants, especially substantially higher than in this alternative variant of capitalism.

Historically, capitalist dictatorship continues and to some degree approaches, even occasionally exceeds and intensifies the exploitation, non-protection and insecurity of lower classes in pre-capitalism, including slavery, caste and feudalism. In some historical accounts, capitalist dictatorship or monopoly capitalism represents the source and sign of 'all of the heaviest exploitations of man by men', just as of 'all the greatest material progresses', and capitalist and pre-capitalist 'social modes of exploitation' complete each other.[112] In short, capitalist dictatorship operates as the economic system of exploitation, compounded with non-protection and insecurity, of labor.

This suggests that actual capitalist dictatorships manifest and realize the inherent tendency to labor exploitation, non-protection, insecurity and coercion, thus unjust and coercive wage distribution. Wieser acknowledges pervasive 'capitalistic exploitation', namely the 'exploitation of workers' resting on 'capitalistic power' and 'domination', the 'tremendous power of wealthy

---

112   This is reported in Braudel (1979) and Perelman (2000).

capitalists' in capitalism, and hence implies that the latter, at least during its late 19th- and early 20th-century expansion, effectively develops and functions as the system of capitalist dictatorship or oppression. Adopting Wieser's insights, Mitchell observes this process and implores the state to protect the 'weak against exploitation' pervasive in American capitalism by the 'despotic might of capital' and thus through 'industrial despotism', implying that 'industrial democracy' would be an antidote of labor exploitation and capitalist 'economic oppression'. In addition, during early capitalism in England between 1780 and 1840 reportedly real wages increased around four times less (12 percent) than real output per worker (46 percent). This indicates intense labor exploitation according to the productivity-wage equation, resulting in a reduction of workers' share of the national income from 60 percent to 45 percent, and that capitalists were the 'big gainers' and workers 'losers' during the Industrial Revolution.[113]

Furthermore, labor coercion and consequently exploitation, as well as nonprotection and insecurity, evidently persisted in later 19th-century England due to its coercive master-servant economic system based on common law and its American variant involving 'employer exploitation of workers' and 'exploitative arrangements' until the New Deal. This includes especially the postbellum South under intense and persistent 'labor repression' and 'monopsonic arrangements' involving capital's monopoly in the labor market and inherently enabling exploitation of workers.[114] Probably in light of such tendencies in pre-New Deal American and British capitalism, supposedly anti-Marxian Parsons attributes to Marx's exploitation theory 'permanent importance' in reintroducing the Hobbesian 'factor of differences of power into social thinking', including 'bargaining power'.

Furthermore, labor exploitation reportedly continues to be 'probably widespread' in contemporary American capitalism, especially under monopsony in labor markets, by applying the Pigou productivity-wage formula. More broadly, in some accounts 'free market ideology' in the US especially since Reaganism has become 'an excuse for new forms of exploitation', with 'rugged individualism and market fundamentalism' leading to 'rampant exploitation of unwary and unprotected individuals'. In particular, an accurate and indeed precise syndrome of labor exploitation by the above formula is the finding of a 'marked

---

113   These findings are from Allen (2008, pp. 965–6).
114   For 19th-century England and America before the New Deal see Fishback (1998), Kimeldorf (2013), Naidu and Yuchtman (2013), Orren (1991), and Steinberg (2003), for the postbellum South, see Acemoglu and Robinson (2008) and Ruef (2014).

disparity between the growth in labor productivity and real wages' substantially lagging behind the first in the US during the last three decades.[115]

Moreover, in comparative terms labor exploitation appears to be rising more in American than other Western capitalism, specifically its major examples in continental Europe. This seems so in light of the observation of the US being the 'only advanced country' experiencing the constant growth of productivity during last several decades but most citizens suffering from stagnating or declining incomes, along with increasing non-protection and economic insecurity. This commits a flagrant violation of the formula in that real wages move in the opposite direction of productive performance. Moreover, such a striking trend might be historically unprecedented or relatively exceptional even within Western capitalism as another 'American exceptionalism' in view of that real wages tended to move in the same direction as labor productivity—rising though less than the latter—during its early stages such as the Industrial Revolution and America's Gilded Age. In particular, the trend to greater labor exploitation seems more persistent and powerful in American than Western European capitalism judging by the 'evidence of a greater direct effect of firm productivity on wages' in Europe than the United States, including its 'much stronger positive effects' on them in France than in the latter. In addition, some observations suggest the presence and indeed 'acceptance' of flexible labor exploitation ('flexploitation'[116]), increasing coercion, non-protection and economic insecurity seem to persist in Great Britain because of its labor contract resting on coercive pro-capital master-servant common law rather than on employment law in contrast to Europe. These observations note in particular the British government under Thatcherism legally permitted labor exploitation and thus allowed distributive injustice by the 'removal of 'fair wages' requirements for government contractors and the abolition of Wages Council protection for lower-paid workers'.[117]

Finally, if labor exploitation, non-protection, economic insecurity and coercion remain widespread in plutocratic American and in part Western capitalism, it is even more pervasive and persistent in non-Western capitalist dictatorships. This holds with the qualification that often Western capitalism as the core transmits by coercion or persuasion these methods and processes

---

115   These findings are from Boal and Ransom (1997, p. 110) and Stiglitz (2010, pp. 275–6, 2016, 45), see also Wodtke (2016).
116   'Flexploitation' is from Bourdieu (1998, p. 85).
117   These findings and observations are from Acemoglu and Robinson (2013), Allen (2008), Atkinson (1997), Beck (2000), Blanchard and Katz (1999), Bourdieu (1998), and Fishback (1998).

of wealth extraction by capital, along with militaristic and related barbarization via arms exports for tribal wars, to the second as the periphery. For example, this trend includes the apparent transmission (ideologically rationalized by the 'libertarian' Chicago School) of these methods to Chile under its 'free market' dictatorship and to Eastern Europe during its domination by oligarchy. In this regard, non-Western capitalist dictatorships form their own oceans or deserts of labor and related group exploitation, non-protection, insecurity, coercion, discrimination, and oppression by both 'dictators and mafias' if Western capitalism forms the lake and even, as with most of Western Europe, above all Scandinavia, an oasis. Most third-world societies are 'highly unequal and exploitative'[118], examples ranging from South Africa during the apartheid regime through Latin American, Caribbean, and African countries under oligarchies and other dictatorial regimes to Eastern Europe during the transition to its own oligarchic capitalism and to most Islamic, including Turkey, Saudi Arabia and other Gulf, states.

In sum, pervasive and intense economic exploitation, non-protection and insecurity of non-capital is yet another indicator and identifier of capitalist dictatorship as the system of distributive economic injustice, coercion and oppression. This process interacts with and complements both the poverty, degradation and deprivation of non-capital classes and the distribution and concentration of wealth and income in capital.

---

118   See Acemoglu and Robinson (2006a, b), Bourdieu (1998), Jomo (2003), and Sen (2009).

CHAPTER 3

Capitalist Dictatorship as a Political Regime

1 Moving from Economy to Polity, Transforming Economic to Political Domination

The second and related element and thus subsystem of capitalist dictatorship as a total/totalistic social system is an authoritarian, repressive and exclusionary polity integrated with its economic subsystem. Capitalist dictatorship also represents a political system or an extension in the polity, although the latter, like the economy, does not exhaust it as a sociological system by forming approximately a quarter of its four-fold structure. Capitalist dictatorship conforms to the tendency for dictatorships, including those of economic character, to be political regimes, structures of power and domination by the ruling class and of repression and submission of subordinate classes. In this sense, it belongs to dictatorial and other repressive political regimes, just as to coercive and anti-egalitarian economic systems.

Historically, pre-capitalist despotism such as slavery, caste and feudalism in Europe, including its ramification, the master-servant economy in England and America through the late 19th and early 20th century, represented not only an old economic system but also the ancient political regime. Analogously, capitalist dictatorship represents a modern political regime in the framework of capitalism and modernity. Specifically, if pre-capitalist despotism in these and other forms involved the old aristocracy or oligarchy in Pareto's sense of power elite or governing class in the ancient regime, capitalist dictatorship involves the new aristocracy or oligarchy, as Mosca's novel ruling class in the modern regime. Like pre-capitalist feudal and other despotism, capitalist dictatorship tends to expand and indeed metastasize beyond economy into polity and society. It therefore conforms to—rather than overcoming, as its 'libertarian' defenders like Chicago and similar economists allege—dictatorships' intrinsic tendency to political expansion and ultimately societal metastasis. Just as the old aristocracy or oligarchy of land estate did as Pareto's ancient elite in pre-capitalism, the new aristocracy of capital and oligarchy of money, simply plutocracy as the modern elite in capitalism expands its rule and dominance from economy to polity and beyond. In Weber's terms, both pre-capitalist and capitalist aristocracy and oligarchy continue and escalate economic domination 'by virtue of a constellation of interests', including as its 'purest' type 'monopolistic domination of the market' or a 'position of monopoly', into political domination 'by virtue of authority' consisting of the 'power to command and the duty to obey'. One can predict[1] that the aristocracy of capital will transform domination 'by virtue of the constellation of interests', particularly that 'originally founded on a position of monopoly', into that by authority consistent with the tendency for 'even mere possession' of wealth to be the 'basis of power in forms other than that of the market'.

Considering this historical continuity, to paraphrase Clausewitz, capitalist dictatorship politically considered is the modernized continuation of the ancient political regime of pre-capitalist despotism, including feudalism, by other means in formal terms and identical mechanisms substantively. Such means include legally free non-capitalist populations versus the legal unfreedom of the pre-capitalist populace, and these mechanisms involve coercion, repression, exclusion and closure in the polity. Consequently, plutocracy as Pareto's governing class in capitalism reinventing itself as 'plutonomy' in American capitalism during conservatism becomes the continuation of aristocracy as the elite in pre-capitalism by other means, wealth or money versus land or estate, and identical mechanisms such as those mentioned above. It is no wonder that Pareto, Michels, Mosca, Weber and other sociologists and economists consider and depict capitalist plutocracy as the new aristocracy and political elite of capital or money, just as identify the tendency of pre-capitalist aristocracies and oligarchies or elites to becoming ever-more plutocratic in capitalism. Overall, capitalist dictatorship, in particular its most essential form and agent, plutocracy as a social class, tends to extend from economy to polity and evolve in a modern political regime, particularly a new ruling group. It therefore substantively resurrects the 'dead hand' of the past of pre-capitalist despotism as the ancient regime and its aristocracy as the old elite.

Within the framework of the sociological system in Pareto's sense, capitalist dictatorship's political regime typically develops and functions in an interaction, complementarity and mutual perpetuation and reinforcement with its economic system, with certain variations. Capitalist dictatorship's authoritarian, repressive and exclusionary polity interacts with, complements, sustains and reinforces its coercive oppressive and anti-egalitarian economic system, while the latter complementing, sustaining and reinforcing the former. On this account, like pre-capitalist despotism before the French Revolution, capitalist dictatorship persists and generalizes globally post-2016 and since the 1990s as a coherent, self-sustaining and self-reinforcing dual economic-political system, a double structure of coercion, oppression, inequality, exclusion and closure

---

1   This is what Weber (1968, pp. 943–5) predicts.

in economy and polity. More broadly, it expresses in an authoritarian form the nature of capitalism as a total self-consistent social system having the 'totality of capitalistic features and their more immediate interrelationships'.[2]

Oligarchy or plutocracy in the economy interacts with, complements, sustains and reinforces that in the polity, and vice versa, producing an effective fusion between the two. This fusion comprises reportedly an oligarchic and plutocratic economy/state and fused economic and political elites in America[3] during the surge and dominance of conservatism, most of South America traditionally and Eastern Europe more recently, which oligarchies and oligarchs, along with autocracy and family dynasty, rule politically and dominate economically. In this regard, capitalist oligarchy or plutocracy and to some degree autocracy or family dynasty in America since the 1980s or post-2016 lives on and expands as a cohesive, entwined and self-perpetuating dual economic-political ruling group both in the economy and polity, just as aristocracy did in feudalism. In sum, by the logic and path of expansion and escalation of dictatorships, including pre-capitalist despotism as the ancient regime and aristocracy as the old elite, capitalist dictatorship such as plutocracy or oligarchy expands and escalates from economy to polity. It thereby develops into a modern political regime and a new elite, which functions in a reciprocal relation, reproduction and reinforcement with its economic system and upper class.

2   Negative Definition and Specification of Capitalist Dictatorship as a Political Regime

In terms of a negative dimension, definition and specification, capitalist dictatorship represents a political regime of negation and suppression of universal freedoms and rights for non-capitalist groups such as non-plutocracy or non-oligarchy, especially the labor and related population. Simply, it negates and suppresses, in Jefferson's words, liberty, equality and justice 'for all' in the polity. Therefore, it manifests its inherent negativity and antagonism to political liberalism, universalism and egalitarianism, and consequently liberal and universalistic democracy, while sharing the syndrome of dictatorships and other repressive political regimes, including pre-capitalist despotism. Capitalist dictatorship inherently operates as a pure negativity for and vehement antagonism toward non-capitalist political, especially non-plutocratic or

---

2   See MacIver (1964, p. 364), also, Bourdieu (1998), Burawoy (2005), Hirschman (1977), Wodtke (2016), and Wright (2013).

3   See Pryor (2002, pp. 364–7).

non-oligarchic, groups such as labor movements, organizations, and parties. In this respect, like all, including pre-capitalist and non-capitalist, dictatorships, it forms a negative compound of anti-liberalism, anti-universalism and anti-egalitarianism and in consequence anti- or non-democracy. At most, it amounts to bogus illiberal conservative, including fascist or theocratic, exclusionary and anti-egalitarian 'democracy', especially from the experience of non-capitalist, non-plutocratic and non-oligarchic social groups.

While granting some formal political freedoms and rights such as legally free labor and the right to vote in elections—yet only partially with a myriad of restrictions, as in the US South—capitalist dictatorship suppresses what Schumpeter would call the universal freedom and right to pursuing—via a 'free competition for leadership'[4]--and holding political power. In reality, it specifically denies such a freedom to non-capitalist and non-plutocratic or non-oligarchic groups, simply those ('people', 'laborers', 'masses', 'peasants', 'plebeians') not born into political power, wealth and social status through wealthy classes and families, and conversely born into lower strata.[5]

First, capitalist dictatorship perpetuates the ancient regime of pre-capitalist despotism such as master-servant feudalism and aristocracy, compounded with theocracy via the plutocratic-theocratic Religious, Christian Right in the 'American regime'.[6] Second, it negates the principle and practice of political democracy as Schumpeter's 'free competition' for power among all, including capitalist and non-capitalist, groups and individuals. By the first tendency, capitalist dictatorship manifests itself as pre-democracy and its ruling group, plutocracy as having what Mannheim[7] denotes an authoritarian and aristocratic preliberal and pre-democratic mind. By the second, it appears as non-democracy and its ruling group as an illiberal and non-democratic force from the standpoint of liberalism and liberal, universalistic and egalitarian

---

4 Schumpeter's (1950, p. 298) concept of 'political leadership' appears to borrow or echo Weber's (1958, pp. 84–6) of the 'leadership of a state or of a party' and more broadly Wieser's (1967, p. 404) of 'social leadership' adopted by Mitchell (1917, p. 107). See also Besley and Kudamatsu (2006), Bollen and Jackman (1985), Fearon (2011), and Mulligan et al. (2004).

5 For expressions 'not born into a wealthy family' and 'born into lower classes', see Alesina and Angeletos (2005, p. 972) and Maas and Leeuwen (2016, p. 839).

6 Expressions the 'Religious Right', the 'Christian Right' and the 'American regime' are from Bénabou et al. (2015, p. 347), plus Domhoff (2013), Hout and Fischer (2002; Jouet (2017), and Manza and Brooks (1997).

7 Mannheim (1967, pp. 181–2) writes that the 'authoritarian, pre-democratic mind shuns the idea of progress and genesis in favour of static, hierarchically ordered models of excellence. The democratic mind stresses the plasticity of man (and) is prone to explain phenomena in terms of contingency rather than essence'.

democracy that Schumpeter's classic, albeit simplistic economistic, definition implies.

In Schumpeter's terms, capitalist dictatorship negatively defined represents the mode of negation and destruction of established and proven liberal, universalistic, egalitarian and thus democratic political structures without the affirmation and creation of new structures. In this respect, it arises and operates as a pure negativity and destructiveness in relation to liberal democracy, just as all dictatorships do, especially conservative-fascist regimes and theocracies, arising and operating in adverse reaction and destructive posture to liberalism. In this context, Schumpeterian capitalism is the process of 'creative destruction' in the economy by destroying its old structures and creating the new through technological, market and organizational innovation, thus 'fruitful capitalist destruction'.[8] By contrast, its authoritarian version through capitalist dictatorship, which he downplays in favor of 'capitalist democracy', is the system of uncreative destruction in the polity by eliminating democracy and universal political freedom without any creation to replace what it destroys: 'new' democracy and liberty.[9]

Relatedly, while 'creative destruction' in the economy involves what Schumpeter following Marx connotes the endogenous 'revolutionizing' of capitalism from within and economic-technological revolution in the means of production starting with the Industrial Revolution, capitalist dictatorship's uncreative destruction in the polity enfolds in the opposite manner. It consists of a counter-revolutionary negation of and attack on democracy and its universal liberty and equality originating in the French Revolution.[10] Capitalist dictatorship thus operates as a political counter-revolution or retrogression and restoration that typifies conservatism, including fascism, beginning with its vehement opposition to the French Revolution and liberalism and becoming the crucial ideological-political source of this and fascist-right dictatorships.

In this connection, Schumpeter fails to identify and differentiate between the two processes, as do later economists enamored by his otherwise derivative notion of creative destruction (essentially borrowed from Marx and implicit in earlier sociologists like Tönnies, Tarde, Simmel, Weber and even Comte and Saint Simon) by innovation. The first process is what he and later economists

---

8   See Samuelson (2004, p. 144), also, Aghion, Akcigit and Howitt (2015), Massey (2009), Phelps (2013), and Rajan and Zingales (2004).
9   The concept of 'new liberty' is in Dahrendorf (1975) and of 'capitalist democracy' in Wright (2013).
10   On the French Revolution, see Acemoglu et al. (2011), Dahrendorf (1979), Habermas (2001), and Knight (1967).

exalt as capitalism's creative destruction and revolution in the economy through entrepreneurial technological and other invention and innovation, simply technical advancement. The second process that Schumpeter and these economists overlook is capitalism's political uncreative destruction of and counterrevolution in democracy precisely as he defines the latter. This negative process unfolds via capitalist dictatorship and plutocratic or oligarchic capitalists destroying the 'free competition for leadership' and monopolizing the latter, thus Weber's 'domination by virtue of authority', for themselves and excluding others from this power contest.

Even within Schumpeterian heroic, essentially unrestrained capitalism with *pax capitalis* as the Panglossian best of all possible worlds for many economists, its authoritarian version through capitalist dictatorship appears as a pure negativity and destructive force to democracy in Schumpeter's own terms. It is the negative obverse of the process of 'free competition' for political power between all individual and collective agents, capitalist and non-capitalist. By such a negativity, notably negating non-capitalist groups' freedom and right of seeking and holding political power, capitalist dictatorship dissolves democracy into the 'free competition for leadership' only among capitalists and cliques of plutocrats and oligarchs, thus perverts it into plutocracy and oligarchy. In short, non-capitalists or non-plutocrats 'need not apply' for political office—this is the credo, injunction or outcome of capitalist dictatorship.

Empirically, all capitalist dictatorships, past and present, exhibit this pattern of negation and suppression of such and related political freedoms and rights for non-capital political subjects. They span from 19th-century England and Gilded-Age America through interwar capitalist-fascist dictatorships in Germany, Italy and Spain and their postwar variations to Latin America and elsewhere to the first two societies déjà vu during Reaganism and Thatcherism and Eastern European oligarchies since the 1990s. Further, they involve America under the post-2016 plutocratic and oligarchic regime and via contagion or confluence other countries from Brazil and Brexit Britain to Hungary and Poland. All these cases, with some variations, deny such liberties and rights, notably the freedom and right of non-capitalist or non-plutocratic and non-oligarchic groups and individuals to seek and hold political power.

Consequently, they represent anti-liberal, exclusionary political regimes and non-democracies, at most ersatz illiberal 'democracies' involving the 'free competition' for office among plutocrats and oligarchs only, thus within the narrow circle of capitalist plutocracy, oligarchy and dynasty. For example, this crucially helps explain and probably predict why most participants and winners in such competition for and thus holders of political power in the US, including Presidents and Congressmen, have historically been and remain at present capitalists, plutocrats and oligarchs. This holds with secondary and transient variations from what is almost an iron Michels-style law of capitalist oligarchy or historical-empirical pattern. The same holds true for most of South America traditionally and Eastern Europe during oligarchic capitalism, let alone most of Africa and Islamic capitalist-theocratic (Gulf and other) states where theocrats join capitalist plutocrats and oligarchs in ruling the polity and excluding and oppressing especially non-plutocrats and less religious groups.

In sum, by way of a negative dimension, definition and specification, capitalist dictatorship constitutes a political regime of negation and suppression of universal political liberties and rights. This involves negating the freedom and right to pursue and hold power to non-capitalist, non-plutocratic and non-oligarchic groups and hence an anti-liberal structure and non-democracy, at most illiberal ersatz 'democracy' as the 'free competition' for office among capitalists or plutocratic and oligarchic cliques only.

3   Positive Definition and Specification of Capitalist Dictatorship as a
       Political Regime

In terms of a positive dimension, definition and specification, capitalist dictatorship is a political regime of distribution, extreme concentration and eventually monopolization of power in capital and its exertion, including its abuse and corruption, by the latter as both a collective plutocratic and an individual autocratic agent versus non-capital groups. Consequently, it is the regime of virtually absolute or unrestrained and arbitrary political power and through its exertion near-total domination of capital over non-capitalist populations within the polity. In this sense, capitalist dictatorship approaches an absolutist and totalistic political regime and expresses absolutism in the polity, which resembles pre-capitalism despotism such as feudalism with its pattern of absolute and arbitrary power and total domination of the pre-capitalist ruling group over the populace. The process of concentration, and monopolization of power in capital typically connects with, complements and sustains that of wealth, both processes representing the dual program of Reaganism and Thatcherism for American and British capitalism.[11]

In this sense, capitalist dictatorship constitutes the political regime of extremely unequal distribution of power in the specific sense of its distribution

---

11   On Reaganism and Thatcherism, see Hodgson (1999), Hung and Thompson (2016), Jacobs and Dirlam (2016), Kristal (2010), and Solow et al. (1987), for general insights see Acemoglu (2005) and Spenkuch and Toniatti 2018).

in favor of capital as the ruling class of the 'powerful' and hence its extreme concentration and ultimately monopolization in the latter. As the modern regime, capitalist dictatorship replicates the pattern of pre-capitalist despotism as the ancient regime of extremely unequal distribution of power in favor of the ruling group, Michels' 'master caste' including slave owners and feudal aristocracy, while manifesting the inner logic and workings of dictatorships as extreme political regimes. Capitalist dictatorship appears as Mitchell's modern 'industrial despotism' in early American capitalism, with its ruling group, the class of capitalists appearing as the new aristocracy of capital, which the infamous robber barons and their proxies embody.[12]

Consequently, capitalist dictatorship extends from an economic system to a political regime in which capital as an upper social class and a collective agent prevails and reigns supreme: the domination of capitalists as a group and sometimes individuals or families and thus autocrats or dynasties in the polity. More precisely, it becomes the rule primarily of certain, usually uppermost fractions of the capitalist class that become the ruling group or power elite, converting in a reverse alchemy money and wealth into power and domination. This holds so long as not all capitalists seek, possess and exert political power and enjoy domination in the polity but instead many confine their activity to the pure accumulation, concentration, and monopolization of wealth and income. Yet they may realize that the first process is necessary and effective for succeeding in the second in capitalist dictatorship, especially autocracy, oligarchy, military dictatorships and theocracy, just as conversely. The result is extremely narrow, exclusive class-as-elite rule and an exclusionary and closed political regime, replicating pre-capitalist despotism, including slavery, caste, feudalism or master-servant oppression, and exemplifying dictatorships in these terms.

Literally, capitalist dictatorship evolves into the modern political regime of 'capitacracy' in the same sense (though not the form) pre-capitalist despotism such as feudalism was the ancient regime of aristocracy mixed with theocracy as the first and second estate—the rule of capital over non-capital populations. Conversely, it is 'capitacracy' and the new aristocracy of capital in the analogous meaning of non-dictatorial and welfare capitalism integrated with a political regime of liberal, secular and universalistic democracy, as in most of Western Europe, particularly Scandinavia.[13] On this account, capitalist dictatorship continues rather than supersedes the ancient regime of pre-capitalist

---

12   On the robber barons, see Acemoglu and Robinson (2015), Merton (1968), and Mizruchi and Marshall (2016).

13   On Scandinavia, especially Sweden, see Hällsten and Pfeffer (2017) and Samuelson (1964, 1983b).

feudal and other despotism and distorts the modern political system of liberal and inclusive democracy. Therefore, it forms a perversion of liberal democracy, as in most non-Western or third-world settings from most of Africa and South America to much of Asia and Eastern Europe, above all Hungary and Poland, during oligarchic capitalism.[14] Alternatively, it operates as a simulation of liberal democracy, including 'placebo reforms', as in America during the Gilded Age, since the 1980s and post-2016, with the ruling group, such as the oligarchy allied with conservatism and merged with theocracy in the 'Bible Belt', simulating 'capitalist democracy'.[15]

In empirical terms, capitalist dictatorships as political regimes, present and past, confirm the above positive dimension, definition and specification. They epitomize the process and regime of distribution, extreme concentration, and monopolization of power in capital and hence the domination and rule of the later over non-capital groups. Cases in point range from 19th-century English and Gilded-Age American capitalism through capitalist-fascist dictatorships in interwar Germany, Italy and Europe overall to South American 'free market' dictatorships and Britain's and America's 'plutonomy' déjà vu since Thatcherism and Reaganism. Additional cases include Eastern European capitalist oligarchies, Turkey under Islamic rule, Saudi Arabia and other Gulf states. The most recent examples are the post-2016 US and by contagion or convergence Brexit Britain, as well as Brazil, Hungary, Poland, and so on. In sum, what positively defines and specifies capitalist dictatorship as a political regime is the process of extreme concentration and monopolization of power in and its exertion by capital and hence the latter's domination over non-capitalist groups in the polity, with most empirical cases conforming to this definition and specification.

4   Political Forms and Agents of Capitalist Dictatorship

With respect to the forms and agents of capitalist dictatorship as a political regime, these are mostly identical or closely interlinked with those of it as an economic system. However, consistent with capitalist dictatorship's extension from being an economic system into becoming a political regime, they extend from economy to polity, market to state, rather than confining themselves to

---

14   For non-Western settings, see Acemoglu and Robinson (2006b), Hoff and Stiglitz (2004), and Huber et al. (2006).
15   On American capitalism and politics, see Baudrillard (1994), Bauman (2001), Pryor (2002), Spiegler (2013), Wodtke (2016), and Wright (2013).

the first domain, thus developing and functioning in both societal domains. Consequently, they transform themselves from economic into political forms and agents of capitalist dictatorship consistent with its transformation into such a regime. Furthermore, capitalist dictatorship's economic and political forms and agents tend to merge or ally with each other to create a cohesive compound of almost undistinguishable components. An example is the fusion of an oligarchic (or oligopolistic) economy and an oligarchic state in America during conservatism fusing elites from both societal domains, joined with 'corporate political unity' and the Religious Right alliance between the rich and religious poor groups in the plutocratic-theocratic 'American regime'.[16]

Such a tendency of these forms and agents stems from and expresses the tendency of systems of economic inequality through sharply unequal wealth distribution to complement, expand into and merge with repressive political regimes involving equivalent power concentration. Consequently, what renders and sustains capitalist dictatorship as a political regime, just as an economic system, is their extension from economy into polity and their transformation into those within the latter and their fusion into double economic-political forms and agents. Moreover, manifesting the tendency of moving from economy to polity or developing and operating in both realms, most forms and agents of capitalist dictatorship acquire an explicit political connotation. In that sense, these forms and agents become politicized—contrary to pro-capitalist economic policy's' 'depoliticized'[17] posture—just as those of pre-capitalist despotism, such as feudal autocracy, and non-capitalist dictatorships. Such politicization reflects that capitalist dictatorship constitutes a political regime, as well as an economic system, thus being continuous and convergent with pre- and non-capitalist dictatorships.

As with most of their economic variants, capitalist dictatorship's political forms and agents range from autocracy and family dynasty to aristocracy, oligarchy, and plutocracy and to kleptocracy, police states, military dictatorships and theocracies within capitalism as distinct from pre- and non-capitalism. Thus, virtually all the forms and agents previously considered have explicit and salient political traits and overtones, except seemingly for predatory, mafia capitalism. Yet even the latter and its capitalists tend to expand from economy to politics by capturing or influencing the state and thus become self-politicized and power-holding, as the robber barons and their variations

---

16   See Bénabou et al. (2015, p. 347), also, Domhoff (2013), Murray (2017), and Pryor (2002).

17   Murray (2017, p. 452) remarks that the 'rising monetarist orthodoxy depoliticized neoliberalism by providing a stamp of scientific respectability to a whole range of conservative policies' (see also Bowles and Gintis 1993; Elsner 2000; Piketty 2014).

TABLE 6   Political forms and agents of capitalist dictatorship

capitalist autocracy as a political regime
capitalist dynasty as a political regime
capitalist plutocracy, aristocracy and oligarchy as a political regime
secondary forms of capitalist dictatorship as political regimes
    kleptocracy and predatory capitalism as a political regime
    capitalist police states, military dictatorships and theocracies as
    political regimes

in America show. Ranging from autocracy and dynasty to plutocracy and oligarchy, they are explicitly political forms and agents, although merged with the economic, within capitalist dictatorship, just as in pre-capitalist dictatorships. In fact, capitalist dictatorship inherits and perpetuates, with some modifications, virtually all of them—except for mafia capitalism as its own invention through its American variant in current accounts—from pre-capitalist despotism such as slavery, caste and feudalism or master-servant oppression where they originate and prevail as political forms and agents.

Consequently, capitalist dictatorship de facto continues, with formal adaptations, the manifestly political and even, as with the 'American regime', religious connotation of pre-capitalist despotism like feudalism, rather than eliminating it through, as 'libertarian' economics alleges for capitalism, apolitical economic processes and standards. In this sense, it reappears as the modern regime and conglomerate of politically manifest or politicized forms and agents descending from pre-capitalist despotism, while fused with their economic variants, just as feudalism was the ancient regime and aggregate of such phenomena. Virtually all its forms and agents reveal capitalist dictatorship as a kind of politics and political rule, thus as 'industrial despotism' continuous with pre-capitalist despotism and convergent with post-capitalist dictatorships, not just a type of pure economy and capitalism. In short, they expose it as the 'political economy' of power and domination of capital versus non-capital.

4.1   Capitalist Autocracy as a Political Regime

Like their versions in pre- and post-capitalism, autocracy and autocrats in capitalism represent a manifestly political form and agent of capitalist dictatorship, albeit merged with the economic, by encompassing and acting in the polity through the capture, control and exercise of state power, just as jointly in the economy. Hence, autocracy in capitalism represents the 'dictatorship' of a rich capitalist in the specific sense of primary personal political rule through the complete and effective control of state power, just as that in pre-capitalism represented the tyranny of a wealthy pre-capitalist monarch or aristocrat in the realm of polity.[18] Such personal political dictatorship merges and mutually reinforces with individual economic domination via controlling—yet perhaps less completely and effectively—the economy.

Like those in pre-capitalism, autocrats in capitalism typically act as political or state, as well as economic-market, dictators and play 'dictator games' in the polity as in the economy, for example, US conservative Presidents- demagogic autocrats[19] since Nixon and Reagan to especially post-2016 days. For illustration, almost all postwar US Presidents, with a single exception of the 1977–1981 President, started offensive wars or launched attacks against other states, with the result of mass murder, notably of civilian populations, from Latin America and Vietnam through Grenada and the former Yugoslavia to Afghanistan, Iraq, Libya and Syria. Overall, by such actions most US postwar Presidents continue a long tradition from Puritanism's and Andrew Jackson's genocide of native Americans—and generally 'Jacksonian nationalism'—through the violent conquest of the Mexican territories to the 'gunboat' mistreatment of the adjacent weak states in Central and South America. By so doing, most US Presidents since the American Revolution deny to and take from other states what US revolutionaries demanded for America—national independence and freedom—displaying what Weber refers to as the Puritan-rooted 'pure hypocrisy' of 'Americanism' as aggressive nationalism or in Pareto's words jingoism. Thereby, they effectively render liberated America a heir and substitute of the

---

18   See Gurvitch (1945, p. 291), also, Acemoglu et al. (2018), Besley and Kudamatsu (2006), and Lee (2007).

19   Mueller (1996, p. 275) implies that many presidents tend to behave in autocratic manner remarking that the US government's 'decision to attack countries like Cambodia, Grenada, or Iraq rests on one man's judgment. Moreover, in times of real war and national crisis the country has been effectively converted into a dictatorship (because of) an expansive interpretation of the powers that the U.S. Constitution grants to the president as commander-in-chief when the nation experiences armed rebellion'. Further, this implies that they commit war crimes or interstate terror and qualify as corresponding offenders by launching offensive wars or attacks against other states and committing mass murder and destruction. Bauman (2001, pp. 208–9) suggests that the US-led 'NATO Kosovo campaign' as an illegitimate attack on the former Yugoslavia on behalf of a group of 'terrorists' (the 'Kosovo Liberation Army') qualifies as a war crime or interstate terror and its President as a war criminal, by concurring with the observation that the latter, along with the British Prime Minister, 'violated simultaneously all forms of decency and the laws of war'.

British empire and seemingly anticipate, as with those prior WW II, or converge with, as those during postwar times, Nazi Germany's wars and conquest. Further, they, especially postwar Presidents, remade America the probably most militaristic and warlike state in modern Western history, along with the British empire, Prussia and Nazi Germany. Fittingly, a militaristic and nationalistic Congress matches most US Presidents' militarism and bellicosity by virtually unlimited, socially irresponsible and reckless military expenditure and thus expansion of the military-capitalist complex and approving all offensive wars, of which its near-unanimous approval of the Vietnam War is only the most notorious, deadly and destructive, followed by that of the second Iraq War.[20]

Alternatively, capitalist autocracy and autocrats are far from being apolitical rule and rulers premised and acting on purely economic processes and criteria like 'efficiency', 'productivity', 'merit', 'performance', 'growth', 'free' enterprise and markets, as neither were pre-capitalist autocracies and autocratic dictators.

Virtually all the past and present cases and proxies of capitalist autocracy and autocrats exemplify this general tendency. For instance, capitalist-fascist autocratic dictatorships in interwar Germany, Italy and Spain were not only or mainly 'corporate-economic' but also political, especially in the first and second country, with their autocrats being dictators primarily in the polity, as secondarily in the economy. Hitler reportedly epitomizes this by acting principally as a state rather than economic dictator and the 'promise of broad coalition' of the political right involving large capitalists a la Krupp et al. and traditional authoritarian conservatives. Hence, the coalition with these capitalists demonstrates that Hitlerism wholly preserved capitalism, including the stock market in which Nazi-connected firms gained the most. The coalition with conservatives reveals Nazism's origin in, alliance and indeed merger—as the 'new conservatism'—with traditional conservatism as intrinsic authoritarianism. This is what especially Mannheim who personally witnessed and recounted these developments and events suggests by stating that dictatorship becomes 'possible' within capitalism under certain conditions in the form of fascism as the 'exponent of bourgeois groups'. In a similar vein, Polanyi identifies the 'fascist solution to the impasse' of capitalism that it essentially preserved rather than supplanted, as both Nazism and Italian fascism show. In this connection,

---

20   On these and related matters, see Adorno (1991), Bonikowski and DiMaggio (2016), Hahl et al. (2018), Kentor and Boswell (2003), Lamont (2018), Mann (2005), Mueller (1996), Murray (2017), Savelsberg and King 2005), Stiglitz (2012), and Shiller (2017).

Mannheim invokes Mussolini as a fascist autocrat adoring capitalism as the 'choice of the fittest, equal opportunities for the most gifted'.[21]

The same, with slight modifications, holds for capitalist or neo-fascist autocratic dictatorships and autocrats in postwar Latin America, with Chile and Pinochet as the exemplar, theocratic autocracies in Gulf and other Islamic states, including Saudi Arabia for long and Turkey at present. This seems to hold for the emerging proxy autocracy of 'free enterprise' capitalism in America post-2016 and via global convergence or contagion in other countries from Brexit Britain to Brazil and Hungary and Poland. In all these instances, with some variations, capitalist autocracies and autocrats function and act as dictatorial political regimes and personal rulers in the polity, just as economic systems and actors in the economy in conjunction and mutual reinforcement. Such a tendency is harmonious with the logic and operation of capitalist dictatorship as the political economy of power and domination of capital over non-capital, not only the pure economics of its profit and wealth. The manifestly political character of autocracies and autocrats in capitalism and pre-capitalism has induced many economists and other scholars to identify autocracy and autocratic rulers as the exact opposite and main opponents of democracy and equate them with dictatorship and dictators overall. Therefore, they overlook dictatorship's non-individual forms and agents such as plutocracy and oligarchy, plutocrats and oligarchs, including military juntas that do not necessarily involve or lead to personal rule.[22]

4.2 Capitalist Dynasty as a Political Regime

The preceding about autocracy in capitalism also applies to capitalist family dynasty, with some qualifications. Even if less manifestly and overly than autocracy, dynasty represents a political form and agent of capitalist dictatorship, or eventually becomes so, while complementing, reinforcing and merging with the economic. It does this by expanding from economy to polity, moving from the acquisition and concentration of wealth to that of power in combination and mutual reinforcement. Dynasty in capitalism manifests itself as the dictatorship of a rich capitalist family and similar primary group in the meaning of dynastic political rule by seizing and controlling the state, in interaction with familial economic domination by wealth concentration and control of the economy, including the market. Capitalist dynasty operates as the family-based political economy of power and wealth by transforming through

21   See Mannheim (1936, p. 146), see also Adorno (2001), Ferguson and Voth (2008), Friedman (1982), Riley and Fernández (2014), and Satyanath et al. (2017).

22   On military juntas and personal rule, see Acemoglu et al. (2009).

a reverse alchemy money and economic control into political authority and domination, just as conversely, coming a full virtuous circle for its members and a vicious cycle for democracy. Just as their precursors and successors in pre- and post-capitalism, capitalist dynastic families behave as repressive and exclusionary political agents and provide state autocrats or dictatorial individuals—simply playing, manipulating and ruling politics—just as coercive and exclusive economic agents accumulating wealth, controlling the economy and monopolizing the market.

Most capitalist and other dynasties, past and present, manifest this dual process. They range in time from 19th-century England (even discounting the royal family) and Gilded-Age America to these same societies during neoconservatism, including post-2016 America seemingly witnessing the resurge of dynastic and autocratic capitalism and politics. In social space, they span from the third and non-Western world, including most of Latin America, Africa and Asia traditionally and Eastern Europe during the transition to dynastic and oligarchic capitalism to some Western and other European societies such as Italy, Spain, and to some degree France and Germany. What is common to these disparate instances is that capitalist dynasty starts as or becomes a political regime and a dynastic family acts as a ruling group in the polity, as well as an economic system and an agent dominant in the economy in combination.

4.3   Capitalist Plutocracy, Aristocracy and Oligarchy as a Political Regime

Plutocracy or plutocratic aristocracy and oligarchy represents the sociologically most important political form and agent of capitalist dictatorship, just as the economic. Like autocracy and dynasty, plutocracy possesses salient political attributes and epitomizes capitalist dictatorship as a specific polity, a structure of politics, power, domination and repression, not just an economic system of capitalism, wealth, market and competition. This is what the cited US President posits by identifying the 'tyranny' of plutocracy through that of its 'mere wealth' in American capitalism and Weber implies witnessing the money acquisition and power and political dominance of 'naked plutocracy' during the Gilded Age and later times. These times particularly include, after the interlude of the Great Deal and WW II, the period after 1980 and the 'conservative revolution' of Reaganism and of its authoritarian ideological and political twin Thatcherism in England. Recent observations vindicate the observations from the Gilded Age by observing the resurgence of plutocracy and the proxy 'tyranny of mere wealth' déjà vu in the form of 'plutonomy' in American and other Anglo-Saxon capitalism during the 21st century.

As the US President and Weber suggest, plutocracy is more than an economic system of accumulation and concentration of wealth and of group domination in the economy and plutocrats more than merely wealthy groups and individuals, as the 'robber barons' of their and later times show. This even more expressly holds for aristocracy or oligarchy that has no manifest economic connotation. Beyond such an economic dimension of wealth, plutocracy intrinsically represents or ultimately becomes a political regime and a system of power and rule in the polity and plutocrats act as agents and rulers in the latter, as the 'robber barons' and their later variations exemplify. Therefore, plutocracy proves to be the most consequential politically salient form and agent of capitalist dictatorship in sociological terms of collective organization and action.

The above holds more explicitly for aristocracy and oligarchy in its plutocratic or capitalist forms, proxies and agents and its classic and prevailing concept and meaning of a political regime and rule. In this context, one can redefine plutocracy in capitalism as the 'dictatorship of the rich' in the sense of group political rule via concentrating and wielding state power, while interacting with, complementing and reinforcing economic domination and wealth concentration. This redefinition hence applies to aristocracy and oligarchy in capitalism so long as they are usually plutocratic, and conversely plutocracy tends to become or claim to be aristocratic, noble, elite, and eventually reduces to an oligarchic size. This is what Pareto, Michels, Mosca and other sociologists theoretically posit and the 'top one percent' or even less such as a small number of family 'dynasties' (e.g., 400–500) in American capitalism empirically indicates. On this account, plutocracy represents a collective functional analogue of autocracy, as do consequently plutocratic, wealthy aristocracy and oligarchy. Plutocracy and autocracy share the unrestrained political rule or dictatorship of the wealthy in the polity, even if the capitalist class in one case and individual capitalists in another.

In sum, like autocracy and dynasty, plutocracy and thus plutocratic aristocracy and oligarchy within capitalism constitutes the structure of politics, concentrated power and domination, both interacting with and extending beyond the economy and wealth concentration. As a result, it becomes the paradigmatic collective and sociologically most consequential political economy of power and domination in capitalist dictatorship.

4.4 Secondary Forms of Capitalist Dictatorship as Political Regimes

In addition, the secondary forms of capitalist dictatorship represent political regimes. The extreme, corrupted variation of plutocracy, oligarchy and aristocracy and its agents, kleptocracy and kleptocrats in capitalism are a manifestly political form and agent of capitalist dictatorship, just as the economic in combination.[23] One can characterize kleptocracy as the dictatorship of robber capitalists in the sense of a system of political rule, in conjunction and mutual reinforcement with economic domination via robbery and fraud, and klepto-crats as dictatorial plutocrats moving from economy to and ruling polity. In this regard, kleptocracy arises and operates as the robbery-driven version of plutocracy, oligarchy and aristocracy and thus of capitalist dictatorship as a political regime, and kleptocrats act as robber plutocrats, oligarchs and aristo-crats seeking and wielding political power rather than only robber-capitalists robbing and defrauding non-capitalists and extorting wealth. For example, kleptocratic, predatory and coercive capitalists in Gilded-Age American cap-italism were not just robber-capitalists as economic agents amassing wealth through robbery, predation, coercion and monopolistic control of the econ-omy. They were also robber-aristocrats cum barons as political rulers or polit-ically dominant actors seeking, acquiring and wielding power and thus dom-inating in the polity. Similarly, combining robbery and fraud with predation and violence, predatory, gangster or mafia capitalism and capitalists extending kleptocracy and kleptocrats and expanding from economy to polity operate as the political forms and agents of capitalist dictatorship, in conjunction with their operation as the economic.[24]

Most capitalist kleptocracies and kleptocrats, predatory and mafia capi-talism and capitalists evince the tendency to evolve from economic systems and agents to political regimes and rulers. Especially kleptocracies and klep-tocrats in non-Western societies tend to become effective dictatorships and dictators within the polity spanning from Africa and most of South America to Eastern Europe under oligarchy. Within the Western world, a paradigmatic historical exemplar is the reported dual economic and political monopoly of the American 'robber barons' during Gilded-Age capitalism and their later incarnations. These include the apparent resurgence and dominance of auto-cratic and dynastic kleptocracy and kleptocrats in the economy and polity of America after 2016 and predatory and mafia capitalism and capitalists which Enron-like and related practices of predation and criminal capitalist financial engineering exemplify. In sum, kleptocracy and predatory/mafia capitalism move from economy to polity, expanding from acquisition of wealth by rob-bery and predation to acquiring and exerting power by coercion and closure,

---

23   The term 'kleptocracy' or 'kleptocratic regimes' is from Acemoglu (2005, p. 1046).
24   The term capitalist 'mafias' is from Bourdieu (1998, p. 76), 'gangster capitalism' from
       (Giddens 2000, p. 35) and 'mafia capitalism' from Pryor (2002, p. 364).

and thus generalize themselves from economic into political forms and agents of capitalist dictatorship.

As a matter of course, police states and their leaders, military dictatorships and dictators, theocracies and theocrats in capitalism represent the most explicit and exemplary political forms and agents or state protectors of capitalist dictatorship, albeit having certain economic dimensions and actors. All these are coercive and violent political regimes and rulers representing capitalist dictatorship and acting as dictators, or enforcing and sustaining it through state terror, militarized repression and religious coercion, respectively. They all arise and function as the dictatorship of the capitalist class, which it exerts directly or indirectly through police states, military dictatorships and theocracies exerting it on behalf of or in association with it, aside from some variations and transient tensions between plutocracy or capitalist oligarchy and the military, theocracy or religion.

Police states and repressive rulers, military dictatorships and dictators and theocracies and coercive theocrats in capitalism more overtly than its other forms and agents reveal the inner logic and working of capitalist dictatorship as a political regime of dictatorial power ('despotic might') of capital in the polity, and not only the economy. This looks like a capitalist-dictatorship variation on the revelation of the dictator's 'new clothes'. In ideological-political terms, all these are invariably conservative/right, including fascist/extreme-right and religious, states and dictatorships. They exemplify the close connection, affinity and congruence of conservatism, including within its extended family fascism, and theocratic religion with capitalist and related dictatorship. In short, they express the observed tendency for conservatism as an ideology and politics and dictatorship to move 'hand in hand'.[25] In a way, they are the most violent, ultimate and, in Pareto's words, 'coward' forms and agents, the last stand of capitalist dictatorship and dictators. They are syndromes of the latter's violence, obstinacy and lack of confidence in the non-coercive operation of the 'spontaneous order" of laissez-faire capitalism as a system of labor coercion and a condition for capitalist dictatorship.

What Pareto predicts as the rise of a 'military dictatorship' among some Western nations due to their wars appear as a dual complex of dictatorships. This is, first, the dictatorship of the existing capitalist elite by itself or on its behalf by the military caste and its twin, the police state (and conceivably of the prospective non-capitalist elite). Second, it is religious dictatorship by harnessing religion in the aim of keeping laboring classes 'subdued'. Most police

---

25   See Mueller (2009, p. ix), also, Bartling et al. (2015), Perelman (2000), and Simpson (1934).

states, military dictatorships and theocracies within capitalism exemplify the capitalist class' pattern of dictatorship exerting it by itself or through these overt and ultimate political and coercive mechanisms. For example, the police states and military and religious dictatorships, which Pareto predicts in inter-war Europe, including Nazi Germany and fascist Italy and Spain, represented or enforced the dictatorship of the capitalist class, namely its political dominance and corporate pro-capital dictatorship. Similarly, their postwar variants show the same tendencies. They include most of Africa, much of Asia, including South Korea, Singapore and Taiwan under military rule, South America, notable Chile's neo-fascist police state and military 'free market' and Catholic-supported dictatorship, and European countries such as Franco's Spain after WW II, Portugal and Greece under militarist and religiously supported regimes.

In addition, Pareto, Scheler, Sombart, and other contemporaries detect the proxy police state[26] and repressive and religiously sanctified, essentially theocratic political regime in 19th-century England and especially Gilded-Age America. Such a state and regime enforced by 'brute force' and 'capitalist militias' the dictatorship of the capitalist class in the sense of economic and political 'oppression' and labor 'exploitation'. Mitchell implies this by imploring the state to protect the 'weak against exploitation' and the 'despotic might of capital' and 'industrial despotism' in America.

Furthermore, what the 1954–62 US President lamented as the surge of the military-industrial complex as a predictor of military dictatorship and a threat to democracy (and the welfare state[27]) in America enforces the power and domination of the capitalist class in the polity, including plutocracy, oligarchy and conceivably autocracy and dynasty post-2016. On this account, it operates as the military-capitalist complex and in that sense the ultimate basis and last resort of the effective or prospective dual dictatorship of the military caste and the capitalist class. It interacts, complements and intertwines with a resurgent policing punitive and theocratic or religiously over-determined coercive state déjà vu descending from the Gilded Age, Puritan theocracy and the European Middle Ages, as Pareto, Sombart, and Scheler suggest. In a word, the warfare state merges with the police state, the two forming or enforcing dual capitalist dictatorship.

---

26 Scheler (1964, pp. 15–6) observes around a century ago that Puritanism's 'fundamental distrust of the bodily drive' resulted in 'an espionage and police system directed against all natural impulses' in the countries that it historically dominated, hence England and especially the US.

27 See Hooks and McQueen (2010) identify the surging military-industrial complex as a major cause of the 'underdeveloped' welfare state in postwar America.

A phenomenon coming full circle to the Gilded Age of brute force against non-capital consists of a resurgent Puritanical police state and theocracy in evangelical America via mass imprisonment, widespread executions of the poor and powerless and other acts of 'political terror'. Further, it coexists, co-functions and entwines with the military-capitalist complex to represent or enforce the 'dictatorial rule' of the capitalist class, including 'plutonomy'. The moralistic and religiously driven police state, including the prison and death-penalty system, in evangelical America, such as the 'Bible Belt' from the 'deep' South to Texas, functions as the political regime or coercive instrument of capitalist dictatorship like plutocracy since Reaganism and autocracy post-2016. In short, this penal system reduces to a prison-capitalist complex by merging 'a dictatorial business class' and 'a hyperactive police and penal state'.[28] In sum, police states, military dictatorships and theocracies in capitalism are the most overt, violent and ultimate political, invariably conservative, including fascist and other extreme-right, forms and agents, as well as mechanisms and enforcers, of capitalist dictatorship.

5   Political Indicators and Proxies of Capitalist Dictatorship

Capitalist dictatorship's indicators and proxies if considering it a political regime are generally equivalent to those of all dictatorships. This reaffirms that the former is just a special case of these latter rather than (as claimed for its American variation) an exceptional, unique phenomenon of 'free enterprise' of capital and of freedom of non-capital strata in the economy and polity, and not really dictatorship but capitalist democracy. These indicators include the suppression of political freedoms and rights reduced to non-existence or minimum, power concentration and consequently sharp political-social inequality, and severe penal repression and punishment within society, in conjunction and mutual perpetuation with militarism versus other societies.

5.1   *Suppression of Political Freedoms and Rights*
Suppression and consequently the non-existence or minimum degree of basic political freedoms and rights provides an essential indicator of capitalist dictatorship politically considered. Negation of these freedoms and rights for non-capital populations and their monopolization and closure by capital typifies capitalist dictatorship as a political regime that hence continues the pattern of

---

28   See Wacquant (2002, p. 1521), also, King et al. (2012).

TABLE 7   Political indicators and proxies of capitalist dictatorship

suppression of political freedoms and rights
    suppression of voting and related political freedoms and rights
    suppression of free political competition for power
    suppression of political 'voice'
concentration of political power
    mistreatment and subordination of non-capital
    denial of equal political freedoms and rights to non-capital
    suppression of political pluralism and imposition of ideological
    monism
    unequal legal treatment
severe penal repression and punishment
    'law and order' for capitalists, lawlessness for capital.
    political terror: mass imprisonment, widespread death sentences and
    executions, violations of human rights
militarism
    military-capitalist complex and aggressive wars
    militarized political repression

pre-capitalist despotism such as feudalism with respect to the non-aristocratic populace and aristocracy. Suppression of the elemental freedom and right of voting in elections and especially of pursuing and holding political power for non-capital propertyless and non-religious groups and its monopolizing by capital as the ruling class characterizes capitalist dictatorship.[29] Consequently, capitalist dictatorship features, with some variations, low electoral and other political participation such as voter turnout mainly due to voting-rights suppression and notably minimal non-capital influence and representation versus capital exclusive power and dominance. It therefore virtually perpetuates, as with regard to the freedom to pursue and hold power, the syndrome of pre-capitalist despotism regarding the populace and aristocracy.

---

29   Alexander (2001, p. 239) remarks that the 'force of capitalist economic institutions encouraged the belief that failure in the market sphere revealed a parallel incompetence in democratic life, hence the long-standing exclusion of the propertyless from full electoral participation and the polluting stereotypes about the irrationality and even animality of the soot covered classes. It is easy to see the conversion of religious into civil competence in much the same way' (see also Giddens 1984; Somerville 2000).

5.1.1   Suppression of Voting and Related Political Freedoms and Rights
Capitalist dictatorship typically, with certain variations, suppresses voting and
related political freedoms and rights for non-capital groups, especially lower
and powerless social strata. It turns out to be the political regime of mostly
unfree, unfair and non-universal elections through the suppression or minimal permission of political freedoms and rights, simply disenfranchisement,
of non-capital groups and related undemocratic methods consistent with
dictatorships. At least, this is what the US South and the conservative pole of
America shows, acting as the sole remaining instance among Western societies in persistent and systematic voting-rights suppression or minimal permission with regard to lower and powerless strata and so unfree, unfair and non-
universal elections, which only dictatorial third-world countries parallel.[30]
By suppressing or minimizing a basic political freedom and process for such
groups and subverting the foundation of inclusive democracy and society,
capitalist dictatorship descends to pre-capitalist and pre-democratic despotism in this region, as does in these other societies. This region hence primarily renders, sustains and penetrates America as such a political regime and
effective theocracy, in Weber's words, 'Bibliocracy' as the 'Bible Belt'. In stark
contrast, such negative practices of disenfranchisement and exclusion of non-
capitalist and related groups from democracy have become virtually extinct
and even inconceivable in Western liberal democracies.[31] Yet, they apparently
persist and resurge in capitalist dictatorships or theocracies such as the South
or conservative America and most Islamic states. These two seemingly opposite political regimes share the property that unrestricted and universal voting
rights and free, fair elections are non-existent or systematically suppressed by
fused plutocratic-theocratic conservative ruling groups as 'proto-totalitarian'
opposites to liberal democracy and individual liberty.[32]

---

30   For the US South, see Amenta et al. (2001), Amenta, Caren and Olasky (2005). for Islamic
     countries Kuran (2018).
31   For contemporary Western liberal democracies especially in Europe, see Bloemraad,
     Korteweg, and Yurdakul (2008) and Marks et al. (2009).
32   The designation 'proto-totalitarian' for the 'Bible Belt' is from Bauman (1997, p. 184), see
     also Bénabou et al. (2015), Domhoff (2013), and McBride (2008). More broadly, Putnam
     (2000, p. 350) describes conservative America during the 1950s as 'proto-fascist', which
     hence especially applies to the US South from Alabama and Tennessee to Oklahoma and
     Texas. These states qualify as such by, first, labor repression though suppressing union-
     ization and the right to collective bargaining and strike (e.g., in the Texas educational
     system) consistent with fascism's, notably Nazism's, suppression of unions and worker
     rights. Second, they do by suppressing voting rights and monopolizing political power for
     capitalist and religious elites and excluding non-capitalist and non-religious groups by

In respect of such voting-rights suppression, the conservative pole of
America, particularly the South, hardly qualifies as factual, full democracy in
terms of basic and universal electoral freedoms and rights, unrestricted franchise for all groups, thus free and fair elections that typify, even if do not necessarily ensure, a democratic regime. Instead, it presents itself as substantively
non-democracy in the sense of a reportedly persistent 'under-democratized'
political system and democratic 'backwardness', or ersatz illiberal and exclusionary, including a limited electoral, 'democracy', as it has been since postbellum, let alone antebellum, times.[33] A 'limited electoral democracy' is a non
sequitur and functionally equivalent to non-democracy from the prism of liberal democracy that features maximal and so unlimited voting rights, simply
the 'universal franchise', under certain conditions, in spite or because of the
perennial attempts of conservative groups to deny or restrict them.[34] This pole
of America does not even pass the basic preliminary test and threshold of rep-
resentative democracy that citizens have a universal or widely permitted right
to vote (franchise) and elect their leaders. Instead, their capitalist and religious
rulers such as Southern and other pro-capital, anti-labor and theocratic conservatives select their voters through voting-rights suppression or minimal permission and other disenfranchising, exclusionary practices (gerrymandering,

---

theocratic 'must recognize divinity' prohibitions also consistent with fascism's and theocracy's power monopolization and exclusion of these strata. Third, they qualify as such
by their moralistic Puritanical 'holy' state terror through mass imprisonment for sins-as-
crimes (drug use, etc.) and widespread executions often of innocent persons consistent
with fascism as the system of terrorism. Fourth, they appear as such by their irrationalism
and anti-rationalism through the preservation of religious superstitions (e.g., beliefs in
'Satan') and hostility to science such as evolution and climate science consistent with
fascism as the irrational and anti-rational system. Taken together, they appear as compounded 'proto-fascist', capitalist and theocratic dictatorships compatible with fascism.
Such 'proto-fascist' conservative forces resurged and indeed exploded and prevailed in
the US South on the eve of and during post-2016 capitalist autocracy which awakens and
intensifies them and which they prefigure and sustain.

33 Amenta et al. (2001, p. 227) point to 'American backwardness in the 20th century, two
    thirds of which was characterized by restricted voting rights in a substantial part of the
    polity' (see also, Acemoglu and Robinson 2008; Piven 2008).

34 Llavador and Oxoby (2005, pp. 1158, 1186) observe that 'in early stages of industrial
    development liberals typically promoted extending the franchise to workers against the
    opposition of conservatives', inferring that 'franchise contractions are mostly fostered by
    conservative governments' and 'there exists a limit to capitalists' support for extending
    the franchise'. Acemoglu and Robinson (2000, p. 1169), however, suggest that 'in Britain,
    France, Germany, and Sweden, the threat of revolution was the major factor in the exten-
    sion of the franchise to the poorer segments of the society' (see also Habermas 2001;
    Marks et al. 2009; Somerville 2000).

prohibition of voting by mail, etc.) in which they persist for long and excel at present.[35]

In comparative terms, by such suppression of universal voting freedoms and rights the conservative pole of America manifests its typical 'American exceptionalism'. This holds in the sense of democratic 'backwardness' in relation to and thus a large substantive distance from Western liberal democracies, including its neighbor Canada, in which such practices are virtually unknown. By contrast, it appears closer to many third-world undemocratic countries, including Islamic theocratic states, yet even some of them like Turkey and Iran apparently do not suppress such rights with the intensity and on the scale the 'Bible Belt' does. Historically, this pole manifests and perpetuates historical atavism in the third millennium.

On one hand, Western liberal democracies move toward maximizing and universalizing voting and related political freedoms and rights by extending them to the widest number of groups, including noncitizens.[36] By stark contrast, the conservative pole of America such as the South does not allow even some of its own citizens such as lower and powerless strata voting rights, let alone noncitizens or immigrants denied any political as well as civil rights. Further, not only does conservative America not grant political and civil liberties and rights to both legal and illegal immigrants but its post-2016 leader completely stopped legal immigration from all countries in 2020 by an executive order seizing on the covid-19 pandemic as the rationale. Therefore, such an order reveals that the conservative campaign against illegal immigrants from a certain country (Mexico) is only the prelude to and cover for a total assault on legal immigration from all countries in a typical revelation and escalation of nativism and xenophobia replicating or reminiscent of Nazi Germany. This seems a move without apparent precedent in American history since the late 18th century and probably without constitutional authority, instead by effectively making laws ruling by decree and usurping the legislative powers of Congress and has been unthinkable until recently—post-2016

---

35   Friedman and Holden (2008, p. 113) observe that the 'much publicized Republican redistricting in Texas in 2003 caused four Democratic congressmen to lose their seats and would have been even more extreme but for the Voting Rights Act, which effectively protected nine Democratic incumbents. Other particularly stark current examples include Florida, Michigan, and Pennsylvania—states that are evenly divided, but whose delegations to the 109th Congress collectively comprised 39 Republicans and 20 Democrats' (see also Jouet 2017).

36   Bloemraad et al. (2008, p. 165) find that 'political rights tend to be those most tied to nation-state citizenship, but countries such as the Netherlands, Sweden, and New Zealand allow noncitizens local voting rights'.

capitalist-conservative autocracy does what no other government or president has done during more than two centuries, illustrating the gravity of the action. Such an unprecedented and probably unconstitutional move of presidential law-making, along with the fact that no other Western government, notably neighboring Canada, has done this, illustrates what many observers note as the post-2016 autocratic threat to the Constitution, the rule of law, democracy and political and civil liberties and rights in the US. It also reaffirms the vehement and implacable nativism and xenophobia of American conservatism and its autocracy that it shares with Nazism and its leader. The fact that no group or individual has mounted a legal and even unofficial challenge to this unprecedented anti-immigration action proves that capitalist-conservative autocracy has succeeded to spread its virulent xenophobia to the nearly entire 'nation of immigrants'.

In this and most other respects, contemporary American conservatism and Nazism and generally European fascism appear as functional equivalents by generating the same effects on or performing identical 'functions' in society, including its polity. So, conservative America need not European fascism because all-American conservatism suffices in that it functions in the same way as the first would if it were transferred in its pure form from Europe. Similarly, evangelical America such as the 'Bible Belt', despite its paranoia about, need not fear, Islamic 'Sharia law', because it already enforces the Christian equivalent of the latter, including the Biblical 'eye for eye' punishment-vengeance driving the use of the death penalty, mass imprisonment, torture and other forms of 'holy' terror. Further, American conservatism reproduces its own brand of native proto- and neo-fascism and neo-Nazism in America, just as traditional German and other European conservatism produced and merged with Nazism and fascism in interwar Europe.

On the other hand, conservative America petrifies in the 'dead past' of their minimization and restriction to the smallest possible numbers, especially disenfranchising lower and powerless social strata, including minorities, poor, former prisoners and others. A formal aspect of this atavism is that liberal democracies are increasingly creative in such an extension of political rights by multiple ways, including compulsory universal voting. Yet, this pole creates ever-new or reinvents the old methods and justifications of suppression, with the US South reinventing those of the *Gone with the Wind* past, for example, justifying the prohibition of voting by mail by preserving the 'integrity of democracy' reminiscent of the justification from the postbellum era. While creating such inventions, including identification and related onerous requirements for lower classes, Southern and similar conservative states reinvent much of the 'creative legislation' they enacted after the civil war, including 'elaborate registration systems', purges of low-class and powerless voters and other mea-sures curtailing such political rights for certain groups. In spite of such 'creative legislation', the conservative-dominated and pro-capital Supreme Court essen-tially abrogated the 1965 Voting Rights Act invoking the ground, as if operating in a parallel universe, that Southern states no longer curtail such rights and the South remakes itself into a region of 'free elections', 'democracy' and 'liberty for all', contrary to its reality.

For instance, during the 2010–20s the conservative 5-to-4 majority of the Supreme Court effectively revoked or repeatedly suspended the 1965 Voting Rights Act exactly when most Southern and other conservative-ruled states escalated and intensified their suppression of voting rights for low and pow-erless social groups. (Further, its conservative supreme judge cynically stated that these states no longer suppress such rights as the ground for revoking the Voting Rights Act!) Therefore, this striking convergence creates the well-founded impression that the conservative-dominated, pro-capital Supreme Court and Southern and other conservative-ruled states act in concert or tacit mutual understanding in the suppression of voting rights for these groups and thus in the contraction and degeneration of democracy in America.

Furthermore, while some liberal democracies in Western Europe institute compulsory universal voting, conservative America attempts to enforce com-pulsory non-voting for certain non-capital and other social strata such as lower classes, racial minorities, liberal, secularist, progressive and non-religious groups when identified or known.[37]

A substantive outcome of such atavism in the suppression or minimal permission of voting rights—for example, for millions current and former prisoners—is reportedly the drastic 'democratic contraction'[38] and distor-tion of democracy, while Western European liberal democracies effecting an

---

37   Borgers (2004, p. 56) notes that 'while in most countries participation in (political) elec-tions is voluntary, some countries (e.g., Belgium, Italy) have tried to make it compulsory', but fails to note that conservative America, particularly the South, has attempted to make instead non-participation in voting compulsory at least for certain targeted groups, espe-cially non-capital lower classes, along with minorities.

38   Uggen and Manza (2002, p. 778) identify 'democratic contraction' as a political conse-quence of 'felon disenfranchisement in the US' finding that 'felon disenfranchisement constitutes a growing impediment to universal political participation in the US because of the unusually severe state voting restrictions imposed upon felons and the rapid rise in criminal punishment since the 1970s'. They elaborate that the 'success of the conservative crime policy agenda over the past three decades has had a remarkable impact, produc-ing an enormous increase in felony convictions and incarceration, and a corresponding increase in rates of felon disenfranchisement', and conclude that the 'results signal a true democratic contraction in the US' (Uggen and Manza 2002, pp. 781–84).

expansion of democracy by extending these rights. This democratic contraction often reportedly reaches the point at which democracy in conservative America hardly remains and operates, especially in egalitarian and universalistic terms.[39] In light of such unparalleled suppression of basic political freedom and rights, it is no wonder that voting turnout has historically been lower in America and continues to be in presidential and especially parliamentary (Congressional) elections, with some transient variations, than in most Western liberal democracies. Such exceptionalism is primarily due to the suppression or minimal permission of voting rights for lower and powerless strata in its conservative and theocratic pole such as the South. Yet, this apparently does not discourage US conservative politicians and presidents to lecture Western European liberal democracies, not to mention third-world countries, about 'free elections', 'democracy' and 'freedom', evoking what Weber refers to as the Puritan-style 'pure hypocrisy of Americanism' or, in Pareto's words, 'jingoism'. In sum, persistently low electoral participation is a testament or first approximation to capitalist dictatorship merged with conservative repression and evangelical theocracy in America under conservatism, with the South as a regional proof showing a strong tendency to national metastasis during recent times.

5.1.2   Suppression of Free Political Competition for Power

Furthermore, capitalist dictatorship typically suppresses free competition for political power by denying such a freedom to and excluding non-capital propertyless social strata from this democratic process and monopolizing it for and including only capital. Consequently, it amounts to a process of unfree political competition for power in favor of capital over non-capital, along with favoring religious over non-religious groups, as the 'American regime' through the plutocratic-theocratic fusion demonstrates since the Gilded Age and Puritan theocracy through these days, especially in the South. Like all others, capitalist dictatorship thus epitomizes non-democracy, violating and reversing Schumpeter's definition of democracy as free and universal 'competition for leadership' as 'competition for a free vote' into an opposite.[40]

Conversely, capitalist dictatorship proves to be a political regime with simulated free, fair and universal elections by rulers selecting electors, as through

---

39   Beck (2000, p. 115) asks referring to the US and apparently answers in the negative whether a democracy with a 30% turnout at elections is still a democracy'.

40   Mulligan et al. (2004, pp. 52–4) note that 'suppression of political competition is an especially important activity for dictators, because it helps them retain their position' (see also Bollen and Jackman 1985; Wimmer, Cederman, and Min 2009).

capital-favoring or conservative voting suppression and arbitrary partisan redistricting (gerrymandering) in the US South, simulating placebo democracy or democratic reforms. Relatedly, just as being at most a limited electoral democracy, it is at the maximum a process of limited and distorted free competition for power only within capital—and the religious in its American version—between its factions, so bogus illiberal, exclusionary 'democracy' as an inner contradiction, impossibility or perversion. This includes capitalist theocracy, as in the 'Bible Belt', Catholic-dominated Poland and Islamic autocratic and plutocratic regimes like Saudi Arabia and other Gulf states. Like a limited electoral democracy, a limited competitive 'democracy' is formally a non sequitur and substantively non-democracy from the angle of liberal democracy: both nonsensical and unsustainable.

In either case, capitalist dictatorship represents a deviation from and indeed degeneration and substitution of Schumpeter's canonical model of democracy as a political regime of both free, fair and universal elections of rulers and of free competition for power between capital and non-capital, as well as religious and secular groups. In Schumpeter's terms, it exposes itself as the process of 'uncreative destruction' of democracy as a political regime, as opposed to capitalism's technological and related 'creative destruction' of the economic system. These form two distinct processes that can coexist and enfold together, as in 19th-century English and American capitalism since the Gilded Age through, with some adaptations, to the present. Due to both exclusionary elections and restricted competition for power, capitalist dictatorship is what Weber would call an 'abomination' of Jefferson's universalistic principle of 'liberty and justice' and equality in politics 'for all'. Instead, it reduces to exclusive and closed 'capitalist freedom' and 'democracy', plus, as in the religiously overdetermined 'American regime, 'Christian liberty', as an ersatz substitute. This holds from the standpoint of universalism and liberal universalistic democracy, although stand-alone and in its own self-deception this regime may look as the 'most democratic' ever in time and space, as the conservative adherents of 'American exceptionalism' claim.[41]

---

41 Yet even 'super-patriotic' and neo-conservative sociologist Lipset (1996) admits of the 'double-edged sword' of 'American exceptionalism'—hence far from being an unmitigated blessing and superiority—compared to Western European societies. Lipset exalts the historical 'resilience' of American democracy—in an invidious distinction from 'non-resilient' Western Europe—which seems groundless or premature in view of its rapid dissolution into effective autocracy post-2016 despite the celebrated 'checks and balances'. More broadly, turned neo-conservative Lipset rebrands neo-conservatism like Thatcherism and Reaganism as a true modern heir of classical liberalism, thus ignoring its inherent illiberalism and strong authoritarianism, including its alliance and eventual

In Schumpeter's terms of free and universal 'competition for leadership' between capital and non-capital, religious and secular groups, the capitalist-theocentric 'American regime' or the conservative pole of America hardly functions and qualifies as liberal or full democracy in the sense of Western European liberal democracies. Hence, such an exception from the Western rule of liberal democracy rather than democratic superiority in space and time seems to be true, non-Western conservative 'American exceptionalism' as a deviation from the West. Instead, because of the perversion of political competition into that within capital and the religious only and the exclusion of non-capital and non-religious groups, conservative America exemplifies capitalist non-democracy or illiberal, exclusionary and theocentric 'democracy'. This also holds for many non-Western countries like most of Latin America, Catholic-dominated Poland and especially capitalist Islamic states like Saudi Arabia and Turkey. The preceding appears as the obverse facet of conservative-reproduced American exceptionalism'—an exceptional convergence with the non-Western world, including Islamic states.

It is no wonder that the propertyless and 'godless', aside from rare exceptions, neither are often legally allowed and socially expected to compete ('need not apply') for nor to hold especially political power in the conservative pole of America. This includes the South as the capitalist 'Bible Belt', where they become a species threatened with extinction with regard to competing for or holding public office. The Southern formula of prohibition and exclusion of the propertyless and 'godless' from power applies to these groups in many non-Western countries, especially Islamic plutocratic states like Saudi Arabia and others. Some Southern and other states continue to prohibit non-believers from seeking and holding public office, and their justifications for such political exclusion of and discrimination against the propertyless and 'godless' revolve around preserving the 'integrity' of democracy and 'Divine design', respectively, thus replicating those of postbellum times and medievalism.

This double feature of effectively treating those not born into power and wealth and displaying 'faith' as outcasts is what precisely typifies and identifies

---

merger with neo-fascism replicating that of conservatism with fascism during the 1930s, let alone conservatism's original and persistent antagonism to liberalism, as Mannheim (1986) classically demonstrates. Lipset also chastises his sociological colleagues for despising capitalism and brand them being 'leftists' but even as a sociologist does not inquire into the societal sources for such attitudes, just as 'libertarian' economist Mises (1956) condemns most intellectuals for an 'anti-capitalist mentality' without inquiring into the causes of the latter. For 'American exceptionalism' as a 'deviant case' from the West see Jouet (2017), Mueller (2009), Norris and Inglehart (2007), for its 'Bible-Belt' proto-totalitarian affinity with the Islamic world such as Iran see Bauman (1997, p. 184).

capitalist and related dictatorship/theocracy and flagrantly deviates from Schumpeter's definition of democracy, as it did pre-capitalist despotism like feudalism. In this light, conservative America in the theocratic South and similar regions appears as the ancient, indeed oldest, atavistic and in that sense darkest political regime among Western democracies rather than the 'new', 'newest' and 'modern'. Hence, there seems to be 'nothing new' in the 'new nation' under conservatism, at least under the Southern sunbelt', compared to pre-capitalist regimes such as feudalism and medieval theocracy with regard to the exclusion of the propertyless and 'godless' from the political process, specifically Schumpeter's 'free competition for leadership'.[42] This definition of democracy hence becomes worthless, hardly worth the paper on which it is written, or a cynical phrase in conservative America and Islamic and other third-world capitalist states—nothing of sorts exists or matters in both settings.

5.1.3   Suppression of Political 'Voice'

Generally, the suppression of and consequently non-existent or minimal freedom in the polity, simply 'voice', for non-capital groups versus capital expresses capitalist dictatorship as an undemocratic political regime. In particular, the weak freedom and right of voting that low voter turnout approximates and other low political participation by these groups is an expression of such a regime, all else being equal. Relatedly, the minimal freedom and right of non-capital and, as in the 'American regime', non-religious groups to pursue and hold political power—what Weber, Wieser and Schumpeter denote 'leadership' and US politicians 'public office' as a euphemism—thus to attain representation in the polity supplies a particularly accurate indication and so diagnosis. It diagnoses capitalist dictatorship not merely as undemocratic in the sense of not all people having 'political voice' through free and universal voting and related democratic participation but as overtly and consistently dictatorial by

---

42   Relatedly, Bourdieu (1998, p. 50) remarks that American and other conservatism since Reagan and Thatcher is 'based on an atavistic faith in historical inevitability' or 'fatalism' and that 'this fatalistic doctrine gives itself an air of a message of liberation, through a whole series of lexical tricks around the idea of freedom (etc.) euphemisms, or ambiguous uses of words (reform)—designated to present a restoration as a revolution in a logic which is that of all conservative revolution' (see also Acemoglu et al. 2011). Further, Bourdieu (1998, p. 35) considers neo-conservatism fundamentally equivalent to fascism in that 'it is characteristic of conservative revolutions, that in (Nazi) Germany in the 1930s, those of Thatcher, Reagan (etc.) that they present restorations as revolutions', adding that 'if this conservative revolution can deceive people, this is because it seems to retain nothing of the old Black Forest pastoral of the conservative revolutionaries (fascists) of the 1930s; it is dressed up in all the signs of modernity'.

a narrow, closed group of capitalist oligarchy merged with theocracy. Merged capitalist oligarchy and theocracy monopolizes this pursuit and rules virtually uncontested and unrestrained, as in the US South and conservative America by mixing with demagogic autocracy post-2016.

Alternatively, capitalist dictatorship exposes itself as an undemocratic and repressive political regime by its minimal political freedoms and rights, including the suppressed freedom and right of non-capital groups for voting and related political participation and especially for pursuing and holding power through free competition. It reveals its nature both by mostly unfree, unfair and non-universal elections of rulers, which the US South epitomizes perennially, and by the unfree or simulated-free competition for leadership by being limited only to that within capital among its factions, which 19th-century England and conservative America exemplify. In consequence, capitalist dictatorship tends to have as a proxy sociological 'iron law' the comparatively lowest degree of political freedoms and rights, including the freedom and right of political participation and representation, among other types of capitalism or forms of government. In particular, its level of political freedoms and rights is drastically lower than that of its opposite, democratic and egalitarian capitalism or liberal democracy.

Overall, most empirical and historical cases of capitalist dictatorship demonstrate its 'law' of minimal liberty and rights in the polity. They range from 19th-century English and Gilded-Age American capitalism through corporate-fascist dictatorships in interwar Germany and Italy to postwar Chile's and South American 'free market' dictatorships to the first two countries déjà vu during Thatcherism and Reaganism and to Eastern Europe under oligarchy, Gulf and most other Islamic states. Further, they continue in America after 2016 and via contagion or plutocratic and extreme-right mobilization in some other countries, including Brexit Britain, Brazil, Hungary, Poland, and so on.

In sum, the suppression and consequently non-existence or minimal level of political freedoms and rights, including the freedom and right to voting and related participation, to holding power and representation in politics and other 'voice' for non-capital groups represents a manifest and salient indicator and identifier of capitalist dictatorship as an undemocratic, repressive and exclusionary form of polity.

5.2 Concentration of Political Power

Another related indicator or proxy of capitalist dictatorship constitutes the concentration and indeed monopolization and exertion of political power by capital versus non-capital. The outcome is sharp, pervasive and persistent political and related social inequality favoring capital and disfavoring non-capital groups. Evidently, such inequality in the polity and society complements, reinforces, connects and ultimately blends with that in the economy, such as extreme wealth and income inequalities characterizing capitalist dictatorship as an economic system. Generally, the unequal distribution of political power, influence and rights is consistent, complementary and mutually reinforcing with the identical distribution of economic resources like property, wealth and income in capitalist dictatorship, as in all dictatorships and other oppressive regimes from slavery and master-servant oppression to their later variations in capitalism.

Concentration, monopolization, and exertion of political power by capital as an agent and ruling group in the polity complements and blends with the same process of wealth privileging it as a production factor and upper class in the economy, just as these two processes enfolded in this way for master-caste and aristocracy in pre-capitalism. To use Weber's words, the positive privilege or monopolistic closure of capital in the polity proceeds hand in hand, with its being a positively privileged class with a position of monopoly in the economy, just as the political domination of aristocracy did with its economic privileges and the monopoly of status groups in pre-capitalism like feudalism. Conversely, the negation of equal or symmetrical power and rights for non-capital political groups within capitalist dictatorship stands in the same relation to the distribution of wealth adverse to labor in the economy, just as these two processes went hand in hand for the non-aristocratic populace in pre-capitalism like peasantry in feudalism, along with slaves and subjugated castes. In Weber's terms, the disprivilege, exclusion and repression of non-capital social groups in the polity move together with their being disprivileged, excluded or oppressed strata in the economy, just as the political subjection of the non-aristocratic populace did with its economic subjugation, as of serfs in feudalism or servants in a master-servant regime and slaves in slavery.

5.2.1 Mistreatment and Subordination of Non-capital Groups

Capitalist dictatorship and its plutocracy—or autocracy and dynasty in non-Western countries, interwar fascist regimes and America post-2016—treats substantively non-capital groups in the polity as pre-capitalist despotism and its aristocracy and autocratic and dynastic rulers treated the non-aristocratic populace like serfs in the ancient regime and lower castes and slaves.[43] This is

---

43   Bourdieu (1998, p. 42) suggests that capital-labor opposition 'is rather like that between
      masters and slaves'. Roemer and Trannoy (2016, p. 1328) remark that the bourgeois revolu-
      tions only 'replaced feudal inequality of opportunity with inequality of opportunity due
      to differential wealth of families'.

treating non-capital in capitalism as effectively an unequal and inferior despised stratum subjected to political exclusion and repression, just as to economic degradation and coercion in reciprocal relation and intensification. This holds even if labor is formally free or not legally treated as a slave or servant caste, as historically was in the master-servant system that England and America retained until the late 19th and early 20th century, let alone the US South.

Capitalist dictatorship's and plutocracy's de facto condition, treatment of and power over non-capital strata in the political system is substantively analogous to pre-capitalist despotism's and aristocracy's de jure status, mistreatment of and dominance over the non-aristocratic populace in the ancient regime, as the postbellum US South reportedly exemplifies.[44] To that extent, contrary to his expectations, Spencer's system of status and 'compulsory cooperation' continues, although in a de facto, substantive form, from pre-capitalist to capitalist dictatorship. The latter rules out or suspends 'voluntary cooperation' between non-capital and capital and confines it only to the latter among particular capitalists and their organizations and associations in the context of their overall unity. This seems analogous to the 'free' cooperation, organization and association within aristocracy between individual aristocrats in pre-capitalist despotism.

Furthermore, capitalist dictatorship often subjects non-capital or non-plutocratic strata to an unequal legal treatment through inequality before the law in relation to capital or plutocracy abandoning any appearance of such equality, just as pre-capitalist despotism subjected the non-aristocratic populace. An exemplar of such unequal legal standards involves differential harsher and milder sanctions, such as long and life prison sentences and usually minimal or no punishment, for lower and upper classes' blue- and white-collar crimes, respectively in conservative America, as Veblen, Merton and other sociologists observe since the Gilded Age through the present. This double legal standard of capital and non-capital law violations makes the legal system ranging from local and state to federal courts up to the Supreme Court, with some variations, in conservative America an instrument of capitalist

---

44 Acemoglu and Robinson (2006b, p. 326) observe that 'although slavery as an economic institution was abolished, Southern elites still possessed considerable de facto power through their control over economic resources, their greater education, and their relative ability to engage in collective action', substituting 'a labor-intensive, low-wage, low-education, and repressive economy that in many ways looked remarkably like that of the antebellum South' and derailing 'political reforms they opposed, and freed slaves were quickly disenfranchised through the use of literacy tests and poll taxes' (see also Amenta et al. 2001; Morck et al. 2005; Ruef 2014).

dictatorship,[45] just as it defined and maintained pre-capitalist despotism like slavery and the feudal master-servant regime.

In general, capitalist dictatorship treats non-capital strata de jure as subordinate in Spencer's system of status with 'successive grades of subordination' within a hierarchy, thus as Weber's negatively privileged political groups in institutional terms versus capital as a positively privileged group in the polity, as pre-capitalist despotism treated the non-aristocratic populace relative to aristocracy. Capitalist dictatorship thus perpetuates, with some adaptations, Spencer's system of status subordination and hierarchy from pre-capitalist despotism and extends it from the non-aristocratic populace to non-capital groups in a legal manner, compromising its pretension to 'equality before the law'. This is what the perpetuation of the master-servant regime based on common law in 19th-century England and America until the early 20th century historically shows through reducing 'free' labor and laborers to legally unfree servitude and servants and subjecting them to severe labor coercion and subordination by law, just as factually.

Accordingly, capitalist dictatorship and its plutocracy retains under some disguises certain legal-institutional aspects of pre-capitalist despotism and its aristocracy by arising and operating as a new anti-egalitarian Paretian aristocratic-like elitist political regime and a ruling group respectively. In this context, it shares with pre-capitalist dictatorship what Wieser names the 'subordination of the masses' to the 'power (of) the leaders', in Simmel's words, 'super-subordination' of non-capital and 'superordination' of capital, simply, as even Durkheim suggests, capitalist 'dominating' members and others 'subordinate' to them.[46]

---

45   Relatedly, Wright (2013, p. 7) observes that no 'capitalist democracy is able to insulate political decision-making from the exercise of power connected to capitalist wealth. In the US this assault on democracy intensified after the Supreme Court's recent decision on the use of corporate funds in political campaigns'. In a similar vein, Spenkuch and Toniatti (2018, pp. 2031–2) remark that 'since the Supreme Court's landmark decision, so-called super PACs may accept unlimited donations from individuals, corporations, and unions to overtly advocate for or against particular candidates', and find that because 'much of super PACs' spending directly relates to campaign advertising, our results reinforce existing concerns about the ability of deep-pocketed donors to influence democratic outcomes'. Further, Formisano (2015, p. 3) suggest that 'Congress and a reactionary Supreme Court majority cater to a hydra-headed plutocracy that enjoys a government of the rich, by the rich, and for the rich'.

46   Habermas (1989, p. 149) registers that the 'separation of the producer from the means of production—the class relationship fully evolved in the industrial capitalism of the nineteenth century—transformed the formally equal legal relationship between capitalists and wage earners into a relationship of factual subordination; its conceptualization in

5.2.2   Denial of Equal Political Freedoms and Rights

Capitalist dictatorship, in conjunction with Puritanical evangelical pro-capital, anti-labor theocracy, especially in conservative America such as the South and similar regions denies equal political freedoms and rights to non-capital and secular 'un-American' groups and monopolizes them for capital/plutocracy and religious believers. Such undemocratic practices continue or resemble pre-capitalist despotism's ancient regime of denying any legal rights to the non-aristocratic populace and monopolizing them for aristocracy and theocracy. These practices include suppressing the basic democratic freedom to vote in especially Presidential elections through constant voting suppression by tactics targeting non-capitalist, non-religious and similar 'un-American' populations (e.g., former prisoners) and especially denying their right to pursue and hold power by excluding them from this process, along with other suppressions of their 'voice'. Both practices, especially the second, cause subverting free, open competition for power as the hallmark of political democracy into its monopolization that marks non-democracy, including dictatorship, or bogus illiberal 'democracy', as the double economic-political monopoly of the robber barons' in early American capitalism shows.

At this point, the subversion of free competition in the political system through denying to non-capital (and non-religious) groups the freedom/ right of seeking and holding power may seem incongruent with and atypical for a 'capitalist' regime presumed to be competitive politically, as capitalism

terms of private law shrouded a quasi-public authority (as) private law secures for the capitalist the exercise of a "delegated public power of command." ' Somerville (2000, p. 7) observes that 'under capitalism, the working class is typically subordinated to a 'dominant political coalition', so that workers are both exploited and oppressed'. Perelman (2000, p. 24) notes that 'contemporary economists such as Milton Friedman gloss over the dark side of capitalism, ignoring the requisite subordination, while celebrating the freedom to dispose of one's property'. Steinberg (2003, pp. 446, 487) suggests that capitalist development does not necessitate "free labor" (as) capitalists can deploy legal frameworks of unfreedom to subordinate labor', for example, English common law 'was a vestige of a feudal past that provided capitalists with the leverage of state authority to subjugate workers', concluding that 'legal unfreedom is wholly compatible with capitalist labor subordination'. In turn, Morrill, Zald, and Rao (2003, p. 392) point to 'challenges by subordinates in capitalist workplaces' during modern times. Piven (2008, p. 7) emphasizes that US capitalist dominant groups, 'drawing on the full range of power resources available to them, inhibit subordinate groups from activating the distinctive power rooted in interdependence'. Kimeldorf (2013, p. 1040) finds in early American capitalism that there was 'workers' dependence on a hostile employing class for their livelihood, their partial subordination to the dominant ideology, and the federal government's long history of opposition to unionism, and the real question is not why workers in the US have generally failed to act in concert with one another but why on some occasions they have'.

supposedly is economically. However, such distortion is consistent with the politically anti-competitive nature and operation of pre-capitalist and all dictatorships, thus typical for their capitalist sequel and variation. This holds even aside from the fact that capitalism is not necessarily a free competitive economic system, the realm of 'pure', 'perfect competition' in the market, as the rise and prevalence of monopoly or oligopoly capitalism, with spurious 'monopolistic competition', demonstrates in America and elsewhere. This is what 'free competitive capitalism' suggests as distinct from other modalities of capitalism, as does the distinction between 'capitalism' and the 'market economy', notably that the first is not invariably the second, as monopoly or state capitalism shows, just as conversely.

In sum, the above confirms that capitalist dictatorship as a political regime in some Western and many non-Western countries follows and conforms to, rather than supersedes and diverges from, the inner logics and workings of pre-capitalist and other dictatorships, just as it does as an economic system. The effect of such negations of equal political rights is the extremely unequal distribution and reproduction of power through its concentration and monopolization in capital and, as in conservative America and plutocratic Islamic states, the religious versus non-capital and non-religious groups in capitalist dictatorship mixed with theocracy. This tendency effectively replicates or evokes the monopolized power of aristocracy over the populace in pre-capitalism. Perpetuating de facto and to some degree de jure the aristocratic-style inequality of political and legal rights, such as the right to seek and hold power monopolizing it for capital and denying it to non-capital strata, in capitalist dictatorship operates as an effective mechanism of coercion, repression, exclusion and discrimination in politics.

Relatedly, capitalist dictatorship negates or restricts additional equal political rights for non-capital groups, such as the right to assembly and collective organization and action in the polity while monopolizing it for capital or plutocracy. For illustration, in America since the Gilded Age and capitalist militias through Reaganism and post-2016, capitalist 'plutonomy' has denied and suppressed non-capitalist political assemblies, parties, actions and activists ultimately by severe and systematic coercion to the point of 'brute force'[47] as

---

47   Kimeldorf (2013, p. 1035) reports that in America 'around the turn of the (20th) century industrial conflicts were routinely decided by brute force, pitting desperate strikers against equally determined employers backed, in most cases, by the courts, police, and newspapers'. In addition, Kimeldorf (2013, p. 1056) notes 'President Regan's decision in 1981 to fire and permanently replace more than 12,000 striking air traffic controllers, destroying their union and dramatically exposing organized labor's heightened vulnerability', as well as that the US under conservatism is 'one of the few industrial democracies in violation of

if following Pareto's Machiavellian and fascism-inspiring statement that domination 'cannot last without the use of force'. Capitalist dictatorship or its proxy
since the Gilded Age has been and remains post-2016 the stage of the operation of the law of the strongest and the jungle and to that extent the Hobbesian
state of nature in the form of anarchy for capital, combined with Leviathan for
non-capital groups via coercion.[48]

5.2.3 Suppression of Political Pluralism and Imposition of Ideological Monism

In general, capitalist dictatorship typically features forcible suppression of
political pluralism and coercive imposition of ideological monism, as a facet of
power concentration and monopolization in capital. In particular, the preceding points to capital's forcible suppression of non-capital political freedom and
coercion operating as probably the principal factor—rather than 'American
exceptionalism' in 'free enterprise' capitalism or harmonious capital-labor
relations without 'class warfare'—in this respect. It crucially helps explain the
virtual non-existence of political and ideological pluralism in the sense of a relevant non-capital party and ideology and the prevalence of capitalist monism.
Specifically, this factor primarily accounts for the absence of an influential
labor, social-democratic or socialist party[49] and the failure of socialism in

---

the International Labour Organization's principles for safeguarding the right to organize'
(see also Hung and Thompson 2016; Isaac 2002; Jacobs and Dirlam 2016).

48   Kimeldorf (2013, p. 1055) points to the US 'pre-modern system of industrial relations
where the only law governing class conflict was that of the jungle, resulting in frequent,
often violent confrontations between workers and employers that were decided by the
ability of one side to outlast the other'.

49   Clawson and Clawson (1999, pp. 100–2) note that the 'US has not had a social democratic
or labor party, and the legal frame creates more difficult conditions for unions here than
in virtually any other democracy (while) the level of employer hostility to labor is unique
to the US', and thus imply that the combination of legal coercion and capitalist antagonism primarily explains this exceptional absence of a non-capital political force. In turn,
echoing Sombart's early insights, Lipset and Marks (2000) propose that the reason 'why
socialism failed in the United States' lies in America being the 'prototype for capitalism',
so for the 'analogous reasons liberal democracy failed in Iran, Saudi Arabia and other
Islamic countries'. Yet they omit that what may well explain this failure is a near-total
system of capital coercion and repression of non-capital and in that sense capitalist dictatorship since the Gilded Age, joined with Puritan-inspired theocracy. (In passing, like
Pareto and Sheller, Sombart identifies Puritan-inspired theocracy or moralistic repression
in America during his time, but still downplays the role of capital and religious coercion as an explanation of why socialism is absent or weak in this country.) Relatedly,
they state that 'rather than being an exception, America (is) actually the model for capitalist countries. Far from being a unique or even only slightly different case, America

sharp contrast to all other major Western countries, including proto-capitalist and aristocratic England. To that extent, it helps decisively, even if not entirely, explain the resulting party duopoly.

The latter deviates from the principle of political and ideological pluralism expressing non-pluralism and subverts free competition for power in Schumpeter's definition—who does not envision such competition as that between only two major political parties with irrelevant ('libertarian', 'green' and other) outsiders and pretenders—and related definitions of liberal-pluralist democracy and society or 'poliarchy'.[50] In this connection, the completion of this book precedes the 2020 US Presidential elections. However, just as those in 2016, the prelude to these elections confirmed the absence or weakness of political pluralism and the prevalence of ideological monism in that they reduced the electoral choice to that between slightly different variations of nationalism cum Americanism: Cold-War militarism and bellicosity and nativist proto-fascism and irrationalism. Whoever wins the elections, both militarism and proto-fascism are likely to persist in some forms and agents. Conversely, whoever losses the elections, this is not likely to cause the end of militarism and especially nativist proto-fascism that, most notably the second, have deeper social roots primarily in conservative America like the South and

was the prototype for capitalism'. Comparatively, this seemingly ethnocentric, if not in Pareto's words jingoistic ('patriotic'), statement denies or overlooks that what exists in contemporary Western and other capitalist countries is not a single 'model' of capitalism but instead its many and different models or varieties, simply not one but many capitalisms, including American, European and others. Historically, it seems inaccurate or imprecise so long as America is a capitalist late-comer by almost a century (like Japan) lagging behind Western Europe, specifically Holland, England and laissez-faire France, that instead represents or qualifies as the 'prototype for capitalism' in historical terms. Acemoglu and Robinson (2015, p. 7) recognize that 'after the end of the US Civil War came the age of the robber barons and the huge concentration of economic ownership and control', but fail to identity the latter and by implication capital coercion of labor as a reason for the failure of socialism or a socialist party ('decline of general laws of capitalism') in America aside from abstract and vague references to an 'evolving institutional equilibrium' or the 'prevailing political institutions at a certain time' without specifying which social groups created, sustained and mobilized these institutions against whom, even if this may be all too obvious—capital versus non-capital. This is what Mizruchi and Marshall II (2016, p. 145) precisely suggest in a sociologically more relevant and historically accurate account that the robber barons 'were able to attain considerable power, not only economically but also politically' and that their relations with workers 'were also extremely conflictual, with corporations actively suppressing, sometimes violently, attempts by workers to organize' both in unions and by implication in an associated labor, social-democratic or socialist political party.

50   The notion of 'poliarchy' is in Dahl (1971), see also Dahrendorf (1959), Esping-Andersen (2003), Mueller (1996), and Munch (2001).

beyond. Hence, in longer terms, the 2020 emanations of American militarism and bellicosity and nativist proto-fascism and irrationalism do not matter greatly, even if, especially that of the second, awoke and legitimized all hidden 'proto-fascist' and irrational forces and energies in conservative America. As noted, some observers describe conservative America during the 1950s as 'proto-fascist'. As in 2016, whoever wins the 2020 elections, it probably will not be because of the stronger attractiveness of the candidate's program or personality but because of the more intense repulsiveness of or dislike for the other's.

Furthermore, such party duopoly especially since Reaganism effectively becomes ideological monopoly in terms of capitalism and the 'free market', theocratic religion, nationalism in the virulent form of what Pareto diagnosed as 'jingoism' and Weber as 'Americanism' ('patriotism'), militarism ('defense spending'), offensive war and imperialism ('bipartisanship'). Thus, despite their growing polarization and 'culture wars', both political parties show a striking ideological monopoly cum 'bipartisanship' with respect to essentially unfettered capitalism, as well as nationalism, militarism, and imperialism and offensive war, not to mention all-present religion, as all-American values. Thus, they or their majorities both reject 'socialism' and even social democracy, including a universal health care system as 'socialist medicine' that the richest country in the world 'cannot afford' even if virtually all capitalist societies, notably Great Britain, already have and obviously can afford such a system. Recent examples are the shared ideological rejection by both parties or their majorities of 'socialism' and even universal health care/Medicare for all in 2020, plus their outrage over the 'Russian interference' in the 2016 elections while virtually all party-ruled governments have routinely interfered and militarily intervened in many, including European and especially Latin American and other third-world, countries since WW II, in an expression of what Weber denotes the Puritan-style 'pure hypocrisy' of 'Americanism'. In addition, both Congress parties tend to indulge in the seeming frenzy of economic and political nationalism, including irrational protectionism,[51] such as trade wars or restrictions and other anti-Chinese and anti-Russian acts (e.g., the 'bipartisan' attempt at delisting Chinese companies from the stock market).

In essence, this represents a bipartisan exercise and near-sadistic indulgence in what Pareto diagnosed a century ago as the pathology of 'jingoism' and Weber as 'Americanism' cum 'patriotism', as the probably most pathological and virulent form of nationalism, judging by its adverse consequences

---

51   On 'US-led protectionism' after 2016, see Head and Mayer (2019), for its 'Brexit' variant, see Fetzer (2019).

on other societies from Native Americans to Latin America, after its German variant ranging from traditional nationalism to Nazism. Relatedly, both parties agree on virtually unlimited, exorbitant and fiscally irresponsible military expenditure that is larger than the combined amount of all the 'enemies', with only few cases challenging or questioning such a fiscal irrationality which already the cited US 1952–1960 President detected in its adverse substitution or reduction effects on civilian spending. Similarly, both parties consent on imperialism and offensive wars, as the near-anonymous Congress vote for the Vietnam as well as the second Iraq war shows, with just few instances of dissent. Lastly, both parties are almost exclusively religious, a kind of 'Christian' rather than liberal-secular political parties essentially maintaining an effective capitalist theocracy of 'in God (and dollar) we trust' and 'one nation indivisible under God' in violation of the Jeffersonian separation of church and state, with hardly any one without religious affiliation or seriously challenging such a theocratic and thus undemocratic mixing of politics and 'faith'.

Such an ideological monopoly rules out alternatives from socialism or social democracy to cosmopolitanism, pacificism and non-imperialist foreign policy as inconceivable and 'un-American'—Reagan's variation on Thatcher's illiberal 'there is no alternative'.[52] This holds with secondary ideological variations and polarizations especially around social issues ('culture wars') not only converging with and reasserting but also diverging from and occasionally questioning this Parsons-style consensus on capitalist, religious, nationalist, militarist, and imperialist 'basic American values'. However, this consensus ultimately reasserts itself when capitalism ('free enterprise') or theocratic religion ('faith'), nationalism ('Americanism'), militarism ('defense spending'), and imperialism ('American interests') face challenges by 'un-American' and 'evil' forces from organized labor through liberal, secular, progressive, cosmopolitan and pacifist groups, to foreign 'enemies'.[53] A recent instance of the bipartisan defense of imperialism and militarism is the anti-Chinese hysteria in US Congress, government and beyond in response to China's apparent economic and military challenge to American imperialism, by targeting, harassing and banning various Chinese companies competing with US firms, while driven

---

52 See Bauman (2001) and Centeno and Cohen (2012).
53 Murray (2017, p. 1618) suggests that 'in contrast to the fractured elite thesis, (US) corporate politics in the 21st century (as of 2006) is largely unified (though) past domestic sources of U.S. corporate unity are less significant in bringing political consensus (but) the transnational aspects of the corporate network are clearly embedded in the domestic context, rather than separate from it' (see also Jouet 2017; Steinmetz 2005; Wacquant 2002; Wright 2013).

by intensive nationalism on grounds of 'national security' even in the apparent lack of such evidence—yet never matters to irrational nationalists—along with military provocations. For instance, both the authoritarian populist government and the opposition House of Representatives banned some Chinese media companies in 2020. Historically, this is just the latest—and probably not the last—nationalist hysteria against a challenger state, following Reagan's incited protectionist hysterics against Japanese car imports, that of his model, McCarthyism, the 'red scare' and many others. Overall, mass hysterias starting with Puritan witch-trials and transcending ideological or party lines are a constant or recurring wave of American politics and society dominated by conservatism and religion—as Americans may say, 'as American as the apple pie'.

While since Reaganism the two major political parties are not equally pro-capitalistic in favor of capital's unrestrained power and in that sense capitalist dictatorship or plutocracy, such ideological monopoly in respect of capitalism reflects or links with capital's fundamental consensus and unity versus non-capital given the absence of a classic labor political party and influence. Consequently, such coercive and related methodical suppression of non-capital parties and movements by capitalist dictatorship as a political regime, in fusion with conservatism and theocracy, rather than a Hayekian market 'spontaneous order' of capitalism, reproduces formal party duopoly and the lack of pluralism. It perpetuates the absence of alternatives and of pluralist democracy and free multi-group competition for power in the way of Schumpeter in American politics.[54] Comparatively, this duopoly stands in stark contrast to most other Western countries, including England. They all feature multi-party systems and democracies, at least relatively relevant and strong 'third' parties (the Liberal-Democratic Party in England, the Green Party in Germany and Austria, etc.) and thus plural political competition among such power-seeking groups, including a two-party coalition government and multiple opposition parties.

Moreover, this formal party duopoly reduces into monopoly in substantive ideological terms in favor of capital and to that extent tends toward capitalist and related dictatorship.[55] This holds so long as both major political parties are explicitly or implicitly capitalist ones, representing capital rather or more

54   Jouet (2017, p. 32) observes that in the US 'there is little alternative under the two-party system. conservative politicians are likelier than liberal ones to overestimate public support for their agenda, which may partly explain why the modern G.O.P. takes hardline positions' (see also Hill 2002).
55   Mueller (1996, p. 274) suggests that 'two-party democracies are probably more prone to dictatorship than are multiparty systems with a weak or nonexistent executive (but) not necessarily more likely to produce dictatorship than is a multiparty system with a strong executive' (see also Domhoff 2014; Wagner-Pacifici and Hall 2012).

than non-capitalist strata, and upper and upper-middle versus lower-middle, working and poor classes, as in the US two-party system. This holds with some rhetorical deceptions in the first case, for example, 'Reagan Democrats'[56] as economically irrational but socially conservative workers and unions, and occasional exceptions or secondary factions in the second like progressives and socialists. Relatedly, it applies insofar as they ardently exalt capitalism as the only alternative and the Panglossian 'best of all possible world' or endorse and pragmatically prefer it to its supposedly radical alternatives, including socialism, social democracy and the comprehensive welfare state, with secondary variations such as minor anarchic, progressive and socialist currents (within the Democratic Party). In brief, both reach by different routes the there is no alternative illiberal destination.

In this sense, while formally different capitalist plutocracy in conservative America substantively perpetuates pre-capitalist despotism's monopolistic closure by aristocracy. It does so through denying and suppressing equal political freedoms and rights to assembly, organization and action for non-capital groups and thus generating party duopoly and ideological monopoly, just as by so doing it resembles one-party systems in dictatorships. Capitalist dictatorship substantively, even if not always formally, proscribes, suppresses or restricts non-capital political organizations and movements, just as fascist dictatorships such as Nazism legally banned all social-democratic, socialist, liberal and related parties and labor unions and persecuted their members. No doubt, the mechanisms and degrees of repression differ, with the second dictatorships being more brutal and total, but the ultimate outcome is nearly identical—the non-existence or extinction of a major labor and liberal-secular party in conservative America like the South and interwar Germany. These dictatorships while appearing structurally different and even institutionally opposite therefore operate as functional equivalents on account of their equivalent consequences ('functions') in this respect, just as 'Bible Belt' evangelicalism and Islamic fundamentalism do against liberal democracy. Relatedly, Mill's comparative 'method of identity' would reveal these dictatorships as substantive equivalents and the 'method of difference' as different in only formal traits

---

56 Martin and Dixon (2010, p. 103) remark that some 'relatively conservative' US labor unions (the Teamsters) 'endorsed Reagan's presidential bid'. Baldassarri and Goldberg (2014, p. 52) suggest that 'Ronald Reagan's success in the 1980s was, at least in some part, attributable to his capacity to appeal to low-income white voters who were traditionally considered part of the Democratic Party's electoral base. These working-class social conservatives, who became known as Reagan Democrats, found themselves in a position whereby each of the two major parties spoke to either their material or cultural interests'.

like mechanisms, agents, scopes and degrees of repression, as well as the latter two as differing only in theology, ritual, and church organization.

It follows that capitalist dictatorship confirms rather than exempts itself, contrary to 'American exceptionalism' in capitalism and democracy, from the Michels-style 'iron law' or historical pattern of dictatorships in respect of party systems. This is that dictatorships represent one-party systems formally by outlawing all other parties or substantively when major nominally different parties are pro-capital and hostile to non-capital groups, as in 19th-century England prior to the formation of the Labour Party and America during most of its history since the Gilded Age and 1920s through the 1980s and post-2016.

On this account, by suppressing these and other equal political rights for non-capitalist groups, capitalist dictatorship perverts pluralism in the polity and thus liberal democracy. Conversely, it imposes what Dahrendorf calls substantive political and ideological 'totalitarian monism'[57] celebrating capital and depreciating non-capital strata and expressing 'totalitarianism' and so anti-democracy.[58] Thus, denying or curtailing, in Dahrendorf's words, the 'political permissibility of organization as the additional intervening prerequisite of conflict group formation' to non-capital political parties and interest-groups like labor unions in American capitalism and politics primarily explains the failure of formation, let alone influence, of socialist or social-democratic parties in America rather than Americans' inner anti-socialism. Apparently, while exalting 'free market' and 'free enterprise', US plutocrats and ruling conservatives detest, fear and suppress the 'free market' and competition of capitalist and non-capitalist ideas and ideologies, as

---

57   Dahrendorf (1959, p. 318) suggests that 'totalitarian monism is founded on the idea that conflict can and should be eliminated. The pluralism of free societies is based on the recognition and acceptance of social conflict. For freedom in society means, above all, that we recognize the justice and the creativity of diversity, difference, and conflict'. (For the Thatcherite 'threat of totalitarianism', see Hodgson 1999, 82). Relatedly, he includes the 'political permissibility of organization as the additional intervening prerequisite of conflict group formation', i.e., into the 'empirical conditions for interest-group formation' such as political parties (Dahrendorf 1959, p. 186). If so, the denied or curtailed 'political permissibility of organization' to non-capital political parties and interest-groups like labor unions in American capitalism and politics accounts for the failure of socialist or social-democratic parties in America rather than Americans' 'natural born' anti-socialism (contrary to Lipset and Marks 2000).

58   Rydgren (2007, pp. 243, 246) remarks that 'political monism of the extreme right is expressed in two ways: as a rejection of the democratic political system and/or a rejection of universalistic and egalitarian, sometimes called democratic, values', while the 'new radical right's longing for ethnic purity, homogeneity, and organic order places them in the same tradition as fascism'.

the violent 'red scare' and other political witch-trials suggest. In a perverse Orwellian logic, to paraphrase Ford's statement about the 'choice' among all-black cars, US plutocrats and conservatives permit the 'free market' and 'competition' of ideas and ideologies—so long as these are only capitalist and conservative, if they are not, they are 'un-American' or 'we cannot afford them'. In a related political perversion of the democratic process, they praise and accept democracy and its results, including free competition for power via 'free elections', only if they win, if not, they cry electoral 'fraud', as one of them stated explicitly during the 2016 Presidential elections and repeatedly threatened afterwards not to accept the result of the 2020 elections in case of electoral loss. On this account, American conservatism remakes America a proxy of 'banana republics' where dictators do not accept electoral results if they lose and generally of a third-world country pervaded with unfree, unfair and rigged elections. For example, the 2000 Presidential election in which a conservative pretender was victorious probably qualified as rigged, as in Florida, as do most congressional and state elections in the South due to conservatism's voting rights suppression, gerrymandering, voter purges and other anti-democratic methods.

A previously noted exemplar of such monism is Thatcherism-Reaganism's common insinuation that 'there is no alternative' to unrestrained and inegalitarian, proxy laissez-faire capitalism—despite what Keynes diagnoses as its chronic 'outstanding faults'—or rather to its ideological and political program which reportedly harbors authoritarian connotations and totalitarian threats, just as what it condemns as socialist monism. Such monism stemming from suppressing equal collective political rights for non-capital strata particularly in the conservative pole of America replicates or resembles the monistic character of pre-capitalist despotism and aristocracy's monopolistic closure versus the populace, with variations in historical time, geographic space and social structure.

5.2.4   Unequal Legal Treatment

In addition to and conjunction with the preceding, capitalist dictatorship denies equal legal treatment, equality before the law, to non-capital or non-plutocratic populations through a myriad of anti-egalitarian, exclusionary and discriminatory practices against them in relation to capital. These practices involve, as in conservative America, drastic differences in negative sanctions for the unlawful actions of these groups. They consist in Draconian punishments of non-capital populations' actions, such as drug non-violent offenses and other sins through 'three strikes' laws (despite their recent mainly cosmetic modifications), and non-punishment of or leniency to the transgressions by the capitalist class, 'blue' versus 'white collar' crimes in criminology or public discourse.

Capitalist dictatorship evokes pre-capitalist despotism's denial of equality before the law to the non-aristocratic populace and subordinate classes versus aristocracy and 'master-caste', including severe sanctions for the offenses of the first and non-sanctioning those of the second stratum in feudalism, slavery and the caste system. As in pre-capitalist regimes with respect to their subordinate strata, the unequal legal treatment of capital and non-capital groups favoring the first, including unequal sanctioning of their unlawful actions, is a norm or tendency in capitalist dictatorship. Conversely, their complete equality before the law, in particular full justice within the penal, especially—as in conservative America—prison and death-penalty, system becomes an exception, rarity, pretense and simulation, including placebo criminal-justice and other 'reforms'.[59]

Furthermore, criminal justice becomes an extremely costly outcome for non-capitalists or non-plutocrats, especially lower middle, working and low classes, let alone the underclass. This applies to these groups when considering the exorbitant financial costs of securing proper legal defense against grave and life-threatening crime accusations, even if unsubstantiated ranging from those accusing of murders and other violent crimes to the near-epidemic of false allegations of 'sexual offenses' in America during recent times. At this juncture, militant feminism especially seems to incite or justify this near-epidemic of bogus 'sexual offenses' evoking Puritan witch-trials in a tacit alliance with its putative enemy, religious-political conservatism.

The two otherwise hostile ideologies and movements apparently find their shared interest and common goal in the mass imprisonment and widespread executions of male 'offenders' as 'natural' criminals for radical feminism and perpetual sinners recommitting (Adam's) 'original sin' for religious conservatism. Both therefore pervert the time-honored legal rule of presumed innocence into presumed guilt, converting mere accusations of 'sexual offenses' into actual proofs and in process ruining the lives of the accused, even if innocent (as often proved by DNA and other evidence after the fact and usually too late). At this point, political-religious conservatism and radical feminism represent the main obstacles to the administration of criminal justice in America and more broadly the major enemies of liberal democracy by denying universal liberty to all groups and of meritocracy by, as the second does, seeking 'equal pay' for unequal performance, work or experience defining injustice rather

---

59   The expression 'placebo reforms' is from Spiegler (2013, p. 1491).

than 'justice' in income distribution. To that extent, they seem to reaffirm and self-justify their character or description as 'proto-fascism' and its equivalent (as US conservatives brand militant feminism), respectively. More broadly, they represent ideologies of what Simmel calls 'social hatred' directed against liberals and the opposite gender, respectively. Relatedly, conservatism proves to be the implacable antagonist of liberalism and thus of liberty, equality and justice, and radical feminism by pretending to be 'liberal' a perversion and eventual decomposition of liberalism. Thus, the main internal problem and even tragedy of liberalism is its being perverted, penetrated, captured and thus decomposed by militant feminism, as especially observed in the liberal pole of America (California, etc.) and parts of Western Europe, above all Scandinavia (Sweden). To that extent, this feminist penetration into and perversion of liberalism portends hard times for sustaining liberal democracy and universal liberty, along with meritocracy, in these settings in the foreseeable future, even apart from the utterly destructive illiberal effects of conservatism, including its offspring fascism, and theocracy.

Moreover, the complete equality of capital and non-capital strata before the law is what Weber calls an 'impossible contradiction' or an 'impossibility theorem' in capitalist dictatorship as dictatorship, as in all dictatorships with respect to the legal balance and distribution of criminal and civil justice between the ruling class and subordinate classes. Consequently, in Weber's 'naked plutocracy' as the main form and agent of capitalist dictatorship in America since the Gilded Age through the present, 'mere money' and generally wealth by purchasing political power and influence effectively purchases legal, including criminal and civil, justice for its proprietors. Furthermore, that 'money buys justice' in this all-American plutocracy applies often regardless of the formal validity of plutocrats' claims to justice and the legal propriety of their actions—whether or not they are innocent or guilty of crimes. This forms a syndrome spanning from what Pareto calls the 'machinations' of US and other capitalists ('men who are out to make money') during his time, seemingly implicating the robber barons, to recent financial crimes by their successors, including Enron's and other accounting frauds and those associated with the Great Recession.[60]

Conversely, by so doing wealth enables and perpetuates an unequal legal treatment in favor of capital and disables and rules out equality before the law for non-capital strata and thus 'justice for all' in the style of Jefferson, especially distorting a system of universal criminal and related justice. In this sense,

---

60   See Akerlof and Shiller (2015), Baumer et al. (2017).

President Roosevelt's 'tyranny' of plutocracy through 'mere wealth' intrinsically involves the privileged legal treatment of capital and the opposite status of non-capital strata. In particular, it entails dispending criminal and other justice for the first and denying it to the second and frequently regardless of the formal validity of their justice claims and the propriety, including the presence or degree of criminality, of their respective actions. Moreover, such a duality often involves the punishing, including life imprisonment and executions, of non-capital groups such as lower and powerless classes without proven guilt or with proven innocence (as by DNA and other evidence), while not sanctioning or simulating punishment of capital for demonstrably criminal actions, usually massive white-collar crimes such as accounting frauds and financial scandals. The first process results in an Orwellian dystopia of no or less crime and more severe punishment of non-capital strata in a typical Draconian Puritan-inspired fashion. The second leads to legalized and thus institutionalized 'mafia capitalism' as the system of capital predation and a predatory case of capitalist dictatorship. Hence, in respect of inequality before the law, as with regard to unequal political rights, for non-capital populations, capitalist dictatorship and its plutocracy especially in America under conservatism represents an anti-egalitarian, near-aristocratic political and legal regime and a ruling group continuing pre-capitalist anti-egalitarianism and its aristocracy in relation to the non-aristocratic populace. That this statement is far from being an exaggeration is what Jefferson implies by detecting 'in its birth the aristocracy of our monied corporations which dare already to challenge our government to a trial of strength and bid defiance to the laws of our country'.

In general, political and related inequality and in extension exclusion and closure are symbiotic with their economic forms in capitalist dictatorship. As a rule, with some secondary exceptions, extensive and severe political-social inequality, exclusion and closure privileging capital over non-capital populations characterize and pervades capitalist dictatorship. In consequence, capitalist dictatorship represents not only an economic system of extreme anti-egalitarianism, but also an extremely anti-egalitarian political regime in an interaction and mutual reinforcement, just as pre-capitalist despotism and all later dictatorships. Capitalist dictatorship invariably features the unequal distribution of political power, influence and rights between capital and non-capital groups through their concentration, monopolization and exertion by the first and their denial, suppression or restriction for the second strata. Therefore, it operates as the political regime of an extreme imbalance or asymmetry of power, influence and rights between capital and non-capital groups in favor of the first over the second, which typifies non-democracy. Conversely, capitalist dictatorship deviates from and violates the proximate balance or asymmetry between these political agents, thus deviating from democracy that such relations characterize.

The preceding justifies and necessitates taking pervasive and severe inequality, exclusion and closure in the polity as an indicator of capitalist dictatorship as an anti-egalitarian, exclusionary and closed political regime with respect to non-capital groups. Alternatively, capitalist dictatorship presents itself as such a political regime by its characteristic inequality, exclusion and closure in the polity. In consequence, capitalist dictatorship as a rule with minor variations tends to have the comparatively highest levels of political and related inequality among comparative social systems and the types of capitalism, notably a drastically higher level than that of liberal, universalistic and open democracy and egalitarian welfare capitalism.

In empirical terms, virtually all capitalist dictatorships manifest the tendency to extreme political-social inequality. Cases span from 19th-century England and Gilded-Age America through capitalist-fascist dictatorships in interwar Europe, South American 'free market' dictatorships, the first two countries since Thatcherism and Reaganism, Eastern Europe under capitalist oligarchy, Gulf Islamic states, and to post-2016 America and via plutocratic radical-right contagion or convergence other countries. Within Western society, an exemplar is extreme political-social inequality between capital and non-capital groups through power concentration and monopolization in the first within 19th-century English and American capitalism during the Gilded Age through the double political-economic monopoly of the robber barons. Another latter, apparently recurring instance is the 'plutonomy' of their later and present reincarnations from Reaganism to post-2016 and Great Britain and other Anglo-Saxon countries since Thatcherism.

In sum, extensive and persistent inequality, exclusion and closure in the polity through the unequal distribution of power, influence and rights in favor of capital over non-capital strata furnishes a relevant indication of capitalist dictatorship as an anti-egalitarian, exclusionary and closed political regime.

5.3 Severe Penal Repression and Punishment

Systematic and severe legal-political coercion, specifically penal repression and severe punishment of non-capital strata is another complementary indicator of capitalist dictatorship to the previous two. Such coercion/repression represents an expression of non-existent or minimal political freedoms and rights for non-capital strata and an effective mechanism for denying and suppressing them. It is the instrument of forcible implementation, imposition and perpetuation of the political unfreedom of these strata and monopolization of such liberty for capital under the guise and pretext of establishing and maintaining 'law and order' as the 'conservative-authoritarian' slogan.[61] In short, it is the means of Leviathan-style control over non-capital and a Hobbesian anarchy and state of nature for capital.

5.3.1   'Law and Order' for Non-capitalists, Lawlessness for Capital
Capitalist dictatorship perversely establishes and maintains 'law and order' by systematically and intensively coercing and repressing non-capital strata through legal-political means while endowing, indeed lavishing capital with anarchic freedom. The latter becomes a 'license to kill' metaphorically and literally, as in 19th-century England's master-servant and Gilded-Age American capitalism resorting to severe labor coercion by, as in the latter, using physical force against and committing murders of workers, often through the alliance of a pro-capital state with violent capitalist militias, according to the primeval law of the strongest/jungle. In a way, capitalist dictatorship is the political regime of stringent 'law and order' enforced on non-capital strata and lawlessness or the law of the strongest and chaos for capital, including autocracy and autocrats acting lawless, as reportedly in the US post-2016 and before, yielding 'lawless capitalism'.[62] Capitalist dictatorship continues, with some modifications, the archetype of pre-capitalist despotism such as slavery, caste and feudalism or the master-servant regime with respect to non-aristocratic strata and aristocracy—enslaved labor, subjugated castes, peasant bondage and servant oppression versus master aristocratic unlimited freedom reaching license. It more broadly epitomizes the tendency of all dictatorships, especially conservative-fascist and religious regimes, to exalt and enforce 'law and order' in a corresponding manner. This is imposing 'law and order' on the masses and

61   Dahrendorf (1979, p. 98) identifies the 'conservative-authoritarian movement by way of law-and-order slogans' as belonging to the 'collectivist threats' to democratic society (for the US see Campbell and Schoenfeld 2013). He elaborates that right conservatism has 'elements of social and political control which do not even stop short of freedom of the press, and general praise for the good old values of authority, discipline, order, punishment (so) finds itself in a position of confrontation with prevailing conditions' (Dahrendorf 1979, p. 103). Perelman (2000, p. 20) identifies 'laissez-faire authoritarianism' in early capitalism in that 'liberty, for capital, depended on the hard work of common people' and within a 'contrived law and order, workers found their rights to organize unions and even to act politically severely restricted'.
62   Simpson (1934, p. 157) reports that in the US the 'whole decade from 1920 to 1930 was a period of conspicuous governmental incompetence, with a consequent increase in lawlessness and crime, the development of vicious types of business organizations and crime, the development of vicious types of business organizations and methods, and the growth of a deep penumbra of racketeering practices around the ragged fringe of corrupt and incompetent government'. The term 'lawless capitalism' is from Ramirez (2013).

granting their leaders the literal license to kill, oppress and other unlawful acts, or those only in accordance with to the primitive 'law' of the strongest, causing legal disorder and chaos.

Widespread and severe penal repression and punishment of non-capital strata complements and reciprocally relates to and reinforces power concentration in capital and thus pervasive and sharp political and related inequality in capitalist dictatorship. In particular, this holds for such repression in relation to the unequal legal treatment of capital and non-capital strata, including differential negative (and positive) sanctioning of their respective activities by privileging capitalists over non-capitalists, notably non-punishment of or lenience for the first and Draconian punishment of the second. Penal repression of non-capital strata expresses inequality before the law in their disfavor in relation to capital and indirectly their unequal political rights, notably the right to seek and hold public office and assembly and collective party organization and action, and thus sustains their minimal power, influence and representation in the polity. The capitalist-plutocratic and conservative-religious mobilization in the US since the 1980s precisely does this through the mass imprisonment, widespread executions, violations of human rights and other penal abuses of low, powerless, non-religious or immoral groups. It does so through the agency of a 'dictatorial business class' in alliance with 'a hyperactive police and penal state' that repressive conservatism creates, and religious fundamentalism perpetuates as moralistic theocracy Puritan-style. The eventual merger of the capitalist class and the conservative-theocratic penal state effectively terrorizes or criminalizes these social strata through creating the 'ambience of terror' for and virtually criminalizing the poor and non-religious,[63] enforcing their unequal legal treatment versus capital and the religious, as the 'Bible Belt' exemplifies.

The above applies to such practices in other capitalist dictatorships, especially in non-Western settings. These include most of Latin America historically, much of Asia like South Korea, Singapore and Taiwan in the past and in part presently and, above all, Islamic autocracies, dynasties, oligarchies and plutocracies such as Turkey during recent years, Saudi Arabia and other Gulf states perpetually. Thus, the 'American regime' of mixed plutocracy-theocracy in evangelical America and Islamic capitalist-theocratic regimes converge at the point of mass imprisonment, widespread executions, violations of human

---

63 A 'Bible Belt' senator and failed Presidential candidate attempted to effectively criminalize non-religious people or those not attending church in America by proposing a law that would enforce mandatory church attendance on the cynical ground that they by so doing would get to know and more appreciate 'faith'.

rights and other abuses of low, powerless and non-religious groups enforcing their inequality before the law versus capital and the religious. Therefore,
they reaffirm the observation that they act as proto-totalitarian equivalents
and objective allies ('brothers in arms')—pretending to be enemies or actually
being contestants for religious dominance—against liberal democracy and
political and individual liberties.

5.3.2 Political Terror: Mass Imprisonment, Executions, Violations of Human Rights

By its nature and tendency to escalation and intensification typifying dictatorships, the systematic and severe legal-political coercion, notably penal
repression of non-capital strata ultimately tends to reach or approach the
ambiance and stage of state terrorism or political terror[64] within capitalist
dictatorship, as reported for conservative America and third-world dictatorial regimes. The 'political terror scale' incorporates the above and similar
practices, thus ranging from mass imprisonment and widespread executions
through police brutality and torture to persecutions of political opponents and
many other violations of political as well as civil rights in capitalist and other
dictatorship.[65] In particular, strong syndromes of 'political terror' in capitalist and conservative-religious dictatorships or authoritarian regimes such as
the US since Reaganism and to some degree Great Britain under Thatcherism
abound and persist. They are mass and long incarceration for sins-as-crimes
such as non-violent drug and other moral offenses and widespread arbitrary
executions American-style frequently of innocent persons, along with police
brutality, murders and torture rampant in conservative America.

Capitalist-conservative dictatorship via the merger of the 'dictatorial business class' and the 'police and penal state' in conservative America occupies
a comparatively high, indeed the highest place (the 'best' in Reagan's words)

---

64   Bauman (2001, p. 43) observe that US conservative politicians cynically use the 'specta-
      cle of execution' in order to 'terrorize a growing underclass', while the 'silent American
      majority' demands such 'terrorization of the underclass'. Specifically, Jacobs, Carmichael,
      and Kent (2005, p. 657) concur with the view that the US Southern states that 'once had
      the highest lynching rates now appear to use the death sentence most often (so that)
      the death penalty was used by powerful groups to protect their privileges with selective
      terror' (see also, Besley and Persson 2009; Gibbs 1989).
65   Besley and Persson (2009, p. 292) define the 'political terror scale' as consisting of wide-
      spread 'civil and political rights violations such as execution, imprisonment and political
      murders/brutality', including 'purges: systematic murders and eliminations of political
      opponents within regimes'.

on the 'political terror scale' within the Western world and beyond judging by the largest prison population and prisoner rate. This is because of the imprisoning much of the mass prison population for drug and related non-violent sins that American conservatism, virtually alone within Western society, redefines as grave crimes through the 'tough' on sin-crime Puritan-style crusade via the 'war on drugs' and other temperance wars since Reaganism and its model Puritanism. Further, it is due to not rarely executing or sentencing to death innocent persons on overt or covert religious grounds ('God's justice', 'Biblical vengeance') in the 'Bible Belt' from Alabama and Tennessee to Oklahoma and Texas. These practices of 'holy terror' provide an accurate hallmark and precise identifier of fundamentalist theocracy fused with capitalist plutocracy through the Religious Right alliance of plutocrats and poor religious groups and the merger of political and religious conservatism in revolt against both liberal democracy and science in evangelical America.

Overall, conservative America's unique record of the largest number of prisoners and highest rate of imprisonment and the most frequent, indeed exclusive executions in the Western world alone suffices, as does widespread, chronic and unrivaled police brutality, indefinite detention, murders and torture, as a diagnostic criterion in terms of the 'political terror scale' in capitalist-conservative dictatorship. Moreover, thanks to the Religious Right alliance of capitalist plutocracy and theocracy and merged political-religious conservatism such an exceptional pattern indicates a comparatively higher, indeed the highest ranking on this scale compared to other comparable societies such as Western Europe within this comparative setting. In this connection, pervasive, perpetual and systematic police brutality, murders and torture directed against non-capital or lower and powerless classes in conservative America is a clear syndrome of capitalist dictatorship and non-democracy overall rather than being incidental and isolated acts by few 'rotten apples'. Conversely, it manifests devaluation, disregard and disrespect of fundamental political, civil and individual liberties and rights for these groups, thus a depreciation of and disdain for democracy. To that extent, conservative America does not function or qualify as genuine democracy on account of its characteristic and even, within Western society, exceptional police brutality to and murders and torture of lower and powerless classes. By contrast, the absence or low incidence of police brutality, murders and torture against lower, powerless and all social classes typifies, ceteris paribus, liberal democracy in most Western societies, especially Scandinavia and Western Europe. Alternatively, by virtue of this these societies function as true liberal democracies. In short, police brutality seems an accurate syndrome of non-democracy and anti-liberalism in conservative America, ceteris paribus, as does the police state overall.[66]

In turn, Islamic capitalist theocracies from Turkey to Iran, Saudi Arabia and other Gulf states epitomize and rank the highest on the 'political terror scale' within the non-Western third-world. This is because of their equivalent practices of mass and long incarceration for sins-crimes—yet their rates are lower than that of the US—especially widespread and summary executions for such offenses exceeding those in the latter. In addition, state terror through mass or large imprisonment and widespread arbitrary executions—though both being less religiously driven and sanctified than in evangelical America and Islamic states—pervades most other capitalist and similar dictatorships. They include those in Asia, for example, Singapore, South Korea, and Taiwan, in the past or present, including China considering it among these, Africa under autocracies and dynasties, South America such as Chile's and other countries' military 'free market' dictatorships. They also comprise to a lesser extent and only for large imprisonment, because of the European Union-wide abolition of the death penalty, most of Eastern Europe (except for Slovenia) during oligarchic capitalism and predominant conservative-religious politics after the 1990s. In comparative terms, with minor variations, these countries, notably evangelical America and Islamic states, feature both the highest prison population and rates of imprisonment and the largest figures of death sentences and executions and to that extent commit the most extensive and intense acts on the 'political terror scale' in the world. (This holds probably along with North Korea and few other remaining non-capitalist dictatorships, plus China if belonging to them in an alternative view.)

Owing to its severe penal repression and punishment of non-capital groups eventually escalating into 'political terror', capitalist dictatorship manifests rather than overcomes the tendency for most modern dictatorships to become ultimately regimes of state terror which Nazi and other fascist/extreme-right dictatorships epitomize. Relatedly, due to this process, capitalist dictatorship evokes and inherits, with some modifications, pre-capitalist tyranny with its ancient regime of coercion, repression and state terror rather than supersedes and assigns the latter to the 'dead past'. It indeed seeks to resurrect this past

---

66   For example, some former police personnel reported to the media in the wake of a wave of police brutality in 2020 that it 'starts with the paramilitary-style police training academy. "The mentality that we're in a war, and the culture of 'us versus them', starts in the academy." Further, many US conservative politicians, including presidents, incite or encourage and condone police brutality, murders and torture by advocating a 'rough' treatment of offenders and suspects.

through fascism as the most 'possible' form of dictatorship within capitalism due to its acting as the 'exponent' of bourgeoisie, as Mannheim personally experiences, including large-scale industrial capital in Nazi Germany.

Hence, to observe that capitalist dictatorship's political coercion and penal repression and, as in conservative America, Draconian and mass punishment of non-capital groups eventuates in state terror of the latter while a strong proposition is just observing that it represents a special case of dictatorships harboring that tendency. This holds unless one claims that capitalist dictatorship, notably plutocratic oligarchy and post-2016 proxy autocracy in America and other Western societies, is different from and even opposite to these dictatorships, as 'libertarianism' does deny its existence in American and Western capitalism which it equates with economic and political 'freedom', including 'capitalist democracy'. In any event, this repression involves such activities as large-scale imprisonment, widespread death sentence and executions, pervasive police brutality, indefinite detention, murders and torture, systematic persecutions and similar treatments of non-capital strata such as lower and powerless classes and other violations of their human rights, all of which reportedly belong to the 'ambiance' and 'scale' of selective political terror.

Generally, with some variations, mass imprisonment, widespread executions, abuse, mistreatment, indefinite detention, torture and other violations of the human rights of non-capital and lower classes typify capitalist dictatorship, just as characterized pre-capitalist dictatorships with respect to subordinate groups like the non-aristocratic populace in feudalism. Couched as conservative and plutocratic 'law and order', such state repression to the point of terrorizing these strata appears as the political hallmark of capitalist dictatorship, which makes it what it becomes ultimately—the regime highly placed on the 'political terror scale', along with other dictatorships. Such repression or terror, most commonly mass imprisonment and extensive executions of non-capitalist low classes for sins-as-crimes in the style of conservative American and Islamic theocratic regimes provides a precise identifier of this dictatorship, just as the same practice with regard to past subordinate strata identified pre-capitalist dictatorships. Alternatively, capitalist dictatorship identifies itself by its systematic and severe penal repression and terror of non-capital strata, including their arbitrary mass imprisonment and sometimes, as in American and Islamic regimes, executions, that it couches in 'law and order' slogans typical of conservative authoritarian regimes, including their fascist totalitarian and theocratic proto-totalitarian variants.

In consequence, capitalist dictatorship, especially pro-capital theocracy like evangelical America and Saudi Arabia, tends to have the greatest levels of legal coercion and penal repression and to rank the highest on the 'political terror scale' in comparative terms, including the largest prison populations and rates and the most numerus death sentences and executions. Notably, these components of coercion and repression are invariably and dramatically higher and larger than those of democratic and egalitarian capitalism combined with liberal and secular democracy.

Empirically, capitalist and related conservative-fascist, dictatorships demonstrate the pattern of most extensive and intense penal repression and state terror, including the highest figures of imprisonment and death sentences and executions. They replicate this pattern in a historical range from 19th-century England and Gilded-Age America to interwar Germany and Europe through postwar South American dictatorial regimes to the first two countries during neo-conservatism, most Islamic states and Eastern Europe under capitalist oligarchy and conservatism. In particular, since Reaganism, with minor recent modifications of a Draconian penal system, including 'three strikes' laws for drug offenses and other sins and non-violent crimes, the 'American regime' of blended plutocracy and theocracy has become and solidified itself as the Western and world leader in mass imprisonment–and for sins-crimes and of sinners-criminals. This is due to its globally highest incarceration total figure (almost 2.3 million) and rate (655) and its continuing religiously driven death sentences and executions of low classes. In terms of large-scale imprisonment, pervasive capital punishment and systematic violations of lower classes' human rights, this regime ranks the highest on the 'political terror scale' among Western societies, along with Britain during and with the legacy of Thatcherism as the repressive twin of Reaganism, when compared to Western Europe,[67] including Scandinavia.

Among non-Western societies only Islamic merged capitalist-theocratic regimes like Turkey, Iran, Saudi Arabia and other Gulf states equal or approach, as with mass imprisonment, and occasionally surpass, as with death sentences and executions, the 'American regime' of plutocracy-theocracy. This reaffirms that the latter approaches more third-world countries than Western liberal-secular democracies and features 'exceptionalism' primarily in this sense rather than as superior 'democracy' and 'freedom' versus European welfare capitalism, liberalism and secularism which American 'libertarianism' and theocratic conservatism construes as 'socialism', 'statism' and 'godlessness'. The capitalist-conservative, including populist and religious, mobilization and dominance since Reaganism through post-2016 has succeeded to remake America a proxy post-Western and in that sense 'third-world' society on account of unparalleled

---

67   Such findings and comparisons see in Sutton (2013) and Uggen and Manza (2002).

imprisonment and death sentences and executions, thus remaking it a deviation from Western liberal democracy. By contrast, in the latter the first practice is drastically more limited through incarceration rates that are multiple times lower than the US rate and the second actually non-existent, as in all Europe, along with Australia, Great Britain, Canada and New Zealand.

The aggregate legal-political outcome in America under political-religious conservatism—especially the South driven by religious fundamentalism making it the 'Bible Belt'—is the prison- and death penalty-capitalist complex as the forcible instrument of political repression and state terror of low and powerless classes. At this point, if one does not know what capitalist dictatorship as a political regime is and even whether it exists, the prison- and death penalty-industrial complex helps to define and identify it in conservative America since Reaganism and post-2016. This complex is the criminal justice mechanism, face and name of such dictatorship through the merger of a dictatorial plutocracy and a totalistic police/penal state within society, just as the military-industrial complex acts as its tool and a direct instrument against 'enemy' societies.

In sum, capitalist dictatorship or theocracy in conservative America since Reaganism ultimately develops into and operates as the prison- and death penalty- industrial complex and as the first in Great Britain during Thatcherism due to the Europe-wide's abolition of capital punishment. It therefore follows the template of all modern, notably fascist, religious and other conservative, dictatorships to function as systems of mass imprisonment and widespread death sentences and executions in the 'law and order' guise. Hence, one cannot claim 'American exceptionalism' in relation to these dictatorships in contrast to that compared to Western welfare capitalism and liberal-secular democracies lacking the prison- and death penalty-industrial complex in the form and on the scale in conservative America since Reaganism and Islamic states. In general, the systematic and severe legal-political repression of non-capital strata to the stage of state terror through t mass imprisonment and, as in conservative America and Islamic states, pervasive executions gives an additional indication and diagnosis of capitalist dictatorship as a coercive, repressive and exclusionary political regime.

5.4   *Militarism*

Militarism is yet another, specifically external inter-societal and indeed, as with 'great' military powers, global indicator of capitalist dictatorship, operating in conjunction and mutual reinforcement with the previous indicators, particularly the penal repression and state terror of non-capital strata. Militarism expands such repression and terror from within capitalist dictatorship to military conquest and subjugation of other societies, while the second process reinforcing and rationalizing—thus obscuring its undemocratic basis—the first under the guise of 'national security', 'war', 'emergency', 'evil enemies'.

5.4.1   The Military-Capitalist Complex and Aggressive Wars
Militarism in capitalist dictatorship is, to paraphrase Clausewitz's definition of war as its consummate element, a continuation and notably escalation of the politics and law of repression and state terror of non-capital strata, as of hostile foreign policy toward other societies, by formally other means like military force and substantively identical instruments such as coercion. What a US President identified as the 'military-industrial complex' expressing militarism and in his opinion threatening democracy continues and escalates capitalist dictatorship's prison-industrial complex of mass imprisonment, widespread executions, mistreatment and torture to other societies subjecting them to the same or worse treatment as its own population. Conversely, it sustains, reinforces and justifies repression, political terror and overall authoritarianism within society[68] in the name of 'national security' and 'patriotism'.

In consequence, capitalist dictatorship's militarism or anti-pacifism and war versus other societies is consistent, complementary and eventually merges with its repression and terror within society, just as negative and destructive in its own right.[69] Aside from secondary exceptions, its military-industrial complex and warfare state move hand in hand and often merge with its prison-industrial complex and police state, including aggressive wars against other

---

68   Steinmetz (2005, pp. 361–2) suggests that 'American empire' through by implication the military-industrial complex involves both 'authoritarian efforts to control social life and dominate foreign societies and cultures', thus sustaining and reinforcing 'domestic authoritarian closure' in America itself.

69   Dahrendorf (1979, p. 95) remarks that a 'foreign policy which is not serving peace is in itself evil'. Centeno (1994, p. 125) pinpoints the neoconservative ('neoliberal')'military authoritarianism of Latin America'. Beck (2000, p. 174) suggests that the neoconservative ('neoliberal') revolt leads into a 'militarization of conflicts between and within individual states'. Acemoglu, Ticchi and Vindigni (2010, p. 1) observe that state repression 'is often exercised by a specialized branch of the state, the military' and so that 'many nondemocratic regimes survive with the support of the military', although 'there are also numerous examples of military dictatorships that have emerged either as a result of a coup against a nondemocratic regime or against the subsequent democratic government'. Slater and Smith (2016, p. 1477) note that conservative counterrevolutions involve 'militarized repression, motivated by tragic cases such as the mass killings of suspected communists in Indonesia in the 1960s or right-wing violence against leftist rebels in El Salvador and Guatemala in the 1980s'. For reviews of US conservative and right-wing movements, see Blee and Creasap (2010). Gross, Medvetz, and Russell (2011).

societies moving together with mass incarceration and executions of non-capital and other strata.[70] This is what the US and to some degree Great Britain demonstrate since the 1980s and during later times. In this respect, what is capitalist dictatorship's repression and terror of non-capital strata within society becomes militarism, including conquest and war, versus other societies. Conversely, the second tendency sustains and reinforces the first, according to Simmel's classical sociological theory of a reciprocal action and intensification between political 'despotism' and 'warlike tendencies'.

Militarism pervades capitalist dictatorship, just as militarily defines colonialism and imperialism as their invariant instrument. Aggressive religious and other nationalism a la 'God's plan', 'true' religion, 'manifest destiny', 'master race', 'Nation first', national 'superiority' or 'exceptionalism' drives all of them into military aggressions, conquests and enslavement or forcible subjugation of 'inferior' and 'godless' societies.[71] High military spending, large armed forces, a massive military-capitalist complex, what Mannheim calls the 'military-bureaucratic mentality'[72] and offensive wars against other societies typically characterize capitalist dictatorship, especially that in 'great' colonial,

---

70   Sutton (2000, p. 377) finds that 'military expansion contributes to the expansion of prisons', although among Western countries since the 1980s 'conspicuous episodes of military growth occurred only in the United States and the United Kingdom'. Mulligan et al. (2004, pp. 51–2) imply that large military spending relates to torture, execution, and censorship. Béland (2005, p. 33) implies a link between the 'maintenance of such a large prison population and the increase in military spending associated with the "war on terrorism" in the US and that both 'could divert resources from other areas of state protection like social policy and environmental protection'. Acemoglu and Yared (2010, p. 83) note that 'despite the increasing reach of globalization, anecdotal evidence suggests that nationalism and militarism are strong around the world, in countries ranging from the US to China, Russia, and India'.

71   Keesing (1981, p. 59) observes that a 'shift toward militarism and expansionism followed theocratic states'. Munch (2001, p. 235) proposes that America's 'manifest destiny or 'civilizing' included not only the 'mastery of nature but also the expulsion of the Indians from their lands, their oppression, and the destruction of their culture'. Savelsberg and King (2005, pp. 586–7) state that in 'America, the early destruction of much of the Native American population during the colonial era was continued, after the foundation of the United States, by further atrocities, wars, broken treaties, forced migration and death marches, and the destruction of livelihood. (i.e.) the annihilation and mistreatment of Native Americans'. Mueller (2009, p. 385) suggests that 'for most of the first two millennia since Christ's birth, however, Christianity and slavery, coexisted quite happily'. Stamatov (2010, p. 617) points to the 'traditional aggressive combination of evangelization and military conquest'.

72   See Mannheim (1936, p. 119), also, Collins (1993), Fershtman, Murphy and Weis (1996), and Kestnbaum (2009).

imperial and nationalist powers, just as most other dictatorships, including pre-capitalist despotic and absolutist states ruled by a military aristocracy.

On this account, capitalist dictatorship continues, even expands and advances via the technologically advanced military-industrial complex in the 'great' Western powers' pre-capitalist militarism, including large military expenditure and aggressive wars, and consequently imperialism. Alternatively, it does not overcome militarism and imperialism, as Schumpeter (1965) and other economists and some sociologists believe by attributing them, along with nationalism, to pre-capitalism and disassociating them from capitalism.[73] In Clausewitz's military terms, capitalist dictatorship appears as the continuation and escalation rather than the supersession and mitigation—contrary to Schumpeter et al.--of the pre-capitalist despotic state's militarism, war, and imperialism by technically other means and substantively by identical instruments. Such means include more advanced technology and ever-more lethal weapons that the modern military-industrial complex produces and delivers in unprecedented mass production and distribution, including global profitable arms exports, and these instruments involve coercion and dominance.[74] Conversely, Clausewitz's offensive war becomes the continuation of capitalist

---

73 Schumpeter (1965, pp. 96–7) states that imperialism and by implication militarism 'would never have been evolved by the 'inner logic' of capitalism itself'. However, Habermas (1989, p. 145) suggests that in 19th-century capitalism large industry took interest 'in an expansion of the military apparatus for the sake of the conquest and protection of privileged markets abroad'. Shaffer (1996, p. 643) objects contra Schumpeter that 'many of the past threats which exploded into military confrontations were nurtured by the marketing efforts of rent-seekers (so) aspects of market behavior could promote conflict'. Further, Chase-Dun (1992, 10) suggests that world wars 'are a necessary, cyclical, and structural component of the expansion and deepening of capitalism'. Relatedly, Berger et al. (2013, p. 889) identify American 'commercial imperialism; during the Cold War in that 'covert CIA interventions increased the influence of the US over foreign governments, and that this was used to increase US exports to the intervened countries'. Dube, Kaplan, and Naidu (2011, p. 1377) suggest that covert operations designed to overthrow foreign governments were usually first approved by the director of the CIA and then subsequently by the president of the US'.

74 Bauman (2001, p. 84) relatedly writes that the 'former civilization centre (is) ever more often in the role of not of pacifying or policing force, but of a supplier of the weapons needed to conduct tribal wars in the innumerable Afghanistans (etc.) of the globe. (This) secondary barbarization best sums up the overall impact of the present-day metropolises on the world periphery' (see also Dell and Querubin 2018; Sutton and Trefler 2016). Torfason and Ingram (2010, pp. 359, 372) identify 'Western military and economic dominance' as an example of 'coercive isomorphism whereby the militarily powerful influence the weak (by) the network of military alliances (that) often involves collective use of force and military aid, which may offer a potent path for coercive influence'.

dictatorship by other, military means or identical mechanisms of coercion. Hence, in inter-societal terms, just as forming a prison-capitalist complex of mass imprisonment and state terror in the intra-societal sense, capitalist dictatorship especially in the 'great' Western powers represents the epitome of militarism and militarist imperialism. This involves a massive and aggressive military-capitalist complex comprising a large military force even in times of peace, exorbitant or high military cum 'defense' expenditure and aggressive 'preemptive' wars or constant threatening alliances (NATO) with 'collective use of force' against other societies.[75]

5.4.2   Militarized Political Repression

Moreover, capitalist dictatorship can become de facto what Pareto predicts as (most probably) plutocratic 'military dictatorship' within society both because of and as the instrument of wars among Western societies, exerting military-style repression of non-capital strata through the military-capitalist complex as by the prison-capitalist system. He accurately predicts capitalist military dictatorships arising in interwar Germany, Italy, and Spain through the alliance of the right, namely the extended family of 'authoritarian rightists', such as conservatives and fascists, along with capitalists and the military. As he would expect, they inflicted non-capital and similar strata, notably labor unions and socialist parties, with violent repression, state terror and mass murder, while launching wars of aggression and destruction against 'inferior' nations. Many postwar cases of capitalist dictatorship from autocracy and dynasty to oligarchy and plutocracy especially in non-Western environments represent military dictatorships exerting militarized repression against non-capital labor and other populations within society. Such instances include South America, most egregiously Chile, most of Africa, much of Asia, including South Korea and Taiwan until recently and Singapore persistently, parts of Europe such as Greece, Portugal, and Spain until the 1970s, and so forth. Conversely, most postwar and contemporary military dictatorships either their personal forms or juntas in non-Western countries, especially in Latin America and Asia, are

---

75   Bauman (2001, p. 218) states that 'to paraphrase Clausewitz (global) war is primarily the 'promotion of free global trade by other means'. However, capitalist dictatorship does not necessarily link with and even delinks from free trade and instead is prone to protectionism and more broadly economic closure and nationalism, as conservative America during Reaganism and post-2016 with its various trade wars or restrictions demonstrates. As a result, American 'free market' capitalism is a comparatively closed economy to free trade while Western European, including Scandinavian, welfare capitalism being more open and globalized by the ratio of imports/exports to GDP. Torfason and Ingram (2010, p. 372) refer to the 'collective use of force' by NATO.

instances of capitalist dictatorship, including militarized autocracies, oligarchies or plutocracies, especially since the 1990s.

Furthermore, in some Western societies, capitalist dictatorship cum 'plutonomy' and more broadly capitalism, even if not becoming Pareto's 'military
dictatorship', tends to become not only militaristic and warlike, or allied and
threatening versus other societies. (This applies to their allying within NATO as
a growingly aggressive military alliance seeking to exert illegitimate coercion
on non-members since the 1990s, as it showed in the offensive Kosovo war that
was illegal by international UN-based norms.[76]) Capitalist dictatorship also
becomes militarized and potentially coercive, repressive and undemocratic
even within society, which is what the US President apparently means by alerting to the surging military-industrial complex due to its intrinsic tendency to
aggressive war and militarism as a potentially serious threat to democracy in
America.

This implies that the ever-expanding military-industrial complex and the
consequent permanent Orwellian imperial war as peace in such 'great' imperial powers, above all the US and Great Britain, has the potential for transforming capitalist plutocracy in these societies into Pareto's plutocratic 'military
dictatorship'. This especially holds in situations of the growing relative power
or unrest of non-capital and related strata and the potential insufficiency of
the prison-capitalist complex as the mechanism of their repression. Capitalist
dictatorship assumes the form of a warfare state where the army exerts militarized repression within society when non-capital gains some political influence
or raises its voice and the police state becomes insufficient for its subjection,
as conservative military dictatorships in Latin America, much of Asia, parts of
postwar Europe and elsewhere show. Conversely, this does not hold so long as
the relative positional and structural power of non-capital strata versus capital remains minimal and further erodes through the decline of their collective
organization and action and their unrest is rare and weak (e.g., strikes) and the
prison-capitalist complex continues to operate as a sufficient mechanism of
their repression. Both conditions hence make the military-industrial complex
and militarized coercion of these groups an unnecessary instrument. Taken
together, the combination of weak, repressed labor and a strong totalistic
police, security and surveillance state renders capitalist dictatorship's warfare
state in which the army also represses non-capital populations redundant, as

---

76   Specifically, Bauman (2001, pp. 209, 217) recommends that 'a charge of aggression (or
      illegitimate violence) to be raised against NATO forces (due to) violent acts perpetrated
      (during) the NATO Kosovo campaign' (see also Giddens 2000; Habermas 2001; Li 2002;
      Torfason and Ingram 2010).

in the US until recently. For instance, just as expected, in the early summer of 2020 when the police or security state proved insufficient to deal with the mass protests against chronic and pervasive police brutality, the US President and other conservative politicians threatened to use and indeed partly used (as in the capital) the active military, not just the national guard, to 'dominate' protesters and streets.

If neither condition persists, the military-industrial complex and militarized coercion of non-capital strata becomes the ultimate resort and final defense and insurance of capitalist dictatorship even in putatively democratic Western societies, as Pareto implies, as does in especially conservative counterrevolutions and right-wing dictatorships with respect to the repression of subordinate groups. In other words, when non-capital groups rise to relative power or challenge capital and the police-security state, however large and encompassing conservative American-style, no longer suffices to terrorize them into submission, the warfare state will likely enter the internal stage of society and defend capitalist dictatorship by terrorizing them as well.

This is a scenario of eliminating or preventing democracy that while typically enfolding in non-Western settings such as Africa, Asia, South America and parts of Southern Europe can potentially materialize in some Western societies, as Pareto predicts, in particular the US, as the above US President alerts. At the end, like all dictatorships or Pareto's aristocracies, capitalist dictatorship in both societies can only last in long terms by the use of coercion, including the 'brute force' of the police state and capitalist militias in American capitalism during the Gilded Aged and Reaganism, ultimately that of the warfare state or military-industrial complex since postwar times. The preceding implies a 'good news' or 'consolation prize' for US non-capital and related lower social strata. This is that the warfare state (e.g., the army, national guard) or military-industrial complex will only enter the stage and exert militarized and thus the most brutal repression of them only if the gigantic and all-embracing police-surveillance state proves 'not good enough' for that purpose and so for the conservation of capitalist dictatorship, including pro-capital theocracy, in conservative America.

Comparatively and historically, this is a tendency and path that fascism, most theocracy and generally authoritarian conservatism also typically adopts and hence invariably operates as a system of militarized repression within society, as of militarism and offensive wars against other societies.[77] This

---

77   Initially, communism follows this path but eventually abandons it, as the relatively peaceful collapse of communist Eastern Europe and the Soviet Union shows, during which the military refrained from conserving the system at any cost and instead joined

suggests that capitalist dictatorship in respect of a warfare state and especially militarized repression of lower and subordinate classes ultimately manifests a Weberian elective affinity, congruence and indeed merger with fascism during all its phases, as merged capitalist-fascist dictatorships in Nazi Germany, fascist Italy and postwar Latin America show. Also, it is similar to communism during its early militaristic stage but not its later stages when the military avoids and even, as in Eastern Europe, resists militarized internal repression.

The preceding justifies adopting militarism and high military spending, a large military force, a massive and aggressive military-industrial complex and offensive wars against other societies in particular as the indicator of capitalist dictatorship, notably an ultimate instrument of repression and terror of non-capital strata, as through military dictatorships or militarized coercion within society. At the minimum, militarism versus other societies provides an indirect indication in this respect. This holds insofar as in capitalist dictatorship militarism typically enfolds together, almost hand in hand, with the political subjection of non-capital strata within society, as especially does in fascist and other conservative dictatorships with regard to such a treatment of subordinate groups. In particular, the military-industrial complex or the warfare state tends to complement and even substitute the prison-industrial system or the police state. This especially holds when the latter proves insufficient in respect of repression of non-capital groups such as lower and powerless classes, along with ethnic-religious minorities, as in many non-Western countries and conceivably some Western societies such as the US during conservatism, where 'military imperialism' relates to 'more authoritarian' political life.[78]

Alternatively, capitalist dictatorship especially in such 'great' Western powers as the US and Great Britain effectively reveals itself by its strong militarism. The latter involves its large military-capitalist complex threatening democracy and its military-style coercion of non-capital strata in association or reciprocal intensification with their penal repression by the prison-capitalist system or independently when the latter proves ineffective.

Accordingly, capitalist dictatorship, ceteris paribus, features the comparatively strongest militarism, including the highest military spending,

---

its opponents, as well as not indulging in foreign interventions for the sake of political deflection or distraction and fabricating nationalist frenzy or solidarity American-style during the Kosovo war and the second Iraq war. Habermas (2001, p. 47) remarks that the Soviet Union abandoned the 'time-honored pattern of deflecting internal conflicts with military adventures abroad', which, however, the 'American empire' apparently continues, as Steinmetz (2005) suggests. For related insights see Fischer (2003), Keesing (1981), and Satyanath et al. (2017).

78   See Steinmetz (2005, pp. 361–2).

the largest military force, including the most numerous military bases, the most massive and aggressive military-industrial complex, and most offensive wars or attacks against other societies among the variates of capitalism and contemporary political regimes. In particular, all these components of militarism drastically exceed their levels in democratic egalitarian welfare capitalism and liberal democracy. Like pre-capitalist despotism and other dictatorships, with some qualifications, capitalist dictatorship becomes militarized under certain conditions stated above in relation to non-capital strata, just as versus other societies, and uses military force as the ultimate mechanism of their repression and its own preservation and, as with 'great' powers, the instrument of war, conquest and empire. In particular, large military expenditure in absolute or relative terms provides a standard, conventional measure or proxy of militarism among contemporary societies, along with military bases, arms exports, and offensive imperial wars[79] against other countries.

Empirically, not all real-life military dictatorships and more broadly militarized and warlike political regimes are capitalist, but also pre- and post-capitalist. However, aside from minor exceptions, most capitalist dictatorships, especially those or their proxies like plutonomy in 'great powers', are militaristic, aggressive and warlike to other societies and military dictatorships spanning from interwar Europe during fascism to postwar South America, Africa, Asia, and Islamic states. Thus, most capitalist dictatorships, like all others, exhibit the syndrome of militarism from high military spending, a large military force, a massive military-industrial complex to offensive wars and attacks against other societies, with many becoming military regimes or exerting militarized coercion of non-capital and related strata.

Instances include 19th-century and later England's capitalist militarism and imperialism, the US 'gun boat diplomacy', interwar Europe, especially Germany, Italy and other, capitalist-military dictatorships, postwar South American and African military dictatorships, those in Greece, Portugal and Spain through the 1970s, Singapore, South Korea, Taiwan, and other Asian countries, Turkey, Saudi Arabia and similar Islamic plutocratic-theocratic states. An additional continuous example involves the growing militarization déjà vu in Great Britain and America since Thatcherism and Reaganism, including the exorbitant and further increasing military expenditure in the second since the 1980s and after 2016 and under the autocratic regime. Apparently, this country since postwar times and especially during conservatism has assumed the place of the leader

---

79   The term 'imperial wars' from Abbott (2005).

or advocate within NATO[80] of militarization in the Western and entire world (along with Saudi Arabia) in all its aspects. These involve the exorbitant, virtually unlimited, economically and politically irresponsible, world-highest military spending, the largest military force and most military bases in other countries, notably as the US President at the time suggested, the most massive and aggressive military-industrial complex and most offensive wars or attacks against other societies ranging from Vietnam[81] to Iraq. This instance demonstrates the linkage and even symbiosis between militarism and capitalist dictatorship, specifically the repression of non-capital strata, including the military-industrial complex with its tendency to aggressive wars against other societies and the prison-capitalist system of mass imprisonment and widespread death sentences and executions of these groups.

In sum, strong and persistent militarism is an additional indication of capitalist dictatorship, especially complementing and reinforcing the political repression of non-capital strata and under some conditions ensuing in their militarized coercion. The latter can operate directly and effectively through military dictatorships in non-Western countries or indirectly and potentially

---

80   During post-2016 the US President and other officials persistently pressure NATO countries to increase and even double military expenditure from around 1 to 2 percent of GDP, while escalating that in America and thus effectively launching yet another arms race in the manner of Reagan's fiscal recklessness and huge budget deficits.

81   Dell and Querubin (2018, pp. 708–9) note that the 'costs of the conflict in Vietnamese lives were staggering (e.g.) more than 3 million total deaths between 1954 and 1975, including over 2 million civilian deaths. A 2008 *British Medical Journal* study estimated a death toll of 3.8 million. The financial costs of the war to the United States were also substantial, (e.g.) over $1 trillion. More firepower was unleashed during the Vietnam War than during any other conflict in human history. More than twice as many tons of explosives were dropped as during World War II (e.g.) about 500 pounds of ordnance per inhabitant. The munitions unleashed equaled the power of 640 Hiroshima-sized atomic bombs, and the amount of ammunition fired per soldier was 26 times greater than in World War II'. Cynics may comment that if this were an 'empire for good', then what an 'evil empire' was; it was the Soviet Union in Reagan's projection of Puritanism's and American conservatism's own negative, including sadistic-masochistic, attributes or intentions onto others (Adorno 2001; Altemeyer 2007; Fromm 1941). In addition, Reagan as a Calvinist, praised the Puritan theocracy as the 'shinning city upon a hill' and so a model for America. Further, this 'all-American', 'sunny' conservative, President implied an equivalence between Nazism and anti-Nazism by visiting the Nazi graves in Germany, which does not seem surprising given that conservatism produced or merged with fascism in interwar Europe, as it does in postwar and present times. Lastly, expressing pathological anti-liberalism Reagan attempted to virtually criminalize liberals in America by declaring them 'un-American', showing the inspiration in and lineage from McCarthyism. On this account, Reagan qualifies as the single main role model for or precursor of the post-2016 and indeed any subsequent capitalist-conservative autocracy and thus dictatorship in America.

by a military-industrial complex in some Western societies. For example, comparative data on levels of military expenditure, along with these other figures, give estimates of the degree of militarism of which they are a standard measure and reliable predictor. They also help predict the possibility of offensive wars against other societies. This applies primarily to such Western 'great' powers' as the US under warlike and imperialist conservatism and Great Britain and France still with the ghost of colonialism, expressing under diverse disguises and realizing in various ways their militaristic impulses within NATO as a classic offensive military alliance versus non-members, while posturing and pretending to be 'defensive'.

CHAPTER 4

Capitalist Dictatorship as Civil Society

1 Capitalist Dictatorship and Civil Society

In addition to representing an economic system and political regime, capitalist dictatorship represents a peculiar civil society, more precisely a perverted form of the latter, through its operation and extension from economy and polity into the civic or private sphere of the social system. Therefore, it manifests its totalistic scope by encompassing both the formal economic-political system of society and its informal 'life-world' of individual liberty and privacy, or everyday personal life and intersubjective social interactions and associations.

Consistent with its nature as an equivalent economic system and pollical regime, capitalist dictatorship constitutes an unfree, coerced civil society. The latter hence ceases to be 'civil' in the sense of civic liberty or individual freedom, a far cry and aberration from Hegel's and even Marx's free, uncoerced classic 'bourgeois' form in early capitalism transcending the absolute and coercive state.[1] Following the logic and method of dictatorships, capitalist dictatorship distorts civil society as the sphere of universal individual liberty, choice and privacy, notably personal moral freedom, by denying such liberties and choices to non-capital strata and monopolizing them for capital, just as it does away with liberal democracy and democratic capitalism.[2]

On this account, capitalist dictatorship proves to be the antithesis of civil society in that it violates the principle of 'liberty for all' in private life, including personal morality, beyond and outside economy and politics. It thereby perverts this subsystem of the social system into the sphere of individual moral and related unfreedom for non-capital strata and of absolute personal freedom for capital. By such a dualism, it distorts and splits this subsystem into a pervasive non-civil society for non-capital strata and a narrow, exclusive and closed, thus ersatz civil society solely for capital, as it subverts democracy into non-democracy and repression for the first and bogus illiberal 'democracy' and exclusive 'freedom' for the second. Such a dualism in civil society

---

1 Habermas (1989, p. 79) suggests that in the middle of the nineteenth century 'civil society as the private sphere emancipated from the directives of public authority to such an extent that at that time the political public sphere could attain its full development in the bourgeois constitutional state' (see also Ku 2000).

2 For instance, on civil society in Chile's Pinochet dictatorship see Huber and Stephens (2005).

complements, corresponds and reinforces that of Hobbesian anarchy for capital and Leviathan-like repression of non-capital strata in the economy and
politics. Moreover, capitalist dictatorship's civil society represents the duality
of anarchy and Leviathan for capital and non-capital, respectively, in terms of
individual liberties, just as its economy and polity do in economic and political
freedoms.

Capitalist dictatorship historically replicates pre-capitalist despotism such
as feudalism with its dualism of individual illiberty for non-aristocratic strata
and absolute personal freedom for aristocracy precluding the emergence of a
true civil society. In comparative terms, it conforms to contemporary dictatorships, especially post-2016 (and earlier) resurging conservative-fascist regimes
and theocracies from America under the radical-right government and Brexit
Britain to Brazil, Hungary and Poland and Saudi Arabia and other Gulf states
and Turkey. They all feature an equivalent pattern with regard to subordinate
and ruling groups and thus eliminate or pervert civil society as the free private sphere. Therefore, capitalist dictatorship shares with pre-capitalist despotism a pre-civil society by refusing to generalize individual freedom, choice
and privacy from plutocracy as the new aristocracy of capital to non-capital
as the modern populace of formally free labor, while sharing pre-democracy,
including a preliberal and 'pre-democratic mind'. In addition, it shares with
conservative-fascist dictatorships and theocracies an anti-civil society by eliminating such and related freedoms for non-capital after liberal democracy for
the first time in history has granted them to the latter, while sharing authoritarian and eventually totalitarian anti-liberalism and anti-democracy that define
conservatism, fascism and theocracy.

Like its prototype in ancient Greek democracy and Hobbes' late medievalism or early modern times—except perhaps for the Renaissance—Hegel's civil
society within capitalism has appeared to observers or outsiders as a relatively
narrow, exclusive, closed and coercive domain.[3] The prime reason for this

---

3 Habermas (1989, p. 125) observes that during that time 'power relationships were not effectively neutralized in the reproduction of social life' and 'civil society itself still rested on
   force' which prevented the full development of democracy, as 'no juridical condition which
   replaced political authority with rational authority could be erected on (the) basis' of civil
   society. Also, Ku (2000, p. 226) notes that in the seventeenth and eighteenth centuries, 'from
   the perspective of the liberal Enlightenment thinkers, it was against this kind of proclaimed
   public authority of the absolute monarchy that the emerging civil society counteracted.
   Alexander (2001, p. 239) remarks that 'capitalist economic institutions' not only 'encouraged
   the belief that failure in the market sphere revealed a parallel incompetence in democratic
   life' but also contributed to the substantively theocratic 'conversion of religious into civil
   competence in much the same way'.

impression was, as he, Marx, Sombart, Weber and Pareto suggest, 'bourgeois' narrowness, in particular petty-bourgeois narrow-mindedness and outlook and middle-class rigid puritanical moralism, exclusiveness and closure in relation to non-bourgeois and non-aristocratic strata, although with a potential or rather promise for an extension beyond bourgeoisie and inclusion of these groups into the free private sphere.[4] Pareto observes that pre-capitalist aristocracy and other old 'higher strata of society' display 'decadent elements' in moral terms but are not narrow-minded, intolerant and rigid. By contrast, he implies that bourgeoisie, especially petty-bourgeoise, shows mostly opposite traits such as moralistic zealotry and discipline, narrow-mindedness, intolerance and rigidity.

In a paradox, it appears that bourgeoisie harbors a 'penchant for laissez-faire' in the economy and market, but not in civil society understood as an evolved and broadened non-economic 'life-world', in particular individual morality and privacy.[5] Instead, it subjects the moral and private sphere to narrow petty-bourgeois and strict religious control, disrespect, constraint and punishment for transgressions, including mass imprisonment for moral sins (e.g., alcohol and drug use, prostitution, etc.) and pervasive executions often of innocent offenders, as conservative America and capitalist Islamic states demonstrate. In that sense, it imposes merged capitalist-puritanical theocracy in the style of the 'American regime' since Puritanism through evangelicalism. As a result, 'bourgeois' civil society hardly ever reaches the stage of moral, private and non-economic 'laissez-faire' and thus universalized individual liberty for all strata,[6] in contrast to its economic version with respect to capital mixed with generalized labor coercion in early capitalism such as 19th-century England and Gilded-Age America. Capitalist dictatorship inherits and carries what Schumpeter calls the 'scheme of bourgeois motivation' in civil society, economic and political activities to the point of submission of non-capital strata in this sphere by restricting their individual liberties and of Weberian monopolistic closure of bourgeoisie by monopolizing them for capital. In these terms, it is an unfree civil and thus pre-civil society in the sense of a life-sphere of individua unfreedom for non-capital strata and a spurious

---

4 Solow (1963, p. 9) identifies the 'moralistic overtones' of the capitalist 'ideological justification for profit' in terms of 'abstinence'. For similar observations see Habermas (1989), Hicks (2006), and Wagner (1997).

5 Samuelson (1983a, p. 8) refers to the 'bourgeois penchant for laissez-faire' but not in civil society (see also Alexander 2001; Giddens 2000; Habermas 1989; Ku 2000).

6 Popper (1973, p. 238) suggests that moral and related 'higher' values ought to be considered a 'non-agenda' of the state and instead left to the 'realm of *laissez-faire*.'

non-liberal, exclusive civil society and personal freedom only for capital, related to non-democracy and bogus illiberal 'democracy' with regard to these two classes, respectively.

2   Negative Definition and Specification of Capitalist Dictatorship as Civil Society

Accordingly, by way of a negative dimension, definition and specification, capitalist dictatorship with respect to civil society as an element of the total social system forms the process and space of negation and suppression of universal individual liberty, choice and privacy for non-capital strata, in particular non-oligarchy and non-plutocracy. In this sense, it becomes and epitomizes a negative civil society, the obverse of the latter as the realm of such liberty and privacy for all strata in capitalism and generally.

Historically, like pre-capitalist despotism and its aristocracy with regard to non-aristocratic groups, capitalist dictatorship and its plutocracy as the ruling group typically, with some variations, does not grant agency and dignity, thus personal freedom, autonomous choice and full privacy, to non-capital and other low strata. It considers the latter as undeserving of such intangible civic, as well as tangible economic and political, entitlements because of their lack of, as Weber put it, of 'qualifications' of great wealth, power and social status and often religious qualities of 'godliness', 'faith' and 'purity'—simply, not born into them—as in Puritan American and Islamic capitalism.

In this regard, capitalist dictatorship in a historical continuity with pre-capitalist despotism manifests itself as a purely and completely negative civil society for non-capital strata, as feudalism and aristocracy fid for the peasantry and other populace. To use Simmel's words, it is a pure negativity of individual liberty, choice and privacy for these strata, their negation and suppression as autonomous, dignified and responsible individual agents, simply free individuals. Comparatively, capitalist dictatorship appears and operates as such negativism of civil society and individual liberty more than the other types of capitalism and polity, showing, for example, the 'negative fallout of the usurers and exploiters' in capitalism.[7] This holds notably by comparison to democratic and egalitarian welfare capitalism and its typical complement liberal-secular democracy that are the opposite in this respect. Conversely, it approaches other contemporary, especially persistent and resurrecting conservative-fascist and

---

7   See Basu (2018, p. 190), also, Akerlof and Shiller (2015).

theocratic, dictatorships since the 1980s and post-2016. These dictatorships tend to be capitalist or plutocratic in economic and class terms, as Pinochet's Chile, evangelical America, Hungary under conservatism, Catholic-dominated Poland, Islamic-ruled Turkey and Saudi Arabia and other Gulf states, show.

In particular, capitalist dictatorship/plutocracy denies and suppresses individual moral liberty and responsibility or personal freedom, choice and privacy ('laissez-faire') in morality, for non-capital strata, just as feudalism/aristocracy did for the populace. In this respect, as negative civil society, capitalist dictatorship appears especially as the process and space of negation and suppression of personal moral, including the most intimate, freedom, choice and privacy for non-capital and other lower social strata. Furthermore, it operates in fusion or alliance with coercive, moralistic religion, as in evangelical America and Islamic countries.

Like pre-capitalist despotism during medievalism and especially conservative-fascist and theocratic dictatorships, capitalist dictatorship, with some variations, tends to be moralistic or puritanical in ethical terms and often religious. Consequently, it is rigid, coercive and repressive in respect of individual moral freedom and privacy in morality for non-capital strata. This is what Weber's Puritan-rooted capitalism in England and especially America— as he witnesses during his visit—demonstrates since Puritanism through 'Puritanical' evangelicalism, along with some Islamic states such as Saudi Arabia perennially and Turkey recently. As a consequence, in these Puritan-evangelical and Islamic versions or underpinnings, capitalist dictatorship arises and operates as a pure and indeed puritanical negativity in terms of individual moral freedom and thus a negative moralistic civil society for non-capital, sinful and nonreligious groups. If laissez-faire capitalism manifests what Keynes describes (and rejects) as self-defeating financial "purism" such as the dogma of non-government intervention leading to the Great Depression, capitalist dictatorship does an analogous property. Thus, especially when merged with theocratic religion in American and Islamic settings, it exhibits and enforces coercive moral, religious and ideological 'purism' on these strata, while lavishing capital with aristocracy-like unrestricted personal freedom and privacy.[8]

---

8   Keynes (1936, p. 173) predicts that a wartime government would lose a war if pursuing financial "purism." Eggertsson (2008, p. 1479) reaffirms that laissez-faire 'policy dogmas' (low government spending and balanced budget, along the gold standard) played a major role in causing or aggravating the Great Depression. In turn, Jouet (2017, pp. 41–2) remarks that some features 'mainly concentrated in conservative America', such as 'profound anti-intellectualism, visceral antigovernmentalism, and Christian fundamentalism', 'foster a purist, far right ideology that is hostile to compromise and impedes rational decision making and problem-solving'.

Furthermore, capitalist dictatorship that is moralistic by enforcing 'bourgeois' puritanical morality and religious by imposing 'godliness' operates as a double negativity in terms of individual freedom. It does this by negating such freedom for these strata because they lack qualifications of wealth, power and status and of 'godliness', simply being neither of plutocracy nor of the 'godly', for example, of the 'elect' in Calvinism and their predestination equivalent in Islam. In this sense, moralistic capitalist dictatorship within civil society is dual and to some degree total by combing the plutocratic or oligarchic with the puritanical or religious suppression of personal moral freedom for non-capital and non-religious groups, oppressing both non-capitalists and the 'ungodly'. Consequently, it functions as both economic-corporate and moralistic-religious dictatorship by capital or plutocracy—in alliance with theocracy or religion thus effectively remaining the 'second estate' as in feudalism—of non-capital strata due to their lack of wealth/power/status qualifications and of 'pure' morality and 'true' religiosity. It therefore expresses its totalistic nature within civil society, as in the social system as a whole.

The usually moralistic and frequently religious connotation of capitalist dictatorship indicates that in ideological terms it typically assumes the form of conservative, including fascist and theocratic, dictatorships in civil society and thus negative civil societies, just as non-democracies within the polity. The observation that virtually all capitalist dictatorships from autocracies and dynasties to oligarchies and plutocracies ideologically are essentially conservative, including fascist and theocratic, and conversely anti-liberal and in that sense anti-civil societies, helps explain why they are usually moralistic and often religious. The aggregate effect in all cases is therefore eliminating or perverting civil society such as individual freedom for non-capital strata.

In sum, negatively defined, capitalist dictatorship due its usual moralistic and often religious undertones represents a negative, illiberal civil society in the sense of a domain of individual unfreedom and the lack of choice and privacy, especially in moral, including the most private, actions and relations for non-capital or lower social strata. The latter especially include those not originating (born) in or belonging to plutocracy, oligarchy and theocracy for capitalist dictatorship's Puritan and Islamic variants. Hence, it manifests itself as a pure and complete, frequently puritanical and totalistic, negativity of civil society as a life-sphere of individual liberty, including personal moral freedom, for all social strata. Civil society, and thus universal individual liberty, becomes an extinct species, non-entity and impossibility theorem, at best a transient rarity, in capitalist dictatorship, as does in all dictatorships, especially resurrecting conservative-fascist or radical-right and theocratic regimes.

3   Positive Definition and Specification of Capitalist Dictatorship as
     Civil Society

In its positive dimension, definition and specification, capitalist dictatorship
as civil society constitutes the social process and space of control and constraint of the private and related life sphere, especially of the corresponding
actions and relations of non-capital and similar strata. Capitalist dictatorship
positively defined and specified represents a capital-controlled, constrained,
dominated and thus distorted civil society, just as an equivalent economic system and political regime do in interaction and mutual reinforcement. It hence
operates as the dictatorship of capital and capitalists playing 'dictator games'
in civil society, just as jointly in the economy and polity, within the total social
system.[9] Despite its prime economic and political connotations, capitalist dictatorship does not remain confined to and satisfied with controlling economy
and polity and instead expands its scope of control further and deeper into
civil society by controlling and constraining the private and related life sphere.
It thereby exhibits its totalistic tendency and exemplifies the syndrome of
most dictatorships.

     In historical terms, capitalist dictatorship and its plutocracy adopts, with
some adaptations, the prototype of pre-capitalist despotism like feudalism
and its aristocracy for controlling, constraining and dominating the private
and entire life sphere, especially personal activities, of non-aristocratic and
similar strata. Just as pre-capitalist despotism and aristocracy, capitalist
dictatorship considers and transforms civil society into the social space of
control, constraint and domination by the ruling class beyond economy and
polity rather than a free private or civic sphere, especially for other classes.
In so doing, it dissolves civil society into the narrow and closed domain of
exclusive individual liberty for capital to the point of the literal or figurative
'license to kill' and oppress—as in the 19th-century English master-servant
system and American capitalism during the Gilded Age, since the 1980s and
post-2016—just as pre-capitalist despotism endowed aristocracy with absolute personal freedom. Consequently, capitalist dictatorship transforms civil
society, just as economy and polity, into Hobbesian anarchy and state of
nature for capital exclusively and into Leviathan for and total control over
non-capital and similar strata and thus perverts it as the generalized free private life sphere. It thereby shares and reinvents pre-capitalist despotism's old

---

9   The capitalist 'dictator game' is from Stiglitz (2012, p. 114), see also Andreoni et al. (2017),
     Henrich et al. (2004), and Opp (2011).

method of anarchic freedom and severe constraint for aristocracy and non-aristocratic classes, respectively.

Just as pre-capitalist despotism was the supreme space of personal freedom exclusively for aristocracy reflecting its equivalent force and dominance, capitalist dictatorship becomes a supremely positive and exclusive, yet partial and spurious, civil society, the pure positivity, blessing of individual liberty, choice and privacy for capital. It therefore expresses and sustains (in Mitchells' words) the 'despotic might' or superior systemic power of capital over non-capital. In Weber's terms, just as pre-capitalist despotism monopolized personal freedom for aristocracy, capitalist dictatorship through such control and constraint of the private and related life sphere attains and sustains monopolistic closure of civil society, thus individual liberty, choice and privacy, as well as monopolizing wealth and power, capital. On this account, capitalist dictatorship develops as the substantive continuation of pre-capitalist despotism, and plutocracy emerges as the true heir—and often an admirer, as with the American 'robber barons'—of aristocracy, by sharing the same archetype of spurious civil society. This is complete individual liberty for the ruling class and strict personal illiberty for other classes.

In comparative terms, capitalist dictatorship forms more a positive space of control, constraint and domination of the private life-sphere by capital and monopolistic closure of civil society by plutocracy than other types of capitalism and polity, especially the complex of welfare capitalism and liberal democracy which Scandinavia and Western Europe epitomizes representing the opposite in these terms. On the other hand, capitalist dictatorship complements and converges in these terms with other contemporary, especially prevailing and surging post-2016 conservative-fascist and theocratic, dictatorships. This complementarity is compatible with the observation that it is primarily a conservative, right regime in political terms, just as these dictatorships are mainly capitalist in the economic sense.

Particularly consistent with its negative definition, capitalist dictatorship is the social process and space of usually moralistic and frequently religious control and constraint of the private, including intimate, life sphere, especially that of non-capital and similar strata, as in conservative America and Islamic states. In consequence of being moralistically and religiously controlled, constrained, and dominated, this sphere degenerates into disfigured civil society, as observed for evangelical America and plutocratic Islamic states sharing the joint plutocratic and moral-religious control and suppression of individual liberty for non-plutocratic and non-religious groups. At this point, one encounters especially the dictatorship of the moralistic and religious capitalist class or its sections characterized with such traits. This involves the domination of 'righteous', 'God-fearing' capitalists and allied agents by acting as dictatorial enforcers of 'righteousness' and 'godliness', thus playing 'dictator games' of moralism and purism in civil society, as in the economy and polity. Consequently, capitalist dictatorship mutates into a system of moralistic and, under some conditions, religious oppression in terms of civil society, just as being the compound of economic and political repression in respect of economy and polity. This is self-consistent with its totalistic tendency and congruent with conservative dictatorships as its ideological analogues.

By its moralistic and especially religious underpinnings, capitalist dictatorship can assume the form of pro-capital theocracy which Jefferson describes as 'religious slavery' while mainly referring to what Weber denotes the Puritan 'theocracy of New England' persisting as the established state religion in revolutionary America through the early and middle 19th century. Jefferson implies and Weber suggests thereby that especially capitalist dictatorship or plutocracy in historically Puritan societies such as America and to some degree England and more broadly capitalism with religious origins in Calvinism tends to be capitalist theocracy or theocratic capitalism, just as its proxies in Islamic countries like Saudi Arabia and other Gulf states and Turkey presently. Capitalist dictatorship's typical moralism and conservatism indirectly and its frequent religious component directly both move it toward pro-capital theocracy and theocrats. The latter represent its additional, indeed prevalent form and agent in certain societies and times, most manifestly the US South as the pro-capital, anti-labor 'Bible Belt' and Saudi Arabia and other Gulf states also mixing capitalism with theocratic oppression, including religion-driven mass imprisonment, torture,[10] and widespread executions

Further, one can positively define and specify capitalist dictatorship in respect of civil society as moral 'fascism' in the sense of extensive and intensive moralistic, often religiously driven, control, constraint and repression of the private life sphere, notably of the individual liberty and privacy of non-capital and other lower social strata. In other words, it moves toward puritanical 'fascism' in civil society in the generic meaning of constraining, repressive and rigid moral purism usually—along with Keynes' 'financial purism'—characterizing capitalist dictatorship or in his opinion laissez-faire capitalism. Another specific sense of puritanical 'fascism' is that of Puritanism. The latter is the extreme instance, together with Islam, of a coercive 'pure' morality and church, indeed theocratic 'unexampled tyranny' deriving from Calvinism's 'absolutely unbearable' control of individuals and sanctified by

---

10   On torture by the US government during the Iraq War, see Einolf (2007).

Calvin's dogma of predestination expressing 'extreme inhumanity' in Weber's words. Moreover, it is the religious analogue of fascism or authoritarian conservatism in Merton's and other accounts.[11] By being moralistic and often religiously driven capitalist dictatorship tends to be over-controlling, extremely constraining and systematically repressive of individual liberty and to that extent morally 'fascist' or totalitarian in the generic sense within civil society. This is what 'Puritanical' repression epitomizes in America under repressive capitalism since Reaganism and revived theocratic evangelicalism transforming much of it into a 'proto-totalitarian' Bibliocracy (Weber's term) named the 'Bible Belt'.[12]

At the minimum, moral control, constraint and repression defines capitalist dictatorship in terms of civil society as the moralistic, puritanical functional equivalent of fascism in the private life sphere, especially with regard to the individual liberty of non-capital and related strata. Such an equivalence seems plausible in view of that many capitalist dictatorships are fascist or extreme-right regimes, as in interwar Germany, Italy and Spain, postwar South America and Southern Europe, including Greece, Portugal and Spain, Eastern Europe such as the Baltic states, Hungary and Poland, the US post-2016 and via contagion Brazil and so on. Generally, virtually all of them are conservative, right regimes, as in moralistic Victorian England and Puritanical America during the 19th century and the Gilded Age, under Thatcherism and Reaganism and during Brexit and post-2016, along with Singapore, South Korea and Taiwan in Asia, Eastern Europe ruled by capitalist oligarchy, Turkey, Saudi Arabia and

---

11   Merton (1939, p. 437) comments that 'American nativism, in the form of anti-Catholic and later of anti-foreign sentiment, was partly rooted in this same Puritanism. The main outlines of this pattern significantly resemble nativist developments in Europe today. The colonial *New England Primer* finds its analogue in the various Nazi primers (viz.) the displacement of aggression against a convenient out-group (especially) marked in periods of economic strain (plus) the impugning of out-group morality (etc.)—all this needs little change to characterize the myths and tactics of nativist movements before and since'. Fromm (1941, p. 77) proposes that 'Calvin's theory of predestination has one implication (that) has found its most vigorous revival in Nazi ideology: the principle of the basic inequality of men'. Adorno 2001, p. 229) alerts to the 'important role played by the religious element in American fascist and anti-Semitic propaganda', with this element by implication being mostly rooted in the 'whole Puritan tradition' of America. Lipset (1955, 180) notes that 'one important factor affecting this lack of tolerance in American life is the basic strain of Protestant puritanical morality'. McLaughlin (1996, p. 249) suggests that Puritanism/Calvinism 'served the same sociological function for Anglo-Saxon countries' as fascism did for Europe in that Protestantism was not only linked with 'political freedoms and economic progress' but also to 'Nazism'.
12   The term the 'Bible Belt' is in Bauman (1997), McBride (2008), Putnam (2000), and Wagner (1997).

other Gulf states. Conversely, redefining capitalist dictatorship in civil society as the moralistic substitute for fascism is consistent with that most fascist and generally conservative dictatorships are, with some minor variations, largely capitalist systems in economic or class terms.

Correspondingly, most past and present capitalist dictatorships conform to the positive definition as equivalents of 'moral fascism' in the sense of puritanical, including Puritan, control, constraint and repression of individual liberty and privacy in morality. Virtually of all them represent moralistic, conservative dictatorships in terms of civil society from Victorian England to America during Prohibition and other temperance wars. The latter include the Reagan puritanical economically irrational 'war on drugs', alcohol and related, for Puritan-inspired conservatives, grave moral sins redefined as crimes—as the logic of the 'tough on crime' crusade—and severely punished, generating the totalitarian Orwellian outcome of no/less crime and more severe punishment.[13] Relatedly, they are under some conditions de facto religious dictatorships and thus capitalist theocracies, as in Puritan-evangelical America such as the Southern and other 'Bible Belt' (plus Mormon-totally ruled Utah), Catholic-dominated Latin America and Poland, Turkey under Islamic rule and Saudi Arabia and other Gulf states.

For example, Pareto observes that the US capitalist government coercively enforces puritanical 'morality by law' and hence becomes 'malignant power' committing 'abuses of power' that are not observable in other, European societies without such moralistic 'restrictions'. His contemporaries Sombart, Scheler and Weber, along with the domestic critic of Puritanism, Mencken, make similar observations.[14] Moreover, Pareto suggests that by so doing such moralistic

---

13   Friedman (1997, p. 194) comments: 'Surely, one reason for the growth in crime is that the number of activities that are classified as crimes has multiplied in recent years. Indeed, it is often asserted that there is hardly an individual in the U.S. who could not be convicted of a crime, if prosecutors made a real effort to do so. There are so many laws covering so many activities that none of us know what they are in full detail. The most promising candidate for decriminalization (represents) is the current prohibition of the consumption, purchase, or sale of a limited number of chemical substances designated as illegal drugs'. However, he fails to mention that it was the ideology and politics to which he subscribes—economically 'libertarian' Reaganism and generally conservatism—that criminalized and prohibited the 'consumption, purchase, or sale of a limited number of chemical substances' and hence produced the Orwellian (or Kafka-style) totalitarian situation in which 'there is hardly an individual in the U.S. who could not be convicted of a crime, if prosecutors made a real effort to do so'. See also Akerlof (2002), Bergemann (2017), Campbell and Schoenfeld (2013), Cooney and Burt (2008), and Roth (2018).

14   Scheler (1964, pp. 15–6) observes that the 'distrust of natural man as completely corrupted by original sin (is) an idea driven to the extreme in all Protestant dogmatics (and) with the purpose of producing a new artificial man', and identifies the 'external espionage

government—which Mencken characterizes as the 'worst'—replicates rather than supersedes the Dark Middle Ages of Europe by enacting a 'mass of hypocritical laws for the enforcement of morality that are replicas of laws of the European Middle Ages'. These laws mix with what he denotes the 'rise of no end of strange and wholly unscientific religions such as Christian Science that are utterly at war with any sort of scientific thinking'. By the latter statement Pareto anticipates the 'Christian Right' alliance between the capitalist rich and the religious poor in revolt against scientific innovation and progress. More directly related to the present context, Pareto by a 'mass of hypocritical laws for the enforcement of morality' precisely diagnoses alcohol Prohibition, anticipates the 'war on drugs' in America and provides an operational definition and accurate identification of moralistic Puritan capitalist dictatorship. This holds so long as the US government's—and supposedly the American people's—'chief business' is precisely the 'business' of capitalists[15] according to a Calvinist-named President (e.g., Calvin Coolidge apparently christened after the French founder of Calvinism, Calvin) during the Gilded Age and up to post-2016.

In this sense, if one does not know what moralistic, Puritan capitalist dictatorship and particularly pro-capital theocracy is or whether it exists in Western society, one can resolve this dilemma by looking at the Constitution-enforced Prohibition. The latter is an act of constitutional change to enforce private morality consistent with and implementing Puritanism but without a precedent or sequel in Western history and a dismal failure of paternalistic coercion, as its repeal indicates. Further, one should look at Prohibition's partial re-imposition in the 'Bible Belt' ('dry' Southern states) and for certain categories at the national level (age groups under 21), the 'war on drugs', abortion rights and other puritanical wars on sins-as-crimes with Draconian punishments, including life sentences and death for immoral offenses (e.g., drug use and trade). By their aims or effects, since Prohibition through the 'war on drugs' these puritanical wars on sins-crimes function as a compounded and

---

system against unchastity, drinking, vice and luxury of all sorts, which has been created in Protestant countries'. In a similar vein, Sombart (1928, p. 62) remarks that Puritanism's restrictions were stronger than those by Catholicism and 'focused primarily on sex life' with the result that 'chastity degenerated into prudery' among Anglo-Saxon peoples. Sombart (1928, p. 62) infers that 'Puritanism has certainly done much to develop in England and in the U.S. states of New England this false modesty and the hypocrisy in sexual matters, which have persisted to this day'. See also Adamczyk and Hayes (2012).

15   See Phelps (2013, p. 136), also, Gorman and Seguin (2018), Lamont (2018), and Shiller (2017).

consistent warfare against individual moral freedom, choice and privacy for lower and powerless strata, including religious and racial minorities.

In particular, the testament in this respect consists of almost 2.3 million prisoners many of whom (between 20 and 44 percent) imprisoned for moral sins such as drug and related non-violent offenses, and the consequent highest prisoner population and rate in the Western and whole world, along with the largest number of death sentences and executions, excluding only but converging with Islamic states.[16] An additional category consists of several millions of former prisoners to whom the US government, alone among Western democracies, denies basic democratic rights and civil liberties and punishes them perpetually Puritan-style after their formal completion of punishment.

These millions of present and former prisoners of de facto ethical conscience, simply moral sinners reclassified Puritan-style as criminals, are living proofs of moralistic and religious capitalist dictatorship, specifically pro-capital theocracy or theocratic capitalism. If one does not know what the latter is or whether it exists in conservative America, looking at these sinful-as-criminal Americans will help settle the matter. It is no wonder that the probability or lifetime risk of imprisonment reportedly 'doubled' in conservative America since Reaganism and is drastically higher than in any Western and OECD country. In view of this trend, such victims of moralistic repression probably will reproduce and the 'astronomical growth of the incarcerated population' continue in the foreseeable future judging by recent tendencies, as will those, including innocent persons, subjected to death sentences and executions whose likelihood is zero in virtually all of these societies because of their abolition of capital punishment.[17] This holds if the medieval-style coercive imposition of puritanical morality that Pareto diagnosed long ago continues via the Leviathan-like police state—which is a 'limited', and the minimal welfare state 'big', government for US conservatives or 'libertarians'. And it evidently does in the 'Bible Belt' and similar regions of conservative America, with the example of persistent and escalating negations and violations of various (including reproductive and related) privacy rights.

---

16   Becky and Western (2004, p. 152) note that in the late 1990s 'more than 60 percent of Federal prisoners were serving time for drug crimes' (see also, Jacobs et al. 2005; Kohler-Hausmann 2013; Mueller 2009; Uggen and Manza 2002). Further, Roth (2018, p. 1633) registers that the Federal Bureau of Prisons 'reports as of January 2018 that 46 percent of all inmates were convicted of drug offenses'.

17   For a sociological and historical account of the abolition of capital punishment see Mathias (2013).

The above holds a fortiori for moralistic Islamic capitalist dictatorships and indeed theocracies, such as Saudi Arabia and other Gulf states for long, featuring total alcohol, abortion, drug, sexual and related prohibitions and even more severe punishments, usually executions, for violations, and to a growing extent in Turkey recently. Yet, its Islamic government attempted but failed for now, under the pressure of the European Union which it aspires to join, to reinstitute the death penalty and ban adultery, while succeeding to enact alcohol restrictions. However, even Islamic-ruled Turkey still has a lower minimum legal drinking age of 18 for alcohol consumption than conservative America since Reaganism that increased it from 18 to 21, making it abnormally, unreasonably and dangerously high,[18] indeed the highest among Western and all OECD countries whose typical figure is 18 and in many cases below.

Alternatively, non-moralistic, non-conservative capitalist dictatorships are non-entities or rare species so that it becomes hard to identify pertinent cases among Western societies, as are often non-religious and non-theocratic instances among them. Even after the formal disestablishment of Puritan theocracy in the early to middle 19th century, American capitalism during the Gilded Age as the mix of the Hobbesian state of nature/anarchy for capital and Leviathan for non-capital hardly exemplifies a non-moralistic, non-conservative, non-religious and non-theocratic, system in terms of civil society, as Pareto and other observers suggest.[19] This holds especially for capitalism in the postbellum South that reinvented itself as moralistic capitalist theocracy through the double systematic repression of formally free labor and

---

18   Carpenter and Dobkin (2011, p. 133) report that the 'Amethyst Initiative, signed by more than 100 college presidents and other higher education officials calls for a reexamination of the minimum legal drinking age in the US. A central argument of the initiative is that the U.S. minimum legal drinking age policy results in more dangerous drinking than would occur if the legal drinking age were lower'. This argument implies that the minimum legal drinking age in the US that Reaganism increased from 18 to 21 is unreasonably and even dangerously high. This is consistent with the ideology and policy of unreason or irrationalism of Puritanical American conservatism; and yet nothing is unreasonable for its enforcement of private morality by coercion on Americans—coercing them in what to and what not to drink—replicating the European Dark Middle Ages, as Pareto prophetically diagnosed a century ago. By virtue of this replication of Mannheim's 'dead past', conservatism remakes America the oldest or most atavistic society among modern Western societies rather than the 'new' and 'youngest' nation versus the 'old' world.

19   Among these observers are Andrews and Seguin (2015), Isaac (2002), Jenness (2004), Mizruchi and Marshall (2016), Simon (1976), Thaler (2018). For instance, Thaler (2018, p. 1282) points to the 'coercion normally associated with paternalistic policies such as Prohibition'.

non-religious groups or religious minorities, as Mencken suggests by inventing the term 'Bible Belt' and using the epithet repressive 'barbarism' for its Puritan-rooted evangelical rulers. Overall, the conservative 'American regime' of capitalist dictatorship or generally capitalism scarcely qualifies as non-moralistic, non-religious or non-theocratic in view of its noted 'Religious Right' alliance between the plutocratic rich and the religious poor against personal moral freedom and science.

Furthermore, given that many capitalist dictatorships are fascist or radical-right regimes, they formally or substantively mutate into moral fascism in respect of civil society. Examples include interwar Germany, postwar Chile and South America and apparently conservative America (at least the South) since the1980s with Reaganism's war on drugs, alcohol and other sins-as-crimes and the post-2016 autocracy which the religiously driven 'fascist' propaganda of the 1950s prefigures.[20]

In sum, positively defined in terms of civil society, capitalist dictatorship forms in general the social space of over-control and extreme constraint of the life sphere and individual liberty, specifically that of non-capital and related strata. Through attaining and sustaining monopolistic closure of civil society and personal freedom for capital, it presents itself as a pure positivity, unmitigated good to the latter. In particular, it is the compound of typically moralistic and frequently religious control and constraint of civil society and liberty for non-capital strata, thus including capitalist theocracy, consistent with that virtually all its cases are conservative regimes ideologically. In that sense, capitalist dictatorship as civil society turns into a moralistic, puritanical equivalent

---

20   Adorno (2001, p. 226) identifies religion-driven 'fascist propaganda' in America during the 1950s. He elaborates that in this propaganda the 'actual shedding of blood is advocated as necessary because the world has supposedly been redeemed by the shedding of Christ's blood', and identifies 'destructiveness as the psychological basis of the fascist spirit' so that the 'promise expressed by fascist oratory is nothing but destruction itself'. (Adorno 2001, pp. 229–30). Adorno (2001, p. 230) adds that 'all fascist agitators dwell upon the imminence of catastrophes of some kind. Whereas they warn of impending danger, they and their listeners get a thrill out of the idea of inevitable doom, without even making a clear-cut distinction between the destruction of their foes and of themselves. This mental behavior (was) clearly observed during the first years of Hitlerism in Germany, and has a deep archaic basis'. Adorno (2001, p. 230) invokes 'one of the West Coast demagogues (who) once said: "I want to say that you men and women, you and I are living in the most fearful time of the history of the world. We are living also in the most gracious and most wonderful time" and comments that 'this is the agitator's dream, a union of the horrible and the wonderful, a delirium of annihilation masked as salvation'. For fascist or radical-right tendencies and the problem of lying demagogues in the US from the 1950s to post-2016 see also Hahl et al. (2018), Lipset (1955), and MacLean (2018).

TABLE 8   Forms and agents of capitalist dictatorship as civil society

---

capitalist autocracy in civil society
capitalist dynasty in civil society
capitalist plutocracy, oligarchy, and aristocracy in civil society
secondary forms of capitalist dictatorship in civil society
    capitalist police states and military dictatorships in civil society
    capitalist theocracies in civil society

---

of 'fascism', compatible with that many of its instances are fascist regimes politically.

4   Forms and Agents of Capitalist Dictatorship as Civil Society

The forms and agents of capitalist dictatorship as civil society are identical to those in its facets as a political regime and economic system, with some additions and variations. They span therefore from capitalist autocracy and dynasty to aristocracy, oligarchy and plutocracy, as well as police states, military dictatorships and theocracies. Aside from minor and uncertain exceptions like kleptocracy and predatory capitalism, most political and economic forms and agents of capitalist dictatorship do not limit themselves to the polity and economy and instead expand from these realms of the social system to civil society and operate in the non-political and non-economic private, including moral and intimate, sphere, invading and colonizing the 'life-world'. Additional forms and agents include theocracy and theocrats and similar theocentric entities and actors within capitalism that especially characterize and often prevail in moralistic or puritanical and religiously driven, 'faith-based' capitalist dictatorship that conservative-American, Catholic-Polish and Islamic regimes exemplify. Altogether, the spectrum of forms and agents of capitalist dictatorship as civil society is as rich, varied and entwined as that in its facets as a political and economic system, with a pertinent addition of capitalist theocracy and theocrats or theocratic capitalism and capitalists, American 'Bible-Belt', Catholic-Polish and Islamic Saudi-Arabia style.

4.1   Capitalist Autocracy and Dynasty in Civil Society
Autocracy and family dynasty in capitalism far from limiting to the polity and economy typically, with some secondary exceptions, move from the two

domains to civil society and operate in the private sphere of social life. They thus effect a kind of autocratic and dynastic—both capitalistic and political—invasion and colonization of the informal non-economic and non-political 'life-world'. Consequently, capitalist autocracy, dynasty and related elite becomes a mode of control and constraint of civil society, especially of the sphere of individual liberty, choice and privacy with regard to outside individuals and groups and generally non-capital social strata, simply outsiders and commoners. Capitalist autocracy or dynasty tends to be overall as coercive, repressive and exclusionary within civil society, thereby effectively eliminating or perverting it into its opposite, as does in the polity and economy. Capitalist autocrats, family dynasties and similar elites seek to control, constraint and coerce civil society in that they negate and suppress individual liberty or privacy for outsiders, just as controlling and constraining the polity and economy by negating and suppressing political and economic freedoms for out-groups.

Furthermore, capitalist autocracy or dynasty aims to attain and sustain Weberian monopolistic closure of civil society, as of the economy and polity. It performs such closure by monopolizing individual liberty, choice and privacy for itself to the point of 'license to kill' literally or figuratively and akin to the unlimited freedom and personal 'fulfilment' of pre-capitalist autocrats or dynasties, while denying the same free sphere to out-groups and non-capital and similar strata generally. It thereby replicates the template of its predecessors like feudal lords who denied such freedom to outsiders and non-aristocratic commoners, English-style.[21] Such monopolistic closure moves toward attaining and perpetuating the compound of the Hobbesian state of nature as anarchy in civil society for capitalist autocracy/dynasty and of Leviathan as control and constraint and coercion for non-capital strata. This dual formula looks functionally equivalent to the duality in this respect between pre-capitalist autocrats or dynasties and outsiders, as in slavery, caste, feudalism or master-servant systems. Like their autocratic predecessors and role models, capitalist autocrats or dynasties reserve individual liberty, autonomous personal development for themselves and negate it to outsiders such as workers and peasants.[22] They do this by imposing by legal coercion their

---

21   Giddens (2000, p. 74) remarks that 'as it stands, the House of Lords is an anachronism in a democratic society'. Piketty (2014, p. 28) more broadly remarks that England retains 'political privileges for the hereditary nobility (reform of the House of Lords is still under discussion, a bit late in the day)' (see also Dow and Reed 2013).

22   Moore (1993, pp. 430–1) suggests that a historical condition of democratic development in Western countries was the 'prevention of an aristocratic-bourgeois coalition against the peasantry and workers'.

norms of conduct on civil society, notably those of proper moral action, what Schumpeter calls 'bourgeois standards' of morality and the 'scheme of bourgeois motivation', on all other social groups, which displays in Mannheim's opinion the 'organizational anomaly' of 'bourgeois' civil society. They express capitalist dictatorship's tendency especially in its moralistic-religious variety to, as Pareto observes for the US plutocratic government, imposing rigid puritanical morality by coercion on civil society, particularly non-capitalist and other out-groups, committing violations of individual freedom 'abuses of power'.

Empirically, capitalist autocracy and dynasty in the context of civil society and generally characterize mostly and often dominate in non-Western societies. These include most of South America historically and to some extent presently, Africa, parts of Asia until recently or presently, including Singapore, South Korea, Taiwan, Thailand, and Philippines, much of Eastern Europe during the transition to autocratic or oligarchic capitalism since the 1990s through the present, especially Hungary and Poland. However, these forms and agents also in part persist and even reemerge in Western societies. This includes syndromes of capitalist autocracy in Great Britain and America during Thatcherism and Reaganism and especially in the second after 2016 and those of family dynasty in France, Italy, Spain and in part Germany, the post-2016 US and Brexit Britain, along with corporate-fascist autocracies and family dynasties in interwar Germany, Italy and Spain.

Still, capitalist autocracy or family dynasty in civil society, as in the polity and economy, tends to become less typical for Western societies—though its reemergence and prominence in the post-2016 US counters this trend—than for non-Western countries and less sociologically relevant than its collective counterparts, oligarchy and plutocracy. In particular, autocracy in civil society, as in the polity, does not exhaust capitalist and any dictatorship and is less frequent and salient among Western societies, aside from post-2016 American exceptionalism, than oligarchy and plutocracy. This casts doubt on many economists' equation of autocracies with dictatorships by reducing the second to the first. In sum, autocracy and family dynasty are particular forms and agents of capitalist dictatorship as illiberal, unfree civil society primarily among non-Western societies, albeit persisting or recurring in some of their Western counterparts such as the post-2016 US and Brexit Britain.

4.2   Capitalist Plutocracy, Oligarchy, and Aristocracy in Civil Society

In addition, plutocracy as capitalist aristocracy or oligarchy typically moves and expands its power and domination from the economy and polity to civil society and operates as the dominant force in the private sphere of the social system and in that sense performs the plutocratic colonizing of the 'life-world' by wealth. In consequence, plutocracy and plutocrats generalize into—by contrast to autocracy as personal, relatively unstable or transient unless hereditary or dynastic—a more stable, enduring and effective collective form and agent of control and constraint of civil society. This specifically entails controlling and constraining the sphere of individual liberty, choice and privacy with respect to non-plutocratic out-groups, simply outsiders or commoners in the English tradition. In this way, like autocracy but collectively and enduringly, plutocracy reshapes civil society after its own mode of coercion and exclusion and eliminates or distorts it as the free private and informal non-economic and non-political realm of the social system.

On this account, plutocracy and thus capitalist aristocracy or oligarchy appears as coercive and exclusionary within civil society converted into the realm of individual unfreedom and exclusion of non-plutocratic strata as does in the economy and polity. This is consistent with plutocracy's nature as the total or comprehensive 'dictatorship of the rich' encompassing all or most realms of the social system. Just as tending to dominate the economy and constrict democracy in that they suppress political and economic liberties for non-plutocrats, plutocrats as capitalist aristocrats or oligarchs aims at dominating and constricting or compressing civil society beyond recognition by suppressing individual liberty for out-groups and outsiders. In President Roosevelt's words, 'all-American' plutocracy and plutocrats such as the robber barons of the Gilded Age exert the 'tyranny of mere wealth' not only over workers in the economy and citizens in the polity, but also, by not stopping in these two realms, over non-plutocratic individuals within civil society. They do so by invading and colonizing the latter's private 'life-world', including literally their homes through Prohibition and the later war on drugs and sexual sins, thus tyrannizing most of the social system, including its cultural subsystem as elaborated in the next chapter.

Moreover, just as autocracy and family dynasty, plutocracy pursues and usually succeeds to reach Weberian monopolistic closure of civil society and thus of the free private or informal domain of the social system, as does that of the economy and polity in interconnection and reciprocal intensification. Equally, it performs this operation by monopolizing individual liberty, choice and privacy for plutocrats and depriving non-plutocratic groups from these elemental entitlements and rights in a liberal-democratic society. The first process approaches the threshold of collective 'license to kill' in the literal sense of use of brutal physical force against non-capital, as in American Gilded- Age capitalism, or in the figurative meaning of the unrestricted liberty to coerce and oppress, and analogous to the unlimited freedom of pre-capitalist aristocrats.

The second process resembles the unfreedom of non-aristocratic populations or commoners in feudalism. Plutocracy reestablishes the aristocratic duality of absolute freedom for pre-capitalist aristocrats and complete unfreedom of the populace in the functionally equivalent form. This is a dual complex in civil society of Hobbesian anarchy and the unconstrained state of nature for the plutocratic stratum and Leviathan-style overarching control and intense constraint of non-plutocratic strata. Plutocrats or capitalist oligarchs appropriate and exalt individual liberty and choice, free personal development and privacy but only for themselves. And they deprive outsiders from the same privileges and rights which they devaluate and even condemn with respect to non-plutocratic and non-oligarchic groups, just as their aristocratic ancestors and role models did.

This process involves coercive imposition of plutocracy's patterns and norms of behavior in civil society on the latter as a whole, in particular appropriate moral conduct ('bourgeois standards' of morality') on non-plutocratic groups, which Pareto implies by observing the US plutocratic government's penchant for enforcing puritanical 'morality by law' on the entire population. By so doing, plutocracy extends and exploits its power and domination from the economy and polity to civil society, as Pareto puts it, commits 'abuses of power' in the latter. In turn, it merges or allies with theocracy as the most extreme coercive enforcement of morality and religion, along with fascism, especially Nazism, that still tends, with minor variations, to be theocratic or extremely religious. As Pareto implies, such an imposition is an abuse of power because it commits a violation of moral freedom and generally incompatible with civil society as a setting impervious or resistant to strict control and constraint, so intrinsically unconstrained. It is a violation because civil society in that sense represents the only true domain of laissez-faire by virtue of being private, informal space without pertinent external adverse effects in contrast to the market and economy as the public realm with frequent negative and destructive externalities making laissez-faire impossible or self-defeating.

In empirical terms, unlike autocracy and dynasty, plutocracy and in that sense capitalist aristocracy or oligarchy in respect of civil society almost equally characterizes and prevail in both Western and non-Western societies. This is contrary to many economists that tend to relegate plutocracy or oligarchy to the third world and absolve or purify the West from this—as they imply by doing so—impurity of capitalism as the presumed pure unmitigated good. Recall that Pareto already identifies plutocracy as the 'ruling power in civilized countries today', notably the 'present plutocratic regime in the civilized countries of the West', and depicts Western democracies as becoming growingly 'demagogic plutocracies', while considering plutocracy the 'new aristocracy and oligarchy' of capital. In a similar vein, his contemporaries US President Roosevelt and Weber point specifically to the American variant of plutocracy with its traits of 'tyranny of mere wealth' and 'naked plutocracy' whose wealth effectively purchases power and thus domination and coercion of non-plutocratic strata. Most notable in terms of civil society's elimination, Pareto identifies moralistic plutocracy in America through the coercive imposition of plutocratic Puritan morality on the population, thus its merger with religiously driven coercion versus personal moral freedom and privacy, along with his contemporaries Sombart, Scheler and Mencken. In addition, capitalist-fascist dictatorships in interwar Germany, Italy and Spain exemplify moralistic plutocracies or oligarchies eliminating civil society, just as autocracies and dynasties, as is, with some qualifications, the case with those in postwar South America, especially Chile.

Further and more recent instances involve parts of Asia, including South Korea, Singapore and Taiwan, along with their autocracies and dynasties, most of Africa, virtually all Eastern European countries after the 1990s as plutocracies or plutocratic oligarchies that tend to be moralistic, theocratic or religiously coercive and conservative, as Hungary and Poland show. Additional cases include Islamic capitalist plutocracies, especially Saudi Arabia and other Gulf states and Turkey, along with Britain and America during neo-conservatism and the second post-2016, and so on. For example, what observers identify as a resurgent plutonomy in these two countries tends to be as moralistic-religious and coercive as was in Pareto's time. It does so by continuing and escalating the enforcement of 'morality by law' through multiple temperance wars on moral sins and personal freedom, choice and privacy of which the Reagan 'war on drugs' is the most egregious instance causing unrivaled levels of mass imprisonment, along with extreme economic irrationality.

In general, in light of the rarity of autocracy and the decline of dynasty in most Western societies, except for the US post-2016, plutocracy or plutocratic oligarchy reasserts itself as the sociologically most important form and agent of capitalist dictatorship in terms of civil society, just as economy and polity, in these and, along with autocracies and dynasties, non-Western settings. What epitomizes and implements capitalist dictatorship in civil society, just as in the economy and polity, is primarily plutocracy or plutocratic oligarchy in most societies. This suggests that economists and other scholars are well-advised to follow Pareto and sociologists in paying more attention to Western and other plutocracies or oligarchies compared to third-world autocracies. In sum, plutocracy or plutocratic oligarchy represents a principal form and agent of capitalist dictatorship as civil society, just as an economic-political structure, especially among Western and comparable societies.

4.3   Secondary Forms of Capitalist Dictatorship in Civil Society
First, police states and military dictatorships and their leaders in capitalism, as
distinct from those in pre- and post-capitalism, represent additional forms and
agents of capitalist dictatorship in its dimension of civil society, as they do in
its facet of a political regime. Like others, capitalist police states suppress and
eventually extinguish civil society through suppressing individual and other
civil liberties and rights for non-capital strata and coercing and repressing
them by mass imprisonment, widespread executions, mistreatment, torture
and other acts of state 'political terror'. These include terrorizing the low and
underclass by the specter of the death penalty as 'selective terror' in conservative America.[23] Similarly, but often more immediately and violently, capitalist
military dictatorships practically destroy civil society by eliminating individual and other civil liberties and rights for these and related groups and their
repression through such practices involving the use of military force or militarized coercion in the private sphere and beyond. On this account, capitalist
police states and military dictatorships function as direct, violent mechanisms
of over-control, severe constraint and elimination of civil society, namely the
free private and related sphere for non-capital and related strata.

Empirically, not all police states and military dictatorships in respect of civil
society are capitalist, with many being pre-capitalist, although the first mostly
as proxies in pre-capitalism, and non-capitalist regimes. However, most capitalist dictatorships as civil societies and political regimes, represent police
states in varying degrees and ways and many are military dictatorships—and
often both. For example, Pareto's observation of the US government's imposition of puritanical morals by coercion and committing 'gross abuses of power'
looks as describing a capitalist moralistic vice-police state. This applies to
other early and latter observations to that effect, including those of police surveillance, brutality and massive unrivaled personnel and resources centering
on policing human vices and sins as 'crimes' through a myriad of puritanical
wars from Prohibition to the 'war on drugs'. At the minimum, this holds for
the US South as the 'Bible Belt' that appears as such a vice-police state in the

---

23   Bauman (2001, p. 39) observes that the 'spectacle of execution is 'cynically used by (US)
politicians to terrorize a growing underclass'. But in demanding the terrorization of the
underclass, the silent American majority attempts to terrorize its own inner demons'.
Jacobs et al. (2005, p. 657) cite the view that in the US the 'death penalty was used by
powerful groups to protect their privileges with selective terror' especially in the Southern
states that 'once had the highest lynching rates (and) now appear to use the death sentence most often'. As noted, Besley and Persson (2009, p. 292) adopt the notion of a
'political terror scale including civil and other human rights violations such as execution,
imprisonment and others.

function of capital domination and theocracy or religious coercion and control of civil society. More broadly, corporate-fascist dictatorships in interwar
Germany, Italy and Spain, were exemplary police states and military dictatorships in an osmosis destroying civil society, as are their postwar variations in
South America, most notoriously Chile,[24] and their reenactments in some for-
merly fascist countries of Eastern Europe such as Hungary.

Additionally, capitalist dictatorships in much of Asia such as South Korea,
Singapore and Taiwan have been or still are police states and military dictatorships in unison, just as are mostly the first and often both in Islamic countries,
including Saudi Arabia and Turkey, and the second in Africa. Also, capitalist
dictatorships in the form of oligarchies or autocracies in many Eastern countries after the 1990s approach police states perverting civil society in the service
of oligarchy or autocracy in Hungary, while conjoined with resurgent theocracy
in Catholic-dominated, conservative-ruled Poland. Lastly, police states and
military dictatorships or militarized coercion within capitalism against civil
society and individual freedom for non-capital strata persist, retrench, even
proliferate and expand in a range of societies. They span from America post-
2016 and Brexit Britain to via global contagion or convergence South America
like Brazil, parts of Asia, and some former fascist European countries such as
Austria, Hungary and the Baltic states, while targeting low classes, including
minority and immigrant populations.

Next, theocracy and more broadly theocentric regimes within capitalism—
as distinct from those in pre-capitalism—manifest an additional, 'new' form
and agent of capitalist dictatorship as civil society, while being already implicit
in its facet as a political regime. As noted, capitalist dictatorship tends to
expand from economic-political to moralistic and, under some conditions,
religious dictatorship within civil society, as in the polity. When it expands into
or merges with religious dictatorship, it effectively becomes or approaches
capitalist theocracy, including 'pure' and 'diluted' theocracies and more
broadly theocentric regimes within capitalism.[25] Consequently, capitalist theocracy arises as the outcome of capitalist dictatorship merging coercion and

---

24   Huber and Stephens (2005, p. 560) observe that 'Chile implemented these reforms (pri-
     vatization, etc.) earlier and to a greater extent than any other country under the military
     dictatorship. Power was highly concentrated in the hands of Pinochet, and opposition
     was dealt with ruthlessly. The neoliberal project was attractive to the military not only for
     economic but also for political reasons, because it would atomize civil society and remove
     the state as a target for collective action'.
25   Sorokin (1970, p. 15) refers to 'pure or diluted theocracy' (see also Bénabou et al. 2015;
     Mueller 2009).

oppression in the economy and polity with moralistic and especially religious control and constraint of civil society, specifically individual liberty, choice and privacy for non-capital and similar strata. Alternatively, and perhaps more frequently in historical terms, pre-capitalist theocracy can precede and render capitalist dictatorship into a moralistic-religious regime within civil society and thus a moralizing and theocratic structure in its own right. This is what Puritan and Islamic theocracies in America (from New England to the South) and Saudi Arabia and other Gulf states demonstrate.

In any event, capitalist theocracy develops and functions as the 'holy' and thus extreme form and agent—the pinnacle and destination—of capitalist dictatorship within civil society, as in the polity. Relatedly, it is the 'godly', ultimate and most effective mechanism of imposing and sustaining capitalist dictatorship especially when all other, secular mechanisms of its imposition and reproduction, including police states and military dictatorships, prove ineffective or insufficient. As a result, like its pre-capitalist precursor, capitalist theocracy tends to be more enduring and obstinate, extensive and intense than most non-religious forms and agents of capitalist and other dictatorship. This is consistent with the tendency for theocratic or religious dictatorial regimes and rulers to endure and persevere longer—in eternity or infinity in their design of eternal 'God's kingdom'—and to be more sanctimonious and uncompromising as 'God's agents' with 'divine rights' than their secular versions. By becoming moralistic-religious or resorting to morality and especially religion as the ultimate weapon of its imposition and preservation, capitalist dictatorship assumes the form of theocracy or theocentric control and constraint within civil society, as in the polity.

Accordingly, capitalist theocracy operates as the 'sacred' and thus the most lethal poison and its theocrats act as 'holy' (Christian, Islamic and other) warriors against civil society, specifically the private and related sphere and individual liberty and choice of non-capital and non-religious strata, just as versus liberal-secular democracy. Like police states and military dictatorships but with 'holy' and so infinite determination, persistence and sanctimony, capitalist theocracy completely extinguishes civil society, especially such a sphere and liberty. Conversely, it creates and imposes the dark space of illiberty and extreme constraint of these strata and in that sense the 'peace of the cemetery'[26] after the image of the secularly lifeless 'Bible Belt'.

---

26 Mises (1951, p. 96) use the expression the 'peace of the cemetery' due to being 'based on an eternal government' in reference to 'socialism' rather than theocracy though disingenuously tries to equate the first with the second, failing to distinguish secular and religious dictatorships, including that in the US South as the 'Bible Belt'. In an apparent failure to

In consequence, civil society, notably individual liberty and choice for non-capital and 'ungodly' strata, becomes an extinct category and taboo, indeed a non sequitur, impossibility theorem in capitalist theocracy. This is what evangelical America and Turkey under Islamic rule and Saudi Arabia and other Gulf states show, along with pre- and non-capitalist theocracies like Iran and Taliban and the Christian 'Dark' Middle Ages. In essence, whenever and wherever capitalist theocracy begins and thrives, civil society and individual liberty for non-capital and non-religious strata in particular ends or decays, as does liberal-secular democracy. Capitalist theocracy develops and functions as the most destructive form and agent of capitalist dictatorship in respect of civil society and thus individual liberty, choice and privacy—the space of personal illiberty 'for all'. This holds except for capitalists-theocrats as of the 'elect', as Weber identifies them in Calvinist capitalism, or 'godly' plutocrats within the American 'Religious Right'.

Hence, if moralistic capitalist dictatorship operates as proxy 'moral fascism' within civil society, it does most manifestly, strongly and persistently in the form and through the agency of capitalist theocracy and related forms and agents. In this regard, capitalist theocracy represents or approaches 'moral-religious fascism' in civil society, namely the fascist-style 'holy' control, constraint, terror and elimination of the latter. It does so by extinguishing the individual liberty, choice and privacy and often life for most groups in, as Pareto sarcastically states, the 'name of the divine master' and committing state and anti-state 'terror in the mind God'. At the minimum, it becomes the religious analogue and

---

predict even medium-term social change Mises fails to notice or realize that 'an eternal government' typifies evangelical theocracy such as both the ante- and post-bellum 'Bible Belt' for more than two centuries rather than 'socialism' that lasted just a few decades as in Eastern Europe and any secular society. Simply, Weber's Southern Bibliocracy almost eternalizes itself while 'socialism' is 'gone with the wind'. Yet, if Mises were sufficiently impartial and lived long enough in the 'Bible Belt' (including Alabama where a namesake institute is established), he would have definitely used the description the 'peace of the cemetery' by being 'based on an eternal government' for the South, especially its sleepy, church-saturated small towns, as for Soviet 'socialism'. More broadly, Jurgeensmeyer (2003, p. 217) observes that the 'absolutism of religion has been revealed especially in the notion of cosmic war. Although left-wing movements subscribe to what may seem a similar idea—the concept of class conflict—ordinarily this contest is thought to take place only on a social plane and within the temporal limitations of history. In fact, in the more humane versions of Marxist conflict theory, persons can be separated from their class roles: capitalists, for instance, can be reeducated, as the leaders in Mao Zedong's Chinese communist regime attempted to do with former landlords and businessmen. Religious concepts of cosmic war, however, are ultimately beyond historical control, even though they are identified with this-worldly struggles. A satanic enemy cannot be transformed; it can only be destroyed'.

covariate of political and ideological fascism in the strict sense, as the description of the Christian Right as 'American fascists' suggests.[27]

Historical and current tendencies and examples support this characterization. Many capitalist as well as pre-capitalist theocracies have been and still are fascist, radical-right and generally conservative dictatorships, at least have elements of fascism. This is what Puritan-evangelical theocracy in America, its Catholic variant in South America and Poland, and its Islamic counterparts in Saudi Arabia and other Gulf states and in part Turkey demonstrate—they are all ultra-conservative regimes. Conversely and more manifestly and indisputably, virtually all fascist or radical-right and other conservative dictatorships have been and are capitalist and pre-capitalist theocracies or theocentric, religiously-overdetermined regimes. Even supposedly non-theocratic and irreligious Nazi dictatorship was theocentric in the sense of being closely linked with religion as its 'sacred' mechanism and support, as were even more manifestly other fascist dictatorships in Italy, Spain, Portugal and Croatia as Catholic theocracies in religious terms. Similarly, neo-fascist dictatorships in South America, most notoriously Chile, represented such Catholic-capitalist theocracies in these terms, and the trend continues at present in some of these countries like Brazil and in part Colombia.

The preceding suggests capitalist theocracy permeates historically and even presently some Western and many non-Western societies. Still, it tends to decline in Western societies since the defeat of theocratic fascism, with the persistent and salient American exceptionalism in the form of evangelical America, decreasingly England and persistently Catholic-overdetermined Ireland with its persistent Draconian abortion prohibitions and other theocratic syndromes. Capitalist and pre-capitalist theocracy persists and even pervades much of the non-Western world, including parts of Eastern Europe such as Poland and Hungary, most of Latin America, and virtually all Islamic states—except for Egypt after its short-lived theocratic regime recently—notably Iran, Turkey and Saudi Arabia and its neighbors. In particular, evangelical America such as the 'Bible Belt' of 'God and money' appears as an exemplar of capitalist theocracy or theocratic capitalism within Western society. Islamic Iran, Taliban, Turkey, Saudi Arabia and other Gulf states seem examples of increasingly capitalist and decreasingly pre-capitalist theocracy, along with Catholic-dominated Poland and Latin America, in the non-Western world. In sum, capitalist theocracy emerges as the outcome of the process of

---

27   'Terror in the mind God' is from Jurgensmeyer (2003), 'American fascists' from Hedges
      (2006), see also Adorno (2001) and Bruce (2004).

moralization and religious over-determination or connotation of capitalist dictatorship. Consequently, it operates as the ultimate and most destructive form and agent of the latter in relation to civil society by eliminating individual liberty, choice, privacy and ultimately, as through 'holy' terror and war, life for non-capital and non-religious strata.

5   Indicators and Proxies of Capitalist Dictatorship as Civil Society

Indicators and proxies of capitalist dictatorship as civil society complement, interrelate with and reinforce, just as are reinforced by, those of it especially as a political regime, as well as an economic system. Capitalist dictatorship indicates itself within the setting of civil society in a manner that is complementary, compatible and mutually reinforcing with its self-indication in the political regime and to some degree the economic system, manifesting its self-coherence and totality. Specifically, these civil-society indicators of capitalist dictatorship entail suppression of individual liberty and other civil liberties, negation and invasion of individual human rights such as privacy, criminalization and severe punishment of moral sins-as-crimes, and consequently, moralistic-religious terror with massive populations of prisoners of ethical conscience, including death sentences and executions for such and related reasons.

5.1   *Suppression of Individual Liberty and Other Civil Liberties*
Suppression and consequently the non-existence or minimum degree of individual liberty and other civil liberties for non-capital represents the foremost indicator and hallmark of capitalist dictatorship as illiberal civil society,

TABLE 9   Indicators and proxies of capitalist dictatorship as civil society

suppression of individual liberty
    denial of personal freedom of moral choice
suppression of other civil liberties
negation of civil and other human rights
    negation and invasion of individual human rights—privacy
criminalization and severe sanctioning of moral offenses
moralistic-religious terror
    massive populations of prisoners of ethical conscience

as of other dictatorships. Therefore, capitalist dictatorship from third-world autocracy and military dictatorships to Western plutocracy and police/security states conforms to and exhibits the blueprint of dictatorships, as of pre-capitalist despotism. This contradicts the allegations of 'American exceptionalism' in authoritarian 'unfettered' capitalism as laissez-faire ('free enterprise') for capital versus oppression for non-capital.)

Suppression of and hence non-existent or minimal individual liberty and other civil liberties for non-capital and related social strata typifies capitalist dictatorship, as it does pre-capitalist dictatorships. Capitalist dictatorship through such suppression of civil liberties forms the process and social space of individual illiberty for non-capital strata, mixed with unlimited aristocratic-style liberty for capital, including autocracy, dynasty, oligarchy and plutocracy, as pre-capitalist despotism does in relation to non-aristocratic groups and aristocracy, respectively. It therefore evolves into the Hobbesian state of nature and individual anarchy for capital and Leviathan for, via over-control, coercion and personal unfreedom of, non-capital social strata, perpetuating the duality of pre-capitalist despotism with regard to aristocracy and the non-aristocratic populace. In this regard, capitalist dictatorship hardly seems new, distinct and original compared to pre-capitalist despotism, in particular plutocracy in capitalism in relation to aristocracy in feudalism and the 'old spirit of master-caste'.

While proclaiming the 'scheme of bourgeois motivation' and the 'bourgeois penchant for laissez-faire' in the economy in theory for all, in reality solely for capital, capitalist dictatorship rejects the same principle in civil society for non-capital strata. Notably, it does this in the realm of private moral action as in effect, because of its typical lack of negative externalities, the only genuine space for the application of laissez-faire in contrast to the market/economy as a public domain with both positive and adverse external effects. Evidently, the 'scheme of bourgeois motivation' and taste for personal freedom and other civil liberties, along with profit and power, does not apply to non-bourgeois individuals and groups—they 'need not apply'—and the 'bourgeois penchant for laissez-faire' stops before civil society, notably private morality, for these outcasts and out-groups. Such tendencies in capitalist dictatorship evidently continue or evoke aristocratic motivations and penchants versus the non-aristocratic populace and commoners, as manifest and persistent especially in English capitalist plutocracy.

5.1.1   Denial of Personal Freedom of Moral Choice
In particular, moralistic and religious capitalist dictatorship such as theocracy or theocentric government denies and suppresses a myriad of individual and other civil liberties and rights, notably personal freedom of choice in moral

action, for non-capital and related social strata. This entails denying the most
private and intimate liberties and rights to these social strata spanning from
the freedom of consumption of alcoholic beverages and related chemical substances, as through puritanical Prohibition and the Reagan 'war on drugs' and
alcohol in conservative America, to reproductive and sexual freedoms and
rights. This process proceeds in conjunction and mutual reinforcement with
the suppression of their political and economic freedoms. In moralistic and
religious capitalist dictatorship conservative-American and Islamic style, non-
capital and non-religious social groups are unfree or controlled, coerced, constrained and monitored even in their home with regard to their private moral
activities and indeed intentions—the 'intent to commit' sin-as-crime in the
US criminal justice system—that the totalistic vice-policing state detects and
deciphers.

Such a tendency renders capitalist dictatorship in its moralistic-religious or
theocratic and generally conservative version closer to an Orwellian perverted
civil society of totalitarian moral control, constraint and high-tech surveillance
than any pre-capitalist dictatorships have been. It generates, as in conservative
America since Reaganism, the dystopian less crime, more severe punishment
condition nearly replicating Puritan theocracy's witch trials and other acts of
'sacrificial violence'.[28] Capitalist dictatorship in such a puritanical rendition
effectively makes non-capital social strata's homes, their lives and generally
civil society a macroscopic open prison, just as the polity/economy is for millions of US former prisoners denied basic political freedoms and rights and
subjected to perpetual Puritan-style punishment, discrimination and hardship
after their release. Relatedly, it converts civil society into an all-encompassing
monastery of saints and sinners punishing the latter with Draconian Puritan
severity, as in conservative America since Reaganism. It therefore acts as if
implementing the Calvinist 'You think you have escaped from the monastery,
but everyone must now be a monk throughout his life' injunction in Weber's
account.[29]

---

28   Gorski and Türkmen-Dervişoğlu (2013, p. 187) alert to 'modern episodes of sacrificial vio-
      lence, such as the (Puritan) New England witch craze (plus) the violent cults of the 1980s,
      such as those in Jamestown and Waco'. See also Bruch et al. (2010), Cable et al. (2008),
      Cooney and Burt (2008), and King et al. (2012).
29   Weber's (1950, pp. 365–6) elaborates that in the Middle Ages in the West the 'monk is the
      first human being who lives rationally, who works methodically and by rational means
      toward a goal, the future life. The economic life of the monastic communities was also
      rational. But the rational mode of life remained restricted to the monastic circles. The
      Reformation made a decisive break with this system (by the injunction) 'You think you
      have escaped from the monastery, but everyone must now be a monk throughout his life'.

Capitalist dictatorship allows non-capital social strata formal individual freedom in product and financial markets as sellers or byers, but not in the labor market as group agents via union organization, action and collective bargaining. Such a freedom is, however, what Simmel[30] denotes a spurious 'compensatory substitute' for their private moral unfreedom and other civil illiberty, simply 'ersatz' liberty.[31] Capitalist dictatorship negates individual, especially moral agency, dignity and responsibility to non-capital actors and monopolizes these capabilities and entitlements for capital—just as their collective action in the economy and polity—thus replicating the pattern of pre-capitalist despotism with respect to non-aristocratic groups and aristocracy, respectively. Consequently, non-capitalists, especially non-plutocrats, become what Tönnies[32] calls 'nonentities' in terms of individual agency or as personal agents within capitalist dictatorship, as do with respect to collective economic and political action or as group actors, evoking the subordinate status of non-aristocratic groups in pre-capitalism.

Suppression of individual liberty and other civil liberties and rights, especially personal freedom of moral choice and privacy, for non-capital and related social strata hence identifies capitalist dictatorship especially in its moralistic and religious conservative rendition in terms of civil society. Conversely, capitalist dictatorship in this rendition reveals itself precisely by its suppression of such and other civil liberties and rights for these groups. In consequence,

---

The wide significance of this transformation of the ascetic ideal can be followed down to the present. It is especially discernible in the import of the religions denominations' in the US' (see also Collins 1980; Parsons 1935).

30   By contrast, Simmel (1955, p. 166) suggests that pre-capitalist despotism denies political freedom to its subjects but permits them some degree of individual moral liberty and privacy as well as economic freedoms stating that early 'tyranny is correlated with and indeed support the most perfect freedom and an utter abandon of all restraint in those personal relations which have no importance to its own purpose. This is an expedient distribution of collective coercion and individual arbitrariness (as a) compensatory substitute'. This implies that capitalist dictatorship in its puritanical American as well as Islamic version by suppressing both political and personal moral freedoms is even more intense and totalistic than and thus hardly a 'progress'—despite the formally free status of non-capital and non-religious strata—compared to pre-capitalist despotism.

31   Relatedly, Adorno (1991, pp. 39, 77) points to 'ersatz satisfaction' in the 'frozen modernity of monopoly and state capitalism'.

32   Tönnies (2001, p. 71) states that 'capitalists—possessors of money which can be increased by double exchange—are the natural lords and masters of commercial Society. *Gesellschaft* exists for their sake and is their tool. All non-capitalists within Society are either themselves like inanimate tools—the very essence of slavery—or they are legally nonentities, deemed incapable of exercising rational choice, therefore unable to make contracts valid within the system'. For the concept of agency see Barnes (2000).

capitalist dictatorship features the lowest degree of individual liberty, notably personal freedom of moral choice, and of other civil liberties in comparative terms among the variants of capitalism and types of social system, particularly, a lower one than that of its opposite, the fusion of egalitarian welfare capitalism with liberal-secular democracy. Especially moralistic-religious capitalist dictatorship tends more to suppress intimate reproductive liberties and rights (birth control, abortion), personal sexual freedoms (premarital sex, homosexuality, prostitution, pornography), the freedom of consumption of alcoholic beverages and related chemical substances (certain medically effective or less harmful recreational drugs). Overall, such capitalist dictatorship suppresses civil liberties for non-capital and related social groups more than other variants of capitalism and types of social system and even all dictatorships, except for allied, conservative-fascist and theocratic regimes

In empirical terms, virtually all past and present capitalist dictatorships especially their moralistic-religious de facto theocratic versions exemplify the tendency to the suppression of individual liberty and other civil liberties and rights. They range from moralistically repressive capitalism in 19th-century Victorian England and neo-Puritan America through capitalist-fascist dictatorships in Germany and Italy and Chile's 'free market' dictatorship to the first two countries during Thatcherism and Reaganism and the second after 2016, Catholic-dominated Poland and Turkey, Saudi Arabia and other Gulf states. All these seemingly disparate examples share the common practice of denying and suppressing basic individual and other civil liberties and rights. This commonality includes the suppression of personal freedom of choice spanning from that of alcohol consumption, as in America and Islamic states, to sexual freedoms especially in these two societies, and reproductive rights, as also in Catholic dictatorships such as those in South America and Poland (plus Ireland even if with some partial moderation).

For example, as Pareto predicts, conservative America's capitalist theocracy long ago enforced puritanical 'morality by law' in the form of alcohol Prohibition through its Constitutional enforcement defining the consumption of alcoholic beverages as a grave sin-crime and the ground to change the Constitution to eradicate it. In this sense, it acted with what he calls Puritan-style sadistic-masochistic 'insanity'.[33] It continues to do so through what Merton identifies as 'dry' Sothern states and various other restrictions, just as

---

33   Pareto (2000, p. 106) apparently anticipating Prohibition remarks that that 'it is not only abuse that (anti-alcoholic groups) wish to combat but even the most moderate use; and it is herein that the religious and sectarian sentiments can be decried'. Further, Pareto (2000, p. 107) notes a symptom of moralistic and religious sadism-masochism in that 'certain men experience great delight in tormenting themselves and others', invoking Puritanism (the Scotch Presbyterian clergy's code) in which 'all the natural affections, all

launching additional puritanical wars on sins-as-crimes. Among these wars, the most notorious is the 'war on drugs' causing an unrivaled explosion of prison populations, along with the recurring warfare on reproductive rights in the 'Bible Belt' and beyond, all applying Draconian sanctions up to life in prison and the death penalty. Among modern Western societies, Prohibition and the 'war in drugs' in America qualify each in its own right as the epitome and pandemonium of the suppression of individual liberty, notably personal freedoms of moral choice, and related civil liberties and rights in capitalist dictatorship, which only equivalent practices in Islamic capitalist theocracies like Saudi Arabia and other Gulf states rival. If one does not know what capitalist dictatorship in its moralistic and religious, indeed theocratic rendition is or whether it exists, taking account of these and related episodes and trends can solve the problem.

In sum, the suppression and consequently non-existence or minimum level of individual liberty, notably personal freedom of moral choice, and other civil liberties and rights for non-capital strata provides a salient indicator and identifier of capitalist dictatorship as civil society. This primarily holds for moralistic and religious capitalist dictatorship as the social space of individual and other civil illiberty, particularly personal unfreedom of choice in moral action, for these groups and hence the unfree sphere abolishing civil society.

5.2   Negation of Civil and Other Human Rights

Relatedly, the negation and violation of civil and other human rights specifically of non-capital and similar social strata constitutes another pertinent feature and syndrome of capitalist dictatorship, as of other dictatorships. It denies in various ways that non-capital and related social strata have civil and other human rights and instead entitles exclusively capital with such rights. In respect of such rights, it treats these social strata as Tönnies' 'nonentities' and thus non-humans comparable, even if not legally identical, to slaves or servants, and affirms capitalists as 'natural lords and masters'. It therefore perpetuates pre-capitalist despotism such as feudalism that treated the non-aristocratic populace as a nonentity and affirmed 'master-caste' such as aristocrats as 'natural' and 'divinely ordained' rulers. Furthermore, by this dual treatment, it is consistent with later dictatorships, especially being convergent with resurgent conservative-fascist regimes that deny civil and other human

the pleasures of society, all the pastimes, all the gay instincts of the human heart were so many sins'. He concludes that 'long before, the monks had carried this kind of (Puritan) insanity to the utmost limit', specifically that 'pleasure and crime were synonyms in the monastic idiom' and they still are to our modern ascetics' (Pareto 2000, p. 107).

rights to subordinate groups and entitle solely the ruling group with them. Such a dual treatment illustrates the duality of Leviathan for non-capital social strata and Hobbesian anarchy for capital in capitalist dictatorship.

The above syndrome of capitalist dictatorship involves the negation and violation of certain core or fundamental civil and other human rights of non-capital social strata. Specifically, it negates those basic civil and other human rights that the UN Universal Declaration of Human Rights establishes and protects. Such adverse practices suggest that capitalist dictatorship usually tends to violate or disregard global conventions, rules and standards concerning civil and human rights. This is what especially conservative America from Reaganism to post-2016 demonstrates by its hostility to the UN and opposition to the Universal Declaration of Human Rights, along with other countries imitating this conduct, including Hungary and Poland under autocracy and conservative-Catholic dominance as the pariah states or deviant regimes within the European Union. Capitalist dictatorship from conservative America to autocratic Hungary and Brazil and theocratic Poland, Turkey and Saudi Arabia hence asserts and defends its sovereign national right to negate and violate global, universally established and recognized fundamental civil and other human rights by targeting non-capital and related social strata for such systematic egregious and indeed self-righteous unapologetic violations.

With regard to such practices, capitalist dictatorship becomes an equivalent of pariah state or deviant regime within the global order in the context of the UN Universal Declaration of Human Rights, as its particular instances like autocratic Hungary and theocratic Poland and Turkey are within regional associations like the European Union and NATO. Like especially conservative-fascist dictatorships, capitalist dictatorship closes itself from and dismisses the global order such as UN-based international conventions and laws about fundamental civil and other human rights, and attains and exerts an absolutely free rein in negating and violating them for non-capital and related social strata. This is what Reagan's and post-2016 conservative America especially shows while in so doing inspiring other imitators in such closure and violations like autocratic Hungary and Brazil and theocratic Poland, Turkey and Saudi Arabia. For capitalist dictatorship such as these instances fundamental civil and other human rights as established in the UN Universal Declaration of Human Rights are not worth the paper on which they are printed, which provides, as especially for conservative America, the 'patriotic' license to negate them for non-capital. This is how the merged autocracy-plutocracy in post-2016 conservative America construes basic civil and other human rights that the US Constitution establishes from due process through free speech to privacy, and consequently acquires its free rein in their violations for non-capitalist and other low and powerless strata.

As a particular facet of the above, capitalist dictatorship usually engages in negation and invasion or violation of such individual human rights as privacy specifically for these strata. Consequently, it accords with the anti-privacy pattern of dictatorships rather than being, as according to 'American exceptionalism' in capitalism, exceptional in relation to the latter. Aside from secondary variations, the negation, invasion and hence complete lack of or extremely weak privacy characterizes capitalist dictatorship ranging from autocracy and dynasty to plutocracy and oligarchy, as well as police states and military dictatorships within capitalism. In particular, the imposition of non-privacy permeates moralistic, religious and generally conservative capitalist dictatorship such as pro-capital theocracy, in which privacy essentially becomes a non-entity or taboo. Such a variant of capitalist dictatorship denies on moralistic and religious grounds the right to privacy to non-capita and similar social strata and invades and suppresses through legal coercion and political repression the free private activities of these groups within civil society. This is what especially conservative America such as the 'Bible Belt' of 'God and money' and Saudi Arabia and other Islamic plutocratic states demonstrate. Specifically, capitalist dictatorship controls, constraints and invades private actions in morality as the inherent sphere of privacy, including those most intimate at home. It permits some public activities, including those in the market through selling and buying as a 'compensatory substitute' or ersatz compensation for personal unfreedom and partly in politics via voting in elections, yet often restricted, as in the US South.

Like pre-capitalist dictatorships, capitalist dictatorship in its moralistic, religious and conservative variant detests, distrusts or fears and invades more non-capital strata's actions in their private domain of morality and intimacy than their activities in the public realm of the market and economy, fearing more what they do in the privacy of their homes than in the openness of the marketplace. This indicates the moralistic perversity, backwardness or excess of such dictatorship so long as actions in the sphere of moral privacy located in Americans' 'home sweet home' typically generate no adverse direct or tangible external consequences for society[34] in contrast to public activities in the economy with their negative and positive externalities. It is perverse or

---

34   Mueller (2013, p. 9) suggest that a non-economic, including moral action 'does no measurable physical damage to an individual, but it makes her angry or sad causing her to seek redress. Religious beliefs are a great source of psychological externalities. The religious person sees someone dressed in a "wanton" manner and becomes offended. Even contemplating an action by others, say two homosexuals having a sexual relationship, can distress a person with strong religious convictions. Thus, religious beliefs have led those

backwards hence because it violates the implicit (Pigouvian) principle[35] that one should not over-control, constrain (including tax) and generally regulate a societal activity or sphere with no relevant negative externalities and leave it to its autonomous operation of freedom, and conversely. This precisely holds for privacy in the civil-society sense of free private moral agency and responsibility. Capitalist dictatorship in its moralistic, religious and conservative variant appears anachronistic by suppressing laissez-faire where it intrinsically belongs, the private moral sphere. Instead, it imposes capitalist dictatorship where it does not belong, the public realm of the economy and solely for capital versus labor coercion resulting in 'laissez-faire authoritarianism'.[36]

On these grounds, the negation and invasion of privacy in the sense of free private moral action indicates and identifies capitalist dictatorship especially its moralistic, religious and conservative, ultimately theocratic variant. Alternatively, capitalist dictatorship exposes itself as a system of intrusion in and elimination of privacy involving free private moral actions for non-capital strata. As a consequence, capitalist dictatorship tends to have the

---

holding them to demand, and often obtain, legislation restricting the freedom to act of other individuals, even when the prohibited actions cause no physical harm'. US conservatives object that free private activities at home such as alcohol consumption, drug use and sexual acts produce negative external effects for society, notably on themselves, for example, health and related costs that they supposedly would incur ('who will pay'?). They by so doing deny or overlook that even normal private activities like excessive home food consumption (e.g., eating too much of their favorite pizza) can also produce through obesity and other conditions health and related costs as negative external effects. In addition, they are oblivious of the fact that these effects in the form of health and related costs primarily apply to conservative-dominated America and not or less to, for example, Great Britain and most other Western countries that have a free universal health care system that mostly absorbs such costs.

35 Kaplow (2004, p. 150) remarks that to solve problems involving negative (economic) externalities, economists favor internalization: Actors should be made to bear the full social costs of their decisions, such as by imposing taxes equal to the marginal external cost of their activities—Pigouvian taxation'. More broadly, Kaplow and Shavell (2007, p. 496) state that the 'moral sentiments can only imperfectly correct behavior that generates (economic) sanctions, because of the cost of inculcating the moral sentiments, limits on the capacity of individuals to experience them, and also the need to instill guilt and virtue at uniform levels over groups of acts that may exhibit heterogeneity', inferring that 'for a variety of reasons, the optimal level of the moral sanctions may be lower or higher than a Pigouvian tax benchmark, under which moral sanctions would be set equal to the level of the relevant expected (economic) externality'. Thus, they suggest that moral sanctions can correct economic externalities, and not that private moral actions generate economic externalities, which Mueller explicitly denies in the previous footnote.

36 'Laissez-faire authoritarianism' is from Perelman (2000, p. 20), see also Bartling et al. (2015).

comparatively lowest degree of privacy with respect to moral actions among the variations of capitalism and types of society, notably a considerably lower one than that of the combination of egalitarian capitalism and liberal-secular democracy.

Empirically, most capitalist dictatorships follow this pattern of negation and invasion of privacy with respect to free moral actions. As before, they range from capitalism in 19th-century Victorian England and neo-Puritan America through corporate-fascist dictatorship in interwar Germany and postwar Latin American 'free market' neo-fascist dictatorships to the first two countries during Thatcherism and Reaganism and the second post-2016 to Catholic-dominated Poland, Turkey and Saudi Arabia and other Gulf states. All they have in common denying and invading privacy in the sense of free private moral actions for non-capital and related, especially non-religious groups. For example, neo-Puritan evangelical America denies any right to privacy for lower and 'godless' groups, and US religious and political conservatives allege that the Constitution provides no assurance of privacy in moral action—no free private sphere of life in the 'land of freedom'—just as Islamic theocracies do. The rationale is that privacy in morality is a luxury that (like universal health care) one cannot afford in 'faith-based' capitalism and undermines the Religious Right's design of 'Christian America' such as the Southern and other 'Bible Belt', and of 'Islamic republics' like Iran and Turkey and monarchies in Saudi Arabia and other Gulf states. In sum, the negation and invasion or violation of privacy in the moral sphere for non-capital and related social strata supplies a complementary indicator of capitalist dictatorship as civil society, especially of its moralistic-religious rendition.

5.3   *Criminalization and Severe Sanctioning of Moral Offenses*

Another related indicator of capitalist dictatorship consists of the criminalization of moral offenses and consequently severe sanctioning of them as crimes for non-capital and related social strata. The equation of moral sins, vices and human pleasures with crimes and their consequent Draconian punishment characterizes and permeates capitalist dictatorship primarily in its moralistic-religious forms and agents such as capitalist theocracy or theocentric 'faith-based' regimes especially in evangelical America and Saudi Arabia and other plutocratic Islamic states. Alternatively, such capitalist dictatorship opposes the distinction between the two categories that liberal-secular democracy and civil society establishes and typically does not redefine and punish moral offenses as crimes.

Instead, proving to be an antithesis of liberal-secular democracy and civil society, moralistic capitalist dictatorship subsumes moral offenses into and punishes them as serious and often deadly or grave crimes. It thereby expands dramatically the scope of criminalizing and harshly punishing human behavior to leave non-criminalized and uncontrolled virtually 'nothing under the sun' of private activities, as in conservative America since Reaganism's war on drugs and other sins-as-crimes.[37] Consequently, capitalist dictatorship eliminates or perverts both liberal-secular democracy and civil society that essentially does not criminalize and harshly punish moral offenses by differentiating them from crimes, while replicating pre-capitalist despotism featuring the equation of sin and crime. If civil society is the free social space of individual liberty and privacy distinguishing moral offenses from and not sanctioning them harshly as crimes, capitalist dictatorship through its moralistic-religious connotation resembles an open prison or overarching monastery from which sinful-as-criminal humans are unable to escape. The outcome is an Orwellian no crime, Draconian punishment dystopia of puritanical and religiously sanctified 'fascism'.[38]

Therefore, the process of criminalizing and severe sanctioning moral offenses and human pleasures as crimes indicates and identifies moralistic-religious capitalist dictatorship as civil society, just as does conservative, including fascist, dictatorships At this juncture, capitalist dictatorship effectively mutates into theocracy within capitalism and converges with conservative-fascist dictatorships that completely erase or violate liberal democracy' line of demarcation between moral sins and social dissent and crimes by treating and punishing the first as the second. In consequence, far from being an advanced, different, exceptional phase of civil-society evolution—as per 'American exceptionalism' in capitalism—capitalist dictatorship descends into the darkest times of religious oppression or theocracy. For illustration, its example in conservative America, as Pareto notes, descends through its coercive enforcement of morality by puritanical hypocritical laws to the European Dark Middle Ages, while moving together with radical-right dictatorships.

Alternatively, capitalist dictatorship in its moralistic-religious variation reveals itself through equating moral sins with serious crimes and punishing them with Draconian severity emulating and occasionally, as in conservative America since Reaganism, exceeding that of pre-capitalist despotism. Such

---

37   This is admitted by conservative economist Friedman (1997), see also Bergemann (2017), Cooney and Burt (2008), Roth (2018) and Wacquant (2002).

38   For the strong historical and persistent link between religion, including especially Puritanism and Puritan-rooted evangelicalism in America, and fascism and right dictatorship overall, see Adorno (2001), Bruce (2004), Fromm (1941), Hedges (2006), McLaughlin (1996), and Mueller (2009).

Draconian punishment entails long and mass imprisonment, police brutality, torture and mistreatment, indefinite detention and continuing widespread death sentences and executions especially targeting non-capital and related lower and powerless social strata. As a consequence, capitalist dictatorship tends to engage in the most intense criminalization and severe sanctioning of moral offenses as crimes for non-capital and related strata among the variations of capitalism and types of society, dramatically more so than the complex of welfare capitalism and liberal democracy.

Empirically, virtually all past and present capitalist dictatorship especially in their moralistic-religious versions manifest the tendency to an equation of pleasures and sins with and their sanctioning as serious, grave and even death-deserving crimes. As usual, instances span from capitalism in 19th-century Victorian England and neo-Puritan America, including the time of Prohibition and the early drug prohibitions, to the same societies under Thatcherism and Reaganism, Turkey recently, and Saudi Arabia and other Gulf Islamic states for longer, and, to a lesser extent, Catholic-dominated regions like South America, Poland and Ireland (mostly on account of criminalization of abortion). Pareto observes that Puritan societies commit the moralistic 'insanity' of equating pleasures/sins with crimes and punishing them harshly, especially pointing to the US government's coercive imposition of puritanical morality through enacting laws that replicate those of the 'European Middle Ages', as do his contemporaries Sombart, Scheler, Mencken and others. A noted early and near-grotesque exemplar of coercive moral enforcement or paternalism is the US Constitutional criminalization of alcoholic beverages—defining their consumption as a grave criminal activity necessitating the change and mobilization of a constitution in eradicating sins—by Prohibition and its Draconian punishment of violations up to life in prison. Its sequel, the conservative 'war on drugs' apparently exceeds Prohibition in extensiveness and intensity, becoming the second more enduring pandemonium of moralistic coercion, which the mass epidemic of religion-driven anti-abortion laws in conservative America with typically Draconian punishments seek to surpass at present.

5.4   *Moralistic-Religious Terror*

As a corollary, massive populations of prisoners of ethical or moral conscience among non-capital and similar social strata, including death sentences and executions, and in that sense moralistic-religious terror is an additional indicator of especially moralistic-religious capitalist dictatorship. A result of the criminalization and Draconian punishment of moral sins-as-crimes for non-capital and related strata is the 'astronomical growth' of mass and long imprisonment, including widespread death sentences and executions, of the latter, especially in conservative America since Reaganism among Western societies, along with Islamic states in the Western world. These strata form within capitalist and related dictatorship, notably its theocratic variant, a vast population of prisoners of ethical and political conscience subjected to severe punishment because of their violations of rigid puritanical morality enforced through legal coercion, just as due to their dissent from or opposition to a repressive state. Through such criminalization and punishment of these offenses moralistic capitalist dictatorship reproduces the category of moral, religious and political crimes and criminals that are unknown in liberal-secular democracy which typically does not criminalize or harshly punish immorality and distinguishes it from criminality.

At this point, capitalist dictatorship's failure to follow liberal democracy's differentiation between immorality and criminality, human sins-vices and crimes and the consequent coercive imposition of strict morality operates as the generator of massive prisoner populations of ethical conscience— imprisoned sinners rather than criminals. This holds from the stance of an enlightened criminal justice system typifying Western liberal modernity and superseding its primitive antecedents, as in Durkheim's classical sociological distinction between premodern penal law with repressive sanctions and modern civil law with restitutive sanctions. So long as it defines and punishes in a Draconian manner moral sins and vices as grave crimes for non-capital and related social groups, moralistic capitalist dictatorship will perpetrate moralistic-religious terror and generate massive populations of prisoners and in part executed persons of ethical and religious conscience among them. It will therefore reproduce contemporary equivalents of the 'witches' and 'heretics' during the Dark Middle Ages.

5.4.1   Massive Populations of Prisoners of Ethical Conscience

Massive populations of prisoners of ethical or moral conscience among non-capital and similar social strata, including their death sentences and executions, typify capitalist dictatorship particularly its moralistic-religious forms and agents culminating in theocracy or theocentric 'faith-based' regimes. Capitalist dictatorship through such prison populations of sinners reduces itself to a system of moralistic and religious terror in civil society, a puritanical 'holy' warfare on and abolition of personal moral freedom and responsibility, as it does to state terror in the political regime via mass imprisonment and executions for dissent and opposition to existing powers.

Consequently, in capitalist dictatorship, moralistic-religious terror within civil society complements, interacts with and reinforces state terror in the polity, prisoners of ethical conscience complementing those of political conscience, sinners going hand in hand with dissenters or heretics. It therefore operates after the model of pre-capitalist despotism, especially Weber's 'unexampled tyranny of Puritanism' in early America ('theocracy of New England') repressing and punishing both groups harshly. Like its conservative-fascist counterpart, capitalist dictatorship tends to expand state terrorism from the polity into civil society and generalize it into moralistic-religious terror in the private life sphere, moving from terrorizing dissenters and 'enemies of the state' to human sinners and 'enemies of moral purity and God'. It thereby commits methodical and multiple acts not only on the 'political terror scale' but also on that of moralistic-religious terror to form a double compound of terrorism or terrorist repression, reaffirming its remarkably comprehensive scope of operation. The second mode of terror thus results from the escalation of the first from the public realm of polity into the private sphere of civil society, moving from visible dissenters and opponents of secular powers to secret sinners and enemies of sacred power. In this regard, far from being different or exceptional, capitalist dictatorship effectively replicates pre-capitalist theocratic despotism, especially Puritan theocracies in England and New England, and converges with contemporary conservative-fascist or radical right dictatorships. They all share the prototype of total oppression and terror of subordinate social strata and large populations of prisoners ('evil enemies' and 'witches') of ethical and political conscience among them and their pervasive executions.

Massive populations of prisoners of ethical conscience or imprisoned sinners among non-capital and similar strata, including their death sentences and executions, hence indicate capitalist dictatorship in terms of civil society, as in American and Islamic settings. These prisoners are faces of capitalist dictatorship within civil society with its moralistic-religious terror in the private sphere, just as those of political conscience like dissenters are emanations of its terrorism in the public realm. Alternatively, capitalist dictatorship in its moralistic-religious rendition exposes itself by massive populations of prisoners of ethical conscience as vast numbers of humans imprisoned and often executed for their moral sins rather than crimes proper according to liberal democracy's differentiation between the two and their differential treatment in terms of sanctions.

In this connection, if one does not know what moralistic-religious capitalist dictatorship is or whether it exists in civil society, considering these tendencies can help answer the question. In consequence, such capitalist dictatorship has the comparatively largest populations of prisoners of ethical conscience and thus ranks the highest on the moralistic-religious terror scale among the variations of capitalism and types of society, along with conservative-fascist dictatorships. In particular, it tends to have invariably and dramatically larger populations of such prisoners and to rank higher on this scale than its opposite, the conjunction of welfare capitalism and liberal-secular democracy. Moralistic-religious capitalist dictatorship is prone to exhibit the highest imprisonment rates for moral sins-as-crimes, including alcohol, drug, sexual, reproductive and related offenses, as those for political acts. It forms an Orwellian world of fictitious, moral crimes—from the standpoint of civil society and liberal democracy but real crimes for illiberal absolutism—and mass prisoners-sinners, as in conservative America since Reaganism and Islamic states.

By such moralistic and religious overdetermination or destination, dictatorship in capitalism effectively becomes a capitalist theocracy or theocentric regime in which moral sins are grave and deadly crimes, so sinners ultimately criminals deserving the desert of justice through massive, long imprisonment, mistreatment, torture and execution. Capitalist theocracy commits all these acts in the 'name of the divine master', thus state terror in the 'mind of and for the glory of God' according to the Calvinist/Puritan and Islamic formula (Weber's 'God of Calvinism'). Puritanical capitalist dictatorship 'receives' the Divine, plutocracy merges with theocracy in the style of the 'American regime' and its Religious Right, as pre-capitalist despotism and aristocracy merged with the second estate and post-2016 fascist/radical-right dictatorships merge with 'faith-based' regimes.

As typical, empirical and historical capitalist dictatorships mostly display the syndrome of massive populations of prisoners of ethical conscience among non-capital and similar strata, including their death sentences and executions. Instances abound spanning from capitalist Victorian England and America during the Gilded Age, including Prohibition and other temperance wars, through moralistic capitalist-fascist dictatorship in interwar Germany and the rest of Europe to postwar 'free market' dictatorships in Chile and other South American countries. They then include the first two societies déjà vu under puritanical neo-conservatism like Thatcherism and Reaganism and the second post-2016, Catholic-dominated Poland, along with Islamic capitalist theocracies in Turkey, Saudi Arabia and other Gulf states. Within Western society, America during resurrected religious conservatism provides a paradigmatic instance owing to the fact that a large proportion of nearly 2.3 million US prisoners in 2020 (20 percent of their total and 44 percent of their federal figures) qualify as those of ethical conscience by being imprisoned for committing moral sins like non-violent drug and related offenses, mostly the possession and use of drugs without negative externalities in the sense of not harming others.[39]

Among non-Western countries, Islamic states are an exemplar by sharing the same trend as conservative America. In addition, the latter remains the only one among Western societies to provide for and potentially apply the death penalty for certain moral sins such as drug trade and possibly (as in the 'Bible Belt') abortion, while Islamic states are the most frequent users of such a punishment among non-Western countries. In sum, massive populations of prisoners of ethical conscience among non-capital social strata, including their death sentences and executions for moral sins-as-crimes, represent an important indicator of capitalist dictatorship, especially its moralistic-religious forms and agents in evangelical America and Islamic states.

---

39   Mueller (2013, p. 9) remarks that 'many of those in jail in the US are guilty of drug-related crimes, and so this latter statistic can be attributed to the draconian nature of US policies with respect to drugs in comparison to other rich democracies. But these draconian policies can also be traced to the much stronger religious beliefs in the United States. Evangelical Americans, a significant fraction of the population, see the world in terms of good and evil. Evil must be punished. Drugs are evil. Send the users and sellers to jail'. More broadly, he suggests that in 'a liberal democracy, people should be free to do as they please unless their actions cause undo harm to others. Harmful actions can be regarded as causing negative externalities. [But] religious beliefs have led those holding them to demand, and often obtain, legislation restricting the freedom to act of other individuals, even when the prohibited actions cause no physical harm' (Mueller 2013, p. 9; see also Roth 2018).

CHAPTER 5

Capitalist Dictatorship as a Cultural System

1   Capitalist Dictatorship and Culture

Furthermore, capitalist dictatorship also constitutes (what Sorokin calls) a cultural system as yet another subsystem of the total social system, just as capitalism as a whole does historically and empirically.[1] Capitalist dictatorship is prone to generalize and indeed universalize from economy, polity and civil society to culture, thus assuming the shape or properties of a peculiar cultural system. By so doing, it attains a totalistic domain and closure by encompassing society as a whole, not just economy as 'capitalist' might convey or polity as 'dictatorship' may suggest. In this regard, capitalist dictatorship has an intrinsic tendency to metastasize from these societal domains into a corresponding culture. It thereby follows the syndrome of pre-capitalist despotism and converges with that of conservative-fascist dictatorships, all sharing this cultural metastasis or metamorphosis.

If economy is the logical and empirical point of origin and departure, in Weber's words, a materialistic beginning for capitalist dictatorship as initially an economic system and subsequently a political regime and degenerate civil society, culture becomes its destination, a spiritual endpoint and fulfilment. This process is historically continuous with pre-capitalist despotism such as slavery, caste and feudalism and comparatively convergent with conservative and fascist dictatorships. Hence, capitalist dictatorship is far from being unique in a broader historical and comparative framework and instead exemplifies dictatorships' common process of metastasizing from economy and polity to culture, as to civil society—and moving back forming a full totalistic circle. Contrary to appearances and economistic theories, like pre-capitalist dictatorships, capitalist dictatorship is also a cultural phenomenon possessing

---

1   For capitalism and more broadly economy as a cultural system or part of it, see Braudel (1979), Collins (1988), Parsons (1967), also, Abrutyn (2009), DiMaggio (1987), Goldberg, Hannan and Kovács (2016), Meyer and Jepperson (2000), Schneiberg and Clemens (2006), and Swidler (1986). Generally, even the neoclassical economist Phelps (2013, p. 194) acknowledges that 'as important as institutions and policies may be, we must recognize that every economy is a culture or mix of cultures, not just policies, laws, and institutions. The economic culture of a nation consists of prevailing attitudes, norms, and assumptions about business, work, and other aspects of the economy'.

culture dimensions and sources, just as is more manifestly an economic and political system.

Specifically, capitalist dictatorship especially its moralistic-religious variant in the style of conservative America, Catholic-dominated Poland and Turkey, Saudi Arabia and other plutocratic Islamic states moves toward an anti-liberal or illiberal type of cultural system with respect to culture freedom. It is in essence a compulsory and narrow cultural system in terms of artistic, scientific, intellectual and other culture liberties and autonomous activities. Especially capitalist dictatorship attributes no independent value to and systematically suppresses these liberties and activities so long as they challenge, threaten or question itself, thus following pre-capitalist despotism and aristocracy and converging with conservative-fascist dictatorships. Conversely, it values and embraces culture, including artistic, scientific and other intellectual, liberties and activities, only so long as they contribute to its perpetuation and solidification, consistent with the same pattern of conservative-fascist dictatorships.

In addition and in conjunction, especially with its moralistic-religious variant manifested in conservative America, Catholic Poland and plutocratic Islamic states, capitalist dictatorship represents an irrational or anti-rationalistic kind of cultural system in terms of culture rationality, notably science rationalism, aside from some variations. It is essentially the culture of anti-science in the sense of opposition or suspicion to the pursuit of science and scientific progress for its own purpose and universal societal purposes, a species of anti-rationalistic antagonism that some apologists of dictatorial as laissez-faire capitalism rationalize as anti-scientism.[2] Alternatively, capitalist dictatorship promotes science, including technology, only in the function of its conservation and expansion, spanning from profits and other vested interests to militarism and imperialism. It thereby reduces science and all intellectual activity into the handmaid of non-scientific entities reminiscent of its being the servant of religion in pre-capitalism such as the Christian and Islamic 'Dark Middle Ages'.[3]

In essence, science or scientific-technological progress is valueless or pointless in its own right, waste of resources and time unless and until it serves as the efficient instrument of establishing and preserving capitalist dictatorship in its internal and external dimensions. The latter hence adopts the identical

---

2   An example within conservative 'libertarian' economics of opposition or suspicion to scientific rationalism construed as scientism is Hayek (1955), along with his followers (Infantino 2003; also, Myerson 2008).

3   On the Christian and Islamic 'Dark Middle Ages' in antagonism to science and reason, see Mueller (2009).

instrumental approach in this respect as conservative-fascist dictatorships do. For illustration, some apologists of capitalist dictatorship as laissez-faire capitalism such as Hayek and his followers attack scientific, Enlightenment-rooted rationalism and progress as a 'counter-revolution of science' and the 'abuse of reason', as well as the resulting French Revolution. Instead, they favor irrational or prerational religiously grounded tradition, essentially medievalism and its ancient regime of feudal despotism that their proto-conservative role model, reactionary Burke exalted as expressing the 'laws of God' and the 'golden past' but critics relegate it to what Mannheim calls the 'dead past'. Even some of his colleagues[4] rebut Hayek's anti-rationalism and laissez-faire ideals of capitalist dictatorship as 'absurd' and 'wishful thinking' and reaffirm the 'triumph of the principles of the Enlightenment and the resulting 'gradual extension of the dual ideal of freedom-and-progress', along with the French Revolution's credo "Liberty, Fraternity, Equality".

Taken together, capitalist dictatorship forms an illiberal and irrational cultural system with regard to culture freedom and rationalism, respectively, which adopts the archetype of pre-capitalist despotism such as medievalism and moves together with conservative-fascist dictatorships and their inherent and profound illiberalism and irrationalism. On this account, its cultural logic and outcome far from being new and unique is that of all past and present dictatorships, by rendering culture, including science, technology and scientific-technological progress, the efficient mechanism of imposition and preservation of dictatorship and dictators.

2   Negative Definition and Specification of Capitalist Dictatorship as a Cultural System

In terms of a negative dimension, definition and specification, capitalist dictatorship as a cultural system represents the process and structure of negation and suppression of universal culture freedom and scientific rationalism. First, it is the system of denial and elimination of artistic, literary, scientific, academic and intellectual, educational, moral, religious, ideological and other cultural liberties for non-capital and related, especially non-religious, social groups. Conversely, it is the system of their monopolization and so closure for

---

4   For instance, even his colleague within Chicago economics, Knight (1960, p. 20; 1967, pp. 791, 794) rebuts Hayek's anti-rationalism and laissez-faire as 'absurd' and 'for the proverbial birds' while noting the 'triumph' of the Enlightenment (see also Acemoglu et al. 2011; Dahrendorf 1979; Habermas 2001).

capital and its religious and related allies, as through the Religious Right alliance between the capitalist rich and religious poor against 'belief-eroding discoveries and ideas' in the 'American regime'.[5]

It is this feature that makes capitalist dictatorship a negative, pre- and anti-liberal, cultural system, the opposite of cultural liberalism in the sense of a principle and realization of universal culture, including artistic and literary, scientific, intellectual, educational, moral, religious and ideological, liberty and agency. Capitalist dictatorship arises as an anti-liberal counterrevolution, including a capitalist-populist mobilization, in cultural and political terms, in a negative reaction to liberal-democratic revolutions, just as all contemporary, particularly conservative-fascist, dictatorships do. This is what Mannheim suggests witnessing that dictatorship in capitalism becomes a possibility when the capitalist class' own devices for resolving and prevailing in class conflicts prove insufficient and develops typically in the form of fascism. He characterizes fascism as 'complete irrationalism' derived from that of its source, conservatism and as the 'exponent' of the capitalist class, just as the latter supported fascist movements in interwar Europe, with Germany's major capitalists like Krupp et al. both financing and benefiting from the rise of Nazism to total power.[6]

As in other respects, in respect of universal liberty in culture from that in art, science and education to morality, religion and ideology capitalist dictatorship hence becomes a pure, unmitigated negativity for non-capital and related social strata, the negation and elimination of their cultural freedom or agency. This negativity to cultural freedom is characteristic for most forms and agents of capitalist dictatorship, including autocracy, dynasty, oligarchy, plutocracy and especially theocracy within capitalism. For example, the blended capitalist-religious 'American regime' reportedly tends to block 'belief-eroding discoveries and ideas' and thus to constrain and suppress the cultural and other liberties and activities of secular groups. Conversely, it favors those of the religious sector through laws and policies that benefit 'religious activities and citizens' in the manner substantively consistent with the 'theocratic regime'.[7]

---

5   See Bénabou et al. (2015, p. 347; also, Darnell and Sherkat (1997), Edgell 2012; Emerson and Hartman 2006; Evans and Evans 2008; Friedland 2002; Gauchat 2012; Hout and Fischer 2002; Keister 2008; Lindsay 2008).

6   On Germany's capitalists financing the rise of Nazism, see Ferguson and Voth (2008).

7   Bénabou et al. (2015, p. 347) observe that the 'American regime' entails 'specific exemptions or other policies (e.g., laws regulating behavior) benefiting religious activities and citizens'. Bénabou et al. (2015, pp. 349–50) also find in the US and elsewhere that 'religiosity (is) consistently associated with more negative views of scientific progress. greater religiosity (is) clearly associated with lower scientific literacy. Across people as well as places, the strength of religious belief is strongly negatively correlated with education (especially for literalist

Second and related, capitalist dictatorship forms the system of negation and obstruction of cultural, notably scientific rationalism and progress in favor of irrationalism and pre-science, including religious and related fanaticism, superstitions and dogmas. This attribute renders capitalist dictatorship a negative, namely pre- and anti-rational, cultural system, the antithesis of cultural or sociological rationalism in the meaning of a principle and societal activation of reason, notably science-based rationality which the Enlightenment epitomizes and whose product is liberal-rational modernity.[8] Science-based rationality is distinct from and often opposite to the utilitarian rationality of self-interest or utility maximization in orthodox economics and its extension 'rational choice theory' that misconstrues all social rationality as 'rational egoism' or 'utility-maximizing'.

Capitalist dictatorship arises as an anti-rationalistic counterrevolution or capitalist-populist mobilization in cultural terms, in a negative reaction to rationalistic revolutions such as the Enlightenment, just as conservative-fascist dictatorships do. It expresses the anti-Enlightenment, just as conservatism and especially fascism does, although capitalism as an economic system, including the Industrial Revolution, has, along with liberal democracy, its roots in the Enlightenment. While capitalism, along with liberal democracy, is the product of the Enlightenment, capitalist dictatorship is, together with conservatism, including fascism, the effect of the counter-Enlightenment, the antipode of reason and science-based rationality. The 'libertarian' (Hayekian) apologetic vision of capitalist dictatorship rationalized as laissez-faire capitalism is essentially that of a system of cultural anti-rationalism, specifically of anti-Enlightenment, and of perpetuation of premodern medieval irrationalism, including ignorance extolled as 'freedom' and by implication 'bliss', rooted in religious 'sacred' tradition.

---

beliefs in miracles, the devil, or the inerrancy of the Bible', concluding that 'greater religiosity was almost uniformly and very significantly associated to less favorable views of innovation'. See also Keister (2008) and Mueller (2013).

8   Mannheim (1986, p. 55) suggests that the basis of 'liberal theory' is the Enlightenment, while conservative theory 'rests primarily' on medievalism like romanticism. Kettler and Volker (1984, p. 78) comment that Mannheim shows 'how conservatism has its roots in strata hostile to capitalist and liberal rationalism'—which, as he implies, dictatorship in capitalism in the form of fascism transforms into 'complete irrationalism'. Schumpeter (1954, p. 111) remarks that 'sociological or economic rationalism' characterize 'all reforming groups who propose 'to apply reason to social phenomena', starting with the 'men of the Enlightenment'. On the latter, see also Dombrowski (2001), Habermas (2001), Mokyr (2009), Mueller (2009), and Squicciarini and Voigtländer (2015).

Capitalist dictatorship as cultural anti-rationalism is the culture of anti-science—justified by its 'libertarian' apologists as prudent anti-scientism—thus the antithesis to scientific rationalism and progress, just as are conservative-fascist dictatorships, albeit capitalism originates in Enlightenment-based science and technology. This confirms it is not only an aberration from liberalism and liberal democracy but also from cultural rationalism and modernism in the form of the Enlightenment and science and scientific rationality. Furthermore, it appears as a deviation from capitalism. This holds so long that the latter originates in Enlightenment rationalism and remains related to the latter in its contemporary variant of democratic, welfare and coordinated capitalism, simply what Cassel denotes, and Keynes envisages, as a 'rationally regulated social economy' to supersede repressive and self-destructive laissez-faire capitalism.

If early capitalism, along with emergent liberal democracy, belongs to the Enlightenment's age of reason and freedom, capitalist dictatorship, together with conservative-fascist dictatorships, is part of the anti-Enlightenment's period of unreason and unfreedom culminating in fascism, most egregiously Nazism's ultimate irrationalism. It is no wonder that some apologists for capitalist dictatorship couched as laissez-faire capitalism such as 'libertarian' economists à la Hayek et al.[9] assault the Enlightenment and its scientific rationalism as the 'abuses of reason' and the 'counterrevolution of science' as if science rather than anti-science, including religious superstition and tradition, were counterrevolutionary. Following this logic, the Enlightenment was a rationalistic counterrevolution, and the Dark Middle Ages of religious superstition and oppression were the revolution of irrationalism and pre-science, the French Revolution the counterrevolution of liberty and equality and feudalism the revolution of illiberty and inequality. Such is the 'absurd(ity)'

---

9   Von Hayek himself was a reactionary aristocrat in the mold of Burke and seemingly a hidden defender, along with also aristocratic von Mises and Schumpeter from Austrian economics, of pan-German Nazism as the best protector against socialism and the Scandinavian and other welfare state. It seems likely that Hayek and Mises would, just as Schumpeter privately did, prefer Austrian-born Hitler and his 'broad coalition of the right', indeed 'authoritarian rightism', including large capitalists a la Krupp et al., against labor unions and liberal democracy to FDR whom they (as apparent for Schumpeter) strongly detested as the incarnation of the American welfare state. It is no wonder that Samuelson (1983 b, p. 59) suggests that Hayek was a false prophet, noting that 'many are called as prophets (and) few are chosen as seers by the scorekeeping historian. Forty years after Friedrich Hayek wrote down his nightmare of the welfare state leading remorselessly to the totalitarian murder of freedom, Scandinavians enjoy freedom second to none that the world has ever seen'.

and 'wishful thinking'[10] of this 'libertarian' apology for capitalist dictatorship through laissez-fare for capital and oppression of non-capital.

Hence, with regard to cultural-scientific rationalism and progress capitalist dictatorship appears as a pure, undiluted negativity for non-capital and related, including non-religious, social strata, the antithesis and abolition of rationality and science. This negativity to cultural rationalism and progress especially characterizes religious forms and agents of capitalist dictatorship, including 'godly' autocracy, dynasty and 'faith-based' oligarchy and plutocracy and, above all, theocracy within capitalism. Thus, the 'American regime' of pure capitalism and diluted theocracy reportedly features the Religious Right alliance that the capitalist rich especially in times of growing economic inequality form with poor religious strata, aiming to obstruct scientific innovation and progress that undermine established dogmas of religion and perpetuate such and related pre- and anti-science superstitions spanning from 'Satan' to 'creationism'. In light of such an alliance, it is hardly a surprise that the vast majority of Americans believe in the 'Satan' superstition or dogma compared to a small minority of Western Europeans and more of them trust 'creationism' or 'intelligent design' than biological evolutionism contrary to these latter. Specifically, as a likely consequence of such joint capitalist-populist anti-science mobilization, almost three quarters of Americans hold in the midst of supposedly rational capitalism the belief in the existence and nefarious actions of 'Satan'[11] and by implication 'witches', as a paradigmatic example of religious superstitions versus only a fraction of other Western nations (19 percent in France, 11 percent in Denmark). This specifically illustrates religious 'American exceptionalism' from the West.

By contrast, this figure is comparable to the proportion of 'Satan' believers in Islamic countries such as Turkey, actually even higher than in the latter, manifesting Islamic-style religious 'American exceptionalism' from Western societies or its convergence with non-Western countries in superstitions. To that extent, this finding illustrates the dismal failure of the US educational system to challenge, let alone discredit and eradicate, what most social scientists see as a case of religious superstition or cultural irrationality, and conversely the success of these European systems in this respect. Assuming that virtually all Puritans in 17th-century America believed in the existence of 'Satan' and 'witches', in light of the exceptionally high percent of Americans still believing

---

10   See footnote 4.
11   Glaeser (2004, p. 408) refers to the finding that '71 percent of Americans believe in the Devil, while only 19 percent of the French and 11 percent of Danes think that there is some sort of Mephistopheles'.

in the 'Devil', it seems as if not much scientific, educational and cultural progress has occurred since the Satan-as-witch trials at Salem. Especially, given
the near-universal belief in the existence and activity of 'Satan' in evangelical
America such as the 'Bible Belt', this region today probably appears and feels
similar to Salem 1692, with some differences in degrees of superstition and irrationalism. This is in the sense that—counterfactually but not unrealistically—
most people in evangelical America would fit in and rejoice at Salem 1692 in
respect of this and related Puritan-rooted beliefs, and conversely 17th-century
superstitious, witch-believing Puritans would find their 'paradise lost' or a new,
Southern home in the 'Bible Belt' and evangelical America overall.

At this point, if one does not know what an anti-rational, in particular anti-
science, capitalist dictatorship is or whether it exists, such persistent anti- and
pre-scientific religious beliefs in conservative America's exceptional theocratic
capitalism and Islamic capitalist theocracies like Saudi Arabia and other Gulf
states can help solve this matter. This shows that capitalist dictatorship can
be as anti-rational in cultural terms, notably pre- and anti-scientific, as pre-
and non-capitalist dictatorships and capitalism while economically rational
in Weber's sense may become under religious conservatism or fascism as nonrational or irrational non-economically as pre-capitalist medievalism.

3   Positive Definition and Specification of Capitalist Dictatorship as a
       Cultural System

Relatedly, in respect of a positive dimension, definition and specification, capitalist dictatorship constitutes a cultural system of reproduction of compulsion
and irrationalism in culture, including religious and other coercion and superstition. First, it represents the system of reproduction of cultural compulsion
for non-capital and related, particularly non-religious, strata, while lavishing
capital and its theocratic allies, as in conservative America and Islamic plutocratic states, with limitless freedom to the point of license.

Such a property defines positively capitalist dictatorship as a compulsory
and illiberal cultural system, the mode of implementation of cultural illiberalism in the sense of a blueprint of culture compulsion and in the primary
form of conservatism, in particular fascism as its extreme variant and the
polar opposite of liberalism. In this regard, far from being historically original and unique it arises as the form of regression into and of restoration of
pre-liberal and pre-democratic culture in relation to subordinate strata, just
as conservative-fascist dictatorships do. It is the desert of cultural and related
societal compulsion of non-capital and related social strata and an oasis of

unlimited freedom for capital, as was pre-capitalist despotism for the populace and aristocracy—Leviathan for non-capitalists and secularists, anarchy/state of nature for capitalists and religionists. Capitalist dictatorship becomes a pure positivity, unmoderated good only for the capitalist class and, as in conservative America and Islamic countries, its ally theocracy, as pre-capitalist despotism was for aristocracy solely and the allied theocratic estate.

This duality of mass compulsion and elite freedom in the domain of culture is typical for most forms and agents of capitalist dictatorship from autocracy and dynasty to oligarchy, plutocracy and especially theocracy within capitalism. For instance, the conservative 'American regime' mixing capitalism with theocracy features systematic, pervasive and large-scale compulsion through mass incarceration and arbitrary widespread executions of non-capital and other lower and powerless social strata. It combines such compulsion with almost unlimited freedom for capitalists and theocratic elites, above all in 'evangelical America' such as the 'Money and God', pro-capital, anti-labor Southern 'Bible Belt'. The same holds for the Islamic theocratic regime in Turkey, Saudi Arabia and other Gulf states and to some degree for Catholic-dominated Poland and Latin America. They feature a similar mix of large-scale compulsion, including mass imprisonment and extensive executions, of subordinate groups, in combination with the despotic-style license for its capitalist or plutocratic and religious rulers. The post-2016 radical-right 'American regime', Turkey's and Saudi Arabia's theocratic regimes, Catholic-dominated Poland, conservative-ruled Hungary, and Brazil under far-right autocracy all indulge in large-scale compulsion of their 'enemies'. By contrast, they endow and lavish their rulers with the license to kill or oppress subordinate groups (e.g., Saudi Arabia's crown prince, Brazilian, Hungarian, Polish, Turkey and US presidents). Moreover, they act in alliance as an extended equivalent of the 'broad coalition of the right', specifically 'authoritarian rightism', in interwar Germany and simultaneously as if in coordination, reciprocal admiration and encouragement. They form a post-2016 radical-right alliance of these capitalist-theocratic and conservative regimes through formal or informal coordination, communication and personal meetings (e.g., invited visits with the US President), which is reminiscent of the alliances between the anti-liberal conservative and fascist powers during WW I and II.

In turn, these regimes merging repressive or oligarchic capitalism with theocracy differ from and oppose via joint 'holy' wars the Western European liberal-secular regime of egalitarian capitalism and liberal democracy, which rules out large-scale compulsion, including mass incarceration and legally prohibits state executions. As typical, pro-capital, anti-labor theocracy that these and related regimes located outside Western Europe exemplify proves to be the most compulsory and expansive form and agent of capitalist dictatorship in culture, as in the polity and civil society. For example, Catholic-dominated Poland under conservatism, along with conservative-ruled Hungary, has become an illiberal, anti-secular and undemocratic outcast or pariah-state within the European Union and is probably less free, democratic or liberal than even during the last years of their socialist regimes of the late 1980s. This makes for a Polish-Hungarian tragedy in the sense of substitution of even a harsher and more total theocratic and conservative for a secular dictatorship.

Second and related, capitalist dictatorship operates as a system of reproduction of irrationalism in culture, including in particular religious and other superstitions. This element defines capitalist dictatorship positively as an irrational cultural system, the mechanism of realization of cultural irrationalism in the meaning of an 'intelligent design'[12] of unreason or irrationality in culture and in the prime shape of conservatism, including fascism as the extreme antithesis of rationalism and reason. If capitalism starting with the Industrial Revolution and liberal democracy beginning with the French Revolution are the age and space of economic, political and cultural reason and rationalism in the sense of the Enlightenment, capitalist dictatorship is the time and site of unreason and irrationalism in culture, as are conservative-fascist dictatorships. In this sense, capitalist dictatorship is born and remains decomposed or disabled in terms of cultural reason and rationalism, namely as an irrational cultural system, replicating pre-capitalist despotism and converging with conservative-fascist dictatorships. As with regard to the compulsion of non-capital strata, it forms the desert of culture irrationalism, including mass religious and other superstitions, unreason and darkness, with only small and isolated spots of reason and light. It is the mix of ignorance and squalor for the religious masses with aristocratic-style refinement and luxury for the ruling class, with exceptions like US plutocrats lacking the aristocratic sense of *noblesse oblige*.[13] On this account, like conservative-fascist dictatorships, it

---

12   Some Chicago-school 'libertarian' economists use, even if as a metaphor, the term 'intelligent design' in a theoretical equivalence with evolution both applied to economics and social science, and thus effectively adopt or echo US conservatives' claim that the first should have the same 'scientific' status as the second (Sargent 2008). Relatedly, others populate economic theory with 'God' as if this were demonstrated or demonstrable empirical hypothesis rather than what Schumpeter connotes an instance of 'extra-empirical cognition' for which scientific rationalism has an intrinsic 'aversion' (Lucas 2009).

13   Fuchs (1996) cites 'a weak sense of noblesse oblige' as one of the main reasons the US has no national health insurance, unlike other Western countries, including Sweden, England, Canada, and others, see also Akerlof (2007).

descends to the Dark Middle Ages of religious superstition, including 'Satan', and fails to reach the Enlightenment.

The preceding primarily typifies the religious forms and agents of capitalist dictatorship, namely theocracy within capitalism, and to a lesser degree their more secular counterparts. For illustration, in the 'American regime' of merged capitalism and theocracy, the capitalist class allies with poor religious strata to form the Christian right alliance obstructing scientific progress and perpetuating cultural irrationalism, including religious superstitions from 'creationism' to 'Satan'. The effect is that the vast majority of Americans believe in the latter superstition or dogma, as do most people in Islamic countries, but only a fraction among Western societies. More broadly, Pareto observes that Christian capitalist theocracies continue to hold various religious superstitions or dogmas from their holy book in spite of a myriad of demonstrated 'scientific errors of the Bible'. At this point, if one doubts what an irrational, religiously superstitious capitalist dictatorship is or whether it exists, what can dispel this doubt is the proportion of American and Islamic populations believing in the existence of 'Satan' and Satanizing and persecuting 'infidels' and the continuing sway of the 'scientific errors of the Bible'. On this account, capitalist dictatorship appears generally as irrational culturally and superstitious religiously as pre-capitalist despotism like medievalism and conservative-fascist dictatorships. A look at capitalist-evangelical America, notably pro-capital, anti-labor 'Bible Belt', along with Islamic capitalist theocracies like Saudi Arabia and other Gulf states, will remove most doubts. Hence, capitalist theocracy that theocratic regimes in these and other societies exemplify proves to be the most irrational, notably fanatical and superstitious, form and agent of capitalist dictatorship as a cultural system, as are conservative-fascist dictatorships among other dictatorial systems.

4   Forms and Agents of Capitalist Dictatorship as a Cultural System

Forms and agents of capitalist dictatorship as a cultural system correspond to those in terms of civil society and polity. Hence, they involve autocracy and dynasty as personal and familial cases and plutocracy, aristocracy, oligarchy, notably theocracy, and in part police states and military dictatorships within capitalism, as its collective, sociologically more important instances. The evident difference is that they extend from civil society and the political-economic system to and operate and dominate in culture, manifesting their comprehensive scope of operation and domination consistent with the totalistic nature and domain of capitalist dictatorship. In addition, most of them become more and indeed explicitly 'cultural' or 'spiritual', notably religious or 'faith-based', by moving to, operating in and pervading culture spanning from art, science and education to morality, religion and spirituality. For this reason, they reinvent themselves as compounded capitalist-spiritual, specifically capitalist-religious, autocracy, dynasty, plutocracy, aristocracy and oligarchy, police states and military dictatorships, together with capitalist theocracy as the consummate exemplar of this spiritualization of capitalist dictatorship. As they move from economy to culture via polity and civil society, in the process they tend to assume increasing 'spiritual' or religious, including theocratic, pretensions, aspirations and functions, just as capitalist dictatorship does in general.

The above tendency especially holds for plutocracy or plutocratic aristocracy and oligarchy as the sociologically most relevant form and agent of capitalist dictatorship as an economic-political system becoming religiously over-determined or overdriven and thus effectively merging with capitalist theocracy within culture, as in civil society. Capitalist theocracy or theocratic 'faith-based' plutocracy presents itself as the most salient cultural form and agent of capitalist dictatorship and hence the most destructive force against culture freedom for non-capital strata and scientific rationalism. Thus, the merged plutocratic-theocratic 'American regime' represents since theocratic Puritanism the most powerful and lasting form and agent of capitalist dictatorship as a cultural system among Western societies. It is the most lethal weapon via the Christian Right alliance between plutocrats and the religious poor against scientific progress and individual freedom and the strongest mechanism of perpetuating religious superstitions and dogmas from 'creationism' and 'intelligent design' to 'Satan' and 'witches'.

This regime of capitalist theocracy primarily explains why most Americans still downgrade science in favor of religion as their primary revealed preference in the midst of third-millennium capitalism, virtually being alone and thus unique among Western societies in this religiously overdetermined irrationalism. In particular, it accounts for that nearly three quarters of Americas

TABLE 10 Forms and agents of capitalist dictatorship as a cultural system

capitalist autocracy in culture
capitalist dynasty in culture
capitalist plutocracy, oligarchy, and aristocracy in culture
secondary forms of capitalist dictatorship in culture

continue to believe in the existence of 'Satan' and by implication 'witches' in spite or because of all scientific, educational and technical progress, prefer 'creationism' and other superstitions (including 'flat earth' centuries after its discredit) to scientific evidence such as biological evolutionism. Conversely, as the most lethal weapon against scientific progress, the regime mainly explains why most Americans, above all in conservative America, oppose evolution as 'just as theory' versus God's 'intelligent design' and the biblical truth of 'genesis as well as climate change evidence as 'unbiblical' and a liberal, secular or progressive 'conspiracy' against the 'godly'.

Overall, the conservative 'American regime' of merged plutocracy and theocracy ('in God we trust' dollar, 'one nation indivisible under God') seems almost as irrational and pre-rational in cultural terms, notably anti- and pre-scientific, just as compulsory, as European medievalism and the Islamic 'theocratic regime' also merging the two, which Saudi Arabia and other Gulf states demonstrate, with secondary differences. At this point, evangelical America and Saudi Arabia and other Gulf states are long-standing allies because of not only geopolitical reasons traced to the Cold War, massive weapon exports to the second and favorable oil imports by the first, but more profoundly in sociological terms due to their shared plutocratic-theocratic regime, capitalist theocracy. For example, like its equivalent, evangelical America, Saudi Arabia as exemplary theocracy not only has a capitalist-style stock market but also the single company with the highest financial valuation in the world that is owned by its theocratic dynasty.

Thus, Pareto implies that the 'American regime' is nearly as irrational culturally, plus compulsory, as European medievalism. He observes in America the rise of ersatz 'Christian Science' (including by implication 'Christian mathematics' at the time, plus 'Christian medicine' through these days) being 'utterly at war with any sort of scientific thinking', together with the theocratic government 's 'mass of hypocritical laws for the enforcement of morality that are replicas of laws of the European (Dark) Middle Ages'. On this account, it would seem to Pareto that the term 'Dark Ages' in the sense of utter cultural irrationalism and violent compulsion might apply to both cases. He implies that the 'American regime' of plutocratic theocracy is unable, due to its obstruction of scientific progress, or unwilling because of its superior 'Americanism' (jingoism in his words) to overcome the darkness and oppression of the European Middle Ages despite its lofty claims to 'exceptionalism'. In short, for Pareto the 'American regime' emerges both as the most zealous defender of the 'scientific errors of the Bible' and so the most fanatical promulgator of irrationalism and anti-science and as the strictest enforcer of hypocritical Puritanical morality and thus the strongest violator of individual liberty. Hence, for Pareto if one does not know what capitalist theocracy or religiously overdriven plutocracy is and whether it exists, the 'American regime' can help solve the conundrum, along with the functionally equivalent Islamic 'theocratic regime'. Both regimes vehemently revolt against and become strong deviations from the Western European secular regime of egalitarian capitalism and liberal democracy promoting culture freedom and scientific rationalism. This hence yields the proper meaning of conservative 'American exceptionalism'—an Islamic-style deviation from the West and thus the first world. Thus, the 'American regime' of capitalist theocracy in conservative America often looks like a 'third-world' nation, at any rate closer to the latter than to the Western world, especially Western Europe. Yet, apparently its conservative apologists enjoy with some perverse pleasure remaking American capitalism resemble less this region of the 'old world' and more non-Western regions like South America, theocratic Islamic states or even Africa.[14]

In addition, autocracy and dynasty become cultural forms and agents of capitalist dictatorship when they expand from economy, polity and other societal realms to and operate and dominate in culture. Capitalist autocrats and family dynasties often seek and succeed to control culture, including art, science, education, philosophy, ideas, morality, religion, and spirituality, just as these other societal realms, thus impeding scientific rationalism and suppressing cultural freedoms for out-groups. Such a tendency mostly typifies non-Western countries such as those in South America, Africa, and Asia traditionally and Eastern Europe, especially Hungary and Poland, during recent times. Still, it persists or resumes in some Western societies such as America during the post-2016 period seeing the rise of autocracy and family dynasty, just as pervaded interwar capitalist-fascist autocracies and dynasties in Germany, Italy, Spain and other parts of Europe.

Similarly, police or penal states and military dictatorships within capitalism may become cultural forms and agents of capitalist dictatorship when expanding from polity and civil society to and operating and dominating in culture. Capitalist police states and military dictatorships may aim and reach control of, along with these other societal spheres, culture from art, science, and philosophy to morality, religion, and spirituality, and consequently suppress cultural freedoms for non-capital and related social groups and impede scientific progress. As the previous, this trend primarily characterizes non-Western environments like South America for long, most egregiously Chile, plus Africa and Asia, and to some degree Eastern Europe, especially the Baltic states, Hungary

---

14   See Jouet (2017) and Mueller (2009).

and Poland, recently in terms of capitalist police states. Still, the trend occasionally manifests in Western societies, such as interwar Nazi Germany and fascist Europe and postwar conservative America and in part, Great Britain during the expanding police and surveillance state in tandem with the further expansion of the military-capitalist complex since Thatcherism and Reaganism and post-2016.

In sum, cultural forms and agents of capitalist dictatorship coincide with its economic, political and civil variants, by extending from economy and polity to and operating and prevailing in culture. As typical, plutocracy or plutocratic oligarchy especially in its religiously over-determined form in conservative-American and Islamic regimes proves to be in sociological terms the most consequent cultural form and agent of capitalist dictatorship that effectively becomes or merges with capitalist theocracy. Hence, capitalist theocracy qua 'faith-based' capitalism and politics functions as the ultimate form of capitalist dictatorship as a cultural system and the most adverse and destructive force to culture freedom and rationalism, ultimately a deadly poison of artistic, scientific, educational, moral, religious and related freedoms and science and progress, as conservative-American and Islamic theocratic regimes demonstrate.

5   Indicators and Proxies of Capitalist Dictatorship as a Cultural System

Indicators and proxies of capitalist dictatorship as a cultural system include suppression of artistic and other cultural liberties for non-capital strata and devaluation of the arts and culture, extreme and compulsory religiosity, obstruction of science and scientific freedom and progress, and widespread superstitions and dogmas.

TABLE 11   Indicators and proxies of capitalist dictatorship as a cultural system

suppression of artistic and cultural liberties and devaluation of the arts and culture
extreme and compulsory religiosity
obstruction and suppression of scientific progress and freedom
persistence of widespread religious superstitions

5.1   *Suppression of Artistic and Cultural Liberties and Devaluation of the Arts and Culture*

Suppression of artistic and other cultural liberties for non-capital strata and devaluation of the arts and culture represent a salient cultural indicator of capitalist dictatorship, including autocracy, oligarchy, plutocracy and especially theocracy within capitalism. What generally characterizes capitalist dictatorship as a cultural system is the suppression and consequently absence or low degree of artistic and related cultural freedoms for non-capital strata and depreciation of the arts and culture or relatedly intellectualism and the presence and prevalence of anti-intellectualism. This holds with some variations such that anti-artistic and anti-intellectual currents are stronger and more pervasive and persistent in capitalist dictatorship's religious forms and agents, for example, conservative, Puritanical America and plutocratic Islamic countries.[15]

In particular, artistic and related cultural liberties for non-capital strata tend to be absent or weak subjected to suppression, as are artists themselves, in capitalist dictatorship on either economic-political or moralistic-religious grounds—or on both. Relatedly, the lack of public appreciation and support, including government funding, of the arts and related free and creative cultural activities pervades especially religious capitalist dictatorship which depreciates, downgrades and deprives them from material funds on these and other grounds. For example, the government spending on and thus proximate public appreciation of the arts in the religiously overdetermined 'American regime' has been historically and continues to be drastically lower than in the 'Western European secularization regime', including France, Germany and Scandinavia.[16]

---

15   Scitovsky (1972, p. 64) laments that Americans 'smile condescendingly over the prejudices of 18th century America, which morally disapproved of the theatre and frowned on wasting time and money on sports and the arts. But this is no smiling matter, because our behavior is still governed by those prejudices'. Jouet (2017, p. 37) observes that 'conservative America is an exception in the modern Western world, since it is dominated by peculiar mindsets that have little to no weight elsewhere, including virulent anti-intellectualism', compounded with 'fervent Christian fundamentalism'. More broadly, Munch (2001, p. 226) remarks that the US 'lacks the kind of intellectual scene that France enjoys'.

16   Throsby 1994, p. 21) reports that public expenditure on arts and museums among Western countries in 1987 ranged from 0.05% of all public expenditure in the US as the lowest to 0.77% France and 0.79% Germany as the highest, thus being over 15 times (not 15 percent) lower in the first country than in these two countries.

Artistic and related cultural liberty for non-capital social strata and even art and culture itself become a luxury, nuisance, economic inefficiency, and waste, indeed an actual or potential enemy, danger and threat in capitalist dictatorship that construes them as anti-capitalistic in both meanings. Specifically, they are anti-capitalistic in the purely economic sense especially in plutocracy cum plutonomy, including kleptocracy and predatory mafia capitalism and in the ideological and other non-economic meaning primarily in theocracy, autocracy, police states and military dictatorships. As a result, most autonomous artists look as useless anti-capitalists in plutocracy and as enemies of the state in capitalist theocracy and autocracy. Capitalist dictatorship hence suppresses artistic liberty for non-capital strata, represses free artists and devaluates and defunds the public arts, while perverting the creations of art masters into private monetary investments, with plutocrats monopolizing them. It does this both for the economic rationale of plutocratic wealth accumulation preferred to art ('we cannot afford it' Puritanical American-style) and for religious reasons of theocratic compulsion and prohibition ('godless' arts for conservative America and Islamic states).

Therefore, capitalist dictatorship exemplifies the tendency of all dictatorships, especially conservative-fascist regimes, to deny and suppress artistic and related cultural liberties for subordinate strata and define artists and other free intellectuals as 'enemies of the state' and 'people'. Relatedly, it manifests their propensity to devaluate and deprive art and related culture from resources, unless it is ersatz conservative, religious or fascist 'art' and 'culture'. This holds with secondary exceptions such as autocratic and plutocratic rulers occasionally financing and indulging in the higher and sometimes popular arts. Still, these instances seem less frequent or famous in capitalist dictatorship than in pre-capitalism or pre-modern capitalism prior to the Industrial Revolution such as Renaissance Europe (Florence) and in modern capitalism.[17] The

17   Bourdieu (1984, p. 395) suggests that 'what is generally meant by popular art, i.e., the art of the peasant classes of capitalist and pre-capitalist societies, is the product of a stylizing intention which is associated with the existence of a hierarchy: locally based, relatively autonomous milieux also have their hierarchies of luxury and necessity, which the symbolic marks, clothing, furniture, jewelry, express and reinforce'. Peterson and Kern (1996, p. 900) propose that 'many high-status persons are far from being snobs and are eclectic, even omnivorous, in their tastes' regarding art. Blau, Blau and Golden (1985, p. 311) state referring to the US that 'in the absence of support from aristocrats, an established church, or substantial subsidies from the government, only the very rich have the resources to create and maintain major art institutions, such as operas or museums, or invest in major commercial art ventures. As a matter of fact, the elite in a capitalist society without an aristocracy may well have particularly strong incentives to become patrons of the arts. Whereas the legitimacy of the nobility as the dominant elite was rooted in a centuries-old

preceding therefore especially applies to religiously overdetermined capitalist dictatorship that arises as a functional equivalent of conservative-fascist
dictatorships in respect of suppression of artistic and other intellectual liberties for such social strata, repression of artists and public devaluation of the
esthetic arts.

At the minimum, the suppression of artistic and intellectual liberties, the
repression of artists and other intellectuals and the depreciation and condemnation of irreligious art pervades capitalist theocracy, even if one allows
that autocracy, dynasty, oligarchy, and plutocracy tolerate and even occasionally support some of these cultural freedoms and activities. An atmosphere
of artistic and non-artistic anti-intellectualism and of intolerance and rigidity envelops and maintains capitalist theocracy or theocentric 'faith-based'
regimes which capitalist dictatorship assumes in highly religious settings such
as Puritan-evangelical America (New England and the postbellum South), to
some degree England, and Islamic countries like Turkey, Saudi Arabia and
other Gulf states.

Still, while capitalist theocracy is the most persistent and destructive force
against artistic and related intellectual freedom, secular art and intellectualism, most forms and agents of capitalist dictatorship exhibit low degrees of
such freedoms, especially when compared to other modalities of capitalism
and liberal democracy. Suppression of artistic and related intellectual liberties for non-capital strata hence helps indicate capitalist dictatorship especially in its theocratic form and agent suppressing them on ultimate 'divine'
nondebatable grounds and to lesser extent its other less explicitly religious
forms and agents. Conversely, capitalist dictatorship as a cultural system
reveals itself through its suppression of such liberties, mistreatment of free

---

value system that defined its members as intrinsically superior to commoners, the values of a capitalist democracy deny that some citizens are inherently superior to others'.
This overstates the role of the capitalist elite in the promotion and expansion of the arts
in American society so long as the latter continues to display artistic and intellectual
backwardness compared to Western Europe where their government financial support is
incomparably stronger (see Munch 2001). Further, this statement overlooks Pareto's and
other observations that the 'elite in a capitalist society' such as the US tends to become
or act as the new aristocracy of capital or money. Relatedly, it ignores the fact that even
if the 'values of a capitalist democracy deny that some citizens are inherently superior
to others', the 'elite in a capitalist society' like the US seeks to define and present itself
precisely as 'inherently superior' to non-elites, namely non-capitalists as what Tönnies
calls 'nonentities'. In turn, Lachmann (1990) invokes 'Florence during the Renaissance' as
one of 'historical cases' of conflicts among 'feudal' rather than capitalist elites, along with
'England in the century leading to the 1640 (Puritan) Revolution, and France from the
16th through the 18 centuries'.

artists and other intellectuals, devaluation and financial deprivation of arts, and relatedly the ambiance of anti-art, anti-creativity and anti-intellectualism or anti-rationalism pervading conservative America among Western societies and Islamic states within the third world. As a consequence, capitalist dictatorship tends to display the lowest degree of artistic and related cultural liberties and relatedly of public valuation and funding of art and culture among the variations of capitalism and types of social system, in particular a drastically lower one than that of welfare capitalism and liberal democracy. Alternatively, its degree approaches those of other, particularly conservative-fascist dictatorships whose degrees of such liberties are as a rule the lowest and their suppression of art and culture the most intense among all societies.

Most contemporary and historical capitalist dictatorships, especially their theocratic or religious forms and agents, epitomize the above template of suppression of artistic and related cultural liberties and the public depreciation of the arts and culture.

Especially indicative contemporary instances include capitalist-evangelical America, in particular the Southern 'Bible Belt', and Islamic plutocratic-theocratic countries like Turkey (recently), Saudi Arabia and other Gulf states. Both share the suppression of artistic and related intellectual liberties, persecution or repression of artists, and the devaluation and economic deprivation of the secular arts and culture, and relatedly the ambiance of anti-art and anti-intellectualism or anti-rationalism, all 'in the name of the divine master' a la Pareto. American capitalism's Puritan-rooted anti-art antagonism and anti-intellectualism has become a case of legend and an expression of striking persistence or path-dependence through the present primarily in conservative America.

Other seemingly less conspicuous cases of plutocratic and theocratic attacks on these and other freedoms involve Catholic-dominated Poland and South America, conservative-ruled and 'Christian' Hungary, and other parts of Eastern Europe under conservatism and oligarchy. Historical exemplars include 19th-century Victorian English and neo-Puritan American Gilded-Age capitalism suppressing, as Pareto suggests, immoral art and artists by legal compulsion evoking the Dark Middle Ages, interwar Germany and South American Catholic dictatorships and the first two countries during Thatcherism and Reaganism. Further, this includes the US post-2016 when artists, journalists and other intellectuals again become 'enemies of the people'. Notably, capitalist-fascist and theocentric ('Christian') dictatorships in interwar Europe, most egregiously Nazi Germany, destroyed artistic and intellectual liberties, persecuted artists and other intellectuals, and devaluated and eliminated genuine 'degenerate' art and culture or exploited some its forms (German music) for totalitarian propaganda while creating their own ersatz-art. This is a pattern that later neo-fascist and neo-Nazi regimes and movements in Europe and America especially post-2016 aim to continue.

Accordingly, if one doubts if capitalist dictatorship suppressing artistic and related intellectual liberties for non-capital strata exists at all—and 'libertarian' economists precisely deny that it does—and what it is, the above instances can dispel such doubt. This most notably applies to conservative America under 'faith-based' plutonomy or autocracy and dynasty and Islamic plutocratic-theocratic states, along with interwar Germany. For example, all these seemingly disparate and even opposite cases share the practice of burning or banning various artistic and other intellectual works like books, paintings and movies that they condemn as 'degenerate', 'immoral', 'indecent', 'blasphemous', 'heretic', 'anti-religious' ('anti-Christian', 'anti-Islamic') and punish their producers and consumers in a Draconian manner to the point of death or imprisonment. As a result, they replicate medieval despotism that destroyed classical 'pagan' cultural creations and usher in the 'New Dark Ages'.[18] In sum, a relevant, although overlooked or downplayed, indicator of capitalist dictatorship as a cultural system is the suppression of artistic and related cultural liberties for non-capital strata and relatedly the public depreciation and low economic support of the arts and culture.

5.2   Extreme and Compulsory Religiosity

Another related indication or approximation of capitalist dictatorship as a cultural system consists of extreme and compulsory religiosity that it spreads to culture and imposes on non-capital and similar social strata, thereby denying to them freedom of choice of and from religion. This relates to the previous so long as the suppression of artistic and related secular intellectual liberties for non-capital and similar social strata complements extreme religiosity within capitalist dictatorship—and conversely, such 'godliness' serving as the 'holy' justification for this practice—and reinforces the denial of freedom for and from religion to these groups. Generally, with secondary variations, extreme, largely compulsory, intolerant and superstitious religiosity characterizes capitalist dictatorship, which therefore approaches conservative-fascist religious

---

18   Bauman (2001, p. 84) refers to the observation of the 'coming of the New Dark Ages'. Emerson and Hartman (2006, p. 132) state that 'from a modern, secular viewpoint, fundamentalists are reactionaries, radicals attempting to grab power and throw societies back into the dark ages of oppression, patriarchy, and intolerance', yet adopt a more traditionalist, religious outlook that makes such fundamentalists appear in a different and even opposite light as 'heroes' fighting for 'religious liberty'.

dictatorships and evokes, with some modifications, pre-capitalist 'divinely ordained' despotism. The aggregate outcome—or alternatively the over-arching source—is therefore 'faith-based' capitalist dictatorship that conservative America, Catholic-dominated Latin America and Poland and Turkey, Saudi Arabia and other Islamic plutocratic states illustrate. Such a regime thus ranges from 'God-fearing' autocracy and family dynasty to 'divine' aristocracy, oligarchy and plutocracy, including 'godly' kleptocracy, police states and military dictatorships, to capitalist theocracy as the ultimate point on this continuum of extension, intensification and cultural domination of religion within capitalism.

Extreme, compulsory and superstitious religiosity therefore primarily typifies capitalist and any theocracy, just as the latter spreads and enforces such religious beliefs, along with strict morality, to culture and imposes them on non-capital strata. Thus, extreme and mostly compulsory religiosity reportedly belongs to the constitutive components of the purely 'theocratic regime' of capitalism characterizing non-Western societies such as Islamic states and most South American countries. In addition, this component permeates the intermediate 'American regime' of substantively theocratic capitalism due to the Religious Right alliance between the capitalist class and religious poor classes, in which the first exploits and sustains via culture wars their extreme religiosity.[19] Islamic and American theocratic regimes exhibit the highest levels of religiosity in the third- and Western world, respectively, and share such superstitious beliefs or dogmas as 'creationism', 'Satan', 'witches', 'miracles', and the like. Recall that reportedly nearly three quarters of Americans believe in the existence and workings of 'Satan' and implicitly 'witches', which is comparable to, just marginally lower than, the corresponding figure of Islamic-ruled Turkey where a vast majority also hold such a belief. Due to such shared beliefs both American and Islamic regimes deviate from and revolt against the 'Western European secularization regime', which lacks and rules out extreme religiosity and instead forms of complex of egalitarian capitalism with liberal democracy. Conversely, recall that only fractions of people in such Western countries as France and Denmark believe in the existence of 'Satan. Furthermore, the US 'believe the Devil exists' figure is the highest (71 percent) among OECD countries judging by the World Values Survey, after that of Turkey, which makes conservative America appear as the most superstitious country among Western

---

19   See Bénabou et al. (2015, p. 347). In addition, Glaeser, Ponzetto, and Shapiro (2005, p. 1322) find 'extreme connections' between religiosity and right-wing political orientation especially in countries with church attendance of about 50 percent.

and comparable societies (Greece is the distant second at 61 percent), along with Islamic states.

Accordingly, extreme, compulsory and superstitious religiosity helps indicate and identity capitalist dictatorship, more precisely its theocratic form and agent. Alternatively, capitalist dictatorship exposes itself as a theocratic cultural system by extreme and compulsory religiosity that one observes in conservative America, Catholic-dominated Poland and Islamic states, and its superstitious forms ('Satan') that they manifest. In consequence, capitalist theocratic dictatorship tends to have the most extreme levels of religiosity (often approaching 70–90 percent in conservative America and Islamic-ruled Turkey) among the variations of capitalism and types of society, notably, a higher level than that of the complex of egalitarian capitalism and liberal democracy. They approach the levels of pre-capitalist theocracies—transforming themselves into capitalist systems, as with Saudi Arabia and other Gulf states—and conservative-fascist dictatorships. All these dictatorships share with capitalist dictatorship extreme, compulsory and superstitious religiosity (e.g., the belief in 'Satan') as the common denominator.

Historical and contemporary capitalist dictatorships in their theocratic forms and agents largely conform to the pattern of extreme, superstitious, compulsory religiosity. Historical instances are, not counting Weber's early Puritan theocratic capitalism, 19th-century Victorian England and highly religious America up to his visit (when he noticed that only 6 percent of Americans have no religious affiliation). Later examples involve capitalist-fascist dictatorships enabled by and allied with religion in Germany, Italy, and Spain through postwar South American Catholic dictatorships and to the US during the revival of evangelicalism. Contemporary cases include evangelical America featuring the highest level of religiosity among Western societies and Catholic-dominated South America and Poland and Islamic states having the most extreme levels among third-world countries. Particularly, more than a century after Weber's 1904 visit, the 'American regime' of Puritan-rooted capitalism continues to excel in extreme, superstitious and compulsory or socially pressured (as in the 'Bible Belt', Utah, etc.), religiosity in the Western and entire world, with only Islamic states, some Catholic and other third-world countries rivaling it. For example, the US figure of 'believing in a personal God' is the highest (68 percent among Western societies and even OECD countries, with only Chile, Greece, Mexico and Turkey having the higher figures.[20]

---

20   See figures in Smith (2012).

In sum, extreme, mostly compulsory and superstitious religiosity represents an additional indicator of capitalist dictatorship as a cultural system, primarily of its religious forms and agents such as theocracy in capitalism.

5.3   *Obstruction and Suppression of Scientific Progress and Freedom*

Obstruction and suppression of scientific progress and freedom for non-capital social strata and the depreciation of science, simply anti-science, from another indicator of capitalist dictatorship, which relates to the previous two. First, the obstruction and indeed reversal of scientific progress and freedom and the depreciation and denial of science, including science-based education and applications, complements and reinforces the suppression of artistic and related intellectual liberties for non-capital strata and the devaluation of the arts and culture. This especially holds for capitalist dictatorship's religiously overdetermined version that conservative America and Islamic plutocratic states exemplify.

In this capitalist dictatorship, the attacks on artistic liberty and artists and the devaluation of art and culture go hand in hand with the assaults on scientific freedom and scientists and the depreciation, obstruction and reversal of science and science-based education and applications. Such capitalist dictatorship as a cultural system tends to suppress and devaluate virtually all forms and elements of intellectual liberty, academic freedom, activity, and products—scientific, educational, artistic and creative—manifesting its consistency and totalistic scope and converging with conservative-fascist dictatorships. It therefore generalizes unfreedom and anti-intellectualism from the arts and similar cultural activities to science and scientific applications, including science-based public education, creating an unfree and anti-intellectual, irrational or anti-rational cultural sphere, and conversely, moving from the second domain of culture to the first.

Capitalist dictatorship especially when religiously overdetermined hence perverts both art and science from cultural realms of liberty, intellectualism and rationalism into exact opposites, thus perverting them from the age or space of reason and freedom to that of their antithesis. In this sense, it is both the anti-Renaissance and the counter-Enlightenment, thus converges with conservative-fascist dictatorships as paradigmatic instances of the antagonism to the Renaissance and especially the Enlightenment. The point is that the suppression of scientific freedom for non-capital strata, the obstruction of scientific rationalism and progress and the depreciation science are not isolated tendencies in capitalist dictatorship. Rather, they enfold in interconnection and mutual reinforcement with suppressing artistic and other cultural liberty and the devaluation of art and related culture, forming elements of a self-consistent and totalistic process of elimination and restrictions of intellectual liberties and activities.

In this sense, the suppression of artistic and cultural liberty and the devaluation of the arts and culture links with and predicts suppressing scientific freedom and devaluating science—anti-art linking with and predicting anti-science, and conversely. Art and culture may be different from science and even impertinent to scientists. Yet, suppressing artistic liberty and artists and depreciating and depriving the arts and culture from material resources typically complements and predicts the suppression of scientific freedom, the repression of scientists and the depreciation of science and science-based education especially in religiously overdetermined capitalist dictatorship in the style of conservative America and Islamic plutocratic states. Simply, anti-art is often the prelude to and harbinger of anti-science, as most historical and contemporary religiously overdetermined capitalist dictatorships demonstrate. This dual tendency spans from 19th-century anti-artistic Victorian England and neo-Puritan America through interwar Nazi Germany and fascist Europe destroying 'degenerate' art and 'liberal' science to postwar South American neo-fascist regimes to the first two countries under anti-artistic and anti-scientific Thatcherism and Reaganism. More recent instances are the US post-2016, including the radical-right regime's violent antagonism to climate, medical and virtually all science, Catholic-dominated Poland and Islamic theocracies.

Second, the suppression and obstruction of scientific freedom and progress and the depreciation of science and science-based education complements and relates to extreme, coercive and fanatical religiosity typifying capitalist dictatorship, especially its theocratic or religiously overdetermined form. Anti-science is consistent with extreme religiosity so long as the latter in this and conservative-fascist dictatorships tends to result in suppressing and obstructing scientific freedom and progress and depreciating science and science-based secular education in favor of its ersatz-religious opposites (Christian and Islamic 'science', 'education', 'medicine').

Conversely, such suppression reaffirms, perpetuates and reinforces extreme religiosity tempered by science but persisting by being anchored in anti-science to form a vicious circle of scientific unfreedom, irrationalism and stagnation and of religious extremism, superstition and fanaticism interacting with and reinforcing each other. In this respect, extreme, coercive, fanatical religiosity is adverse and destructive not only to liberty of conscience characterizing freedom of/from religion but to scientific freedom, rationalism, innovation and progress and the public valuation, including government funding, of science and science-based education. Such a degree of religiosity acts as a strong predictor of the suppression and obstruction of scientific freedom and progress

and the degradation of science and science-based education in religious capitalist dictatorship, as especially conservative America and Islamic states show.

Thereby, far from being original and unique, capitalist dictatorship evokes
pre-capitalist despotism and converges and merges or allies with conservative-
fascist dictatorships. All these share the identical dual model of extreme,
coercive, fanatical religiosity and scientific unfreedom, irrationalism and stagnation and the devaluation of science or creation of their own ersatz 'science'.
Like pre-capitalism and conservative-fascist dictatorships, capitalist dictatorship in its theocratic form is antagonistic and destructive to scientific freedom
and progress and depreciating of science and education, just as artistic and
cultural liberty, art and culture. The underlying reason for its antagonism is
that it features extreme, coercive and fanatical religiosity or religious extremism, coercion and fanaticism as the 'holiest', strongest and implacable species
of anti-science and irrationalism. While conservative US apologists of capitalist theocracy exalt extreme, coerced ('expected'), and fanatical religiosity
as the supreme virtue of "faith' and 'Americanism', this feature not only violates individual liberty of conscience or freedom of/from religion. It is also
instrumental—and instrumentalized by anti-science 'holy warriors'—in suppressing and obstructing scientific freedom and progress and devaluating science and education.

In general, like the suppression of artistic and cultural liberty and the devaluation of art and culture, extreme and compulsory religiosity in capitalist dictatorship has manifest and enduring pernicious consequences for scientific
freedom and progress, science and science-based education as opposite to
non-scientific religious 'education'. (The latter included religion-based 'home
schooling' in opposition to public secular education and pervading conservative America on a scale unknown in Western society.) Alternatively, the
suppression of scientific freedom and the depreciation, degradation and mal-
treatment of science and scientists in the style of conservative America and
Islamic states is not accidental, sporadic and transient, but intertwined with
that of artistic liberty and culture and rooted in and sanctified by extreme,
fanatical religiosity. Hence, on both accounts, it is intrinsic and fundamental
to capitalist dictatorship, above all its theocratic form that that these two societies epitomize today.

In any event, the suppression and obstruction of scientific freedom, rationalism and progress and the public depreciation and degradation of science
and scientists, science-based education and educators generally characterizes capitalist dictatorship, with some secondary deviations and variations.
A vehement anti-science stand primarily holds for capitalist theocracy and
other 'faith-based' theocentric regimes in capitalism such as conservative

America, Catholic-dominated Latin America and Poland and Islamic states. Nevertheless, its other forms and agents are also prone in varying degrees and ways to this repressive, anti-science and anti-rationalist tendency. Thus, capitalist autocracy, dynasty, oligarchy and plutocracy in their pure, non-religious types can also suppress and obstruct scientific freedom, rationalism and progress. Relatedly, they can depreciate and degrade science and scientists and science-based education and educators, even technology and occasionally medicine—as conservative America showed during the Covid-19 pandemic and other occasions—for their narrow anti-social economic and political interests, even if abstracting from their religious motivations.

For illustration, a case in point is the vehement opposition of most US large capitalist corporations (including but not limited to oil and other energy companies) against the rational collective action on environmental disasters like climate change. In the process, they obstruct or retard the innovation, adoption and diffusion of 'clean' and more advanced sciences and technologies in America compared to other Western and non-Western societies.[21] These instantiations of capital thereby sacrifice science, scientific advancement and non-capital social strata and most of American society, let alone the environment, to their own narrow short-term private gains displaying short-sightedness,[22] although their adoption of 'clean' and related advanced technologies would better serve their long-term interests, thus being more rational. Capital's hyper-rational but ultimately irrational sacrifice of non-capital strata to its own benefit is consistent with the ruling class' tendency in all dictatorships for sacrificing subordinate classes' wellbeing and lives to their own exclusive benefit. The American capitalist class apparently sacrifices non-capital strata's welfare and lives—as through the opposition to rational climate-change solutions, let alone the destruction of the environment—to its own profit and power, just as European pre-capitalist aristocracy sacrificed the populace to its

---

21   Gauchat (2012, p. 172) identifies US transnational corporations as one of the 'two key constituencies' of the anti-science new right, the other being the religious right, and suggests that 'each have vested interests in scientific outcomes. Corporations subject to government regulation often challenge science to undermine federal controls and protect their profit margins'. For the climate-change 'environment disaster' under laissez-faire capitalism, see Acemoglu et al. (2012) and Stern (2013), as the 'ultimate challenge', see Nordhaus (2019), for the transition to 'clean' technology Acemoglu et al. (2016).

22   Nordhaus (2019, p. 2012) implies this by invoking 'short-sightedness among those who discount the interests of the future' among the obstacles to slowing the 'ominous march of climate change', along with 'ignorance, the distortions of democracy by anti-environmental interests and political contributions, free-riding among those looking to the interests of their country'.

benefit and dignity. In essence, judging by its opposition to the societal action on climate change, American capital appears and acts to be ready and willing to destroy both the natural environment and society in the sense of non-capital social strata (99 percent of the population)—ultimately physical and social life—for the sake of its own profit and power. It therefore acts as short-term hyper-rational but utterly irrational in longer terms by effectively making capitalism unviable as the outcome of such destruction. By so doing, capital evokes the 'deluge' pattern of pre-capitalist aristocracy, as Pareto notes,[23] and resembles the apocalyptic tendency of US evangelical cults and sects to mass suicide, including both themselves and eventually all society.

Still, capitalist theocracy remains the most vehement, consistent and lasting form and agent that is adverse and ultimately destructive to scientific freedom, rationalism and progress and thus to science and science-based secular education, technology and medicine, simply the most intense anti-science engine, as pre-capitalist theocracies do. It does this because as 'holy' religious capitalist dictatorship it implacably opposes and obstructs scientific freedom, rationalism and progress and devaluates, degrades and eliminates science and scientists and science-based secular education and educators, technology and medicine as 'enemies of God' when questioning sacred 'divine truths' and challenging non-negotiable theocratic 'godly' politics. This contrasts to some degree with capitalist autocracy, dynasty, oligarchy and plutocracy in their non-religious forms that can be more adaptable, flexible or pragmatic because of being driven by 'profane' more negotiable and transient economic-political interests. The above holds unless they blend these interests with 'faith' to sanctify their opposition to science and obstruction of scientific progress, as in conservative America since Reaganism or post-2016 and Saudi Arabia and other plutocratic Islamic states.

For instance, as in many previous occasions, during the 2020 Covid-19 virus pandemic, American conservatism manifests its virulent anti-science antagonism, specifically its self-destructive hostility to scientific medicine, and generally its irrationalism and anti-rationalism, along with anti-humanism and inhumanity, in full deadly force and acts accordingly by causing hundreds of thousands of deaths of Americans in conservative America such as the South and similar regions. It once again displays its lethal syndrome of devaluation and suppression of science and scientific rationalism, including scientific medicine, in favor of religion and superstition (and 'conspiracy theory') and

---

23   Pareto (2000, pp. 67–8) notes that the 'bourgeoisie of today does not look to the future; it exploits the present and thereafter—the deluge. Its sensibility gives vent in words, often concealing base profits'.

of sacrifice of human life and humans to 'higher' causes such as capitalism and 'God' as 'more important things' than living (as a Texas ultra-conservative official urged). By devaluating and sacrificing human life to capitalism—effectively capitalist dictatorship in the form of autocracy—and 'God', 'Bible Belt' and other American conservatism acts as or resembles a religious suicidal cult bent on committing mass suicide and causing widespread death in America.

Comparatively, no cultural and social forces and agents among Western and even other societies acts more anti-science, specifically anti-medicine, and superstitious, thus anti-rational and irrational and indeed inhuman during the global Covid-19 virus pandemic than do American conservatism and conservatives, so conservative America in the South and beyond. Compared to American conservatism and conservatives, even extremist Islamic fundamentalism and fundamentalists in Iran and other countries looks pro-science, including pro-medicine, and non-superstitious, rational or reasonable and humane during the pandemic. Most Southern and other US conservatives dismiss this deadly medical pandemic, just as potentially catastrophic climate change, as 'liberal conspiracy' (something that the 'left' invented) and act accordingly—refusing to respect public-health measures, endangering their and other people's lives and indirectly killing themselves and others. Further, during this pandemic, ultra-conservative governors in Southern states such as Alabama, Florida, Georgia, Tennessee and others aim to please their capitalist autocrat rather than to save human lives via rational medical and other measures, thus indirectly causing widespread death and suffering, with rare exceptions (e.g., the Texas governor followed a more intelligent, independent and reasonable approach provoking the rage of extreme conservatives who seemingly prefer the opposite). It is no wonder, the news in the summer of 2020 reported 'America's anti-science coronavirus crisis' and Southern conservative states Florida, Georgia and Texas had the most virus cases per capita due to the extreme irrationalism of conservatism.

Most US conservatives' actions therefore amount to those of an evangelical suicidal cult that commits suicide to reach 'rapture' and causes in the process mass deaths and destruction of other Americans. These US conservatives in their religion-grounded 'blissful ignorance' are not aware that by acting so they pose the main threat to the survival of modern civilization within the Western world and beyond. No other social group in the Western and whole world proves more unreasonable and irrational about the global Covid-19 pandemic and climate change, thus potentially more destructive to human life and civilization survival, than do US conservatives using destruction as the path to their salvation. As Adorno predicted a half century ago, US religious conservatives enjoy 'a delirium of annihilation masked as salvation'. Overall, American conservatism continues to be driven even during the most severe life and death situations by ideological-religious fanaticism, Puritanical 'insanity' (which Pareto diagnosed for its root Puritanism) and so utter irrationalism that creates ever new or aggravates serious crises rather than as pragmatism that solves them. This creation of pragmatic solutions to crises and other problems is what liberalism with its rationalism and progressivism tends to do, economically, for instance, since the Great Depression and its resolution by the New Deal and Keynesianism to its Great Recession and its equivalent liberal solution.

The 'theocratic regime' of capitalism in Islamic countries and Catholic-dominated Latin America and Poland with its extreme religiosity suppresses and obstructs scientific freedom and progress and devaluates science and science-based secular education, just as denies individual liberties for non-religious groups and favors the religious sector. Further, the substantively theocratic 'American regime' of capitalism operates through the Religious Right alliance between the capitalist class and religious low classes to obstruct scientific innovation and progress such as discoveries challenging established religious beliefs and to regulate moral activities to favor religious groups over others.[24] In both cases, the effect is suppressed and obstructed scientific freedom and progress and degraded science and science-based secular education in the name of 'divine' truth and 'faith', in conjunction and mutual reinforcement with discrimination against non-religious groups and favoritism of the religious, as typical of theocratic regimes.

By doing so, both Islamic and American regimes reside at the opposite pole of the Western European secular regime[25] of egalitarian capitalism and liberal democracy. This regime instead promotes scientific freedom, innovation and progress and thus highly values and cultivates science and scientists, science-based secular education and educators, just as applies equal treatment to religious and non-religious groups with regard to individual moral activities. This regime represents the strongest and most effective antidote—or for their adherents, the poison—to these two regimes in terms of scientific freedom and progress, science and science-based education, as well as individual liberty. At this point, the 'American regime' reappears as deviational or exceptional by comparison to the Western secular regime rather than in relation to Islamic and other third-world theocratic regimes, which qualifies conservative-sustained 'American exceptionalism' accordingly. The latter manifests itself as

---

24   See Bénabou et al. (2015, p. 347).
25   See Bénabou et al. (2015, p. 347).

Islamic-style exceptionalism in relation to the Western model of liberal-secular democracy and culture. Alternatively, it displays convergence with the Islamic, Catholic Latin-American/Polish and other third-world 'theocratic regimes', which makes conservative America appear as a proxy non- or post-Western society in these and related terms.

Suppression of scientific freedom, the obstruction of rationalism and progress and the public devaluation of science and science-based education, briefly anti-science, help indicate capitalist dictatorship primarily in its theocratic form and secondarily in its other forms, just as it does conservative-fascist, dictatorships. These tendencies inhere to capitalist theocracy and related theocentric regimes that perpetually condemn and eliminate scientific freedom and progress as 'enemies' of God and eternal divine 'truth'. They also characterize capitalist autocracy, oligarchy and plutocracy in their non-religious types that restrict them while being driven by mundane, more negotiable and transient economic or political interests. If not capitalist dictatorship, then its theocracy form perverts and eventually poisons scientific freedom and progress, science and science-based education, technology and medicine, just as all other elements of culture, including artistic and cultural liberty, art and freedom of religion.

Alternatively, capitalist theocracy exposes itself by its suppression and obstruction of scientific freedom, rationalism and progress and the public devaluation and degradation of science and science-based education. Predictably, it does all this in the 'name of the divine master', specifically the 'God of Calvinism' in historically Puritan societies like England and America and the theological functional equivalent in Islam—with both religions sharing the concept of absolutely powerful God—among Islamic plutocratic theocracies such as Saudi Arabia and other Gulf states.[26] Consequently, capitalist dictatorship in its theocratic or religious forms and agents shows the highest degree of suppression, obstruction and devaluation of scientific freedom and progress among the variations of capitalism and types of society, in particular drastically exceeding that in the complex of egalitarian capitalism and liberal-secular democracy. Further, its degree of suppression approaches that of conservative-fascist dictatorships.

---

26   Gauchat (2012, p. 172) finds that US religious groups 'clash with science over moral, epistemological, and ontological issues, such as Darwinian evolution, stem cell research, and AIDS research'. Gauchat (2012, p. 184) concludes that US 'conservatives were far more likely to define science as knowledge that should conform to common sense and religious tradition' and that 'conservatives' unfavorable attitudes are most acute in relation to government funding of science and the use of scientific knowledge to influence social policy'.

In empirical terms, most capitalist dictatorships, notably their theocratic forms and agents, exemplify the preceding tendency with respect to scientific freedom, rationalism and progress, science and science-based education. Historical cases include Weber's Calvinist-Puritan capitalist theocracies in 19th-century Victorian England and especially America suppressing scientific freedom via 'Monkey trials' or perverting science and rationalism into the theocratic instrument of glorification of God and of reproduction of oppression in society. Subsequent instances are corporate-fascist religious Catholic and Protestant dictatorships in interwar Italy, Germany and Europe, effectively destroying scientific freedom and abusing science, postwar Catholic 'free market' dictatorships in Latin America suppressing these and all freedoms, and the UK and the US déjà vu under anti-science neo-conservatism. Contemporary examples replicate the historical and involve, among Western societies, especially capitalist-evangelical America where the above processes continue and intensify through new 'Monkey and witch trials' of scientific freedom, science and science-based education. Among non-Western societies, instances are most Islamic capitalist theocracies like Saudi Arabia and other Gulf states where scientific and artistic liberties are non-entities and taboos, along with Catholic-dominated South America and Poland in which science and all culture becomes the servant of Catholicism reminiscent of the Dark Middle Ages.

In sum, suppressing and obstructing scientific freedom, rationalism and progress and devaluating science and science-based education, thus manifesting anti-science, is an additional indicator of capitalist dictatorship, especially its theocracy form, and to a lesser degree its other forms such as autocracy and plutocracy in non-religious types. For example, the suppression and obstruction of scientific freedom and progress in fields ranging from biological evolution and stem-cell research to climate science and alternative energy sources may indicate capitalist dictatorship, in particular its theocracy from, condemning such activities and scientists as 'enemies of God' and eternal 'divine truths', and partially autocracy and plutocracy in capitalism. More precisely, perpetual suppressions of biological evolutionism help identity capitalist theocracy, as in evangelical America and Saudi Arabia and other Islamic states. In addition, climate change denials serve to detect autocracy, dynasty, oligarchy and plutocracy especially in the US, apparently pursuing narrow anti-social but more transient vested interests of wealth preservation through irrational, self-destructive economic actions in longer terms.

5.4   *Persistence of Widespread Religious Superstitions*

Persistence of widespread religious superstitions and dogmas constitutes yet another related indicator or proxy of capitalist dictatorship as a cultural system. Evidently, this tendency closely connects with obstructing scientific progress and devaluating science and science-based education and extreme religiosity featuring capitalist dictatorship. In a sense, the persistence of widespread religious superstitions and dogmas is a positive equivalent of the obstruction of scientific progress—while the devaluation of science involving negativity—and an extension and intensification of extreme religiosity. Such persistent and pervasive beliefs epitomize the cultural irrationalism of capitalist dictatorship, while the obstruction of scientific progress and the devaluation science and science-based education epitomizing its anti-rationalism, in particular anti-science. The first process completes capitalist dictatorship as a coherent cultural compound of both anti-rationalism and irrationalism, including anti-science and religious superstition.

With some variations, persistent and pervasive religious superstitions and dogmas and corresponding practices manifesting cultural irrationalism permeate capitalist dictatorship. In this regard, the latter far from being novel replicates pre-capitalist despotism like medievalism and pre-modernism and converges with conservative-fascist dictatorships, all featuring such irrational beliefs and practices. In particular, the enduring persistence and methodical perpetuation of mass religious superstitions and corresponding practices primarily typify capitalist theocracy or theocentric regimes compared the other forms and agents of capitalist dictatorship, including autocracy and plutocracy in their non-religious types. This process is the special cultural irrational essence of capitalist theocracy, as is of pre-capitalist despotism and conservative-fascist dictatorships.

Hence, if not capitalist dictatorship as a whole, including plutocracy assuming its non-religious type, at the minimum, capitalist theocracy replicates in this respect rather overcomes medievalism and other pre-capitalist irrationalism and despotism, and resembles conservative-fascist dictatorships. Pareto implies this observing in capitalist America during the Gilded Age the 'rise of no end of strange and wholly unscientific religions such as Christian Science that are utterly at war with any sort of scientific thinking' that; along with 'a mass of hypocritical laws for the enforcement of morality', represent 'replicas' of those of the 'European Middle Ages'. He thus depicts capitalist theocracy in this and other societies as the New Dark Ages in respect of its ersatz 'science' and as renewed despotism with regard to its coercive imposition of morals. Such a depiction hence corresponds in both respects to the darkness of conservative and fascist dictatorships commonly portrayed, especially those in the postbellum US South and interwar Germany, respectively, as Dark Ages. In Pareto's depiction, capitalist theocracy in the 'new nation' seems as plagued with and as much inflicts its subjects with religious superstitions and dogmas cum 'Christian science' (including Christian 'education' and 'medicine') as the European 'old world' did and conservative-fascist dictatorships do in various societies. In a word, capitalist theocracy remains a 'flat earth society' in a generic and figurative sense of religious superstition and even in a specific and literal meaning of a true belief, as in sections of the US 'Bible Belt'.

The 'theocratic regime' of capitalism both obstructs scientific progress and perpetuates and imposes religious superstitions and dogmas, with the result of 'knowledge stagnation' and privileging the religious sector.[27] This regime primarily characterizes non-Western, notably Islamic and Catholic South American societies and some European countries like post-socialist Poland under Catholicism and helps explain their lack of substantial scientific progress and permeation with superstitions. In addition, the 'American regime' of capitalism while formally different has substantively theocratic attributes or effects. It thus impedes 'belief-eroding discoveries and ideas' ranging from evolution and stem-cell research to climate science, perpetuates superstitious religious beliefs through the Christian Right alliance of the capitalist wealthy and religious non-capitalist strata, and favors 'religious activities and citizens'.[28] In the process of such an alliance, plutocracy mutates into capitalist theocracy as 'faith-based' culture and society, and conversely, the theocratic regime contaminates and saturates the plutocratic elite and capitalism, which evangelical America, and the 'Bible Belt' within it, demonstrates.

Both non-Western and American regimes of capitalism share superstitious or 'literalist beliefs in miracles, the devil, or the inerrancy of the Bible (or Koran)', which all have negative views of and effects on scientific progress.[29] It follows that these beliefs are religious superstitions and dogmas because they impede—and are compromised by—'belief-eroding discoveries and ideas' and thus scientific innovation and progress, not because, as adherents of both regimes allege, of anti-religious 'bias' and 'hostility'.

Among these beliefs, the belief in 'Satan' qualifies probably as the supreme exemplar of all religious superstitions and dogmas within religions like Christianity and Islam. This is the belief that the vast majority of Americans share with equivalent Islamic populations, along with many other aspects of the 'inerrancy' of the Bible and Koran such as 'creationism', 'intelligent design', 'all-mighty God', and 'predestination' ('heaven and hell'). At this point, 'Satan' in the sense of a negative belief in and condemnation of the 'enemy'— yet in a perverse logic, the personal creation—of 'God' (not 'satanism' as

---

27   See Bénabou et al. (2015, p. 347).
28   See Bénabou et al. (2015, p. 347).
29   See Bénabou et al. (2015, p. 347).

counter-religion) typifies, embodies and saturates capitalist theocracy among these religions, as did its pre-capitalist forms in medievalism.

Notably, probably more than any other religious superstitions and dogmas the belief in 'Satan' blocks 'belief-eroding discoveries and ideas' and obstructs scientific innovation and progress in Islamic and American regimes. For example, it perhaps helps explain the widespread opposition or suspicion to biological evolution by recurring 'monkey trials', stem-cell research and in part climate science in evangelical America condemning these and other sciences and scientists as 'associates of Satan', so 'witches' déjà vu, and thus 'enemies of God'. Both Islamic and American theocratic regimes stand in vehement opposition against the 'Secularization or Western-European regime' that cultivates 'unimpeded scientific progress'[30] and features weak religious superstitions or literalist beliefs, including 'Satan', 'creationism' and related 'inerrancy' of the holy books. For example, only between one tenth and fifth of the Western European population (Denmark, France) maintain the belief in 'Satan', which is multiple times lower than the corresponding proportion of American and Islamic populations. The same holds, with some variations, for 'creationism', the overall 'inerrancy of the Bible' and levels of religiosity.

Therefore, the perpetuation and further diffusion of mass religious superstitions and dogmas and corresponding practices helps indicate capitalist dictatorship as a cultural system, at the minimum its theocracy form or theocentric regimes. Furthermore, this minimum becomes a proxy maximum so long as capitalist theocracy infuses and saturates capitalist dictatorship, including its merging or allying with plutocracy and prevailing within this merger. This is what the 'American regime' demonstrates through the Religious Right alliance between plutocratic elites and religious low classes in the function of preserving religious superstitions and dogmas and impeding scientific innovation, just the Islamic 'theocratic regime' does. In a way, capitalist dictatorship or whatever its proxy is in America since Puritanism through evangelicalism has been primarily theocracy merged or allied with plutocracy and dominating in this merger. For example, the long-standing Puritan 'blue laws' against Sunday business and other secular activity indicate the dominance of theocracy within this alliance, even if recently repealed in New England but apparently persisting in some forms in the 'Bible Belt', not to mention Prohibition and the war on drugs.

The preceding holds as a prevalent tendency, albeit with some occasional transient frictions and tensions between theocratic and plutocratic elites—but

---

30   See Bénabou et al. (2015, p. 347).

still not seriously endangering their basic unity—within the extended family of authoritarian conservatism and its main political organization. Consequently, a myriad of religious superstitions and dogmas from 'creationism' through 'Satan' to 'flat earth' persisting up to the present has pervaded and plagued capitalist dictatorship or American exceptional capitalism, as they did European pre-capitalist despotism like medievalism. The same holds for capitalist and pre-capitalist dictatorship in Islamic counties like Saudi Arabia and other Gulf states, which is axiomatically and invariably theocracy within capitalism or pre-capitalism. More broadly, to the extent that theocracy immerses into and merges with, as in conservative America and the Islamic world, most other forms and agents of capitalist dictatorship, the present indicator applies to the latter as a whole and not just its theocratic form and agent.

Alternatively, capitalist dictatorship as a cultural system, notably its theocracy form, reveals itself through mass religious superstitions and corresponding practices enforcing them. These range from 'creationism' and 'intelligent design'—which the US court system has consistently defined as a superstition/religion by defining it as non-science—and 'flat earth' to 'Satan' and 'exorcism'. Comparatively, especially Islamic and American evangelical theocratic regimes share these beliefs. This is consistent with Weber's treatment of Islam and Puritanism as structural equivalents in theological terms, including the dogmas of absolute 'all-mighty' God, predestination and the elect, and in political respects such as the merger of religion with politics, legal or de facto theocracy, religious revolution, and 'holy' war.

As a consequence, capitalist dictatorship, in particular its theocracy form, tends to exhibit the most extensive and enduring religious superstitions such as 'Satan' and others among the varieties of capitalism and types of modern society, especially when compared to the composite of welfare capitalism and liberal-secular democracy in Western Europe, notably Scandinavia. Conversely, it approaches conservative-fascist dictatorships in which religious superstitions and corresponding practices dominate. In particular, capitalist theocracy is essentially identical with conservative/religious dictatorship in this and other respects, as Islamic and American regimes demonstrate. Further, it often fuses with fascism, as Latin American Catholic neo-fascist regimes show, along with corporate-fascist dictatorships in interwar Germany, Italy and Spain.

As the preceding suggests, most past and present capitalist dictatorships, notably their theocratic or theocentric forms and agents, follow the above path. Among past cases, mass superstitious beliefs and practices, including 'Satan', 'witches', human sacrifices via exorcism and witch-crazes and trials—of which those at Salem are just the most notorious episode—consumed and obsessed Weber's proto-capitalist Calvinist, especially Puritan, theocracies and theocrats in England and early America, as they did Catholic pre-capitalist despotism like European medievalism. They therefore rendered both settings and times truly Dark Ages.

Moreover, Pareto by the cited observation suggests that this tendency to the prevalence and resurrection of religious superstition and anti-science (cum 'Christian science') continues in America through the early 20th century, thus effectively predicting the 1925 'Monkey Trial' in Mencken's 'Bible Belt' against evolution and similar religious attacks on science and scientists, science-based educations and educators then, later and now. In addition, the 'godliness' of corporate-fascist dictatorships in interwar Catholic-Lutheran Germany and Catholic Italy, Spain and Portugal imbued them with superstitious beliefs and practices like 'miracles' and the 'devil'. In essence, all these dictatorships in Italy, Spain, Portugal and other Catholic countries, including Nazi-allied Austria, Croatia, and Hungary, were capitalist and in part pre-capitalist Vatican-controlled theocracies and more broadly conservative regimes featuring such superstitious beliefs and practices. This applies, with some variations, to neo-fascist dictatorships in postwar Latin America, especially Chile, as they represented Catholic theocracies or theocentric regimes with such religious features.

Among contemporary examples, capitalist-evangelical America such as the 'Bible Belt and beyond continues to be in the Puritan style consumed and obsessed with 'Satan', as the above figure indicates, human sacrifices via cult mass suicides and sectarian exorcism, by implication 'witches' and witch-trials, 'creationism', in part 'flat earth' déjà vu, up to the present. This also applies to Turkey recently, Saudi Arabia and other Islamic capitalist-theocratic states. The fact[31] that 7 out of 10 Americans believe in the existence and operation of 'Satan' as the utmost 'enemy of God' and so probably willing to engage in the exorcism of 'evil' or to Satanize and eliminate 'infidels' as 'un-American'—liberals, secularists, progressives, rationalists, scientists—is telling and unparalleled among contemporary Western societies and only compares with such a belief in Islamic states. As additional instances, resurging capitalist-Catholic dictatorship in Poland, former-fascist European countries such as Croatia,

---

31   In methodological terms, this fact is perhaps one of those cases defying Parsons (1967, pp. 10, 698) who cautions, invoking the neoclassical economist Marshall, that facts do not 'speak for themselves' and 'do not tell their own story; they must be cross-examined'. Alternatively, the fact does not really speak for itself and requires, as Parsons would suggest, to be cross-examined in the context of persistent, widespread religious superstitions within capitalist dictatorship as a cultural system, especially its theocracy form in Puritan-rooted conservative America and plutocratic Islamic states.

Hungary and some Baltic states and parts of South America like Brazil and Colombia retrieve and sustain beliefs in 'miracles', the 'devil' and related religious superstitions and dogmas. Further examples include capitalist and similar dictatorships, in particular theocracies, in most of Africa and much of Asia, which perpetuate and enforce their own superstitious beliefs and practices, including, as in the first, the literal belief in witches and witch-hunting and killing rituals[32]. In sum, an additional indicator of capitalist dictatorship as a cultural system, in particular of its theocratic forms and agents, comprises persistent and mass superstitions and dogmas and corresponding coercive and violent practices enforcing them.

32   For witch-killing rituals in today's Africa, see Duflo (2012, p. 1055).

Degrees of Capitalist Dictatorship for Contemporary Societies

This chapter calculates the degrees of capitalist dictatorship for contemporary Western and comparable societies such as OECD countries. It calculates these degrees based on the preceding societal, including economic, political, civil-society and cultural, indicators of capitalist dictatorship and their specifications and measures. In sociological terms, it calculates the degrees of capitalist dictatorship as a total social system by aggregating these four sets of indicators which the following section summarizes and specifies.

1   Summary and Specification of Societal Indicators of Capitalist Dictatorship

1.1   Economic Indicators

Suppression of unionization. Suppression and consequently a low level and indeed non-existence of unionization of non-capital classes constitutes an inherent feature and accurate economic indicator of capitalist dictatorship. Suppressed and extremely low labor unionization inheres to and diagnoses, ceteris paribus, capitalist dictatorship in all its forms and agents ranging from autocracy and dynasty to plutocracy or plutocratic aristocracy and oligarchy, including kleptocracy and predatory capitalism, and to police states, military dictatorships and theocracies. In these terms, capitalist dictatorship develops and functions as the economic system of negation and suppression of unionization and thus collective organization of non-capital classes to the lowest possible level, asymptotically to zero or so. It historically continues the pre-capitalist despotic ancient regime of prohibition and suppression of collective organization of lower classes such as slaves, subjugated castes and servants. More broadly, it exemplifies the tendency of all past and contemporary dictatorships to negate and suppress the collective organization of subordinate production factors or social classes. Comparatively, its labor unionization level invariably tends to be lower than that in the alternative egalitarian and democratic variations of capitalism and types of society or polity, specifically welfare capitalism and liberal democracy. A standard specification or equivalent of the level of labor unionization is union density.

Restriction of the scope of unionization. Another related built-in property and accurate indicator of capitalist dictatorship, as an economic system is the restriction of and hence narrow scope of unionization of non-capital classes. Restricted economy-wide scope of unionization and of labor collective action, including negotiation with capital, typifies and identifies, all else being equal, capitalist dictatorship in its diverse forms and agents, including autocracy/dynasty, plutocracy/oligarchy and others. On this account, capitalist dictatorship emerges and persists as the economic system of systematic and intensive limitation of the scope of unionization of non-capital classes to the lowest possible level, asymptotically to zero or so. In historical terms, it perpetuates the pre-capitalist ancient regime of maximal limitation of the scope of collective action of slaves, subjugated castes, servants and other ruled classes. Generally, it illustrates dictatorships' tendency to systematically and intensely limit the scope of collective action of subordinate production factors or classes to the lowest possible level, ultimately to zero or so. In comparative terms, its scope of unionization is as a rule invariably lower than that in welfare capitalism and liberal democracy. Union or collective bargaining coverage is the standard specification or equivalent of the economy-wide scope of unionization.

Suppression of collective bargaining. Yet another related intrinsic trait and accurate indicator of capitalist dictatorship as an economic system consists of the suppression and consequently non-existence or rarity of collective bargaining between capital and non-capital. Suppressed and non-existent negotiations between capital and non-capital as social classes and thus collective (as opposite to individual) agents intrinsically characterize and accurately indicate capitalist dictatorship in its various forms and agents from autocracy/dynasty to plutocracy/oligarchy and others. In this regard, capitalist dictatorship appears and operates as the economic system of denial and suppression of the collective bargaining between capital and non-capital to a minimum point, asymptotically to zero. It replicates, with some alterations, the pre-capitalist ancient regime of prohibition of any collective negotiations between ruling and ruled classes, such as slave masters and slaves, dominant and subjugated castes, aristocrats and servants. Generally, it conforms to dictatorships' syndrome—especially of conservative-fascist and theocratic regimes—of denying and suppressing the collective bargaining between the ruling class and subordinate classes to the minimum, asymptotically to zero. Comparatively, the presence and spread of collective bargaining between capital and non-capital in capitalist dictatorship tends be invariably lesser than in welfare capitalism and liberal democracy. One can specify and measure collective bargaining directly and exactly by its incidence and frequency subject to data availability or indirectly and approximately by collective bargaining coverage as its proxy.

Suppression of codetermination. Suppression and consequently the absence or scarcity of labor collective participation in firm management, simply co-determination, provides an additional related inherent characteristic and accurate indicator of capitalist dictatorship as an economic system. Suppressed and absent labor codetermination in corporate governance inheres to and accurately diagnoses capitalist dictatorship in its particular forms and agents, including both autocracy/dynasty and plutocracy/oligarchy. On this account, capitalist dictatorship manifests itself as the economic system of negation and suppression of labor codetermination in management to the minimal level, asymptotically to zero. Consequently, it continues, with some adaptations, the pre-capitalist despotic ancient regime of prohibition of any participation of lower classes, including slaves, subjugated castes, and servants, in economic and related decision making, however different from that in capitalism. The point is these two systems exclude pre- and non-capitalist subordinate classes, respectively, from business management/power despite its historical varia-tions. More broadly, capitalist dictatorship accords with the penchant of dic-tatorships, especially conservative-fascist and theocratic regimes, to deny and suppress the participation of subordinate classes in economic governance to the minimal level, asymptotically to zero. In comparative terms, labor codeter-mination in capitalist dictatorship is as a rule invariably scarcer and weaker than in welfare capitalism and liberal democracy. Works councils and board-level employee representation are typical specifications and measures of codetermination.

Extreme concentration of wealth. Extreme concentration of wealth rep-resents an intrinsic attribute and salient economic indicator of capitalist dictatorship. Wealth concentration and ultimately monopolization in capital typifies and identifies capitalist dictatorship in all its forms and agents, espe-cially autocracy, dynasty and axiomatically plutocracy, plutocratic aristocracy and oligarchy, including kleptocracy and mafia capitalism. On this account, capitalist dictatorship constitutes the dictatorship of the wealthy within capi-talism, as distinct from that in pre-capitalism, including slavery, caste and feu-dalism. Hence, in historical terms, it provides a paradigmatic instance of dic-tatorships of the rich or plutocracies, their continuation by identical means, such as invariably wealth even if in new, primarily financial and industrial forms as distinct from land property prevailing in pre-capitalism. In compar-ative terms, it remains the only existing exemplar of the dictatorship of the wealthy within contemporary society in light of the effective disappearance or irrelevance of pre-capitalism like slavery, caste and feudalism as defunct cases of such dictatorship. Specifically, its level of wealth concentration as a whole tends to higher than in the other variations of capitalism and types of society, specifically welfare capitalism and liberal democracy. A specification and measure of wealth concentration is the wealth share of the top one per-cent of society.

Extremely unequal income distribution. Extremely unequal income distribu-tion and especially concentration in capital is another inherent feature and salient indicator of capitalist dictatorship as an economic system, operating in reciprocal relation ad reinforcement with wealth concentration (at least in moderate correlation with the latter). As with that of wealth, extreme income inequality or concentration characterizes and detects capitalist dictatorship in all its forms and agents, including plutocracy or plutocratic oligarchy. Since unequal income distribution is typically both the source and result of wealth concentration, it forms an integral element of capitalist dictatorship as the dictatorship of the wealthy in capitalism. Thus, the capitalist 'dictatorship of the rich' involves the latter by virtue of their wealth and monetary income. This appears to be a historical novelty and specificity of such a dictatorship so long as its pre-capitalist precedent involved the rich mostly because of their wealth in the form of estate property and just secondarily money income. Comparatively, capitalist dictatorship is the only example of the dictatorship of the rich with an economic basis in income and wealth in contemporary society. Particularly, the inequality of its income distribution as a rule tends to be higher than in welfare capitalism and liberal democracy. Among the con-ventional specifications or measures of unequal income distribution is the Gini coefficient.

Material degradation, deprivation and hardship. Material degradation, deprivation and hardship, including poverty, of non-capital form an additional intrinsic property and important economic indicator of capitalist dictatorship mostly resulting from wealth concentration and unequal income distribution. As with the previous indicators, persistent and extensive material degradation, deprivation and hardship to the point of poverty typifies and indicates capital-ist dictatorship in all its forms and agents from autocracy and dynasty to plu-tocracy or plutocratic oligarchy. If it is the dictatorship of the wealthy from the standpoint and interest of capital, it operates as the system of material depri-vation, degradation, hardship and impoverishment from the viewpoint and experience of non-capitalists, especially lower and powerless social classes. This includes pervasive and chronic adult and child poverty and hence, ceteris paribus, misery, combined with labor hardship such as hard long work and short or no (paid) vacation. In historical terms, capitalist dictatorship is just one instance of such systems, thus perpetuating them with some quantitative differences in the (usually lower) degrees of deprivation, hardship and poverty of low social classes compared to pre-capitalism. In comparative terms, capitalist dictatorship becomes the economic system with the most persistent and extensive material deprivation, deprivation, hardship and poverty among the variations of capitalism and types of polity, especially as compared to welfare capitalism and liberal democracy. General and child poverty rates specify and measure material degradation deprivation, and hardship of non-capital, along with hard long work and short or no paid vacation.

Economic exploitation. A related and typical attribute and accurate economic indicator of capitalist dictatorship is the extensive and high exploitation of non-capital classes generating or exacerbating their degradation, deprivation and poverty and contributing to, just as stemming from, extreme wealth and income concentration in capital. Widespread and intense labor exploitation typically characterizes and accurately identifies capitalist dictatorship in its various forms and agents, including both autocracy and plutocracy or oligarchy. While being an oasis of universal justice and meritocracy for capital, capitalist dictatorship is to an economic system of systematic exploitation and thus injustice, and its autocracy or plutocracy appears as exploitative and predatory kleptocracy, for non-capital. Capitalist dictatorship inherits and continues, with some modifications, the pre-capitalist despotic ancient regime of universal and severe exploitation of subordinate classes like slaves, subjugated castes, and servants, with plutocracy effectively continuing aristocracy's exploitative template as the immediate model or precursor. Generally, it epitomizes rather than overcomes the tendency of all dictatorships, especially conservative-fascist and theocratic regimes, to systematically exploit laboring and subordinate classes. Comparatively, the level of exploitation of non-capital classes in capitalist dictatorship tend to be as a whole more pervasive and intensive than in its opposites, welfare capitalism and liberal democracy. The rate of labor exploitation serves to specify and measure the level of exploitation of non-capital.

Economic non-protection and insecurity. Weak and even non-existent economic and related protection and security represents yet another intrinsic feature and accurate economic indicator of capitalist dictatorship that derives from and connects with the previous indicators, especially extreme wealth and income concentration in capital and labor exploitation. Pervasive and chronic non-protection and intense insecurity of non-capital intrinsically permeates and accurately indicates capitalist dictatorship in its diverse forms and agents from autocracy and dynasty to plutocracy and oligarchy. This includes weak employment protection or high economic insecurity, low unemployment benefits or insurance, weak social protection or high social

insecurity and the like. While representing a supreme mechanism of protection and security of capital in the sense if its property and power (e.g.,
property rights), capitalist dictatorship represents a system of non-protection
and insecurity of non-capital, with some secondary variations. In historical
terms, it resembles the pre-capitalist despotic ancient regime of universal
economic non-protection and intense insecurity of slaves, subjugated castes,
servants and other subordinate classes subjected to the arbitrariness of their
masters. Thus, plutocracy essentially seeks to recreate the same ambiance
of existential fear and uncertainty for non-capital as aristocracy did for the
non-aristocratic populace. More broadly, capitalist dictatorship exemplifies
dictatorships', particularly conservative-fascist and theocratic regimes', typical inclination to provide weak economic protection and security for subordinate classes and induce and sustain their non-protection and insecurity.
In comparative terms, the economic protection and security of non-capital
classes in capitalist dictatorship tends to be weaker—and conversely, their
non-protection and insecurity stronger—than in welfare capitalism and liberal democracy. Several measures serve to specify economic non-protection
and insecurity of non-capital: employment protection, unemployment benefits and economic-social protection.

1.2   *Political Indicators*

Suppression of political freedoms and rights. Suppression of political freedom
is a characteristic trait and pertinent indicator of capitalist dictatorship as a
political regime, usually deriving from or connecting with the extreme concentration of power in capital. Non-existent or minimal political freedom of
non-capital groups characterizes and identifies capitalist dictatorship as a corresponding system in all its forms and agents, including both autocracy and
oligarchy. While forming a system of virtually unrestricted political freedom
for capital, capitalist dictatorship appears as a regime with opposite properties to the point of unfreedom for non-capital. It tends to deny both electoral
freedoms and rights and especially the freedom and right to seek and hold
power for non-capital and thus suppress free political competition for power.
To that extent, it historically perpetuates past systems of (complete) political
unfreedom for subordinate groups. Comparatively, it exemplifies rather than
overcomes political regimes of absent or limited freedom for lower and powerless strata among contemporary societies, especially allying or converging
with conservative-fascist and theocratic dictatorships. Specifically, its degree
of political freedom tends to be the lowest among the variations of capitalism
and types of polity, notably lower than that in welfare capitalism and liberal
democracy.

What exemplifies and measures the suppression of political freedom is suppressing voting freedoms and rights, which low voter turnout approximates. Another related specification or measure is the suppression of voice. Suppression of voice in the polity and society overall represents another typical element and relevant political indicator of capitalist dictatorship, while also being the effect or correlate of the extreme concentration of power in capital. Absent or weak voice for non-capital intrinsically features and accurately expresses capitalist dictatorship in all its forms and agents from autocracy to oligarchy. Capitalist dictatorship while being an exclusive area of voice and expression for capital and its interests is a wide space of largely voiceless or silenced non-capital groups especially with regard to critical and overarching political, economic and other social matters, for example, type of polity and capitalism or economy. In historical terms, capitalist dictatorship appears as an instance and, with some modifications, continuation of past political regimes of non-existent voice in the polity and society for lower and powerless strata rather than their outgrowing. Comparatively, it belongs to rather than substantively differs from their contemporary versions, above all, linking and merging with conservative-fascist and theocratic regimes. Especially, its level of voice in the polity and society tends as a rule to be lower than that in welfare capitalism and liberal democracy.

Concentration of political power. Power concentration and ultimately monopolization constitutes an inherent element and essential political indicator of capitalist dictatorship typically in interconnection and mutual reinforcement with that of wealth. The extreme concentration and indeed monopolization of power in capital politically defines and indicates capitalist dictatorship in all its forms and agents from autocracy and family dynasty to plutocracy and oligarchy. In this respect, capitalist dictatorship represents the system of superior structural power and domination of capital over non-capital, as distinct from but substantively continuous with the pre-capitalist ancient regime with the same structure for aristocracy and non-aristocracy. Historically, it forms a special case of past systems of power concentration in and domination of the ruling group or elite over subordinate groups, their continuation or evocation by both identical and different means such as repression and formal freedom, respectively, of non-capital. Comparatively, it belongs to rather than overgrows such systems of power concentration and domination among contemporary societies, especially conservative-fascist and theocratic dictatorships. Particularly, its degree of power concentration tends to be higher as compared to welfare capitalism and liberal democracy. One specification and measure of power concentration is the absence or weakness of constraints on state or government powers. Additional specifications, measures or proxies include the negative reciprocal or inverse of political pluralism, of political stability and absence of violence, of the rule of law, of control of corruption, and of open government.

Severe penal repression and punishment. Mainly as a consequence of the concentration of power in capital, the severe penal repression and punishment of non-capital groups forms an intrinsic element and accurate indicator of capitalist dictatorship as a political regime. Systematic penal repression and Draconian punishment of non-capital groups for even their mildest criminal and, as in its moralistic and religious forms, sinful transgressions typifies and accurately diagnoses capitalist dictatorship ranging from autocracy and dynasty to plutocracy and oligarchy and to police states and military dictatorships. While being the foremost mechanism of non-repression and non-punishment, even for gravest financial and often personal crimes, for capital, it represents the political regime of crime—and as in its theocratic forms of no crime in the ordinary sense distinct from sin—and severe punishment for non-capital groups. In historical terms, it continues, with secondary alterations, the pre-capitalist despotic ancient regime featuring pervasive penal repression and severe punishment of subordinate groups, including slaves, subjugated castes and servants, in particular aristocracy's punitive treatment of the populace which plutocracy effectively applies to non-capital. In general, it expresses the classic and enduring proclivity of all, especially conservative-fascist and theocratic, dictatorships, to systematically repress and severely punish subordinate political groups for their even slightest crimes and sins, along with dissent, that they criminalize. In comparative terms, the political repression and punishment of non-capital groups is as a rule more pervasive and severe in capitalist dictatorship than in the complex of welfare capitalism and liberal democracy. Penal repression and punishment measures are imprisonment, death sentences and executions, and other 'political terror'.

Militarism. Another typical property and reliable indicator of capitalist dictatorship is militarism, including a large military-capitalist complex, aggressive wars against other states and militarized political coercion of non-capital groups within society. Militarism in both of these manifestations usually characterizes and reliably indicates capitalist dictatorship in its various forms and agents, from autocracy to plutocracy, especially military dictatorships, including personal rule and juntas within capitalism. While being an instrument of safety, national security and 'peace' for capital, capitalist dictatorship effectively functions as the militaristic, warlike and coercive political regime for non-capital and 'enemy' states. It historically retrieves and expands the pre-capitalist despotic ancient regime of militarism, including militarized political coercion and war, such as that of feudalism, with militaristic plutocracy essentially inheriting the feudal military caste or aristocracy. More broadly, capitalist dictatorship demonstrates rather than supersedes the propensity of all, especially conservative-fascist and theocratic, dictatorships for militarization, including militarized political coercion of subordinate groups within society and aggressive wars against other states. Comparatively, the intensity of militarism in its various forms tends to be higher in capitalist dictatorship than in the compound of welfare capitalism and liberal democracy. A conventional quantitative measure or proxy of militarism is large military expenditure.

1.3   Civil-Society Indicators

Suppression of individual liberty. Suppression of individual liberty or personal freedom represents an additional characteristic and indicator of capitalist dictatorship as a civil society, deriving from or linking with the extreme concentration of power in capital, such as the absence or weakness of constraints on its government powers. Limited and even, under certain conditions, nonexistent individual liberty for non-capitalists permeates and precisely diagnoses capitalist dictatorship in all its forms and agents, including autocracy and oligarchy. While lavishing capital with almost unrestrained personal freedom capitalist dictatorship appears as a system of individual unfreedom for and from the experience of non-capitalists, especially lower and powerless strata. Capitalist dictatorship historically resembles, and to some extent continues, ancient regimes of individual unfreedom for subordinate groups, specifically plutocracy treats non-capitalists, with respect to their personal freedom, in a way reminiscent of aristocracy's treatment of the populace. Comparatively, it exemplifies but does not transcend such contemporary political systems of individual unfreedom for these groups, especially showing an elective affinity with conservative-fascist and theocratic dictatorships. Specifically, the degree and scope of individual liberty tends to be lower and narrower in capitalist dictatorship than in welfare capitalism or liberal democracy.

Suppression of other civil liberties. Suppression of other civil liberties is a usual feature and pertinent indicator of capitalist dictatorship as a (perverted) civil society, ensuing from or associating with the extreme concentration of power in capital, particularly the absent or weak constraints on its government powers. Non-existent or minimal civil liberties typify and identify capitalist dictatorship in all its forms and agents, including both autocracy and oligarchy. Capitalist dictatorship while being the realm of virtually unlimited civil and related liberties for capital is the sphere of their denial or violation, simply of proxy illiberty, for non-capital groups. Historically, capitalist dictatorship replicates ancient regimes of non-existent civil liberties for subordinate groups, thus plutocracy in capitalism adopting versus non-capital the method of aristocracy in pre-capitalism against the populace, with some modifications. In comparative terms, it exemplifies but does not outgrow such contemporary systems, especially allying or converging with conservative-fascist and theocratic dictatorships. Particularly, its degree of civil liberties tends as a whole to be lower than that in the complex of welfare capitalism and liberal democracy. This syndrome of capitalist dictatorship also includes suppression of particular civil liberties such as media or press freedom.

Negation of civil and other human rights. The negation or violation of civil and other human rights is another related attribute and indicator of capitalist dictatorship as a civil society, which results from or connects with the extreme concentration of power in capital, in particular the absence or weakness of constraints on its state powers. Weak civil and other human rights for non-capital groups pervade and accurately indicate capitalist dictatorship in all its forms and agents from autocracy and dynasty to oligarchy and plutocracy. While endowing capital with generous and extensive rights capitalist dictatorship amounts to a system of their denial, suppression or violation in respect of non-capital groups. In historical terms, it evokes and, with certain adaptations, perpetuates the pre-capitalist ancient regimes of negation of human rights for subordinate groups, in particular plutocracy acts toward non-capital almost in the manner aristocracy acted versus the populace, with some modifications. Comparatively, it forms a peculiar example and not an opposite of contemporary political systems with weak human rights, especially connecting and often blending with conservative-fascist and theocratic dictatorships. In particular, human rights tend as a rule to be weaker and fewer in capitalist dictatorship than in the complex of welfare capitalism and liberal democracy. A composite measure of the negation of civil and other human rights is the violation of certain fundamental, core rights such as those that the UN Universal Declaration of Human Rights establishes. Another specific measure consists of negating or invading privacy as an exemplary and inviolable individual human right consistent with the inviolability of the person in liberal democracy and modernity.

Criminalization and severe sanctioning of moral offenses. This indicator forms the special, moralistic component of the severe penal repression and punishment of non-capital groups in capitalist dictatorship. Repression and punishment of non-capital groups for sins-as-crimes involves the criminalization and severe sanctioning of moral offenses and offenders as grave criminal acts and criminals deserving appropriate negative sanctions up to mass imprisonment and death sentences and executions. This practice particularly pervades and identifies moralistic-religious capitalist dictatorship or theocracy within capitalism. Theocratic capitalist dictatorship while absolving capital or theocrats from virtually any vice and sin or applying mild sanctions for transgressions, is a political regime of criminalizing all human vices and sins for non-capital groups. It sanctions these moral offenses of non-capital accordingly, in a typical Draconian manner of punishment to the point of death or mass long imprisonment. Consequently, it historically reiterates the pre-capitalist despotic ancient regime of criminalizing and harshly sanctioning moral offenses with respect to subordinate groups (but not the ruling group), specifically medieval and other pre-modern theocracy. Relatedly, it converges and ultimately merges or allies with contemporary conservative-fascist and theocratic dictatorships that especially engage in such practices. Comparatively, the criminalization and sanctioning of moral offenses tends to be more extensive and severe in capitalist dictatorship than in the compound of welfare capitalism and liberal democracy. Its measures are accordingly the moralistic aspects of imprisonment, death sentences and executions, and other 'political terror', for example, the use or threat of application of the death penalty for drug offenses.

Moralistic-religious terror. Moralistic and religiously driven terror or repression of non-capital sinful groups is the ultimate outcome of the criminalization and sanctioning of moral offenses and offenders in capitalist dictatorship in its theocratic forms and agents. It is hence a moralistic and religious complement of state 'political terror', namely of mass imprisonment, widespread death sentences and executions, and other serious violations of human rights. Moralistic and religiously driven terror or repression of non-capital groups typifies and accurately identifies capitalist dictatorship especially in its theocratic forms and agents. The latter continues, with some adaptations, the 'holy' terror of the pre-capitalist despotic ancient regime, such as medieval Christian Catholic and Protestant, Islamic and other pre-modern theocracies. Furthermore, it equals contemporary conservative-fascist and theocratic dictatorships in their invariant tendency to and practice of moralistic and religiously driven terror of subordinate sinful groups. In comparative terms, the moralistic and religiously driven terror or repression of non-capital groups tends to be more extensive and intensive in religious or theocratic capitalist dictatorship than in the complex of welfare capitalism and liberal democracy where it is as a rule unknown or exceedingly rare and disappearing. Similar to the previous, one can measure or approximate moralistic-religious terror by the moralistic components of state 'political terror', including mass imprisonment and widespread death sentences and executions, such as massive populations of prisoners and executed persons of moral conscience as a share of the total prison population. Specifically, a measure is the share of those imprisoned, sentenced to death or executed and terrorized due to their sins-as-crimes, for example, the percent of drug offenders of the prison population.

1.4   *Cultural Indicators*

Suppression of artistic and other culture liberties and devaluation of the arts and culture. Suppression of artistic and related cultural liberties for non-capital strata and the devaluation of the arts and culture belong to the typical attributes and reliable indicators of capitalist dictatorship especially in its moralistic-religious or theocratic forms and agents, while linking with those concerning its operation in civil society. In particular, it links with the suppression of individual liberty and other civil rights, the negation of civil and other human rights, especially privacy, and the criminalization and severe sanctioning of moral offenses. Suppressing artistic and other culture liberties for non-capital strata and repressing artists from the latter typifies and indicates capitalist dictatorship in its moralistic-religious forms and agents, simply capitalist theocracy. While some capitalist may enjoy and even sponsor the higher arts and culture, moralistic-religious capitalist dictatorship is a cultural system of suppression of artistic and other culture liberties and activities for non-capitalists and generally of the societal, including government, devaluation of the arts and culture. It does so through minimal investment of resources on the latter that it devaluates either as economically wasteful or as immoral, irreligious and politically dangerous. Historically, such capitalist dictatorship probably represents the most anti-artistic or anti-aesthetic cultural system, together with its theocratic equivalent, ancient Puritan, as distinct from Catholic more art-friendly, theocracy, as Pareto, Weber and other sociologists and historians shows. Further, it emulates contemporary conservative-fascist and theocratic dictatorships as anti-artistic or anti-aesthetic cultural systems. In comparative terms, the suppression of artistic liberties for non-capital strata and generally the depreciation of the arts is more intense in moralistic-religious capitalist dictatorship than in the complex of welfare capitalism and liberal democracy where the opposite tendency prevails. A measure or proxy of the suppression of artistic and related liberties and the devaluation of the arts and culture is the low public spending on the arts and other cultural activities.

Extreme and compulsory religiosity. Extreme and compulsory religiosity and thus week freedom of or rather from religion for non-capital strata is among the usual features and valid indicators of capitalist dictatorship specifically in its theocratic or religious forms. Extremely intense, essentially fanatical, largely compulsory religious beliefs and week freedom from religion for non-capital and related lower strata permeates and identifies capitalist dictatorship in these forms. Such capitalist dictatorship while featuring moderation or free choice of religion for capital and its theocratic allies is a cultural system of religious extremism and fanaticism, especially compulsion for these strata. As a corollary, it historically descends from rather than transcends the pre-capitalist despotic ancient regime of medieval theocracy, featuring extreme, fanatical and compulsory religiosity among lower strata. Contemporaneously, it equals contemporary conservative-fascist and theocratic dictatorships belonging to a wider family of cultural systems of religious extremism, fanaticism, and compulsion and lack of freedom from religion for subordinate strata. Comparatively, religiosity tends to be more extreme, fanatical and compulsory in religious capitalist dictatorship than in the complex of welfare capitalism and liberal democracy in which it has opposite features. A measure or proxy of extreme and compulsory religiosity is the widespread belief in God on the assumption that this to some degree derives from religious extremism and compulsion or wider social control,[1] pressures and expectations of religiosity ('faith', 'godliness', 'belief'). Additional related measures are the extremely high importance of religion in life and extreme incidence of daily prayer for the same or similar reasons.

Obstruction and suppression of scientific progress and freedom. As a corollary extreme and compulsory religiosity of non-capital groups, cultural anti-rationalism, in particular antagonism to science, simply anti-science, is an integral property and manifest indicator of capitalist dictatorship as culture in some of its forms and agents. It exists in interconnection and mutual reinforcement with religiously overdetermined capitalist dictatorship's inherent irrationalism of which it is a negative derivative. For example, the beliefs in 'Satan', 'witches', 'creationism', intelligent design', 'and 'flat earth' predict anti-science, including opposition to scientific biology, evolutionism, astronomy and even, as in conservative America, climate science.

Cultural anti-rationalism, including anti-science couched as anti-scientism, pervades and accurately identifies capitalist dictatorship especially in its theocratic or religious forms and agents. While being extremely rational in economic terms of profit making and income and wealth concentration for capital,

---

1   Ruiter and Tubergen (2009, pp. 883, 888) suggest that the 'religious context of the nation during people's childhood has an enduring role in their religious practice [so that] religious behavior is a social phenomenon, in which people are socialized, controlled, and possibly sanctioned by their environment'. They especially observe that in the US and other 'religious nations, not only are there more people who were raised by religious parents, but the religious norms people internalize are strongly reinforced and controlled by others, such as family members, neighbors, peers, and colleagues at work' (Ruiter and Tubergen 2009, p. 888). Specifically, Voas and Chaves (2016, p. 1520) find that 'American religiosity is substantially overreported [and] indicates sociability more than religious belief [and] American religion is in some sense internally secularized', which is an indirect proof that it is to some degree socially compulsory, controlled or pressured and hence external and ritualized rather than truly internalized.

capitalist dictatorship in these forms and agents is a system of extreme cultural irrationality and consequently anti-rationalism, including religious superstition and its consequence anti-science. In historical terms, it manifests itself as just a newer instance of ancient religiously dominated regimes of irrationalism and superstition, thus continuing them, specifically the Christian and Islamic 'Dark Middle Ages' in which science and all culture became subservient to and dissolved into religion. In comparative terms, it belongs to a wider family of contemporary systems of cultural anti-rationalism or anti-science, especially aligning and merging with conservative-fascist and theocratic dictatorships. Notably, the intensity of cultural anti-rationalism or anti-science tends to be higher and more enduring in capitalist dictatorship in its religious forms and agents than in the composite of welfare capitalism and liberal-secular democracy. A specific measure or proxy of cultural anti-rationalism, particularly anti-science, is the opposition to biological evolutionism and its substitution by and coercive imposition (through 'monkey trials' in the 'Bible Belt' and conservative America overall, plus Islamic states) of its antithesis, such as 'creationism' or 'intelligent design' on society's science and education system.

Persistence of widespread religious superstitions. Resulting largely from extreme and compulsory religiosity, the persistence of mass religious superstitions and dogmas, thus cultural irrationalism is a characteristic trait and valid indicator of capitalist dictatorship especially in its theocratic forms and agents. Persistent and widespread religious superstitions and dogmas and generalized irrationalism among both capital and non-capital, theocratic leaders and masses characterize and indicate capitalist dictatorship in these forms. A case in point consists of the persistent and widespread beliefs in 'Satan' and by association 'witches' in religious capitalist dictatorship. The latter amounts to a cultural system of generalized irrationalism (e.g., the US 'Bible Belt' and Saudi Arabia), specifically a vast desert of old and new superstitions and dogmas (and 'conspiracy theories'), with some rare and small oases of reason and rationality among few capitalists and non-capitalists. In historical terms, it resembles the Dark Middle Ages thus characterized precisely by the rise and persistence of widespread religious superstitions, including 'Satan', 'witches' and many others. In contemporaneous terms, it emulates contemporary conservative-fascist and theocratic dictatorships forming cultural systems of irrationalism, including old and new superstitions and dogmas (and 'conspiracy theories'). In comparative terms, religious superstitions and dogmas are as a rule more persistent and widespread in capitalist dictatorship in its theocratic forms than in the composite of welfare capitalism and liberal-secular democracy where they disappear or decline. The present measure of religious superstitions and dogmas are the beliefs in 'Satan' and by association 'witches'.

2   Measures of Capitalist Dictatorship

2.1   *Economic Measures*

(1) *Suppression of unionization—inverse of trade union density.* The measure is the negative reciprocal or inverse of trade union density. Trade union density data are available for OECD countries during 2017 or latest year. The source is OECD Labour Force Statistics that defines trade union density as the percentage of 'wage and salary earners that are trade union members, divided by the total number of wage and salary earners' and estimates it by 'using survey data, wherever possible and administrative data adjusted for non-active and self-employed members otherwise'. While having a possible range from 0 to 100, union density among OECD countries ranges from a minimum in Estonia at just over 4 percent to a maximum in Iceland at 90 percent (see Table A1 in Appendix 2). Therefore, to derive estimates for the suppression of unionization or the inverse of trade union density requires subtracting these density figures from 100. This results in a reverse range from Estonia's unionization suppression maximum of 95 percent to Iceland's minimum of 10 percent.

(2) *Restriction of the scope of unionization—inverse of collective bargaining coverage.* The measure is the inverse of trade union or collective bargaining coverage. Trade union coverage data are available for OECD countries during 2017 or closest year. The source is OECD Labour Force Statistics that defines collective bargaining coverage as the percentage of total numbers of employees with the 'right to bargain collectively with employers' and to be covered by union employment agreements. While theoretically ranging from 0 to 100 collective bargaining coverage among OECD countries has a range from a minimum in Turkey at 7 percent to a maximum in France at 98.5 percent (see Table A2). Consequently, for deriving estimates for the restriction of the scope of unionization or the inverse of trade union coverage one needs to subtract these coverage figures from 100. This produces a reverse range from Turkey's restriction maximum of 93 percent to France's minimum of 1.5 percent. They therefore serve also as estimates or proxies for the suppression of collective bargaining, thus ranging from a suppression minimum in France at 1.5 percent to a maximum in Turkey at 93 percent.

(3) *Suppression of codetermination—inverse of works councils.* A measure is the inverse of the presence of works councils. Works councils' data are available for OECD countries during various years. The source is the European Trade Union Institute, along with additional sources.[2] Works councils' frequency

---

2   These sources Baker and Mckenzie International (2009), Flanagan (1999), and Rogers and Streeck (1995).

within OECD ranges from a minimum in the US and some other countries of zero in the sense of non-existence or unimportance to a maximum in Germany and others in the meaning of being common and important (see Table A3). Hence, to obtain estimates for the suppression of labor codetermination such as the inverse of works councils presuppose deducting works councils' frequency data (transformed into scores on a 0–100 scale) from 100. This produces a reverse range from the US and some other countries' works councils' suppression maximum of 100 percent to Germany and others' minimum of 0 percent. One first creates a 0–100 scale by assigning the maximum score to the country or countries with the greatest frequency of works councils and proportionate scores to others depending on their own frequencies, and one deducts these scores from 100 to obtain the inverse.

(4) *Suppression of codetermination—inverse of board-level employee representation.* Another measure is the inverse of board-level employee representation. Board-level employee representation data are available for OECD countries during various years. The source is OECD: Collective Bargaining in OECD and Accession Countries, Board-Level Employee Representation, along with additional sources.[3] Board-level employee representation incidence within OECD spans from a minimum in the US and some other countries at zero presence to a maximum in Germany and others at a level of the entire economy (see Table A4). It follows that estimates for the suppression of labor codetermination such as the inverse of board-level employee representation result from subtracting representation incidence data (transformed into scores on a 0–100 scale) from 100. This generates a reverse range from the US and some other countries' board-level employee representation suppression maximum of 100 percent to Germany and others' minimum of 0 percent. One first constructs a 0–100 scale by giving the maximum score to the country/countries with the highest board-level employee representation incidence and proportionate scores to others according to their own incidences, and one subtracts these scores from 100 to derive the inverse.

(5) *Extreme wealth concentration—share of the top one percent.* The measure is the wealth share of the top one percent of the population. This measure pertains to OECD countries during 2016 or latest available year. The source is OECD Statistics on distribution of wealth. Among OECD countries, the wealth share of the top one percent ranges from Greece's minimum of just over 9 percentage

---

3   The full description of the sources is as follows: The European Trade Union Institute, Gold and Waddington (2019); OECD's Collective Bargaining In OECD And Accession Countries, Board-Level Employee Representation (2016) and OECD's Ownership And Governance Of State-Owned Enterprises: A Compendium Of National Practices (2018).

to the United States' maximum of over 42 percentage (see Table A5). One creates a full 0–100 scale by assigning the maximum score to the country with the largest wealth share and proportionate scores to other countries depending in their own shares. (An alternative is using standardized wealth shares or standard z-scores as standard deviations from the mean with no definite range, a mean of 0 and a standard deviation of 1, but they seem less intuitive or convenient to grasp or interpret than a 0–100 scale with 'natural' units.)

(6) *Unequal income distribution—Gini coefficient.* The measure is the Gini coefficient or index. Gini coefficients on disposable household income are available for OECD countries in 2018 or nearest year. Their source is OECD Social and Welfare Statistics: Income distribution. Gini indexes or coefficients theoretically range from 0 to 100 or 0 to 1, respectively, and among these countries, Slovak Republic displays the minimum of 24 and Chile the maximum of 46 (see Table A6). To create a full 0–100 scale, the country with the largest Gini coefficient receives the maximum score and other countries proportionate scores according to their own coefficients.

(7) *Material degradation, deprivation and hardship—general poverty rate.* An overarching measure is the general poverty rate. General poverty or working-age poverty rates after taxes and transfers, age group 17–66 years, are available for OECD countries during 2018 or nearest year. Their source is OECD Data on inequality/poverty defining the general poverty rate as the 'percentage of people whose income falls below the poverty line taken as half the median household income of the total population'. Among OECD countries, general poverty rates have a minimum in Iceland at just over 5 and the maximum in Israel and the United States with nearly 18 (see Table A7). On a full 0–100 scale, the country with the largest poverty rate receives the maximum score and other countries proportionate scores according to their own rates.

(8) *Material degradation, deprivation and hardship—child poverty rate.* A particular measure is the child poverty rate. Child poverty rates after taxes and transfers, age group 0–17 years are available for OECD countries during 2018 or closest year. The source is OECD Data on inequality/poverty that defines the child poverty rate as the 'percentage of children 0–17 years old living in families whose income falls below the poverty line taken as half the median household income of the total population'. Child poverty rates among OECD countries find the minimum in Denmark at below 4 and the maximum in Turkey at over 25 (see Table A8). On the full 0–100 scale, one assigns the maximum score to the country with the largest child poverty rate and proportionate scores to other countries depending on their own rates.

(9) *Material degradation, deprivation, and hardship—hard long work.* A specific measure of especially material degradation or physical hardship and often

a correlate of poverty is hard long work in annual hours. Annual work hours data are available for OECD countries during 2018 or closest year. The source is OECD employment *statistics that calculate* 'average annual hours actually worked' by dividing the 'total number of hours worked over the year' by the 'average number of people in employment', including both full-time and part-time workers. Annual work hours among OECD countries attain a minimum in Germany of 1363 and a maximum in Mexico of 2148 (see Table A9). On a 0–100 scale, one assigns the maximum score to the country with the highest annual work hours and proportionate scores to other countries in accordance with their own figures.

(10) *Material degradation, deprivation, and hardship—inverse of paid vacation.* As a mirror image of hard long work, a corollary measure or proxy material degradation or physical hardship and sometimes a correlate of poverty is the inverse of paid vacation. Data on statutory minimum and collectively agreed paid annual leave in working days are available for OECD countries during 2016 or latest year. The source is OECD Family Database *on* leave entitlements of working parents. Paid annual leave in working days among OECD countries features a minimum[4] in the US of 0 and a maximum in Denmark and Germany of 30 (see Table A10). To create a 0–100 scale, one designates the maximum score to the country/countries with the longest paid vacation and proportionate scores to others based on their own figures. Obtaining the inverse of paid vacation proceeds by deducting paid annual leave figures (transformed into scores on a 0–100 scale) from 100. This produces a reverse range from the US's

---

4   Zero statutory minimum or collectively agreed paid annual leave in working days for US workers is an indicative, even if seemingly peripheral, symptom of capitalist dictatorship or 'plutonomy' in conservative America. No other Western society and even OECD country (including Mexico) denies to its workers statutory minimum or collectively agreed paid annual leave. And the way the radical-right alliance of capital and American conservatism justifies this denial and vehemently opposes granting such entitlements to workers is a classic exercise in Pareto's irrational 'derivations', including deliberate deceptions and self-deceptions, and Mannheim's ideologies expressing the class 'collective unconscious', simply what Samuelson (1983a, p. 6) calls 'mental gymnastics of a peculiarly depraved type'. Such a 'mental gymnastics' characterizes generally the conservative-capitalist justifications of the suppression of basic labor collective liberties and rights, such as suppressing the right to unionization, collective bargaining and strikes, for example, for public sector workers in the US South from Alabama to Texas. The comparative proof that this is ideological gymnastics is that virtually all Western societies in the sense of Western Europe permit and promote such collective liberties and rights, including the right to unionization, collective bargaining and strikes, which is what makes them 'Western' while the above suppression making conservative America closer to the non-Western 'third world' of capitalism.

hardship non-vacation maximum of 100 to Denmark's and Germany's minimum of 0.

(11) *Economic exploitation—rate of labor exploitation.* The measure is the rate of labor exploitation. Labor exploitation rates are available for OECD countries in 2016. Labor exploitation rates result from the differences between labor productivity and wages and calculated according the formula: Labor Exploitation = (Real GDP per Hour—Hourly Wages)/Hourly Wages. The source of real GDP per hour is OECD Data and that of hourly wages (hourly compensation costs in manufacturing) the Conference Board International Labor Comparisons Program. Labor exploitation rates among OECD countries have a minimum in Switzerland of under -4 percent which means absence of exploitation and that Swiss are paid nearly 4 percent above their productivity and a maximum in Turkey at 504 percent signifying that Turkish workers are paid 500 percent or five times less than what they produce (see Table A11). On a 0–100 scale, one designates the maximum score to the country with the highest labor exploitation rate and proportionate scores to others according to their own rates.

(12) *Economic non-protection and insecurity—inverse of employment protection.* A measure is the inverse of employment protection or job security. Coefficients of the strictness of employment protection legislation for overall, regular and temporary employment, including individual and collective dismissals, are available for OECD countries during 2014 or closest year. The source is OECD Statistics on employment protection legislation. Employment protection coefficients among OECD countries show a minimum in the US at .26 and a maximum in Portugal at 3.18 (see Table A12). On the 0–100 scale, one imputes a maximum score to the country with the highest employment protection coefficient and proportionate scores to other countries using their own coefficients. To derive estimates for economic non-protection and insecurity or the inverse of employment protection entails subtracting employment protection coefficients (converted into scores on a 0–100 scale) from 100. This results in a reverse range from the US's non-protection and insecurity maximum of 100 to Portugal's minimum of 0.

(13) *Economic non-protection and insecurity—inverse of unemployment benefits.* Another corollary measure is the inverse of unemployment benefits or insurance. Data on the 'average of net replacement rates over 60 months of unemployment' (for single persons without children) that indicate the 'proportion of net income in work that is maintained after job loss' are available for OECD countries during 2018 or closest year. The source is OECD Benefits and Wages Statistics. With a possible 0–100 range, such replacement rates among OECD countries display a minimum in Italy, Mexico, and Turkey of 0 percent

and a maximum in Denmark of 75 percent (see Table A13). Therefore, deducting these replacement rates from 100 serves to obtain the inverse of unemployment benefits and a reverse range from Mexico's non-protection and insecurity maximum of 100 to Denmark's minimum of 0.

(14) *Economic non-protection and insecurity—inverse of economic-social protection.* An additional related measure is the inverse of economic-social protection. Data on central government spending on social protection including welfare and related assistance as a percentage of GDP, are available for OECD countries during 2015 or latest year. The source is OECD Data, National Accounts Statistics. Government spending on social protection among OECD countries spans from a minimum in Chile at just over 6 percentage of GDP (which sheds light on the mass protests against inequality and related issues in this country recently) to a maximum in Finland at nearly 25 percent (see Table A14). On a full 0–100 scale, the country with the highest percentage of social protection spending has the maximum score and other countries proportionate scores in proportion to their own percentages. Hence, the inverse of economic-social protection results from subtracting government spending figures for social protection (converted into scores on a the 0–100 scale) from 100, which makes for a reverse range from Chile's social non-protection maximum of 100 to Finland's minimum of 0.

2.2   *Political Measures*

(15) *Suppression of political freedoms and rights—inverse of voting rights.* A measure is the suppression or negative reciprocal, simply inverse of electoral/voting rights proxied by voter turnout. Voter turnout data for parliamentary elections, as percentage of the voting age population, are available for OECD countries during 2019 or nearest year. The source is the International Institute for Democracy and Electoral Assistance. With a theoretical 0–100 range, voter turnout among OECD countries exhibits a minimum in Chile at 46.5 percent and a maximum in Australia of 91 percent (see Table A15). To obtain the proxy inverse of voting rights one subtracts voter turnout figures from 100, yielding a reverse range from Chile's proxy suppression maximum of 53.5 to Australia's minimum of 9.

(16) *Suppression of political freedoms and rights—inverse of voice.* A related measure is the suppression or inverse of voice in the polity and society. 'Voice and accountability' rankings are available for OECD countries in 2018. The source is the World Bank's Worldwide Governance Indicators project that provides such ranking as percentile ranks among all world countries and defines 'voice and accountability' as a reflection of 'perceptions of the extent to which a country's citizens are able to participate in selecting their government, as

well as freedom of expression, freedom of association, and a free media'. Voice and accountability rankings on the original 0–100 scale among OECD countries attain a minimum in Turkey of just over 25 and an absolute maximum in Norway of 100 (see Table A16). Subtracting these figures from 100 gives estimates of the suppression of voice and a reverse range from Turkey's voice suppression maximum of just under 75 to Norway's minimum of 0.

(17) *Power concentration—inverse of power constraints*. A measure consists of the inverse of constraints on state powers. Scores for constraints on government powers are available for OECD countries in 2018. The source is the World Justice Project Rule of Law Index that supplies 'factor *scores' on* constraints on government powers that it defines as a 'measure of the 'extent to which those who govern are bound by law. It comprises the means, both constitutional and institutional, by which the powers of the government and its officials and agents are limited and held accountable under the law. It also includes non-governmental checks on the government's power, such as a free and independent press'. *Scores* for constraints on government powers among OECD countries reach a minimum in Turkey at 29 and a maximum in Norway at 95 (converted to a 0–100 scale by multiplying them by 100) (see Table A17). Therefore, obtaining power concentration estimates or proxies involves subtracting these scores from 100. This yields a reverse range from Turkey's power concentration maximum of 71 to Norway's minimum of 5.

(18) *Power concentration—inverse of electoral freedom and political pluralism*. An additional related measure or proxy represents the inverse of electoral freedom and political pluralism. Indexes of electoral process and political pluralism are available for OECD countries during 2019. The source is the Economist Intelligence Unit's Democracy Index 2019 that defines political pluralism as the freedom of 'citizens to form political parties that are independent of the government' and so on, while defining electoral process by free and fair elections. Within OECD, political pluralism and electoral process indexes attain the minimum in Turkey at barely 31 and the maximum in Australia, Denmark, Iceland, Ireland, Luxembourg, New Zealand and Norway all at 100 (transformed to a 0–100 scale by multiplying them by 10) (see Table A18). To obtain estimates or proxies for the suppression or inverse of electoral freedom and political pluralism requires subtracting these indexes from 100. This generates a reverse range from Turkey's electoral unfreedom and non-pluralism maximum of 69 to these countries' minimum of 0.

(19) *Power concentration—inverse of political stability and absence of violence*. Another measure or proxy includes the inverse of political stability and absence of violence. Percentile ranks among all UN nations on 'political stability and absence of violence/terrorism' are available for OECD countries in

2018. The source is the World Bank's Worldwide Governance Indicators project defining this measure by 'perceptions of the likelihood of political instability and/or politically-motivated violence, including terrorism'. Such ranks among OECD countries display a minimum in Turkey of 10 and a maximum in Iceland of 99 (see Table A19). Deducting these percentile ranks from 100 helps derive the inverse of political stability and absence of violence. A resulting reverse range is from Turkey's instability and violence maximum of 90 to Iceland's minimum of 0.

(20) *Power concentration—inverse of the rule of law.* Yet another measure or proxy involves the inverse of the rule of law. Percentile ranks among all UN nations on the rule of law are available for OECD countries in 2018. The source is the World Bank's Worldwide Governance Indicators project that defines the rule of law by 'perceptions of the extent to which agents have confidence in and abide by the rules of society, and in particular the quality of contract enforcement, property rights, the police, and the courts, as well as the likelihood of crime and violence'. These ranks among OECD countries range from a minimum in Mexico at just over 27 to a maximum in Finland at 100 (see Table A20). One obtains the inverse of the rule of law by subtracting its percentile ranks from 100. The result is a reverse range from Mexico's lawlessness maximum of nearly 73 to Finland's minimum of 0.

(21) *Power concentration—inverse of the control of corruption.* A corollary measure or proxy is the inverse of the control of corruption. Percentile ranks among all UN nations on the control of corruption are available for OECD countries during 2018. The source is the World Bank's Worldwide Governance Indicators project defining this measure by 'perceptions of the extent to which public power is exercised for private gain, including both petty and grand forms of corruption, as well as "capture" of the state by elites and private interests'. Such percentile ranks among OECD countries have a range from the minimum in Mexico at around 19 to the maximum in Finland at 100 (see Table A21). The control of corruption inverse derives through subtraction of its percentile ranks from 100. This generates a reverse range from Mexico's uncontrolled corruption maximum of just over 81 to Finland's minimum of 0.

(22) *Power concentration—inverse of open government.* An additional related measure or proxy is the inverse of open government. Estimates of the latter such as factor *scores* on open government are available for OECD countries in 2018. The source is the World Justice Project Rule of Law Index that furnishes factor *scores on* open government measuring the 'openness of government defined by the extent to which a government shares information, empowers people with tools to hold the government accountable, and fosters citizen participation in public policy deliberations'. This factor measures whether basic

laws and information on legal rights are publicized and evaluates the quality of information published by the government'. These factor *scores* among OECD countries (transformed to a 0–100 scale) reach a minimum and maximum in Turkey and Norway of 41 and 88, respectively (see Table A22). One subtracts such factor *scores* from 100 to derive the inverse of open government and a reverse range from Turkey non-open government maximum of 59 to Norway's minimum of 12.

(23) *Severe penal repression and punishment—mass imprisonment.* A conventional measure is the level and rate of specifically mass imprisonment. Prison population rates (per 100,000 persons) are available for OECD countries in 2019 or nearest year. The source is International Centre for *Prison* Studies. Prison population rates among OECD countries reveal a minimum in Iceland at 37 and a maximum in the US at 655 (see Table A23). On a 0–100 scale, one attributes the maximal score to the country with the highest prison population rate and corresponding scores to other countries in view of their own rates.

(24) *Severe penal repression and punishment—death sentences and executions.* Another conventional, more precisely ultimate measure is the application and frequency of death sentences and executions. Data on the numbers of death sentences and executions are available for OECD countries in 2018 or nearest year. The source is Amnesty International Global Report, Death Sentences and Executions. Since only three OECD countries used death sentences or executions during the period, this punishment has a zero minimum and a mode in 34 member states and a maximum in the US of 2724 counting 'recorded executions, recorded death sentences and people known to be under sentence of death at the end of 2018', while Japan having 135 and South Korea 61 (with no executions in 2018) (see Table A24). For consistency and in view of the gravity of this measure of penal repression and punishment despite its rare or decreasing application, one constructs a 0–100 scale by attaching a maximum score to the country with the largest number of death sentences and executions, minimal and proportionate scores to those with zero and intermediate numbers.

(25) *Severe penal repression and punishment—other political terror.* An additional broader and residual measure is other state or political terror. Scores on the 'political terror scale' are available for OECD countries in 2018 or nearest year. The source is the Political Terror Scale, specifically its larger scores from Amnesty International or Human Rights Watch. The Political Terror Scale defines political terror as 'state-sanctioned killings, torture, disappearances and political imprisonment'.[5] Among OECD countries, political terror scale levels with a possible 1–5 range have a minimum in most cases of 1 and a

---

5   See Gibney et al. (2019).

maximum in Israel, Mexico and Turkey of 4 (see Table A25). On a 0–100 scale, one assigns a maximum score to the country with the highest political terror scale level and proportionate scores to others given their own levels.

(26) *Militarism—large military expenditure.* A standard measure or proxy of militarism is large military expenditure so long as it tends or threatens to become the spending of vast societal resources on offensive and continuous wars. Data on military expenditure as percentage of GDP are available for OECD countries during 2019. The source is Stockholm International Peace Research Institute. Military expenditure figures for OECD countries show a minimum in Iceland at 0 percent and a maximum in Israel at over 5 percent (see Table A26). On a 0–100 scale, one attributes the maximum score to the country with the largest military expenditure percentage and proportionate scores to other countries after their own percentages.

2.3   Civil-Society Measures

(27) *Suppression of individual liberty—inverse of individual liberty.* The measure is the negative reciprocal or inverse of individual liberty. Personal freedom indexes[6] are available for OECD countries in 2017. These indexes for OECD countries span from a minimum in Turkey of just over 57 and a maximum in Sweden of 94.5 (transformed to a 0–100 scale by multiplying them by 10) (see Table A27). One derives estimates of the suppression or inverse of individual liberty by subtracting these indexes from 100. This generates a reverse range from Turkey's personal-freedom suppression maximum of around 43 to Sweden's minimum of 5.5.

(28) *Suppression of other civil liberties—inverse of civil liberties.* The obvious measure is the negative or inverse of civil liberties. Civil liberties indexes are available for OECD countries in 2019. The source is the Economist Intelligence Unit's Democracy Index that includes among civil liberties 'free' media, 'freedom of expression and protest', 'open and free discussion of public issues', the 'opportunity to petition government to redress grievances', lack of the 'use of torture by the state', the judiciary's independence of government influence, etc. Such indexes among OECD countries have a minimum in Turkey at 23.5 and an absolute maximum[7] in Australia, Ireland and New Zealand at 100 (converted

---

6   The source of personal freedom indexes is Vásquez and Porčnik (2019) who incorporate personal freedom indexes into the 'human freedom index' as a 'global measurement of personal, civil, and economic freedom'.

7   Ireland's maximal civil liberties index seems strikingly exaggerated in view of its continuing prohibition or harsh restriction and sanctioning of abortion or reproductive and various other liberties and rights on anachronistic religious grounds (see Mueller 2013). Alternatively, one can only 'justify' the index by a defective or partial concept of civil liberties that does

to a 0–100 scale by multiplying them by 10) (see Table A28). Estimating the suppression or inverse of civil liberties necessitates subtracting their indexes from 100. This yields a reverse range from Turkeys' civil-liberties suppression maximum of 76.5 to Australia's, Ireland's and New Zealand's minimum of 0.

(29) *Suppression of particular civil liberties—inverse of media freedom.* The measure is the inverse of media or press freedom. World press freedom indexes are available for OECD countries in 2019. The source is *Reporters without Borders whose index is a score on* 'Abuses and Acts of Violence against Journalists and Score on Pluralism, Media Independence, Environment and Self-Censorship, Legislative Framework, Transparency, Infrastructure'. These indexes represent the inverse of press freedom in that they are estimates of abuses and violence against journalists, reaching among OECD countries a minimum in Norway of around 8 and a maximum Turkey of about 53 (see Table A29). On a 0–100 scale, the maximum score hence attaches to the country with the largest index and proportionate scores to other countries after their indexes.

(30) *Negation of civil and other human rights—inverse of fundamental human rights.* The measure is the inverse of human rights. *Scores* for core or fundamental human rights are available for OECD countries during 2018. The source is the World Justice Project Rule of Law Index that provides 'factor *scores' on* 'a relatively modest menu of rights that are firmly established under the Universal Declaration of Human Rights and are most closely related to rule of law concerns'. *Scores* for fundamental human rights among OECD countries range from a minimum in Turkey at 32 and maximum in Denmark and Finland at 92 (transformed to a 0–100 scale by multiplying them by 100) (see Table A30). Deducting these figures from 100 produces estimates of the negation or inverse of human rights with a reverse range from Turkey's human-rights negation maximum of 68 to Denmark's and Finland's minimum of 5.

(31) *Negation of individual human rights—inverse of privacy.* A measure is the negation or inverse of the human right to privacy. National privacy rankings and scores are available for OECD countries in 2007. The source is Privacy International whose National Privacy Ranking considers 'Constitutional protection, Statutory protection, Privacy enforcement, Identity cards and biometrics, Data-sharing, Visual surveillance, Communication interception, Workplace monitoring, Government access to data, Communications data

---

not include abortion or reproductive and related private liberties and rights, as seems the case with the Economist Intelligence Unit's Democracy Index. In addition, Australia's civil liberties index appears largely overstated in view of the repressive or exclusionary (including xenophobic) tendencies of its consecutive conservative governments during recent times (a partial 'Anglo-Saxon' bias seems to permeate such indexes overall).

retention, Surveillance of medical, financial and movement, Border and trans-
border issues, Leadership, Democratic safeguards'. National privacy scores
with an apparent 0–4 range have among OECD countries a minimum in the
UK of 1.4 and a maximum in Greece of just over 3 (see Table A31). On a 0–100
scale, one attributes the highest score to the country with the highest privacy
score and proportionate scores to other countries. To derive the negation or
inverse of privacy one subtracts privacy scores from 100. This yields a reverse
range from the UK privacy-negation maximum of around 55 to Greece's minimum of 0.

(32) *Negation of human rights to life and safety—inverse of civic peace.*
A measure is the negation or inverse of human right to civic peace. Global
peace indexes are available for OECD countries during 2019. The source is
Institute for Economics and Peace whose Global Peace Index 'measures the
state of peace using three thematic domains: the level of Societal Safety and
Security; the extent of Ongoing Domestic and International Conflict; and the
degree of Militarisation'. As actually peace-disturbance indexes and hence the
inverse of civic peace, they display a minimum in Iceland at around 1 and a
maximum Turkey at just over 3 (see Table A32). On a 0–100 scale, one attributes a maximum score to the country with the highest peace-disturbance
index and corresponding scores to other countries.

(33) *Criminalization and severe sanctioning of moral sins—the death penalty
for drug offenses.* A measure is the application or provision of the death penalty
for nonviolent drug offenses, including the use of or trade in illicit drugs. Data
on the 'death penalty for drug offences' are available for OECD countries during
2018. The source is the International Harm Reduction Association. According
to Harm Reduction International, the 'death penalty for drug offences is a clear
violation of international human rights law. Numerous international authorities and legal scholars have reaffirmed this point, including the UN Human
Rights Committee as recently as 2018'. Only two OECD countries, South Korea
and the US, apply or provide for the 'death penalty for drug offences' through
'symbolic application' (see Table A33). For consistency and in light of the gravity of applying or providing for the death penalty for non-violent drug moral
offenses, one creates a binomial 0–100 scale by imputing the maximum to the
countries that apply or provide for this punishment and minimal scores to
other countries that do not.

(34) *Moralistic-religious terror—prisoners and on-death row and executed
persons of ethical conscience.* A corollary measure or proxy is the existence and
large number of prisoners and on-death row and executed persons of moral
conscience as a share of the total prison population and of death sentences
and executions. Percentages of drug offenders of the total prison population

are publicly available and widely known only for some OECD countries such as the US in which they make almost half of all federal prisoners, for example.[8] This is because the mass imprisonment of drug users (and prostitution offenders) and the potential death penalty for drug offenses like trade in drugs are a unique American phenomenon especially since Reaganism or its model Puritanism among Western societies. Hence, the percentage of drug users and similar moral (prostitution) offenders of the total prison population reaches a probable but indeterminate minimum in most Western European countries especially in long-term imprisonment and a determinate maximum in the US, with long prison terms and even life in prison due to the Draconian 'three strikes' laws. Due to the lack of data for most other countries, one can take the US's share of drug offenders of the total prison population to tentatively estimate theirs in a proportionate manner. For example, if this share is 20 percent at a prisoner rate of 655, it will be 10 percent at a rate half of it, 5 percent at a rate quarter of it, 2 percent at rates ten times lower, and so on (see Table A34). This is an imprecise procedure but is the most convenient way to estimate this share for OECD countries other than the US because of the lack of full data for them. Moreover, these estimates may overstate their shares so long as most OECD, especially Western European, countries do not imprison drug users in mass numbers and for long time in the manner that conservative America does. An even starker contrast exists for the percentage of on-death row or executed persons for drug offenses: all Western societies abolish the death penalty for such and any crimes, while the US government still provides for and continuously, as during post-2016, threatens to use this punishment for trading in illicit drugs. On a 0–100 scale, one attaches the maximum score to the country with the largest share of drug offenders of the total prison population and proportionate scores to other countries after their own shares as approximated by the above procedure.

2.4   *Cultural Measures*

(35) *Suppression of artistic and other cultural liberties and devaluation of the arts and culture—inverse of public spending on the arts and culture.* A measure or proxy is the negative or inverse of government expenditure on the arts and culture as a whole. Data on the latter such as general government expenditure on art and culture as percentage of GDP are available for OECD countries during 2018 or closest year. The source is OECD National Accounts that provide

---

8   Recall Roth (2018, p. 1633) referring to the Federal Bureau of Prisons report that '46 percent of all inmates were convicted of drug offenses' as of January 2018.

data on government spending on 'recreation, culture and religion', along with additional sources. Government expenditure on culture among OECD countries features a minimum in the US at nearly 0 percent and a maximum in Iceland at just over 3 percent (see Table A35). Transforming these figures to a 0–100 scale involves designating the maximum score to the country with the largest percent and corresponding scores to other countries. Deducting these figures (on a 0–100 scale) from 100 permits deriving the inverse of public expenditure on art and culture and estimating the suppression and devaluation of artistic and cultural liberties and activities.

The preceding in particular involves suppression of specifically artistic liberties and devaluation of the arts, of which a measure or proxy is the negative reciprocal or inverse of government spending on the arts. Data on 'public expenditure on arts and museums'[9] are available, however, for only several OECD, specifically Western, countries, during certain years. For instance, among these Western countries during 1987 the public expenditure on arts and museums as a proportion of GDP attains a minimum in the US at .02 percent and a maximum in Sweden at .24 percent. To estimate the suppression of artistic liberties and devaluation of the arts or derive the inverse of public art spending requires subtracting the latter's figures (transformed to a 0–100 scale) from 100. This yields a reverse range from the US artistic liberties suppression and the arts devaluation maximum of around 100 to Sweden's minimum of 0. However, this procedure is not applicable to most OECD countries because of the lack of the data on government spending specifically on the arts.

(36) *Extreme and compulsory religiosity—mass and enforced beliefs in 'God'*. A measure or proxy involves mass or widespread, intensive and socially enforced, pressured or expected beliefs in 'God'. Proportions of people 'believing in a personal God or higher power' are available for OECD countries during various years.[10] Such proportions among OECD countries reach a minimum in Czech Republic of 16 percent and a maximum in Mexico and Turkey of 94 percent (see Table A36).

(37) *Extreme and compulsory religiosity—extremely high importance of religion in daily life*. A corollary measure or proxy includes the extremely high,

---

9   A source is Throsby (1994) who provides data on public expenditure on arts as proportion of all public expenditure and of GDP and per head, however only for several OECD countries such as United States, Canada, United Kingdom, West Germany, France, Netherlands, Sweden and Australia.

10   The main source for the data on 'believing in a personal god or higher power' is Smith (2012); additional sources are Clarke and Beyer (2009), Angus Reid Institute, Eurobarometer survey, and Pew Research Center.

pervasive and enforced or expected importance of religion in everyday human life. Proportions of people agreeing with the statement that religion is 'very important' in their daily life are available for OECD countries during 2018. The source is the Pew Research Center that reports the comparative importance of religion in the world. Among OECD countries, proportions of people agreeing with the preceding statement have a minimum in Estonia at 16 percent and a maximum in Turkey at 82 percent (see Table A37).

(38) *Extreme and compulsory religiosity—extreme incidence of daily prayer.* Yet another corollary measure or proxy consists of the extreme and to some degree compulsory incidence of daily prayer especially when performed as a religious public, and not only private, ritual. Proportions of people praying daily publicly or privately are available for OECD countries during 2018. The source is the Pew Research Center that reports the comparative incidence of daily prayer in the world. Proportions of people praying daily among OECD countries show a minimum in the United Kingdom of 6 percent and a maximum in Turkey of 60 percent (see Table A38).

(39) *Obstruction and suppression of scientific progress and freedom—inverse of biological evolutionism.* The measure or proxy is the inverse of scientific rationalism or simply science, for example, biological evolutionism. Figures for the 'public acceptance of evolution' are available for OECD countries during the 2005–14 period.[11] 'Public acceptance of evolution' among OECD countries spans from a minimum in Turkey at 25 percent to a maximum in Iceland at 82. Estimates for the opposition or suspicion to biological evolutionism and the inverse of scientific rationalism result from deducting 'public acceptance of evolution' figures from 100. This yields a reverse range from Turkey's anti-evolution maximum of 75 percent to Iceland's minimum of 18 (see Table A39).

(40) *Persistence of widespread religious superstitions—pervasive beliefs in 'Satan' and 'witches'.* The measure comprises the mass or pervasive and persistent beliefs in 'Satan' and by association 'witches' as the 'associates'. Proportions of people who believe in the existence and nefarious operation of 'Satan' or the 'Devil'—and hence conceivably are prone to 'satanize' or associate those of different or no religion—are available for OECD countries during various years. The chief source is the World Values Survey 1995–98 that asked the question if people 'believe the Devil exists', together with additional sources.[12]

---

11   The source is Miller, Scott, and Okamoto (2006), along with Australian Academy of Science (2010), Canada—Angus Reid Polls (2012), Pew Research Center (2014), International Social Survey Programme (2000), IPSOS (2011), and UMR Research (2007), also listed at the bottom of Table A39.

12   Additional sources are Gallup Poll, Tiffen and Gittins (2009), and Lacy (2000).

The percent of people among OECD countries who believe that 'Satan' and by association 'witches' exist exhibits a minimum in Denmark of 10 percent and a maximum in the US of 71 percent among Western societies and in Turkey of 73 percent among others, the first and the last two thus appearing as the respective least and most superstitious or the most and least rational members in this regard (see Table A40). In turn, the beliefs in the existence of 'Satan' and by association 'witches' strongly correlate with the belief in 'God'.[13]

3   Calculation of the Degrees of Capitalist Dictatorship

Altogether, the degrees or indices of capitalist dictatorship represent the aggregate or average of the preceding four sets of measures.

One first calculates total degrees of capitalist dictatorship for OECD countries by aggregating the above measures. One then calculates average degrees or composite indices (on a 0–100 scale) of capitalist dictatorship for these countries through dividing their total degrees by the number of measures. As a corollary, this results in ranking OECD countries in average degrees or composite indices of capitalist dictatorship from the highest to the lowest. Alternatively, it allows ranking them in average degrees or composite indices of capitalist democracy from the highest to the lowest by subtracting their dictatorship figures from 100. A caveat or disclaimer is that such a calculation is an approximation to and exercise in determining the degrees of capitalist dictatorship, aiming to see whether and to what extent a quantification of it as a total social system is possible and plausible. Hence, one should take these calculated degrees as only approximate, illustrative, tentative and provocative figures to arouse further calculation, estimation and discussion.

---

13   The correlation between the beliefs in the existence of 'Satan' and the belief in 'God' is around .8 for 36 OECD countries. This signifies that virtually the same persons who believe in the existence/operation of 'God' believe in that of 'Satan' and by association 'witches'. At the upper end, in Turkey 94 percent believe in 'God' and 73 percent in 'Satan', around 68 percent of Americans believe in 'God' and 71 percent in 'Satan', and so on. (Judging by personal self-reports, both believers believe that 'God' both created and will ultimately defeat 'Satan' and the associated 'witches' or 'infidels' as proof of absolute 'divine' power.) At the lower end, in Denmark 28 percent believe in 'God' and 10 percent in 'Satan', in Sweden 19 and 16 percent hold these beliefs, respectively, and so forth. In sum, 'Satan' and 'God' go hand in hand for most religious believers, especially those in Islamic Turkey and evangelical America.

TABLE 12   A summary of the above measures of capitalist dictatorship

---

I Economic Measures

---

(1) suppression of unionization—inverse of trade union density

(2) restriction of the scope of unionization—inverse of collective bargaining coverage

(3) suppression of labor codetermination—inverse of works councils

(4) suppression of labor codetermination—inverse of board-level employee representation

(5) extreme wealth concentration—share of the top one percent of wealth

(6) extremely unequal income distribution—Gini coefficient

(7) material deprivation, hardship and poverty—general poverty rate

(8) material deprivation, hardship and poverty—child poverty rate

(9) material deprivation, hardship and poverty—hard long work

(10) material deprivation, hardship and poverty—inverse of paid vacation

(11) economic exploitation—rate of labor exploitation

(12) economic non-protection and insecurity—inverse of employment protection

(13) economic non-protection and insecurity—inverse of unemployment benefits

(14) economic non-protection and insecurity—inverse of economic-social protection

---

II Political Measures

---

(15) suppression of political freedoms and rights—inverse of voting rights

(16) suppression of political freedoms and rights—inverse of voice

(17) power concentration—inverse of power constraints

(18) power concentration—inverse of electoral freedom and political pluralism

(19) power concentration—inverse of political stability and absence of violence

(20) power concentration—inverse of the rule of law

(21) power concentration—inverse of the control of corruption

(22) power concentration—inverse of open government

(23) severe penal repression and punishment—mass imprisonment

(24) penal repression and punishment—death sentences and executions

(25) penal repression and punishment—other political terror

(26) militarism—large military expenditure

TABLE 12   A summary of the above measures of capitalist dictatorship (*cont.*)

III Civil-Society Measures

(27) suppression of individual liberty—inverse of individual liberty
(28) suppression of other civil liberties—inverse of civil liberties
(29) suppression of particular civil liberties—inverse of media freedom
(30) negation of civil and other human rights—inverse of fundamental human rights
(31) negation of individual human rights—inverse of privacy
(32) negation of human rights to life and safety—inverse of civic peace
(33) criminalization and severe sanctioning of moral sins—the death penalty for drug offenses
(34) moralistic-religious terror—prisoners and on-death row and executed persons of ethical conscience

IV Cultural Measures

(35) suppression of artistic and other cultural liberties and devaluation of the arts and culture—inverse of public spending on the arts and culture
(36) extreme and compulsory religiosity—mass and enforced beliefs in 'God'
(37) extreme religiosity—extremely high importance of religion in life
(38) extreme religiosity—extreme incidence of daily prayer
(39) obstruction and suppression of scientific progress and freedom—inverse of biological evolutionism
(40) persistence of widespread religious superstitions—pervasive beliefs in 'Satan' and 'witches'.

Specifically, one calculates, with the above caveat in mind, the total and average degrees of capitalist dictatorship as the sum and average, respectively, of the following:

1 inverse of trade union density + 2 inverse of collective bargaining coverage + 3 inverse of works councils + 4 inverse of board-level employee representation + 5 wealth share of the top one percent + 6 Gini income coefficient + 7 general poverty rate + 8 child poverty rate + 9 hard long work + 10 inverse of paid vacation + 11 labor exploitation rate + 12 inverse of employment

protection + 13 inverse of unemployment benefits + 14 inverse of economic-social protection + 15 inverse of voting rights + 16 inverse of voice + 17 inverse of power constraints + 18 inverse of electoral freedom and political pluralism + 19 inverse of political stability and absence of violence + 20 inverse of the rule of law + 21 inverse of the control of corruption + 22 inverse of open government + 23 mass imprisonment + 24 death sentences and executions + 25 other political terror + 26 large military expenditure + 27 inverse of individual liberty + 28 inverse of civil liberties + 29 inverse of media freedom + 30 inverse of fundamental human rights + 31 inverse of privacy + 32 inverse of civic peace + 33 death penalty for drug offenses + 34 prisoners and on-death row and executed persons of ethical conscience + 35 inverse of public expenditure on the arts and culture + 36 mass and enforced beliefs in 'God' + 37 extremely high importance of religion in life + 38 extreme incidence of daily prayer + 39 inverse of biological evolutionism + 40 pervasive beliefs in 'Satan' and 'witches'.

4   Degrees of Capitalist Dictatorship for Western and Comparable Societies

This section presents the degrees or indices of capitalist dictatorship for Western and comparable societies, specifically OECD countries (with the above caveat). Formally, capitalist dictatorship degrees or indices (on a 0–100 scale) for these countries derive as the average of 40 measures (as Table 13 and Figure 1 demonstrate).

Their possible range is from a 0 to 100 given the equivalent scale. Thus, one first aggregates these 40 items (all transformed to a 0–100 scale) and then calculates their averages, which indicate the degrees or indices of capitalist dictatorship for OECD countries (which Table 14 ranks in these terms). A higher average indicates an equivalent degree of capitalist dictatorship and conversely.

Conversely, subtracting these indices of capitalist dictatorship from 100 yields indexes of liberal or capitalist democracy for OECD countries (as Table 15 and Figure 2 show).

Substantively, the degrees of capitalist dictatorship with a 0–100 range are the highest in the following OECD countries ranked from 1 to 10. These ten countries are 1. Turkey (67.95), 2. United States (63.49), 3. Mexico (59.89), 4. Israel (50.07), 5. Chile (47.71), 6. South Korea (45.05), 7. Lithuania (43.20), 8. Greece (42.98), 9. Latvia (41.13), and 10. Poland (39.75). On this account, these top-ten countries most closely instantiate or approximate capitalist dictatorship, although with certain differences between the top three and the rest.

TABLE 13 Measures and degrees of capitalist dictatorship, OECD countries

Country	1	2	3	4	5	6	7	8	9	10	11	12	13	14
Australia	85.30	40.80	100	100	35.31	71.74	67.60	49.41	77.51	33.33	7.07	47.48	48.00	58.67
Austria	73.30	2.00	0	0	60.10	61.74	54.75	45.45	70.34	16.67	9.56	25.47	21.33	18.34
Belgium	48.10	4.00	0	100	28.39	57.83	54.19	48.62	71.93	33.33	7.32	40.57	26.67	21.78
Canada	70.60	69.70	90	100	36.49	67.39	67.60	45.85	79.52	66.67	12.41	71.07	56.00	29.70
Chile	83.90	79.10	100	100	40.96	100	92.18	84.98	90.36	50.00	53.60	17.30	94.67	74.72
Czech Republic	88.30	53.70	50	20	21.94	55.00	31.28	33.60	83.43	16.67	44.05	8.18	38.67	51.23
Denmark	33.90	16.00	0	0	55.60	56.74	32.40	14.62	64.80	.00	8.26	30.82	.00	11.03
Estonia	95.70	81.40	50	100	49.98	68.26	87.71	37.94	81.38	33.33	34.02	43.08	54.67	47.12
Finland	37.80	10.70	0	20	31.33	57.83	35.20	14.23	72.39	16.67	8.39	31.76	18.67	.00
France	91.10	1.50	0	50	43.90	63.26	46.37	45.45	70.76	16.67	11.24	25.16	36.00	1.42
Germany	83.30	44.00	0	0	55.70	63.91	58.10	48.62	63.44	.00	7.68	15.72	36.00	21.15
Greece	79.80	60.00	50	80	21.56	72.39	80.45	69.57	91.06	33.33	21.98	33.33	70.67	21.23
Hungary	91.90	77.20	50	0	40.56	61.30	43.58	30.43	81.06	33.33	51.65	50.00	80.00	43.85
Iceland	10.20	10.00	0	100	54.14	55.43	30.17	22.92	68.39	20.00	6.29	45.60	28.00	59.84
Ireland	75.50	66.50	90	80	33.38	67.17	51.40	39.53	82.96	20.00	25.11	55.97	17.33	63.55
Israel	75.00	73.90	100	50	52.97	74.78	100	93.68	88.92	63.33	11.10	35.85	69.33	54.81
Italy	65.70	20.00	0	100	27.52	71.30	76.54	68.38	80.20	16.67	9.28	15.72	100	15.82
Japan	82.90	83.30	100	100	25.35	73.70	87.71	54.94	78.21	66.67	11.27	56.92	22.67	34.49
Korea	89.50	88.20	50	80	70.62	77.17	97.21	57.31	92.78	50.00	8.56	25.47	57.33	72.67
Latvia	87.80	86.20	100	100	50.35	75.22	93.85	52.17	79.10	33.33	46.05	15.41	57.33	52.87
Lithuania	92.30	92.90	90	100	50.35	82.17	94.41	69.96	75.23	33.33	57.03	23.90	68.00	51.11

	1	2	3	4	5	6	7	8	9	10	11	12	13	14
Luxembourg	67.90	45.00	0	20	44.28	66.09	62.01	51.38	70.11	16.67	17.18	29.25	21.33	27.17
Mexico	86.10	87.50	100	100	40.96	99.57	92.74	78.26	100	80.00	75.01	36.16	100	69.49
Netherlands	83.20	21.40	0	0	65.51	61.96	46.37	43.08	66.71	16.67	15.82	11.32	12.00	37.27
New Zealand	82.70	84.10	100	100	56.50	75.87	60.89	55.73	81.75	33.33	11.92	56.29	40.00	23.20
Norway	50.70	33.00	0	0	47.39	56.96	46.93	31.62	65.94	16.67	12.51	26.73	37.33	22.43
Poland	87.30	85.30	50	50	27.61	61.74	57.54	36.76	83.43	33.33	55.96	29.87	57.33	33.32
Portugal	83.90	27.70	50	50	33.99	71.96	69.83	61.26	80.17	26.67	44.04	.00	69.33	30.69
Slovak Republic	89.10	75.60	50	20	21.94	52.39	47.49	55.34	79.05	16.67	47.01	42.14	70.67	41.79
Slovenia	80.40	35.00	0	0	54.21	53.04	48.60	28.06	74.62	33.33	19.45	32.08	37.33	32.39
Spain	85.80	26.90	0	80	38.42	74.13	86.59	86.96	79.19	26.67	19.93	35.53	57.33	32.59
Sweden	34.40	10.00	0	0	47.39	61.30	51.96	36.76	68.62	16.67	9.72	17.92	21.33	20.73
Switzerland	85.10	50.80	0	80	55.70	64.35	50.84	37.55	72.67	33.33	-.74	49.69	5.33	46.04
Turkey	91.40	93.00	100	100	40.96	87.83	96.09	100	85.29	60.00	100	27.36	100	49.21
United Kingdom	76.80	73.70	50	100	48.26	77.61	66.48	50.99	71.60	6.67	17.23	65.41	36.00	39.01
United States	89.70	88.00	100	100	100	84.78	99.44	83.79	83.15	100	12.43	91.82	89.33	69.41

Key: 1 inverse of trade union density, 2 inverse of collective bargaining coverage, 3 inverse of works councils, 4 inverse of board-level employee representation, 5 share of the top one percent of wealth, 6 Gini coefficient, 7 general poverty rate, 8 child poverty rate, 9 hard long work, 10 inverse of paid vacation, 11 rate of labor exploitation, 12 inverse of employment protection, 13 inverse of unemployment benefits, 14 inverse of economic-social protection

TABLE 13 Measures and degrees of capitalist dictatorship, OECD countries (cont.)

Country	15	16	17	18	19	20	21	22	23	24	25	26
Australia	8.99	4.43	17.00	.00	17.14	7.21	7.21	18.00	25.80	.00	40	35.85
Austria	24.40	6.90	16.00	4.20	19.05	2.40	8.65	28.00	14.50	.00	20	13.21
Belgium	11.60	5.91	17.00	4.20	40.48	11.54	9.62	23.00	14.50	.00	20	16.98
Canada	32.30	3.94	15.00	4.20	15.24	5.29	5.29	19.00	16.34	.00	20	24.53
Chile	53.50	17.73	28.00	4.20	38.57	16.35	18.27	28.00	31.91	.00	40	33.96
Czech Republic	39.20	21.67	27.00	4.20	12.86	18.27	30.77	34.00	29.62	.00	20	22.64
Denmark	15.40	1.97	5.00	.00	17.62	3.37	1.44	14.00	10.84	.00	20	24.53
Estonia	36.30	10.34	16.00	4.20	33.81	13.46	10.10	20.00	27.79	.00	20	39.62
Finland	31.30	1.48	8.00	.00	18.10	.00	.00	13.00	8.09	.00	20	28.30
France	57.40	11.82	26.00	4.20	48.10	11.06	12.02	21.00	15.88	.00	20	35.85
Germany	23.80	4.93	15.00	4.20	33.33	8.65	4.81	21.00	11.76	.00	20	24.53
Greece	42.10	24.63	31.00	4.20	50.00	40.87	44.23	39.00	16.18	.00	40	49.06
Hungary	30.30	41.38	59.00	12.50	26.67	27.88	40.38	54.00	25.50	.00	40	22.64
Iceland	18.80	5.42	6.00	.00	3.33	6.73	6.25	12.00	5.65	.00	20	.00
Ireland	34.90	7.88	16.00	.00	13.81	10.10	9.13	20.00	11.30	.00	20	5.66
Israel	30.20	30.05	31.00	8.30	84.76	19.23	20.67	39.00	35.73	.00	80	100
Italy	27.10	18.23	29.00	4.20	42.38	38.46	37.98	37.00	13.74	.00	40	26.42
Japan	47.30	19.70	29.00	12.50	11.90	9.62	10.58	31.00	5.95	4.96	20	16.98
Korea	42.00	26.11	28.00	8.30	34.76	13.94	27.88	31.00	16.18	.00	40	50.94
Latvia	45.42	25.12	27.00	4.20	39.05	20.19	35.58	34.00	27.33	.00	20	37.74
Lithuania	49.36	22.17	27.00	4.20	27.14	20.67	31.25	34.00	33.74	.00	20	37.74

	15	16	17	18	19	20	21	22	23	24	25	26
Luxembourg	10.30	3.45	17.00	.00	3.81	4.33	2.88	23.00	16.03	.00	20	11.32
Mexico	36.80	54.19	53.00	21.70	74.29	72.60	81.25	39.00	24.12	.00	80	7.55
Netherlands	18.10	2.96	14.00	4.20	21.90	3.85	3.85	18.00	9.62	.00	20	24.53
New Zealand	20.20	.49	15.00	.00	.95	1.92	.48	19.00	30.38	.00	20	28.30
Norway	21.80	.00	6.00	.00	9.52	.48	2.40	12.00	9.16	.00	20	32.08
Poland	38.30	28.08	42.00	8.30	34.29	33.17	25.48	37.00	28.85	.00	40	37.74
Portugal	51.40	11.33	21.00	4.20	10.48	14.90	19.71	33.00	16.79	.00	20	35.85
Slovak Republic	40.20	23.15	27.00	4.20	27.62	29.81	33.65	34.00	29.31	.00	20	33.96
Slovenia	47.40	20.69	35.00	4.20	20.00	17.31	19.23	35.00	10.53	.00	20	20.75
Spain	28.20	17.24	28.00	4.20	44.76	19.71	27.40	30.00	18.93	.00	40	22.64
Sweden	12.80	2.46	13.00	4.20	19.52	1.44	1.92	14.00	9.31	.00	20	20.75
Switzerland	51.60	.99	13.00	4.20	4.76	.96	3.37	21.00	12.21	.00	20	13.21
Turkey	13.80	74.88	71.00	69.20	90.00	57.69	56.25	59.00	52.52	.00	80	50.94
United Kingdom	32.40	6.40	16.00	4.20	51.90	8.17	6.73	20.00	20.46	.00	20	32.08
United States	43.20	18.72	27.00	8.30	38.10	10.58	11.54	23.00	100	100.00	60	64.15

Key: 15 inverse of voting rights, 16 inverse of voice, 17 inverse of power constraints, 18 inverse of electoral freedom and political pluralism, 19 inverse of political stability and absence of violence, 20 inverse of the rule of law, 21 inverse of the control of corruption, 22 inverse of open government, 23 mass imprisonment, 24 death sentences and executions, 25 other political terror, 26 military expenditure

TABLE 13 Measures and degrees of capitalist dictatorship, OECD countries (*cont.*)

Country	27	28	29	30	31	32	33	34	35	36	37	38	39	40	Degree*
Australia	8.40	.00	31.34	21.00	29.03	47.06	.00	25.80	77.28	28.50	18.00	18.00	21.00	44.00	34.33
Austria	7.50	11.80	29.03	15.00	25.81	42.82	.00	14.50	63.68	27.40	12.00	8.00	42.00	23.00	23.47
Belgium	9.30	14.70	22.86	16.00	12.90	50.85	.00	14.50	60.61	21.50	11.00	11.00	21.00	19.00	25.07
Canada	7.80	2.90	29.71	27.00	6.45	44.01	.00	16.34	77.28	67.00	27.00	25.00	39.00	43.00	35.91
Chile	15.90	8.80	48.57	17.00	29.03	54.20	.00	31.91	88.81	71.80	41.00	39.00	31.00	59.00	47.71
Czech Republic	10.80	14.70	47.13	22.00	19.35	45.61	.00	29.62	53.12	16.10	7.00	9.00	36.00	13.00	29.49
Denmark	7.60	8.80	18.69	8.00	35.48	43.65	.00	10.84	49.39	28.20	9.00	10.00	19.00	10.00	17.43
Estonia	9.80	14.70	23.23	17.00	9.68	57.28	.00	27.79	38.51	18.00	6.00	9.00	37.00	22.00	34.66
Finland	7.30	2.90	14.96	8.00	19.35	49.35	.00	8.09	53.93	33.00	10.00	18.00	37.00	41.00	19.65
France	13.10	14.70	42.06	26.00	38.71	62.75	.00	15.88	56.69	18.70	11.00	10.00	20.00	20.00	27.89
Germany	7.50	5.90	27.65	15.00	9.68	51.31	.00	11.76	67.06	32.00	10.00	9.00	27.00	14.00	23.94
Greece	19.30	14.70	55.07	34.00	.00	64.11	.00	16.18	75.15	79.00	56.00	30.00	48.00	61.00	42.98
Hungary	19.60	29.40	57.64	42.00	6.45	51.08	.00	25.50	.00	30.90	14.00	16.00	31.00	24.00	36.57
Iceland	9.20	2.90	27.85	10.00	12.90	35.56	.00	5.65	.78	31.00	19.00	18.00	18.00	10.00	19.90
Ireland	11.00	.00	28.40	18.00	19.35	46.10	.00	11.30	83.36	64.00	22.00	19.00	35.00	55.00	33.25
Israel	23.00	41.20	58.32	34.00	29.03	90.71	.00	35.73	52.55	66.50	36.00	27.00	46.00	40.00	50.07
Italy	13.30	20.60	47.15	27.00	9.68	58.18	.00	13.74	76.15	54.00	21.00	21.00	30.00	40.00	35.34
Japan	13.00	11.80	55.60	22.00	29.03	45.41	.00	5.95	87.81	24.00	10.00	33.00	20.00	12.00	36.68
Korea	11.90	17.60	47.23	26.00	29.03	61.92	100	16.18	72.99	54.00	16.00	32.00	59.00	20.00	45.05
Latvia	11.50	11.80	36.98	22.00	29.03	56.98	.00	27.33	49.17	38.10	11.00	18.00	52.00	36.00	41.13
Lithuania	12.40	8.80	41.77	22.00	29.03	57.31	.00	33.74	65.12	47.00	16.00	15.00	50.00	42.00	43.20

	27	28	29	30	31	32	33	34	35	36	37	38	39	40	*
Luxembourg	7.40	2.90	29.65	16.00	9.68	50.85	.00	16.03	60.80	46.00	11.00	11.00	36.00	19.00	24.17
Mexico	36.20	38.20	88.58	46.00	29.03	86.24	.00	24.12	88.81	94.00	45.00	40.00	36.00	53.00	59.89
Netherlands	7.20	8.80	16.72	16.00	32.26	50.75	.00	9.62	63.40	24.40	20.00	20.00	31.00	18.00	23.51
New Zealand	7.30	.00	20.36	20.00	25.81	40.50	.00	30.38	77.28	34.20	18.00	18.00	25.00	30.00	33.65
Norway	7.40	2.90	14.81	10.00	32.26	50.95	.00	9.16	46.29	25.70	19.00	18.00	22.00	27.00	21.18
Poland	16.80	26.50	54.71	34.00	25.81	54.86	.00	28.85	58.16	59.60	30.00	29.00	35.00	34.00	39.75
Portugal	9.80	8.80	23.92	21.00	9.68	42.26	.00	16.79	74.52	58.10	36.00	38.00	36.00	35.00	33.70
Slovak Republic	14.60	20.60	44.65	22.00	32.26	51.41	.00	29.31	66.78	51.00	23.00	31.00	42.00	34.00	36.87
Slovenia	12.20	17.60	42.25	27.00	9.68	44.94	.00	10.53	55.69	26.90	12.00	8.00	32.00	25.00	27.56
Spain	13.10	11.80	41.64	22.00	25.81	56.35	.00	18.93	65.18	39.10	22.00	23.00	19.00	35.00	35.10
Sweden	5.50	5.90	15.74	14.00	32.26	50.85	.00	9.31	59.89	45.00	10.00	11.00	19.00	16.00	20.27
Switzerland	7.60	8.80	19.92	15.00	22.58	45.87	.00	12.21	74.21	19.10	9.00	8.00	36.00	28.00	27.06
Turkey	42.60	76.50	100	68.00	29.03	100	.00	52.52	72.74	94.00	68.00	60.00	75.00	73.00	67.95
United Kingdom	11.50	8.80	42.09	18.00	54.84	59.73	.00	20.46	81.35	26.90	10.00	6.00	21.00	33.00	34.79
United States	12.80	17.60	48.65	28.00	51.61	79.64	100	100	91.32	67.50	53.00	55.00	67.00	71.00	63.49

* average of 1–40

Key: 27 inverse of individual liberty, 28 inverse of civil liberties, 29 inverse of media freedom, 30 inverse of fundamental human rights, 31 inverse of privacy, 32 inverse of civic peace, 33 the death penalty for drug offenses, 34 prisoners and on-death row and executed persons of ethical conscience, 35 inverse of public spending on the arts and culture, 36 mass and enforced beliefs in 'God', 37 extremely high importance of religion in life, 38 extreme incidence of daily prayer, 39 inverse of biological evolutionism, 40 pervasive beliefs in 'Satan' and 'witches'

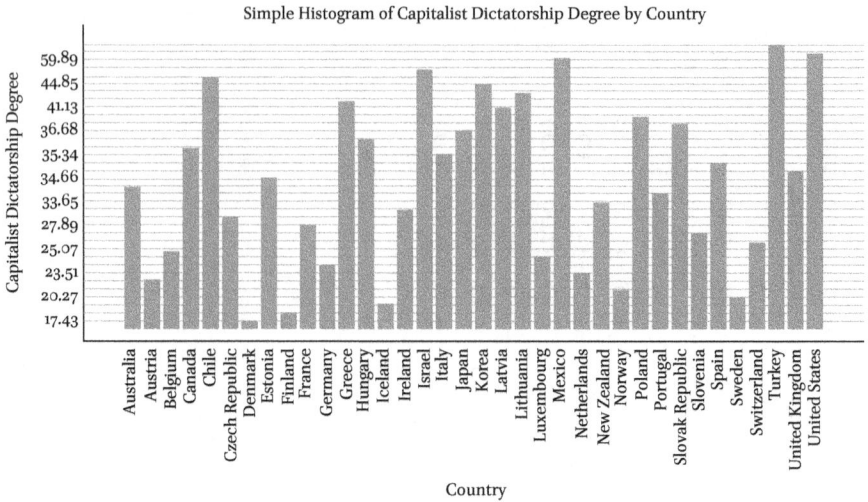

FIGURE 1   Degrees of capitalist dictatorship, OECD countries

Thus, judging by their capitalist dictatorship degrees especially three countries appear as outstanding exemplars in this respect: Turkey, United States and Mexico. First, Turkey features the highest degree of capitalist dictatorship that is due to its ranking the first or high on a large number of measures. These are: union density and collective bargaining coverage inverse, councils and board-level employee representation inverse, Gini coefficients, general and child poverty rates, work hours, vacation inverse, labor exploitation, benefits inverse, voice inverse, power constraints inverse, pluralism inverse, stability inverse, rule of law inverse, control of corruption inverse, open government inverse, prisoner rates, political terror, military expenditure, and beliefs in Satan. Additional measures include personal freedom inverse, civil liberties inverse, press freedom inverse, human rights inverse, peace inverse, moralistic-religious terror, art and culture spending inverse, extreme and compulsory religiosity (all dimensions), and evolutionism inverse. Conversely, Turkey ranks comparatively low on a few capitalist dictatorship indicators and measures such as wealth concentration, employment protection and *social protection* inverse, voter turnout inverse, death sentences and executions, privacy inverse (but mainly before Islamic rule), and death penalty for drug offenses. The preceding finding reaffirms the widespread observations that Turkey has emerged and consolidated as capitalist autocracy and theocracy or autocratic and theocratic capitalism under Islamic governance during recent times.

Next, the United States is the second-ranked and hence exhibits the highest degree of capitalist dictatorship among Western societies, which thus

TABLE 14   Ranking in capitalist dictatorship by average degrees, OECD countries

Ranking	Country	Average degree
1	Turkey	67.95
2	United States	63.49
3	Mexico	59.89
4	Israel	50.07
5	Chile	47.71
6	South Korea	45.05
7	Lithuania	43.20
8	Greece	42.98
9	Latvia	41.13
10	Poland	39.75
11	Slovak Republic	36.87
12	Japan	36.68
13	Hungary	36.57
14	Canada	35.91
15	Italy	35.34
16	Spain	35.10
17	United Kingdom	34.79
18	Estonia	34.66
19	Australia	34.33
20	Portugal	33.70
21	New Zealand	33.65
22	Ireland	33.25
23	Czech Republic	29.49
24	France	27.89
25	Slovenia	27.56
26	Switzerland	27.06
27	Belgium	25.07
28	Luxembourg	24.17
29	Germany	23.94
30	Netherlands	23.51
31	Austria	23.47
32	Norway	21.18
33	Sweden	20.27
34	Iceland	19.90
35	Finland	19.65
36	Denmark	17.43

TABLE 15   Indexes of capitalist/liberal democracy, OECD countries

Country	Average index*
Australia	65.67
Austria	76.53
Belgium	74.93
Canada	64.09
Chile	52.29
Czech Republic	70.51
Denmark	82.57
Estonia	65.34
Finland	80.35
France	72.11
Germany	76.06
Greece	57.02
Hungary	63.43
Iceland	80.10
Ireland	66.75
Israel	49.93
Italy	64.66
Japan	63.32
Korea, South	54.95
Latvia	58.87
Lithuania	56.80
Luxembourg	75.83
Mexico	40.11
Netherlands	76.49
New Zealand	66.35
Norway	78.82
Poland	60.25
Portugal	66.30
Slovak Republic	63.13
Slovenia	72.44
Spain	64.90
Sweden	79.73
Switzerland	72.94
Turkey	32.05
United Kingdom	65.21
United States	36.51

* 100—CAPITALIST DICTATORSHIP INDEX

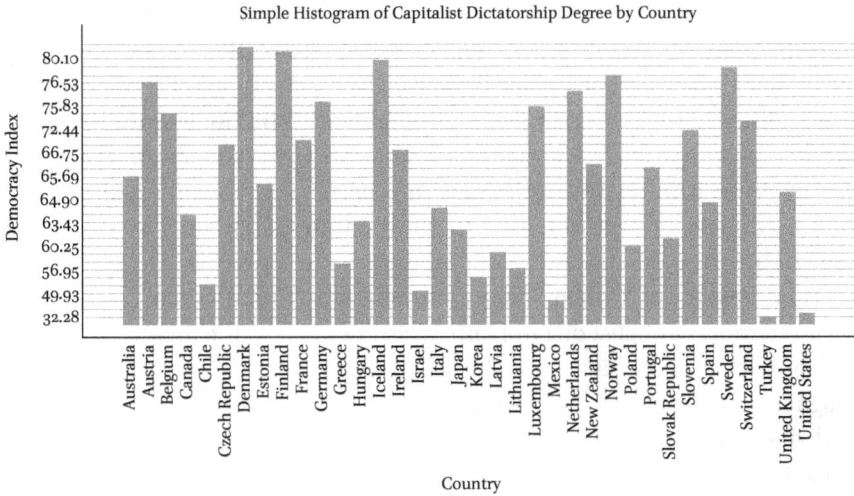

FIGURE 2   Indexes of liberal/capitalist democracy, OECD countries

excludes Turkey and the other eight countries of the top ten. The reason for such a degree is the US's ranking the first or second and otherwise comparatively high on a wide spectrum of capitalist dictatorship measures among Western societies and all OECD countries. For example, it ranks the first on councils and board-level employee representation inverse (along with some other countries), wealth concentration, vacation inverse and employment protection inverse. Further, it occupies the first rankings on prisoner rates, death sentences and executions, death penalty for drug offenses (with another country), moralistic-religious terror (share of drug offenders of prisoners), art and culture spending inverse, and beliefs in Satan (among Western and Christian societies). In addition, it ranks the second and generally high on additional measures. These are union density and collective bargaining coverage inverse, Gini coefficients, general and child poverty rates, work hours, benefits inverse, *social protection* inverse, voter turnout inverse, pluralism inverse, stability inverse, political terror, military expenditure, civil liberties inverse, press freedom inverse, human rights inverse, privacy inverse, peace inverse, extreme and compulsory religiosity (all dimensions, especially mass beliefs in 'God' and daily prayer), and evolutionism inverse. For example, the post-2016 radical-right US government continued and further intensified typical conservative American militarism by continually and drastically increasing military expenditure that is the highest by far among Western societies. As part of this tendency, it launched space militarization by creating the 'space force' as the new branch of the military, thus following and perhaps eventually fulfilling Reagan's fantasy of 'star wars'. This confirms that the main and most lethal enemy of the conservative militarist government and thus America is—itself, because any launching of space or other wars with weapons of mass destruction almost certainly will result in one definite outcome: MAD (mutually assured destruction). In short, it reaffirms the extreme irrationalism of American conservatism manifested in what Adorno diagnoses as it proneness to the 'delirium of annihilation masked as salvation'.

Alternatively, the United States ranks relatively (but not dramatically) low on just several capitalist dictatorship measures, namely the inverse of the rule of law, control of corruption and open government. The result confirms the diagnoses of the resurgence of American capitalist plutocracy qua 'plutonomy' and theocracy or plutocratic and theocratic capitalism under conservatism since Reaganism, hence in predominant conservative America, and to some degree of autocracy and dynasty post-2016. For instance, during the US 2020 Presidential campaign, one candidate accused another one for seeking to 'hurt the Bible, hurt God' (sic), suggesting that this was the supreme and ultimate disqualification for seeking and holding the Presidency and generally political power in America in an echo of early Puritan theocracy repressing and excluding the 'godless'. One might expect that in a Western democracy, the accused and supposed liberal candidate would respond that the US Constitution prohibited 'establishment of religion', disestablished the Puritan theocracy, and instead erected a 'wall separation of church and state' and did not require what Weber calls religious qualifications for holding political power, notably the Presidency. Instead, the candidate responded by extoling the devout 'faith' as defining and indeed having more of it than the accuser, thus revealing the possession of the foremost qualification for the US Presidency. Similarly, the opposition (House of Representatives leader) responded to the autocratic actions of a President effectively disposing of the Constitution by a 'faith'-based' solution—'pray' for the perpetrator as if this were the most effective cure, indeed more efficacious than any secular or medical alternative. If, as Weber suggests, what defines theocracy is precisely the application of religious qualifications like 'faith' and 'godliness' for holding political power, American formal democracy under conservatism meets this definition, just as does the Islamic 'Republic of Iran' also staging presidential elections. Simply, if one does not know what theocracy is and whether it exists, one knows it when seeing it, as during US Presidential and virtually any political elections in which religious 'faith' is the supreme qualification and those without it simply 'need not apply'. This provides an American and Western functional equivalent to presidential elections and other processes in Islamic theocracies such as Iran and

Turkey, in which 'faith' determines who will be elected president and to other positions.

In turn, Mexico evinces the third highest degree of capitalist dictatorship. This is because of Mexico's ranking the first, second or generally high on various capitalist dictatorship indicators and measures. These include collective bargaining coverage inverse, councils and board-level employee representation inverse (with some other countries), Gini coefficients, general and child poverty rates, work hours, vacation inverse, labor exploitation, benefits inverse, *social protection* inverse. Other measures are voice inverse, power constraints inverse, pluralism inverse, stability inverse, rule of law inverse, control of corruption inverse, open government inverse, political terror (with others), personal freedom inverse, civil liberties inverse, press freedom inverse, human rights inverse, peace inverse, art and culture spending inverse, extreme and compulsory religiosity (all dimensions, especially mass beliefs in 'God'), and belief in Satan. Mexico ranks comparatively lower on only a few capitalist dictatorship measures like wealth concentration, employment protection inverse, death sentences and executions, military expenditure, privacy inverse, death penalty for drug offenses, and evolutionism inverse. The finding illustrates the common impression that capitalist oligarchy, along with political instability, the weak rule of law, corruption, and religious traditionalism, continues to pervade Mexico as its long-standing prevalent form at least prior to the recent changes in government and attempted democratic and egalitarian reforms.

Regarding the other seven countries from the top-ten, for example, Israel ranks the first on councils' inverse (with other countries), general poverty rates (with another country), political terror (with others) and military expenditure. Chile also ranks the first on councils and board-level employee representation inverse (with other countries), Gini coefficients, *social protection* inverse, and voter turnout inverse (with another country). Chile's highest ranking on Gini coefficients and *social protection* inverse helps explain the mass protests during recent times and reflects the disastrous effects of Chicago economics' laissez-faire and massive privatization economic policy that its dictator Pinochet adopted from Friedman and Hayek during their personal visits of counsel and encouragement to enact 'free market' fascist dictatorship, which apparently persists. For example, Chile's 2019 mass protests against rampant economic inequality, insecurity and poverty illustrates the enduring dismal failure and legacy (and 'science') of Chicago economics' laissez-faire dogma that its exponents Friedman, Hayek and their students 'Chicago boys' personally presented to the dictator Pinochet as a supposed antidote against socialism but effectively becoming a lethal poison of both egalitarian capitalism and liberal democracy.[14] In turn, what perhaps mainly accounts for Israel's overall rank and in particular, its highest ranking on general poverty rates is its relatively long rule by an ultra-conservative, right-wing government as opposed to its previous labor, social-democratic governments.

In addition, South Korea ranks the first or high overall on union density and collective bargaining inverse, wealth concentration, Gini coefficients, general poverty rates, work hours, *social protection* inverse, military expenditure, press freedom inverse, death penalty for drug offenses, art and culture spending inverse, extreme religiosity (belief in God), and evolutionism inverse. (Strikingly, South Korea ranks the third highest on general poverty rates despite its spectacular economic growth and development, thus seeming emulating American capitalism's model of widespread persistent poverty and concentrated wealth.) Greece ranks generally high on Gini coefficients, child poverty rates, work hours, labor exploitation, benefit inverse, stability, rule of law and open government inverse, military expenditure, press freedom inverse, human rights inverse, art and culture spending inverse, extreme religiosity (all dimensions), and belief in Satan. These rankings leave the impression that South Korea has not fully overcome the experience of military capitalist dictatorship compounded with the infiltration of anti-science evangelicalism. They also suggest that the recent reforms have only in part transformed Greece's social structure, including economic system, political regime and traditionalist religion, less than expected, so that its ranking is somewhat surprising. (Greece's consolation prize is its unexpectedly highest privacy score, but this is insufficient to compensate for its other rankings.)

Baltic states Lithuania and Latvia rank comparatively high on union density and collective bargaining inverse, councils and board-level employee representation inverse, Gini coefficients, general and child poverty rates, labor exploitation, benefit inverse, *social protection* inverse, voter turnout inverse, control of corruption inverse, open government inverse, prisoner rates, military expenditure, press freedom inverse and evolutionism inverse. These striking and seemingly surprising rankings make Lithuania and Latvia appear to have just substituted capitalist-conservative dictatorship or repressive oligarchic capitalism—rather than liberal democracy—for their postwar communist

---

14   Rodrik (2010, p. 34) points to the 'disastrous policies of the Chicago boys' in Chile under Pinochet's military and neo-fascist dictatorship that the conservative US government, as typical during the Cold War, installed and sustained for about two decades with the 'collateral damage' of thousands murdered and many more imprisoned and tortured in the name of 'free enterprise' and 'God' consecrated by Catholicism—an exemplary case of religious capitalist dictatorship.

dictatorships in seeming path-dependence on, if not partial restoration of, their interwar fascist or radical-right regimes.

Poland ranks comparatively high on union density and collective bargaining coverage inverse, work hours, labor exploitation, power constraints inverse, pluralism inverse, stability inverse, rule of law inverse, open government inverse, prisoner rates, military expenditure, civil liberties inverse, press freedom inverse, human rights inverse, and extreme religiosity, especially belief in God. For example, Polish ruling religious conservatives in the Parliament proclaimed Jesus Christ the 'honorary king of Poland' even if such an influential historical individual had died more than 2000 years ago and the country itself has no monarchy. Such are what Merton would call the 'perversities' of religious conservatism and its 'divinely ordained' design of theocracy cum the 'Catholic tradition' in Poland and elsewhere. Historically, this suggests that religious conservatism in Poland and beyond in Eastern Europe proves to be even more irrational, unreasonable and implacable that late communism that at least showed rationality by prudent self-termination, consistent what Mannheim classically diagnoses as the 'complete irrationalism' of conservatism, including fascism.[15] In light of such rankings, Poland looks as it has substituted not liberal democracy but just one form of dictatorial regime for another: capitalist-conservative dictatorship, specifically capitalist theocracy or theocratic and oligarchic capitalism, for its communist variant in apparent path-dependence on its theocratic or religious (Catholic) tradition or inheritance.

Moreover, along with Hungary under authoritarian populism, Poland during conservative-religious dominance has become what Weber would call a pariah state within the European Union (EU). A 2020 report by the EU Parliament's Committee on Civil Liberties, Justice and Home Affairs reported the 'continuing deterioration of democracy, rule of law and fundamental rights in Poland' under the ruling ultra-conservative, theocratic 'Law and Justice' party. Apparently, along with democracy and human rights, the rule of law has deteriorated under a populist 'Law and Justice' party whose name claims the opposite. This contradiction illustrates the penchant of today's ultra-conservative, radical-right, including neo-fascist, parties and forces in Europe and America to claim and use 'rule of law', 'freedom' (the 'Freedom Party'), 'liberty' (the 'Liberty Caucus', the 'Liberty University') and 'democracy' to effectively destroy or pervert rule of law, freedom, liberty, and democracy. Such a negative report is highly ironic from the standpoint of the European Union

---

15   See Merton (1968, p. 477) and Mannheim (1936, p. 127).

because the latter (along with NATO) accepted Poland with a hope of its high democratic potentials or promises manifested during the late 1980s, which yet has become the major impediment, along with Hungary, to 'democracy, rule of law and fundamental rights' in the EU. In the context of Poland, it amounts to a true sociological tragedy of replacing one form of dictatorship with another one that seems even more severe and enduring, consistent with the fact that conservative-religious dictatorships tend to be more obstinate and long-lasting than their secular opposites.

Overall, Poland's theocratic and generally 'authoritarian rightism' tragedy, along with that of Hungary, illustrates a broader tendency in central, Eastern and Southern Europe, including the Balkans. The disintegration of communism while necessary for democracy has marked the return, resurgence, eventually triumph and dominance of the social forces that suffered defeat and discredit during WW II—essentially of fascism and generally authoritarian conservatism or 'rightism'. Neo-fascist and related radical-right forces resurrected from the WW II death of fascism and now prevail in former fascist states such as Hungary, most of the Baltics and to some degree Austria and Italy, along some non-OECD (but NATO) countries or provinces previously ruled by fascism (Albania, Bulgaria, Croatia, Kosovo).

More broadly, authoritarian religious-political conservatism or 'rightism' revitalized from its the WW II discredit as the creator or ally of fascism and how rules Catholic-dominated Poland, Turkey during Islamic governance, along with various non-OECD countries, especially South America. The WW II fascist-conservative losers seek and indeed succeed to become today's winners in their societies and the post-1990s signal the return of mixed capitalist-conservative-religious dictatorships rather than establishing liberal democracies, as Poland and Hungary show most egregiously within the EU. These defeated forces strategically infiltrated into or masked as anti-communist democratic movements and revolutions in Poland, Hungary and elsewhere in the region (Albania, the Baltics, Croatia, Kosovo) and once seized state power they immediately proved their fascist and extreme conservative, including theocratic, character, just as Islamic theocrats used the same strategy during the Iranian revolution and the Arab Spring. In essence, by so doing post-WW II fascists-conservatives in these countries used democratic processes and institutions to eliminate or pervert what they promised as 'democracy' into compounded capitalist-conservative-religious dictatorship, just as Islamic theocrats did by imposing theocracy in Iran, Turkey and other Muslim countries.

The above EU Parliament's compliant of the 'continuing deterioration of democracy, rule of law and fundamental rights in Poland' is a special proof of such a striking anti-democratic and illiberal reversal in this and other countries. And German, American and British governments are especially instrumental in such resurrection from death or rehabilitation of the defeated ww ii fascist forces in the Balkans and beyond (the Baltics, Ukraine, etc.). The German conservative government is instrumental in this trend in that after the reunification it basically continues the Nazi Balkans policy by allying with Germany's ww ii allies ((Albania, Croatia, Kosovo, Slovenia) and attacking, under the NATO cover, its enemies from ww i and ii (Serbia). US and British governments are instrumental by supporting the secessionist regions (Croatia, Muslim Bosnia, Kosovo, Slovenia) in the Yugoslavia civil war—which is equivalent to the British or French empire siding with the Southern Confederacy in the American civil war—and even attacking the latter (Serbia) on behalf of an 'ethic terrorist army' that was a descendant of a ww ii Nazi movement (*Bali combatar*), thus launching a fantasy or proxy war with Russia in the Balkans of which millions of civilians are a 'collateral damage' in death, destruction and suffering. In sum, fascism and conservatism overall may have been defeated and discredited in ww ii but neo-fascism and the new conservatism have won later local wars and revitalized during postwar times in the Balkans and much of Eastern and Central Europe mostly thanks to German, American and British governments, with the first continuing the Nazi foreign policy and the other two waging a fantasy war against Russia in this region. (This parallels and continues the tendency of the US postwar conservative government to enlist and use Nazi scientists during the Cold War, as well as Reagan's equivalence between fascist and anti-fascist ww ii forces, which illustrates the elective affinity and indeed fatal attraction between American conservatism and European fascism.)

Alternatively, their highest capitalist dictatorship degrees suggest (subtracting them from 100) that these countries have the lowest indexes of liberal or capitalist democracy (as shown in Table 16 ranking OECD states in these terms).

Thus, the top-ten countries in capitalist dictatorship become the bottom-ten in liberal or capitalist democracy with corresponding indexes of the latter: 36. Turkey (32.05), 35. United States (36.51), 34. Mexico (40.11), 33. Israel (49.93), 32. Chile (52.29), 31. South Korea (54.95), 30. Lithuania (56.80), 29. Greece (57.02), 28. Latvia (58.87), and 27. Poland (60.25).

Conversely, the degrees or indices of capitalist dictatorship are the lowest in these OECD countries in a reverse ranking from 36–27. They are Denmark (17.43), Finland (19.65), Iceland (19.90), Sweden (20.27), Norway (21.18), Austria (23.47), Netherlands (23.51), Germany (23.94), Luxembourg (24.17), and Belgium (25.07). In this regard, these countries most fully depart from and transcend capitalist dictatorship and instead epitomize or approach its obverse liberal or capitalist democracy because of their economic system being fundamentally

TABLE 16   Ranking in capitalist/liberal democracy by average indexes, OECD countries

Ranking	Country	Average index
1	Denmark	82.57
2	Finland	80.35
3	Iceland	80.10
4	Sweden	79.73
5	Norway	78.82
6	Austria	76.53
7	Netherlands	76.49
8	Germany	76.06
9	Luxembourg	75.83
10	Belgium	74.93
11	Switzerland	72.94
12	Slovenia	72.44
13	France	72.11
14	Czech Republic	70.51
15	Ireland	66.75
16	New Zealand	66.35
17	Portugal	66.30
18	Australia	65.67
19	Estonia	65.34
20	United Kingdom	65.21
21	Spain	64.90
22	Italy	64.66
23	Canada	64.09
24	Hungary	63.43
25	Japan	63.32
26	Slovak Republic	63.13
27	Poland	60.25
28	Latvia	58.87
29	Greece	57.02
30	Lithuania	56.80
31	South Korea	54.95
32	Chile	52.29
33	Israel	49.93
34	Mexico	40.11
35	United States	36.51
36	Turkey	32.05

capitalism even if a regulated and egalitarian or welfare rather than laissez-faire inegalitarian type.

It is especially striking that the degrees of capitalist dictatorship are the lowest in the five Scandinavian or Nordic countries that therefore qualify primarily as antipodes of capitalist dictatorship and models of liberal democracy, thus as most advanced capitalist democracies—'social democracies' within capitalism. Particularly, Denmark reveals the single lowest degree of capitalist dictatorship followed by the other four Scandinavian countries. Such degrees of these countries as a whole are due to their lowest or comparatively low ranking, singly or as a group, on virtually all four sets of capitalist dictatorship measures, with some variations. For example, they, with minor exceptions, rank the lowest or exceptionally low on a wide spectrum of economic measures. These are union density and collective bargaining coverage inverse, councils and board-level employee representation inverse, Gini coefficients, general and child poverty rates, work hours, vacation inverse, labor exploitation, employment and *social protection* inverse, and benefits inverse (except for and only in part the wealth share of the top one percent). Their rankings are also the lowest, or among them, on capitalist dictatorship's political measures, including voter turnout inverse, voice inverse, power constraints inverse, pluralism inverse, stability inverse, rule of law inverse, control of corruption inverse, open government inverse, prisoner rates, mass imprisonment, political terror, and military expenditure. In addition, they rank the lowest or among them and exceptionally low on its civic-society measures, such as personal freedom inverse, civil liberties inverse, press freedom inverse, human rights inverse, privacy inverse, peace inverse, the death penalty for drug offenses and moralistic-religious terror. Finally, their rankings are the lowest or so on its cultural measures from art and culture spending inverse through extreme and compulsory religiosity (all dimensions) o evolutionism inverse and belief in Satan.

The preceding reaffirms the widespread and indeed near-universal observations and experiences that Scandinavian/Nordic countries are at the minimum most remote from capitalist and any dictatorship and indeed models and most advanced instances of liberal or capitalist democracy—a fusion of a fully democratic regime and regulated welfare capitalism. This holds even if they are not yet perfect in all respects, for example, the wealth share of the top one percent in Denmark remains comparatively high and social protection in Iceland unusually low.

As regards the remaining five countries from this bottom-ten group, while usually not ranking lower than their Scandinavian/Nordic counterparts they rank comparatively low on the above sets of measures of capitalist dictatorship. For example, Austria and Germany rank among the lowest on a large variety of measures. These are collective bargaining coverage inverse, councils and board-level employee representation inverse, the wealth share of the top one percent and general poverty rates, work hours, vacation inverse, labor exploitation, employment and *social protection* inverse, and benefits inverse, as well as on most political, civil society and cultural measures, with some partial exceptions like stability and open government inverse. These degrees/rankings confirm that Austria and Germany have moved away from the inter-war merged capitalist-fascist dictatorship (Hitler-Krupp alliance) toward liberal democracy, however fragile and under the constant threat of neo-fascist and other ultra-conservative forces. This applies to Germany in domestic terms not considering its foreign policy especially toward Eastern Europe and the Balkans that is reminiscent, especially after its reunification, of that of its WW I imperial and WW II Nazi governments.

Thus, just a few years after the reunification, the German conservative government in the Fall of 1991 first unilaterally without consultation within the EU and ahead of the US granted dependence to Nazi Germany's WW II allies Croatia and Slovenia as Nazi-puppet regimes, thus effectively ending the former Yugoslavia (the same day its prime minister resigned) its victorious enemy during this war. It described this decision as a Christmas gift to its WW II allies and implied it was a death blow to its enemy. Further, to add injury to insult, this government abundantly armed and otherwise militarily supported its Nazi-era allies, especially Croatia and thus enabled its neo-Nazi regime's massacre and expulsion of the non-Croatian population reminiscent of its WW II infamous atrocities. Moreover, the German government directly attacked its WW II enemy in that it enthusiastically joined, for the first time after 1945, the NATO s attack on behalf of an 'ethnic terrorist army' (as US secretary of state admitted) against the former Yugoslavia in 1998 on the ground of 'protection of human rights' but more plausibly as an apparent belated act of vengeance for the lost war in the region, just as the Nazi military attacked the latter in 1941, although it eventually suffered a humiliating defeat. In doing so, it defended another Nazi-era ally (Albanian *Bali Combatar*), recognized among the first, together with the US and Turkey and other Islamic states, the creation of a neo-fascist, Islamic and mafia state of Kosovo which it has armed and otherwise supported ever since. Overall, after the reunification, the German long-ruling conservative ('Christian Democratic') government—this thus excludes its social-democratic counterpart or partner—has consistently favored Germany's Nazi-era Balkans allies Croatia and Slovenia, as well as Albania and Kosovo, over its wartime enemies like the former Yugoslavia (e.g., Serbia in WW I and II). In this respect, to paraphrase Prussia's military strategist Clausewitz, its activity is the continuation of the Nazi policy to the region by other or identical means such as military force under the cover of NATO.

In a broader historical context, this is not surprising because the conservative parties in the German Parliament helped pass Hitler's 1933 'enabling law' imposing Nazi totalitarian dictatorship and generally authoritarian conservatism or rightism formed the 'broader family' to which Nazism belonged. This demonstrates that Germany's Nazi-style nationalistic and expansionist foreign policy especially to the Balkans and Eastern Europe neither started with Hitler—but with Bismarck, Prussia and pan-German conservatism as WW I and prior times showed—nor ended with his death but continued under (NATO) covers through its conservative governments after its reunification. It is perhaps naïve to expect that the same conservative government whose ruling party supported Hitler's 1933 'enabling law' would abandon Nazism's and German conservatism's Balkans and Eastern Europe 'divide and rule' policy and expansionism. Apparently, the German conservative government's Balkans and Eastern Europe policy manifests its path-dependence on that of Nazism during WW II and of German conservatism in WW I and before, as well as perhaps Germans' old and partly persistent '*folkgeist*' of superiority and supremacy over the neighbors.

The Netherlands, Luxembourg and Belgium feature among the lowest rankings on various measures. These include union density and especially collective bargaining coverage inverse, councils and board-level employee representation inverse, the wealth share of the top one percent, in part Gini Coefficients, general and child poverty rates, work hours, vacation inverse, labor exploitation, employment and *social protection* inverse and benefits inverse, just as on most political, civil society and cultural measures, aside from rare exceptions, such as stability inverse for Belgium. These results affirm the observations or impression that the Netherlands, Luxembourg and Belgium continue to transcend capitalist and related, radical-right, dictatorship, including capitalist Calvinist theocracy in the first historically, and to consolidate liberal-secular democracy in fusion with mostly regulated, welfare capitalism and in that sense forming capitalist democracy.

Overall, the lowest capitalist dictatorship degrees (subtracted from 100) of this group indicate that, alternatively, these countries have the highest indexes of liberal or capitalist democracy. Hence, the bottom-ten countries in capitalist dictatorship turn out to be the top-ten in liberal or capitalist democracy with its corresponding indexes: 1. Denmark (82.57), 2. Finland (80.35), 3. Iceland (80.10), 4. Sweden (79.73), 5. Norway (78.828), 6. Austria (76.53), 7. Netherlands (76.49), 8. Germany (76.06), 9. Luxembourg (75.83), and 10. Belgium (74.93) (as Table 16 also shows).

In turn, the degrees of capitalist dictatorship are intermediate between these two extremes in most other OECD countries. In this sense, these countries occupy generally an intermediate location between, or mix elements of, capitalist dictatorship and liberal democracy. Specifically, on one hand, capitalist dictatorship degrees are closer in a descending order to the top-ten group in countries such as Slovak Republic (36.87), Japan (36.68), Hungary (36.57), Canada (35.91), Italy (35.34), Spain 35.10), United Kingdom (34.79), Estonia (34.66) and Australia (34.33). In this regard, their degrees make these countries appear closer in varying extents to capitalist dictatorships than to liberal democracies. They confirm the observations or perceptions that, for example, Slovak Republic and in part Estonia approach capitalist or conservative oligarchy rather than liberal democracy and indeed that Hungary moves toward capitalist-conservative dictatorship, specifically pro-capital radical-right populist autocracy. They also reaffirm that Japan tends to be closer to capitalist plutocracy than to Western-style liberal or inclusive democracy and that Italy and Spain mostly remain dominated by capitalist dynasty and oligarchy and experience democratic regression under recurring conservative, right-wing governments. Further, they support the identification of resurgent 'plutonomy' as a form or proxy of capitalist dictatorship or a variation of undemocratic plutocracy in Canada, the United Kingdom and Australia following the US as the plutonomic leader. In turn, the degrees of capitalist dictatorship help derive the indexes or levels of liberal or capitalist democracy for these countries in a descending order: Australia (65.67), Estonia (65.34), United Kingdom (65.21), Spain (64.90), Italy (64.66), Canada (64.09), Hungary (63.43), Japan (63.32) and Slovak Republic (63.13).

On the other hand, capitalist dictatorship degrees are closer in an ascending order to the bottom-ten group in countries like Switzerland (27.06), Slovenia (27.56), France (27.89), Czech Republic (29.49), Ireland (33.25), New Zealand (33.65), and Portugal (33.70). Judging by their degrees these countries, more precisely the first four, look closer to liberal-capitalist democracy than capitalist dictatorship. For instance, they reaffirm the impression that Switzerland and France approach liberal or capitalist democracy rather than capitalist dictatorship. They also support the perception that Slovenia and Czech Republic are the rare success stories of Eastern Europe's transition to capitalism and democracy by approaching liberal democracy and overcoming the authoritarian scenario of capitalist/conservative dictatorship, including oligarchy and theocracy within capitalism, plaguing especially most Baltic states, Hungary, Poland and Slovak Republic. In turn, they are inconclusive as to whether Ireland and in part Portugal have moved away from a proxy capitalist theocracy and oligarchy or a Catholic-dominated political regime to liberal and inclusive democracy combined in varying degrees with welfare capitalism, so if the first has become an outlier among English-speaking countries and the second distinct from Spain. Still, the overall trend or climate in both countries seems to be in a more democratic and/or secular direction. In addition, these rankings are inconclusive with regard to New Zealand's possible exclusion from or inclusion into 'plutonomy' making it difficult to infer whether this country during recent times has become a minor outlier among the other Anglo-Saxon countries or moved in tandem with them as the 'key plutonomies'. The second possibility seems probably more plausible in view of New Zealand's own emulation of anti-egalitarian and repressive Reaganism (e.g., pro-capital, anti-labor policies, 'three strikes' laws) or Thatcherism since the 1980s. Alternatively, these countries' degrees of capitalist dictatorship serve to obtain their indexes of liberal or capitalist democracy from higher to lower: Switzerland (72.94), Slovenia (72.44), France (72.11), Czech Republic (70.51), Ireland (66.75), New Zealand (66.35) and Portugal (66.30).

Overall, these figures are just preliminary, tentative estimates but still are generally indicative and provide some suggestive evidence of the degrees of capitalist dictatorship—and alternatively of capitalist democracy—in contemporary Western and comparable societies during the 2010s, especially post-2016.

CHAPTER 7

Conclusion

It seems to be the right time to introduce explicitly the concept and expression of capitalist dictatorship and indeed to formally establish it in sociology and related social science and perhaps to conceivably popularize it or make it present in public discourse, alongside the idea of capitalist or liberal democracy. This holds especially in light of post-2016 societal developments and events in the US and via global contagion or convergence in many other countries and regions in the world from Brexit Britain through sections of South America (Brazil, Colombia) and parts of Europe (Austria, Hungary, Poland) to Islamic countries (Saudi Arabia, Turkey). Moreover, these tendencies in post-2016 predominant conservative—as distinct from and opposed to secondary liberal— America and beyond compel such a sociological introduction and the establishment of capitalist dictatorship as a concept, for the purpose of its study, as this book has attempted, and to its conceivable popularization or presence in public discourse.

In essence, the post-2016 period feels and qualifies as the resurgence and 'spirit of the time' of capitalist dictatorship, including autocracy, dynasty, plutocracy and theocracy in capitalism, along with allied conservative-fascist and theocratic dictatorships, in these settings starting with the US as the leader and model of this 'brave' old world forming an alliance against democratic capitalism or liberal democracy. Perhaps post-2016 times feel like the 1930s in Europe seeing the rise and prevalence of merged capitalist-fascist dictatorships via capitalism's degeneration into or alliance and eventual merger with fascism, and like the Gilded Age in America featuring the unconstrained power of capital over non-capitalist strata.

While history probably does/will not repeat itself and these are distinct developments, events and times, they share the common overarching property of capitalist dictatorship (even if not so called) merged with fascism during the 1930s and post-2016 years and with theocracy or coercive religion in America since the Gilded Age and Puritanism. Alternatively, history in the shape of capitalist-fascist dictatorship or the unrestrained power of capital may well repeat itself if one neglects the tragedy of the 1930s and the lessons of the Gilded Age. Especially, the history of capitalist-fascist autocracy from interwar Germany and Italy may replicate even if in a semi-grotesque form in Western societies such as post-2016 America and to some degree Brexit Britain, just as is effectively replicating in non-Western countries like Brazil,

Hungary, Poland and others. It is no wonder that actual or potential (would-be) capitalist-fascist autocrats in these settings at present look comparable and indeed are often compared and similar to or reminiscent of those in Nazi Germany and fascist Italy. Thus, combined with exerting or wishing absolute personal rule reminiscent of the autocrats of the 1930s, they create a 'broad coalition of the right' and thus an extended family of 'authoritarian rightism' involving capital, conservatism and neo-fascism in their societies, just as Hitler did in Nazi Germany, and exalt capitalism in the manner of Mussolini's fascist exaltation of it as the 'choice of the fittest'. Further, their legacy or vestige of capitalist-fascist autocracy may continue and last even after their personal demise or decline (e.g., 2020 and later elections) through family dynasty and inheritance of wealth and power, as well as the residue of mass fanatical followers, in a process equivalent to Weber's societal 'routinization of charisma' in the succession of especially religious leaders. In this scenario, the end or fall of these autocrats would not necessarily signify the termination of capitalist-fascist autocracy and dynasty. Rather, it would initiate a process of autocratic or dynastic succession (the latter partly happened in the 2000 US Presidential elections), just as the death of Hitler and Mussolini did not make Nazism and fascism dead as an ideology and politics, as the postwar and current surge of neo-Nazism and neo-fascism shows.

More broadly, the history of merged capitalist, conservative and fascist oligarchy and plutocracy such as the 'broad coalition of the right', indeed the 'broader family of authoritarian rightists' in Nazi Germany and interwar Europe may repeat or echo itself irrespective of autocracy and dynasty. This may happen through the resurgence of 'plutonomy' and the radical right in the US and Great Britain and the persistence of oligarchy in most non-Western countries and its reappearance in Eastern Europe. Recurrence of capitalist-fascist autocracy or oligarchy from the 1930s into post-2016 times even if in different faces and shapes especially holds in view of long-term tendencies. Namely, it does insofar as the tendency to capitalist dictatorship is historically continuous and persistent in long terms since primitive laissez-faire capitalism in England and the 19th century such as the Gilded Age in America up to the New Deal as a transient interruption of this process.

Even if interwar capitalist-fascist dictatorship, including both autocracy and oligarchy, certainly does/will not replicate itself exactly in post-2016 times, one can underestimate as 'impossible' its reinvention and reassertion even in different forms only at the peril[1] of democratic capitalism or liberal

---

1 Altemeyer's (2006, pp. 246–7) earlier warning seems even more urgent today: the 'threat [of] fascist dictatorship is growing. Our societies presently produce millions of highly

democracy and sociology and social science itself, as happened with underestimating fascism as 'unthinkable' in the 1930s. In short, one can hardly
dismiss the post-2016 trend to and spirit of the time of capitalist dictatorship mixed, as in the 1930s, with fascism and religion with impunity. In this
respect, post-2016 times even if not entirely replicate are continuous with or
evocative of the fascist 1930s in Europe and the capital-dominated Gilded
Age in America, thus being yet another stage of a long process of capitalist
dictatorship.

It is therefore the occasion and time to express and translate this reemerging social reality and *zeitgeist* dominating the post-2016 US and spreading
beyond as if by contagion into an explicit concept of capitalist dictatorship in
sociological and related theory and research. Alternatively, it is an opportunity
for sociology and other social science to capture, document and do full justice
to such a social reality and climate by adopting and establishing the concept of
capitalist dictatorship as theoretically legitimate and empirically valid as that
of capitalist democracy that prevails in theory and research.

Moreover, the explicit introduction of 'capitalist dictatorship' to and its formal establishment in sociology, economics and related social science seems
long overdue in longer terms. This holds in the context of long-term societal
developments and events since the formation and expansion of modern capitalism and democracy during the 18th and 19th century through the 1930s to
postwar times, the 1980s and post-2016 days.

First, at the point of origin, primitive laissez-faire capitalism or its
approximation developed and functioned as proto-typical capitalist dictatorship in the sense of absolute power and total domination of capital or
the unrestrained rule of the capitalist class, in substitution of and eventual
alliance with pre-capitalist aristocracy, versus non-capital. At this point,
to capture and do justice to this reality, classical political economy since
Smith should have introduced and established 'capitalist dictatorship' as
a legitimate and valid concept as that of capitalist democracy, in fact even
more given the latter's absence or underdevelopment during this forma-
tive, heroic age of industrial capitalism during the late 18th and early 19th
century.

---

authoritarian personalities as a matter of course, enough to stage the Nuremberg Rallies over
and over and over again. Turning a blind eye to this could someday point guns at all our
heads, and the fingers on the triggers will belong to right-wing authoritarians. We ignore this
at our peril'.

However, classical political economy[2] omitted to do this, not counting Marx[3] or rather counting him as a dissident heterodox figure dissenting from orthodox economic theory. This holds despite some intimations of capitalist dictatorship in Smith's detection of capitalists' 'conspiracy against the public', Ricardo's denunciation of the 'wealthy aristocracy' and 'Oligarchy' in capitalism, J. S. Mill's characterization of the distribution of wealth as determined by the 'ruling portion of the community', and Cairnes' repudiation of laissez-faire capitalism. In addition, one would expect that early classical sociology since Comte adopted and established the concept in order to capture and do justice to the reality of original laissez-faire capitalism as initial capitalist dictatorship, yet it did not. This holds in spite of some implications like Comte's references to 'dictatorship', including religious and economic dictatorships in England and France, for example the 'English oligarchy', even envisioning the 'normal dictatorship' of capitalist bankers and Spencer's disapproval of the capitalist 'maintainers of class power' in the service of 'keeping the masses in thralldom' as in feudalism. Apparently, Comte envisioned primitive capitalism as a 'normal [financial] dictatorship' and Spencer identified its facet of dictatorial 'class power' but both came short of an explicit concept of capitalist dictatorship and its introduction to sociology.

Further, most of later, mature capitalism during the later 19th century evolved into and operated as proto-typical capitalist dictatorship in the above sense. For example, this holds for 19th-century England due to unrestrained capital power and severe labor coercion through the capitalist rendition of the despotic master-servant system based on feudal common law and maintained until the later part of the century. Later English classical political economy (ending during the 1870s) should have done justice to this persistent reality but

---

2 Perelman (2000, 20) suggests that since Smith classical political economy 'frequently couched its recommendations in a rhetoric of individual liberty, but its conception of liberty was far from all-encompassing. Liberty, for capital, depended on the hard work of common people'—the result was 'laissez-faire authoritarianism'.

3 Marx identifies (in *The Eighteenth Brumaire Of Louis Napoleon*) the 'dictatorship of the bourgeois republicans' in France 1848, providing this historical account: 'June 25 to December 10, 1848. Dictatorship of the pure bourgeois republicans. Drafting of the constitution. Proclamation of a state of siege in Paris. The bourgeois dictatorship set aside on December 10 by the election of Bonaparte as President'. To that extent, Marx identifies a short-lived historical example of capitalist dictatorship rather than expounding or elaborating an explicit and general concept of the latter applicable to other societies adopting capitalism. Even if supposing that Marx expounds it, such a concept is either absent or latent in other strands of economics and sociology, and this book aims to help explicitly introduce it to the latter.

did not introduce and establish capitalist dictatorship as a concept or expression that is as legitimate as or more than that of capitalist democracy in light of the latter's continuing underdevelopment and exclusionary character even in England. This holds with some implications like Ricardo's complaint that in England the 'really efficient power of Government' is in the 'hands of the wealthy aristocracy', the 'King, and the Oligarchy' and his advocacy to 'extend the right of voting for members of Parliament to every class of the people'. It continues to hold despite Mill's misgiving about (Comte's vision of) financial 'dictatorship' that reserves 'political power to the rich' in capitalist societies and Cairnes' deploring the 'harsh and hopeless destiny' of labor in capitalism, as both late classical economists came close to but did not use the concept.

In addition, despite this persisting reality of the 'wealthy aristocracy' in capitalist England and beyond, English and other neoclassical economics (beginning from the early 1870s) refrained from introducing and establishing the concept of 'dictatorship' in capitalism in the form of capitalists' arbitrary power over and severe coercion of labor. This holds in spite of some intimations to that effect such as Marshall detecting 'a few powerful capitalists' in England and imploring them not to be 'extravagant' by keeping their 'horses or slaves overworked or underfed'. Generally, this applies to other early neoclassical economists in Europe, although Wieser comes most closely to developing (in an apparent echo of Marx) the concept by such expressions as 'capitalistic despotism', 'capitalistic power', 'capitalistic despots', 'capitalistic exploitation', 'a lasting, physical and moral degradation of the proletarian strata', and the like.

In another example, American 'unfettered capitalism' during the Gilded Age essentially represented or approximated proto-typical capitalist dictatorship for the same reasons: unrestrained capital power and severe labor coercion, including the capitalist master-servant, common law system perpetuated through the early 20th century, until the New Deal. Yet, early American neoclassical and even institutional economics avoided using and establishing the concept or term. This applies to them in spite of J. B. Clark's identification of the 'strategic inequality between capitalists and laborers' and especially Mitchell's observation of the 'despotic might of capital', 'economic oppression', 'industrial despotism' and the 'physical and moral degradation of the lower classes' as the 'socially irrational, anti-economic phenomena' of American capitalism. Notably, it also holds even if Veblen implied the concept by the 'industrial dictatorship of the captain of finance' since this looks narrower and less enduring ('held on sufferance of the engineers and is liable at any time to be discontinued at their discretion, as a matter of convenience') than capitalist dictatorship as presently understood. Ironically, US President at the time, Theodore Roosevelt, came the closest to inventing substantively the concept of capitalist dictatorship by detecting and deploring the 'tyranny of mere wealth, the tyranny of a plutocracy' in American unfettered capitalism during the Gilded Age.

Moreover, just as neoclassical economics, later classical sociology refrained from explicitly introducing and establishing the concept of capitalist dictatorship in spite of some implications to that effect. These are Tonnies' depiction of capitalists as the 'natural lords and masters' of capitalism, Durkheim's description of the latter as the stage of the 'law of the strongest', Simmel's observation of the capitalist 'oppression' of workers, and Weber's imagery of the capitalist 'iron cage' and indeed the 'masterless slavery' of non-capitalists. Other implications are Michels' observation of the 'unrestricted power [and corruption] of capital' especially in the US, Pareto's diagnosis of plutocracy as the 'ruling power' in Western nations and prediction of 'military dictatorship' among them, and notably Mosca's notion of 'plutocratic dictatorship'. The latter still seems broader than capitalist dictatorship as its particular variant within capitalism by virtue of being also pre-capitalist.

Next, capitalism in interwar Europe, particularly Italy, Germany and Spain, mutated into dictatorship that allied and ultimately merged with fascism, including Nazism, thus mutating into blended capitalist-fascist dictatorship. Conversely, after and despite some initial anti-capitalist 'socialist' proclamations and pretensions, fascism in interwar Europe represented fundamentally a fused capitalist-conservative dictatorship, which the alliance and ultimate fusion of Nazism with major capitalists (Krupp et al.) and traditional conservatism within the 'broad coalition of the right', notably the extended family of 'authoritarian rightism' in Germany and beyond, epitomized. This might have seemed finally the right time and compelling rationale for sociology and economics to introduce and establish the concept of capitalist dictatorship and thus capture and do justice to the developing reality and *zeitgeist* of society. However, this did not happen, even though Mannheim came most closely to explicitly introducing the concept by 'dictatorship' in the bourgeois political regime in the form of fascism as the exponent of capitalist classes. In addition, the concept remained dormant, although Schumpeter admitted bourgeois democracy's 'apparent ease' to surrender to 'dictatorship', Polanyi identified fascism as the undemocratic 'solution to the impasse' of *laissez-faire* capitalism by reforming rather than vanquishing it, and Moore observed that the latter passing through reactionary conservatism culminates in fascism.

Similarly, capitalism especially in non-Western settings like South America, most egregiously Chile under Pinochet, and continuously in parts of Europe such as Portugal and Spain during postwar times degenerated into dictatorship mixed with neo-fascism, and in that sense into blended capitalist-neo-fascist dictatorship. Alternatively, neo-fascism in these settings represented a mixed capitalist-conservative dictatorship, which South America, especially Chile under Pinochet, exemplifies. In spite of this continuous degeneration of capitalism into capitalist dictatorship, postwar sociology and economics did not explicitly introduce and establish the concept, except for the cited single and secondary or occasional mention of 'capitalist dictatorships' and 'noncommunist dictatorships' with apparent reference to non-Western settings only.

Furthermore, the reappearance of proxy laissez-faire unregulated, repressive and antiegalitarian ('neoliberal') capitalism in some Western and other societies, especially the US, the UK and to some extent other Anglo-Saxon countries, during the 1980s marked essentially the return of capitalist dictatorship, including oligarchy, plutocracy and to some degree pro-capital theocracy. Thatcherism and Reaganism emerged and prevailed in these countries fundamentally as the neoconservative program and indeed counter-revolution of capitalist dictatorship, including plutocracy and, as with the second, theocracy, which also applies to their emulations and sequels through the early 21st century. At this point, contemporary sociology, economics and other social science probably should have definitely introduced and established the concept and expression for theory and research and contributed to making it common in public discourse. However, this expectation did not materialize, in spite of some implications. These include the observation of Reaganomics' 'redistribution of wealth in favour of the wealthy and of power in favour of the powerful', the detection of symptoms of authoritarianism and even totalitarianism in Thatcherism and Reaganism and the rediscovery of 'Plutonomy' in the US and the UK. A further instance is the identification of 'workplace dictatorships', 'authoritarian firms' and 'a dictatorial business class' in American capitalism. Altogether, the concept of capitalist dictatorship remained at most latent and unstated in sociology while economics relegated 'capitalist dictatorships' and 'noncommunist dictatorships' to non-Western countries and disregarded them for Western societies, especially the US and the UK, and thus overlooked or denied the mutation or linkage of laissez-faire, unregulated capitalism to such dictatorships.

Finally, post-2016 developments and events in the US and through global contagion many other societies signaled the resurgence, even literal eruption of capitalist dictatorship in alliance and ultimate merger with neo-fascist and other conservative, right dictatorships and pro-capital theocracies. Post-2016 years seem the time of surge and explosion of capitalist autocracy/dynasty and of oligarchy, plutocracy and theocracy, of demagogic, incompetent autocrats and predatory family dynasties and of exclusionary oligarchs, power-seeking plutocrats, and oppressive pro-capital theocrats in the US and via contamination or confluence, with some variations, other countries. These countries range from Brexit Britain, Brazil through Austria, Hungary and Poland to Saudi Arabia, other Gulf states and Turkey. On this account, capitalist dictatorship through these forms and agents reinvents and reasserts itself and prevails in the major segment of Anglo-Saxon capitalism déjà vu, much of South America again, certain former fascist countries, growingly Eastern Europe, most of the plutocratic Islamic world, and so forth.

Still, in spite of these growing tendencies, post-2016 sociology, economics and related social science is yet to explicitly introduce and establish capitalist dictatorship as a concept for the purpose of theory and analysis. This holds with intimations such as the sociological and other observations of 'authoritarian politics and exclusionary policies', 'populist rhetoric', 'nativist and racist claims', 'fake news stories', the 'lying demagogue' and the like in the post-2016 US,[4] along with some capitalist members' 'concern about the destabilizing concentration of wealth and power in America' during this time. In a charitable interpretation, all of them imply but none explicitly states capitalist dictatorship which precisely authoritarianism, exclusion, right-wing populism, nativism, racism, mass deceptions and lies, demagogy, and, most notably and specifically, the 'concentration of wealth and power' in capital typify. Apparently, the time has come to simply state what is implied—the post-2016 rise of capitalist dictatorship, including autocracy and plutocracy, American capitalism and via contagion beyond.

Evidently, post-2016 developments in the US and beyond form just the latest stage of this long-term process of capitalist dictatorship spanning from primitive laissez-faire capitalism and its later phase through interwar fascism and postwar neo-fascism to Thatcherism and Reaganism and their ramifications. Hence, far from being accidental and unusual, they are continuous and consistent with this process, including their immediate precursor Reaganism (Thatcherism in Britain), interwar fascism and in extension their distant archetype, Gilded-Age American capitalism. They hence mark essentially the second postwar eruption of capitalist dictatorship in the post-2016 US and to some degree Brexit Britain, emulating, indeed escalating via proxy autocracy, the first that occurred through the conservative revolution of Reaganism and Thatcherism.

More broadly, they signal the third surge of capitalist dictatorship among Western societies since merged capitalist-fascist dictatorships in interwar

---

4   For example, Allcott and Gentzkow (2017), Bonikowski (2016), Hahl et al. (2018), Kranton and Sanders (2017), and Lamont (2018).

Europe, including Germany and Italy. It is no wonder that the post-2016 period in the US and beyond has the noted déjà vu ambiance or echo of the 1930s in Europe, although it is not likely to exactly replicate the interwar outcome or that the latter repeats itself in the same form. Specifically, it has the social feeling and spirit of capitalist autocracy blended with plutocracy and pro-capital theocracy emulating or evoking that in interwar Germany through Hitler's 'coalition of the right' with major capitalists, traditional conservatism and religion, thus forming a wider family of 'authoritarian rightism', and Mussolini's fascist exaltation of capitalism for the 'fittest' and alliance with the Catholic church. In this sense, post-2016 developments, events and figures in the US and beyond leave a taste of déjà vu in relation to those in Europe during the 1930s, Reaganism and Thatcherism and in extension Gilded-Age American capitalism, even if do not exactly replicate them. Such a taste reaffirms that they are just the latest stage and face of a long process culminating in interwar capitalist-fascist dictatorships and initiated in Gilded-Age American as well as primitive laissez-faire capitalism.

The preceding requires situating post-2016 developments in America in a longer historical perspective and broader comparative framework, including capitalist-fascist dictatorships in interwar Europe and Gilded-Age American capitalism. It particularly necessitates placing post-2016 capitalist autocrats in the extended family of capitalist-fascist autocracy (including Hitler and Mussolini) and in the company of the Gilded-Age robber barons and other early despotic capitalists. Conversely, by failing to do so, one risks missing the historical sequence and notably sociological continuity between post-2016 developments and figures and their earlier tendencies and precursors and indeed declared or secret role models of the 1930s, as well as the Gilded-Age, even if not being exactly the same. It is no accident that effective capitalist or conservative autocrats from the US through Brazil to Austria and Hungary express admirations for their fascist precursors from the 1930s (including Hitler and Mussolini) or postwar times (military dictators) and adopt elements or symbols of fascism, including Nazism. In sum, post-2016 developments, events and figures in the US and beyond show such a manifest and strong tendency to capitalist or conservative dictatorship that they inevitably resemble or evoke capitalist-fascist dictatorships and their autocratic rulers in interwar Europe, including Germany and Italy.

Furthermore, post-2016 developments are likely to have an enduring and pervasive impact in terms of capitalist dictatorship and conservative-fascist dictatorships comparable to that of their fascist antecedents in interwar Europe, especially Germany, and of Reaganism and Thatcherism. The vision of capitalist dictatorship, including autocracy, plutocracy and pro-capital theocracy, is not likely to end with the demise of its leaders, as possibly in the US 2020 elections, just as Nazism and fascism did not end with the death of Hitler and Mussolini nor did the design of Puritan evangelical theocracy in America with that of Calvin or Winthrop. Instead, it is likely to undergo a process of evolution and adaptation analogous to Weber's 'routinization of charisma' following the demise of a charismatic leader, including capitalist-fascist autocrats and religious rulers, and involving autocratic succession or dynastic dilution conjoined with the residual mass of fervent and armed followers determined to preserve the image and legacy of their ruler. Consequently, even if its autocratic rulers lose power or leave the stage, capitalist dictatorship is likely to continue as a social system or ideological vision in the face of another dynastic hereditary autocrat or the form of oligarchy, plutocracy and pro-capital theocracy routinizing the charismatic leader, as in conservative America and Saudi Arabia and other Gulf states.

However, the post-2016 autocracy apparently attempts to rig or distort the US 2020 Presidential elections by various tactics, for example, de-legitimizing certain forms of voting (mail-in vote) and defunding the agencies responsible for facilitating it (the US Post Office, etc.) with the open or tacit support of the conservative-dominated Senate, Supreme Court and other institutions within the celebrated yet suspended constitutional 'separation of powers'. These actions, first, confirm the penchant of actual or would-be autocrats for rigging or distorting elections in their favor. Second, they effectively suspend and reduce American democracy to a 'banana republic' or third-world state where rigged elections are rampant. Third, they illustrate that what was unthinkable just a few years ago such as pre-2016 becomes both possible and real in post-2016 America under autocracy and its principal support conservatism. Fourth, it suggests that conservatism continues to rig or distort elections and thus democratic processes directly or indirectly by complicity, following its apparent rigging of the 2000 Presidential elections (from a conservative-controlled state to the Supreme Court conservative majority) as a successful precedent. The US founders and Constitution apparently could probably the least imagine the power constellation in which the autocratic executive, in alliance or complicity with majority conservative legislative and judicial powers, would try to overly rig elections by violating voting rights and thus subvert democracy and the rule of law. Obviously, what was unimaginable for Jefferson et al. two centuries ago has become possible and real in America post-2016 due to the capitalist autocracy seeking to rule by 'executive actions' and cultivated via a cult of personality and protected by conservatism, including evangelicalism, just as it did in Germany after 1933 because of an autocrat that authoritarian 'rightism' enabled to rule by decree.

At any rate, post-2016 developments, events and powers resurrected—after Reaganism/Thatcherism and fascism opened twice in the 20th century—the ghost or specter of capitalist dictatorship, specifically autocracy, dynasty, plutocracy and pro-capital theocracy, in the US and via global contagion beyond. It seems difficult to return the ghost to the 'dead past' in the foreseeable future especially in light of the continuous predominance of the pro-capital conservative-repressive and religious pole of America over its liberal-democratic and secular opposite. Relatedly, post-2016 times uncovered, after Reaganism's and McCarthyism's initial uncovering, the societal basis and setting of capitalist dictatorship from autocracy to plutocracy and pro-capital theocracy—conservative, religious America as the growingly dominant pole of the US since the 1980s. In a way, they have awaked all those social forces, potentials, resources and persons seeking to establish capitalist dictatorship in association and ultimate merger with fascism or theocracy, as through the Religious Right alliance between plutocracy and poor religious groups versus liberal democracy and science. That is why post-2016 developments in conservative America have an ambiance and feeling of the 1930s in fascist Europe, which reaffirms that contemporary American and British conservatism like Reaganism and Thatcherism while not being substantively identical displays a functional equivalence with European fascism in respect of their equivalent effects on capitalist dictatorship and alternatively on liberal democracy—reproduction of the first, elimination of the second. In this regard, they resurrect in post-2016 conservative America the ghost of merged capitalist-fascist dictatorship from the 1930s Europe.

The post-2016 resurrecting of the ghost of capitalist dictatorship—or merged capitalist-fascist dictatorship—in the US and beyond should compel or motivate sociology and related social science to finally adopt and establish the concept for sociological and other study. Alternatively, sociology and other social science acquires the probably strongest rationale or motivation to do so during post-2016 times after Reaganism/Thatcherism and interwar fascism, although Mannheim came extremely close to doing this then. Hence, in light of these dramatic and momentous tendencies, contemporary sociology and related social science can no longer afford to operate in its theory and research without an explicit concept of capitalist dictatorship when analyzing these and related social phenomena—or can do so at its own theoretical and empirical risk. While being perilous times reminiscent of the 1930s in Europe and McCarthyism in America, post-2016 years signal the perfect timing, ideal opportunity or urgent need to introduce, establish, face and study capitalist dictatorship as a legitimate sociological concept in the same right as capitalist democracy and in the context of dictatorships and democracies. In short, capitalist dictatorship arises and persists in social reality and enters and comes 'alive' in sociological research.

If the preceding provides a compelling rationale for it, the introduction, establishment and study of capitalist dictatorship as a sociological concept with theoretical plausibility and empirical relevance would proceed along these lines. One can introduce, establish and study capitalist dictatorship as a valid and legitimate sociological concept in the same right as and the mirror image of that of capitalist democracy. A broad justification is that capitalism can, has been and still is both democratic and undemocratic, thus has two opposite faces, forms or elements, as sociological and historical studies and experience show—simply, it is Janus-faced in terms of democracy and dictatorship. In other words, capitalism fuses or associates with both democratic and undemocratic ideologies and regimes, including political liberalism and liberal democracy versus anti-liberal conservatism, fascism and theocracy or bogus illiberal 'democracies'. Consequently, capitalism can evolve in capitalist democracy or may degenerate into capitalist dictatorship depending on the social conditions and historical conjunctures of its development and functioning. For example, during early postwar times following the defeat of fascism and discredit of its parent conservatism through the late 1970s, capitalism generally, with some variations, fused with or resigned to liberal democracy and the democratic welfare state, yielding capitalist democracy. By contrast, since the early 1980s with the rise and dominance of Thatcherism and Reaganism it has largely, with certain exceptions, merged or allied with repressive conservatism, including fascism, as well as religion and theocracy, and thus degenerated into capitalist-conservative and religious dictatorship. In this context, post-2016 developments, events and ruling powers such as the radical-right regime in the US manifest themselves as a culmination of the above trend.

A related specific justification is that most contemporary societies adopting capitalism qualify more as capitalist and related conservative dictatorships or ersatz illiberal 'democracies' than as genuine liberal or capitalist democracies. While primarily applying to non-Western capitalist countries from Africa and Asia to Latin America and much of Eastern Europe under oligarchic capitalism, this apparently applies to some degree to the post-2016 US and Brexit Britain judging by their degrees of capitalist dictatorship and alternatively their derivative indexes of capitalist democracy. For example, the US features the second highest degree of capitalist dictatorship or the 35th lowest index of capitalist democracy among 36 OECD countries and the UK the 17th and 19th indices, respectively. In addition, other OECD countries from Turkey and Mexico through Chile and South Korea to most Baltic states and Poland look closer to capitalist dictatorships than to liberal democracies considering their rankings on capitalist dictatorship.

Conversely, only a small minority of contemporary capitalist societies appear to represent liberal democracies—probably, around 20 corresponding to Western countries, along with rare marginal cases in non-Western settings. Moreover, just over half of the 36 OECD supposedly democratic countries seemingly qualify as liberal or capitalist democracies, these being primarily located in Western Europe, especially Scandinavia. For instance, they seem to be the five Scandinavian countries (Denmark, Finland, Iceland, Sweden, Norway), along with Austria, the Netherlands, Germany, Luxembourg and Belgium, plus probably Switzerland, Slovenia, France and Czech Republic, and possibly Ireland, New Zealand and Portugal, judging by their derivative rankings on capitalist democracy. If capitalist or genuine liberal democracies are a small majority even among OECD countries representing the first world and its additions, they are probably a minor rarity in third-world settings, as most global democracy rankings suggest by the democratic dominance of Western societies. Hence, at the minimum, capitalist dictatorship looks as a valid, necessary and legitimate sociological concept as that of capitalist democracy.

An additional empirical justification for introducing capitalist dictatorship as a legitimate sociological concept is that most current, including post-2016, dictatorships are precisely 'capitalist dictatorships' or 'noncommunist dictatorships'. In this sense, what strongly justifies the concept is that 'capitalist dictatorships' or 'noncommunist dictatorships' have become a multiplying or persistent form of dictatorship and their opposites a diminishing and largely extinct species. Hence, the concept fully captures and does justice to this reality of prevailing and multiplying 'capitalist dictatorships' in relation to their alternatives within the extended family of such regimes. Like other adequate concepts, it helps illuminate, understand, make sense and demystify such dictatorships that tend to use various deceptions and disguises claiming 'democracy' and 'freedom'.

The concept expresses the fact that the recent global triumph of capitalism over its alternatives comprises not just the victory of capitalist democracy and freedom but also the resurgence and even prevalence of capitalist dictatorship or plutocracy. This especially holds for non-Western social environments such as South America, Africa, much of Asia, most of Eastern Europe, Islamic states and even some Western societies such as the US post-2016 and since Reaganism judging by its exceptional high degree of capitalist dictatorship. For example, in Eastern Europe capitalism primarily triumphed over and replaced socialism in the form of capitalist dictatorship or repressive, oligarchic and theocratic capitalism (especially in Hungary, Poland and most Baltic states) and just secondarily as capitalist democracy (only in Czech Republic and Slovenia), judging by these indices. In this regard, most of Eastern Europe just substituted one form of dictatorship for another—capitalist for communist—with Hungary and Poland as the most egregious examples of such a substitution and even by being conservative autocracy and theocracy, respectively, appearing less liberal and democratic during post-2016 times than in the waning days of communism. Their enfolding sociological tragedy, path-dependent on their recent fascist and distant theocratic or religious past, respectively, suggests that the abolition of non-capitalism and the adoption of capitalism is not the sufficient, even if the necessary, condition of capitalist or liberal democracy. Moreover, it implies that capitalist dictatorship is no substantial improvement over and even is in some respects more intransigent and severe—especially when merged with neo-fascist dictatorships in former fascist states like Hungary and the Baltics or with theocracy in Poland—than communist dictatorship that eventually performed its own peaceful euthanasia ('velvet' revolutions). Further, capitalism in most of South America and especially Saudi Arabia and other Gulf Islamic states has traditionally functioned as capitalist dictatorship, including autocracy, oligarchy and pro-capital military rule, and hardly ever as capitalist democracy.

Generally, most post-2016 dictatorships are capitalist by virtue of the fact of arising and operating within capitalism as the dominant economic and social system—and indeed an exclusive one among Western and OECD countries—albeit 'libertarian' economics tries to obscure this reality by continuing to alert to and obsess with their extinct or rarified non-capitalist versions. Alternatively, the dominance and even proxy-monopoly of capitalism as such a system necessarily makes most such dictatorships capitalist ones that 'libertarian' economics evades as if they were non-existent and even impossible, aside from rare and diminishing non-capitalist exceptions. It follows that the dominance and proxy-monopoly of capitalism yields not only that of capitalist democracy as in most Western societies, especially Western Europe and within it Scandinavia, judging by their respective rankings on it. It also generates the prevalence and indeed near-monopoly of capitalist dictatorship in many non-Western societies, including even some OECD countries from Turkey and Mexico to the US and Poland considering their respective rankings on it.

Introducing and establishing the sociological concept of capitalist dictatorship entails considering it a total social system, as this study has done. What is sociological and holistic about the concept of capitalist dictatorship is that it treats the latter as a complex of at least four interconnected social systems: an economic system, political regime, civil society and cultural system. More precisely, this involves considering capitalist dictatorship a totalistic social system in the sense of encompassing control, coercion and repression of society as a whole, including its economy, polity, civil society and culture. In turn, the sociological concept of capitalist dictatorship is distinct from and broader and more adequate than its implicit reductive concepts as only an economic system or a political regime in economics.

Inauguration of the sociological concept of capitalist dictatorship also involves applying it to its both historical and present forms, elements and agents. The concept applies to both extinct capitalist dictatorships from the 19th and 20th centuries and to their reincarnations during the early 21st century, particularly post-2016 times. For example, it is applicable to the 'despotic might of capital', 'economic oppression' and the 'physical and moral degradation of the lower classes' in Gilded-Age American capitalism, the merger of capitalism and conservatism/fascism through the 'broad coalition of the right', indeed the extended family of 'authoritarian rightism' in interwar Germany and elsewhere in Europe. It also applies to Reaganism's 'redistribution of wealth in favour of the wealthy and of power in favour of the powerful' and the US post-2016 capitalist autocracy, dynasty and plutocracy. Such an application thus corrects and extends some economic and other theories' incorrect limitation and relegation of capitalist dictatorship in the sense of coercion and repression by capital only to the past, such as 19th-century England and Gilded-Age American capitalism, and hence dubious omission of its later forms, elements and agents. In this historical context, capitalist dictatorship is hence not just the 'dead past' or 'gone with the wind' but also the persistent present and 'well and alive'.

A comparative advantage of introducing, establishing and studying it is that the sociological concept of capitalist dictatorship is applicable to all of its contemporary forms, elements and agents. It applies to both non-Western and Western instances, first-world and third-world variants or proxies of capitalist dictatorship. For example, it applies to post-2016 capitalist and related autocracies and more broadly dictatorships in Brazil, Hungary, Poland, Turkey, Saudi Arabia and other Gulf states and third-world countries as in conservative America and Brexit Britain. Such a wide comparative application corrects and extends some economic and other theories that implausibly restrict and relegate capitalist dictatorship to non-Western settings and thus overlook or deny its existence or relevance in parts of the Western world exonerated from such a regime. Within this comparative framework, capitalist dictatorship from autocracy and dynasty to oligarchy and plutocracy appears as not merely a non-Western, third-world peculiarity but also in part a Western, first-world phenomenon at least in the form of post-2016 'American exceptionalism'. In this respect, capitalist dictatorship is a global and generalized phenomenon in certain social settings paralleling the globalizing and generalization of capitalism. Thus, the diffusion of capitalist dictatorship occurred through global contagion from or convergence with post-2016 America to other parts of the world, including Western and non-Western countries. And if capitalist dictatorship such as autocracy or oligarchy and plutocracy in capitalism is an emergent, salient and expanding social reality or current during post-2016 times, sociology and related social science has both the opportunity and obligation to adopt and establish the concept and to face and study the phenomenon that it expresses.

Social developments and events in post-2016 conservative—as opposed to liberal—America and via contagion Brexit Britain and other, especially non-Western societies already generate fateful and even probably fatal societal consequences, offer sobering lessons and allow corresponding predictions. As a first consequence and lesson, what was inconceivable just in 2016 or earlier nearly materialized in post-2016 conservative America, Brexit Britain and beyond, just as the unthinkable happened in Germany and most of Europe during the 1930s. The inconceivable in pre-2016 America and other Western democratic societies was capitalist dictatorship—excepting Reaganism and Thatcherism mainly discredited by that time—specifically autocracy mixed with dynasty, plutocracy and theocracy within capitalism, just as the unthinkable in pre-1933 Germany was merged capitalist-fascist autocratic, plutocratic dictatorship. In this respect, post-2016 years in conservative America, Brexit Britain and beyond mark the times of implementation or approximation of the inconceivable scenario of capitalist autocracy and thus dictatorship, just as the 1930s in Germany and Europe formed the period of realization of the unthinkable specter of merged capitalist-fascist dictatorships.

More broadly, post-2016 times witnessed capitalism's degeneration into capitalist dictatorship in the shape of autocracy, plutocracy and neo-fascism or generally conservatism, just as the 1930s saw its degenerating (as Mannheim experienced in Germany) into autocratic 'dictatorship' in the form of fascism, including Nazism, as the exponent of capitalist classes. In this sense, the history of authoritarian capitalism virtually repeats itself today even if in different ways and especially social settings—conservative America, Brexit Britain and non-Western societies in contrast to interwar Germany and continental Europe—and figures: post-2016 autocratic leaders versus Hitler, Mussolini, Franco, etc. Evidently, the triumph and dominance of capitalism post-2016 and since the 1980–90s generates the resurgence and prevalence of capitalist dictatorship in an autocratic, plutocratic and neofascist form in conservative America, Brexit Britain and non-Western societies—and not just of capitalist democracy and freedom—just as it did in Germany and continental Europe

during the 1920–30s. In short, the post-2016 surge of autocratic and plutocratic capitalist dictatorship in these settings renders nothing inconceivable
in contemporary capitalism, just as interwar capitalist-fascist dictatorships
made nothing unthinkable. If capitalist dictatorship emerged at least twice in
Western and other settings over less than a century, it is likely to reemerge in
the foreseeable feature even if its present autocrats suffer electoral and other
defeats or setbacks and leave the stage, which especially holds for conservative
America.

As a second consequence and lesson, post-2016 capitalist dictatorship manifests a tendency and trajectory from a wide capitalist and conservative, including neo-fascist or populist, reactionary movement to autocratic, dynastic and
oligarchic rule, just as merged capitalist-fascist dictatorships did during the
1930s. In other words, it begins as a relatively widespread counterrevolution—
for example, approximately half of America such as its conservative pole—
against liberal democracy and ends as an autocracy, dynasty or oligarchy in
capitalism, as also capitalist-fascist dictatorships did in interwar Germany and
Europe. In conservative America, capitalist dictatorship moves from a merged
capitalist-conservative, including neo-fascist or populist and theocratic, mobilization in 2016 to attempted autocratic rule during post-2016 years, just as
merged capitalist-fascist dictatorships in Germany and Europe moved from
the 'broad coalition of the right' and the extended family of 'authoritarian
rightism' to Hitler's and other autocracy. Such autocratic rule escalates in every
year of the post-2016 period and eventually assumes the form of almost 'total'
presidential power, including effectively creating laws without constitutional
authority via executive orders on countless issues and the legislature's participation, thus seeking to rule by decree, just as Hitler did thanks to the 'enabling
law' that the Nazi and conservative parties passed on request.

For example, the post-2106 conservative-dominated Congress (the Senate
after 2018) and the Supreme-Court and district-courts conservative majority
have approved virtually all these apparently autocratic decrees creating law,
thus evoking the role of the German Parliament (minus the Social Democratic
Party) and judiciary in approving Hitler's rule by decree thanks to its passing of
the 'enabling law'. Therefore, these conservative-dominated major legislative
and judiciary institutions have willingly, indeed enthusiastically, as with Senate
and Supreme-Court and district-courts conservatives, become enablers or
tools of the post-2016 autocracy, just as did those in Germany after 1933, albeit
if history does not repeat itself in the same form. Even in the rare cases when
the Supreme Court decides to defend the rule of law and democracy rather
than protect the lawlessness and authoritarianism of the post-2016 autocracy,
the latter effectively defies and dismisses these decisions and thus disables and

ignores any legal constraints on its power, treating the Constitution as if it were a non-entity and enabled by the conservative-ruled Congress such as the post-2018 Senate.

The above confirms the old experience since at least ancient Rome that autocracy or other dictatorship, no matter how brutal, corrupt or inept, always finds its enablers or tools within the existing capitalist and other elite, just as mass support among the rank and file who as fanatical followers are to be eventually sacrificed in their freedom, wellbeing and lives for the wealth, power and honor of the dictator. Within American history, this striking alliance reaffirms that even the US founders were unable to predict the power constellation in which the same, radical political party ('faction' in their terms) will seize and control all state power, making the celebrated constitutional checks and balances of the separation of powers worthless or helpless, which is what precisely happened after 2016 (for further historical insights see Mueller 1996). In comparative terms, the above confirms that conservatism or rightism is the primary source and enabling force and ally of neo-fascist and fascist autocracy in both post-2016 America and interwar Germany.[5]

The same or similar trend as above occurs to some degree in Brexit Britain and especially non-Western countries like Brazil, Hungary, Poland, Turkey, Saudi Arabia and other Gulf states—moving from capitalist-conservative resurgence and the coalition of the right and the broader family of 'authoritarian rightists' to autocracy or oligarchy in capitalism. Therefore, post-2016 capitalist dictatorship replicates or resembles merged capitalist-fascist dictatorships during the 1930s in that capitalist-conservative mobilization and the coalition of the right, notably the wider family of 'authoritarian rightism', is the starting point and autocracy a destination, combined with dynasty, oligarchy, plutocracy and even theocracy, as in conservative America, much of South America, Poland, Turkey, and Saudi Arabia. That helps explain why post-2016 conservative America, Brazil, Hungary, Poland, and other countries under capitalist autocracy, oligarchy, plutocracy and theocracy have the almost same ambiance or feeling as Germany and Europe ruled by capitalist-fascist autocrats, oligarchs, plutocrats and theocrats during the 1930s. The above does not necessarily mean that autocracies and autocrats are or will become the most important forms and agents of post-2016 capitalist dictatorship especially in Western countries in longer periods, since they derive either from or evolve into oligarchy and plutocracy as group rule and thus sociologically more consequential.

---

5   See MacLean (2018) and Mann (2005).

As a third consequence and lesson, capitalist dictatorship post-2016 shows deep and relatively broad roots and support in society even if remaining a minority rule, as most dictatorships do. Thus, capitalist autocracy and dynasty post-2016 unleashes and legitimizes all extreme illiberal, anti-democratic and exclusionary, notably proto-fascist, nationalist, xenophobic and theocratic, energies and forces previously hidden in conservative America such as the South and similar regions, just as Hitlerism unleashed and legitimized such and related currents in interwar Germany. Similarly, capitalist and similar actual or potential autocrats perform such an operation in Britain during conservatism and conservative non-Western societies such as Brazil, Hungary, Poland, Turkey, Saudi Arabia and other Gulf states and so on. In socio-psychological terms, this reaffirms the finding that US and other religious-political conservatives are 'authoritarian personalities' with a sadistic-masochistic 'character structure' by willingly and totally submitting to capitalist, fascist and theocratic dictators while enjoy abusing subordinate, lower and powerless social strata and seeking destruction as 'salvation'.[6]

In sociological terms, it indicates that capitalist dictatorship while, like most dictatorships, remaining a minority rule even beyond autocracy and dynasty has its fanatical, reliable, mass and strong rank-and-file or base especially in conservative America and to some degree Brexit Britain, just as capitalist-fascist dictatorships had such extensive grassroots in interwar Germany and Europe. This predicts that capitalist dictatorship is likely to recur even after its current autocratic leaders leave the stage through electoral processes or otherwise, as its base will seek and find readily and quickly such a leader due to its authoritarian sadistic-masochistic and destructive proclivities, as precisely happened in America post-2016 and probably will in the future.

As a fourth and probably most salient consequence and lesson, capitalist dictatorship post-2016 exposes the fragility and non-resilience of modern democracy to dictatorial and generally authoritarian tendencies, including autocratic and dynastic figures or pretenders, as well as to oligarchic, plutocratic and theocratic trends, in some Western societies, as in many non-Western countries. Thus, post-2016 effective or developing capitalist autocracies and dynasties, along with oligarchies, plutocracies and theocracies, essentially suspend or drastically upend democracy in America, Brexit Britain and many non-Western societies. Conversely, democracy in these and other settings has proven fragile, vulnerable and non-resilient in facing such autocratic,

---

6   See Altemeyer (2007) and *Adorno* (2001), for broader insights, see *Fromm* (1941), Miller, Slomczynski, and Kohn (1987).

dynastic, oligarchic figures and other authoritarian tendencies, and consequently becomes a simulation or placebo, as witnessed especially in conservative America and non-Western countries like Hungary, Poland and Turkey. In particular, capitalist (from would-be to actual) autocracy and dynasty in post-2016 conservative America disables virtually all celebrated constitutional 'checks and balances' by perverting the legislature (Senate after 2018) and the judicial system (including the Supreme Court and the Department of Justice) into tools of 'total' presidential power. This suggests that constitutional 'checks and balances' are insufficient to prevent autocratic, dynastic and oligarchic capitalist dictatorship, as their creators were far from omniscient and not able to predict the Weberian power constellation in which the same political 'faction' controls executive, legislative and judicial powers and exert near-total political control, as precisely happened in post-2016 conservative America.

Alternatively, virtually no relevant institutional resources and structures (except for the partial restraint by the post-2018 House of Representatives) remain in place to check and balance such proclaimed 'total' presidential power turned into and continuing to operate as unrestricted autocratic rule by decree emulating or echoing Nazi Germany's 'enabling law'. In this connection, the US founders could not also predict the situation in which a President effectively rules by decree, as during 2017–2020, and the conservative-controlled Congress (the Senate after 2018) and Supreme Court enable such rule even without passing and approving an 'enabling law' such that German conservatism in alliance with Nazism passed on Hitler's request in the 1933 German Parliament session. They thus overlooked a scenario in which the legislative and judicial branches of the American state would be either enablers of or mostly helpless (e.g., the House of Representatives after 2018) to 'check and balance' Presidential autocracy ruling by decree and making law in defiance to and violation of the Constitution.

As a related detail, they also did not envision certain conflicts of personal and national interests, as when the family member of a Congress leader is a part of the executive branch, as during 2017–2020, which apparently provides strong incentives for that leader to protect this particular position in the administration rather than to apply the constitutional 'checks and balances' on an autocratic or other President. It is no wonder that the post-2016 Senate leader would defend an autocratic President ruling by decree against the 'enemies' from the other party and thus protect the member in the administration rather than defending Congress as an institution, the Constitution and the rule of law from lawless autocracy. (Even some members of the same 'faction' deplored such autocratic executive actions as 'unconstitutional slop' but not the Senate leader determined to protect the position in the executive branch and promote the party and ideology over democratic institutions and national wellbeing.) Further, the founders could not anticipate the nepotism of the post-2016 executive branch and thus dynastic government. Even more gravely, they did not envision the power constellation in which most members of the conservative-controlled Congress and Supreme Court, along with other conservatives, would display total dedication and loyalty to—and create the apology and cult of—an autocratic executive from the same political 'faction' requesting adoration and devotion rather than to democracy, the rule of law, including the Constitution, and the country, as it happened after 2016.

And the mostly secular founders like Jefferson could not anticipate the scenario in which religious conservatives such as evangelicals both in Congress/Supreme Court (along with state governments) and outside would effectively restore the 'divine rights' of kings by divinizing and consecrating such an autocratic executive as 'chosen' and 'sent by God' who reenacts 'Lord's commandments' by executive orders and rules by decree abolishing the rule of law that US conservatism declaratively cherishes but actually eliminates or perverts into 'law and order' repression.

The preceding exposes the 'resilience' of American democracy to dictatorial subversions like autocratic pretenders as a myth or premature conclusion, and indicates an inclination to easily succumb (as Schumpeter would expect) to even what it seems as a dilettante attempt at autocratic rule rendering virtually all constitutional and other institutional democratic defenses helpless and worthless. In a similar vein, through emulation or contagion of the US post-2016 apparent model, capitalist and other autocrats or autocratic pretenders in Brexit Britain and especially Brazil, Hungary, Poland, Turkey and Saudi Arabia disable constitutional and any institutional constraints on their power and pervert them into instruments of their rule.

At the end, if capitalism proves to be what Marx implies and Weber describes as the 'most fateful force in our modern life', capitalist dictatorship may well prove to be the most fatal development in contemporary society during post-2016 times given the extinction or extreme rarity of non-capitalist dictatorships. Especially capitalist autocracy, conjoined with oligarchy, plutocracy and theocracy, post-2016 has already demolished or perverted most social, including egalitarian economic, political, judicial, and cultural, institutions in conservative America and in part Brexit Britain and almost reversed any democratic reforms in many non-Western societies from Brazil and the rest of South America through Hungary and Poland to Turkey and Saudi Arabia. Based on these early post-2016 outcomes, a post-2020 iteration of capitalist autocracy will likely be fatal by causing the end or grave crisis of a functioning American society, including its economy, democracy, civil society and culture such as science and education, nationalistic closure in Brexit Britain and complete anti-democratic reversals in these non-Western societies. Given the post-2016 syndrome, these post-2020 consequences are predictable with almost mathematic precision or high statistical probability, just as were those of the comparable developments, events and figures during the 1930s, for example, the Nazi 1933 (partial) electoral victory and Hitler's 'enabling law' and 1936 reelection by plebiscite. Still, it remains to wait and see if capitalist dictatorship via autocracy and/or plutocracy will sooner or later prove to be the most fatal force in contemporary society, as it promises to do through its post-2016 emanations in the above societal settings. In the meanwhile, just as adopting and operating with Marx-Weber's notion of capitalism for long, sociology and other social science can finally adopt and operate with the explicit concept of capitalist dictatorship as not just a possibility implicit in it but also a salient empirical phenomenon in some Western societies, above all post-2016 conservative America and Brexit Britain, and many non-Western societies today.

Capitalist Dictatorship in the Literature

> The Reagan administration cares about the distribution of wealth and power and its program is and has always been in favour of the redistribution of wealth in favour of the wealthy and of power in favour of the powerful
>
> (SOLOW ET AL. 1987, p. 182).

This appendix surveys in more detail how the economics, sociological, and related literature defines and conceptualizes capitalist dictatorship and its structural equivalents such as authoritarian, repressive capitalism and its proxies or particular forms like plutocracy, oligarchy, and the like. It places focus on the substantive category or underlying concept of capitalist dictatorship broadly understood rather than just the term itself.

1 Identification of Capitalist Dictatorship

Starting with the opening statement of this appendix, Solow et al. posit and identify by implication, by referring to the US 'Conservative Revolution' in the form of Reaganism, capitalist dictatorship (while not using the term). Further, they provide its working definition or first approximation as the program and process of the 'redistribution of wealth in favour of the wealthy and of power in favour of the powerful'. More precisely, the redistribution and thereby concentration and application or use of wealth in favor of the wealthy would define or approximate capitalist dictatorship as the form of repression by capital in the economy. In turn, the redistribution and thus concentration and exertion of power in favor of the powerful would constitute conservative, extreme-right and in that sense 'proto-fascist'[1] dictatorship, so non-democracy such as the mode of repressive rule by conservatism in alliance with the capitalist class in the polity, simply oligarchy. However, Solow et al. apparently propose that the redistribution, concentration and application of wealth and the same process of power proceed in tandem simultaneously, or the second follows the first with a certain political lag, consistent with social-cultural lags in relation to the economy and technology. They

---

1 'Proto-fascist' is from Putnam (2000, p. 350).

thus implicitly conceive capitalist dictatorship in terms of both outcomes resulting from the 'Conservative Revolution'.

In this context, the latter generates capitalist and conservative dictatorships, so economic and political oppression, via the unequal distribution, concentration and use of wealth for the wealthy as an upper class and of power for the powerful as a ruling group, thus what Weber classically observed as American 'plutocracy' and oligarchy, respectively. Hence, their implied concept represents a fusion of capitalist dictatorship in the strict sense of economic compulsion and repression and of conservative dictatorship in the form of political coercion and oppression, including by implication that religiously driven through theocracy opposing and perverting liberal-secular democracy and scientific rationalism.

Specifically, it involves the US blend of Reaganomics with Reaganism. Reaganomics is a repressive anti-labor and pro-capital plutocratic anti-egalitarian economic policy—successful for Reaganite economists, failed for others—in the economy. Reaganism as a political, ideological and religious project of moralistic repression, as exemplified by Reagan's economically and legally irrational Puritanical 'war on drugs' and various other sins-as-crimes, all joined with militarism via exorbitant military spending, in politics and ideology. In this context, Reaganomics' program is the redistribution, concentration and application of wealth in favor of the wealthy in the US and that of Reaganism the same process with respect to power favoring the powerful, while both operating in fusion and mutual reinforcement. In sum, in Solow et al.'s framework, Reaganomics operates as the economic policy of capitalist plutocracy fused and mutually reinforced with Reaganism as the politics and ideology as well as Puritanical religion and morality of conservative oligarchy, including evangelical theocracy ('I am one of you' evangelicals).

In this connection, Cohen and Blanchard[2] refer to and generally concur with Solow et al., restating that the 'constituency' of conservatism (the right) in the US is 'wealthy and powerful and does not need the government's protection that the poor and the weak want so much'. In addition, reminiscent of Solow et al. King[3] implicates Reaganomics/Reaganism in suggesting that, contrary to the latter, economic and social institutions should possess 'political legitimacy and an acceptance that they will not redistribute income and wealth in favor of some groups rather than others at the expense of the objective given to them'. Also, similarly to Solow et al., Pryor[4] conceives implicitly capitalist dictatorship (without using the term) in the US as the fusion and reciprocal intensification of plutocratic oligarchy via oligopoly in the economy and of a conservative oligarchic state, thus fusing business and political elites. Further, in his

2   See Cohen and Blanchard (1988, p. 196).
3   See King (2004, p. 5).
4   See Pryor (2002, p. 364).

prediction, it tends to move, to 'Hobbesian anarchy' or 'mafia capitalism', and to inflict the population with systematic and growing repression. Likewise, and by implication, Pryor attributes the fusion of political and economic domination though the 'oligarchical control of both the state and the economy' mainly to the conservative revolution and dominance enfolding since the 1980s.

More recently, Piketty evokes and extends Solow et al. by characterizing capitalist dictatorship (without referring to it by name) and even capitalism in general by the unequal distribution and concentration of wealth and consequently power for capital versus labor and associating this process and outcome with resurgent conservatism such as neo-conservative Thatcher and Reagan counterrevolutions. Generally, Piketty[5] argues evoking Keynes (see below) that capitalism as such tends to 'automatically' generate 'arbitrary and unsustainable inequalities' of wealth and hence power, in turn 'radically' undermining the 'meritocratic values' at the basis of modern democratic societies, thus subverting political democracy. In this context, Piketty suggests that the 'history of the distribution of wealth has always been deeply political, and it cannot be reduced to purely economic mechanisms', with its inequality being conditioned by 'economic, social, and political actors' and their definitions of justice and injustice, notably their 'relative power' and the resulting 'collective choices'. In particular, he locates the phenomenon of a 'spectacular increase' in wealth and income and by implication power inequality 'mainly in the US and to a lesser degree in Britain' and suggest an explanation of it 'in terms of the history of social and fiscal norms in those two countries over the past century). In addition, he finds that this tendency is less noticeable in 'other wealthy countries (such as Japan, Germany, France, and other continental European states), but the trend is in the same direction'.

Notably, like Solow et al. Piketty associates and even directly attributes the 'concentration' of income and wealth, especially of capital, to neo-conservative counterrevolutions observing that the 'growth of capital's share accelerated with the victories of Margaret Thatcher in England in 1979 and Ronald Reagan in the US in 1980, marking the beginning of a conservative revolution'. Piketty, like Solow et al. do by implication, explicitly warns and concludes that the 'unlimited growth of global inequality of wealth' indicating and inherently resulting from authoritarian and inegalitarian, including 'globalized, patrimonial', capitalism threatens and subverts democracy. He suggests that instead the latter is the only way of regaining 'control of capitalism' by making it democratic and egalitarian, thus ending or mitigating capitalist dictatorship.

---

5   See Piketty (2014, pp. 3, 22, 24–25, 35, 399).

2   Anticipations of Capitalist Dictatorship

In retrospect, Solow et al.'s as well as Piketty's is not the first and best-known identification and working definition or close approximation of capitalist dictatorship and
its structural equivalents such as oppressive capitalism and plutocracy in the US and
elsewhere. Outside of the sociological, economics and related scientific literature, US
President Theodore Roosevelt in the wake and in repudiation of the Gilded Age and
its 'robber barons' perhaps provides the most explicit identification and definition
of capitalist dictatorship. He does so by identifying and defining it as the 'tyranny of
mere wealth, the tyranny of a plutocracy' and even describing it the 'most vulgar' of
'all forms of tyranny'. In American and other capitalism in which 'mere wealth' primarily constitutes that of the capitalist class, including remnants of the old aristocracy
merging into it, this amounts to the 'tyranny' of capital through, as in Solow et al.'s
framework, the redistribution, concentration and use of wealth and consequently of
power in its favor. At this juncture, Roosevelt anticipates Solow et al. whose implicit
definition in terms of distribution, concentration and by implication exertion of superior material and political power seems just a modern or economic term for the older
word 'tyranny'.

    Around the same time as Roosevelt, in the scientific literature early US institutional
economist Mitchell comes most closely to an explicit identification and definition of
the concept of capitalist dictatorship, i.e., undemocratic capitalism. Mitchell[6] identifies the 'despotic might of capital' as leading to its 'industrial despotism' and 'oppression', as another old name for capitalist dictatorship, which he opposes to 'industrial
democracy' and by implication political democracy. What Roosevelt and Mitchell
denote in their time capital's 'tyranny' and 'despotism' in the US during and in the
wake of the Gilded Age today's scholars would call it capitalist and other dictatorship
or authoritarian capitalism in this country since the 1980s, so the first regime is substantively equivalent to the second.

    A decade or so later, on the eve and in the midst of the Great Depression as the histor-
ically gravest crisis of laissez-faire capitalism, Keynes, at his young age a contemporary
of President Roosevelt and Mitchell, also prefigures Solow et al.'s characterization of
capitalist dictatorship. This holds explicitly for its economic facet of the redistribution
and concentration of wealth in privilege of the upper class and implicitly for its political aspect of such a process power privileging the ruling group. Certainly, like Solow
et al., as well as his contemporaries President Roosevelt and Mitchell, Keynes is well-
aware and acknowledges that the unequal distribution and concentration of wealth
in favor of the wealthy in capitalism, far from being an isolated and self-contained

---

6   See Mitchell (1917, p. 108).

phenomenon, proceeds in conjunction and mutually reinforcement with that of power in in favor the powerful. More precisely, he is aware that the latter process inevitably or ultimately, with a certain delay and adjustment—probably shorter than the cultural lag from technological progress—results from or accompanies as well as sustains the former, as do contemporary economists and sociologists.

Thus, apparently writing during the late 1920s and before the Great Depression Keynes[7] identifies and strongly denounces what he connotes the 'evils of unjust distribution' explicitly of wealth and by implication and in consequence of power in laissez-faire capitalism. He hence characterizes the latter as intrinsically being or ultimately becoming capitalist dictatorship or authoritarian capitalism immediately in Solow et al.'s purely economic dimension favoring the wealthy class, and eventually in the social-political component privileging the powerful. Then, writing at the onset and in the height of the Great Depression which in 1930 he describes as 'one of the greatest economic catastrophes of modern history', Keynes[8] continues to detect and deplore the 'arbitrary and inequitable distribution of wealth and incomes'—and in consequence or by implication of power—between diverse social classes. He treats this as one of the two inherent grave defects ('outstanding faults') of laissez-faire capitalism, together with its inability to secure full employment to production factors (labor) due to its inherent tendency to generate such catastrophic crises. In so doing, Keynes implies that laissez-faire capitalism inherently constitutes or subsequently develops into capitalist dictatorship or authoritarian capitalism, just as it is an economic catastrophe-prone or crisis-plagued type of economy. It does this directly in its economic core of the unequal distribution and concentration of wealth in favor of the upper class, and indirectly in its political essence of such a process of power favoring the ruling group,

Moreover, probably in view of the first defect primarily regardless of the second, even prior to the Great Depression, as during the extremely inegalitarian and 'glorious' 1920s, Keynes diagnoses the 'end of laissez-faire' capitalism as an anti-egalitarian economic system and by implication a repressive political regime due to its 'unjust distribution' of wealth and so power. In addition, Keynes during the 1930s repudiates what he sees as Hayek's rigid and misguided alternative between either—professing a fervent belief in—laissez-faire capitalism as a 'spontaneous (market) order' of freedom or socialism. Keynes rejects Hayek including the latter, along with his colleague Mises, not only Soviet communism but also the emerging European welfare state and the US New Deal, condemning it as the 'road to serfdom' on account of greatly underestimating the 'practicality of the middle course'.[9] By the latter, Keynes means the movement from laissez-faire capitalism's 'economic anarchy to a regime, which deliberately aims at controlling

7   See Keynes (1936, p. 162).
8   See Keynes (1960, p. 381; 1972, pp. 326, 275).
9   Cited in Hodgson (1999, p. 207).

and directing economic forces in the interest of social justice and social stability'.[10] He thus suggests what his European contemporary Cassel proposes in the eve of the Great Depression as 'a rationally regulated social economy'. Further, Samuelson[11] and other Keynesians consider the latter the 'successful development of the Mixed Economy'—which in his view both Marx and Schumpeter failed to predict—during postwar times, and today's analysts regard as coordinated and egalitarian/welfare capitalism and the like. Crucially and contrary to Hayek, Mises, Friedman and other later 'libertarian' economists within Austrian, Chicago and cognate dogmatic schools, Keynes persuasively argues the following. The alternative of choosing between capitalist or communist dictatorships by making a choice between either laissez-faire' capitalism as a form of 'economic anarchy' or socialism is false and almost equally pernicious, analogous to one being forced to choose the proverbial poison[12]. Instead, Keynes implies and thus would definitely urge 'outgrowing communist and capitalist dictatorships' alike.[13]

Akin to Keynes, around the same time Myrdal[14] states that the social-political choice is never between 'a number of abstract, logically coherent social orders', such as laissez-faire capitalism or free competition versus communism. As Cassel does explicitly and Myrdal implicitly, Keynes proposes that a rational, practical solution consists of a dual model of capitalism. This is that the latter is both regulated, egalitarian, just and stable, thus superseding by 'social justice and social stability' laissez-faire capitalism and its 'economic anarchy', and liberal-democratic, so by 'personal liberty' and 'individualism' transcending socialism, as an efficient or pragmatic 'middle' path between and overcoming the two. Keynes diagnoses the demise of laissez-faire capitalism and thus, ceteris paribus, of capitalist dictatorship at least in its strictly economic core of unjust and arbitrary wealth concentration, and predicts its regulated, egalitarian, and democratic version as the face of future. Yet, cynics or critics may comment that the rumors of the death of the first are grossly exaggerated, as Keynesians Solow et al. suggest for America during Reaganomics as largely the program of laissez-faire déjà vu and of such redistribution favoring capital.

More broadly, Knight mostly—perhaps surprisingly if deemed the founder or at least precursor of the laissez-faire and ant-egalitarian Chicago School—concurs with Keynes, evokes Mitchell and anticipates Solow and others. Knight[15] does this in that

---

10   See Keynes (1972, pp. 304–5).
11   See Samuelson (1967, p. 623).
12   Bauman (2001, p. 111) states that as the 'principal antagonists' in social design the 'now defunct Marxism and the now ruling' laissez-faire capitalism ('economic liberalism') each produced 'as much, if not more, misery than happiness' and 'in equal measure'.
13   See Olson (2000).
14   See Myrdal (1953, p. 198).
15   Knight (1967, p. 791) adds that generally but especially in laissez-faire capitalism inequality 'tends to grow, especially economic; for one who at a moment possesses more wealth

he implicitly characterizes capitalist and related dictatorship by the unequal distribution, concentration and hence exertion of wealth and power in that a 'great inequality of power' under various forms in capitalism in general ('exchange and other formally free relations') 'gives the stronger party some control over the weaker and may mean his helplessness'. Moreover, he implies—almost shockingly for a founder or precursor of the Chicago School—that laissez-faire, anarchic capitalism eventually mutates into capitalist dictatorship in these terms, dismissing Hayek's ideal of such an economic system as 'wishful thinking', 'simply absurd', even downright ludicrous ('it is for the proverbial birds') in favor of the French Revolution's principles as 'important ideals'. Knight[16] admits that the 'defects' of laissez-faire capitalism cum the 'free system' are 'numerous and diverse beyond enumeration', in particular that its unrestrained functioning intrinsically produces 'excessive inequality' in wealth and consequently in power (thus causing 'to him that hath shall be given'). He adds that 'still worse, this tendency goes on operating from generation to generation through various forms of inheritance'.[17]

Most ominously for democracy and liberty in society, Knight predicts that the redistribution, concentration and use or abuse of wealth in the economy will lead to those of power. This holds so long as economic distribution is—concurring with Keynes on this point—'arbitrary to any large degree', it will not only subject the 'allocation of resources' to 'authoritative fiat' but even cause 'general social freedoms' to 'undoubtedly contract or disappear'. Lastly, Knight opposes to conservative revolutions or revolts of various forms and times from its medieval to Hayek's 'libertarian' variant the 'liberal revolution' transforming medievalism to modernism and occurring at the 'epochs of the Renaissance and the Enlightenment'. Especially he emphasizes the 'triumph of the principles of the Enlightenment' and the consequent 'advent of liberalism' as a revolutionizing force in relation to 'primitive', including medieval, society and its 'sacred' law and authority.

Echoing Keynes and anticipating Solow at al., another early leading Keynesian Samuelson[18] identifies unequal 'class distribution' in terms of wealth, while rejecting the Marxian (surplus value) explication, and implicitly of power as the intrinsic trait or eventual outcome of laissez-faire ('competitive') capitalism in general. Samuelson thus implies that the latter hence effectively operates as or at least verges to capitalist dictatorship in this sense and so an anti-egalitarian and by implication undemocratic

---

is in a better position to acquire still more. And free inheritance continues the tendency over generations'.

16   See Knight (1960, pp. 32–4, 19–21).

17   Later on, this is what Piketty (2014) also emphasizes generally and Stiglitz (2016) specifically for the US.

18   See Samuelson (1983a, pp. 253, 582).

economic-political system. In addition, Samuelson suggests that the 'monopolization' of the market and in consequence, as Mitchell within economics and Weber in sociology predict, that of wealth and power relates to the 'measure of support' (sic) for capitalism among social groups. An interpretation of this statement is that it probably implies that such support normally limits to capitalists as the holders of monopoly conventionally judged as 'evil' (yet recommending that such judgments be 'reversed'), and thus 'monopoly power' tends to resort to extortion. One can invoke the financial sector as a case in point 'especially in the United States' prior and leading to the Great Recession.[19] A complementary interpretation is that monopolistic capitalism eventually escalates, as Mitchell explicitly proposes above, into capitalist dictatorship cum 'industrial despotism', as also Weber hints by the 'monopolistic domination of the market'.[20]

Within interwar and early contemporary sociology, Mannheim is probably (among) the first to identify or predict capitalist dictatorship in general, and indeed to witness and suffer blended corporate-fascist dictatorships in Germany in particular, as well as Italy, Spain and other European countries during that period. Thus, Mannheim[21] (predicts that when the capitalist class' self-devised mechanisms for prevailing in conflicts against other classes such as parliamentarian democracy turn out to be 'insufficient', a 'dictatorship' typically in a conservative, including fascist, form becomes a possibility in capitalism so long as the latter persists, as he personally witnessed in Nazi Germany. Mannheim characterizes fascism as the 'exponent of bourgeois groups' that seeks only to substitute 'one ruling group for another within the existing class arrangements', just as 'a complete irrationalism', citing Mussolini's exaltation of capitalism as the choice of the fittest, equal opportunities for the most gifted, a more developed sense of individual responsibility'. Therefore, Mannheim implies that fascism, including Nazism he personally witnessed in Germany, if not initially arises, then ultimately develops and functions as merged capitalist-conservative dictatorship 'living in the blind glare of the irrational'.

Akin to Mannheim Moore and Dahrendorf identify explicitly or implicitly capitalist and related, i.e., conservative or fascist dictatorship. Moore[22] explicitly detects capitalist or fascist dictatorship resulting from the tendency of capitalism under certain historical circumstances ('absence of a strong revolutionary urge') for passing through 'reactionary political forms' such as conservatism and culminating in 'fascism', simply of 'abortive bourgeois revolutions'. Dahrendorf[23] (1979, 102–3) implicitly identifies

---

19   This is what Stiglitz (2010) does.
20   See Weber (1968, 942–3).
21   See Mannheim (1936, pp. 143, 146, 145).
22   See Moore (1993, pp. xvii-xxiii, 413).
23   See Dahrendorf (1979, pp. 102–3).

CAPITALIST DICTATORSHIP IN THE LITERATURE

capitalist as well as socialist dictatorship through societal constraint by proposing that the 'freedom from the constraints of a capitalist or socialist society bent on expansion' constitutes the 'new liberty'. Relatedly, within capitalism he alerts to the authoritarian threat to this liberty that 'right conservatism' poses due to its 'social and political control' transgressing political liberties such as freedom of the press and exalting the 'good old values of authority, discipline, order, punishment', thus staging a confrontation with 'prevailing conditions' of liberal democracy.

3 Other Contemporary Ideas and Intimations of Capitalist Dictatorship

Among contemporary economists, as seen, it is somewhat surprising that a hard-line laissez-faire (and rational-choice) economist, Olson is probably the first to explicitly use the word 'capitalist dictatorships', but does not explicitly define or elaborate the concept. Also, he considers it of secondary theoretical and empirical importance to that of non-capitalist dictatorship such as 'communist' dictatorships, and inapplicable or impertinent to US and other Western capitalism— a far cry from Roosevelt and Mitchell—relegating it to non-Western third-world countries. Olson[24] suggests transcending capitalist as well as communist dictatorships by 'secure, right respecting democracies' as the 'best political environment' for the economy and its growth, thus for capitalism as an economic system with social-political preconditions and effects alike. Also, Kornai[25] admits the reality or possibility of capitalist dictatorship due to that democracy does not represent a 'necessary condition' of functioning capitalism, because the latter can function 'under dictatorial regimes as well' insofar as these are 'friendly to private property, free enterprise and freedom of contract between individuals' while abolishing their political, civil and individual liberties. However, Lucas[26] only acknowledges and deplores 'communist dictatorships' such as former 'socialist countries', thus rules out on dogmatic a priori grounds capitalist dictatorships, just as does the latter Chicago School as a whole.

Among its earlier exponents, Friedman implicitly admits that capitalist dictatorship (without using the name) is still possible in the sense of a 'fundamentally capitalist' economic system coexisting with an unfree political regime, but downplays this possibility, by insisting on capitalism as 'a necessary condition for political freedom'

---

24   Olson (2000, p. 198) characterizes democracies by that 'institutions are structured in a way that gives authoritative decision making as much as possible to encompassing interests'.

25   See Kornai (2000, p. 27).

26   See Lucas (2009, p. 3).

and thus democracy. Friedman[27] implies as historical cases of capitalist dictatorship 'Fascist Italy and Fascist Spain, Germany at various times in the last seventy years, Japan before World Wars I and II, tzarist Russia in the decades before World War I' in that all these societies adopt private enterprise as the 'dominant form of economic organization' while being politically unfree. Yet, unlike Solow et al. and Roosevelt and Mitchell, Friedman refuses to include American capitalism during the 'Conservative Revolution' of Reaganism and even the Gilded Age of capital's 'tyranny' or 'despotism' among such cases, apparently refusing to see at these historical points and dogmatically (or ethnocentrically) ruling out capitalist dictatorship in this society. Lastly, among later economists Gompers, Joy, and Andrew implicitly define capitalist dictatorship as a sort of managerial 'dictatorship'[28] against shareholders, which, since the latter represent capitalists, large and small, appears more as a corporate one. Most other contemporary economists reportedly do not adopt the term in their published works, although many suggest and imply the concept and especially its equivalents or proxies such as autocracy, oligarchy, plutocracy and aristocracy within capitalism, as distinct from pre-capitalism such as feudalism, a master-servant regime, caste, and slavery.

3.1   Sociological Concepts of Capitalist Dictatorship

Even contemporary sociologists while often implying the concept rarely use the term, with especially Burawoy suggesting the existence of capitalist dictatorship in historical terms from early to contemporary capitalism, and Wright being the probably sole sociologist known to explicitly use the name. Burawoy[29] conceives (while not using the term) capitalist dictatorship or authoritarianism after the image of Marx's 'satanic mills', identifies its 'economic elements' merged with its 'political and ideological institutions', thus by implication the concentration and exertion of wealth and power. He historically illustrates the merger of authoritarian factory regimes and the repressive

---

27   See Friedman (1982, p. 9).
28   Gompers et al. (2003, p. 107) elaborate that 'corporations are republics. The ultimate authority rests with voters (shareholders). These voters elect representatives (directors) who delegate most decisions to bureaucrats (managers). As in any republic, the actual power-sharing relationship depends upon the specific rules of governance. One extreme, which tilts toward a democracy, reserves little power for management and allows shareholders to quickly and easily replace directors. The other extreme, which tilts toward a dictatorship, reserves extensive power for management and places strong restrictions on shareholders' ability to replace directors. Presumably, shareholders accept restrictions of their rights in hopes of maximizing their wealth, but little is known about the ideal balance of power'. Gompers et al. [2003, p. 108) infer that a 'Governance Index' is a 'proxy for the balance of power between shareholders and managers' while apparently excluding workers from governance and republic.
29   See Burawoy (1984, p. 247).

politics of the state during early capitalism in England, the US, and Russia. In addition, he implies that the Soviet and in extension Eastern European transition from socialism to capitalism represents, in essence, a movement from communist to capitalist dictatorship in the form of oligarchic 'merchant capitalism' deepening 'economic under-development' rather than to modern bourgeois capitalism with liberal democracy.[30]

Wright explicitly adopts the concept/term in the sense of capitalist dictatorship in the production process. Generally, Wright[31] argues that capitalism tends to generate 'severe deficits in realizing democratic values' in the economy by establishing 'workplace dictatorships' and in the polity by causing 'private wealth' to determine 'access to political power' and removing 'crucial decisions from public deliberation'. Regarding capital-labor employment relations in capitalist enterprises, Wright suggests that such relations do not actually constitute "capitalism between consenting adults' to the extent that workers have no free choice between 'democratically organized workplaces and authoritarian firms'. Concerning the wealth-power connection, Wright proposes that 'capitalist democracy' fails to shield political decisions from the exercise of power grounded in 'capitalist wealth', citing as an exemplar the intensifying plutocratic 'assault on democracy' in the US after the Supreme Court's decision allowing the unrestricted use of corporate funds for financing political campaigns. He infers that this persistent and even growing problem of the capitalist subversion of democracy in the polity as in the economy is 'inherent in capitalism's inequalities of wealth and the structural power of capital', rather than being 'peculiar to the institutional design of the political game in the US'. This holds in spite of 'symbiotic strategies' such as via social democracy in its 'most successful instances' leading to 'a more humane capitalism, with less poverty, less inequality, and less insecurity'.[32]

Similarly, Wacquant[33] depicts American capitalism as a proxy capitalist dictatorship because of its being composed of 'a dictatorial business class, a disciplining welfare-workfare state, and a hyperactive police and penal state' performing 'the new division of labor of domestication of the poor'. More broadly, Walder and Lu[34] characterize dictatorships, including implicitly capitalist and communist ones, as 'harshly punitive' regimes to their populations, adding that some can also impose 'harsh discipline on its

---

30   See Burawoy and Krotov (1992).

31   See Wright (2013, pp. 6, 7, 21).

32   Wright (2013, p. 21) explains that 'symbiotic strategies' through social democracy 'have done so in ways that stabilize capitalism and leave intact the core powers of capital. Historically, any advance of symbiotic strategies that appeared to potentially threaten those core powers was massively resisted by capital. The reaction of Swedish capitalists to proposals for serious union involvement in control over investments in the late 1970s is one of the best known examples'.

33   See Wacquant (2002, p. 1521).

34   See Walder and Lu (2017, p. 1148).

own functionaries', as in China. In addition, like economists, while not using the term many other sociologists harbor and intimate the concept of capitalist dictatorship or undemocratic capitalism.

4   Functional Equivalents of Capitalist Dictatorship

Overall, the sociology, economics and related literature mostly refers to capitalist dictatorship's equivalents and proxies or special cases such as authoritarian capitalism, plutocracy, oligarchy, and the like. Evidently, the closest functional-structural equivalent, essentially a substantive identity to capitalist dictatorship constitutes authoritarian—i.e., undemocratic, oppressive, or coercive—capitalism, and this study uses these terms interchangeably as synonyms. Its other equivalents and proxies or particular forms in the literature include capitalist aristocracy, i.e., the aristocracy of capital or money, plutocracy, oligarchy, plutocratic autocracy, kleptocracy, and so on.

Thus, Jefferson) two centuries ago in America identifies and seeks to 'crush in its birth the aristocracy of our monied corporations which dare already to challenge our government to a trial of strength and bid defiance to the laws of our country'. If not knowing the time and space, one may easily take this as historically a description of unfettered capitalism in America during the Gilded Aged which it therefore prophetically predicts, as well as during Reaganomics and after the 2016 elections and today that it also anticipates, and comparatively of pre-capitalism such as feudalism and aristocracy in Europe. Jefferson thereby implies what various scholars have explicitly argued and observed since. This is that supposedly exceptional American capitalism and the unique capitalist class represents, after removing its disguises and embellishments, the new world's slightly modified and adapted version of European feudalism or patrimonialism and aristocracy and to that extent 'belated feudalism', 'neo-feudalism' and the 'new patrimonial capitalism'.[35] An indication is the continuation of a feudal master-servant economy dominated by the aristocracy of money and legally enforced by medieval common law in America, as Britain, into the late 19th and early 20th century until the 1930s with the New Deal's National Labor Relations Act granting to labor, for the first time in the US, legal rights.[36]

Evoking Jefferson and using another name, plutocracy, for the aristocracy of money, as noted, President Roosevelt detects and deplores the 'tyranny of a plutocracy' through its 'mere wealth' in the US during the Gilded Age. Around the same time Weber[37]

---

35   See Binmore (2001), Cohen (2003), Orren (1991), and Piketty (2014).
36   See Hirsch (2008), Kimeldorf (2013), Naidu and Yuchtman (2013), Orren (1991) and Steinberg (2003).
37   See Weber (1976, p. il).

first-hand witnesses the 'naked plutocracy' as, in Jefferson-Roosevelt's sense, a ruling class as well as a political structure in which 'mere' money 'purchases power'—although not social status—and prevailing in America during his visit in the early 1900s. More broadly, their contemporary Pareto[38] observes that putative Western democracies tend to become increasingly 'demagogic plutocracies' as forms of non-democracy and in that sense equivalents or cases of capitalist dictatorships. Moreover, Pareto predicts that such plutocracies will escalate into capitalist 'military dictatorship(s)' because of wars erupting between militaristic Western nations, especially Germany due to its militarism, thus predicting WW I and anticipating WW II.

Relatedly, Pareto proposes that nominal democracies become oligarchies as forms of non-democracy equivalent to plutocracies and aristocracies and thus—since composed of capitalists or the wealthy—of capitalist dictatorship through an aristocracy/oligarchy circulation with the new 'arising, ready to defeat and replace the one in power'. In the same vein, Michels[39] postulates that democracy results in oligarchy because it 'necessarily' entails an 'oligarchical nucleus', and generally the 'law' that an 'essential characteristic of all human aggregates' is to form 'cliques and sub-classes', while describing it, 'like every other sociological law, beyond good and evil' a la Weber. Michels elaborates that democracy inherently contains an 'aristocratic content', just as aristocracy seeks to have 'a democratic form', thus the 'tendency toward aristocracy or rather oligarchy is inherent in all (democratic) organization' as a facet of the 'existence of immanent oligarchical tendencies in every kind of human organization which strives for the attainment of definite ends'. Thence, he infers *'Who says organization says oligarchy"* as the iron law'. As a consequence, he infers that the 'existing economic and social conditions' in capitalism and society and the resulting 'state of dependence' cause 'ideal', 'logical' democracy to become impossible and actually 'never' established despite various democratic and other revolutions.

Furthermore, some contemporary economists apply Michels' 'iron law' of oligarchy, such as monopolizing political power by a narrow group because of the persistence of undemocratic institutions, to explain the evolution and functioning of capitalism in the US South after the Civil War, Latin American, Caribbean, and African countries. Acemoglu and Robinson[40] find after the abolition of slavery a 'labor-intensive, low-wage, low-education, and repressive economy that in many ways looked remarkably like that of the antebellum South (as) its elites preserved their political domination through blocking economic reforms potentially undermining their power and disrupting political reforms by disenfranchising former slaves using literacy tests and poll

---

38 See Pareto (1963, pp. 1587; 2000, 101, 39), also, Acemoglu et al. (2011), Benhabib and Bisin (2018).
39 See Michels (1968, pp. 6, 50–1, 71 342, 365).
40 See Acemoglu and Robinson (2006b, p. 326; 2008, pp. 268–9, 286–7).

taxes'. They elaborate that the Civil War the South mostly retained its pre-Civil War regime of 'labor repression' which persisted through the 'exercise of de facto power', including 'monopsonistic arrangements, policies designed to impede labor mobility, political disenfranchisement, intimidation, violence and lynching', with the effect of the 'continuation of the pre–Civil War economic order'.

In sum, this line of research thereby finds the continuation and transformation of a de jure into a de facto slave Southern economy—which dominant evangelicalism religiously sanctified it in both forms as 'divinely ordained', just as medieval religion did feudalism. Consequently, since this process occurred within American capitalism, it involves the continuation and transformation of, in Weber's terms, formal-legal into substantive or effective capitalist dictatorship, entwined and mutually reinforced with evangelical theocracy, simply Bibliocracy—for example, in what Bauman and others call the Southern 'Bible Belt'—just as was feudal bondage with medieval Christian Catholic and Protestant theocracies. This indicates a continuity of capitalist dictator-ship in the sense of Mitchell's 'despotic might of capital' in the postbellum South and America during the Gilded Age with pre-capitalist despotism through aristocratic rule in Europe, showing that economic-political oppression is continuous and does not, like nature, make 'great leaps' (or rather 'great falls') from pre-capitalism to capitalism. Probably in light of the postbellum American South and related cases of the contin-uation of a de jure into de facto slave economy, Morck et al.[41] generalize that sharper wealth inequality, joined with the 'legally codified inequality intrinsic to slavery', fos-tered the 'evolution of institutions' protecting the wealthy and powerful, 'even after the abolition of slavery'.

In extension beyond the South, Pryor[42] diagnoses and predicts, as a facet of non-sunny 'skies for the future of US capitalism', a 'greater oligarchical control of both the state and the economy', so the fusion of economic and political oligarchs, in the US as a whole, thus extending the Southern historical syndrome to the entire nation. Moreover, Pryor envisions 'Hobbesian anarchy or mafia capitalism' as the possible future outcomes of American capitalism, along with the ever-harsher 'repression of the population'. The outcome is what he connotes an 'authoritarian' economy characterized with further more 'extensive governmental security measures' due to the oligarchy's 'fear of anarchy' resulting from 'heightened social tensions' because of 'widening income inequalities'. Pryor concludes that American capitalism will move 'in many different ways toward a capitalism with an inhuman face', effectively capitalist dictatorship while not calling it by name in the form of either Hobbesian anarchy for capitalists or mafia capitalism. This includes more pitiless' economic

41   See Morck et al. (2005, p. 705).
42   See Pryor (2002, pp. 364, 367).

life and the deteriorating quality of Americans' lives, along with their repression being evermore severe, if that is even possible, given its already extraordinary unrivaled levels under dominant conservatism, within or congruent with the Western 'free' world.

In addition, scholars identify plutocratic autocracy exerted by a single plutocrat, rich person as an equivalent or peculiar form of capitalist dictatorship, along with familial and other dynasty and related authoritarian, dictatorial systems.[43] For instance, while Schumpeter[44] regards the 'autocratic state' as one of 'pre-capitalist forces' and thus disassociates it from capitalism, Besley and Kudamatsu define autocracy as a 'dictatorship of the rich', hence capitalists within capitalism, versus democracy as 'a dictatorship of the poor or middle classes'. In this connection, Michels implies that autocracy thus understood does not differ greatly from capitalist dictatorship in an oligarchic shape, stating that 'little difference' exists between 'individual dictatorship and the dictatorship of a group of oligarchs'. Further, Acemoglu et al. define elite as well as conservative/right dictatorship by that 'all political decisions are made by the rich'. This is in essence a definition of capitalist dictatorship so long as the latter is the axiomatic form that elite dictatorship assumes within capitalism, as distinct from pre-capitalism—in both cases, it defines plutocracy.

Furthermore, some economists pinpoint kleptocracy in the sense of robber plutocracy as the probably most brazen, overt form of the latter or oligarchy and a peculiar proxy or form of capitalist dictatorship when occurring within capitalism. Acemoglu[45] observes that capitalist and other 'kleptocratic regimes' repress and impoverish their citizens and remain in political power for long in the 'absence of strong institutions' by applying the 'divide and rule' strategy, as with kleptocratic rulers defusing opposition to their rule by using bribery as a tool against the 'pivotal groups'. He suggests that this is a tendency witnessed in third-world countries and the US during the 'monopoly of the Robber Barons'. In this connection, as one of the envisioned outcomes of American capitalism, 'mafia capitalism' looks as a pure capitalist version of kleptocracy, just as the expected harsher repression of US labor being a syndrome of capitalist dictatorship through fused oligarchic economic and political controls. More broadly, Acemoglu et al. suggest that an invariant or typical combination of 'relative poverty and dictatorship' exists.

---

43 See Atkinson (1997), Hällsten and Pfeffer (2017), Besley and Kudamatsu (2006), Dixit et al. (2000), Frey and Stutzer (2010) and Rodrik (2014).

44 See Schumpeter (1965, pp. 96–7), Besley and Kudamatsu (2006, p. 303), Michels (1968), p. 348), and Acemoglu et al. (2018, p. 1043).

45 See Acemoglu (2005, p. 1046), (Acemoglu and Autor 2012), and Acemoglu et al. (2008).

5   Capitalist Dictatorship, Other Dictatorships and Democracy

Alternatively, the literature contrasts capitalist and other dictatorship to political democracy, in particular democratic decisions such as social choices, considering the first an antithesis and violation of the second, at the minimum of non-dictatorship. Thus, Pareto[46] posits non-dictatorship as implicitly the axiomatic condition of democracy and explicitly of the social optimum, i.e., general economic equilibrium, defined by reaching the maximum of welfare or utility (*ophélimité*) for society. Pareto specifies that such an optimum obtains when society's members without coercion 'enjoy at a certain position the maximum of *ophélimité* when it is impossible to find some means to depart very little from this position so that the ophélimité which each of the individuals of this community enjoys increases or decreases'.

Following Pareto, Arrow (includes non-dictatorship, along with citizens' sovereignty, into the conditions for the 'social welfare maximum' and by implication of political democracy. Arrow opposes dictatorship to 'capitalist democracy' whose two distinct methods of making 'social choices' include the market in respect of economic decisions and voting with regard to political decisions, suggesting that both are 'methods of amalgaming the tastes of many individuals in the making of social choices'. Similarly, Sen conceives capitalist and related dictatorship as 'an extreme example' of the 'arbitrariness' of power and suggests that the Pareto principle and the 'conditions of nondictatorship' must apply to 'social choices'. Further, in agreement with Marx, Sen suggests that while being a 'huge improvement' compared to a 'system of slave labour' capitalism (wage labour) shares with slavery some common properties such as oppression and exploitation of labour and so distributive injustice, which hence implies the emergence or potential of capitalist dictatorship analogous to its capitalist forms.[47]

In turn, Mulligan et al.[48] while allow, following Machiavelli, that the 'concept of dictatorship' may move 'a step closer' to democracy if dictators are 'sensitive to popular support', point out the 'suppression of political competition' as their 'especially important activity' in the function of retaining power. In particular, they find that dictatorships, i.e., authoritarian political systems, commit more torture, executions, suppression of religious freedom, censorship of the press and spending large resources on the military. Furthermore, Acemoglu et al. imply that capitalist and other dictatorship is both anti-democratic and economically inefficient. They envisage that societies theoretically may follow divergent economic and political development trajectories, such as 'relative prosperity and democracy' versus 'relative poverty and dictatorship

46   See Pareto (1927, p. 354).
47   See Arrow (1969, pp. 154–60, 147), Sen (1995, p. 5; 2009, pp. x–xi, 22).
48   See Mulligan et al. (2004, pp. 52–4).

(or repression)', finding that some countries historically have followed the first path and others the second. Similarly, Frey and Stutzer distinguish authoritarian and dictatorial from democratic political systems, including capitalist and other dictatorships or undemocratic capitalism from democracy.[49]

Alternatively, the literature, while equating capitalist and other dictatorship with plutocratic autocracy defined as a dictatorship or rule of the rich, links it to some extent with theocracy as another mode of non-democracy in the form of religious authoritarianism or totalitarianism via total repression. Regarding the second link, Bénabou et al.[50] imply that capitalist dictatorship merges or allies with a substantively 'theocratic regime' in America. This occurs in that the plutocratic wealthy enter into 'a Religious-Right alliance with the religious poor' in opposition to and obstruction of scientific progress ('belief-eroding discoveries and ideas') and by implication liberal-secular democracy such as the 'secularization or Western-European regime'. Likewise, Mueller[51] identifies the threat that religious extremism such as 'Puritanical' evangelicalism poses to liberal-secular democracy and thus liberty in America, as well as orthodox Catholicism and Islamic fundamentalism in countries like Poland, in part Ireland, Turkey, Iran, Saudi Arabia and other Gulf capitalist-theocratic states and others.

In addition, the literature equates or links capitalist and other dictatorship with other political dictatorships, aside from plutocratic autocracy in third-world countries and evangelical theocracy in America under conservatism (Mueller 2009). Bowles, Franzini, and Pagano 1999, 1) join the 'rise of dictatorship', capitalist and other, with that of conservatism through rising nationalism and the exclusion of minorities, which manifests the linkage between authoritarian processes in capitalism and the subversions of democracy and generally 'economic and political factors'. Acemoglu associates capitalist dictatorship or repression with its political form in that inegalitarian economic institutions by generating a 'very unequal distribution of income and wealth' tend to be 'only consistent with a similarly unequal distribution of political power, i.e., with dictatorships and other repressive regimes', inferring that a 'clear complementarity' exists between the two types of social institutions. Alternatively, he alerts that capitalist dictatorship and generally oppression in the economy is fundamentally inconsistent with democracy in the polity such that economic systems like slavery and forced labor are unsustainable in a democratic society. In this connection, as noted, Acemoglu[52] identifies capitalist and related 'kleptocratic regimes' that by using 'the

---

49   See Acemoglu et al. (2008, pp. 812, 836) and Frey and Stutzer (2010, p. 112).

50   See Bénabou et al. (2015, p. 347), also, Manza and Brooks (1997).

51   See Mueller (2009, pp. ix, 392; 2013), also, Acemoglu et al. (2012), Bauman (1997) and Kuran (2018.).

52   Acemoglu (2005, p. 1046) adds that 'owing to the absence of strong institutions, rulers can deploy strategies, in particular divide-and-rule, to defuse opposition to their regime. The logic of the divide-and-rule strategy is to (ensure) that he can remain in power against

divide-and-rule strategy' seek to maintain power for long and neutralize opposition to their rule while in the process oppressing and impoverishing their citizens. More broadly, Esteban, Morelli, and Rohner point to 'effective dictatorship' in capitalist and related forms especially among third-world countries[53]. In this connection, Dessí finds that dictators, capitalist and non-capitalist, highly value material and symbolic investments stabilizing their 'totalitarian regimes'.

6   Capitalist and Other Dictatorship in Historical and Comparative Frameworks

Further, the literature often places and analyzes capitalist and other dictatorship in historical and comparative frameworks. In terms of a historical framework for analyzing the subject, Comte[54] refers to and distinguishes 'a temporary dictatorship' and a 'permanent and long dictatorship' during the 17th century, including royal aristocratic dictatorship or power in France and England, respectively. He thus focuses on the 'operation of dictatorship' in England and France, in particular on the 'temporary dictatorship' of Catholicism and Protestantism, respectively in these two countries, emphasizing that especially its Protestant variant merged the 'theological and military system', while also registering the 'English oligarchy'. As noted, Pareto predicts the imposition of 'a military dictatorship on some European nation' as the probable effect of wars among the 'civilized nations' of Europe, thus seemingly predicting both WW I and II during the 20th century. Although he regards the relationship of such a dictatorship to capital or other elites as indeterminate, Pareto implies that it is likely to be in a capitalist form. This especially holds for societies such as late-capitalist comers Germany and the US where the rule of capitalists still preserves 'considerable vigor' while showing 'signs of profound decline' in France at that time. Pareto thereby intimates that the rise and influence of fascism as a culmination of capitalism or conservatism will be stronger in these more vigorous capitalist dictatorships, as witnessed in Germany during interwar times and the US since the 2016 elections or even the 1980s with neo-conservatism, as Mannheim[55] confirms later.

---

challenges. By providing selective incentives and punishments, the divide-and-rule strategy exploits the fragility of social cooperation in weakly-institutionalized polities: when faced with the threat of being ousted, the kleptocratic ruler intensifies the collective action problem and destroys the coalition against him by bribing the pivotal groups'.

53   See Esteban, Morelli, and Rohner (2015, p. 1089) and Dessí (2008, p. 536).

54   See Comte (2000 (1896), II, p. 249, III, pp. 136–44).

55   Mannheim (1936, p. 127) personally witnesses—in light of being denied citizenship on no 'German blood and soil' grounds by Germany's pre-Nazi conservative government in the 1920s—that conservatism falls into a 'complete irrationalism', just as does fascism

On the other hand, within a longer historical frame, Steinmetz[56] considers these 'civilized nations', namely Western colonial states, including Britain, France and Germany, while putative democracies at home, in essence, capitalist and related 'dictatorships' over indigenous populations and European settlers alike, citing the East Indian company as especially notorious in this regard. In turn, Go notes that the US while establishing military bases throughout the world rather than 'long-term colonies' sustains 'dictatorial regimes' friendly to its interests, along with cultivating 'a network of client states using covert operations, threats of force, embargoes, and economic leverage', and often military interventions 'into the affairs of weaker countries'.

Among historical sociologists, as noted, Moore historically identifies 'a democratic version of capitalism' involving a 'combination of capitalism and Western democracy', namely combining the first with parliamentary democracy, after a historical 'series of revolutions', including the Puritan, the French, and the American Civil War. However, recall that Moore also identifies its undemocratic version and in that sense capitalist dictatorship in that capitalism as an economic system in some situations culminates in fascism by historically passing through 'reactionary political forms'—which implicates conservatism as such a form of politics and ideology—due to the 'absence of a strong revolutionary urge'. As seen, even Friedman unwittingly admits that 'Fascist Italy and Fascist Spain', as well as Nazi and pre-Nazi conservative Germany were effectively capitalist dictatorships due to merging 'private enterprise' as the 'dominant form of economic organization' with political repression, which contradicts US conservatives' penchant to label them as 'socialist' and even 'communist' dictatorships.

7   Capitalist Dictatorship and Fascist, Conservative and Neo-Fascist Dictatorships

Among these dictatorships, scholars especially pinpoint Nazi effective capitalist, i.e., pro-capital, anti-labor, as well as conservative dictatorship and generally totalitarianism, along with that of Italian fascism, as supplying a paradigmatic instance of this fascist culmination and reactionary evolution of capitalism under certain conditions. These are interwar Germany and Europe, especially during the capitalist as well as democratic crisis of the 1930s.

---

by linking itself with 'irrationalist philosophies and political theories', including that of Pareto, even if fascist 'complete irrationalism' is not totally the same as, but rather an intensification of, the conservative 'kind'.

56   See Steinmetz (2008, p. 607) and Go (2008, p. 202).

For example, Ferguson and Voth[57] provide a kind of quantitative proof or statistical evidence of impending Nazi-capitalist dictatorship. They find that 'weighted by capitalization in 1932, more than half of listed firms on the Berlin stock exchange enjoyed close links with the Nazi movement', thus even before Nazism's seizure of power, with such 'affiliated firms' outperforming the stock market 'by 5% to 8%' and investors rewarding firms with such Nazi 'preestablished ties'. They list 'influential' capitalist industrialists like Alfried Krupp, and others convicted in the Nuremberg trials as indicating that 'major German firms had financed the Nazi party's rapid rise after 1930', citing Fritz Thyssen's payment to Hitler. Furthermore, Ferguson and Voth offer a substantive proof or qualitative evidence that Nazism once seizing power constituted a merged conservative-capitalist dictatorship in that 'promising a broad coalition of the right (i.e., conservatism), Hitler was appointed as head of government by the President on January 30, 1933'. Afterwards, reportedly under the 'pretext of the Reichstag fire', the Nazi government 'suspended civil liberties', then the 'unions were dissolved in early May, and numerous members jailed'—which exposed the 'National Socialist German Workers' Party' as ultimately a deception or misnomer—and finally by the summer of 1933, 'all parties except the (Nazi Party) had been dissolved'. Ferguson and Voth conclude that capitalism merged or allied with and benefited from Nazism, just as the second being financed by the first, in that capitalist firms that 'had bet on Hitler benefited substantially (as) the stock market bid up the share prices of (Nazi) connected firms'. They thus portray a model of capitalist-conservative dictatorship, and a far cry from a 'socialist' one, as later US conservatives allege seeking to disguise this osmosis or alliance of German and other fascism with conservatism and capitalism.

Overall, this economic study reaffirms what sociological and other previous studies show. This is that Nazism not only did not abolish capitalism—for example, not abolishing or nationalizing large capitalist firms and the stock market—but merged with the latter and conservatism to impose capitalist-conservative dictatorship. This is instructive to emphasize in view of conservatives rewriting its history and construing German and all fascism as anti-capitalism, socialism, communism, and the like. They do so in an apparent attempt to disguise the inherently authoritarian nature of their Weltanschauung and regime and to absolve it from breeding and then allying with fascist, including Nazi, totalitarianism, against liberalism, including both liberal democracy/civil society/culture and democratic egalitarian capitalism, as Mannheim shows in his seminal study of conservatism. In this connection, Adena et al. report that media, specifically radio propaganda functioned as Nazism's key mechanism for recruiting 'new party members' in the process of 'consolidation of dictatorship' as a blend of capitalist and conservative dictatorships.[58] This anticipates, if not inspires,

57   See Ferguson and Voth (2008, pp. 101–6, 131).
58   See Adena et al. (2015, p. 1885) and DellaVigna and Kaplan (2007, pp. 1189–90).

what DellaVigna and Kaplan find as the corresponding activity of conservatism in the US through the 'conservative slant of Fox News' exerting the 'sizeable impact' on the 'vote share' (for Republicans) in the 2000 elections. They infer that its 'viewers do not sufficiently account for media bias and are subject to nonrational persuasion', just as evidently most Germans did not and were during the 1930s, while such effects on the 2016 election being even stronger.[59] This sequence from the radio propaganda of Nazism as the 'new conservatism' to Fox News' conservative 'slant' only demonstrate what has been evident but somehow disguised by postwar conservatives. This is that despite being defeated in WW II and discredited during postwar times totalitarian fascism and inherently authoritarian conservatism in general displays an essential continuity and persistence, actually resurrecting from death since the 1980s with the rise of neo-fascism and neo-conservatism such as illiberal and repressive Thatcherism and Reaganism. More broadly, Satyanath et al.[60] report that Nazism arose as a blended conservative, extreme-right and religious, theocentric and implicitly capitalist dictatorship in that Nazi victory 'correlated with religion' that hence, along with other 'dense networks of associations', greatly contributed to the 'eventual collapse of democracy' and the rise of 'one of history's most destructive regimes. Relatedly and recently, religion, as seen in Mueller's account, seeks especially through religious extremism, including evangelicalism in America and Islamic fundamentalism, to cause the collapse of modern liberal democracies and the resurgence of dictatorships.

In addition to the Nazi exemplary case, Riley and Fernández detects two instances of capitalist dictatorship[61] in interwar and in part postwar Europe. These are, first, totalitarian dictatorships, as in Mussolini's Italy during 1922–43, and, second, authoritarian 'economic-corporate dictatorships', as in Rivera's Spain in the 1920–30s and continuing under Franco over 1939–75. More broadly, as implied, Mueller infers that throughout history and up to the present conservatism ('traditionalism') and dictatorship move together to a large degree, as do the first and religion, especially religious extremism and terrorism, as he observes in particular for America during its entire history since Puritanism, as well as for Islamic countries.

---

59 This is what Allcott and Gentzkow (2017, p. 232) find, namely that the 'average US adult read and remembered on the order of one or perhaps several fake news articles during the election period, with higher exposure to pro-Trump articles than pro-Clinton articles'.

60 See Satyanath et al. (2017, pp. 479, 520).

61 Riley and Fernández (2014, p. 433) characterize dictatorships in general as 'nonliberal democratic regimes', while dividing types of dictatorship into totalitarian and authoritarian, which while apparently treating them as 'democracies' contrary to the common view implies that liberal democracy is the sole genuine type of democracy in modern society. In this sense, capitalist and other dictatorships represent spurious illiberal "democracies". See also Riley (2005, p. 288).

Next, the literature also analyzes or implicates capitalist and non-capitalist dictatorship in a comparative framework involving multiple societies. Thus, Myrdal identifies 'two dictatorships', one evidently anti-capitalist in Russia and the other, capitalist or fascist in Italy, sharing 'conscious', 'calculated political indoctrination', and furthermore compares them with the US in this regard. He observes that the US, 'next to Russia and Italy', uses 'most consciously political indoctrination', by instilling the young with 'more uniform and standardized convictions and attitudes' than in 'hardly another nation in the world', excepting these 'two dictatorships'.[62]

More recently, Foran registers capitalist 'personalist, exclusionary military dictatorships' in third-world countries, especially South America, such as those of Stroessner in Paraguay and Pinochet in Chile, as does Muller 'a harshly repressive military dictatorship' in Argentina, Chile, and Uruguay.[63] Habermas adds to these capitalist military dictatorships a 'developmental dictatorship' in South Korea and the 'other dictatorships of developing nations' such as Singapore, Malaysia, Taiwan, and China, as does Rodrik[64] citing the 'Korean military dictator President Park Chung-Hee' since 1961. Still among all these dictatorships, Pinochet's capitalist-conservative, essentially neo-fascist, military dictatorship is the probably foremost and most brutal, notorious and 'disastrous' exemplar. It apparently implemented 'libertarian' economics' ideas and policies, namely those of the Chicago School, just as being reportedly helped ('Chicago boys') and supported by the latter, including the personal visit and support of Friedman, Hayek, etc.[65] For example, Barro and Ursúa[66] invoke Chile during 1972–1976 as the 'only nonwar case' of 20th century economic disasters that relates to 'revolution' but without further specification. This leaves the puzzle if this signifies Pinochet's capitalist, 'free-market' dictatorship imposed after a military coup in 1973 and if Allende's democratic election and short governance reportedly overthrown with the critical help by the US government would not qualify as 'revolution'.

---

62   Myrdal (1953, p. 205) adds that 'this may seem odd, for America is, in a sense, the most individualistic nation in the world (as) there is hardly another nation in the world, with the exception of Russia and Italy, where, in spite of great differences of cultural heritage and of large geographical distances and social gulfs, the young grow up with more uniform and standardized convictions and attitudes. At the same time adult opinion is also worked upon. The development of advertising techniques and the need to maintain domestic morale in the war have led to the refinement of propaganda. Every channel of communication (is) for exercising political influence'.
63   See Foran (1993, p. 4) and Muller (1995, p. 967).
64   See Habermas (2001, pp. 40, 124). Rodrik (2014, p. 205) recounts that the 'Korean military dictator President Park Chung-Hee threw the country's leading businessmen in jail when he came to power in 1961; they were released only after Park extracted promises from them that they would each undertake specific industrial investments'.
65   See Barber (1995) and Rodrik (2010).
66   See Barro and Ursúa (2008, p. 60).

More broadly, Acemoglu et al. consider 'military dictatorships' primarily capitalist ones and define them as undemocratic systems relying on 'repression against competing groups', which the military as a 'specialized branch' of the state in turn exercises. In turn, they associate democracy with 'redistributive policies' in the manner of the welfare state, especially the 'provision of public goods' benefiting all citizens but costing the plutocratic elite that hence impedes a 'transition to democracy' from oligarchy endowing capitalists with disproportionate power and in that sense capitalist dictatorship. Conversely, they link the latter with military repression in that the capitalist elite creates and uses the military in order to suppress 'demands for democratization'.[67]

The above treatment of capitalist dictatorship or its equivalents and proxies in the extant literature has served as the background and impetus for conducting its sociological study in this book.

---

67   Acemoglu et al. (2010, 3) add that 'when inequality is low, the society is likely to become democratic rapidly; but the amount of redistributive spending is relatively low, and most of it is in the form of public goods. As the level of inequality increases and the society remains democratic, the size of the government (the amount of public goods provision) increases. In societies with very high levels of inequality, however, the society is more likely to be nondemocratic (either oligarchic or a military dictatorship), and, in these cases, there will be little spending on public goods and greater (perhaps substantial) spending on the military.

Data on Capitalist Dictatorship Measures

1   Economic Measures

TABLE A1   Trade union density and inverse, OECD countries, 2017 or nearest year

Country	Density %	Density inverse %
Australia	14.70	85.30
Austria	26.70	73.30
Belgium	51.90	48.10
Canada	29.40	70.60
Chile	16.10	83.90
Czech Republic	11.70	88.30
Denmark	66.10	33.90
Estonia	4.30	95.70
Finland	62.20	37.80
France	8.90	91.10
Germany	16.70	83.30
Greece	20.20	79.80
Hungary	8.10	91.90
Iceland	89.80	10.20
Ireland	24.50	75.50
Israel	25.00	75.00
Italy	34.30	65.70
Japan	17.10	82.90
Korea, South,	10.50	89.50
Latvia	12.20	87.80
Lithuania	7.70	92.30
Luxembourg	32.10	67.90
Mexico	13.90	86.10
Netherlands	16.80	83.20
New Zealand	17.30	82.70
Norway	49.30	50.70
Poland	12.70	87.30
Portugal	16.10	83.90

TABLE A1   Trade union density and inverse, OECD countries, 2017 or nearest year (*cont.*)

Country	Density %	Density inverse %
Slovak Republic	10.90	89.10
Slovenia	19.60	80.40
Spain	14.20	85.80
Sweden	65.60	34.40
Switzerland	14.90	85.10
Turkey	8.60	91.40
United Kingdom	23.20	76.80
United States	10.30	89.70

SOURCE: OECD LABOUR FORCE STATISTICS. 2018. TRADE UNION DENSITY. HTTPS://STATS.
OECD.ORG/INDEX.ASPX?DATASETCODE=TUD

Trade union density inverse % = 100—Trade union density %

TABLE A2   Collective bargaining coverage and inverse, OECD countries, 2017 or nearest year

Country	Collective bargaining coverage %	Collective bargaining coverage inverse %
Australia	59.20	40.80
Austria	98.00	2.00
Belgium	96.00	4.00
Canada	30.30	69.70
Chile	20.90	79.10
Czech Republic	46.30	53.70
Denmark	84.00	16.00
Estonia	18.60	81.40
Finland	89.30	10.70
France	98.50	1.50
Germany	56.00	44.00
Greece	40.00	60.00
Hungary	22.80	77.20
Iceland	90.00	10.00
Ireland	33.50	66.50
Israel	26.10	73.90
Italy	80.00	20.00
Japan	16.70	83.30
Korea, South	11.80	88.20
Latvia	13.80	86.20
Lithuania	7.10	92.90
Luxembourg	55.00	45.00
Mexico	12.50	87.50
Netherlands	78.60	21.40
New Zealand	15.90	84.10
Norway	67.00	33.00
Poland	14.70	85.30
Portugal	72.30	27.70
Slovak Republic	24.40	75.60
Slovenia	65.00	35.00
Spain	73.10	26.90
Sweden	90.00	10.00
Switzerland	49.20	50.80
Turkey	7.00	93.00

TABLE A2   Collective bargaining coverage and inverse, OECD countries, 2017 or nearest year
(*cont.*)

Country	Collective bargaining coverage %	Collective bargaining coverage inverse %
United Kingdom	26.30	73.70
United States	12.00	88.00

SOURCE: OECD LABOUR FORCE STATISTICS. 2018. COLLECTIVE BARGAINING COVERAGE.
HTTPS://STATS.OECD.ORG/INDEX.ASPX?DATASETCODE=CBC

Collective bargaining coverage inverse % = 100—Collective bargaining coverage

TABLE A3   Works councils and councils' inverse, OECD countries, various years

Country	Councils' score	Councils' inverse
Australia	0	100
Austria	100	0
Belgium	100	0
Canada	10	90
Chile	0	100
Czech Republic	50	50
Denmark	100	0
Estonia*	50	50
Finland*	100	0
France	100	0
Germany	100	0
Greece	50	50
Hungary	50	50
Iceland*	100	0
Ireland	10	90
Israel	0	100
Italy	100	0
Japan	0	100
Korea, South	50	50
Latvia	0	100
Lithuania	10	90
Luxembourg*	100	0
Mexico	0	100
Netherlands	100	0
New Zealand	0	100
Norway*	100	0
Poland	50	50
Portugal	50	50
Slovak Republic	50	50
Slovenia	100	0
Spain	100	0
Sweden*	100	0
Switzerland*	100	0
Turkey	0	100

TABLE A3 Works councils and councils' inverse, OECD countries, various years (*cont.*)

Country	Councils' score	Councils' inverse
United Kingdom	50	50
United States	0	100

SOURCES: BAKER & MCKENZIE INTERNATIONAL. 2009. *WORLDWIDE GUIDE TO TRADE UNIONS AND WORKS COUNCILS*. HTTPS://DIGITALCOMMONS.ILR.CORNELL.EDU/LAW-FIRMS?UTM_SOURCE=DIGITALCOMMONS.ILR.CORNELL.EDU%2FLAWFIRMS%2F49&UTM_MEDIUM=PDF&UTM_CAMPAIGN=PDFCOVERPAGES
EUROPEAN TRADE UNION INSTITUTE. 2019. NATIONAL INDUSTRIAL RELATIONS. HTTPS://WWW.WORKER-PARTICIPATION.EU/NATIONAL-INDUSTRIAL-RELATIONS
FLANAGAN, ROBERT. 1999. MACROECONOMIC PERFORMANCE AND COLLECTIVE BARGAINING: AN INTERNATIONAL PERSPECTIVE. *JOURNAL OF ECONOMIC LITERATURE* 37, 1150–1175.
ROGERS, JOEL AND WOLFGANG STREECK (EDS.). 1995. *WORKS COUNCILS: CONSULTATION, REPRESENTATION, AND COOPERATION IN INDUSTRIAL RELATIONS*. CHICAGO: UNIVERSITY OF CHICAGO PRESS.
* Equivalents of Works councils
Scores: No Works councils = 0; Few, Uncommon, Voluntary = 10; Limited or Secondary = 50; Common, Important = 100
Works councils' inverse = 100—Works councils

TABLE A4   Board-level employee representation (BLER) and inverse, OECD countries, 2019 or
            nearest year

Country	BLER score	BLER inverse
Australia	0	100
Austria	100	0
Belgium	0	100
Canada	0	100
Chile	0	100
Czech Republic	80	20
Denmark	100	0
Estonia	0	100
Finland	80	20
France	50	50
Germany	100	0
Greece	20	80
Hungary	100	0
Iceland	0	100
Ireland	20	80
Israel	50	50
Italy	0	100
Japan	0	100
Korea, South	20	80
Latvia	0	100
Lithuania	0	100
Luxembourg	80	20
Mexico	0	100
Netherlands	100	0
New Zealand	0	100
Norway	100	0
Poland	50	50
Portugal	50	50
Slovak Republic	80	20
Slovenia	100	0
Spain	20	80
Sweden	100	0
Switzerland	20	80
Turkey	0	100

TABLE A4   Board-level employee representation (BLER) and inverse, OECD countries, 2019 or nearest year (*cont.*)

Country	BLER score	BLER inverse
United Kingdom	0	100
United States	0	100

SOURCES: GOLD, MICHAEL AND JEREMY WADDINGTON. 2019. BOARD-LEVEL EMPLOYEE REPRESENTATION IN EUROPE: STATE OF PLAY. *EUROPEAN JOURNAL OF INDUSTRIAL RELATIONS* 25, 1–14.
OECD. 2016. COLLECTIVE BARGAINING IN OECD AND ACCESSION COUNTRIES, BOARD-LEVEL EMPLOYEE REPRESENTATION. HTTPS://WWW.OECD.ORG/EMPLOYMENT/EMP/BOARD-LEVEL%20EMPLOYEE%20REPRESENTATION.PDF
OECD. 2018. OWNERSHIP AND GOVERNANCE OF STATE-OWNED ENTERPRISES: A COMPENDIUM OF NATIONAL PRACTICES. HTTPS://WWW.OECD.ORG/CORPORATE/CA/OWNERSHIP-AND-GOVERNANCE-OF-STATE-OWNED-ENTERPRISES-A-COMPENDIUM-OF-NATIONAL-PRACTICES.PDF
EUROPEAN TRADE UNION INSTITUTE 2019. BOARD-LEVEL EMPLOYEE REPRESENTATION. HTTPS://WWW.ETUI.ORG/CONTENT/SEARCH?KEYS=BOARD-LEVEL+EMPLOYEE+REPRESENTATION+

Scores: BLER in the entire economy= 100, BLER throughout the public sector and private companies with 50+ employees = 80, BLER restricted to the public sector = 50, BLER only in specified state-owned companies= 20, no BLER = 0
BLER inverse = 100—BLER

TABLE A5   Share of top one percent of wealth and wealth concentration scores, OECD
            countries, 2016 or nearest year

Country	Wealth share %	Wealth concentration score
Australia	15.00	35.31
Austria	25.53	60.10
Belgium	12.06	28.39
Canada	15.50	36.49
Chile	17.40	40.96
Czech Republic*	9.32	21.94
Denmark	23.62	55.60
Estonia	21.23	49.98
Finland	13.31	31.33
France	18.65	43.90
Germany	23.66	55.70
Greece	9.16	21.56
Hungary	17.23	40.56
Iceland**	23.00	54.14
Ireland	14.18	33.38
Israel***	22.50	52.97
Italy	11.69	27.52
Japan	10.77	25.35
Korea, South****	30.00	70.62
Latvia	21.39	50.35
Lithuania*	21.39	50.35
Luxembourg	18.81	44.28
Mexico*	17.40	40.96
Netherlands	27.83	65.51
New Zealand*****	24.00	56.50
Norway	20.13	47.39
Poland	11.73	27.61
Portugal	14.44	33.99
Slovak Republic	9.32	21.94
Slovenia	23.03	54.21
Spain	16.32	38.42
Sweden*	20.13	47.39
Switzerland*	23.66	55.70

TABLE A5   Share of top one percent of wealth and wealth concentration scores, OECD
countries, 2016 or nearest year (*cont.*)

Country	Wealth share %	Wealth concentration score
Turkey*	17.40	40.96
United Kingdom	20.50	48.26
United States	42.48	100.00

SOURCES: OECD STATISTICS ON DISTRIBUTION OF WEALTH. 2016. HTTPS://STATS.OECD.
ORG/INDEX.ASPX?DATASETCODE=WEALTH

* Estimated values from comparable cases: Czech Republic from Slovak Republic, Lithuania
from Latvia, Mexico and Turkey from Chile, Sweden from Norway, Switzerland from Germany.
** https://www.ruv.is/frett/rikasta-prosentid-a-naer-fjordung-audsins
*** https://ref-inst.org/en/wealth-distribution-in-israel/
**** The Credit Suisse Global Wealth Report 2019
***** OECD Statistics and Data Directorate, Inequalities in Household Wealth across OECD
Countries: Evidence from the OECD Wealth Distribution https://www.oecd.org/officialdocu-
ments/publicdisplaydocumentpdf/?cote=SDD/DOC(2018)1&docLanguage=En
Wealth concentration score = 100/42.48 = 2.3540489642184557 x Wealth share %

TABLE A6   Gini coefficient on disposable household income and income inequality scores,
OECD countries, 2018 or latest available

Country	Gini coefficient x 100	Income inequality score
Australia	33.00	71.74
Austria	28.40	61.74
Belgium	26.60	57.83
Canada	31.00	67.39
Chile	46.00	100.00
Czech Republic	25.30	55.00
Denmark	26.10	56.74
Estonia	31.40	68.26
Finland	26.60	57.83
France	29.10	63.26
Germany	29.40	63.91
Greece	33.30	72.39
Hungary	28.20	61.30
Iceland	25.50	55.43
Ireland	30.90	67.17
Israel	34.40	74.78
Italy	32.80	71.30
Japan	33.90	73.70
Korea, South	35.50	77.17
Latvia	34.60	75.22
Lithuania	37.80	82.17
Luxembourg	30.40	66.09
Mexico	45.80	99.57
Netherlands	28.50	61.96
New Zealand	34.90	75.87
Norway	26.20	56.96
Poland	28.40	61.74
Portugal	33.10	71.96
Slovak Republic	24.10	52.39
Slovenia	24.40	53.04
Spain	34.10	74.13
Sweden	28.20	61.30
Switzerland	29.60	64.35

TABLE A6   Gini coefficient on disposable household income and income inequality scores, OECD countries, 2018 or latest available (*cont.*)

Country	Gini coefficient x 100	Income inequality score
Turkey	40.40	87.83
United Kingdom	35.70	77.61
United States	39.00	84.78

SOURCE: OECD DATA. 2019. OECD SOCIAL AND WELFARE STATISTICS: INCOME DISTRIBUTION. HTTPS://DATA.OECD.ORG/INEQUALITY/INCOME-INEQUALITY.HTM

Note: 0 = complete income equality; 1 or 100 = complete income inequality
Income inequality score = 100/46 = 2.1739130434782609 x Gini coefficient x 100

TABLE A7　General poverty rates after taxes and transfers, age group 17–66 years, and general poverty scores, OECD countries, 2018 or latest available

	General poverty rate %	General poverty score
Australia	12.10	67.60
Austria	9.80	
Belgium	9.70	54.19
Canada	12.10	67.60
Chile	16.50	
Czech Republic	5.60	31.28
Denmark	5.80	32.40
Estonia	15.70	87.71
Finland	6.30	35.20
France	8.30	46.37
Germany	10.40	58.10
Greece	14.40	80.45
Hungary	7.80	43.58
Iceland	5.40	30.17
Ireland	9.20	51.40
Israel	17.90	100.00
Italy	13.70	76.54
Japan	15.70	87.71
Korea, South	17.40	97.21
Latvia	16.80	93.85
Lithuania	16.90	94.41
Luxembourg	11.10	62.01
Mexico	16.60	92.74
Netherlands	8.30	46.37
New Zealand	10.90	60.89
Norway	8.40	46.93
Poland	10.30	57.54
Portugal	12.50	69.83
Slovak Republic	8.50	47.49
Slovenia	8.70	48.60
Spain	15.50	86.59
Sweden	9.30	51.96

TABLE A7   General poverty rates after taxes and transfers, age group 17–66 years, and general poverty scores, OECD countries, 2018 or latest available (*cont.*)

	General poverty rate %	General poverty score
Switzerland	9.10	50.84
Turkey	17.20	96.09
United Kingdom	11.90	66.48
United States	17.80	99.44

SOURCE: OECD DATA. 2019. HTTPS://DATA.OECD.ORG/INEQUALITY/POVERTY-RATE.HTM

The general poverty rate is the 'percentage of people whose income falls below the poverty line taken as half the median household income of the total population' (OECD Data)

General poverty score = 100/17.90 = 5.5865921787709497 x General poverty rate

TABLE A8   Child poverty rates after taxes and transfers, age group 0–17 years, and child
poverty score OECD countries, 2018 or latest available

Country	Child poverty rate %	Child poverty score
Australia	12.50	49.41
Austria	11.50	45.45
Belgium	12.30	48.62
Canada	11.60	45.85
Chile	21.50	84.98
Czech Republic	8.50	33.60
Denmark	3.70	14.62
Estonia	9.60	37.94
Finland	3.60	14.23
France	11.50	45.45
Germany	12.30	48.62
Greece	17.60	69.57
Hungary	7.70	30.43
Iceland	5.80	22.92
Ireland	10.00	39.53
Israel	23.70	93.68
Italy	17.30	68.38
Japan	13.90	54.94
Korea, South	14.50	57.31
Latvia	13.20	52.17
Lithuania	17.70	69.96
Luxembourg	13.00	51.38
Mexico	19.80	78.26
Netherlands	10.90	43.08
New Zealand	14.10	55.73
Norway	8.00	31.62
Poland	9.30	36.76
Portugal	15.50	61.26
Slovak Republic	14.00	55.34
Slovenia	7.10	28.06
Spain	22.00	86.96
Sweden	9.30	36.76
Switzerland	9.50	37.55
Turkey	25.30	100.00

TABLE A8   Child poverty rates after taxes and transfers, age group 0–17 years, and child poverty score oecd countries, 2018 or latest available (*cont.*)

Country	Child poverty rate %	Child poverty score
United Kingdom	12.90	50.99
United States	21.20	83.79

SOURCE: OECD DATA. 2019. HTTPS://DATA.OECD.ORG/INEQUALITY/POVERTY-RATE.HTM

The child poverty rate is the 'percentage of children 0–17 years old living in families whose income falls below the poverty line taken as half the median household income of the total population'. (OECD Data)

Child poverty score = 100/25.30 = 3.9525691699604743 x Child poverty rate

TABLE A9   Average annual hours actually worked per worker and annual work hours scores, OECD countries 2018 or latest available

Country	Annual work hours	Annual work hours score
Australia	1665.00	77.51
Austria	1511.00	70.34
Belgium	1545.00	71.93
Canada	1708.00	79.52
Chile	1941.00	90.36
Czech Republic	1792.00	83.43
Denmark	1392.00	64.80
Estonia	1748.00	81.38
Finland	1555.00	72.39
France	1520.00	70.76
Germany	1362.60	63.44
Greece	1956.00	91.06
Hungary	1741.10	81.06
Iceland	1469.00	68.39
Ireland	1782.00	82.96
Israel	1910.10	88.92
Italy	1722.60	80.20
Japan	1680.00	78.21
Korea, South	1993.00	92.78
Latvia	1699.00	79.10
Lithuania	1616.00	75.23
Luxembourg	1506.00	70.11
Mexico	2148.00	100.00
Netherlands	1433.00	66.71
New Zealand	1756.00	81.75
Norway	1416.40	65.94
Poland	1792.00	83.43
Portugal	1722.00	80.17
Slovak Republic	1698.00	79.05
Slovenia	1602.80	74.62
Spain	1701.00	79.19
Sweden	1474.00	68.62
Switzerland	1561.00	72.67

TABLE A9   Average annual hours actually worked per worker and annual work hours scores,
OECD countries 2018 or latest available (*cont.*)

Country	Annual work hours	Annual work hours score
Turkey	1832.00	85.29
United Kingdom	1538.00	71.60
United States	1786.00	83.15

SOURCE: OECD DATA. 2019. EMPLOYMENT STATISTICS. HTTPS://DATA.OECD.ORG/EMP/
HOURS-WORKED.HTM

'Average annual hours worked is defined as the total number of hours actually worked per year
divided by the average number of people in employment per year' (OECD Data).
Annual work hours score = 100/2148 = 0.0465549348230912 x Annual work hours

TABLE A10   Statutory minimum and collectively agreed paid annual leave and vacation
inverse, OECD countries 2016 or latest available

Country	Paid annual leave, working days	Vacation score	Vacation
Australia	20	66.67	33.33
Austria	25	83.33	16.67
Belgium	20	66.67	33.33
Canada	10	33.33	66.67
Chile	15	50.00	50.00
Czech Republic*	25	83.33	16.67
Denmark*	30	100.00	0
Estonia	20	66.67	33.33
Finland	25	83.33	16.67
France	25	83.33	16.67
Germany*	30	100.00	0
Greece	20	66.67	33.33
Hungary	20	66.67	33.33
Iceland	24	80.00	20.00
Ireland*	24	80.00	20.00
Israel	11	36.67	63.33
Italy*	25	83.33	16.67
Japan	10	33.33	66.67
Korea, South	15	50.00	50.00
Latvia	20	66.67	33.33
Lithuania**	20	66.67	33.33
Luxembourg	25	83.33	16.67
Mexico	6	20.00	80.00
Netherlands*	25	83.33	16.67
New Zealand	20	66.67	33.33
Norway*	25	83.33	16.67
Poland	20	66.67	33.33
Portugal	22	73.33	26.67
Slovak Republic*	25	83.33	16.67
Slovenia	20	66.67	33.33
Spain	22	73.33	26.67
Sweden	25	83.33	16.67
Switzerland	20	66.67	33.33

TABLE A10   Statutory minimum and collectively agreed paid annual leave and vacation inverse, OECD countries 2016 or latest available (*cont.*)

Country	Paid annual leave, working days	Vacation score	Vacation
Turkey	12	40.00	60.00
United Kingdom	28	93.33	6.67
United States***	0	0	100.00

SOURCE: OECD. 2016. FAMILY DATABASE, ADDITIONAL LEAVE ENTITLEMENTS FOR WORKING PARENTS. HTTPS://WWW.OECD.ORG/ELS/SOC/PF2_3_ADDITIONAL_LEAVE_ENTITLEMENTS_OF_WORKING_PARENTS.PDF

Statutory minimum 'generally reflect(s) those for full-time, full-year private sector employees, working a five-day week, who have been working for their current employer for one year' (OECD Family Database).

* Collectively agreed
** Estimated from Latvia.
*** 'In the private sector, the offer of paid leave remains at the discretion of the employer' (OECD Family Database).
Vacation score = 100/30 = 3.3333 x Paid annual leave
Vacation inverse = 100—Vacation score

TABLE A11   Real GDP per hour, hourly wages (US dollars) and labor exploitation rates and
scores, OECD countries, 2016

Country	GDP/hour $	Hourly wages $	Exploitation rate %	Exploitation score
Australia	51.80	38.19	35.64	7.07
Austria	58.60	39.54	48.20	9.56
Belgium	64.70	47.26	36.90	7.32
Canada	48.90	30.08	62.57	12.41
Chile*	23.70	6.40	270.31	53.60
Czech Republic	34.50	10.71	222.13	44.05
Denmark	64.20	45.32	41.66	8.26
Estonia	31.50	11.60	171.55	34.02
Finland	55.10	38.72	42.30	8.39
France	59.10	37.72	56.68	11.24
Germany	59.90	43.18	38.72	7.68
Greece	33.10	15.70	110.83	21.98
Hungary	31.00	8.60	260.47	51.65
Iceland***	54.90	41.68	31.72	6.29
Ireland	82.10	36.23	126.61	25.11
Israel	35.30	22.63	55.99	11.10
Italy	47.70	32.49	46.81	9.28
Japan	41.50	26.46	56.84	11.27
Korea, South	32.90	22.98	43.17	8.56
Latvia**	29.40	8.85	232.20	46.05
Lithuania***	34.30	8.85	287.57	57.03
Luxembourg**	80.60	43.19	86.62	17.18
Mexico	18.70	3.91	378.26	75.01
Netherlands	62.20	34.60	79.77	15.82
New Zealand	37.90	23.67	60.12	11.92
Norway	79.30	48.62	63.10	12.51
Poland	32.60	8.53	282.18	55.96
Portugal	35.30	10.96	222.08	44.04
Slovak Republic	39.00	11.57	237.08	47.01
Slovenia**	37.40	18.88	98.09	19.45
Spain	47.00	23.44	100.51	19.93
Sweden	62.10	41.68	48.99	9.72
Switzerland	58.10	60.36	-3.74	-.74

TABLE A11   Real GDP per hour, hourly wages (US dollars) and labor exploitation rates and
scores, OECD countries, 2016 (*cont.*)

Country	GDP/hour $	Hourly wages $	Exploitation rate %	Exploitation score
Turkey	36.80	6.09	504.27	100.00
United Kingdom	53.10	28.41	86.91	17.23
United States	63.50	39.03	62.70	12.43

SOURCES: REAL GDP PER HOUR: OECD DATA. 2016. HTTPS://DATA.OECD.ORG/LPRDTY/
GDP-PER-HOUR-WORKED.HTM

'GDP per hour worked is a measure of labour productivity. it measures how efficiently labour input is combined with other factors of production and used in the production process. labour input is defined as total hours worked of all persons engaged in production. labour productivity only partially reflects the productivity of labour in terms of the personal capacities of workers or the intensity of their effort. the ratio between the output measure and the labour input depends to a large degree on the presence and/or use of other inputs (e.g., capital, intermediate inputs, technical, organisational and efficiency change, economies of scale). this indicator is measured in USD (constant prices 2010 and PPPS) and indices' (OECD Data).

Hourly wages hourly compensation costs in manufacturing: The Conference Board. International labor comparisons program, February 2018 https://www.conference-board.org/ilcprogram/index.cfm?id=38269

* https://tradingeconomics.com/chile/wages-in-manufacturing (Chile pesos converted in US dollars)

** 2016 Eurostat (euros converted in US dollars)

*** Estimated values from comparable cases: Iceland from Sweden, Lithuania from Latvia.

Exploitation rate % = (Real GDP per hour—Hourly wages)/Hourly wages

Exploitation score = 100/504.27 = 0.1983064628076229 x Exploitation rate %

TABLE A12   Coefficients of strictness of employment protection, individual dismissals
(regular contracts) and protection inverse, OECD countries, 2014 or latest
available

Country	Protection coefficient	Protection score	Protection inverse
Australia	1.67	52.52	47.48
Austria	2.37	74.53	25.47
Belgium	1.89	59.43	40.57
Canada	.92	28.93	71.07
Chile	2.63	82.70	17.30
Czech Republic	2.92	91.82	8.18
Denmark	2.20	69.18	30.82
Estonia	1.81	56.92	43.08
Finland	2.17	68.24	31.76
France	2.38	74.84	25.16
Germany	2.68	84.28	15.72
Greece	2.12	66.67	33.33
Hungary	1.59	50.00	50.00
Iceland	1.73	54.40	45.60
Ireland	1.40	44.03	55.97
Israel	2.04	64.15	35.85
Italy	2.68	84.28	15.72
Japan	1.37	43.08	56.92
Korea, South	2.37	74.53	25.47
Latvia	2.69	84.59	15.41
Lithuania	2.42	76.10	23.90
Luxembourg	2.25	70.75	29.25
Mexico	2.03	63.84	36.16
Netherlands	2.82	88.68	11.32
New Zealand	1.39	43.71	56.29
Norway	2.33	73.27	26.73
Poland	2.23	70.13	29.87
Portugal	3.18	100.00	0
Slovak Republic	1.84	57.86	42.14
Slovenia	2.16	67.92	32.08
Spain	2.05	64.47	35.53
Sweden	2.61	82.08	17.92

TABLE A12   Coefficients of strictness of employment protection, individual dismissals (regular contracts) and protection inverse, OECD countries, 2014 or latest available (*cont.*)

Country	Protection coefficient	Protection score	Protection inverse
Switzerland	1.60	50.31	49.69
Turkey	2.31	72.64	27.36
United Kingdom	1.10	34.59	65.41
United States	.26	8.18	91.82

SOURCE: OECD STATISTICS. 2018. HTTPS://STATS.OECD.ORG/INDEX.ASPX?DATASET-CODE=EPL_OV

Data range from 0 to 6 with higher scores representing stricter regulation of individual dismissal of employees on regular/indefinite contracts (OECD Statistics).

Protection score = 100/3.18 = 31.4465408805031447 x Protection index

Protection inverse = 100- Protection score

TABLE A13   Unemployment benefits, net replacement rates in unemployment (single person
without children, duration of 60 months), and benefit inverse, OECD countries,
2018 or latest available

Country	Replacement rate %	Benefits score	Benefits inverse
Australia	39.00	52.00	48.00
Austria	59.00	78.67	21.33
Belgium	55.00	73.33	26.67
Canada	33.00	44.00	56.00
Chile	4.00	5.33	94.67
Czech Republic	46.00	61.33	38.67
Denmark	75.00	100.00	0
Estonia	34.00	45.33	54.67
Finland	61.00	81.33	18.67
France	48.00	64.00	36.00
Germany	48.00	64.00	36.00
Greece	22.00	29.33	70.67
Hungary	15.00	20.00	80.00
Iceland	54.00	72.00	28.00
Ireland	62.00	82.67	17.33
Israel	23.00	30.67	69.33
Italy	0	0	100.00
Japan	58.00	77.33	22.67
Korea, South	32.00	42.67	57.33
Latvia	32.00	42.67	57.33
Lithuania	24.00	32.00	68.00
Luxembourg	59.00	78.67	21.33
Mexico*	0	0	100.00
Netherlands	66.00	88.00	12.00
New Zealand	45.00	60.00	40.00
Norway	47.00	62.67	37.33
Poland	32.00	42.67	57.33
Portugal	23.00	30.67	69.33
Slovak Republic	22.00	29.33	70.67
Slovenia	47.00	62.67	37.33
Spain	32.00	42.67	57.33
Sweden	59.00	78.67	21.33

TABLE A13 Unemployment benefits, net replacement rates in unemployment (single person without children, duration of 60 months), and benefit inverse, OECD countries, 2018 or latest available (*cont.*)

Country	Replacement rate %	Benefits score	Benefits inverse
Switzerland	71.00	94.67	5.33
Turkey	0	0	100.00
United Kingdom	48.00	64.00	36.00
United States	8.00	10.67	89.33

SOURCE: OECD. 2019. BENEFITS AND WAGES STATISTICS. HTTPS://STATS.OECD.ORG/INDEX. ASPX?DATASETCODE=NRR

* OECD Employment Outlook. 2018. https://www.oecd-ilibrary.org/sites/empl_outlook-2018-9-en/index.html?itemId=/content/component/empl_outlook-2018-9-en
Benefits score = 100/75 = 1.3333333333333333 x Replacement rate %
Benefits inverse = 100—Benefit score

TABLE A14   Government spending on social protection as % of GDP and social protection
inverse, OECD countries, 2018 or latest available

Country	Protection % of GDP	Protection score	Protection inverse
Australia	10.19	41.33	58.67
Austria	20.13	81.66	18.34
Belgium	19.28	78.22	21.78
Canada	17.33	70.30	29.70
Chile	6.23	25.28	74.72
Czech Republic	12.02	48.77	51.23
Denmark	21.93	88.97	11.03
Estonia	13.03	52.88	47.12
Finland	24.65	100	0
France	24.30	98.58	1.42
Germany	19.44	78.85	21.15
Greece	19.42	78.77	21.23
Hungary	13.84	56.15	43.85
Iceland	9.90	40.16	59.84
Ireland	8.98	36.45	63.55
Israel	11.14	45.19	54.81
Italy	20.75	84.18	15.82
Japan	16.15	65.51	34.49
Korea, South	6.74	27.33	72.67
Latvia	11.62	47.13	52.87
Lithuania	12.05	48.89	51.11
Luxembourg	17.95	72.83	27.17
Mexico	7.52	30.51	69.49
Netherlands	15.46	62.73	37.27
New Zealand*	18.93	76.80	23.20
Norway	19.12	77.57	22.43
Poland	16.44	66.68	33.32
Portugal	17.09	69.31	30.69
Slovak Republic	14.35	58.21	41.79
Slovenia	16.67	67.61	32.39
Spain	16.62	67.41	32.59
Sweden	19.54	79.27	20.73
Switzerland	13.30	53.96	46.04

TABLE A14   Government spending on social protection as % of GDP and social protection inverse, OECD countries, 2018 or latest available (*cont.*)

Country	Protection % of GDP	Protection score	Protection inverse
Turkey	12.52	50.79	49.21
United Kingdom	15.04	60.99	39.01
United States	7.54	30.59	69.41

SOURCE: OECD DATA. 2019. NATIONAL ACCOUNTS STATISTICS: NATIONAL ACCOUNTS AT A GLANCE. HTTPS://DATA.OECD.ORG/GGA/GENERAL-GOVERNMENT-SPENDING.HTM

* Social expenditure (cash benefits, direct in-kind provision of goods and services, and tax breaks with social purposes). OECD Data. 2019. https://data.oecd.org/socialexp/social-spending.htm

Protection score = 100/24.65 = 4.0567951318458418 x Protection % of GDP

Protection inverse = 100—Protection score

2   Political Measures

TABLE A15   Voter turnout, parliamentary elections, as % of voting age population, and voter
turnout inverse, OECD countries, 2019 or most recent elections

Country	Voter turnout %	Voter turnout inverse %
Australia	91.01	8.99
Austria	75.60	24.40
Belgium	88.40	11.60
Canada	67.70	32.30
Chile	46.50	53.50
Czech Republic	60.80	39.20
Denmark	84.60	15.40
Estonia	63.70	36.30
Finland	68.70	31.30
France	42.60	57.40
Germany	76.20	23.80
Greece	57.90	42.10
Hungary	69.70	30.30
Iceland	81.20	18.80
Ireland	65.10	34.90
Israel	69.80	30.20
Italy	72.90	27.10
Japan	52.70	47.30
Korea, South	58.00	42.00
Latvia*	54.58	45.42
Lithuania*	50.64	49.36
Luxembourg	89.70	10.30
Mexico	63.20	36.80
Netherlands	81.90	18.10
New Zealand	79.80	20.20
Norway	78.20	21.80
Poland	61.70	38.30
Portugal	48.60	51.40
Slovak Republic	59.80	40.20
Slovenia	52.60	47.40
Spain	71.80	28.20

TABLE A15   Voter turnout, parliamentary elections, as % of voting age population, and voter turnout inverse, OECD countries, 2019 or most recent elections (*cont.*)

Country	Voter turnout %	Voter turnout inverse %
Sweden	87.20	12.80
Switzerland	48.40	51.60
Turkey	86.20	13.80
United Kingdom	67.60	32.40
United States	56.80	43.20

SOURCE: THE INTERNATIONAL INSTITUTE FOR DEMOCRACY AND ELECTORAL ASSISTANCE. 2019. HTTPS://WWW.IDEA.INT/DATA-TOOLS/REGIONAL-ENTITY-VIEW/OECD/40

* https://www.idea.int/data-tools/data/voter-turnout
Voter turnout inverse % = 100—Voter turnout %

TABLE A16   Voice and accountability ranking and voice inverse, OECD countries, 2018

Country	Voice percentile rank	Voice inverse
Australia	95.57	4.43
Austria	93.10	6.90
Belgium	94.09	5.91
Canada	96.06	3.94
Chile	82.27	17.73
Czech Republic	78.33	21.67
Denmark	98.03	1.97
Estonia	89.66	10.34
Finland	98.52	1.48
France	88.18	11.82
Germany	95.07	4.93
Greece	75.37	24.63
Hungary	58.62	41.38
Iceland	94.58	5.42
Ireland	92.12	7.88
Israel	69.95	30.05
Italy	81.77	18.23
Japan	80.30	19.70
Korea, South	73.89	26.11
Latvia	74.88	25.12
Lithuania	77.83	22.17
Luxembourg	96.55	3.45
Mexico	45.81	54.19
Netherlands	97.04	2.96
New Zealand	99.51	.49
Norway	100.00	0
Poland	71.92	28.08
Portugal	88.67	1.33
Slovak Republic	76.85	23.15
Slovenia	79.31	20.69
Spain	82.76	17.24
Sweden	97.54	2.46
Switzerland	99.01	.99
Turkey	25.12	74.88

TABLE A16   Voice and accountability ranking and voice inverse, OECD countries, 2018 (*cont.*)

Country	Voice percentile rank	Voice inverse
United Kingdom	93.60	6.40
United States	81.28	18.72

SOURCE: WORLD BANK, THE WORLDWIDE GOVERNANCE INDICATORS (WGI). 2018. HTTPS:// INFO.WORLDBANK.ORG/GOVERNANCE/WGI/

Percentile rank among all countries (ranges from 0 (lowest) to 100 (highest) rank)

Voice and accountability 'reflects perceptions of the extent to which a country's citizens are able to participate in selecting their government, as well as freedom of expression, freedom of association, and a free media' (WGI)

'The worldwide governance indicators (WGI) are a research dataset summarizing the views on the quality of governance provided by a large number of enterprise, citizen and expert survey respondents in industrial and developing countries. these data are gathered from a number of survey institutes, think tanks, non-governmental organizations, international organizations, and private sector firms. the worldwide governance indicators (WGI) project reports aggregate and individual governance indicators for over 200 countries and territories over the period 1996–2018, for six dimensions of governance: voice and accountability, political stability and absence of violence, government effectiveness, regulatory quality, rule of law and control of corruption. these aggregate indicators combine the views of a large number of enterprise, citizen and expert survey respondents in industrial and developing countries. they are based on over 30 individual data sources produced by a variety of survey institutes, think tanks, non-governmental organizations, international organizations, and private sector firms' (WGI).

Voice inverse = 100—Voice percentile rank

TABLE A17   Constraints on government powers and constraints inverse, OECD countries, 2018

Country	Factor score x 100	Factor score inverse
Australia	83	17
Austria	84	16
Belgium	83	17
Canada	85	15
Chile	72	28
Czech Republic	73	27
Denmark	95	5
Estonia	84	16
Finland	92	8
France	74	26
Germany	85	15
Greece	69	31
Hungary	41	59
Iceland*	94	6
Ireland*	84	16
Israel*	69	31
Italy	71	29
Japan	71	29
Korea, South	72	28
Latvia*	73	27
Lithuania*	73	27
Luxembourg*	83	17
Mexico	47	53
Netherlands	86	14
New Zealand	85	15
Norway	94	6
Poland	58	42
Portugal	79	21
Slovak Republic*	73	27
Slovenia	65	35
Spain	72	28
Sweden	87	13
Switzerland*	87	13
Turkey	29	71

TABLE A17   Constraints on government powers and constraints inverse, OECD countries, 2018 (*cont.*)

Country	Factor score x 100	Factor score inverse
United Kingdom	84	16
United States	73	27

SOURCE: THE WORLD JUSTICE PROJECT RULE OF LAW INDEX 2017–2018 HTTPS://WORLD-JUSTICEPROJECT.ORG/SITES/DEFAULT/FILES/DOCUMENTS/WJP-ROLI-2019-SINGLE%20 PAGE%20VIEW-REDUCED_0.PDF

Constraints on government powers' factor score 'measures the extent to which those who govern are bound by law. It comprises the means, both constitutional and institutional, by which the powers of the government and its officials and agents are limited and held accountable under the law. It also includes non-governmental checks on the government's power, such as a free and independent press' (The World Justice Project Rule of Law Index, p. 36).
* Estimated values from comparable countries: Iceland from Norway, Ireland from United Kingdom, Israel from Greece, Latvia and Lithuania from Estonia, Luxembourg from Belgium, Slovak Republic from Czech Republic, Switzerland from Germany.
Factor score inverse = 100—Factor score x 100

TABLE A18   Electoral process and political pluralism indexes and inverse, OECD
             countries, 2019

Country	Pluralism index x 10	Pluralism inverse
Australia	100.00	0
Austria	95.80	4.20
Belgium	95.80	4.20
Canada	95.80	4.20
Chile	95.80	4.20
Czech Republic	95.80	4.20
Denmark	100.00	0
Estonia	95.80	4.20
Finland	100.00	0
France	95.80	4.20
Germany	95.80	4.20
Greece	95.80	4.20
Hungary	87.50	12.50
Iceland	100.00	0
Ireland	100.00	0
Israel	91.70	8.30
Italy	95.80	4.20
Japan	87.50	12.50
Korea, South	91.70	8.30
Latvia	95.80	4.20
Lithuania	95.80	4.20
Luxembourg	100.00	0
Mexico	78.30	21.70
Netherlands	95.80	4.20
New Zealand	100.00	0
Norway	100.00	0
Poland	91.70	8.30
Portugal	95.80	4.20
Slovak Republic	95.80	4.20
Slovenia	95.80	4.20
Spain	95.80	4.20
Sweden	95.80	4.20
Switzerland	95.80	4.20

TABLE A18 Electoral process and political pluralism indexes and inverse, OECD countries, 2019 (*cont.*)

Country	Pluralism index x 10	Pluralism inverse
Turkey	30.80	69.20
United Kingdom	95.80	4.20
United States	91.70	8.30

SOURCE: THE ECONOMIST INTELLIGENCE UNIT. 2019, DEMOCRACY INDEX 2019.

* Electoral process and pluralism pertain to:

1. Are elections for the national legislature and head of government free?
2. Are elections for the national legislature and head of government fair?
3. Are municipal elections both free and fair?
4. Is there universal suffrage for all adults?
5. Can citizens cast their vote free of significant threats to their security from state or non-state bodies?
6. Do laws provide for broadly equal campaigning opportunities?
7. Is the process of financing political parties transparent and generally accepted?
8. Following elections, are the constitutional mechanisms for the orderly transfer of power from one government to another clear, established and accepted?
9. Are citizens free to form political parties that are independent of the government?
10. Do opposition parties have a realistic prospect of achieving government?
11. Is potential access to public office open to all citizens?
12. Are citizens allowed to form political and civic organisations, free of state interference and surveillance? (Democracy Index 2019, pp. 55–56)

Pluralism inverse = 100—Pluralism index

TABLE A19   Political stability and absence of violence/terrorism, percentile ranks and inverse,
            OECD countries, 2018

Country	Stability percentile rank	Stability inverse
Australia	82.86	17.14
Austria	80.95	19.05
Belgium	59.52	40.48
Canada	84.76	15.24
Chile	61.43	38.57
Czech Republic	87.14	12.86
Denmark	82.38	17.62
Estonia	66.19	33.81
Finland	81.90	18.10
France	51.90	48.10
Germany	66.67	33.33
Greece	50.00	50.00
Hungary	73.33	26.67
Iceland	96.67	3.33
Ireland	86.19	13.81
Israel	15.24	84.76
Italy	57.62	42.38
Japan	88.10	11.90
Korea, South	65.24	34.76
Latvia	60.95	39.05
Lithuania	72.86	27.14
Luxembourg	96.19	3.81
Mexico	25.71	74.29
Netherlands	78.10	21.90
New Zealand	99.05	.95
Norway	90.48	9.52
Poland	65.71	34.29
Portugal	89.52	10.48
Slovak Republic	72.38	27.62
Slovenia	80.00	20.00
Spain	55.24	44.76
Sweden	80.48	19.52
Switzerland	95.24	4.76
Turkey	10.00	90.00

TABLE A19 Political stability and absence of violence/terrorism, percentile ranks and inverse, OECD countries, 2018 (*cont.*)

Country	Stability percentile rank	Stability inverse
United Kingdom	48.10	51.90
United States	61.90	38.10

SOURCE: THE WORLD BANK WORLDWIDE GOVERNANCE INDICATORS (WGI) PROJECT. HTTP://INFO.WORLDBANK.ORG/GOVERNANCE/WGI/

Percentile rank among all countries (ranges from 0 (lowest) to 100 (highest) rank)
'Political stability and absence of violence/terrorism measures perceptions of the likelihood of political instability and/or politically-motivated violence, including terrorism' (WGI).
Stability inverse = 100—Stability percentile rank

TABLE A20   Rule of law percentile ranks and inverse, OECD countries, 2018

Country	Rule of law percentile rank	Rule of law inverse
Australia	92.79	7.21
Austria	97.60	2.40
Belgium	88.46	11.54
Canada	94.71	5.29
Chile	83.65	16.35
Czech Republic	81.73	18.27
Denmark	96.63	3.37
Estonia	86.54	13.46
Finland	100.00	0
France	88.94	11.06
Germany	91.35	8.65
Greece	59.13	40.87
Hungary	72.12	27.88
Iceland	93.27	6.73
Ireland	89.90	10.10
Israel	80.77	19.23
Italy	61.54	38.46
Japan	90.38	9.62
Korea, South	86.06	13.94
Latvia	79.81	20.19
Lithuania	79.33	20.67
Luxembourg	95.67	4.33
Mexico	27.40	72.60
Netherlands	96.15	3.85
New Zealand	98.08	1.92
Norway	99.52	.48
Poland	66.83	33.17
Portugal	85.10	14.90
Slovak Republic	70.19	29.81
Slovenia	82.69	17.31
Spain	80.29	19.71
Sweden	98.56	1.44
Switzerland	99.04	.96
Turkey	42.31	57.69

TABLE A20   Rule of law percentile ranks and inverse, OECD countries, 2018 (*cont.*)

Country	Rule of law percentile rank	Rule of law inverse
United Kingdom	91.83	8.17
United States	89.42	10.58

SOURCE: THE WORLDWIDE GOVERNANCE INDICATORS (WGI) PROJECT. HTTP://INFO.WORLDBANK.ORG/GOVERNANCE/WGI/

Percentile rank among all countries (ranges from 0 (lowest) to 100 (highest) rank)
Rule of law 'reflects perceptions of the extent to which agents have confidence in and abide by the rules of society, and in particular the quality of contract enforcement, property rights, the police, and the courts, as well as the likelihood of crime and violence' (WGI),
Rule of law inverse = 100—Rule of law percentile rank

TABLE A21   Control of corruption percentile ranks and inverse, OECD countries, 2018

Country	Control of corruption percentile rank	Control of corruption inverse
Australia	92.79	7.21
Austria	91.35	8.65
Belgium	90.38	9.62
Canada	94.71	5.29
Chile	81.73	18.27
Czech Republic	69.23	30.77
Denmark	98.56	1.44
Estonia	89.90	10.10
Finland	100.00	0
France	87.98	12.02
Germany	95.19	4.81
Greece	55.77	44.23
Hungary	59.62	40.38
Iceland	93.75	6.25
Ireland	90.87	9.13
Israel	79.33	20.67
Italy	62.02	37.98
Japan	89.42	10.58
Korea, South	72.12	27.88
Latvia	64.42	35.58
Lithuania	68.75	31.25
Luxembourg	97.12	2.88
Mexico	18.75	81.25
Netherlands	96.15	3.85
New Zealand	99.52	.48
Norway	97.60	2.40
Poland	74.52	25.48
Portugal	80.29	19.71
Slovak Republic	66.35	33.65
Slovenia	80.77	19.23
Spain	72.60	27.40
Sweden	98.08	1.92
Switzerland	96.63	3.37
Turkey	43.75	56.25

TABLE A21   Control of corruption percentile ranks and inverse, OECD countries, 2018 *(cont.)*

Country	Control of corruption percentile rank	Control of corruption inverse
United Kingdom	93.27	6.73
United States	88.46	11.54

SOURCE: THE WORLDWIDE GOVERNANCE INDICATORS (WGI) PROJECT. HTTP://INFO.WORLDBANK.ORG/GOVERNANCE/WGI/

Percentile rank among all countries (ranges from 0 (lowest) to 100 (highest) rank)
Control of corruption 'reflects perceptions of the extent to which public power is exercised for private gain, including both petty and grand forms of corruption, as well as "capture" of the state by elites and private interests' (http://info.worldbank.org/governance/wgi/)
Control of corruption inverse = 100—Control of corruption percentile rank

TABLE A22   Open government factor scores and inverse, OECD countries, 2018

Country	Open government factor score x 100	Open government inverse
Australia	82	18
Austria	72	28
Belgium	77	23
Canada	81	19
Chile	72	28
Czech Republic	66	34
Denmark	86	14
Estonia	80	20
Finland	87	13
France	79	21
Germany	79	21
Greece	61	39
Hungary	46	54
Iceland*	88	12
Ireland*	80	20
Israel*	61	39
Italy	63	37
Japan	69	31
Korea, South	69	31
Latvia*	66	34
Lithuania*	66	34
Luxembourg*	77	23
Mexico	61	39
Netherlands	82	18
New Zealand	81	19
Norway	88	12
Poland	63	37
Portugal	67	33
Slovak Republic	66	34
Slovenia	65	35
Spain	70	30
Sweden	86	14
Switzerland*	79	21

TABLE A22 Open government factor scores and inverse, OECD countries, 2018 (*cont.*)

Country	Open government factor score x 100	Open government inverse
Turkey	41	59
United Kingdom	80	20
United States	77	23

SOURCE: THE WORLD JUSTICE PROJECT RULE OF LAW INDEX 2017–2018. HTTPS://WORLD-JUSTICEPROJECT.ORG/SITES/DEFAULT/FILES/DOCUMENTS/WJP-ROLI-2019-SINGLE%20 PAGE%20VIEW-REDUCED_0.PDF

Open government factor score 'measures the openness of government defined by the extent to which a government shares information, empowers people with tools to hold the government accountable, and fosters citizen participation in public policy deliberations. This factor measures whether basic laws and information on legal rights are publicized and evaluates the quality of information published by the government' (The World Justice Project Rule of Law Index 2017–2018, p. 38).

* Estimated values from comparable countries: Iceland from Norway, Ireland from United Kingdom, Israel from Greece, Latvia and Lithuania from Estonia, Luxembourg from Belgium, Slovak Republic from Czech Republic, Switzerland from Germany.

Open government inverse = 100—Open government factor score

TABLE A23   Prison population rates (per 100,000) and scores, OECD countries, 2019

Country	Prison population rate	Prison population score
Australia	169	25.80
Austria	95	14.50
Belgium	95	14.50
Canada	107	16.34
Chile	209	31.91
Czech Republic	194	29.62
Denmark	71	10.84
Estonia	182	27.79
Finland	53	8.09
France	104	15.88
Germany	77	11.76
Greece	106	16.18
Hungary	167	25.50
Iceland	37	5.65
Ireland	74	11.30
Israel	234	35.73
Italy	90	13.74
Japan	39	5.95
Korea, South	106	16.18
Latvia	179	27.33
Lithuania	221	33.74
Luxembourg	105	16.03
Mexico	158	24.12
Netherlands	63	9.62
New Zealand	199	30.38
Norway	60	9.16
Poland	189	28.85
Portugal	110	16.79
Slovak Republic	192	29.31
Slovenia	69	10.53
Spain	124	18.93
Sweden	61	9.31
Switzerland	80	12.21
Turkey	344	52.52

TABLE A23   Prison population rates (per 100,000) and scores, OECD countries, 2019 (*cont.*)

Country	Prison population rate	Prison population score
United Kingdom	134	20.46
United States	655	100.00

SOURCE: INTERNATIONAL CENTRE FOR PRISON STUDIES. 2019. THE WORLD PRISON BRIEF.
HTTPS://WWW.PRISONSTUDIES.ORG/HIGHEST-TO-LOWEST/PRISON_POPULATION_RATE?-
FIELD_REGION_TAXONOMY_TID=ALL

Prison population score = 100/655 = 0.1526717557251908 x Prison population rate

TABLE A24   Death sentences and executions numbers and scores, OECD countries, 2018

Country	Death sentences/ executions	Death sentences/ executions score
Australia	0	0
Austria	0	0
Belgium	0	0
Canada	0	0
Chile	0	0
Czech Republic	0	0
Denmark	0	0
Estonia	0	0
Finland	0	0
France	0	0
Germany	0	0
Greece	0	0
Hungary	0	0
Iceland	0	0
Ireland	0	0
Israel	0	0
Italy	0	0
Japan	135	4.96
Korea, South	61	2.24
Latvia	0	0
Lithuania	0	0
Luxembourg	0	0
Mexico	0	0
Netherlands	0	0
New Zealand	0	0
Norway	0	0
Poland	0	0
Portugal	0	0
Slovak Republic	0	0
Slovenia	0	0
Spain	0	0
Sweden	0	0
Switzerland	0	0
Turkey	0	0

TABLE A24   Death sentences and executions numbers and scores, OECD countries, 2018 (*cont.*)

Country	Death sentences/ executions	Death sentences/ executions score
United Kingdom	0	0
United States	2724	100

SOURCE: AMNESTY INTERNATIONAL. 2019. GLOBAL REPORT, DEATH SENTENCES AND EXECUTIONS 2018. HTTPS://WWW.AMNESTY.ORG/DOWNLOAD/DOCUMENTS/ ACT5098702019ENGLISH.PDF

'Recorded executions, recorded death sentences and people known to be under sentence of death at the end of 2018' (Amnesty International. 2019).

Death sentences/executions score= 100/2724 = 0.0367107195301028 x Death sentences/ executions

TABLE A25   Political terror scale and scores, OECD countries, 2018 or nearest year

Country	Terror scale level	Terror scale score
Australia	2	40
Austria	1	20
Belgium	1	20
Canada	1	20
Chile	2	40
Czech Republic	1	20
Denmark	1	20
Estonia	1	20
Finland	1	20
France	1	20
Germany	1	20
Greece	2	40
Hungary	2	40
Iceland	1	20
Ireland	1	20
Israel	4	80
Italy	2	40
Japan	1	20
Korea, South	2	40
Latvia	1	20
Lithuania	1	20
Luxembourg	1	20
Mexico	4	80
Netherlands	1	20
New Zealand	1	20
Norway	1	20
Poland	2	40
Portugal	1	20
Slovak Republic	1	20
Slovenia	1	20
Spain	2	40
Sweden	1	20
Switzerland	1	20
Turkey	4	80

TABLE A25 Political terror scale and scores, OECD countries, 2018 or nearest year *(cont.)*

Country	Terror scale level	Terror scale score
United Kingdom	1	20
United States	3	60

SOURCE: THE POLITICAL TERROR SCALE. 2019. HTTP://WWW.POLITICALTERRORSCALE.ORG/DATA/DOWNLOAD.HTML

GIBNEY, MARK, LINDA CORNETT, REED WOOD, PETER HASCHKE, DANIEL ARNON, ATTILIO PISANÒ, AND GRAY BARRETT. 2019. THE POLITICAL TERROR SCALE 1976–2018. DATE RETRIEVED, FROM THE POLITICAL TERROR SCALE WEBSITE: HTTP://WWW.POLITICALTERRORSCALE.ORG.

'The "terror" in the PTS refers to state-sanctioned killings, torture, disappearances and political imprisonment that the Political Terror Scale measures' (The Political Terror Scale).

Political Terror Scale Levels

Level Interpretation

1 Countries under a secure rule of law, people are not imprisoned for their views, and torture is rare or exceptional. Political murders are extremely rare.

2 There is a limited amount of imprisonment for nonviolent political activity. However, few persons are affected, torture and beatings are exceptional. Political murder is rare.

3 There is extensive political imprisonment, or a recent history of such imprisonment. Execution or other political murders and brutality may be common. Unlimited detention, with or without a trial, for political views is accepted.

4 Civil and political rights violations have expanded to large numbers of the population. Murders, disappearances, and torture are a common part of life. In spite of its generality, on this level terror affects those who interest themselves in politics or ideas.

5 Terror has expanded to the whole population. The leaders of these societies place no limits on the means or thoroughness with which they pursue personal or ideological goals.

Larger score from Amnesty International or Human Rights Watch

Terror scale score = 100/5 = 20 x Terror scale level

TABLE A26   Military expenditure as a percentage of GDP and scores, OECD countries, 2019

Country	Military expenditure % GDP	Military expenditure score
Australia	1.90	35.85
Austria	.70	13.21
Belgium	.90	16.98
Canada	1.30	24.53
Chile	1.80	33.96
Czech Republic	1.20	22.64
Denmark	1.30	24.53
Estonia	2.10	39.62
Finland	1.50	28.30
France	1.90	35.85
Germany	1.30	24.53
Greece	2.60	49.06
Hungary	1.20	22.64
Iceland	0	0
Ireland	.30	5.66
Israel	5.30	100.00
Italy	1.40	26.42
Japan	.90	16.98
Korea, South	2.70	50.94
Latvia	2.00	37.74
Lithuania	2.00	37.74
Luxembourg	.60	11.32
Mexico	.40	7.55
Netherlands	1.30	24.53
New Zealand	1.50	28.30
Norway	1.70	32.08
Poland	2.00	37.74
Portugal	1.90	35.85
Slovak Republic	1.80	33.96
Slovenia	1.10	20.75
Spain	1.20	22.64
Sweden	1.10	20.75
Switzerland	.70	13.21
Turkey	2.70	50.94

TABLE A26 Military expenditure as a percentage of GDP and scores, OECD countries, 2019 (*cont.*)

Country	Military expenditure % GDP	Military expenditure score
United Kingdom	1.70	32.08
United States	3.40	64.15

SOURCE: STOCKHOLM INTERNATIONAL PEACE RESEARCH INSTITUTE. 2020. MILITARY EXPENDITURE DATABASE. HTTPS://WWW.SIPRI.ORG/DATABASES/MILEX

Military expenditure score = 100/5.3 = 18.8679245283018868 x Military expenditure % GDP

3   Civil-Society Measures

TABLE A27   Personal freedom indexes and inverse, OECD countries, 2017

Country	Personal freedom index x 10	Personal freedom inverse
Australia	91.60	8.40
Austria	92.50	7.50
Belgium	90.70	9.30
Canada	92.20	7.80
Chile	84.10	15.90
Czech Republic	89.20	10.80
Denmark	92.40	7.60
Estonia	90.20	9.80
Finland	92.70	7.30
France	86.90	13.10
Germany	92.50	7.50
Greece	80.70	19.30
Hungary	80.40	19.60
Iceland	90.80	9.20
Ireland	89.00	11.00
Israel	77.00	23.00
Italy	86.70	13.30
Japan	87.00	13.00
Korea, South	88.10	11.90
Latvia	88.50	11.50
Lithuania	87.60	12.40
Luxembourg	92.60	7.40
Mexico	63.80	36.20
Netherlands	92.80	7.20
New Zealand	92.70	7.30
Norway	92.60	7.40
Poland	83.20	16.80
Portugal	90.20	9.80
Slovak Republic	85.40	14.60
Slovenia	87.80	12.20
Spain	86.90	13.10
Sweden	94.50	5.50
Switzerland	92.40	7.60

TABLE A27 Personal freedom indexes and inverse, OECD countries, 2017 (*cont.*)

Country	Personal freedom index x 10	Personal freedom inverse
Turkey	57.40	42.60
United Kingdom	88.50	11.50
United States	87.20	12.80

SOURCE: VÁSQUEZ, IAN AND TANJA PORČNIK. 2019. THE HUMAN FREEDOM INDEX: A GLOBAL MEASUREMENT OF PERSONAL, CIVIL, AND ECONOMIC FREEDOM. THE CATO INSTITUTE, THE FRASER INSTITUTE, AND THE FRIEDRICH NAUMANN FOUNDATION FOR FREEDOM.

Personal freedom inverse = 100—Personal freedom index x 10

TABLE A28   Civil liberties indexes and inverse, OECD countries, 2019

Country	Civil liberties index x 10	Civil liberties inverse
Australia	100.00	0
Austria	88.20	11.80
Belgium	85.30	14.70
Canada	97.10	2.90
Chile	91.20	8.80
Czech Republic	85.30	14.70
Denmark	91.20	8.80
Estonia	85.30	14.70
Finland	97.10	2.90
France	85.30	14.70
Germany	94.10	5.90
Greece	85.30	14.70
Hungary	70.60	29.40
Iceland	97.10	2.90
Ireland	100.00	0
Israel	58.80	41.20
Italy	79.40	20.60
Japan	88.20	11.80
Korea, South	82.40	17.60
Latvia	88.20	11.80
Lithuania	91.20	8.80
Luxembourg	97.10	2.90
Mexico	61.80	38.20
Netherlands	91.20	8.80
New Zealand	100.00	0
Norway	97.10	2.90
Poland	73.50	26.50
Portugal	91.20	8.80
Slovak Republic	79.40	20.60
Slovenia	82.40	17.60
Spain	88.20	11.80
Sweden	94.10	5.90
Switzerland	91.20	8.80
Turkey	23.50	76.50

TABLE A28 Civil liberties indexes and inverse, OECD countries, 2019 (*cont.*)

Country	Civil liberties index x 10	Civil liberties inverse
United Kingdom	91.20	8.80
United States	82.40	17.60

SOURCE: THE ECONOMIST INTELLIGENCE UNIT 2019. DEMOCRACY INDEX 2019. HTTP://
WWW.EIU.COM/HANDLERS/WHITEPAPERHANDLER.ASHX?FI=DEMOCRACY-INDEX-2019.
PDF&MODE=WP&CAMPAIGNID=DEMOCRACYINDEX2019

Civil liberties encompass: 'Is there a free electronic media? Is there a free print media? Is there freedom of expression and protest (Bar only generally accepted restrictions, such as banning advocacy of violence)? Is media coverage robust? Is there open and free discussion of public issues, with a reasonable diversity of opinions? Are there political restrictions on access to the internet? Do institutions provide citizens with the opportunity to petition government to redress grievances? The use of torture by the state. The degree to which the judiciary is independent of government influence. The degree of religious tolerance and freedom of religious expression. The degree to which citizens are treated equally under the law. Do citizens enjoy basic security? Extent to which private property rights are protected and private business Is free from undue government influence. Extent to which citizens enjoy personal freedoms. Popular perceptions on protection of human rights; Proportion of the population that think that basic human rights are well-protected. There is no significant discrimination on the basis of people's race, colour or religious beliefs. Extent to which the government invokes new risks and threats as an excuse for curbing civil liberties' (The Economist Intelligence Unit 2019, p. 62–64).
Civil liberties inverse = 100—Civil liberties index

TABLE A29   World Press freedom indexes and scores, OECD countries, 2019

Country	Press freedom inverse index	Press freedom inverse score
Australia	16.55	31.34
Austria	15.33	29.03
Belgium	12.07	22.86
Canada	15.69	29.71
Chile	25.65	48.57
Czech Republic	24.89	47.13
Denmark	9.87	18.69
Estonia	12.27	23.23
Finland	7.90	14.96
France	22.21	42.06
Germany	14.60	27.65
Greece	29.08	55.07
Hungary	30.44	57.64
Iceland	14.71	27.85
Ireland	15.00	28.40
Israel	30.80	58.32
Italy	24.90	47.15
Japan	29.36	55.60
Korea, South	24.94	47.23
Latvia	19.53	36.98
Lithuania	22.06	41.77
Luxembourg	15.66	29.65
Mexico	46.78	88.58
Netherlands	8.83	16.72
New Zealand	10.75	20.36
Norway	7.82	14.81
Poland	28.89	54.71
Portugal	12.63	23.92
Slovak Republic	23.58	44.65
Slovenia	22.31	42.25
Spain	21.99	41.64
Sweden	8.31	15.74
Switzerland	10.52	19.92
Turkey	52.81	100.00

TABLE A29   World Press freedom indexes and scores, OECD countries, 2019 (*cont.*)

Country	Press freedom inverse index	Press freedom inverse score
United Kingdom	22.23	42.09
United States	25.69	48.65

SOURCE: REPORTERS WITHOUT BORDERS. 2019. WORLD PRESS FREEDOM INDEX. HTTPS:// RSF.ORG/EN/RANKING

Inverse index is 'score on abuses and acts of violence against journalists and score on pluralism, media independence, environment and self-censorship, legislative framework, transparency, infrastructure' (Reporters without Borders).

A higher (lower) index means more (less) abuses and violence against journalists

Press freedom inverse score = 100/52.81 = 1.893580761219466 x Press freedom inverse index

TABLE A30   Fundamental human rights factor and inverse scores, OECD countries, 2018

Country	Human rights factor score x 100	Human rights inverse score
Australia	79	21
Austria	85	15
Belgium	84	16
Canada	73	27
Chile	83	17
Czech Republic	78	22
Denmark	92	8
Estonia	83	17
Finland	92	8
France	74	26
Germany	85	15
Greece	66	34
Hungary	58	42
Iceland*	90	10
Ireland*	82	18
Israel*	66	34
Italy	73	27
Japan	78	22
Korea, South	74	26
Latvia*	78	22
Lithuania*	78	22
Luxembourg*	84	16
Mexico	54	46
Netherlands	84	16
New Zealand	80	20
Norway	90	10
Poland	66	34
Portugal	79	21
Slovak Republic*	78	22
Slovenia	73	27
Spain	78	22
Sweden	86	14
Switzerland*	85	15
Turkey	32	68

TABLE A30 Fundamental human rights factor and inverse scores, OECD countries, 2018 (*cont.*)

Country	Human rights factor score x 100	Human rights inverse score
United Kingdom	82	18
United States	72	28

SOURCE: THE WORLD JUSTICE PROJECT RULE OF LAW INDEX 2017–2018. HTTPS://WORLD-JUSTICEPROJECT.ORG/SITES/DEFAULT/FILES/DOCUMENTS/WJP-ROLI-2019-SINGLE%20PAGE%20VIEW-REDUCED_0.PDF

Factor score 'recognizes that a system of positive law that fails to respect core human rights established under international law is at best "rule by law," and does not deserve to be called a rule of law system. Since there are many other indices that address human rights, and as it would be impossible for the index to assess adherence to the full range of rights, this factor focuses on a relatively modest menu of rights that are firmly established under the universal declaration of human rights and are most closely related to rule of law concerns' (The World Justice Project Rule of Law Index 2017–2018, p. 39).

* Estimated values from comparable countries: Iceland from Norway, Ireland from United Kingdom, Israel from Greece, Latvia and Lithuania from Estonia, Luxembourg from Belgium, Slovak Republic from Czech Republic, Switzerland from Germany.

Human rights inverse score = 100—Human rights factor score

TABLE A31   National privacy rankings, indexes and inverse, OECD countries, 2007

Country	Privacy score	Privacy index	Privacy inverse
Australia	2.2	70.97	29.03
Austria	2.3	74.19	25.81
Belgium	2.7	87.10	12.90
Canada	2.9	93.55	6.45
Chile*	2.2	70.97	29.03
Czech Republic	2.5	80.65	19.35
Denmark	2.0	64.52	35.48
Estonia	2.8	90.32	9.68
Finland	2.5	80.65	19.35
France	1.9	61.29	38.71
Germany	2.8	90.32	9.68
Greece	3.1	100.00	0
Hungary	2.9	93.55	6.45
Iceland	2.7	87.10	12.90
Ireland	2.5	80.65	19.35
Israel	2.2	70.97	29.03
Italy	2.8	90.32	9.68
Japan	2.2	70.97	29.03
Korea, South*	2.2	70.97	29.03
Latvia	2.2	70.97	29.03
Lithuania*	2.2	70.97	29.03
Luxembourg	2.8	90.32	9.68
Mexico	2.2	70.97	29.03
Netherlands	2.1	67.74	32.26
New Zealand	2.3	74.19	25.81
Norway	2.1	67.74	32.26
Poland	2.3	74.19	25.81
Portugal	2.8	90.32	9.68
Slovak Republic	2.1	67.74	32.26
Slovenia	2.8	90.32	9.68
Spain	2.3	74.19	25.81
Sweden	2.1	67.74	32.26
Switzerland	2.4	77.42	22.58
Turkey*	2.2	70.97	29.03

TABLE A31 National privacy rankings, indexes and inverse, OECD countries, 2007 (*cont.*)

Country	Privacy score	Privacy index	Privacy inverse
United Kingdom	1.4	45.16	54.84
United States	1.5	48.39	51.61

SOURCE: PRIVACY INTERNATIONAL. 2007. NATIONAL PRIVACY RANKING 2007.HTTP://
OBSERVATORIODESEGURANCA.ORG/FILES/PHRCOMP_SORT.PDF

* Estimated values from comparable countries: Chile and Turkey from Mexico, Lithuania from
Latvia, Korea, South from Japan.
Privacy score on 'Constitutional protection, Statutory protection, Privacy enforcement,
Identity cards and biometrics, Data-sharing, Visual surveillance, Communication intercep-
tion, Workplace monitoring, Government access to data, Communications data retention,
Surveillance of medical, financial and movement, Border and trans-border issues, Leadership,
Democratic safeguards' (Privacy International).
Higher (lower) scores, better (worse) privacy
Privacy index = 100/3/1 = 32.2580645161290323 x Privacy scores
Privacy inverse = 100—Privacy index

TABLE A32   Global Peace Index and peace inverse score, OECD countries, 2019

Country	Peace index	Peace inverse score
Australia	1.419	47.06
Austria	1.291	42.82
Belgium	1.533	50.85
Canada	1.327	44.01
Chile	1.634	54.20
Czech Republic	1.375	45.61
Denmark	1.316	43.65
Estonia	1.727	57.28
Finland	1.488	49.35
France	1.892	62.75
Germany	1.547	51.31
Greece	1.933	64.11
Hungary	1.540	51.08
Iceland	1.072	35.56
Ireland	1.390	46.10
Israel	2.735	90.71
Italy	1.754	58.18
Japan	1.369	45.41
Korea, South	1.867	61.92
Latvia	1.718	56.98
Lithuania	1.728	57.31
Luxembourg*	1.533	50.85
Mexico	2.600	86.24
Netherlands	1.530	50.75
New Zealand	1.221	40.50
Norway	1.536	50.95
Poland	1.654	54.86
Portugal	1.274	42.26
Slovak Republic	1.550	51.41
Slovenia	1.355	44.94
Spain	1.699	56.35
Sweden	1.533	50.85
Switzerland	1.383	45.87
Turkey	3.015	100.00

TABLE A32   Global Peace Index and peace inverse score, OECD countries, 2019 (*cont.*)

Country	Peace index	Peace inverse score
United Kingdom	1.801	59.73
United States	2.401	79.64

SOURCE: INSTITUTE FOR ECONOMICS AND PEACE. 2019. GLOBAL PEACE INDEX 2019. HTTP://VISIONOFHUMANITY.ORG/APP/UPLOADS/2019/06/GPI-2019-WEB003.PDF

* Estimated values from comparable countries: Luxembourg from Belgium.
A lower (higher) index indicates greater (lesser) peace in society
The Global Peace Index 'measures the state of peace using three thematic domains: the level of Societal Safety and Security; the extent of Ongoing Domestic and International Conflict; and the degree of Militarisation' (Institute for Economics and Peace).
Peace inverse score = 100/3.015 = 33.1674958540630182 x Peace index

TABLE A33   Death penalty for drug offenses, OECD countries, 2018

Country	Death penalty for drug offenses	Death penalty for drug offenses score
Australia	N	0
Austria	N	0
Belgium	N	0
Canada	N	0
Chile	N	0
Czech Republic	N	0
Denmark	N	0
Estonia	N	0
Finland	N	0
France	N	0
Germany	N	0
Greece	N	0
Hungary	N	0
Iceland	N	0
Ireland	N	0
Israel	N	0
Italy	N	0
Japan	N	0
Korea, South*	Y	100
Latvia	N	0
Lithuania	N	0
Luxembourg	N	0
Mexico	N	0
Netherlands	N	0
New Zealand	N	0
Norway	N	0
Poland	N	0
Portugal	N	0
Slovak Republic	N	0
Slovenia	N	0
Spain	N	0
Sweden	N	0
Switzerland	N	0
Turkey	N	0

TABLE A33   Death penalty for drug offenses, OECD countries, 2018 (*cont.*)

Country	Death penalty for drug offenses	Death penalty for drug offenses score
United Kingdom	N	0
United States*	Y	100

SOURCE: HARM REDUCTION INTERNATIONAL. GIADA GIRELLI. 2018. THE DEATH PEN-ALTY FOR DRUG OFFENCES: GLOBAL OVERVIEW 2018. HTTPS://WWW.HRI.GLOBAL/DEATH-PENALTY-DRUGS-2018

Harm reduction international states that the 'death penalty for drug offences is a clear violation of international human rights law. Numerous international authorities and legal scholars have reaffirmed this point, including the un human rights committee as recently as 2018'.

* Symbolic Application according to Harm Reduction International. Harm Reduction International reports that the 'USA is one of a handful of retentionist (death penalty) countries in the Americas, and the only one to execute. Federal law allows the imposition of the death penalty for trafficking of substantial quantities of controlled substances (amongst others, 60kg of heroin or 60,000kg of cannabis),399 but there is no record of a person being sentenced to death for drug offences in the country—insomuch that the provision was broadly understood as a symbolic relic. In 2018, however, President Donald Trump called for the imposition of the death penalty against drug traffickers, as part of a plan to confront the opioid crisis in the country' (Harm Reduction International, p. 37).

Death penalty for drug offenses score Y = 100, N = 0.

TABLE A34   Share of drug offenders of total prisoners, estimates, OECD countries, 2019

Country	Prisoner rate	US/Prisoner rate	% of Drug offenders (estimate)	Drug offenders score
Australia	169	3.88	5.12	25.80
Austria	95	6.89	2.88	14.50
Belgium	95	6.89	2.88	14.50
Canada	107	6.12	3.24	16.34
Chile	209	3.13	6.34	31.91
Czech Republic	194	3.38	5.88	29.62
Denmark	71	9.23	2.15	10.84
Estonia	182	3.60	5.52	27.79
Finland	53	12.36	1.61	8.09
France	104	6.30	3.15	15.88
Germany	77	8.51	2.33	11.76
Greece	106	6.18	3.21	16.18
Hungary	167	3.92	5.06	25.50
Iceland	37	17.70	1.12	5.65
Ireland	74	8.85	2.24	11.30
Israel	234	2.80	7.10	35.73
Italy	90	7.28	2.73	13.74
Japan	39	16.79	1.18	5.95
Korea, South	106	6.18	3.21	16.18
Latvia	179	3.66	5.43	27.33
Lithuania	221	2.96	6.70	33.74
Luxembourg	105	6.24	3.18	16.03
Mexico	158	4.15	4.79	24.12
Netherlands	63	10.40	1.91	9.62
New Zealand	199	3.29	6.03	30.38
Norway	60	10.92	1.82	9.16
Poland	189	3.47	5.73	28.85
Portugal	110	5.95	3.34	16.79
Slovak Republic	192	3.41	5.82	29.31
Slovenia	69	9.49	2.09	10.53
Spain	124	5.28	3.76	18.93
Sweden	61	10.74	1.85	9.31
Switzerland	80	8.19	2.43	12.21
Turkey	344	1.90	10.43	52.52

TABLE A34 Share of drug offenders of total prisoners, estimates, OECD countries, 2019 (*cont.*)

Country	Prisoner rate	US/Prisoner rate	% of Drug offenders (estimate)	Drug offenders score
United Kingdom	134	4.89	4.06	20.46
United States	655	1.00	19.86	100.00

SOURCE: THE PRISON POLICY INITIATIVE. 2020. MASS INCARCERATION: THE WHOLE PIE 2020. HTTPS://WWW.PRISONPOLICY.ORG/REPORTS/PIE2020.HTML

The prison policy initiative reports that in the us 'police, prosecutors, and judges continue to punish people harshly for nothing more than drug possession. Drug offenses still account for the incarceration of almost half a million people, and nonviolent drug convictions remain a defining feature of the federal prison system. Police still make over 1 million drug possession arrests each year, many of which lead to prison sentences. Drug arrests continue to give residents of over-policed communities criminal records, hurting their employment prospects and increasing the likelihood of longer sentences for any future offenses'.

The prison policy initiative estimates that in the US in 2020 there are 450,180 people incarcerated for drug offenses out of 2,267.000, i.e., 'almost '2.3 million people in 1,833 state prisons, 110 federal prisons, 1,772 juvenile correctional facilities, 3,134 local jails, 218 immigration detention facilities, and 80 indian country jails as well as in military prisons, civil commitment centers, state psychiatric hospitals, and prisons in the U.S. territories (at) the staggering rate of 698 per 100,000 residents'.

US drug offenders as % of total prisoners 450,180/2,267.000 = 19.86% Drug offenders as % of federal prisoners 100,000/226,000= 44.25%

% of drug offenders (estimate) = 19.86/(655/prisoner rate)

Drug offenders score = 100/19.86 = 5.0352467270896274 x % of drug offenders

4   Cultural Measures

TABLE A35   Government spending on culture as % of GDP and inverse, 2018 or latest available

Country	Spending % of GDP	Culture spending score	Culture spending inverse
Australia	.73	22.72	77.28
Austria	1.16	36.32	63.68
Belgium	1.26	39.39	60.61
Canada*	.73	22.72	77.28
Chile	.36	11.19	88.81
Czech Republic	1.50	46.88	53.12
Denmark	1.62	50.61	49.39
Estonia	1.96	61.49	38.51
Finland	1.47	46.07	53.93
France	1.38	43.31	56.69
Germany	1.05	32.94	67.06
Greece	.79	24.85	75.15
Hungary	3.19	100.00	0
Iceland	3.17	99.22.	78
Ireland	.53	16.64	83.36
Israel	1.51	47.45	52.55
Italy	.76	23.85	76.15
Japan	.39	12.19	87.81
Korea, South	.86	27.01	72.99
Latvia	1.62	50.83	49.17
Lithuania	1.11	34.88	65.12
Luxembourg	1.25	39.20	60.80
Mexico*	36	11.19	88.81
Netherlands	1.17	36.60	63.40
New Zealand*	.73	22.72	77.28
Norway	1.71	53.71	46.29
Poland	1.34	41.84	58.16
Portugal	.81	25.48	74.52
Slovak Republic	1.06	33.22	66.78
Slovenia	1.41	44.31	55.69
Spain	1.11	4.82	65.18
Sweden	1.28	40.11	59.89

TABLE A35 Government spending on culture as % of GDP and inverse, 2018 or latest available (*cont.*)

Country	Spending % of GDP	Culture spending score	Culture spending inverse
Switzerland	.82	25.79	74.21
Turkey**	.87	27.26	72.74
United Kingdom	.60	18.65	81.35
United States	.28	8.68	91.32

SOURCE: OECD 2019. NATIONAL ACCOUNTS AT A GLANCE. HTTPS://DATA.OECD.ORG/GGA/GENERAL-GOVERNMENT-SPENDING.HTM#INDICATOR-CHART

Includes government spending on 'recreation, culture and religion'

* Estimated from comparable countries: Canada and New Zealand from Australia, Mexico from Chile.

** https://knoema.com/OECDNA2014/national-accounts-at-a-glance-2014?tsId=1047510

Culture spending score = 100/3.191 = 31.3381385145722344 x Spending % of GDP

Culture spending inverse = 100—Culture spending score

TABLE A36   Beliefs in 'God', OECD countries, various years

Country	% 'Believing in a personal God'
Australia	28.5
Austria	27.4
Belgium*	21.5
Canada**	67.0
Chile	71.8
Czech Republic	16.1
Denmark	28.2
Estonia***	18.0
Finland***	33.0
France	18.7
Germany (West)	32.0
Greece***	79.0
Hungary	30.9
Iceland***	31.0
Ireland	64.1
Israel	66.5
Italy	54.0
Japan	24.0
Korea, South****	54.0
Latvia	38.1
Lithuania***	47.0
Luxembourg***	46.0
Mexico*****	94.0
Netherlands	24.4
New Zealand	34.2
Norway	25.7
Poland	59.6
Portugal	58.1
Slovakia	51.0
Slovenia	26.9
Spain	39.1
Sweden	19.1
Switzerland	45.0
Turkey***	94.0

TABLE A36 Beliefs in 'God', OECD countries, various years (*cont.*)

Country	% 'Believing in a personal God'
UK	26.9
United States	67.5

SOURCES: SMITH, TOM W. 2012. *BELIEFS ABOUT GOD ACROSS TIME AND COUNTRIES.* CHICAGO: NORC/UNIVERSITY OF CHICAGO.

* Clarke, Peter and Peter Beyer (eds.). 2009. *The World's Religions: Continuities and Transformations.* New York: Routledge.
** Angus Reid Institute. 2012. Public Opinion Polls. http://angusreid.org/britons-and-canadians-more-likely-to-endorse-evolution-than-americans/
*** Eurobarometer 2010. Special Eurobarometer 341, Biotechnology Report https://ec.europa.eu/commfrontoffice/publicopinion/archives/ebs/ebs_341_en.pdf
**** Estimated as equal to people with religious affiliation, Pew Research Center. 2014a. 6 Facts About South Korea's Growing Christian Population. https://www.pewresearch.org/fact-tank/2014/08/12/6-facts-about-christianity-in-south-Korea, South/
***** Pew Research Center. 2014b. Religious Beliefs. https://www.pewforum.org/2014/11/13/chapter-3-religious-beliefs/

TABLE A37   Importance of religion In daily life, OECD countries, 2018

Country	% 'Religion very important'
Australia	18
Austria	12
Belgium	11
Canada	27
Chile	41
Czech Republic	7
Denmark	9
Estonia	6
Finland	10
France	11
Germany	10
Greece	56
Hungary	14
Iceland*	19
Ireland	22
Israel	36
Italy	21
Japan	10
Korea, South	16
Latvia	11
Lithuania	16
Luxembourg*	11
Mexico	45
Netherlands	20
New Zealand*	18
Norway	19
Poland	30
Portugal	36
Slovak Republic	23
Slovenia*	12
Spain	22
Sweden	10
Switzerland	9
Turkey	68
United Kingdom	10

TABLE A37   Importance of religion In daily life, OECD countries, 2018 (*cont.*)

Country	% 'Religion very important'
United States	53

SOURCE: PEW RESEARCH CENTER 2018. RELIGIOUS COMMITMENT BY COUNTRY. HTTPS://
ASSETS.PEWRESEARCH.ORG/WP-CONTENT/UPLOADS/SITES/11/2018/06/12094011/
APPENDIX-B.PDF

* Estimated from comparable countries: Iceland from Norway, Luxembourg from Belgium, New
Zealand from Australia, Slovenia from Austria.

TABLE A38   Daily prayer, OECD countries, 2018

Country	% 'Pray daily'
Australia	18
Austria	8
Belgium	11
Canada	25
Chile	39
Czech Republic	9
Denmark	10
Estonia	9
Finland	18
France	10
Germany	9
Greece	30
Hungary	16
Iceland*	18
Ireland	19
Israel	27
Italy	21
Japan	33
Korea, South	32
Latvia	18
Lithuania	15
Luxembourg*	11
Mexico	40
Netherlands	20
New Zealand*	18
Norway	18
Poland	29
Portugal	38
Slovak Republic	31
Slovenia*	8
Spain	23
Sweden	11
Switzerland	8
Turkey	60

TABLE A38   Daily prayer, OECD countries, 2018 (*cont.*)

Country	% 'Pray daily'
United Kingdom	6
United States	55

SOURCE: PEW RESEARCH CENTER. 2018. RELIGIOUS COMMITMENT BY COUNTRY. HTTPS://
ASSETS.PEWRESEARCH.ORG/WP-CONTENT/UPLOADS/SITES/11/2018/06/12094011/
APPENDIX-B.PDF

* Estimated from comparable countries: Iceland from Norway, Luxembourg from Belgium, New Zealand from Australia, Slovenia from Austria.

TABLE A39   Public acceptance of evolution and evolution inverse, OECD countries, various
            years

Country	% Accept evolution	Evolution inverse %
Australia*	79	21
Austria	58	42
Belgium	79	21
Canada**	61	39
Chile	69	31
Czech Republic	64	36
Denmark	81	19
Estonia	63	37
Finland	63	37
France	80	20
Germany	73	27
Greece	52	48
Hungary	69	31
Iceland	82	18
Ireland	65	35
Israel***	54	46
Italy	70	30
Japan	80	20
Korea, South****	41	59
Latvia	48	52
Lithuania	50	50
Luxembourg	64	36
Mexico*****	64	36
Netherlands	69	31
New Zealand******	75	25
Norway	78	22
Poland	65	35
Portugal	64	36
Slovak Republic	58	42
Slovenia	68	32
Spain	81	19
Sweden	81	19
Switzerland	64	36

TABLE A39   Public acceptance of evolution and evolution inverse, OECD countries, various years (*cont.*)

Country	% Accept evolution	Evolution inverse %
Turkey	25	75
United Kingdom	79	21
United States*****	33	67

SOURCES: MILLER, JON. EUGENIE SCOTT, AND SHINJI OKAMOTO. 2006: PUBLIC ACCEPTANCE OF EVOLUTION. *SCIENCE* 313, 765–766.

* Australian Academy of Science. 2010. Science literacy in Australia.
** Angus Reid Polls. 2012.
*** ISSP Research Group. 2000. International Social Survey Programme.
**** IPSOS 2011. Supreme Being, The Afterlife, And Evolution. https://www.ipsos.com/en-us/news-polls/ipsos-global-dvisory-supreme-beings-afterlife-and-evolution
***** Pew Research Center 2015.
****** UMR research. 2007. Morality, Religion and Evolution. https://openparachute.files.word-press.com/2007/10/finalmorality-religion-evolution-nz_uscomparison-sep07.pdf
Evolution inverse % = 100—% Accept evolution

TABLE A40   Belief in the existence of 'Satan', OECD countries, various years

Country	% 'Believe the Devil exists'
Australia	44
Austria	23
Belgium	19
Canada	43
Chile	59
Czech Republic	13
Denmark	10
Estonia	22
Finland	41
France	20
Germany	14
Greece*	61
Hungary	24
Iceland**	10
Ireland	55
Israel**	61
Italy	40
Japan	12
Korea, South***	20
Latvia	36
Lithuania**	42
Luxembourg**	19
Mexico	53
Netherlands	18
New Zealand	30
Norway	27
Poland**	34
Portugal**	35
Slovak Republic	34
Slovenia	25
Spain	35
Sweden	16
Switzerland	28
Turkey	73

TABLE A40   Belief in the existence of 'Satan', OECD countries, various years (*cont.*)

Country	% 'Believe the Devil exists'
United Kingdom	33
United States	71

SOURCES: WORLD VALUES SURVEY. 1995–1998. WORLD VALUES SURVEY WAVE 3. HTTP://
WWW.WORLDVALUESSURVEY.ORG/WVSDOCUMENTATIONWV3.JSP
TIFFEN, RODNEY AND ROSS GITTINS. 2009. *HOW AUSTRALIA COMPARES.* MELBOURNE: CAM-
BRIDGE UNIVERSITY PRESS.

* Gallup Poll. 1968.
** Estimated from comparable countries: Iceland from Denmark, Israel from Greece, Luxembourg from Belgium, Poland from Slovak Republic, and Portugal from Spain.
For Iceland see also Lacy, Terry G. 2000. *Ring of Seasons: Iceland, Its Culture and History.* Ann Arbor: University of Michigan.
*** Estimated as equal to the percent of Protestants based on Pew Research Center. 2014a. https://www.pewresearch.org/fact-tank/2014/08/12/6-facts-about-christianity-in-south-Korea, South/

References

Abbott, Andrew. 2005. Linked Ecologies: States and Universities as Environments for Professions. *Sociological Theory* 23, 245–274.

Abrutyn, Seth. 2009. Toward a General Theory of Institutional Autonomy. *Sociological Theory* 27, 449–465.

Acemoglu, Daron. 2005. Constitutions, Politics, and Economics: A Review Essay on Persson and Tabellini's The Economic Effects of Constitutions. *Journal of Economic Literature* 43, 1025–1048.

Acemoglu, Daron. 2010. Institutions, Factor Prices, and Taxation: Virtues of Strong States? *American Economic Review* 100, 115–19.

Acemoglu, Daron and James A. Robinson. 2000. Why Did the West Extend the Franchise? Democracy, Inequality, and Growth in Historical Perspective. *Quarterly Journal of Economics* 115, 1167–1199.

Acemoglu, Daron and James A. Robinson. 2006a. *Economic Origins of Dictatorship and Democracy*. New York: Cambridge University Press.

Acemoglu, Daron and James A. Robinson. 2006b. De Facto Political Power and Institutional Persistence. *American Economic Review* 96, 325–330.

Acemoglu, Daron and James A. Robinson. 2008. Persistence of Power, Elites, and Institutions. *American Economic Review* 98, 267–293.

Acemoglu, Daron and James A. Robinson. 2013. *Why Nations Fail: The Origins of Power, Prosperity, And Poverty*. New York: Crown Business.

Acemoglu, Daron and David Autor. 2012. What Does Human Capital Do? A Review of Goldin and Katz's *The Race between Education and Technology*. *Journal of Economic Literature*, 50, 426–63.

Acemoglu, Daron and James A. Robinson. 2015. The Rise and Decline of General Laws of Capitalism. *Journal of Economic Perspectives* 29, 3–28.

Acemoglu, Daron, Simon Johnson, James Robinson, and Pierre Yared. 2008. Income and Democracy. *American Economic Review* 98, 808–42.

Acemoglu, Daron, Georgy Egorov, and Konstantin Sonin. 2009. Do Juntas Lead to Personal Rule? *American Economic Review* 99, 298–303.

Acemoglu, Daron, Georgy Egorov, and Konstantin Sonin. 2012. Dynamics and Stability of Constitutions, Coalitions, and Clubs. *American Economic Review* 102, 1446–76.

Acemoglu, Daron, Davide Ticchi and Andrea Vindigni. 2010. A Theory of Military Dictatorships. *American Economic Journal: Macroeconomics* 2, 1–42.

Acemoglu, Daron, and Pierre Yared. 2010. Political Limits to Globalization. *American Economic Review* 100, 83–88.

Acemoglu, Daron, Davide Cantoni, Simon Johnson, and James Robinson. 2011. The Consequences of Radical Reform: The French Revolution. *American Economic Review* 101, 3286–3307.

Acemoglu, Daron, Philippe Aghion, Leonardo Bursztyn, and David Hemous. 2012. The Environment and Directed Technical Change. *American Economic Review* 102, 131–66.

Acemoglu, Daron, Ufuk Akcigit, Douglas Hanley, and William Kerr. 2016. Transition to Clean Technology. *Journal of Political Economy* 124, 52–104.

Acemoglu, Daron, Georgy Egorov, and Konstantin Sonin. 2018. Social Mobility and Stability of Democracy: Reevaluating De Tocqueville, *Quarterly Journal of Economics* 133, 1041–1105.

Adamczyk, Amy and Brittany E. Hayes. 2012. Religion and Sexual Behaviors: Understanding the Influence of Islamic Cultures and Religious Affiliation for Explaining Sex Outside of Marriage. *American Sociological Review* 77, 723–746.

Adorno Theodor W. 1991. *The Culture Industry: Selected Essays on Mass Culture.* New York: Routledge.

Adorno Theodor W. 2001. *The Stars Down To Earth and Other Essays on The Irrational in Culture.* New York: Routledge.

Aghion, Philippe, Ufuk Akcigit and Peter Howitt. 2015. Lessons from Schumpeterian Growth Theory. *American Economic Review,* 105, 94–99.

Akerlof, George. 2002. Behavioral Macroeconomics and Macroeconomic Behavior. *American Economic Review* 92, 411–33.

Akerlof, George. 2007. The Missing Motivation in Macroeconomics. *American Economic Review* 97, 5–36.

Akerlof, George and Robert J. Shiller 2015. *Phishing for Phools: The Economics of Manipulation and Deception.* Princeton, NJ, US: Princeton University Press.

Allais, Maurice. 1997. An Outline of My Main Contribution To Economic Science. *American Economic Review* 87, S3-S12.

Allcott, Hunt, and Matthew Gentzkow. 2017. Social Media and Fake News in the 2016 Election. *Journal of Economic Perspectives* 31, 211–36.

Alesina, Alberto and George-Marios Angeletos. 2005. Fairness and Redistribution. *American Economic Review* 95, 960–80.

Alexander, Jeffrey. 2001. Theorizing the Modes of Incorporation: Assimilation, Hyphenation, and Multiculturalism as Varieties of Civil Participation. *Sociological Theory* 19, 237–49.

Allen, Robert C. 2008. A Review of Gregory Clark's A Farewell to Alms: A Brief Economic History of the World. *Journal of Economic Literature* 46, 946–73.

Altemeyer, Bob. 2007. *The Authoritarians.* Winnipeg: University of Manitoba.

Alvaredo, Facundo, Anthony B. Atkinson, Thomas Piketty, and Emmanuel Saez. 2013. The Top 1 Percent in International and Historical Perspective. *Journal of Economic Perspectives* 27, 3–20.

Alvaredo, Facundo, Lucas Chancel, Thomas Piketty, Emmanuel Saez, and Gabriel Zucman. 2017. 'Global Inequality Dynamics: New Findings from WID World'. *American Economic Review* 107, 404–09.

Amenta, Edwin, Chris Bonastia, and Neal Caren. 2001. US Social Policy in Comparative and Historical Perspective: Concepts, Images, Arguments, and Research Strategies, *Annual Review of Sociology* 27, 213–34.

Amenta Edwin, Neal Caren, and Sheera Joy Olasky. 2005. Age for Leisure? Political Mediation and the Impact of the Pension Movement on U.S. Old-Age Policy. *American Sociological Review* 70, 516–538.

Andreoni, James, Justin M. Rao, and Hannah Trachtman 2017. Avoiding the Ask: A Field Experiment on Altruism, Empathy, and Charitable Giving. *Journal of Political Economy* 125, 625–653.

Andrews Kenneth T. and Charles Seguin. 2015. Group Threat and Policy Change: The Spatial Dynamics of Prohibition Politics, 1890–1919. *American Journal of Sociology* 121, 475–510.

Arendt, Hannah. 1951. *The Origins of Totalitarianism.* New York: Harcourt Brace Jovanovich.

Arrow, Kenneth. 1969. A Difficulty in The Concept of Social Welfare. In Arrow, Kenneth and Tibor Scitovsky (Eds.). *Readings in Welfare Economics* (pp. 147–168). London: George Allen and Unwin.

Ashenfelter, Orley. 2012. Comparing Real Wage Rates: Presidential Address. *American Economic Review* 102, 617–42.

Atkinson, Anthony. 1997. Bringing Income Distribution in from the Cold. *The Economic Journal* 107, 297–321.

Atkinson, Anthony, Thomas Piketty, and Emmanuel Saez. 2011. Top Incomes in the Long Run of History. *Journal of Economic Literature* 49, 3–71.

Auclert, Adrien, and Matthew Rognlie. 2017. Aggregate Demand and the Top 1 Percent. *American Economic Review* 107, 588–92.

Autor, David, David Dorn, Lawrence F. Katz, Christina Patterson, and John Van Reenen. 2017. Concentrating on the Fall of the Labor Share. *American Economic Review* 107, 180–85.

Ayres, C. E. 1933. The Basis of Economic Statesmanship. *The American Economic Review* 23, 200–216.

Baker & McKenzie International. 2009. *Worldwide Guide to Trade Unions and Works Councils.* https://digitalcommons.ilr.cornell.edu/lawfirms?utm_source=digitalcommons.ilr.cornell.edu%2Flawfirms%2F49&utm_medium=PDF&utm_campaign=PDFCoverPages.

Baldassarri, Delia, and Amír Goldberg. 2014. Neither Ideologues nor Agnostics: Alternative Voters' Belief System in an Age of Partisan Politics. *American Journal of Sociology* 120, 45–95.

Baran, Paul and Paul Sweezy. 1966. *Monopoly Capital. An Essay on the American Economic and Social Order.* New York: Modern Reader Paperbacks.

Barber, William J. 1995. Chile Con Chicago: A Review Essay. *Journal of Economic Literature* 33, 1941–949.

Barnes, Barry. 2000. *Understanding Agency: Social Theory and Responsible Action*. London Sage Publications.

Barro, Robert and Rachel McCleary. 2005. Which Countries Have State Religions? *Quarterly Journal of Economics* 120, 1331–1370.

Barro, Robert and José Ursúa. 2008. Consumption Disasters in the Twentieth Century. *American Economic Review* 98, 2, 58–63.

Bartling, Björn, Roberto A. Weber, and Lan Yao. 2015. Do Markets Erode Social Responsibility? *Quarterly Journal of Economics* 130, 219–266.

Basu, Kaushik. 2018. 'Markets and Manipulation: Time for a Paradigm Shift?' *Journal of Economic Literature* 56, 185–205.

Baxter, Vern and A. V. Margavio. 2000. Honor, Status, and Aggression in Economic Exchange. *Sociological Theory* 18, 399–416.

Baudrillard, Jean. 1994. *The Illusion of the End*. Stanford University Press.

Bauman, Zygmunt. 1997. *Postmodernity and its Discontents*. New York: New York University Press.

Bauman, Zygmunt. 2001. *The Individualized Society*. Cambridge: Polity Press.

Baumer, Eric P., J. W. Andrew Ranson, Ashley N. Arnio, Ann Fulmer, and Shane De Zilwa. 2017. Illuminating a Dark Side of the American Dream: Assessing the Prevalence and Predictors of Mortgage Fraud across U.S. Counties, *American Journal of Sociology* 123, 549–603.

Baumol, William. 2000. What Marshall Didn't Know: On the Twentieth Century's Contributions to Economics. *Quarterly Journal of Economics* 115, 1–44.

Bourdieu, Pierre. 2000. Pascalian Meditations. Stanford: Stanford University Press.

Bowles, Samuel, Maurizio Franzini, and Ugo Pagano (eds.). 1999. The Politics and Economics of Power. London: Routledge.

Beck, Ulrich. 2000. *The Brave New World of Work*. Cambridge: Polity Press.

Becky, Pettit and Bruce Western. 2004. Mass Imprisonment and the Life Course: Race and Class Inequality in U.S. Incarceration, *American Sociological Review* 69, 151–169.

Béland, Daniel. 2005. Insecurity, Citizenship, And Globalization: The Multiple Faces of State Protection. *Sociological Theory* 23, 25–41.

Bénabou, Roland, and Tirole Jean. 2006. Belief in a Just World and Redistributive Politics. *Quarterly Journal of Economics* 121, 699–746.

Bénabou, Roland, Davide Ticchi and Andrea Vindigni. 2015. Religion and Innovation. *American Economic Review* 105, 346–51.

Benhabib, Jess, and Alberto Bisin. 2018. Skewed Wealth Distributions: Theory and Empirics. *Journal of Economic Literature* 56, 1261–91.

Benhabib, Jess, Alberto Bisin, and Mi Luo. 2019. Wealth Distribution and Social Mobility in the US: A Quantitative Approach. *American Economic Review* 109, 1623–47.

Bergemann, Patrick. 2017. Denunciation and Social Control. *American Sociological Review* 82, 384–406.

Berger, Daniel, William Easterly, Nathan Nunn, and Shanker Satyanath. 2013. Commercial Imperialism? Political Influence and Trade during the Cold War. *American Economic Review* 103, 863–96.

Besley, Timothy and Masayuki Kudamatsu. 2006. Health and Democracy. *American Economic Review* 96, 313–318.

Besley, Timothy, and Torsten Persson. 2009. Repression or Civil War? *American Economic Review* 99, 292–97.

Bhaskar V., Alan Manning and Ted To. 2002. Oligopsony and Monopsonistic Competition in Labor Markets. *Journal of Economic Perspectives* 16, 155–174.

Bils, Mark, Peter J. Klenow, and Benjamin A. Malin. 2018. Resurrecting the Role of the Product Market Wedge in Recessions. *American Economic Review* 108, 1118–46.

Binmore, Ken. 2001. The Breakdown of Social Contracts. In Durlauf Steven And Peyton Young (Eds.). *Social Dynamics* (pp. 213–236). Cambridge: MIT Press.

Bivens, Josh, and Lawrence Mishel. 2013. The Pay of Corporate Executives and Financial Professionals as Evidence of Rents in Top 1 Percent Incomes'. *Journal of Economic Perspectives* 27, 57–78.

Blanchard, Olivier. 2004. The Economic Future of Europe. *Journal of Economic Perspectives* 18, 3–26.

Blanchard, Olivier and Lawrence F. Katz. 1999. Wage Dynamics: Reconciling Theory and Evidence. *American Economic Review* 89, 69–74.

Blau, Francine and Kahn Lawrence 2000. Gender Differences in Pay. *The Journal of Economic Perspectives* 14, 75–99.

Blau, Judith, Peter Blau and Reid Golden. 1985. Social Inequality and the Arts. *American Journal of Sociology* 91, 309–31.

Blee, Kathleen and Kimberly Creasap. 2010. Conservative and Right-Wing Movements. *Annual Review of Sociology* 36, 269–286.

Blinkhorn, Martin (ed.). 2003. *Fascists and Conservatives*. London: Taylor & Francis.

Bloemraad, Irene, Anna Korteweg, and Gokce Yurdakul. 2008. Citizenship and Immigration: Multiculturalism, Assimilation, and Challenges to the Nation-State. *Annual Review of Sociology* 34, 153–79.

Boal, William and Michael Ransom. 1997. Monopsony in the Labor Market. *Journal of Economic Literature* 35, 86–112.

Bohm-Bawerk, Eugen. 1959. *Capital and Interest: A Critical History of Economic Theory*. South Holland: Libertarian Press.

Bolle, Friedel, Jonathan H. W. Tan and Daniel John Zizzo. 2014. Vendettas. *American Economic Journal: Microeconomics* 6, 93–130.

Bollen, Kenneth and Robert Jackman. 1985. Political Democracy and the Size Distribution of Income. *American Sociological Review* 50, 438–57.

Bonica, Adam, Nolan McCarty, Keith T. Poole, and Howard Rosenthal. 2013. 'Why Hasn't Democracy Slowed Rising Inequality?' *Journal of Economic Perspectives* 27, 103–24.

Bonikowski, Bart. 2016. Nationalism in Settled Times. *Annual Review of Sociology* 42, 427–449.

Bonikowski, Bart and Paul DiMaggio. 2016. Varieties of American Popular Nationalism. *American Sociological Review* 81, 949–980.

Borgers, Tilman. 2004. Costly Voting. *American Economic Review* 94, 57–66.

Boulding, Kenneth. 1957. A New Look at Institutionalism. *American Economic Review* 47, 1–12.

Bourdieu, Pierre. 1984. *Distinction: A Social Critique of the Judgement of Taste.* Cambridge, Mass: Harvard University Press.

Bourdieu, Pierre. 1998. *Acts of Resistance: Against the Tyranny of the Market.* New York: Free Press.

Bowles, Samuel. 1974. Economists as Servants of Power. *American Economic* Review 64, 2: 129–32.

Bowles, Samuel and Herbert Gintis. 1993. The Revenge of Homo Economicus: Contested Exchange and The Revival of Political Economy. *Journal of Economic Perspectives* 7, 83–102.

Bowles, Samuel and Herbert Gintis. 2000. Walrasian Economics in Retrospect. *Quarterly Journal of Economics* 115, 1411–1439.

Brady, David, Regina S. Baker, and Ryan Finnigan. 2013. When Unionization Disappears: State-Level Unionization and Working Poverty in the US. *American Sociological Review* 78, 872–896.

Braudel, Fernand. 1979. *Civilisation, économie et capitalisme: XVe-XVIIIe siècle.* Paris: Armand Colin.

Brender, Adi, and Allan Drazen. 2009. Consolidation of New Democracy, Mass Attitudes, and Clientelism. *American Economic Review* 99, 304–09.

Bruce, Steve. 2004. Did Protestantism Create Democracy? *Democratization* 11, 3–20.

Bruch, Sarah, Myra Marx Ferree, and Joe Soss. 2010. From Policy to Polity: Democracy, Paternalism, and the Incorporation of Disadvantaged Citizens. *American Sociological Review* 75, 205–226.

Bruni, Luigino, and Robert Sugden. 2013. Reclaiming Virtue Ethics for Economics. *Journal of Economic Perspectives* 27, 141–64.

Buchanan, James. 1975. *The Limits of Liberty: Between Anarchy and Leviathan.* University of Chicago Press.

Buchanan, James. 1991. *The Economics and the Ethics of Constitutional Order.* Ann Arbor: University of Michigan Press.

Burawoy, Michael. 1984. Karl Marx and the Satanic Mills: Factory, Politics Under Early Capitalism In England, The US, And Russia, *American Journal Of Sociology* 90, 247–282.

Burawoy, Michael. 2005. For Public Sociology. *American Sociological Review* 70, 4–28.

Burawoy, Michael and Pavel Krotov. 1992. The Soviet Transition from Socialism to
   Capitalism: Worker Control and Economic Bargaining in the Wood Industry,
   American Sociological Review 57, 16–38.

Cable, Sherry, Thomas Shriver, and Tamara Mix. 2008. Risk Society and Contested
   Illness: The Case of Nuclear Weapons Workers. *American Sociological Review* 73,
   380–401.

Campbell, Michael and Schoenfeld, Heather. 2013. The Transformation of America's
   Penal Order: A Historicized Political Sociology of Punishment. *American Journal of
   Sociology* 118, 1375–1423.

Carpenter, Christopher and Carlos Dobkin. 2011. The Minimum Legal Drinking Age
   and Public Health. *Journal of Economic Perspectives* 25, 133–56.

Cascio, Elizabeth and Ebonya Washington. 2014. Valuing the Vote: The Redistribution
   of Voting Rights and State Funds following the Voting Rights Act of 1965. *Quarterly
   Journal of Economics* 129, 379–433.

Cassel, Gustav. 1927–8. The Rate of Interest, The Bank Rate, and the Stabilization of
   Prices. *Quarterly Journal of Economics* 42, 511–29.

Centeno, Miguel. 1994. Between Rocky Democracies and Hard Markets: Dilemmas of
   the Double Transition. *Annual Review of Sociology* 20, 125–47.

Centeno, Miguel and Joseph Cohen. 2012. The Arc of Neoliberalism. *Annual Review of
   Sociology* 38, 317–340.

Chamberlin, Edward. 1957. On the Origin of Oligopoly. *The Economic Journal*, 67,
   211–218.

Chase-Dun, Christopher. 1992. *Global Formation: Studies in the World Economy.*
   Cambridge, Mass.: Blackwell.

Chetty, Raj, Nathaniel Hendren, Patrick Kline, and Emmanuel Saez. 2014. Where is the
   land of Opportunity? The Geography of Intergenerational Mobility in the United
   States. *Quarterly Journal Of Economics* 129, 1553–1623.

Cherry, Todd, Peter Frykblom, and Jason Shogren. 2002. Hardnose the Dictator.
   American Economic Review 92, 1218–21.

Clarke, Peter and Peter Beyer (eds.). 2009. The World's Religions: Continuities and
   Transformations. New York: Routledge.

Clawson, Dan and Mary Clawson. 1999. What Has Happened to the US Labor
   Movement? Union Decline and Renewal. *Annual Review of Sociology* 25, 95–120.

Cohen, Daniel. 2003. *Our Modern Times: The New Nature of Capitalism in the Information
   Age*. Cambridge, Mass. MIT Press.

Cohen, Daniel, and Olivier Jean Blanchard. 1988. What Caused the Rise of
   Conservatism: A French View. *Economic Policy* 3, 196–219.

Cole, Wade. 2005. Sovereignty Relinquished? Explaining Commitment to the
   International Human Rights Covenants, 1966–1999. *American Sociological Review*
   70, 472–495.

Collins, Randall. 1980. Weber's Last Theory of Capitalism: A Systematization. *American Sociological Review* 45, 924–42.

Collins, Randall. 1986. Is 1980s Sociology in the Doldrums? *American Journal of Sociology* 91, 1336–1355.

Collins, Randall. 1993. Maturation of the State-Centered Theory of Revolution and Ideology. *Sociological Theory* 11, 116–28.

Collins, Randall. 1988. *Theoretical Sociology*. San Diego: Harcourt Brace Jovanovich.

Commons, John. 1931. Institutional Economics. *American Economic Review* 21, 648–657.

Comte, Auguste. 2000 (1830–42). *The Positive Philosophy of Auguste Comte*. https://socialsciences.mcmaster.ca/econ/ugcm/3ll3/comte/Philosophy1.pdf

Cooney, Mark and Callie Harbin Burt. 2008. Less Crime, More Punishment. *American Journal of Sociology* 114, 491–527.

Corak, Miles. 2013. Income Inequality, Equality of Opportunity, and Intergenerational Mobility. *Journal of Economic Perspectives* 27, 79–102.

Cox, Donald. 2007. Biological Basics and the Economics of the Family. *Journal of Economic Perspectives* 21, 91–108.

Dahl, Robert. 1971. *Poliarchy: Participation and Opposition*. New Haven: Yale University Press.

Dahl, Robert. 1985. *A Preface to Economic Democracy*. Berkeley: University of California Press.

Dahrendorf, Ralph. 1959. *Class and Class Conflict In Industrial Society*. Stanford: Stanford University Press.

Dahrendorf, Ralph. 1975. *The New Liberty*. London: Routledge And Kegan Paul.

Dahrendorf, Ralph. 1979. *Life Chances. Approaches to Social and Political Theory*. Chicago: Chicago University Press.

Dal, Bó Ernesto, Frederico Finan, Olle Folke, Torsten Persson, and Johanna Rickne. 2017. Who Becomes a Politician?, *Quarterly Journal of Economics* 132, 1877–1914.

Darnell, Alfred and Darren Sherkat. 1997. The Impact of Protestant Fundamentalism on Educational Attainment. *American Sociological Review* 62, 306–15.

Davis, Kingsley and Wilbert Moore. 1945. Some Principles of Stratification. *American Sociological Review* 10, 242–249.

Dell, Melissa and Pablo Querubin. 2018. Nation Building Through Foreign Intervention: Evidence from Discontinuities in Military Strategies, *Quarterly Journal of Economics* 133, 701–764.

DellaVigna, Stefano, and Kaplan Ethan. 2007. The Fox News Effect: Media Bias and Voting. *The Quarterly Journal of Economics* 122.3: 1187–234.

Dessí, Roberta. 2008. Collective Memory, Cultural Transmission, and Investments, *American Economic Review* 98, 534–560.

Dewey, John. 1940. Freedom and Culture. London: Allen & Unwin.

DiMaggio, Paul. 1987. Classification in Art. *American Sociological Review* 52, 440–55.

Dixit, Avinash, Grossman Gene and Gul Faruk. 2000. The Dynamics of Political Compromise. *Journal of Political Economy* 108, 531–68.

Dombrowski, Daniel. 2001. *Rawls and Religion*. New York: State University Of New York Press.

Domhoff, William. 2013. *Who Rules America? Power, Politics and Social Change*. New York McGraw Hill.

Dow, Gregory K. and Reed, Clyde G. 2013. The Origins of Inequality: Insiders, Outsiders, Elites, and Commoners. *Journal of Political Economy* 121, 609–641.

Dube, Arindrajit, Ethan Kaplan, and Suresh Naidu. 2011. Coups, Corporations, and Classified Information. *Quarterly Journal of Economics* 126, 1375–1409.

Duflo, Esther. 2012. Women Empowerment and Economic Development. *Journal of Economic Literature* 50, 1051–79.

Durkheim, Emile. 1965 (1893). *The Division of Labor in Society*. New York: The Free Press.

Dustmann, Christian, Bernd Fitzenberger, Uta Schönberg, and Alexandra Spitz-Oener. 2014. From Sick Man of Europe to Economic Superstar: Germany's Resurgent Economy. *Journal of Economic Perspectives* 28, 167–88.

Earl, Jennifer, John Mccarthy, and Sarah Soule. 2003. Protest Under Fire? Explaining The Policing Of Protest. *American Sociological Review*, 68, 581–606.

Edgell, Penny. 2012. A Cultural Sociology of Religion: New Directions. *Annual Review of Sociology* 38, 247–265.

Eggertsson, Gauti B. 2008. Great Expectations and the End of the Depression. *American Economic Review* 98, 1476–1516.

Eggertsson, Gauti. 2012. Was The New Deal Contractionary?. *American Economic Review* 102, 524–55.

Einolf, Christopher. 2007. The Fall and Rise of Torture: A Comparative and Historical Analysis. *Sociological Theory* 25, 101–121.

Ellman, Matthew, and Paul Pezanis-Christou. 2010. Organizational Structure, Communication, and Group Ethics. *American Economic Review* 100, 2478–91.

Elsner, Wolfram. 2000. An Industrial Policy Agenda 2000 and Beyond—Experience, Theory and Policy, in Elsner, Wolfram and John Groenewegen (eds.), *Industrial Policies after 2000* (pp. 411–486). Boston: Kluwer.

Emerson, Michael and David Hartman. 2006. The Rise of Religious Fundamentalism. *Annual Review of Sociology* 32, 123–141.

Esping-Andersen Gosta. 2003. *Social Foundations of Postindustrial Economies*. Oxford: Oxford University Press.

Esteban, Joan, Massimo Morelli, and Dominic Rohner. 2015. Strategic Mass Killings. *Journal of Political Economy* 123, 1087–1132.

Evans, John and Michael Evans. 2008. Religion and Science: Beyond the Epistemological Conflict Narrative. *Annual Review of Sociology* 34, 87–105.

Farhi, Emmanuel, and Werning Iván. 2007. Inequality and Social Discounting. *Journal of Political Economy* 115, 365–402.

Feagin, Joe. 2001. Social Justice and Sociology: Agendas for the Twenty-First Century. *American Sociological Review* 66, 1–20.

Fearon, James 2011. Self-Enforcing Democracy. *Quarterly Journal of Economics* 126, 1661–1708.

Ferguson, Thomas, and Voth Hans-Joachim. 2008. Betting on Hitler: The Value of Political Connections in Nazi Germany. *Quarterly Journal of Economics* 123, 101–37.

Fershtman, Chaim, Kevin Murphy and Yoram Weis. 1996. Social Status, Education and Growth, *Journal of Political Economy* 104, 108–32.

Fetzer, Thiemo. 2019. Did Austerity Cause Brexit? *American Economic Review* 109, 3849–86.

Fishback, Price. 1998. Operations of Unfettered Labor Markets: Exit And Voice In American Labor Markets at the Turn of the Century. *Journal of Economic Literature* 36, 722–765.

Fischer Stanley. 2003. Globalization and Its Challenges. *American Economic Review* 93, 1–30.

Flanagan, Robert. 1999. Macroeconomic Performance And Collective Bargaining: An International Perspective. *Journal Of Economic Literature*, 37, 1150–1175.

Fligstein, Neil. 2001. *The Architecture of Markets: An Economic Sociology of 21st Century Capitalist Societies*. Princeton: Princeton University Press.

Foran, John. 1993. Theories Of Revolution Revisited: Toward A Fourth Generation. *Sociological Theory*, 11, 1-20.

Formisano, Ronald. 2015. Plutocracy in America: Baltimore: Johns Hopkins University Press.

Frank, Robert. 2007. Plutonomics. https://blogs.wsj.com/wealth/2007/01/08/pluto-nomics/.

Frey, Bruno and Alois Stutzer. 2010. *Happiness and Economics: How the Economy and Institutions Affect Human Well-Being*. Princeton: Princeton University Press.

Friedland, Roger. 2001. Religious Nationalism and the Problem of Collective Representation, *Annual Review Of Sociology* 27, 25–52.

Friedland, Roger. 2002. Money, Sex, and God: The Erotic Logic of Religious Nationalism. *Sociological Theory* 20, 381–425.

Friedman, Milton. 1982. *Capitalism and Freedom*. Chicago: University of Chicago Press.

Friedman, Milton. 1997. Economics of Crime. *Journal of Economic Perspectives* 11, 194.

Friedman, John and Richard Holden. 2008. Optimal Gerrymandering: Sometimes Pack, but Never Crack. *American Economic Review* 98, 113–144.

Fromm, Erich. 1941. *Escape from Freedom*. New York: Holt, Rinehart And Winston.

Fuchs, Victor. 1996. Economics, Values, and Health Care Reform. *American Economic Review* 86, 1–24.

Garrido, Marco. 2017. Why the Poor Support Populism: The Politics of Sincerity in Metro Manila, *American Journal of Sociology* 123, 647–685.

Gastil, Raymond. 1989. *Freedom in the World: Political Rights and Civil Liberties 1988–1989*. New York: Freedom House.

Gauchat, Gordon. 2012. Politicization of Science in the Public Sphere: A Study of Public Trust in the US, 1974 to 2010. *American Sociological Review* 77, 167–187.

Gorman, Brandon and Charles Seguin. 2018. World Citizens on the Periphery: Threat and Identification with Global Society. *American Journal of Sociology* 124, 705–761.

Gibbs Jack. 1989. Conceptualization of Terrorism. *American Sociological Review* 54, 329–40.

Gibney, Mark, Linda Cornett, Reed Wood, Peter Haschke, Daniel Arnon, Attilio Pisanò, and Gray Barrett. 2019. The Political Terror Scale 1976-2018. http://www.politicalter-rorscale.org.

Giddens, Anthony. 1979. *Central Problems in Social Theory. Action, Structure and Contradiction In Social Analysis*. Berkeley: University of California Press.

Giddens, Anthony. 1981. *A Contemporary Critique of Historical Materialism*. Berkeley: University of California Press.

Giddens, Anthony. 1984. *The Constitution of Society. Outline of the Theory of Structuration*. Berkeley: University of California Press.

Giddens, Anthony. 2000. *The Third Way: The Renewal of Social Democracy*. Malden. Blackwell Publishers.

Glaeser, Edward and Andrei Shleifer. 2002. Legal Origins. *Quarterly Journal of Economics* 117, 1193–1229.

Glaeser, Edward. 2004. Psychology and the Market. *American Economic Review* 94, 408–13.

Glaeser, Edward, Giacomo Ponzetto, and Jesse Shapiro. 2005. Strategic Extremism: Why Republicans and Democrats Divide on Religious Values. *Quarterly Journal of Economics*, 120, 1283–1330.

Glass Jennifer, Robin W. Simon, and Matthew A. Andersson. 2016. Parenthood and Happiness: Effects of Work-Family Reconciliation Policies in 22 OECD Countries, *American Journal of Sociology* 122, 886–929.

Goldberg Amir, Michael T. Hannan, and Balázs Kovács.2016. What Does It Mean to Span Cultural Boundaries? Variety and Atypicality in Cultural Consumption. *American Sociological Review* 81, 215–241.

Goldschmidt, Deborah, and Johannes F. Schmieder. 2017. The Rise of Domestic Outsourcing and the Evolution of the German Wage Structure. *Quarterly Journal of Economics* 132, 1165–1217.

Goldstein, Adam. 2012. Revenge of the Managers: Labor Cost-Cutting and the Paradoxical Resurgence of Managerialism in the Shareholder Value Era, 1984 to 2001. *American Sociological Review* 77, 268–294.

Gompers, Paul, Ishii Joy, and Andrew Metrick. 2003. Corporate Governance and Equity Prices. *Quarterly Journal of Economics* 118, 107–55.

Gorski, Philip and Gülay Türkmen-Dervişoğlu. 2013. Religion, Nationalism, and Violence: An Integrated Approach. *Annual Review of Sociology* 39, 193–210.

Grampp, William D. 2000. What Did Smith Mean by the Invisible Hand? *Journal of Political Economy* 108, 441–65.

Granovetter, Mark. 2017. *Society and Economy: Framework and Principles.* Cambridge: Harvard University Press.

Gross, Neil, Thomas Medvetz, and Rupert Russell. 2011. The Contemporary American Conservative Movement. *Annual Review of Sociology* 37, 325–354.

Gurvitch, Georges. 1945. Social Control. In Gurvitch, Georges and Wilbert Moore (eds.). *Twentieth Century Sociology* (pp. 267–296). Freeport: Books for Libraries Press.

Habermas, Jürgen. 1989. *The Structural Transformation of the Public Sphere: An Inquiry into a Category of Bourgeois Society.* Cambridge, Mass.: MIT Press.

Habermas Jürgen. 2001. *The Postnational Constellation: Political Essays.* Cambridge: MIT Press.

Hahl, Oliver, Minjae Kim, and Ezra W. Zuckerman Sivan. 2018. The Authentic Appeal of the Lying Demagogue: Proclaiming the Deeper Truth about Political Illegitimacy. *American Sociological Review* 83, 1–33.

Halac, Marina. 2012. Relational Contracts and the Value of Relationships. *American Economic Review* 102, 750–79.

Hall, Peter and David Soskice. 2001. *Varieties of Capitalism.* Oxford: Oxford University Press.

Hallock, Kevin F. 2009. Job Loss and the Fraying of the Implicit Employment Contract. *Journal of Economic Perspectives* 23, 69–93.

Hällsten, Martin and Fabian T. Pfeffer. 2017. Grand Advantage: Family Wealth and Grandchildren's Educational Achievement in Sweden. *American Sociological Review* 82, 328–360.

Hamm, Patrick, Lawrence P. King, and David Stuckler. 2012. Mass Privatization, State Capacity, and Economic Growth in Post-Communist Countries. *American Sociological Review* 77, 295–324.

Harrod, Roy. 1956. *Towards A Dynamic Economics.* London: Macmillan.

Hart, Oliver. 2017. Incomplete Contracts and Control. *American Economic Review* 107, 1731–52.

Hayek, Friedrich von. 1955. *The Counter-Revolution of Science. Studies on the Abuse of Reason.* New York: Free Press of Glencoe.

Hayek, Friedrich von. 1991. *Economic Freedom.* Oxford: Basil Blackwell.

Head, Keith, and Thierry Mayer. 2019. Brands in Motion: How Frictions Shape Multinational Production. *American Economic Review* 109, 3073–3124.

Hedges, Chris. 2006. *American Fascists: The Christian Right and the War on America.* New York Free Press.

Henrich, John, Robert Boyd, Samuel Bowles, Colin Camerer, Ernst Fehr, and Herbert Gintis (eds.). 2004. *Foundations of Human Sociality: Economic Experiments and Ethnographic Evidence from Fifteen Small-Scale Societies.* Oxford, UK: Oxford University Press.

Hicks, Alexander. 2006. Free-Market and Religious Fundamentalists versus Poor Relief. *American Sociological Review* 71, 503–510.

Hill, Steven. 2002. Fixing Elections: The Failure Of America's Winner Take All Politics. New York: Routledge.

Hirsch, Barry T. 2008. Sluggish Institutions In A Dynamic World: Can Unions And Industrial Competition Coexist? *Journal Of Economic Perspectives*, 22, 153–176.

Hirschman, Albert. 1977. *The Passions and the Interests: Political Arguments for Capitalism before its Triumph.* Princeton: Princeton University Press.

Hodgson, Geoffrey. 1999. *Economics and Utopia: Why the Learning Economy Is Not the End of History.* New York: Routledge.

Hodgson, Geoffrey. 2000. Economic Sociology-Or Econology? Economic Sociology Editorial Series http://www.Gsm.Uci.Edu/Econsoc/Essays.html

Hoff, Karla and Joseph Stiglitz. 2004. After The Big Bang? Obstacles To The Emergence Of The Rule Of Law In Post-Communist Societies. *American Economic Review*, 94, 753–63.

Hooks, Gregory and Brian McQueen. 2010. American Exceptionalism Revisited: The Military-Industrial Complex, Racial Tension, and the Underdeveloped Welfare State. *American Sociological Review* 75, 185–204.

Hout, Michael and Claude Fischer. 2002. Why More Americans Have No Religious Preference: Politics and Generations. *American Sociological Review* 67, 165–190.

Huber, Evelyne and John D. Stephens. 2005. Welfare States and the Economy. In Smelser, Neil and Richard Swedberg (eds). 2005. *The Handbook of Economic Sociology.* (pp. 552–574). Princeton: Princeton University Press.

Huber, Evelyne, François Nielsen, Jenny Pribble, and John Stephens. 2006. Politics and Inequality in Latin America and the Caribbean. *American Sociological Review* 71, 943–963.

Hung, Ho-fung and Daniel Thompson. 2016. Money Supply, Class Power, and Inflation: Monetarism Reassessed. *American Sociological Review* 81, 447– 466.

Infantino, Lorenzo. 2003. *Ignorance and Liberty.* New York: Routledge.

Isaac, Larry. 2002. To Counter the Very Devil and More: The Making of Independent Capitalist Militia in the Gilded Age. *American Journal of Sociology* 108, 53–405.

Jacobs, David, Jason Carmichael, and Stephanie Kent. 2005. Vigilantism, Current Racial Threat, and Death Sentences. *American Sociological Review* 70, 656–677.

Jacobs, David and Jonathan C. Dirlam, 2016. Politics and Economic Stratification: Power Resources and Income Inequality in the United States, *American Journal of Sociology* 122, 469–500.

Jenness, Valerie. 2004. Explaining Criminalization: From Demography and Status Politics to Globalization and Modernization. *Annual Review of Sociology* 29, 147–71.

Jomo, K. S. 2003. Rethinking Economic Discrimination. *American Economic Review* 93, 338–342.

Jouet, Mugambi. 2017. *One Nation, Divisible: Exceptional America.* Berkeley: University of California Press.

Juergensmeyer, Mark. 2003. *Terror in the Mind of God: The Global Rise of Religious Violence.* Berkeley: University of California Press.

Kalleberg, Arne. 2009. Precarious Work, Insecure Workers: Employment Relations in Transition. *American Sociological Review* 74, 11–22.

Kaplow, Louis. 2004. On the (Ir)Relevance of Distribution and Labor Supply Distortion to Government Policy. *Journal of Economic Perspectives* 18, 159–175.

Kaplow, Louis, and Shavell Steven. 2007. Moral Rules, the Moral Sentiments, and Behavior: Toward a Theory of an Optimal Moral System. *Journal of Political Economy* 115, 494–514.

Kapur, Ajay, Niall Macleod, Narendra Singh. 2005. Plutonomy: Buying Luxury, Explaining Global Imbalances, New York: Citigroup, Equity Strategy, Industry Note: October 16.

Kaufman, Jason. 2008. Corporate Law and the Sovereignty of States. *American Sociological Review* 73, 402–425.

Keesing, Roger 1981. *Cultural Anthropology: A Contemporary Perspective.* Fort Worth: Holt, Rinehart and Winston Inc.

Kentor, Jeffrey and Terry Boswell. 2003. Foreign Capital Dependence and Development: A New Direction. *American Sociological Review* 68, 301–313.

Kestnbaum, Meyer. 2009. The Sociology of War and the Military. *Annual Review of Sociology* 35, 235–54.

Keister, Lisa. 2008. Conservative Protestants and Wealth: How Religion Perpetuates Asset Poverty. *American Journal of Sociology* 113, 1237–71.

Kerrissey, Jasmine. 2015. Collective Labor Rights and Income Inequality. *American Sociological Review* 80, 626–653.

Kettler, David and Volker Meja. 1984. Karl Mannheim and Conservatism: The Ancestry of Historical Thinking. *American Sociological Review* 49, 71–85.

Keynes, John M. 1936 (1930). *A Treatise on Money.* London: Macmillan.

Keynes, John M. 1972 (1931). *Essays In Persuasion.* London: Macmillan St. Martin's Press.

Keynes, John M. 1960 (1936). *The General Theory of Employment, Interest and Money.* London: Macmillan.

Kimeldorf, Howard. 2013. Worker Replacement Costs and Unionization: Origins of the U.S. Labor Movement. *American Sociological Review* 78, 1033–1062.

King, Ryan, Michael Massoglia, and Christopher Uggen. 2012. Employment and Exile: U.S. Criminal Deportations, 1908–2005. *American Journal of Sociology* 117, 1786–1825.

King, Mervyn. 2004. The Institutions of Monetary Policy. *American Economic Review* 94, 1–13.

Knight, Frank H. 1923. The Ethics of Competition. *Quarterly Journal of Economics* 37, 579–624.

Knight, Frank H. 1960. Social Economic Policy. *The Canadian Journal of Economics and Political Science / Revue canadienne d'Economique et de Science politique* 26, 19–34.

Knight, Frank H. 1967. Laissez Faire: Pro and Con. *Journal of Political Economy* 75, 782–795.

Kohler-Hausmann, Issa. 2013. Misdemeanor Justice: Control without Conviction. *American Journal of Sociology* 119, 351–393.

Kornai, Janos. 2000. What the Change of System from Socialism to Capitalism Does and Does Not Mean. *Journal of Economic Perspectives* 14, 27–42.

Kranton, Rachel and Seth Sanders. 2017. Groupy versus Non-Groupy Social Preferences: Personality, Region, and Political Party. *American Economic Review* 107, 65–69.

Kremer, Michael. 1997. How Much Does Sorting Increase Inequality? *Quarterly Journal of Economics* 112, 115–39.

Kristal, Tali. 2010. Good Times, Bad Times: Postwar Labor's Share of National Income in Capitalist Democracies. *American Sociological Review* 75, 729–763.

Kristal, Tali. 2013. The Capitalist Machine: Computerization, Workers' Power, and the Decline in Labor's Share within U.S. Industries. *American Sociological Review* 78, 361–389.

Krugman, Paul. 2009. How Did Economists Get It So Wrong? NYT 09/02.

Ku, Agnes S. 2000. Revisiting the Notion of Public in Habermas's Theory—Toward a Theory of Politics of Public Credibility. *Sociological Theory* 18, 216–40.

Kuran, Timur. 2004. Why the Middle East is Economically Underdeveloped: Historical Mechanisms of Institutional Stagnation. *Journal of Economic Perspectives* 18, 71–90.

Kuran, Timur. 2010. Islam and Mammon: The Economic Predicaments of Islamism. Princeton: Princeton University Press.

Kuran, Timur. 2018. Islam and Economic Performance: Historical and Contemporary Links. *Journal of Economic Literature* 56 1292–1359.

Lachmann, Richard. 1990. Class Formation without Class Struggle: An Elite Conflict Theory of rhe Transition to Capitalism. *American Sociological Review* 55, 398–414.

Lacy, Terry G. 2000. *Ring of Seasons: Iceland, Its Culture and History*. Ann Arbor: University of Michigan.

Lamont, Michèle. 2018. Addressing Recognition Gaps: Destigmatization and the Reduction of Inequality. *American Sociological Review* 83, 419–444.

Lamont, Michele and Virag Molnar. 2002. The Study of Boundaries in the Social Sciences. *Annual Review of Sociology* 28, 167–95.

Lange, Oscar. *1935*. Marxian Economics and Modern Economic Theory. The *Review of Economic Studies* 2, 189–201.

La Porta, Rafael, Florencio Lopez-De-Silanes, and Andrei Shleifer. 2008. The Economic Consequences of Legal Origins. *Journal of Economic Literature* 46, 285–332.

Laski, Harold J. 1936. *The Rise of Liberalism: The Philosophy of a Business Civilization.* New York: Harper & Brothers.

Lee, Cheol-Sung. 2007. Labor Unions and Good Governance: A Cross-National, Comparative Analysis. *American Sociological Review* 72, 585–609.

Lenski, Gerhard. 1984. *Power and Privilege: A Theory of Social Stratification.* Chapel Hill: University of North Carolina Press.

Lenski, Gerhard. 1994. Societal Taxonomies: Mapping the Social Universe. *Annual Review of Sociology* 20, 1–26.

Lerner, Aba. 1955. *Economics of Control.* New York: Macmillan.

Levitt, Steven. 1997. Using Electoral Cycles in Police Hiring to Estimate the Effect of Police on Crime. *American Economic Review*, 87, 270–90.

Levy, Gilat, and Ronny Razin. 2017. The Coevolution of Segregation, Polarized Beliefs, and Discrimination: The Case of Private versus State Education. *American Economic Journal: Microeconomics* 9, 141–70.

Li, Jieli. 2002. State Fragmentation: Toward a Theoretical Understanding of the Territorial Power of the State. *Sociological Theory* 20, 139–56.

Lin, Ken-Hou and Tomaskovic-Devey, Donald. 2013. Financialization and U.S. Income Inequality, 1970–2008. *American Journal of Sociology* 118, 1284–1329.

Lindbeck, Assar, 1971. *The Political Economy of the New Left.* Harper & Row, New York.

Lindsay, Michael. 2008. Evangelicals in the Power Elite: Elite Cohesion Advancing a Movement. *American Sociological Review* 73, 60–82.

Lipset, Seymour Martin. 1955. The Radical Right: A Problem for American Democracy. *The British Journal of Sociology* 6, 176–209.

Lipset, Seymour Martin. 1996. *American Exceptionalism: A Double-Edged Sword.* New York: Norton.

Lipset, Seymour Martin and Gary Marks. 2000. *It Didn't Happen Here: Why Socialism Failed in the United States.* New York: W.W. Norton.

Llavador, Humberto and Robert J. Oxoby, 2005. Partisan Competition, Growth, and the Franchise. *Quarterly Journal of Economics* 120, 1155–189.

Lloyd, Richard. 2012. Urbanization and the Southern US. *Annual Review of Sociology* 38, 483–506.

Long, Jason, and Joseph Ferrie. 2013. Intergenerational Occupational Mobility in Great Britain and the US since 1850. *American Economic Review* 103, 1109–37.

Lucas, Jr. Robert. 2009. Trade and the Diffusion of the Industrial Revolution. *American Economic Journal: Macroeconomics* 1, 1–25.

Luhmann, Niklas. 1995. *Social Systems*. Stanford: Stanford University Press.

Lyness, Karen., Janet Gornick, Pamela Stone, and Angela Grotto. 2012. It's All About Control: Worker Control Over Schedule and Hours in Cross-National Context. *American Sociological Review* 77, 1023–1049.

Maas, Ineke and Marco H. D. van Leeuwen, 2016. Toward Open Societies? Trends in Male Intergenerational Class Mobility in European Countries during Industrialization, *American Journal of Sociology* 122, 838–885.

MacIver, R. M. 1964. *Social Causation*. New York: Harper & Row.

Mailath, George, Larry Samuelson, and Avner Shaked. 2000. Endogenous Inequality in Integrated Labor Markets with Two-Sided Search. *American Economic Review* 90, 46–72.

Mann, Michael. 2004. *Fascists*. New York: Cambridge University Press.

Mann, Michael. 2005. *The Dark Side of Democracy: Explaining Ethnic Cleansing.* New York: Cambridge University Press.

Mannheim, Karl. 1936. *Ideology and Utopia. An Introduction to the Sociology of Knowledge*. New York: Harcourt, Brace & World.

Mannheim, Karl. 1967. *Essays on the Sociology of Culture*. London: Routledge & Kegan Paul.

Mannheim, Karl. 1986. *Conservatism*. London: Routledge & Kegan Paul.

Manza, Jeff and Clem Brooks, 1997. The Religious Factor in U.S. Presidential Elections, 1960–1992; *American Journal of Sociology* 103, 38–81.

Marks, Gary, Heather Mbaye, and Hyung Min Kim. 2009. Radicalism or Reformism? Socialist Parties before World War I. *American Sociological Review* 74, 615–635.

Martin, Andrew and Marc Dixon. 2010. Changing to Win? Threat, Resistance, and the Role of Unions in Strikes, 1984–2002. *American Journal of Sociology* 116, 93–129.

Martin, Isaac. 2010. Redistributing toward the Rich: Strategic Policy Crafting in the Campaign to Repeal the Sixteenth Amendment, 1938–1958. *American Journal of Sociology* 116, 1–52.

MacLean, Nancy. 2018. *Democracy in Chains: The Deep History of the Radical Right's Stealth Plan for America*. Durham: Duke University Press.

Marcuse, Herbert. 1960 (1941) *Reason and Revolution. Hegel and the Rise of Social Theory*. Boston: Beacon Press.

Massey Douglas S. 2009. *Return of the L Word: A Liberal Vision for the New Century*. Princeton: Princeton University Press.

Mathias, Matthew D. 2013. The Sacralization of the Individual: Human Rights and the Abolition of the Death Penalty. *American Journal of Sociology* 118, 1246–1283.

Mauss, Marcel. 1967 (1925). *The Gift. Forms and Functions of Exchange in Archaic Societies*. New York: W.W. Norton & Co.

McBride, Michael. 2008. Religious Pluralism and Religious Participation: A Game Theoretic Analysis. *American Journal of Sociology* 114, 77–108.

McDonnell, Erin Metz. 2017. Patchwork Leviathan: How Pockets of Bureaucratic Governance Flourish within Institutionally Diverse Developing States. *American Sociological Review* 82, 476–510.

McGrattan, Ellen R., and Edward C. Prescott. 2014. A Reassessment of Real Business Cycle Theory. *American Economic Review* 104, 177–82.

McGuire, Martin and Mancur Olson. 1996. The Economics of Autocracy and Majority Rule: The Invisible Hand and the Use of Force. *Journal of Economic Literature* 34 (1): 72–96.

McLaughlin, Neil. 1996. Nazism, Nationalism, and the Sociology of Emotions: Escape from Freedom Revisited. *Sociological Theory*, 14, 3, 241–261.

McMurtry, John. 1999. *The Cancer Stage of Capitalism*. London: Pluto Press.

Merrill, Louis. 1945. The Puritan Policeman. *American Sociological Review* 10, 766–776.

Merton, Robert K. 1939. Review. *The Rise of Puritanism; or, the Way to the New Jerusalem as Set Forth in Pulpit and Press from Thomas Cartwright to John Lilburne and John Milton, 1570–1643.* by William Haller. *American Sociological Review* 4, 436–438.

Merton, Robert K. 1968. *Social Theory and Social Structure*. New York: The Free Press.

Merton, Robert K. 1998. Foreword. In Brinton Mary and Victor Nee (eds.). *The New Institutionalism in Sociology* (pp. xi-xiii). New York: Russel Sage Foundation.

Mesquita, Bruce Bueno de, Alastair Smith, Randolph M. Siverson and James D. Morrow. 2005. *The Logic of Political Survival*. Cambridge, Mass.: The MIT Press.

Meyer John W. and Ronald L. Jepperson. 2000. The Actors of Modern Society: The Cultural Construction of Social Agency. *Sociological Theory* 18, 100–20.

Michels, Robert. 1968 (1911). *Political Parties. A Sociological Study of the Oligarchical Tendencies of Modern Democracy*. New York: The Free Press.

Milanovic, Branko. 2014. The Return of Patrimonial Capitalism: A Review of Thomas Piketty's Capital in the Twenty-First Century. *Journal of Economic Literature* 52, 519–34.

Miller, Joanne, Kazimierz Slomczynski, and Melvyn Kohn. 1987. Authoritarianism as Worldview and Intellectual Process: Reply to Ray, *American Journal of Sociology* 93, 442–4.

Miller, Jon. Eugenie Scott, and Shinji Okamoto. 2006. Public Acceptance of Evolution. *Science* 313, 765–766.

Mills, C. Wright. 1957. *The Power Elite*. New York: Harper.

Mises, Ludwig Von. 1951. *Socialism: An Economic and Sociological Study*. New Haven: Yale University Press.

Mises, Ludwig Von. 1956. *The Anti-Capitalistic Mentality*. Princeton: Van Nostrand Co.

Mises, Ludwig Von. 1957. *Theory and History*. New Haven: Yale University Press.

Mises, Ludwig von. 1966. *Human Action. A Treatise on Economics*. Chicago: Henry Regnery Company.

Mitchell, Wesley C. 1917. Wieser's Theory of Social Economics. *Political Science Quarterly*, 32, 95–118.

Mizruchi, Mark and Linroy Marshall II. 2016. Corporate CEOs, 1890–2015: Titans, Bureaucrats, and Saviors. *Annual Review of Sociology* 42, 143–163.

Mokyr, Joel. 2009. Intellectual Property Rights, The Industrial Revolution, and the Beginnings of Modern Economic Growth. *American Economic Review* 99, 349–55.

Moore, Barrington Jr. 1993. *Social Origins of Dictatorship and Democracy*. Boston: Beacon Press.

Morck, Randall, Daniel Wolfenzon, and Bernard Yeung. 2005. Corporate Governance, Economic Entrenchment, And Growth. *Journal of Economic Literature* 43, 655–720.

Morgan Kimberly J. and Monica Prasad. 2009. The Origins of Tax Systems: A French-American Comparison. *American Journal of Sociology* 114, 1350–94.

Morrill, Calvin, Mayer N. Zald, and Hayagreeva Rao. 2003. Covert Political Conflict in Organizations: Challenges from Below. *Annual Review of Sociology* 29, 391–415.

Mosca, Gaetano. 1939. *The Ruling Class*. New York: McGraw-Hill.

Muller, Edward. 1995. Economic Determinants Of Democracy. *American Sociological Review*, 60, 966–982.

Mueller, Dennis. 1996. *Constitutional Democracy*. New York: Oxford University Press.

Mueller, Dennis. 2009. *Reason, Religion, and Democracy*. Cambridge: Cambridge University Press.

Mueller, Dennis. 2013. The State and Religion. *Review of Social Economy* 71, 1–19.

Mueller, Holger and Thomas Philippon. 2011. Family Firms and Labor Relations. *American Economic Journal: Macroeconomics* 3, 218–45.

Mulligan, Casey, Ricard Gil and Xavier Sala-i-Martin. 2004. Do Democracies Have Different Public Policies than Nondemocracies? *Journal of Economic Perspectives* 18, 51–74.

Munch, Richard. 2001. *The Ethics of Modernity: Formation and Transformation in Britain, France, Germany, and the United States*. Lanham: Rowman & Littlefield.

Murray, Joshua. 2017. Interlock Globally, Act Domestically: Corporate Political Unity in the 21st Century, American Journal of Sociology 122, 1617–1663.

Musgrave, Richard. 1997. Reconsidering the Fiscal Role of Government. *American Economic Review* 87, 156–168.

Myerson, Roger. 2008. Perspectives on Mechanism Design In Economic Theory. *American Economic Review* 98, 586–603.

Myrdal, Gunnar. 1953 (1930). *The Political Element in the Development of Economic Theory*. London: Routledge & Kegan Paul.

Naidu, Suresh and Noam Yuchtman. 2013. Coercive Contract Enforcement: Law and the Labor Market in Nineteenth Century Industrial Britain. *American Economic Review* 103, 107–44.

Nelson Julie A. and Steven M. Sheffrin. 1991. Economic Literacy or Economic Ideology?. *The Journal of Economic Perspectives* 5, 157–165.

Newman, Katherine and Rebekah Peeples Massengill. 2006. The Texture of Hardship: Qualitative Sociology of Poverty, 1995–2005. *Annual Review of Sociology* 32, 423–446.

Nickell, Stephen. 1997. Unemployment and Labor Market Rigidities: Europe Versus North America. *Journal of Economic Perspectives* 11, 55–74.

Nickell, Stephen. 2008. Is the U.S. Labor Market Really That Exceptional? A Review of Richard Freeman. *Journal of Economic Literature* 46, 384–95.

Nordhaus, William. 2019. Climate Change: The Ultimate Challenge for Economics. *American Economic Review* 109, 1991–2014.

North, Douglas. 1990. Institutions And Their Consequences For Economic Performance. In Karen Schweers Cook and Margaret Levi (Eds). *The Limits Of Rationality* (pp. 383–401). Chicago: The University Of Chicago Press.

Norris, Pippa and Ronald Inglehart. 2007. Uneven Secularization in the United States and Western Europe. In Banchoff, Thomas (ed.), *Democracy and the New Religious Pluralism* (pp. 31–58). New York: Oxford University Press.

Ó'Gráda, Cormac. 2007. Making Famine History. *Journal Of Economic Literature* 45, 5–38.

Opp, Karl-Dieter. 2011. Modeling micro-macro relationships: problems and solutions. *Journal of Mathematical Sociology* 35, 209–34.

Olson, Mancur. 2000. *Power and Prosperity: Outgrowing Communist And Capitalist Dictatorships*. New York: Basic Books.

Orren, Karen. 1991. *Belated Feudalism: Labor, the Law, and Liberal Development in the United States*. New York: Cambridge University Press.

Parkin Frank. 1980. Reply to Giddens. *Theory and Society* 9, 891–894.

Palley, Thomas I. 2006. Milton Friedman: The Great Laissez-faire Partisan. *Economic and Political Weekly* 41, 5041–5043.

Pareto, Vilfredo. 1927 (1909). *Manuel D'économie Politique*. Paris: Marcel Girard.

Pareto, Vilfredo. 1932 (1916). *Traité De Sociologie Generale*. Paris, Payot.

Pareto, Vilfredo. 1963 (1916). *The Mind and Society. A Treatise on General Sociology*. New York: Dover Publications.

Pareto, Vilfredo. 2000 (1901). *The Rise and Fall of Elites: An Application of Theoretical Sociology*. New Brunswick: Transaction Publishers.

Parsons, Talcott. 1935. Sociological Elements in Economic Thought. *Quarterly Journal of Economics* 49, 414–453.

Parsons, Talcott. 1949. *Essays in Sociological Theory*. New York: The Free Press.

Parsons, Talcott. 1951. *The Social System*. New York: The Free Press.

Parsons, Talcott. 1967. *The Structure of Social Action. A Study in Social Theory with Special Reference to a Group of Recent European Writers*. New York: McGraw-Hill.

Patriotic Millionaires. https://patrioticmillionaires.org/about/.

Perelman, Michael. 2000. *Classical Political Economy and the Secret History of Primitive Accumulation*. Durham: Duke University Press.

Peterson, Richard and Roger Kern. 1996. Changing Highbrow Taste: From Snob to Omnivore. *American Sociological Review* 61, 900–7.

Phelps, Edmund. 2013. *Mass Flourishing: How Grassroots Innovation Created Jobs, Challenge, and Change*. Princeton: Princeton University Press.

Pigou, Arthur. 1960 (1920). *Economics of Welfare*. London: Macmillan.

Piketty, Thomas, Gilles Postel-Vinay, and Jean-Laurent Rosenthal. 2006. Wealth Concentration in a Developing Economy: Paris and France, 1807–1994. *American Economic Review* 96, 236–56.

Piketty, Thomas. 2014. *Capital In The Twenty-First Century*. Cambridge: Harvard University Press.

Piketty, Thomas, Emmanuel Saez, and Gabriel Zucman, 2018. Distributional National Accounts: Methods and Estimates for the United States, *Quarterly Journal of Economics* 133, 553–609.

Piven, Frances Fox. 2008. Can Power from Below Change the World? *American Sociological Review* 73, 1–14.

Polanyi, Karl. 1944. *The Great Transformation*. New York: Farrar & Rinehart.

Popper, Karl. 1973. *The Open Society and Its Enemies*. Princeton: Princeton University Press.

Pryor, Frederic. 2002. *The Future of U.S. Capitalism*. New York: Cambridge University Press.

Putnam, Robert. 2000. *Bowling Alone: The Collapse and Revival of American Community*. New York: Simon & Schuster.

Rajan, Raghuram. 2009. Rent Preservation and the Persistence of Underdevelopment. *American Economic Journal: Macroeconomics* 1, 178–218.

Rajan, Raghuram and Luigi Zingales. 2004. *Saving Capitalism from the Capitalists*. Princeton: Princeton University Press.

Ramirez, Steven A. 2013. *Lawless Capitalism: The Subprime Crisis and the Case for an Economic Rule of Law*. New York: NYU Press.

Rao, Hayagreeva, Lori Qingyuan Yue, and Paul Ingram. 2011. Laws of Attraction: Regulatory Arbitrage in the Face of Activism in Right-to-Work States. *American Sociological Review* 76, 365–385.

Ravallion, Martin. 2018. Inequality and Globalization: A Review Essay. *Journal of Economic Literature* 56, 620–42.

Redbird, Beth and David B. Grusky. 2016. Distributional Effects of the Great Recession: Where Has All the Sociology Gone? *Annual Review of Sociology* 42, 185–215.

Riley, Dylan. 2005. Civic Associations and Authoritarian Regimes in Interwar Europe: Italy and Spain in Comparative Perspective. *American Sociological Review* 70, 288–310.

Riley, Dylan, and Juan Fernández. 2014. Beyond Strong and Weak: Rethinking Postdictatorship Civil Societies. *American Journal of Sociology* 120, 432–503.

Rodrik, Dani. 1999. Democracies Pay Higher Wages. *Quarterly Journal of Economics* 114, 707–38.

Rodrik, Dani. 2010. Diagnostics before Prescription. *Journal of Economic Perspectives* 24, 33–44.

Rodrik, Dani. 2014. When Ideas Trump Interests: Preferences, Worldviews, and Policy Innovations. *Journal of Economic Perspectives* 28, 189–208.

Roemer, John E., and Alain Trannoy. 2016. Equality of Opportunity: Theory and Measurement. *Journal of Economic Literature* 54, 1288–1332.

Roland, Gerard. 2002. The Political Economy of Transition. *Journal of Economic Perspectives* 16, 29–50.

Roth, Alvin E. 2018. Marketplaces, Markets, and Market Design. *American Economic Review* 108, 1609–58.

Ruef, Martin. 2004. The Demise of an Organizational Form: Emancipation and Plantation Agriculture in the American South, 1860–1880. *American Journal of Sociology* 109, 1365–1410.

Ruef Martin. 2014. *Between Slavery and Capitalism: The Legacy of Emancipation in the American South.* Princeton: Princeton University Press.

Ruef, Martin, Howard Aldrich and Nancy Carter. 2003, The Structure of Founding Teams: Homophily, Strong Ties, and Isolation among US Entrepreneurs. *American Sociological Review* 68, 195–222.

Ruiter Stijn and Frank van Tubergen. 2009. Religious Attendance in Cross-National Perspective: A Multilevel Analysis of 60 Countries. *American Journal of Sociology* 115, 3, 863–95.

Rutherford, Malcolm. 2001. Institutional Economics: Then and Now, *Journal of Economic Perspectives* 15, 173–194.

Rydgren, Jens. 2007. The Sociology of the Radical Right. *Annual Review of Sociology* 33, 241–62.

Saez, Emmanuel and Zucman, Gabriel. 2016. Wealth Inequality in the United States Since 1913: Evidence from Capitalized Income Tax Data. *Quarterly Journal of Economics* 131, 519–578.

Samuelson, Paul. 1964. Personal Freedoms and Economic Freedoms in the Mixed Economy. In: Cheit, E. F. (Ed.), *The Business Establishment* (pp. 193–227). New York: Wiley.

Samuelson, Paul. 1967. Marxian Economics as Economics. *The American Economic Review* 57, 616–623.

Samuelson, Paul. 1983a. *Foundations of Economic Analysis*. Cambridge, Mass.: Harvard University Press.

Samuelson, Paul. 1983b. The World Economy at Century's End. In: Tsuru, S. (Ed.), *Human Resources, Employment and Development* (pp. 58–77). Macmillan, London.

Samuelson, Paul. 1994. The Classical Classical Fallacy. *Journal of Economic Literature* 32, 620–39.

Samuelson, Paul. 2004. Where Ricardo and Mill Rebut and Confirm Arguments of Mainstream Economists Supporting Globalization. *Journal of Economic Perspectives* 18, 135–146.

Sandler, Todd. 2001. Review of *Power and Prosperity: Outgrowing Communist and Capitalist Dictatorships* by Mancur Olson, *Journal of Economic Literature* 39, 1280–1282.

Sargent, Thomas. 2008. Evolution and Intelligent Design. *American Economic Review* 98, 5–37.

Satyanath, Shanker, Nico Voigtländer, and Hans-Joachim Voth. 2017. Bowling for Fascism: Social Capital and the Rise of the Nazi Party. *Journal of Political Economy* 125, 478–526.

Savelsberg, Joachim and Ryan King. 2005. Institutionalizing Collective Memories of Hate: Law and Law Enforcement in Germany and the US. *American Journal of Sociology* 111, 579–616.

Scheler, Max. 1964 (1914). The Thomist Ethic and the Spirit of Capitalism. *Sociological Analysis* 25, 4–19.

Schelling, Thomas. 2006. An Astonishing Sixty Years: The Legacy of Hiroshima. *American Economic Review* 96, 929–937.

Schilke, Oliver and Gabriel Rossman. 2018. It's Only Wrong if It's Transactional: Moral Perceptions of Obfuscated Exchange. American Sociological Review 83, 1079–1107.

Schneiberg, Marc and Elisabeth Clemens. 2006. The Typical Tools for the Job: Research Strategies in Institutional Analysis. *Sociological Theory* 24, 195–227.

Schumpeter, Joseph. 1950. *Capitalism, Socialism and Democracy*. New York: Harper and Brothers.

Schumpeter, Joseph. 1954. *History of Economic Analysis*. New York: Oxford University Press.

Schumpeter, Joseph. 1956. *Ten Great Economists*. London: Allen And Unwin.

Schumpeter, Joseph. 1965. *Imperialism*. Cleveland: Meridian Books.

Scitovsky, Tibor. 1972. What's Wrong with the Arts Is What's Wrong with Society. *American Economic Review* 62, 62–69.

Segal, Uzi. 2000. Let's Agree that All Dictatorships Are Equally Bad. *Journal of Political Economy* 108, 569–89.

Sen, Amartya. 1995. Rationality and Social Choice. *American Economic Review* 85, 1–24.

Sen, Amartya. 1999. The Possibility of Social Choice. *American Economic Review* 89, 349–78.

Sen, Amartya. 2009. *The Idea of Justice*. Cambridge, Mass: The Belknap Press of Harvard University Press.

Shaffer, Edward. 1996. Peace, War And The Market. *The Canadian Journal Of Economics*, 29, 639–643.

Shleifer, Andrei. 2009. The Age of Milton Friedman. *Journal of Economic Literature* 47, 123–35.

Shiller, Robert. 2017. Narrative Economics. *American Economic Review* 107, 967–1004.

Simmel, Georg. 1950. (1908). *The Sociology of Georg Simmel*. New York: The Free Press.

Simmel, Georg. 1955 (1923). *Conflict. The Web of Group Affiliations*. New York: The Free Press.

Simon, Herbert. 1976. *Administrative Behavior. A Study of Decision-Making Processes in Administrative Organization*. New York: The Free Press.

Simmons, Henry. 1951. *Economic Policy for a Free Society*. Chicago: The University of Chicago Press.

Simpson, Herbert D. 1934. The Problem of Expanding Governmental Activities. *The American Economic Review* 24, 151–160.

Slater, Dan and Nicholas Rush Smith, 2016. The Power of Counterrevolution: Elitist Origins of Political Order in Postcolonial Asia and Africa. *American Journal of Sociology* 121, 1472–1516.

Smeeding, Timothy. 2006. Poor People In Rich Nations: The United States In Comparative Perspective. *Journal Of Economic Perspectives* 20, 69–90.

Smith, Adam. 1937 (1776). *An Inquiry into the Nature and Causes of the Wealth of Nations*. New York: Random House, Inc.

Smith, Tom W. 2012. *Beliefs about God across Time and Countries*. Chicago: NORC/University of Chicago.

Sombart, Werner. 1928 (1913). *Le Bourgeois: Contribution à l'histoire Morale et Intellectuelle de l'homme Économique Moderne*. Paris: Éditions Payot.

Solow, Robert M. 1963. *Capital Theory and the Rate of Return*. Amsterdam: North-Holland Pub. Co.

Solow, Robert, Alan Budd, and Christian von Weizsacker. 1987. The Conservative Revolution: a Roundtable Discussion. *Economic Policy* 2, 181–200.

Somers, Margaret and Fred Block. 2005. From Poverty to Perversity: Ideas, Markets, and Institutions over 200 Years of Welfare Debate. *American Sociological Review* 70, 260–287.

Sorokin, Pitirim. 1970. *Social and Cultural Dynamics*. Boston: Porter Sargent Publisher.

Sorokin, Pitirim. 1975. *Hunger as a Factor in Human Affairs*. Gainesville: University of Florida Press.

Squicciarini, Mara and Nico Voigtländer. 2015. Human Capital and Industrialization: Evidence from the Age of Enlightenment. *Quarterly Journal of Economics* 130, 1825–1883.

Spenkuch, Jörg L, and David Toniatti. 2018. Political Advertising and Election Results, *Quarterly Journal of Economics* 133, 1981–2036.

Spiegler, Ran. 2013. Placebo Reforms. *American Economic Review* 103, 1490–1506.

Stamatov, Peter. 2010. Activist Religion, Empire, and the Emergence of Modern Long-Distance Advocacy Networks. *American Sociological Review* 75, 607–628.

Steinberg, Marc. 2003. Capitalist Development, the Labor Process, and the Law. *American Journal of Sociology* 109, 445–95.

Steinfeld, Robert J. 2001. *Coercion, Contract, and Free Labor in the Nineteenth Century*. Cambridge: Cambridge University Press.

Steinmetz, George. 2005. Return To Empire: The New U.S. Imperialism In Comparative Historical Perspective. *Sociological Theory* 23, 339–367.

Steinmetz, George. 2008. The Colonial State as a Social Field: Ethnographic Capital and Native Policy in the German Overseas Empire before 1914. *American Sociological Review*, 73, 589–612.

Stern, Nicholas. 2013. The Structure of Economic Modeling of the Potential Impacts of Climate Change: Grafting Gross Underestimation of Risk onto Already Narrow Science Models. *Journal of Economic Literature* 51, 838–59.

Stiglitz, Joseph. 2010. Lessons from the Global Financial Crisis of 2008. *Seoul Journal of Economics* 23, 321–38.

Stiglitz, Joseph. 2012. *The Price of Inequality*. New York: W. W. Norton & Company.

Stiglitz, Joseph. 2016. How to Restore Equitable and Sustainable Economic Growth in the United States. *American Economic Review* 106, 43–47.

Sutton, John. 2000. Imprisonment and Social Classification in Five Common-Law Democracies, 1955–1985. *American Journal of Sociology* 106, 350–86.

Sutton, John. 2013. The Transformation of Prison Regimes in Late Capitalist Societies. *American Journal of Sociology* 119, 715–746.

Sutton, John and Daniel Trefler, 2016. Capabilities, Wealth, and Trade, *Journal of Political Economy* 124, 826–878.

Swedberg, Richard. 1991. *Schumpeter: A Biography*. Princeton: Princeton University Press.

Swedberg, Richard. 1998. *Max Weber and the Idea of Economic Sociology*. Princeton: Princeton University Press.

Swidler Ann. 1986. Culture in Action: Symbols and Strategies. *American Sociological Review* 51, 273–86.

Taine, Hippolyte. 1885. *Notes on England*. New York; Henry Holt and Company.

Tetlock, Philip E., Barbara A. Mellers, and J. Peter Scoblic. 2017. Sacred versus Pseudo-sacred Values: How People Cope with Taboo Trade-Offs. *American Economic Review* 107, 96–99.

Thaler, Richard H. 2018. From Cashews to Nudges: The Evolution of Behavioral Economics. *American Economic Review* 108, 1265–87.

Throsby, David. 1994. The Production and Consumption of the Arts: A View of Cultural Economics. *Journal of Economic Literature* 32, 1–29.

Tiffen, Rodney and Ross Gittins. 2009. *How Australia Compares*. Melbourne: Cambridge University Press. Gallup Poll. 1968. Gallup, Inc.: Washington, D.C.

Tilly, Charles. 2000. Processes and Mechanisms of Democratization. *Sociological Theory* 18, 1–16.

Tilman, Rick. 2001. *Ideology and Utopia in the Social Philosophy of the Libertarian Economists*. Westport: Greenwood Press.

Tirole, Jean. 2015. Market Failures and Public Policy. *American Economic Review* 105, 1665–82.

Torfason Magnus Thor and Paul Ingram. 2010. The Global Rise of Democracy: A Network Account. *American Sociological Review* 75, 355–377.

Tönnies, Ferdinand. 2001 (1887). *Community and Civil Society*. Cambridge: Cambridge University Press.

Toynbee, Arnold. 2002 (1884). *Lectures on The Industrial Revolution in England*. Cambridge: Cambridge University Press.

Trigilia, Carlo. 2002. *Economic Sociology: State, Market, and Society in Modern Capitalism*. Malden: Blackwell Publishers.

Uggen, Christopher and Jeff Manza. 2002. Democratic Contraction? Political Consequences of Felon Disenfranchisement in the US. *American Sociological Review* 67, 777–803.

Vásquez Ian and Tanja Porčnik. 2019. The Human Freedom Index: A Global Measurement Of Personal, Civil, And Economic Freedom. The Cato Institute, the Fraser Institute, and the Friedrich Naumann Foundation for Freedom.

Voas, David and Mark Chaves. 2016. Is the United States a Counterexample to the Secularization Thesis? *American Journal of Sociology* 121, 1517–1556.

Wacquant, Loÿc. 2002. Scrutinizing the Street: Poverty, Morality, and the Pitfalls of Urban Ethnography. *American Journal of Sociology* 107, 6, 1468–1532.

Wagner, David. 1997. *The New Temperance: The American Obsession with Sin and Vice*. Boulder: Westview Press.

Wagner-Pacifici, Robin and Meredith Hall. 2012. Resolution of Social Conflict. *Annual Review of Sociology* 38, 181–199.

Walder, Andrew and Qinglian Lu. 2017. The Dynamics of Collapse in an Authoritarian Regime: China in 1967. *American Journal of Sociology* 122, 1144–1182.

Wallerstein, Immanuel. 1974. *The Modern World-System*. New York: Academic Press.

Walker, Edward, Andrew Martin, and John McCarthy. 2008. Confronting the State, the Corporation, and the Academy: The Influence of Institutional Targets on Social Movement Repertoires. *American Journal of Sociology* 114, 35–76.

Webb, Sidney and Beatrice Webb. 1902. *Industrial Democracy*. London: Longmans, Green and Co.

Weber, Max. 1950 (1927). *General Economic History*. Glencoe, IL: Free Press.

Weber, Max. 1958. *From Max Weber: Essays in Sociology*. New York: Oxford University Press.

Weber, Max. 1976 (1904). *The Protestant Ethic and the Spirit of Capitalism*. New York: Charles Scribner's Sons.

Weber, Max. 1968 (1920). *Economy and Society*. New York: Bedminster Press.

Western, Bruce and Beckett, Katherine. 1999. How Unregulated Is the U.S. Labor Market? The Penal System as a Labor Market Institution. *American Journal of Sociology* 104, 1030–61.

Western, Bruce and Jake Rosenfeld. 2011. Unions, Norms, and the Rise in U.S. Wage Inequality. *American Sociological Review* 76, 513–537.

Wieser, Friedrich. 1967 (1914). *Social Economics*, New York: A. M. Kelley.

Wieser, Friedrich. 1967 (1914). *Social Economics*, New York: A. M. Kelley.

Wimmer, Andreas, Lars-Erik Cederman, and Brian Min. 2009. Ethnic Politics and Armed Conflict: A Configurational Analysis of a New Global Data Set. *American Sociological Review* 74, 316–337.

Wodtke, Geoffrey. 2016. Social Class and Income Inequality in the United States: Ownership, Authority, and Personal Income Distribution from 1980 to 2010, *American Journal of Sociology* 121, 1375–1415.

Wolff, Edward. 2002. *Top Heavy*. New York: New Press.

Wright, Erik Olin. 2002. The Shadow of Exploitation In Weber's Class Analysis. *American Sociological Review* 67, 832–53.

Wright, Erik Olin. 2013. Transforming Capitalism through Real Utopias. *American Sociological Review* 78, 1–25.

Index

absolutism   102, 186n26, 202

America post-2016   6, 26n27, 109, 127, 184, 305, 314

American exceptionalism   26, 37, 39, 59, 75, 94, 119, 123n41, 123–124, 132, 138, 151, 179, 187, 189, 195, 198, 210, 217, 232, 310

American regime   34, 38, 42, 44–45, 51, 99, 99n6, 105–106, 122–125, 145, 150, 164, 176, 202, 207, 207n7, 210, 212, 214–216, 219, 224–225, 232, 236–237

anarchy   16n4, 16–17, 18n9, 20, 20n16, 42, 42n52, 74, 81, 132, 144, 163, 168, 175, 178, 181, 189, 194, 212, 321, 323–324, 332

Anglo-Saxon   5n10, 18, 29, 36, 67, 70, 73–75, 82, 87, 91, 110, 143, 171n11, 173n14, 265n7, 295, 302–303

apologetic economics   4n8, 4–5, 19, 30, 69, 80

arbitrariness   79–80, 191n30, 246, 334

aristocracy   4n8, 20, 23t4, 23–24, 27, 29, 31–36, 39, 41, 43–44, 47, 52, 62–63, 68, 70, 75–77, 84, 86, 91, 96–99, 103, 105, 106t6, 110–111, 116, 127–131, 137, 139–140, 142, 144, 154, 163–166, 168–169, 177, 177t8, 179–181, 189, 191, 202, 205, 212, 214–215, 215t10, 220n17, 224, 229, 241, 243, 245–250, 298–300, 322, 328, 330–331

artistic liberties   234, 252, 268

arts   218t11, 219n15, 219n16, 218–220, 220n17, 222–223, 226–227, 252, 267–268, 268n9, 272t12, 272–273, 279

Australia   1n3, 35, 57, 67, 82, 151, 260–261, 264, 265n7, 268n9, 274t13, 276, 279, 281t14, 282t15, 290t16, 294, 342ta1, 344ta2, 346ta3, 348ta4, 350ta5, 352ta6, 354ta7, 356ta8, 358ta9, 360ta10, 362ta11, 364ta12, 366ta13, 368ta14, 370ta15, 372ta16, 374ta17, 376ta18, 378ta19, 380ta20, 382ta21, 384ta22, 386ta23, 388ta24, 390ta25, 392ta26, 394ta27, 396ta28, 398ta29, 400ta30, 402ta31, 404ta32, 406ta33, 408ta34, 410ta35, 411n*, 412ta36, 414ta37, 415n*, 416ta38, 417n*, 418ta39, 419n*, 420ta40

Austria   37–38, 59, 81, 136, 184, 239, 274t13, 276, 279, 281t14, 282t15, 288–289, 290t16, 290–291, 293, 296, 303–304, 308, 342ta1, 344ta2, 346ta3, 348ta4, 350ta5, 352ta6, 354ta7, 356ta8, 358ta9, 360ta10, 362ta11, 364ta12, 366ta13, 368ta14, 370ta15, 372ta16, 374ta17, 376ta18, 378ta19, 380ta20, 382ta21, 384ta22, 386ta23, 388ta24, 390ta25, 392ta26, 394ta27, 396ta28, 398ta29, 400ta30, 402ta31, 404ta32, 406ta33, 408ta34, 410ta35, 412ta36, 414ta37, 415n*, 416ta38, 417n*, 418ta39, 420ta40

authoritarianism   8n18, 11n28, 21, 47, 52, 108, 123n41, 144n61, 152, 152n69, 196, 196n36, 299n2, 302–303, 312, 328, 335

autocracy   3, 10, 11n27, 23t4, 22–31, 33–37, 39, 43–44, 46–47, 52, 68, 70, 74–75, 77, 82, 98, 103, 105–106, 106t6, 108–111, 114–115, 118n32, 120, 123n41, 126–127, 144, 149, 155, 160n81, 177t8, 176–182, 184, 189, 194–195, 207, 210, 212, 214, 215t10, 217, 219–221, 223–224, 229–231, 233–235, 241–250, 280, 284, 294, 296–297, 302–306, 309–316, 328, 330, 333, 335

Baltic states   37, 54, 56, 59, 66, 87, 171, 184, 217, 240, 286, 294, 307–308

Bible Belt   40, 42, 44–47, 51, 55–56, 64, 104, 115, 117, 117n32, 119–120, 123–124, 137, 145, 145n63, 147, 151, 171n12, 170–174, 176, 183, 185, 185n26, 187, 193, 195, 197, 203, 211–212, 214, 222, 225, 231, 236–237, 239, 254, 332

Bibliocracy   42, 47, 117, 171, 186n26, 332

board-level employee representation   65, 243, 256, 271t12, 271–272, 274, 280, 283, 285–286, 291–293, 349ta4, 349ta4

Brazil   24–25, 34, 37, 40, 81, 101, 104, 109, 126, 163, 171, 184, 187, 194, 212, 240, 296, 303–304, 310, 313–314, 316

Brexit   6, 24, 82, 101, 104, 109, 126, 134n51, 163, 171, 179, 184, 296, 303, 307, 310–311, 313–314, 316, 431

Britain   2, 5–6, 17, 24, 31, 35, 37–39, 49, 51,
    54, 64, 67, 73, 75, 81–82, 89, 94, 101, 104,
    109, 118n34, 126, 134, 143, 146, 150–151,
    153, 156, 158–159, 161, 163, 179, 182, 184,
    196n34, 218, 296–297, 303, 307, 310–311,
    313–314, 316, 321, 330, 337, 437, 440

Canada   1n3, 35–36, 57, 67, 82, 119–120, 151,
    213n13, 268n9, 269n11, 274t13, 276,
    279, 281t14, 282t15, 290t16, 294, 342ta1,
    344ta2, 346ta3, 348ta4, 350ta5, 352ta6,
    354ta7, 356ta8, 358ta9, 360ta10, 362ta11,
    364ta12, 366ta13, 368ta14, 370ta15,
    372ta16, 374ta17, 376ta18, 378ta19,
    380ta20, 382ta21, 384ta22, 386ta23,
    388ta24, 390ta25, 392ta26, 394ta27,
    396ta28, 398ta29, 400ta30, 402ta31,
    404ta32, 406ta33, 408ta34, 410ta35,
    411n*, 412ta36, 414ta37, 416ta38,
    418ta39, 420ta40
capitalism   1n1, 1–3, 3n7, 4n8, 6n14, 7n18,
    9n19, 11n27, 4–13, 13n29, 13t2, 16n3,
    17n6, 17n7, 18n10, 18n11, 18n9, 15–22,
    22n18, 23n19, 23t4, 28n30, 38n46,
    23–39, 42n51, 42n52, 41–49, 55n64,
    55n65, 58n67, 61n75, 63n77, 69n82,
    74n93, 51–78, 82n98, 80–84, 86–90,
    92–94, 96–98, 104n15, 106t6, 112n24,
    100–115, 123, 124n41, 126–128, 129n46,
    129–132, 132n49, 138n57, 134–139,
    142–144, 144n61, 144n62, 148–151, 154,
    154n73, 155n75, 155–157, 159, 162–166,
    168–170, 174–175, 177, 179–181, 183–184,
    186–187, 189, 191n31, 191–192, 195,
    197–199, 202, 204n1, 208n8, 204–215,
    217–222, 224–226, 228, 229n21, 229–234,
    236, 238, 241–254, 258n4, 280, 284–287,
    291, 293–294, 299n3, 296–304, 307–
    313, 316, 319, 324n12, 324n15, 329n32,
    321–338
  authoritarian capitalism   43–44, 87, 311,
    322–323
  crony capitalism   40, 49
  gangster capitalism   42
  global capitalism   11, 50, 89
  mafia capitalism   42–43, 47, 49, 52, 73,
    105–106, 112, 112n24, 332–333
capitalist class   1–3, 6, 16n3, 28, 62, 71, 73–74,
    76, 80, 83–85, 90, 103, 111, 113–115, 140,

    145, 169, 207, 212, 214, 224, 229, 232, 298,
    319, 322, 326, 330
capitalist democracy   x, 2n4, 2–3, 5, 8, 100,
    100n9, 104, 115, 129n45, 149, 221n17, 270,
    273, 283f2, 289, 291, 293–295, 298, 300,
    306–309, 311, 329, 334
caste   20–21, 34, 41, 70, 74, 76, 84–86, 88,
    91–92, 96, 103, 106, 113–114, 127–128,
    140, 144, 178, 189, 193, 204, 243,
    249, 328
charisma   27, 31, 297, 305
Chicago School   9, 11n27, 95, 324, 327, 340
Chile   11n27, 24, 36, 40, 42, 44–46, 49, 54,
    59, 64, 82, 87, 95, 109, 114, 126, 148, 155,
    162n2, 166, 176, 182, 184, 184n24, 187, 192,
    202, 217, 225, 239, 257, 260, 273, 274t13,
    276, 279, 281t14, 282t15, 285, 286n14,
    289, 290t16, 301, 307, 340, 342ta1,
    344ta2, 346ta3, 348ta4, 350ta5, 351n*,
    352ta6, 354ta7, 356ta8, 358ta9, 360ta10,
    362ta11, 363n*, 364ta12, 366ta13,
    368ta14, 370ta15, 372ta16, 374ta17,
    376ta18, 378ta19, 380ta20, 382ta21,
    384ta22, 386ta23, 388ta24, 390ta25,
    392ta26, 394ta27, 396ta28, 398ta29,
    400ta30, 402ta31, 403n*, 404ta32,
    406ta33, 408ta34, 410ta35, 411n*,
    412ta36, 414ta37, 416ta38, 418ta39,
    420ta40, 424
Christian Right   18, 44, 99, 99n6, 173, 187, 215,
    236, 433
circulation of elites   28, 34, 34n43, 38
civil rights   119, 146, 252
civil society   x, 9, 12t1, 11–14, 162n1, 162n2,
    163n3, 164n5, 162–172, 177t8, 177t8,
    177t8, 184n24, 175–186, 188t9, 188–191,
    193, 195, 197–198, 200–201, 204, 213–
    215, 217, 249–250, 252, 292–293, 309,
    316, 338
Civil War   25, 89, 133n49, 331, 337, 426
class system   16, 16n3
climate change   18, 216, 229, 229n22,
    231, 234
closure   26–27, 29, 37, 64–65, 67, 70, 75, 77–
    79, 84, 86, 97–98, 112, 115, 127, 137, 139,
    142–143, 152n68, 155n75, 164, 169, 176,
    178, 180, 194, 204, 206, 317
codetermination   52t5, 52–53, 65–67, 243,
    255–256, 271t12

coercion   6, 8–9, 16, 21–22, 27, 35, 46, 52t5,
    52–54, 56–58, 60, 63–67, 79–80, 88–89,
    91–95, 97, 112–113, 128–129, 131–132,
    132n49, 143–144, 146, 148–149, 152, 154,
    156–160, 164, 173, 175n18, 175n19, 178, 180,
    182–184, 189, 191n30, 195–196, 199–200,
    211, 228, 248, 299–300, 310, 320, 334
collective action   18, 57–59, 62–64, 128n44,
    184n24, 191, 229, 242, 336n52
collective bargaining   16, 52t5, 52–53, 57–64,
    67, 117n32, 191, 242, 255, 258n4, 271t12,
    271–272, 274, 280, 283, 285–287, 291–
    293, 345, 345ta2, 347ta3, 349ta4
collective bargaining power   61
communism   4, 157n77, 157–158, 287–288,
    309, 323–324, 338
competition   20, 69n84, 71, 73, 99, 101–102,
    110, 116t7, 122n40, 122–126, 130, 133, 136,
    138, 246, 324, 334
compulsion   3, 33, 35, 53, 211–213, 216, 220,
    222, 252, 320
concentration of income   77–79, 81–82
Concentration of political power   247
concentration of wealth and power   1, 1n3, 3,
    8, 71, 86, 303
Congress   32, 108, 119, 119n35, 129n45, 134–
    135, 312, 315–316
conquest   107, 152–153, 153n71, 154n73, 159
conservatism   2, 7, 7n18, 8n18, 11n27, 24–26,
    28, 28n30, 32, 36–37, 40, 43–46, 49–51,
    55n64, 54–56, 59, 64, 66, 70, 70n85,
    75–77, 81–82, 87–88, 91, 99–100, 105n17,
    107, 110, 113, 115, 117n32, 118n32, 118n34,
    121n37, 121n38, 123n41, 125n42, 125n42,
    117–126, 128, 130–131, 133–134, 136n54,
    136–137, 137n56, 139–140, 144n61,
    146n64, 148n66, 144–151, 152n69,
    155n75, 155–158, 160n81, 166n8, 163–167,
    169–172, 174–177, 182–184, 187, 190–196,
    196n34, 198n37, 205n2, 208n8, 198–209,
    211–214, 219n15, 216–233, 235–236,
    238–239, 239n31, 242–243, 245–254,
    258n4, 258n4, 265n7, 267, 283–284,
    286n14, 286–289, 292–294, 296–297,
    301–307, 309–317, 319–321, 325–326,
    333, 336n55, 337n55, 336–340
conspiracy   73, 77–79, 216, 230–231, 254, 299
Constitution   25, 107n19, 120, 173, 192, 194,
    197, 284, 305, 313, 315, 432

consumption   32, 35, 172n13, 175, 190, 192,
    196n34, 199
contagion   9, 12, 24, 53–54, 81–82, 89, 101,
    104, 109, 126, 143, 171, 184, 296, 298, 302–
    303, 306, 311, 316
contract   4n8, 21, 57–58, 58n67, 60–61, 63–
    64, 94, 262, 325, 327, 381
corporate governance   16, 19, 65, 67, 243
corruption   xi, 32, 43, 48, 52, 72–73, 102, 248,
    262, 271t12, 273, 276, 280, 284–286, 291,
    301, 373, 382ta21, 382ta21, 382–383
counterrevolution   49, 101, 207–209, 312
creationism   210, 214–216, 224, 236–239,
    253–254
criminalization   188, 188t9, 197, 199, 250–252,
    272t12
cults   18, 190n28, 230
cultural liberties   206, 218t11, 218–220, 222–
    223, 252, 267, 272t12
cultural pattern   10–11
Czech Republic   66, 268, 274t13, 276, 279,
    281t14, 282t15, 290t16, 294, 308–309,
    342ta1, 344ta2, 346ta3, 348ta4, 350ta5,
    351n*, 352ta6, 354ta7, 356ta8, 358ta9,
    360ta10, 362ta11, 364ta12, 366ta13,
    368ta14, 370ta15, 372ta16, 374ta17,
    375n*, 376ta18, 378ta19, 380ta20,
    382ta21, 384ta22, 385n*, 386ta23,
    388ta24, 390ta25, 392ta26, 394ta27,
    396ta28, 398ta29, 400ta30, 401n*,
    402ta31, 404ta32, 406ta33, 408ta34,
    410ta35, 412ta36, 414ta37, 416ta38,
    418ta39, 420ta40

Darwinism   6
death sentences   116t7, 148, 150–151, 160,
    174, 188, 199–203, 248, 250–251, 263,
    266, 271t12, 273, 276, 280, 283, 285, 389,
    389ta24
deceptions   47, 137, 258n4, 303, 308
degradation   33, 36, 43, 52, 52t5, 62, 68, 82–
    87, 89–90, 95, 128, 228, 233, 244–245,
    257–258, 300, 310
degrees of capitalist dictatorship   x, 14, 241,
    270, 272–273, 274t13, 291, 294–295, 307
demagogue   25, 28, 28n29, 31, 70, 303
deprivation   52, 52t5, 55n65, 62, 68, 81–87,
    90, 95, 222, 244–245, 257–258, 271t12,
    271t12

despotism   6, 20n16, 19–21, 25–26, 26n26,
    29, 33, 37, 54, 68, 72, 74, 76, 80, 84–86,
    91, 93, 96–99, 102–103, 105–106, 114,
    116–117, 125, 127–130, 137, 139–140, 142,
    144, 153, 159, 163, 165–166, 168–169, 189,
    191, 191n30, 193, 198, 201–202, 204–206,
    212–214, 223–224, 228, 235, 238–239,
    300, 322, 326, 328, 332
detention   147, 149, 199, 391, 409
distribution   4n8, 18n10, 18–19, 52t5, 69n82,
    70n85, 68–71, 74–84, 86, 90–92, 95, 102,
    104–105, 127, 131, 141–143, 154, 191n30,
    244, 256–257, 271t12, 299, 319–323, 325,
    335, 351n***, 351ta5
distributive injustice   88, 92, 94, 334
divine rights   41, 44, 185, 316
domination   3, 8, 14, 20, 24, 32–33, 40–41,
    71, 78–80, 83, 89–92, 95–96, 101–104,
    106–107, 109–112, 114, 127, 132, 168–170,
    179, 181–182, 184, 214, 224, 247, 298, 321,
    326, 331
Draconian punishment   56, 145, 197–199, 248
dynasty   3, 11n27, 24–30, 33, 35–37, 39,
    43–44, 46–47, 52, 68, 70, 75, 77, 98, 101,
    105, 106t6, 109–111, 114, 127, 155, 177t8,
    177–182, 189, 195, 207, 210, 212, 214,
    215t10, 215–217, 221, 223–224, 229–230,
    234, 241–245, 247–248, 250, 284, 294,
    296–297, 302, 306, 310–315, 333

Eastern Europe   17, 29, 31, 35–36, 38, 45,
    48, 54–56, 58, 62–64, 66, 75, 82, 95,
    98, 102, 104, 110, 112, 126, 143, 148, 150,
    157n77, 157–158, 171, 179, 184, 186n26,
    186–187, 217, 222, 287, 292–294, 297,
    303, 307–308
economic approach to human behavior   9
economic democracy   55–57, 59–60, 62,
    64–65, 67
economic inequality   11n27, 52, 52t5, 68, 75–
    77, 81–82, 84–85, 87, 105, 210, 285
economic system   10–11, 14–15, 19, 22, 29, 36,
    49, 65, 69, 76, 80–81, 84, 87–88, 92–93,
    96–98, 103–105, 110–111, 123, 127, 131, 142,
    162, 168, 177, 188, 204, 208, 214, 241–245,
    286, 289, 309, 323, 325, 327, 337
economic, sociology   10
economism   9, 9n20, 15
egalitarianism   52, 76, 98, 142

elections   xi, 29, 45n54, 81, 99, 116–118,
    121n37, 122n39, 121–123, 126, 130, 133–
    134, 139, 195, 260–261, 284, 297, 305, 330,
    336, 339, 370ta15, 377
elite   4n8, 27–29, 37, 46, 62, 84, 86, 96–98,
    103, 111, 113, 135n53, 178, 212, 220n17, 236,
    247, 313, 333, 341
employer associations   59
enabling law   293, 312, 315, 317
Enlightenment   163n3, 206, 206n4, 208n8,
    208–209, 213, 226, 325, 445
European regime   42, 45, 51, 237, 335
evangelicalism   42, 46, 49, 137, 164, 166, 171,
    198n38, 225, 237, 286, 305, 332, 335, 339
evolutionism   210, 216, 234, 253–254, 269,
    272t12, 272–273, 279–280, 283, 285–
    286, 291
exclusion   27, 35, 57, 60, 62, 64–65, 91, 97,
    116n29, 116–117, 118n32, 124–125, 127–128,
    131, 142–143, 180, 295, 303, 335
executions   xi, 40, 46, 50, 56, 115, 116t7,
    118n32, 140, 142, 145–153, 160, 164, 170,
    174–175, 183, 188, 199–203, 212, 248, 250–
    251, 263, 266, 271t12, 273, 276, 280, 283,
    285, 334, 388ta24, 388ta24, 388–389,
    389ta24
executive orders   312, 316
exploitation   xi, 43, 52t5, 68, 87–95, 114, 245,
    259, 271t12, 271–272, 274, 280, 285–287,
    291–293, 300, 334, 362ta11
extremism   21, 46, 227–228, 252, 335, 339

fanaticism   208, 227–228, 232, 252
fascism   6–7, 7n18, 11n28, 18n9, 21, 28, 28n30,
    38, 55n64, 55–56, 100, 108, 113, 117n32,
    120, 124n41, 125n42, 132–133, 138n58,
    141, 149, 157, 159, 160n81, 163, 171n11,
    170–172, 176–177, 181, 186–187, 198,
    198n38, 208n8, 207–209, 211, 213, 238,
    287–289, 296, 298, 301, 303–307, 310–
    311, 326, 337n55, 336–338
feudalism   21, 34, 41, 55, 69–70, 74, 76, 82,
    85n103, 84–86, 88–89, 91–92, 96–99,
    102–103, 106, 116, 125, 127, 140, 144, 149,
    163, 165–168, 178, 181, 189, 193, 204, 209,
    243, 248, 299, 328, 330, 332
France   6n16, 29, 31, 33, 35, 54, 59, 94, 110,
    118n34, 133n49, 161, 179, 210, 219, 219n15,
    219n16, 221n17, 224, 237, 255, 268n9,

274t13, 276, 279, 281t14, 282t15, 290t16, 294, 299, 299n3, 308, 321, 336–337, 342ta1, 344ta2, 346ta3, 348ta4, 350ta5, 352ta6, 354ta7, 356ta8, 358ta9, 360ta10, 362ta11, 364ta12, 366ta13, 368ta14, 370ta15, 372ta16, 374ta17, 376ta18, 378ta19, 380ta20, 382ta21, 384ta22, 386ta23, 388ta24, 390ta25, 392ta26, 394ta27, 396ta28, 398ta29, 400ta30, 402ta31, 404ta32, 406ta33, 408ta34, 410ta35, 412ta36, 414ta37, 416ta38, 418ta39, 420ta40, 440, 442

free enterprise   19n13, 19–20, 58, 79–80, 109, 115, 132, 135, 138, 189, 286n14, 327

genocide   107

Germany   24, 29, 31, 33, 35–38, 40, 42, 46, 49, 54, 56, 59, 64, 101, 104, 108, 110, 114, 118n34, 118–119, 125n42, 125–126, 136–137, 149–150, 155, 158–159, 160n81, 171, 176, 176n20, 179, 182, 184, 192, 197, 202, 207, 207n6, 212, 217–219, 219n16, 222–223, 225, 227, 234–235, 238–239, 256, 258, 268n9, 274t13, 276, 279, 281t14, 282t15, 289, 290t16, 290–293, 296–297, 301, 304–305, 308, 310–315, 321, 326, 328, 331, 336n55, 336–337, 342ta1, 344ta2, 346ta3, 348ta4, 350ta5, 351n*, 352ta6, 354ta7, 356ta8, 358ta9, 360ta10, 362ta11, 364ta12, 366ta13, 368ta14, 370ta15, 372ta16, 374ta17, 375n*, 376ta18, 378ta19, 380ta20, 382ta21, 384ta22, 385n*, 386ta23, 388ta24, 390ta25, 392ta26, 394ta27, 396ta28, 398ta29, 400ta30, 401n*, 402ta31, 404ta32, 406ta33, 408ta34, 410ta35, 412ta36, 414ta37, 416ta38, 418ta39, 420ta40, 430–431, 440, 444

Gilded Age   16, 21–23, 26, 32, 38, 48–49, 70, 73, 77–78, 81–82, 84, 94, 104, 110, 114–115, 122–123, 128, 131, 132n49, 138, 141, 143, 168, 171, 173, 175, 180, 202, 235, 296–298, 300, 322, 328, 330, 332, 434

Gini coefficients   81, 257, 280, 283, 285–286, 291

Great Depression   11n27, 17n8, 17–18, 166, 166n8, 232, 322–323

Great Recession   18, 141, 232, 326, 442

Greece   29, 40, 44, 49, 114, 155, 159, 171, 225, 256, 266, 273, 274t13, 276, 279, 281t14,

282t15, 286, 289, 290t16, 342ta1, 344ta2, 346ta3, 348ta4, 350ta5, 352ta6, 354ta7, 356ta8, 358ta9, 360ta10, 362ta11, 364ta12, 366ta13, 368ta14, 370ta15, 372ta16, 374ta17, 375n*, 376ta18, 378ta19, 380ta20, 382ta21, 384ta22, 385n*, 386ta23, 388ta24, 390ta25, 392ta26, 394ta27, 396ta28, 398ta29, 400ta30, 401n*, 402ta31, 404ta32, 406ta33, 408ta34, 410ta35, 412ta36, 414ta37, 416ta38, 418ta39, 420ta40, 421n**

hardship   52t5, 62, 68, 82–87, 190, 244, 257–258, 271t12, 271t12

hierarchy   129, 220n17

Hitler   7, 7n17, 28, 30, 30n35, 54, 64, 108, 209n9, 292–293, 297, 304–305, 311–312, 315, 317, 338, 431

human rights   xi, 116t7, 145–146, 149–150, 183n23, 188, 188t9, 193–195, 250–252, 265–266, 272t12, 272t12, 272–273, 279–280, 283, 285–287, 291–292, 397, 400ta30, 400–401, 407

Hungary   24–25, 34, 37, 40, 42, 46, 54, 56, 66, 81, 101, 104, 109, 126, 163, 166, 171, 179, 182, 184, 187, 194, 212–213, 217–218, 222, 239–240, 274t13, 276, 279, 281t14, 282t15, 287–288, 290t16, 294, 296–297, 303–304, 308, 310, 313–316, 342ta1, 344ta2, 346ta3, 348ta4, 350ta5, 352ta6, 354ta7, 356ta8, 358ta9, 360ta10, 362ta11, 364ta12, 366ta13, 368ta14, 370ta15, 372ta16, 374ta17, 376ta18, 378ta19, 380ta20, 382ta21, 384ta22, 386ta23, 388ta24, 390ta25, 392ta26, 394ta27, 396ta28, 398ta29, 400ta30, 402ta31, 404ta32, 406ta33, 408ta34, 410ta35, 412ta36, 414ta37, 416ta38, 418ta39, 420ta40

imperialism   11n27, 25, 46, 49, 134–135, 153–154, 154n73, 158–159, 205

indicators of capitalist dictatorship   188, 241, 252

individual liberty   12, 12t1, 13t2, 42, 46, 56, 117, 162, 164–165, 167–172, 176, 178, 180, 185–186, 188t9, 188–189, 191–193, 198, 216, 228, 232, 249, 252, 264, 272t12, 272–273, 279, 299n2

industrial democracy   12, 13t2, 33, 53, 59,
      60n70, 67–68, 72, 93, 322
industrial non-democracy   12, 12t1, 52–53, 61
industrial relations   58–59, 63, 65, 132n48,
      347, 347ta3, 349
insecurity   52t5, 68, 83, 87–95, 245, 259–260,
      271t12, 271t12, 285, 329
institutionalism   10, 10n25
Ireland   67, 82, 187, 192, 199, 261, 264, 264n7,
      274t13, 276, 279, 281t14, 282t15, 290t16,
      294, 308, 335, 342ta1, 344ta2, 346ta3,
      348ta4, 350ta5, 352ta6, 354ta7, 356ta8,
      358ta9, 360ta10, 362ta11, 364ta12,
      366ta13, 368ta14, 370ta15, 372ta16,
      374ta17, 375n*, 376ta18, 378ta19,
      380ta20, 382ta21, 384ta22, 385n*,
      386ta23, 388ta24, 390ta25, 392ta26,
      394ta27, 396ta28, 398ta29, 400ta30,
      401n*, 402ta31, 404ta32, 406ta33,
      408ta34, 410ta35, 412ta36, 414ta37,
      416ta38, 418ta39, 420ta40
irrationalism   17–18, 18n9, 43, 118n32, 133,
      175n18, 208n8, 206–209, 211, 213–216,
      227–228, 230–232, 235, 253–254, 284,
      287, 326, 336n55
Islamic countries   34, 38, 45n53, 56, 58,
      117n30, 132n49, 166, 170, 184, 210, 212,
      214, 219, 221, 232, 296, 339
Islamic rule   40, 54, 104, 172, 186, 280
Italy   24, 29, 33, 35–36, 38, 40, 42, 46, 48–49,
      59, 81, 101, 104, 108, 110, 114, 121n37, 126,
      155, 158–159, 171, 179, 182, 184, 187, 192,
      217, 225, 234, 238–239, 259, 274t13, 276,
      279, 281t14, 282t15, 288, 290t16, 294,
      296, 301, 304, 326, 328, 337, 339–340,
      340n62, 342ta1, 344ta2, 346ta3, 348ta4,
      350ta5, 352ta6, 354ta7, 356ta8, 358ta9,
      360ta10, 362ta11, 364ta12, 366ta13,
      368ta14, 370ta15, 372ta16, 374ta17,
      376ta18, 378ta19, 380ta20, 382ta21,
      384ta22, 386ta23, 388ta24, 390ta25,
      392ta26, 394ta27, 396ta28, 398ta29,
      400ta30, 402ta31, 404ta32, 406ta33,
      408ta34, 410ta35, 412ta36, 414ta37,
      416ta38, 418ta39, 420ta40, 442

Japan   28–29, 57, 133n49, 263, 274t13, 276,
      279, 281t14, 282t15, 290t16, 294, 321, 328,
      342ta1, 344ta2, 346ta3, 348ta4, 350ta5,

      352ta6, 354ta7, 356ta8, 358ta9, 360ta10,
      362ta11, 364ta12, 366ta13, 368ta14,
      370ta15, 372ta16, 374ta17, 376ta18,
      378ta19, 380ta20, 382ta21, 384ta22,
      386ta23, 388ta24, 390ta25, 392ta26,
      394ta27, 396ta28, 398ta29, 400ta30,
      402ta31, 403n*, 404ta32, 406ta33,
      408ta34, 410ta35, 412ta36, 414ta37,
      416ta38, 418ta39, 420ta40

kleptocracy   3, 23t4, 39, 41, 42n51, 42–43, 47–
      48, 52, 73, 85, 105, 106t6, 111–112, 112n23,
      177, 220, 224, 241, 243, 245, 330, 333

labor   xi, 3, 7n17, 16–17, 19, 21, 32, 35, 42, 52t5,
      54n64, 52–68, 69n82, 72–73, 75, 79–81,
      84, 87–94, 98–99, 113–114, 117n32, 117–
      118, 127n43, 128n44, 127–130, 130n46,
      131n47, 131–132, 132n49, 137n56, 135–138,
      138n57, 144, 155–156, 163–164, 170, 175,
      191, 196, 209n9, 212, 214, 241–245, 256,
      258n4, 258–259, 271t12, 271t12, 271–272,
      274, 280, 285–287, 291–293, 295, 299–
      300, 320–321, 323, 329–331, 333, 335,
      337, 362ta11, 362–363
laissez-faire   3, 3n7, 4n8, 6–7, 7n18, 11n27,
      18n10, 18n11, 18n9, 17–21, 24, 28n30, 30,
      39–40, 55n65, 74, 79–80, 82, 113, 133n49,
      139, 144n61, 164, 164n5, 164n6, 166,
      166n8, 170, 181, 189, 196, 205–206, 206n4,
      208–209, 229n21, 297–299, 299n2, 301–
      304, 324n12, 324n15, 322–325, 327
law and order   116t7, 144, 144n61, 149, 151, 316
law of the strongest   20n16, 20–21, 74, 80,
      132, 144, 301
Lawlessness   144
leadership   25–26, 26n26, 43, 72, 78, 86, 99,
      99n4, 101, 122, 124–126
legal treatment   116t7, 128, 139–141, 145
Leviathan   16, 16n4, 132, 144, 163, 168, 174–175,
      178, 181, 189, 194, 212, 427, 439
liberal democracy   x, 7, 12, 13t2, 40, 42–44,
      56, 100, 104, 117–118, 123–124, 126,
      132n49, 137–138, 140, 146–147, 151, 159,
      162–163, 169, 198–202, 203n39, 208–209,
      209n9, 212–213, 217, 221, 224–225, 232,
      241–253, 282t15, 286–287, 290t16, 290–
      292, 294, 296, 298, 306–307, 309, 312,
      327, 329, 338, 339n61

liberalism   80, 98–100, 123n41, 141, 148, 150,
     160n81, 163, 207, 209, 211, 232, 307,
     324n12, 324–325, 338
libertarianism   4–5, 149–150

Machiavellian   132
manifest destiny   46–47, 153, 153n71
mass incarceration   40, 50, 153, 212, 409ta34
master-servant   34, 54, 74, 85, 87–89, 93–94,
     96, 99, 103, 106, 127–129, 144, 168, 178,
     299–300, 328, 330
McCarthyism   55n65, 84, 136, 160n81, 306
measures of capitalist dictatorship   x,
     271t12, 291
meritocracy   80, 140, 245
Mexico   57–59, 66, 82, 87, 119, 225, 258n4,
     258–259, 262, 264, 268, 273, 274t13,
     276, 279–280, 281t14, 282t15, 285,
     289, 290t16, 307, 309, 342ta1, 344ta2,
     346ta3, 348ta4, 350ta5, 351n*, 352ta6,
     354ta7, 356ta8, 358ta9, 360ta10, 362ta11,
     364ta12, 366ta13, 368ta14, 370ta15,
     372ta16, 374ta17, 376ta18, 378ta19,
     380ta20, 382ta21, 384ta22, 386ta23,
     388ta24, 390ta25, 392ta26, 394ta27,
     396ta28, 398ta29, 400ta30, 402ta31,
     403n*, 404ta32, 406ta33, 408ta34,
     410ta35, 411n*, 412ta36, 414ta37,
     416ta38, 418ta39, 420ta40
militarism   18, 21, 46, 49, 51, 108, 115, 116t7,
     133–135, 152, 153n70, 153n71, 153–154,
     154n73, 156–160, 205, 248, 264, 271t12,
     283, 320, 331
military expenditure   108, 135, 154, 159,
     160n80, 160–161, 249, 264, 271t12, 273,
     276, 280, 283, 285–287, 291, 393, 393ta26
military juntas   3
military-capitalist complex   18, 21, 49, 108,
     114–115, 116t7, 153, 155, 158, 218, 248
militias   73, 114, 131, 144, 157
modernity   8n18, 51, 96, 125n42, 191n31, 200,
     208, 250
monism   116t7, 132–133, 138n57, 138n58, 138–139
monopolistic   19, 26, 70–73, 77–79, 85, 96,
     112, 127, 131, 137, 139, 164, 169, 176, 178,
     180, 326
monopolization   19, 31, 70–71, 73, 75–78,
     102–104, 115, 118n32, 126–127, 130–132,
     142–143, 206, 243, 247, 326

monopsony   72, 79, 88, 93
moral choice   188t9, 191, 193
moralistic-religious terror   188, 188t9, 199–
     202, 251, 272t12, 280, 283, 291
murder   49, 54n64, 54–55, 107, 107n19, 155,
     209n9, 391
Mussolini   6, 28, 109, 297, 304–305, 311,
     326, 339
mutually assured destruction   18, 284

national security   136, 152, 248
nationalism   11n27, 18, 46, 107, 133–135,
     153n70, 153–154, 155n75, 335
nativism   119, 171n11, 303
Nazism   7, 7n17, 11n28, 30, 30n35, 64, 108,
     117n32, 120, 135, 137, 160n81, 171n11, 181,
     207, 207n6, 209, 209n9, 293, 297, 301,
     304–305, 311, 315, 326, 338, 439
nepotism   316
New Deal   3n7, 23, 25, 36, 54, 70, 84, 89, 93,
     93n14, 232, 297, 300, 323, 330, 430
New Zealand   35, 57, 67, 82, 119n36, 151, 261,
     264, 274t13, 276, 279, 281t14, 282t15,
     290t16, 294, 308, 342ta1, 344ta2, 346ta3,
     348ta4, 350ta5, 352ta6, 354ta7, 356ta8,
     358ta9, 360ta10, 362ta11, 364ta12,
     366ta13, 368ta14, 370ta15, 372ta16,
     374ta17, 376ta18, 378ta19, 380ta20,
     382ta21, 384ta22, 386ta23, 388ta24,
     390ta25, 392ta26, 394ta27, 396ta28,
     398ta29, 400ta30, 402ta31, 404ta32,
     406ta33, 408ta34, 410ta35, 411n*,
     412ta36, 414ta37, 415n*, 416ta38, 417n*,
     418ta39, 420ta40
non-protection   52t5, 68, 87–95, 245, 259–
     260, 271t12, 271t12

oligarchy   3, 4n8, 4–5, 5n10, 8, 10, 11n27, 17,
     23t4, 28n29, 28n31, 23–37, 39, 43–44,
     46–48, 52, 55, 58, 66, 68, 70, 72–73, 75,
     77, 82, 87, 95–96, 98, 101, 103–105, 106t6,
     109–114, 126, 143, 149–150, 155, 165, 167,
     171, 177, 177t8, 179–182, 184, 189, 195, 207,
     210, 212, 214–215, 215t10, 218–219, 221–
     222, 224, 229–230, 233–234, 241–250,
     285, 294, 297, 299, 302, 305, 309–310,
     312–313, 316, 319–320, 328, 330–333,
     336, 341
oligopoly   19, 72, 88, 131, 320

oppression 3, 6, 8, 22, 27–28, 33, 37, 43–44,
    52t5, 52–53, 56–57, 59–60, 62, 65, 72, 81,
    83–84, 86, 89–91, 93, 95, 97, 103, 106, 114,
    127, 144, 153n71, 170, 185, 189, 198, 201,
    209, 216, 223n18, 234, 300–301, 310, 320,
    322, 332, 334–335
ownership 75–76, 78, 81, 90–91, 133n49,
    349ta4

pathology 43, 134
patrimonialism 20, 85, 85n103, 330
Penal Repression 143
Pinochet 11n27, 24, 40, 44–45, 54, 54n64,
    55n65, 64, 109, 162n2, 166, 184n24, 285,
    286n14, 301, 340
Pluralism 132, 265, 376ta18, 376–377,
    439, 441
plutocracy 1n3, 3, 4n8, 4–5, 5n10, 8, 11n27,
    20–22, 23t4, 28n29, 30n33, 30n35, 23–
    37, 39, 42–44, 46–47, 51–52, 68–77, 82,
    91, 96–99, 101, 105, 106t6, 109–111, 113–
    115, 129n45, 127–131, 136–137, 141–142,
    145, 147, 150–151, 155–156, 163, 165–170,
    177, 177t8, 179–182, 189, 194–195, 202,
    207, 210, 212, 215t10, 214–221, 224, 229–
    230, 233–237, 241–245, 247–250, 284,
    294, 296–297, 301–304, 306, 308, 310–
    311, 313, 316, 319–320, 322, 328, 330, 333
plutonomy 1, 3, 5n10, 27, 30n33, 36, 70, 74,
    76–77, 91, 97, 104, 110, 115, 131, 143, 156,
    159, 182, 220, 223, 258n4, 284, 294–
    295, 297
Poland 24–25, 34, 37, 40, 46, 51, 56, 59, 81,
    101, 104, 109, 123–124, 126, 163, 166, 171–
    172, 179, 182, 184, 187, 192, 194, 197, 199,
    202, 205, 212–213, 217–218, 222, 224–225,
    227, 229, 232, 234, 236, 239, 273, 274t13,
    276, 279, 281t14, 282t15, 287–289, 290t16,
    294, 296–297, 303, 307–310, 313–316,
    335, 342ta1, 344ta2, 346ta3, 348ta4,
    350ta5, 352ta6, 354ta7, 356ta8, 358ta9,
    360ta10, 362ta11, 364ta12, 366ta13,
    368ta14, 370ta15, 372ta16, 374ta17,
    376ta18, 378ta19, 380ta20, 382ta21,
    384ta22, 386ta23, 388ta24, 390ta25,
    392ta26, 394ta27, 396ta28, 398ta29,
    400ta30, 402ta31, 404ta32, 406ta33,
    408ta34, 410ta35, 412ta36, 414ta37,
    416ta38, 418ta39, 420ta40, 421n**

police 6, 6n14, 23t4, 39–41, 43–44, 46–47,
    49–52, 105, 106t6, 114n26, 113–115,
    131n47, 145–147, 148n66, 148–149, 151–
    152, 156–158, 174, 177, 177t8, 183–185, 189,
    195, 199, 214, 217, 220, 224, 241, 248, 262,
    329, 381, 409
police states 23t4, 39–41, 43–44, 46–47, 49,
    51–52, 105, 106t6, 113–115, 177, 177t8, 183–
    185, 195, 214, 217, 220, 224, 241, 248
political democracy 12, 13t2, 16, 17n5, 20, 22,
    24, 33, 36, 53, 57, 99, 130, 321–322, 334
political freedoms 99, 101, 115, 116t7, 116t7,
    116–117, 119, 126, 130, 137, 143, 163, 171n11,
    190, 246, 260, 271t12
political non-democracy 12, 12t1, 17
political regime 11, 14–15, 15n1, 36, 96–98,
    102–105, 106t6, 106t6, 110–115, 117, 122–
    123, 125–126, 129, 131, 136, 142–144, 151,
    162, 168, 177, 183–184, 188, 200, 204, 246,
    248, 251, 286, 294, 301, 309, 323, 327
political terror 115, 116t7, 146n65, 146–150,
    152, 183, 183n23, 201, 248, 251, 263, 271t12,
    273, 276, 280, 283, 285, 291, 391ta25
populism 55n64, 55–56, 287, 303
populist 25, 27–28, 54, 81, 136, 150, 207–208,
    210, 287, 294, 303, 312
Portugal 40, 44, 49, 114, 155, 159, 171, 187,
    239, 259, 274t13, 276, 279, 281t14, 282t15,
    290t16, 294, 301, 308, 342ta1, 344ta2,
    346ta3, 348ta4, 350ta5, 352ta6, 354ta7,
    356ta8, 358ta9, 360ta10, 362ta11,
    364ta12, 366ta13, 368ta14, 370ta15,
    372ta16, 374ta17, 376ta18, 378ta19,
    380ta20, 382ta21, 384ta22, 386ta23,
    388ta24, 390ta25, 392ta26, 394ta27,
    396ta28, 398ta29, 400ta30, 402ta31,
    404ta32, 406ta33, 408ta34, 410ta35,
    412ta36, 414ta37, 416ta38, 418ta39,
    420ta40, 421n**
poverty x, xi, 43, 68, 74, 82–87, 90, 95, 244–
    245, 257–258, 271t12, 271t12, 271–272,
    274, 280, 283, 285–286, 291–293, 329,
    333–334, 354ta7, 354ta7, 354–355,
    355ta7, 356ta8, 356ta8, 356–357, 357ta8
pre-capitalism 26, 30, 32, 34, 41, 60, 68, 70–
    71, 89, 96–97, 107, 109, 127, 184, 205, 238,
    243, 250, 328, 330, 332–333
predation 43, 47, 52, 73–74, 79, 112, 142
Presidency 25–26, 284

prisoners of ethical conscience 50, 188, 188t9, 201–203

privacy xi, 162–167, 169–170, 172, 174, 178, 180, 182, 185–186, 188, 188t9, 191, 191n30, 194–198, 250, 252, 265, 272t12, 272–273, 279–280, 283, 285–286, 291, 402ta31, 402–403, 403ta31

production factors 15–16, 19, 53, 59–60, 62–64, 80, 83, 87, 241–242, 323

production regime 16

Prohibition 21, 40, 47, 50, 50n61, 172–173, 175n19, 180, 183, 190, 192, 192n33, 199, 202, 237, 424

propertyless 116, 116n29, 122, 124–125

punishment 50n60, 50–51, 115, 116t7, 120, 121n38, 128, 139, 142–143, 144n61, 144–145, 148–151, 164, 172, 174, 174n17, 188, 190, 200, 203, 248, 250, 263, 266–267, 271t12, 271t12, 327

Puritanism 42, 50–51, 107, 114n26, 147, 160n81, 164, 166, 170, 171n11, 171–173, 173n14, 192n33, 198n38, 201, 215, 232, 237–238, 267, 296, 339, 439

racism 303

radical right 138n58, 201, 297

rationalism 18, 118n32, 205n2, 205–206, 206n4, 208n8, 208–210, 213, 213n12, 215, 217–218, 222, 226–228, 230, 232–235, 253, 269, 320

rationalistic culture 12, 13t2

Reaganism 16, 21, 27, 32, 40–42, 44, 48–50, 53–54, 58, 63–64, 67, 70, 70n85, 73–74, 76–77, 80–82, 84, 87, 93, 101–102, 102n11, 104, 110, 115, 123n41, 126, 131, 134, 136, 139, 143, 146–147, 150–151, 155n75, 157, 159, 171, 172n13, 175n18, 174–176, 179, 190, 192, 194, 197–200, 202, 218, 222, 227, 230, 267, 284, 295, 302–304, 306–308, 310–311, 319–320, 328, 339

redistribution 69–70, 70n85, 73–77, 79–83, 302, 310, 319–320, 322, 324–325

religiosity 167, 207n7, 218, 218t11, 224n19, 223–228, 232, 235, 237, 253n1, 252–254, 268–269, 272t12, 272t12, 280, 283, 285–287, 291

religious superstitions 118n32, 210, 214–215, 218t11, 234–238, 239n31, 239–240, 254, 269, 272t12

rightism 7n18, 28, 28n30, 30, 55n64, 64, 209n9, 212, 288, 293, 297, 301, 304–305, 310, 312–313

robber barons 26, 32, 40, 43, 47, 49, 71–72, 78, 103, 103n12, 105, 111–112, 130, 133n49, 141, 143, 169, 180, 304, 322

ruling class 27, 31, 41, 70, 76, 79, 84–85, 90, 96, 103, 116, 141, 168–169, 213, 229, 242, 331

Satan xii, 118n32, 210, 214–216, 224–225, 236–239, 253–254, 269, 270n13, 272t12, 272–273, 279–280, 283, 285–286, 291, 420ta40

Scandinavia 17, 17n8, 35, 37, 43, 51, 74, 95, 103, 103n13, 141, 147, 150, 169, 219, 238, 308–309

scientific progress 42, 205, 207n7, 214–217, 218t11, 226, 230, 235–237, 253, 269, 272t12, 335

sects 18, 230

secularization 219, 224, 335

separation of church and state 135, 284

slavery 19, 19n15, 34, 41, 54, 61, 63, 68–70, 72, 74, 76, 80, 82, 84–86, 88–89, 91–92, 96, 103, 106, 127, 128n44, 128–129, 140, 144, 153n71, 170, 178, 191n32, 204, 243, 301, 328, 331–332, 334–335

Slovenia 55, 66, 148, 274t13, 276, 279, 281t14, 282t15, 289, 290t16, 292, 294, 308–309, 343ta1, 344ta2, 346ta3, 348ta4, 350ta5, 352ta6, 354ta7, 356ta8, 358ta9, 360ta10, 362ta11, 364ta12, 366ta13, 368ta14, 370ta15, 372ta16, 374ta17, 376ta18, 378ta19, 380ta20, 382ta21, 384ta22, 386ta23, 388ta24, 390ta25, 392ta26, 394ta27, 396ta28, 398ta29, 400ta30, 402ta31, 404ta32, 406ta33, 408ta34, 410ta35, 412ta36, 414ta37, 415n*, 416ta38, 417n*, 418ta39, 420ta40

social democracy 3n7, 7, 16, 81, 134–135, 137, 329, 329n32

social economy 17, 17n8, 209, 324

social strata 3, 8, 13–14, 17, 63, 76, 117, 120–122, 145, 157, 166–167, 170, 178, 189–191, 193–195, 197, 199–201, 203, 207, 210–212, 220–221, 223, 226, 229, 314

socialism 1n1, 3, 7, 7n17, 35, 59, 77, 132, 132n49, 134–135, 137–138, 138n57, 150, 185n26, 209n9, 285, 308, 323–324, 329, 338 sociological economics   10

sociological system   9n19, 9–10, 12, 15, 96–97

South America   11n27, 17, 24, 31, 34, 36, 38,
    40, 44–45, 48–49, 51, 58, 63–64, 81–82,
    98, 102, 104, 107, 112, 114, 148, 155, 157,
    159, 171, 176, 179, 182, 184, 187, 192, 199,
    217, 222, 225, 234, 240, 288, 296, 301,
    303, 308, 313, 316, 340

South Korea   28–29, 40, 54, 59, 66, 82, 87, 114,
    145, 148, 155, 159, 171, 179, 182, 184, 263,
    266, 273, 281t14, 286, 289, 290t16, 307,
    340, 413n****

Spain   24, 29, 35–38, 40, 42, 44, 46, 49, 101,
    108, 110, 114, 155, 159, 171, 179, 182, 184,
    187, 217, 225, 238–239, 274t13, 276, 279,
    281t14, 282t15, 290t16, 294–295, 301, 326,
    328, 337, 339, 343ta1, 344ta2, 346ta3,
    348ta4, 350ta5, 352ta6, 354ta7, 356ta8,
    358ta9, 360ta10, 362ta11, 364ta12,
    366ta13, 368ta14, 370ta15, 372ta16,
    374ta17, 376ta18, 378ta19, 380ta20,
    382ta21, 384ta22, 386ta23, 388ta24,
    390ta25, 392ta26, 394ta27, 396ta28,
    398ta29, 400ta30, 402ta31, 404ta32,
    406ta33, 408ta34, 410ta35, 412ta36,
    414ta37, 416ta38, 418ta39, 420ta40,
    421n**, 442

state of nature   16, 20, 132, 144, 168, 175, 178,
    181, 189, 212

state terror   40, 113, 118n32, 148–152, 155,
    200, 202

status groups   32, 71, 127

stratification   16, 68

subjugation   127, 152–153

subordination   116t7, 129, 129n46

suicide   230–231

Supreme Court   32, 121, 128, 129n45, 305, 312,
    315–316, 329

surveillance   50, 156–157, 183, 190, 218, 265,
    377, 403

Sweden   17n7, 39, 59, 103n13, 118n34, 119n36,
    141, 213n13, 264, 268, 268n9, 270n13,
    274t13, 276, 279, 281t14, 282t15, 289,
    290t16, 293, 308, 343ta1, 344ta2, 346ta3,
    348ta4, 350ta5, 351n*, 352ta6, 354ta7,
    356ta8, 358ta9, 360ta10, 362ta11,
    363n***, 364ta12, 366ta13, 368ta14,

    371ta15, 372ta16, 374ta17, 376ta18,
    378ta19, 380ta20, 382ta21, 384ta22,
    386ta23, 388ta24, 390ta25, 392ta26,
    394ta27, 396ta28, 398ta29, 400ta30,
    402ta31, 404ta32, 406ta33, 408ta34,
    410ta35, 412ta36, 414ta37, 416ta38,
    418ta39, 420ta40, 433

Thatcherism   54, 64, 73, 75, 77, 80–82, 87, 94,
    101–102, 102n11, 104, 110, 123n41, 126, 139,
    143, 146, 150–151, 159, 171, 179, 192, 197,
    199, 202, 218, 222, 227, 295, 302–304,
    306–307, 311, 339

theocracy   10, 17, 37–38, 40–47, 49, 51–52,
    56, 64, 100, 105, 106t6, 113–115, 117, 148,
    163, 172, 175, 177, 177t8, 184–187, 193, 197,
    201–202, 211, 214, 225, 227, 230, 233–234,
    239–241, 251, 284, 302, 314, 332

third world   5, 11n27, 29, 58, 62, 181,
    222, 258n4

top one percent   x, 76–77, 111, 244, 256,
    271t12, 271–272, 274, 291–293, 350ta5

torture   120, 146–147, 148n66, 148–149, 152,
    153n70, 170, 170n10, 183, 199, 202, 263–
    264, 334, 391, 397

totalitarianism   6, 28n30, 138, 138n57, 302,
    335, 337–338

Turkey   24–25, 29, 34–35, 38, 40, 45–46, 51,
    54, 56–59, 63–64, 66, 82, 87, 95, 104,
    109, 119, 124, 145, 148, 150, 159, 163, 166,
    170–172, 175, 182, 184, 186–187, 192, 194,
    197, 199, 202, 205, 210, 212, 221–222,
    224–225, 239, 255, 257, 259, 261–266,
    268–270, 270n13, 273, 274t13, 276,
    279–280, 281t14, 282t15, 282–283, 285,
    288–289, 290t16, 292, 296, 303, 307,
    309–310, 313–316, 335, 343ta1, 344ta2,
    346ta3, 348ta4, 351n*, 351ta5, 353ta6,
    355ta7, 356ta8, 359ta9, 361ta10, 363ta11,
    365ta12, 367ta13, 369ta14, 371ta15,
    372ta16, 374ta17, 377ta18, 378ta19,
    380ta20, 382ta21, 385ta22, 386ta23,
    388ta24, 390ta25, 392ta26, 395ta27,
    396ta28, 398ta29, 400ta30, 402ta31,
    403n*, 404ta32, 406ta33, 408ta34,
    411ta35, 412ta36, 414ta37, 416ta38,
    419ta39, 420ta40

tyranny   6, 16, 22, 27, 33, 36, 44, 72, 107, 110, 142, 148, 170, 180, 182, 191n30, 201, 301, 322, 328, 330

union coverage   54, 57–60, 62, 255
union density   x, 52t5, 52–57, 67, 241, 255, 271t12, 271–272, 274, 280, 283, 286–287, 291, 293, 342ta1, 342–343, 343ta1
union organizations   16
unionization   52t5, 52–60, 117n32, 241–242, 255, 258n4, 271t12
universalism   98, 123
US Presidential elections   2, 133, 297
US South   19, 19n15, 23, 23n20, 61–62, 62n76, 66, 72, 99, 117, 117n30, 117n32, 120, 123, 126, 128, 170, 183, 185n26, 195, 235, 258n4, 331

voice   xi, 116t7, 125–126, 130, 156, 247, 260, 271t12, 273, 276, 280, 285, 291, 372ta16, 372–373
voting   xi, 116t7, 117n32, 118n33, 119n36, 116–121, 121n37, 121n38, 123, 125–126, 130, 139, 195, 247, 260, 271t12, 273, 276, 300, 305, 334, 370ta15

wages   xi, 57, 69n82, 83, 88–91, 93–94, 259, 362ta11, 362–363, 363n*, 367ta13

war on drugs   21, 40, 50, 147, 172–173, 176, 180, 182–183, 190, 193, 198–199, 237, 320
wars   18, 40, 42–43, 46–47, 47n57, 49–51, 69n82, 95, 107, 107n19, 113, 116t7, 134–135, 147, 153n71, 154n73, 154n74, 152–155, 155n75, 159n79, 157–161, 172–173, 182–183, 193, 202, 212, 224, 248, 264, 284, 289, 331, 336
welfare capitalism   3, 16–17, 22, 42, 59, 77, 81–82, 86, 143, 155n75, 159, 165, 169, 192, 199, 202, 222, 238, 241, 243–247, 249–251, 295, 324
Western Europe   17, 22, 43, 51, 57, 62, 66, 74, 77, 95, 103, 121, 123n41, 133n49, 141, 147, 150, 169, 212, 217, 221n17, 238, 258n4, 308–309, 441
Western societies   2, 5, 5n10, 8, 11n27, 15, 24–25, 29–30, 31n36, 33, 35–37, 39–40, 42, 46, 48–49, 51, 58, 63, 66, 70, 75–77, 82–83, 87, 87n105, 112, 117, 147, 149–150, 155–158, 161, 175, 175n18, 179, 181–182, 187, 193, 200, 203, 210, 214–215, 217–218, 222, 224–225, 229, 234, 239, 258n4, 267, 270, 280, 296, 302–303, 308–309, 311, 314, 316
worker participation   16
works councils   59, 65–67, 255, 271t12, 271–272, 274, 347

xenophobia   56, 119

www.ingramcontent.com/pod-product-compliance
Lightning Source LLC
Chambersburg PA
CBHW070858030426
42336CB00014BA/2247